MW01132441

A THEORY OF GOAL SETTING & TASK PERFORMANCE

Edwin A. Locke
University of Maryland

Gary P. Latham
University of Washington

with contributions by

KEN J. SMITH   **ROBERT E. WOOD**

PRENTICE HALL, Englewood Cliffs, New Jersey 07632

Library of Congress Cataloging-in-Publication Data

Locke, Edwin A.
    A theory of goal setting and task performance / Edwin A. Locke,
Gary P. Latham with contributions by Ken J. Smith, Robert E. Wood.
        p.   cm.
    Includes bibliographical references.
    ISBN 0–13–913138–8
    1. Goal (Psychology)   2. Performance.   I. Title.
BF503.L63   1990
153.8—dc20   89–16372
                                                  CIP

Editoral/production supervision and
      interior design by Anne Pietropinto
Cover by Lundgren Graphics, Ltd.
Manufacturing buyer: Ed O'Dougherty

 © 1990 by Prentice-Hall, Inc.
A Division of Simon & Schuster
Englewood Cliffs, NJ 07632

Printed in the United States of America
10   9   8   7   6   5   4   3   2   1

ISBN 0-13-913138-8

Prentice-Hall International (UK) Limited, *London*
Prentice-Hall of Australia Pty. Limited, *Sydney*
Prentice-Hall of Canada Inc., *Toronto*
Prentice-Hall Hispanoamericana, S.A., *Mexico*
Prentice-Hall of India Private Limited, *New Delhi*
Prentice-Hall of Japan, Inc., *Tokyo*
Simon & Schuster Asia Pte. Ltd., *Singapore*
Editora Prentice-Hall do Brasil, Ltda., *Rio de Janeiro*

To Thomas A. Ryan and W. W. Ronan

CONTENTS

8. Goals and Feedback (Knowledge of Results) 173

9. Other Moderators: Ability, Demographic Variables, Personality, Task Complexity, and Situational Constraints 206

10. Goals and Affect 226

11. Integration: The High Performance Cycle 252

PART II: APPLICATIONS

12.   Applications: The Role of Goal Setting in Human Resource Management   269

PART III: THEORETICAL EXTENSIONS

13.   Goal Setting and Strategy Effects on Complex Tasks   293

14.   Macro vs. Micro Goal Setting Research: A Call for Convergence   320

Appendix A   Studies Showing Significant or Contingently Significant Relationships between Goal Difficulty and Performance   337

FOREWORD

We are often reminded that the psychological franchise has become heavily cognitive. For years the attention of the discipline has centered on issues of how the mind works in processing, representing, organizing, and retrieving information. More recently, efforts have been made to invest this austere cognitivism with some affect and passion. So the contemporary cognitive theories of human behavior are taking on an emotional tinge. The present volume addresses itself to motivators of action, which represents a further dimension that is central to the understanding of human functioning.

The mechanisms governing the translation of thought into action have been a continuing major problem in psychology. Some of the transformational processes are concerned with how thought guides the construction of skilled action. But knowing what to do is only part of the story. A comprehensive theory of human functioning must also encompass motivational mediators that govern the selection, activation, and sustained direction of behavior. The long overdue efforts to link cognition to action gives prominence to motivational functions.

Human motivators take two broad forms. One class of motivators is biologically rooted in cellular deficits and physically aversive instigators. The second major source of motivators is cognitively based. In cognitively generated motivation, people motivate themselves and guide their actions through the exercise of forethought. They anticipate likely outcomes of prospective actions; they set goals for themselves and select courses of action designed to realize valued futures. One can distinguish three different forms of cognitive motivators around which different theories have been built. These include casual attributions, outcome expectancies, and cognized goals.

Through the past several decades, Locke has been the foremost spokesman for goal theory. The psychological literature has been enriched by his thoughtful treatises and experimental investigations on the nature of goal systems, their functions, and the mechanisms through which they produce their motivational effects. He was later joined by Latham, a masterful field reseacher, in what has proven to be a highly productive collaboration. In this volume they bring together the vast body of knowledge on the different facets of goal theory and its practical applications. I cannot think of a better scholarly duo to undertake this valuable task. The material reviewed in this volume is an insightful combination of theoretical analyses, empirical tests, and practical applications. The authors not only provide massive testimony that goal theory has withstood stringent empirical tests, but they identify conditional factors that bring order to seemingly conflicting findings and suggest fruitful directions for further inquiry. These conceptual analyses will serve as a major impetus for continuing progress in the understanding of how goal systems work.

The regulation of motivation by goal setting is a remarkably robust phenomenon. Converging lines of evidence from laboratory and field studies involving heterogeneous task domains reveal goal effects to be highly reproducible and of substantial magnitude. Despite this unprecedented level of empirical support, goal theory has not been accorded the prominence it deserves in mainstream psychology. Perhaps it is because this line of theorizing and research has been featured mainly in publications in the organizational field. Whatever the reasons might be, the present volume should go a long way toward rectifying this relative neglect.

The authors of this book have made a masterful contribution toward the understanding of goal systems and the influential role they play in human attainments. It should have a place on the bookshelf of every person who is interested in motivation, whether as a theoretical issue or as a practical matter.

Albert Bandura
Stanford University

PREFACE

THE EVOLUTION OF MOTIVATION THEORY
IN PSYCHOLOGY

Motivation theory in psychology has undergone several marked changes during this century. In essence, broad, all-encompassing, noncognitive theories have gradually been replaced by narrower, "limited domain," or middle-range theories, most of which include key cognitive components.

Freud's theory of psychoanalysis was one of the first all-encompassing theories developed in psychology. Freud claimed that all human action was energized by two broad classes of unconscious instincts: sex and aggression (later termed the life and death instincts). This theory is not viable because, among other reasons, there is no evidence that people possess any such instincts in the sense of inborn drives leading them to pursue preset ends in the absence of learning. Sex and aggression are only potentialities in people, as are thousands of other types of activities. Whether these potentialities become actualized depends on the premises and values that people acquire through experience and thought and on their appraisal of the circumstances in which they find themselves.

Parallel with the rise of psychoanalysis in Europe (which was always more influential in psychiatry than psychology), the theory of behaviorism was developed and popularized by John B. Watson (1924) and others in North America. The early version of behaviorism was called stimulus-response psychology, because it purported to explain human action with reference only to external stimuli, i.e., conditioning. It banished consciousness (mental contents and processes) and introspection from psychology altogether, claiming that they were incompatible with a scientific approach to psychology. In a later version of behaviorism, B. F. Skinner claimed that all human (operant) behavior was controlled by external reinforcements, defined as events that followed the response which made subsequent, similar responses more probable. Again consciousness was banned from psychology—on the grounds that the mind was an epiphenomenon and possessed no causal efficacy (Locke, 1977). "The environment," claimed Skinner, "determines the individual" (1953, p. 448).

Like psychoanalysis, behaviorism does not yield an adequate explanation of human action, because behavior cannot be explained without reference to consciousness. For example, so-called reinforcers do not change behavior unless people want or value them (Dulany, 1968); are aware of the connection between the response and the reinforcers (Brewer, 1974; Dulany, 1968; Levine, 1971); and believe they can make the required responses (Bandura, 1986). Furthermore, learning and performance can occur without any external reinforcement through vicarious reinforcement, modeling, and self-reinforcement (Bandura, 1986; Locke, 1972).

Behaviorism and psychoanalysis, while seemingly at odds with one another, are firmly united on one fundamental issue. They agree that people are not rational beings in that their thinking does not in any fundamental sense regulate their choices and actions. Freud granted that man had an ego, or reason, but it was relatively impotent compared with the id or instincts. For the behaviorists, reasoning is reduced to conditioned verbal behavior. By denying the efficacy of reason, these two theories forfeit all claims to scientific objectivity (Locke, 1980b).

Another scientifically popular, all-encompassing theory, which represented a partial synthesis of behaviorism and psychoanalysis, was Hull's drive theory. This theory argued that all behavior was energized by physiological need deprivation. This state of deprivation, according to the theory, led to a state of drive that prompted the organism to heightened and, at first, random, activity. When by chance an action was taken that reduced the need state (e.g., eating), this response was gradually stamped in (reinforced) while other responses were extinguished. When the need deficit, and therefore the drive state, was reduced, activity ceased.

This theory too has foundered. All action (e.g., exploration) cannot be traced to physiological need deficits (White, 1959). All need deficits do not lead to heightened activity levels (Cofer & Appley, 1967). All reinforcers do not satisfy a need (e.g., saccharin). Drive reduction does not always lead to reduced activity (as in the case of hungry rats fed a snack before running a maze). And drive increases such as sexual activity and brain self-stimulation can even be rewarding (Olds, 1958). The theory is not only hopelessly simplistic but again omits the whole cognitive realm.

While psychoanalysis, behaviorism, and drive theory still have some influence today, their influence is clearly on the decline. They are being replaced by a host of less grandiose theories that do not seek to explain all human action but rather to account for only a limited set of phenomena. Such theories are not deduced from arbitrary premises or formed by overgeneralizations from very limited observations. Rather these theories are constructed painstakingly from accumulated evidence. These theories are generally cognitive and situationally specific.

For example, there are theories designed to explain motivational phenomena only in the realm of work (Hackman & Oldham, 1980). Equity theory (Adams, 1965) is concerned only with the effects of a single value as it operates in one specific (social) domain. Miner's (1977) role motivation theory is concerned with motives affecting the success of line managers in large organizations.

There are still rather broad scale theories such as expectancy theory (Vroom, 1964), which asserts that one's choices in general are a function of the perceived value (valence) of the outcomes of the contemplated action, the probability that the action will lead to those outcomes, and the expectancy that one can, with effort, take the requisite action. However, the measurements used to predict and explain action are always based on the individual's perception of each specific situation. Bandura's (1986) social-cognitive theory, while broad in scope, focuses on conscious, situationally specific regulators of action rather than generalized drive states.

The trend toward cognitive theories has been especially marked within the past two decades as a result of the "cognitive revolution" in psychology (Dember, 1975). Observe that expectancy theory is cognitive in that all the key variables pertain to conscious judgments or estimates, based on introspection. Similarly, as the name implies, social-cognitive theory relies heavily on the concept of cognitive self-regulation (Bandura, 1986). Weiner's (1986) attribution theory is based on conclusions that people reach about the causes of their actions and accomplishments.

Goal setting theory, which is limited in scope, situationally specific, and cognitively based, is congruent with the above trends in motivation theory. These trends are eminently reasonable. It is a hopeless task to try to develop a grand theory of human motivation in the absence of much more extensive knowledge. Furthermore, it is worse than futile to try to understand human beings without acknowledging that they possess a reasoning mind. One's mind is the means by which one gains knowledge, appraises the value significance of that knowledge, and guides actions accordingly. No theory that denies this can hope to explain human action.

All psychological theories (and scientific theories) rest on some philosophical base, either explicitly or implicitly. The first author was heavily influenced by the philosophy of Objectivism (e.g., see Rand, 1964, 1969), especially the premises that people are rational beings who survive by the use of their minds, that they possess volition (the power to think or not to think), and that their actions are regulated by their thinking and their conscious or subconscious ideas. These premises formed the foundation of goal setting theory, but not the details of its content. The content had to be discovered through systematic study.

We believe that psychological theories, including theories of motivation, must be developed gradually, based on accumulated research findings. Deducing or inducing a formal set of propositions from very limited evidence at the early stages of theory building, aside from being scientifically arbitrary, has other disadvantages. It can rigidify thinking so that the researcher only looks at whether the hypothesis is supported and ignores more significant results. It can subtly direct thinking along a single track when an entirely different track might be more appropriate. It can imply that when the formal hypotheses have been tested, theory development stops. There can be severe disadvantages to concluding too much too soon and overformalizing one's ideas at the early stage of theory building. Perhaps when psychology becomes a mature science, with a large body of proven findings at its base, this type of theorizing will be more successful. Thus far, in the realm of motivation theory, it has not worked.

Even many current theories, despite their limited domains, are based on gross overgeneralizations from a paucity of data and a limited number of methods or measures (sometimes only one). As a result, after the proponents of such theories make their "hit," they are forced to "run" from their original version, due to subsequent negative findings by others, and to formulate a revision, again based on only a few studies. This may happen repeatedly, accompanied by constant *post hoc* reinterpretations of nonconfirming studies until the research community (except for a small but devout following) finally loses interest. In contrast to the "hit and run" theorists, developers of other theories based on scant data may refuse to make any revisions at all; they simply defend the original version to the end. These "barricade" theorists deny the validity of disconfirming studies. Again the research community loses interest in such theories relatively quickly.

In contrast to both "hit and run" and the "barricade" theories, goal setting theory was not induced from miniscule amounts of data and then patched and repatched or defended against all comers. It evolved gradually, based on the findings of hundreds of studies. The content of goal setting theory was developed inductively over a twenty-five-year period. We did not start by making a long list of formal propositions and then testing them one by one. At the beginning we only knew enough to ask one simple question, based on a single, core hypothesis, "Do goals affect action?" More specifically, we asked, "Does goal setting work, that is, does it affect task performance?" Once we found that it worked, research proceeded in several different directions. There were attempts to *generalize* the initial findings by determining whether goal setting worked with different tasks and in different settings. At the same time there were attempts at *lateral integration*, which involved connecting goal setting with related concepts at the same level of abstraction, such as feedback, participation, incentives, self-efficacy and satisfaction. Similarly there were attempts at *vertical integration,* through tying goal setting to broader concepts such as values and personality. The theory also underwent *elaboration* through attempts to specify the mechanisms by which goal setting affected performance. And finally attempts were made to identify *moderators* or *boundary conditions* for goal setting.

Studies relevant to these issues were not done in any particular order; nor were they guided by any grand plan or design. The studies were planned only insofar as each one had a purpose, and each one built on previous research. But within those constraints there were (and still are) literally hundreds of options. Since all these options could be exercised, goal setting theory is by no means a complete or closed theory. But we have learned enough in twenty-five years to justify writing this book. In fact, very few theories in the field of psychology or organizational behavior have had as much research support as this one (Pinder, 1984; Miner, 1980, 1984).

In reviewing the goal setting literature, we have reviewed not only our own work in this area but nearly every published goal setting study that we could find, in addition to unpublished studies and doctoral dissertations that we knew about. While we undoubtedly missed some studies, we believe that our literature search was comprehensive; it included a computer search using key words such as goal setting, standard, objective, and intention.

We have included sections of previous articles in a number of places in this book, simply because such material was appropriate to the topic at hand and because we could not find a way to say it better than we had previously. Some of these previous pieces were coauthored. We have given these authors due credit in various places in the book. Despite our use of previous work, this book includes at least two hundred studies that have not been reviewed elsewhere, as well as many new theoretical integrations. The totality of the goal setting literature, not including the literature on Management by Objectives, now amounts to about five hundred books, chapters, and articles, with new ones appearing almost daily.

The present book represents the first comprehensive statement of goal setting theory in contrast to our previous book (Locke & Latham, 1984a), which focused on goal setting as a technique. A shorter and very preliminary version of the theory can be found in Lee, Locke, and Latham (1989; see also Locke, 1968b; Latham & Locke, 1979; Locke & Latham, 1984b). Even now, however, we consider it to be an "open" rather than a "closed" theory. We believe that future revisions of the theory are not only inevitable but desirable. At the same time we are confident that the basic core of the theory will remain intact, since it is based on extensive experimental data derived from numerous sources and obtained in a variety of settings using many different tasks (see Chapter 2). Future modifications, we believe, will primarily involve refinements and elaborations rather than fundamental reformulations.

ACKNOWLEDGMENTS

We would like to thank the following people who read and commented on individual chapters: Jim Austin, William K. Balzar, Al Bandura, Dave Barry, Steve Carroll, Greg Dess, Chris Earley, Miriam Erez, John Hollenbeck, Dan Ilgen, Susan E. Jackson, Jane L. Pearce, Bob Pritchard, T. A. Ryan, Dave Schweiger, Pat Smith, and Susan Taylor. We found the comments to be very helpful. Chris Earley and Robert Wood did an excellent job of critiquing the entire manuscript. We also gratefully acknowledge the help of the University of Maryland General Research Board, which provided a research grant to the first author to enable him to work full time on this book during the summer of 1988, and of the Ford Motor Affiliate research fund, which supported the second author. The authors are especially grateful to Dong Ok Chah, who made all the figures for the book, and to both Dong Chah and Dawn Winters, who did most of the work on the references. We also thank Chul Moon, who helped with the references, and Susan Crandall, who developed the research questions in Appendix G.

E. A. Locke
G. P. Latham

CHAPTER

1

GOAL SETTING THEORY:
An Introduction

In this chapter we present the conceptual base of goal setting theory, the history of the concept of goal and related concepts in psychology and management, and the relationship between goal setting theory and other work motivation theories.

GOALS AS REGULATORS OF ACTION

As budding industrial/organizational psychologists in the 1960s, we were interested in the topic of motivation because this concept provided, in principle, a partial answer to the question, Why do some people perform better on work tasks than others? We agreed with the conventional assumption that human action is determined by both cognitive (e.g., knowledge) and motivational factors.

In approaching the study of motivation, however, we were faced with the problem of how to study it. Since motivation is something within the individual, it can only be observed directly within ourselves. While introspective observation is of scientific importance, motivation in other people cannot be observed directly but must be inferred. While inference is epistemologically abhorrent to some psychologists and leads them to reject internal states as explanatory concepts, it is not to us or to cognitive psychologists in general. As Arnold (1960) pointed out, to do away with inference in science, if one hopes to understand the world, is never possible—even in the hard sciences.

Given our belief that it was legitimate to look for explanations of action within the individual, the next question became, What should we look at? There

A portion of this chapter has been taken from E. A. Locke (1978), "The Ubiquity of the Technique of Goal Setting in Theories of and Approaches to Employee Motivation." *Academy of Management Review, 3*, 594–601. Reprinted by permission of the Academy of Management.

1

were many competing concepts in the field: drives, needs, values, attitudes, motives, instincts, and so on. We were greatly influenced here by T. A. Ryan (1970), who was working on his treatise *Intentional Behavior* while the first author was a doctoral student at Cornell between 1960 and 1964. Ryan, who had in turn been influenced by the Wurzburg school, by Lewin (a Gestalt psychologist), and by C. A. Mace (1935), argued that the most immediate and simplest way to explain, from a motivational standpoint, an individual's action in a specific situation was to look at what the person was trying to do in that situation.

Ryan (1970) observed that "to the layman it seems a simple fact that human behavior is affected by conscious purposes, plans, intentions, tasks and the like" (p. 18). At about the same time, Locke observed that "the man in the street, taking for granted the causal efficacy of purposes, uses this term every day to explain goal-directed action. He explains his changing jobs by his consciously held *purpose* to further his career and . . . his son's going to college by his conscious *purpose* to get an education" (1969b, p. 991). In short, goal setting theory had its ultimate roots in the simplest type of introspection, the kind that can be peformed by anyone. Furthermore, also based on introspective evidence, it unapologetically assumes that goals (ideas of future, desired end states) play a causal role in action. Such assumptions were virtually banned from psychology when behaviorism was the dominant American school, but with the cognitive revolution of the 1970s, such views have become respectable and properly so.

Consider now the question posed earlier as to why some people perform better on work tasks than others. Of course, there are many answers to this question. People differ greatly in their ability, their knowledge, and the strategies they use to perform tasks. However, another important but frequently overlooked reason why people perform differently is that they have different goals. They try for different outcomes when they work on a task. We use the term *goal* as the generic concept that encompasses the essential meaning of terms such as intention, task, deadline, purpose, aim, end, and objective. All of these have in common the element that there is something that the person wants to achieve. (The differences between these concepts are explained later in this chapter.)

The concept of goal-directed action, however, has wider significance. Goal directedness is "a cardinal attribute of the behavior of living organisms. . . . It may be observed at all levels of life: in the assimilation of food by an amoeba, in the root growth of a tree or plant, in the stalking of prey by wild animals, and in the activities of a scientist in a laboratory" (Locke, 1969b, p. 991).

Among living organisms there are two categories of goal-directed action (Binswanger, 1986; Locke, 1969b): (a) nonconsciously goal-directed or vegetative actions such as photosynthesis, digestion, and blood circulation; and (b) consciously goal-directed or purposeful actions such as hunting for food and productive work. The former can be found at all levels of life from plants on up, whereas the latter only occur in animals and human beings.

Binswanger (1986) argued that both types of goal-directed action share three common features that justify calling the action goal-directed:

(1) *Self-generation.* The actions of living organisms are fueled by energy sources integral to the organism as a whole, i.e., the energy source is not "put into it" as the motor into a torpedo but is integral to every cell. Furthermore, this

energy is available for many different actions—depending on environmental circumstances and the organism's needs.

(2) *Value-significance.* A living organism can go out of existence; its survival is conditional. To maintain its existence, every living organism must take specific actions to fulfill its needs. If it does not take such actions, it dies. Life maintenance is the ultimate explicit or implicit end of such action and the standard of successful action. Thus all goal-directed action has value significance for the organism. In contrast, the continued existence of inanimate objects does not require them to take any action; they will remain "as is" unless changed or destroyed by external forces. Their movements have no value significance.

(3) *Goal-causation.* There has been much confusion since the time of Aristotle about the cause of goal-directed or teleological action. For example, it has been claimed that final causation, that is, causation by the goal of the action, is a contradiction in terms in that it suggests that the future is the cause of the present. Actually, there are two types of goal causation and neither one involves a contradiction.

In purposeful action, it is the individual's *idea* of and desire for the goal or end that causes action. The idea serves as the efficient cause, but the action is aimed toward a future state.

In nonconsciously goal-directed action (e.g., the actions of the heart and lungs), the principle is the same, but the explanation is more complex. Binswanger (1986) observed that natural selection explains the adaptation of actions to survival in the same way that it explains the adaptation of structural features of the organism to survival:

> For example, my heart will be able to beat tomorrow only if I am alive tomorrow. But I will survive only if my blood is circulated today. The present blood circulation is thus an indirect cause of the future heartbeat. And since blood circulation is the *goal* of the heartbeat, this means that subsequent heartbeats are caused by the survival value of that action's goal, as attained in earlier instances of that very action.... The vegetative actions of living organisms are teleological—i.e., goal directed—because these actions have been naturally selected for their efficacy in attaining ends having survival value for the agent. ... in vegetative action a *past instance* of the "final cause" functions as the efficient cause. (pp. 4–5)

To summarize, *the ultimate biological basis of goal-directed action is the organism's need to sustain its life by taking the actions its nature requires.* In the lower organisms such as plants, these actions are automatic and nonconscious. In people and animals, some of the required actions must be consciously goal-directed. Purposefully goal-directed actions, which are the concern of this theory, are a subcategory of goal-directed action in which goal attainment is caused by consciousness (e.g., by the individual's desire, vision, expectation, anticipation, imagination, aspiration).

The denial of the causal efficacy of consciousness is a fundamental reason why behaviorism failed as a model for explaining human action (Bandura, 1986; Locke, 1977, 1980b). Behaviorists argued that behavior was controlled by past reinforcements, by events that followed previous responses or actions. They never explained, however, the nature of the link between the past and the future. The so-called law of effect or law of reinforcement was at best descriptive, namely: a reinforcer is something that follows a response and somehow makes subsequent responses more likely. When pressed, behaviorists will claim that the connecting events are strictly physiological, but this reductionist argument has never been proven.

The actual explanation of what is called the reinforcement effect is that every consequent that has a subsequent effect becomes an antecedent in that it generates expectations about the future, which in turn regulate action (Bandura, 1977; 1986). To offer as an explanation, as the behaviorists do, that "the behavior changed because it was reinforced" simply cuts off search for the actual causes of the action. For example: Why does a reinforcer reinforce and by what means? What is a reinforcer? What makes it work? Behaviorists have at best a superficial technology of behavior rather than a science of behavior.

The concept of purposeful action applies to both people and animals, although not to the same extent. People share the perceptual level of awareness with the lower animals but unlike them have the power to regulate their own consciousness. Animals are guided by sensory-perceptual mental contents and processes (i.e., desires for specific objects); their time frame is limited to the immediate past, immediate future, and the present. The capacity to grasp the language of even the most "intelligent" species is not even remotely close to the capacity of human children in this respect (see Terrace, 1979).

Human beings have the capacity to go beyond sensory material. They possess the capacity for reason. They can form concepts based on sensory information and go on to form higher-order concepts based on integrations of lower-order concepts (Rand, 1969). They can project thoughts backward in time and forward through millennia; they can detect objects that no human eye can see; they can imagine things being different from what they are; they can project what might be and what ought to be; they can infer and deduce theories and conclusions; they can count and measure from milliseconds to light years; they can make machines and write documents that change the course of history; and they can study themselves. None of this is possible to animals.

Depending on the amount and quality of people's thinking, they may program their minds with few goals or with many, with clear goals or vague ones. They may set goals that either further their happiness and well-being or undermine and negate them. They can also fail to focus their minds and try to exist in an unfocused or drugged stupor. Thus people have a choice as to whether they set goals, and as to what type of goals they set. But since rational, goal-directed action is essential for happiness and survival, we can say that purposeful action is action that is quintessentially human.

Goal setting theory assumes that human action is directed by conscious goals and intentions. However, it does not assume that all human action is under fully conscious control. Furthermore, there are degrees of conscious self-regulation. For example, some actions are not consciously intended, such as sneezing, tics, and mannerisms. There are also actions that reflect a conflict between conscious intent and subconscious desire, as in a person who feels subconscious hostility toward another person but consciously tries to be polite.

An insulting or critical comment may slip out in a conversation. Such actions may be more common among people with severe psychological problems but are certainly not confined to such people.

We agree with Ach (Ryan, 1970) and more recently with Klinger (1987) that a goal or purpose does not have to be in conscious awareness every second during goal-directed action in order for it to regulate action. Klinger noted, for example, that a student pursuing a Ph.D. degree does not think of that goal every minute. Once the student begins the doctoral program, he or she will normally focus on subgoals such as mastering the material in a given course, finding a thesis topic, or developing plans for reaching those subgoals (e.g., how to study; how to carry out the dissertation research). Getting the degree is the integrating goal behind those subgoals and plans. While not always in conscious awareness, the end goal is easily called into awareness—e.g., the student's asking himself or herself, Why am I here? Furthermore, it may go in and out of awareness at different times. For example, a student who is tired and wants to avoid homework one evening may remind himself or herself that studying is necessary to get the degree. Focusing on the end goal all the time would actually be disruptive to performance in many situations, because it would distract the individual from taking the actions needed to reach it, especially actions requiring new learning. Usually, a goal, once accepted and understood, will remain in the background or periphery of consciousness, as a reference point for guiding and giving meaning to subsequent mental and physical actions leading to the goal.

In habitual action, there is some degree of conscious initiation of the action, but once initiated, the action flows with minimal (but not zero) conscious regulation. A case in point would be driving to work using the same route day after day and year after year. After a while, only minimal attention needs to be paid to the action. In fact, more conscious control would be needed to break the pattern (e.g., take a different route) than to maintain it.

In the case of learned skills, aspects of an action sequence (such as dribbling and shooting a basketball) that were originally conscious may become automatized through repeated practice. The individual only needs to focus on the component motions if something goes wrong. Otherwise he or she is free to focus on the performance outcome desired and the means to attain it, such as game strategy.

Goal theory does not assume that every aspect of a consciously intended action is consciously intended. For example, if one has an intent to lift one's arm, the arm normally goes up even though there is no conscious intent to move each muscle involved, nor to send specific electric signals to the brain and back down to the arm. The end result is intended, but the means, which in this case are physiological, involve automatized processes that do not require direct conscious control in order to operate. Control over such actions is indirect.

There are also actions that, although consciously initiated, do not correspond to the intended action or do not achieve the desired goal (Locke, 1968b). This can be due to many reasons, including lack of sufficient knowledge or ability, external blocks to performance, illness, subconscious conflicts (as noted above), or changed circumstances. Such actions could be called goal-directed, but unsuccessful. It is an empirical question as to just what circumstances facilitate or prevent goal-performance correspondence. Many of these circumstances are described in this book.

Nor does goal setting theory assume that every performance outcome is consciously foreseen. For example, a businessperson with a goal to double sales will not necessarily intend or foresee all the consequences of achieving such a goal (e.g., greater strains on company resources and on family life). People can, in crucial respects, foresee and plan for the future, but they are not omniscient.

Caveats aside, goal setting theory does assume that the goals people have on a task influence what they will do and how well they will perform. Goal setting theory specifies the factors that affect goals, and their relationship to action and performance.

THE CONCEPT OF GOAL AND RELATED CONCEPTS

Since we have chosen to use the term *goal* in preference to other related concepts such as intention, task, or purpose, it will be useful to give our reasons and to show the relationship between the term *goal* and these other concepts.

Figure 1–1 shows our classification of these concepts. First, we distinguish between concepts that stress the conscious or psychological element and those that stress the nonconscious or external element, even though in each case the other is implied. Next we classify on the basis of whether the term stresses behavior or

FIGURE 1–1 Classification of Goal-Related Concepts

Type of Concept	Conscious aspect stressed; external aspect implied	Borderline	Nonconscious (external or physiological) aspect stressed; conscious aspect implied
Emphasis on behavior or action	intent, intention	norm	task
Emphasis on the end or aim of action	level of aspiration purpose ↑ ↓	goal (personal goal) aim end objective standard	budget deadline bogey assigned goal quota
Emphasis on the motivational element underlying goals	purpose value motive desire wish attitude		drive need instinct

action itself, the end or aim of the action, or the motivational force underlying the aim or goal.

Starting in the upper-left cell, the term *intention* refers specifically to a psychological state. It may refer to a goal (e.g., I intend to score twenty points in this basketball game), but it more often refers to a determination to take a certain action (e.g., I intend to mail this letter, get dressed, go to work, call my lawyer).[1] The term *norm* is placed between the two top cells because it refers to an appropriate or desirable way of acting shared by a group of people; thus it refers to what the actor feels is appropriate, but it also stresses what other people believe to be acceptable behavior. In the upper right cell, the term *task* refers to a piece of work to be accomplished. The emphasis is on the work (the external), but it is implied that the work is intended to be accomplished by somebody.

Moving to the left cell in the second row, *level of aspiration* refers clearly to the level of performance one is trying to attain on a task (but see Chapter 5 for different meanings of this concept). *Purpose* refers unambiguously to a consciously held goal, but it may also refer to a motive underlying a goal (what is your purpose in trying to buy out company X?); thus the arrow to the bottom cell.

The term *goal* (the aim or end of an action) is placed between the left and right columns because we usually think of goals as something we consciously want to attain, yet the thing we want to attain is usually something outside us (my goal is to increase sales by 10%). The term *personal goal* distinguishes between assigned and actual (operative) goals. Similarly, the term *aim* also suggests a conscious desire (I am aiming for a scholarship) but also indicates there is something out there we are aiming for. The terms *end* and *objective* place emphasis on the end result of our planned efforts or the place where we are going, but there is a strong implication that somebody is deliberately trying for them. In the same way the term *standard* (something set up as a rule to measure or evaluate things) implies an internalized concept of appropriate action but also may refer to an external criterion (company standard—often a minimal level of acceptable performance).

Turning to the next cell to the right, the emphasis is more external. A *budget* specifies a limit on the amount of money to be spent by an individual, department, or organization. The stress is on the "out there," although it is implied that somebody is trying to meet it. Similarly, a *deadline* refers to a time goal, the time by which some task is supposed to be completed. The focus is on the external (time) aspect, but again the deadline is implicitly somebody's deadline. A *bogey* is a somewhat outdated term referring to an amount of production expected of the employees by management. The bogey is out there, but it is expected that the workers will accept it as their personal goal. The terms *assigned goal* and *quota* are similar in meaning.

Turning to the last row, the concepts of *value, motive, desire, wish* and *attitude* can be viewed as concepts that underlie an individual's choice of goal or decision to accept a goal (e.g., I am trying to increase sales by 10% because I want to please the boss, get promoted, prove that I can do the job, see myself as a good

---

[1]Kuhl (1986) defined *intention* as "an activated plan to which an actor has committed herself or himself" (p. 282). If one takes "plan" to mean a behavior or sequence of behaviors and "committed" to mean entailing a determination to act, then his definition is equivalent to ours (which is based on typical dictionary definitions).

person, etc.). Fishbein and Azjen's (1975) model explicitly used attitudes as predictors of intentions. All these terms refer to consciousness (although values and motives can be subconscious as well as conscious). In contrast, terms in the bottom-right cell such as *drive, need,* and *instinct* (disregarding the issue of whether they are all valid concepts) most typically refer to physiologically based energizers that could affect goal choice, although some theories that rely on such concepts would claim that they control action directly (e.g., Hull).

Combined terms such as "task goal" have occasionally been used in the literature, but such terms seem unnecessarily complicated and redundant. Goal or personal goal would do just as well. Some researchers use the term *intentions* to refer to personal goals in order to distinguish them from assigned goals, but the term *personal goal* seems more consistent.

Why, then, did we choose the term *goal* as the key concept in our theory? First, we were interested in how people perform on tasks so we wanted a term that stresses the end result rather than the behavior alone. Thus our preference for goal over intention. The term *task,* used by Ryan (1958), had too much of an external focus for our needs. *Purpose* was a less than desirable choice because of its frequent reference to underlying motives. The term *level of aspiration* was too narrow because it ruled out goals that did not involve a specific level of performance, and yet which we frequently studied (e.g., try to do your best). *Aim* and *end* also seemed a bit narrow, as did *standard*, which focuses mainly on a minimum amount of work. *Objective* was already widely used in the Management by Objectives literature and, for our purposes, put too much focus on end results (e.g., profits) and too little on shorter-range ends that could guide actions. *Budget, deadline,* and *bogey* had narrower meanings and focused mainly on the external. Thus we found that the term *goal* was the most appropriate concept while recognizing that there were many other terms whose meanings were highly similar. Thus it is not surprising that in the literature one often sees many of these concepts used interchangeably.

LEVELS OF EXPLANATION

Explaining human actions by specifying a person's goal does not constitute a full explanation of that action. Explanations, including explanations of human action, exist on different levels (Ryan, 1970). Goal setting theory provides an immediate or first-level explanation of action. Goals and intentions are viewed as immediate precursors and regulators of much, if not most, human action.

A second-level explanation of action would deal with the question, Where do the goals come from? At this level we would try to account for the goals themselves by reference to other motivational concepts as well as to events and conditions outside the person. We would look, for example, at the individual's motives or values (what he or she seeks to gain and/or keep, considers desirable, beneficial, etc.; Locke, 1976). Values are more general, than goals; goals are more situationally and task specific. For example, one might value ambition, whereas one's goal would be to become a company president or a full professor within fifteen years. We could also look at value or personality syndromes that would predispose individuals to set certain types of goals in certain classes of situations.

McClelland (1961) argued that people high in the achievement motive are prone to set moderately challenging goals in situations where they have immediate feedback, and can control the outcome, and where external incentives are not stressed. The Type A personality is characterized as a compulsive goal setter who will try to do more and more in less and less time, especially when threatened by competition from others (see Chapter 9).

Situational factors would include such influences as the demands or requests of authority figures, peer pressure, role models, cultural standards, incentives, rewards, and punishments. An individual's task-specific goals might also be connected to other, longer-range goals such as "I want to double sales this year because I want this to be the biggest company in the U.S. in ten years."

A third-level explanation would attempt to identify the sources and roots of the individual's values, motives, and personality. The only motivational concept broader and more fundamental than that of values is that of needs: the objective requirements of the individual's survival and well-being. For example, the goal to go shopping for specific dinner items could be tied to the value of nutritious food, which would in turn derive (motivationally) from the individual's need for food. As Nuttin (1984) observed, "a subject's motivational direction toward a specific object [goal] should be conceived as the concretization or canalization of a more general need" (p. 67).

The concept of needs does not account for individual differences, however, because people have the same basic needs (everyone needs food, water, sleep, self-esteem, etc.) But the concept of needs is necessary to explain why people act at all, and to explain why certain broad categories of action (e.g., eating) are universal.

One assumption of this division into levels is that the higher-level factors (second and third levels) affect action through the lower levels—i.e., that needs affect action through their effect on values and values through their effect on goals (Locke & Henne, 1986). This assumption has seldom been tested, and it may not even be true as stated. Subconscious values may affect action without the individual's having conscious awareness of any goals based on such values. Our assumption appears somewhat plausible, however, if only because immediate level theories, focusing on task-specific motives and perceptions (e.g., goal setting theory, turnover intention theory, and social-cognitive theory) seem to have been far more successful in accounting for human action than the more general value theories such as McClelland's "need" achievement theory (Locke & Henne, 1986).

THE DOMAIN OF GOAL SETTING THEORY

Goal setting theory, as developed in this book, is confined mainly to the first level of explanation and goes somewhat into the second. At the first level we ask the fundamental question, What is the relationship between goals and action, or more specifically, goals and task performance? And what factors affect this relationship? Cognitive factors, especially feedback and expectancy/self-efficacy and, to an increasing degree, task strategies, play a major role in the theory (see Chapters 3, 4 and 8). At the second level we look at some of the factors that may affect goal choice and goal commitment, and also briefly at the relation of goal choice to personality (see Chapters 5 and 9).

As noted earlier, the reason for developing the theory was our interest in understanding work motivation. We wanted to explain why some people worked harder than others or performed better than others on a task independently of their ability and knowledge. The most direct way to explain it seemed to be to look at the goals people were trying to attain. From there we looked at how such factors as feedback, participation, commitment, and incentives combined or interacted with goals (see Chapters 6, 7, and 8).

We could, of course, have made our theory "look better" by making predictions regarding only direction rather than level of performance. For example, we could have predicted that people with an intention to go to work are more likely to go there rather than to the ball game. This procedure would certainly have produced very good results (e.g., see Locke, Bryan, & Kendall, 1968, experiments 3, 4 and 5), but it would not have explained differences in performance on the job. (Intention-behavior theories are now well developed in social psychology, as we shall see below.)

COGNITION AND MOTIVATION

At all levels of explanation, cognitive factors play a role in explaining both the choice of action and its degree of success. For example, goals, if chosen by people themselves, are based on such factors as their beliefs about what they can achieve, their recollections of past performance, their beliefs about consequences, and their judgments of what is appropriate to the situation (see Chapter 5). And their degree of success will depend on knowing if they are, in fact, performing in line with the goals (feedback) and their knowledge of appropriate task strategies. At the second level, value choice would depend on the individual's conscious or subconscious philosophy (e.g., What is the good? What values should a person have?) At the third level, cognition is relevant to needs in that how people go about satisfying their needs depends on whether they correctly identify their needs, on their beliefs about what actions will satisfy them, and again on their philosophical premises. .

Although cognition and motivation can be separated by abstraction for the purpose of scientific study, in reality they are virtually never separate. All knowledge or beliefs are appraised automatically by the subconscious and can be appraised consciously (by choice) as well (e.g., Is this fact good for me or bad for me or irrelevant?) This is how knowledge is translated into action. On the other side of the same coin, all motivation is based on conscious or subconscious cognitive input (e.g., "I want high-fiber cereal because it is good for my health"). Most action is guided cognitively ("What is the best way to attain this goal?") as well as motivationally.

Another aspect of cognition, alluded to earlier, must be mentioned here, and that is *volition*. We view volition as involving the choice to raise one's level of cognitive focus from the perceptual level to the conceptual level. To quote Rand (1964, pp. 20–21):

> Man's sense organs function automatically; man's brain integrates his sense data into percepts automatically; but the process of integrating percepts into concepts—the process of abstraction and of concept-information—is *not* automatic.
> The process of concept-formation does not consist merely of grasping a few

simple abstractions. . . . It is not a passive state of registering random impressions. It is an actively sustained process of identifying one's impressions in conceptual terms, of integrating every event and every observation into a conceptual context, of grasping relationships, differences, similarities in one's perceptual material and of abstracting them into new concepts, of drawing inferences, of making deductions, of reaching conclusions, of asking new questions and discovering new answers and expanding one's knowledge into an ever-growing sum. The faculty that directs this process . . . is: reason. The process is *thinking*.

   Reason is the faculty that identifies, and integrates the material provided by man's senses. It is a faculty that man has to exercise *by choice*. Thinking is not an automatic function. In any hour and issue of his life, man is free to think or to evade that effort. . . . The act of focusing one's consciousness is volitional. Man can focus his mind to a full, active, purposefully directed awareness of reality—or he can unfocus it and let himself drift in a semi-conscious daze, merely reacting to any chance stimulus of the immediate moment, at the mercy of his undirected sensory-perceptual mechanism and of any random, associational connections it might happen to make.

In terms of its connection to action, the nature of an individual's thinking, as noted earlier, will affect whether he or she sets specific or vague goals, long-range or short-range goals, consistent or contradictory goals, personally meaningful or meaningless goals, and realistic or unrealistic goals. It will also affect the degree of commitment to goals and the degree to which rational plans are developed for achieving them. Thinking is also pertinent after goals have been formulated. The individual also has to *choose* to take action in accordance with each chosen goal by keeping in focal awareness what is to be achieved, the means needed to achieve it, and the reasons for or benefits of such action.

GOAL SETTING THEORY: A BRIEF HISTORY

As we have noted, the most direct precursor of and direct influence on goal setting theory was the work of T. A. Ryan (1970). But goal setting theory has precursors that go back at least to the turn of the century. Broadly, there are two strands of influence, one connecting the theory to the academic world and the other to the world of business. More specifically, the strands tie into experimental psychology and management theory. These strands of influence are shown in Figure 1–2. This dual heritage, while only coincidental, seems especially appropriate for a theory of work motivation. It is also fortunate, especially in retrospect, that one of the present authors is especially comfortable with laboratory experiments and theorizing while the other author is especially comfortable with field experiments and applying psychological theories to work organizations.

Academic Precursors

The academic strand began with the Wurzburg school in Germany in the early 1900s, directed by O. Kulpe (see Ryan, 1970, for an overview). He and his colleagues were interested in the study of mental processes. They used the term *task* to refer to that which the subject was asked to do. One member of the school, Ach, used the term *determining tendency* to describe the fact, identified by Watt, that a task assigned earlier could affect later action without the individual's being

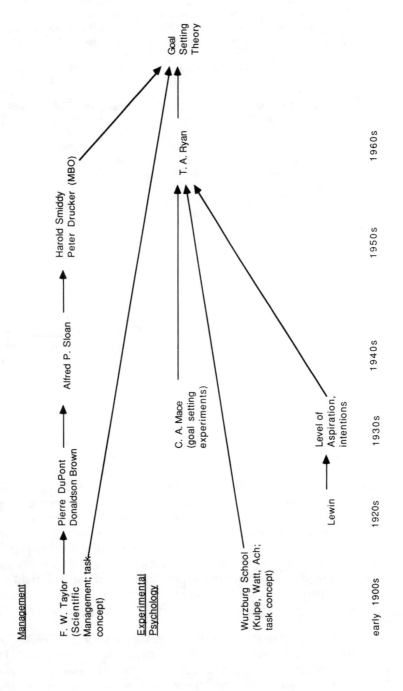

FIGURE 1–2 Historical Precursors of Goal Setting Theory

consciously aware of the task at the time of action. For example, if the task was "to add" when presented with the numbers "4 and 6," the subjects will say "10" without conscious deliberation. Ryan incorporated the concept of determining tendency into his 1970 model (Figure 2–1, p. 25) to describe the fact that intentions may affect action even when separated in time from the relevant action.

It is doubtful whether Ach was correct in asserting that there was no awareness at all of the intent at the time of action. The individual must have retained the task in memory or else could not have responded appropriately to the numbers 4 and 6. The concept of determining tendency is most logically interpreted as a memory of a previously assigned task held, perhaps, in peripheral awareness.

Another contribution of Ach (and his student Hillgruber) was the formulation of the "difficulty law of motivation," which stated that volitional effort increased as the difficulty of a task or action increased (Ach, 1935).[2] This law is clearly the precursor of the "goal difficulty function" presented in Chapter 2.

Lewin, a Gestalt psychologist, criticized some of Ach's work on the grounds that the effect of the task on performance was even stronger than Ach had acknowledged. Ach had pitted the laws of association (e.g., repetition) in word association experiments against the effect of the task.

Lewin also seems to have introduced the specific term *intention* to the field. His work gave it respectability as a psychological concept. Lewin (1961) argued that an intention was a quasi-need and was associated with a state of tension that was maintained until reduced by the performance or completion of the intended activity or a substitute activity. Lewin's work led to experiments on the resumption of interrupted tasks (the Ovsiankina effect), on the recall of interrupted tasks (the Zeigarnik effect), to voluminous studies of the effect of intention on learning (intentional vs. incidental learning), to studies of "mental set," and—most importantly for goal setting theory—to studies of level of aspiration (i.e., goal setting; Ryan, 1970). Unlike goal setting theory, however, level-of-aspiration research focused almost exclusively on the determinants rather than the effects of level of aspiration. (This work is reviewed along with the more recent work on determinants of goals in Chapters 5 and 9.) Lewin's work, including his later studies of group decision making, influenced the studies of goal setting and participation in factory settings by French and his colleagues at both the Harwood Manufacturing Company and the General Electric Company (e.g., Coch & French, 1948; French, Kay, & Meyer, 1966).

Another academic influence on our work was the series of experiments conducted in England by Mace (1935). It is not clear what had influenced Mace to do this research, but so far as we know, his were the earliest experimental studies ever done of goal setting as an independent variable. He was the first to compare the effects of specific, challenging goals with goals such as "do your best," and to compare the effects of goals differing in level of difficulty. The results of one of his most successful experiments were reported in Ryan and Smith's (1954) early industrial psychology textbook, which the present first author was assigned to read as a graduate student. Mace also suggested that task liking and enjoyment

---

[2]The authors are indebted to Dr. Uwe Kleinbeck of the University of Wuppertal for making them aware of this law and translating it into English.

were affected by degree of success in relation to performance goals or standards. Finally, he suggested that incentives such as praise, criticism, feedback, supervision, and assigned standards affected performance through their effects on the individual's personal goals. While Mace did not perform any statistical tests on his experimental data, his work was certainly an important impetus to goal setting theory. The first known study to statistically show a relationship between goals and subsequent performance was that by Bayton (1943).

Applied Precursors

The strand of thought stemming from the field of management started with Frederick W. Taylor, the father of Scientific Management. He published his major work, the *Principles of Scientific Management,* in 1911, which was about the same time that the Wurzburg school was flourishing. This book focused on how to select, train, and motivate shop workers. For Taylor, the two key motivational devices were the task and the bonus. Taylor wrote:

> Perhaps the most important law belonging to this class, in its relation to scientific management, is the effect which the task idea has upon the efficiency of the workman. This, in fact, has become such an important element of the mechanism of scientific management, that by a great number of people scientific management has come to be known as "task management."
>
> There is absolutely nothing new in the task idea. Each one of us will remember that in his own case this idea was applied with good results in his schoolboy days. No efficient teacher would think of giving a class of students an indefinite lesson to learn. Each day a definite, clear-cut task is set by the teacher before each scholar, stating that he must learn just so much of the subject; and it is only by this means that proper, systematic progress can be made by the students. The average boy would go very slowly if, instead of being given a task, he were told to do as much as he could . . . the average workman will work with the greatest satisfaction, both to himself and to his employer, when he is given each day a definite task which he is to perform in a given time, and which constitutes a proper day's work for a good workman. This furnishes the workman with a clear-cut standard, by which he can throughout the day measure his own progress, and the accomplishment of which affords him the greatest satisfaction. (Taylor, 1967 edition, pp. 120–22)

Under Taylor's system, a large bonus was paid if the worker succeeded in attaining his assigned task. While Taylor's classic book was published not long after many of the Wurzburg school publications, there is no evidence that Taylor had ever heard of them. Thus his use of the same key concept (task), while remarkable, seems coincidental.

Taylor's ideas, through a circuitous route, played a role in the emergence of Management by Objectives, or MBO (Greenwood, 1981; Locke, 1982a; Wren, 1987). MBO is a system of motivating and integrating the efforts of business managers by setting goals for the organization as a whole and then cascading these objectives down through each management level, so that goal attainment at each level helps attain goals at the next-highest level and ultimately the goals of the whole firm (Carroll & Tosi, 1973). Greenwood (1981) and Wren (1987) outlined the history of MBO as follows: Pierre DuPont adapted some of Taylor's ideas on accounting and cost control (another aspect of his theory of

Scientific Management) at the DuPont Power Company. For example, ROI (return on investment) was developed as a measure of organizational performance. One of DuPont's subordinates, Donaldson Brown, further adapted this concept so that it could be used to evaluate the performance of various departments or divisions within the DuPont Company. When Pierre DuPont later became head of General Motors, he took Brown with him and hired Alfred P. Sloan, who eventually succeeded him as president of GM. Sloan institutionalized the ROI concept as a means of maintaining some centralized control when he decentralized GM. It appears that Sloan was the first executive to actually use MBO to motivate and evaluate managers, although he did not call it by that name. Sloan claimed that "the guiding principle was to make our standard [goals] difficult to achieve, but possible to attain, which I believe is the most effective way of capitalizing on the initiative, resourcefulness, and capabilities of operating personnel" (cited in Odiorne, 1978, p. 15). This claim turned out to foreshadow, in part, the empirical findings of goal setting research that emerged in our own work.

The name and formal concept of MBO came some years later (Greenwood, 1981). Harold Smiddy had been a partner in the consulting firm of Booz, Allen and Hamilton and while there had learned of the concept of the "manager's letter." Each manager was required to submit to his superior each month a list of the goals he planned to achieve and the means he would use to achieve them. In 1948 Smiddy joined the General Electric Company and introduced the idea of the manager's letter there. *His* outside consultant, Peter Drucker (later to become the famous writer on management), convinced him to develop it into a management philosophy that Drucker named Management by Objectives (Drucker, 1954). Drucker apparently knew about Sloan's prior use of MBO at GM (Greenwood, 1981; Odiorne, 1978), even though Sloan did not use the term or develop MBO into a philosophy of management. MBO can be viewed as goal setting applied to the macro or organizational level.

GOAL SETTING IN CONTEMPORARY
WORK MOTIVATION THEORY

Aside from being a motivation theory in its own right, the concept of goal setting has been incorporated sooner or later, explicitly or implicitly, into a number of work motivation theories. Consider, for example, Human Relations theory, which stresses an approach to motivating employees based on cohesive work groups, considerate supervision, two-way communication, and employee participation in decision making. Especially in its early years, Human Relations theories denigrated top-down styles of leadership, as well as incentives as a means of motivating employees to accept goals (e.g., Whyte, 1955).

Eventually, Human Relations theory, possibly as a result, in part, of Lewin's influence, incorporated both goal setting and money into its body of techniques, even if not into its theory, by combining them with participation. In the famous Harwood studies (Marrow, Bowers, & Seashore, 1967), goal setting in the form of work standards, plus incentives and participation, were all used.

Today Human Relations advocates more openly concede the importance of goals and monetary incentives. A well-known book on the Scanlon Plan, a participative, Human Relations-oriented plan that entails the use of economic rewards to motivate employees, asserts that " . . . standards are not inconsistent with a Scanlon Plan if they are used as a tool for meeting the cost and not for restrictive control. Everyone needs a benchmark and a set of criteria to evaluate himself" (Frost, Wakeley, & Ruh, 1974, p. 121).

Similarly, Likert, while emphasizing the importance of managers acting supportively toward subordinates, acknowledges that "superiors in System 4 organizations . . . should have high performance aspirations, but this is not enough. Every *member* should have high performance aspirations as well" (Likert, 1967, p. 51). This emphasis is taken seriously in practice, as demonstrated in a report of the application of System 4 at GM's Lakewood assembly plant (Dowling, 1975). Management set explicit goals for such areas as production, scrap, grievances, and labor costs and then had employees set their own goals on the basis of higher-management input and as well as their own knowledge of the operation. With respect to feedback concerning goal accomplishment, "employees at Lakewood were given more information about how they were doing and were given it more frequently than ever before" (p. 36).

Organizational development (OD), an outgrowth of the Human Relations movement, considers MBO to be an OD technique (French & Bell, 1984) because, in theory, goals are to be set participatively when MBO is used. Another OD technique, survey feedback, typically involves goal setting in practice in that its aim is to identify specific problem areas in the organization by means of attitude surveys and then take specific steps to eliminate those problems.

Goal setting has also been incorporated into another major work motivation theory: VIE, or valence-instrumentality-expectancy theory. The major premise of VIE theory is that in making choices, an individual mentally sums the expected pleasures to be derived from each possible alternative, subtracts the sum of the expected pains, and chooses the alternative with the highest positive net value. VIE theory did not recognize the importance of goal setting in its original, organizational psychology version (Vroom, 1964), probably due to VIE theory's hedonistic emphasis. Its major focus was on the way in which people's beliefs and feelings allegedly lead them to choose a particular course of action.

The hedonistic and other assumptions of VIE theory have been criticized in detail elsewhere (Locke, 1975). Suffice it to say that some revised models have put less stress on hedonism and, more pertinent to the present discussion, have expanded VIE theory to include an explicit goal setting stage (Campbell, Dunnette, Lawler, & Weick, 1970). One possible way to integrate some of the VIE constructs with goal setting is to view values and expectancies as factors that influence the goals an individual chooses or accepts while viewing goals themselves as the more direct determinants of action (Hollenbeck & Klein, 1987; see also Chapter 5 in this volume). As we shall see in Chapter 3, however, expectancies also influence performance directly.

Two other work motivation theories have never shown any explicit theoretical recognition of the importance of goal setting to employee motivation. Both schools, however, have recognized its importance implicitly, since when these theories are put into practice, goal setting is virtually always involved.

The Cognitive Growth school, associated mainly with Herzberg and to an extent Maslow (1954), promulgated in the early 1960s, emphasized people's psychological or growth needs (e.g., knowing more, integrating one's knowledge, being creative, being effective in ambiguity, developing a genuine sense of self-worth, etc.). It was asserted that these needs could best be satisfied through one's work. According to Herzberg, jobs that did not allow for such growth needed to be enriched by providing the employee with increased responsibility and autonomy.

Herzberg never mentioned goal setting as an element of job enrichment. In fact, the idea was explicitly rejected by him (Herzberg, 1975, pp. 98–99) and his followers (Ford, 1969, p. 28). This may have been due to its association with Scientific Management, whose emphasis on extreme division of labor Herzberg (1966) disparaged. In practice, goal setting was unwittingly incorporated into the procedure of job enrichment under the name of feedback. The explicit purpose of feedback in job enrichment programs is to increase the employee's feeling of achievement and to provide him or her with a sense of personal responsibility for the work. Two obvious questions that arise in this context are, How does an employee know when he or she has achieved something? and How does that employee know when he or she has adequately or successfully fulfilled his or her responsibility? The answer must be, When the feedback is compared, by management or by the employee, with some standard of appropriate performance, i.e., when the feedback is appraised in terms of some goal. Thus whenever management gives its employees feedback, one can be confident that some performance standard is involved, implicitly if not explicitly.

Numerous studies have shown that feedback in itself does not have the power to motivate performance directly (Annett, 1969; Latham, Mitchell, & Dossett, 1978; Locke, Cartledge, & Koeppel, 1968). It has been argued that feedback motivates action only indirectly, through its relationship to goal setting. For example, if the feedback shows that one's prior performance was below the desired standard, one can increase one's subsequent effort, or change one's tactics, in order to meet the standard in the future (for details, see Chapter 8 of this volume).

In practice, job enrichment has involved so many different types of job changes, often within the same study, that isolating specific effects of the different elements is virtually impossible (Locke, 1975). Noticeable progress in this direction was made in a simulated field study by Umstot, Bell, and Mitchell (1976). They found that job enrichment procedures from which goal setting elements had been specifically deleted led to increased job satisfaction but failed to improve productivity. In contrast, assigning the employees explicit, challenging goals accompanied by feedback led to higher productivity even in the absence of job enrichment. When goal setting and job enrichment were combined, both productivity and satisfaction improved. In some studies alleged to involve job enrichment, employee goal setting has been advocated explicitly (Walters, 1975).

It is probable, therefore, that increases in the quantity or quality of productivity found in job enrichment studies (Ford, 1969; Lawler, 1970) are at least partially attributable to an implicit goal setting element. Locke, Sirota, and Wolfson (1976), in their field study of job enrichment, attributed some of the performance improvement found to goals and feedback. They also suggested that productivity might increase under such programs as a result of the elimination of unnecessary tasks or of a more efficient use of labor. This could occur when employees are allowed to work where they are needed rather than where they are arbitrarily assigned by a supervisor (see also Locke, Feren, McCaleb, Shaw, & Denny, 1980).

If the incorporation of goal setting has been subtle among advocates of the Cognitive Growth school, it is much more obvious among advocates of a more recent school, Organizational Behavior Modification (OBM), which became popular in the 1970s as a method of motivating employees. The OBM technique of goal smuggling consists of openly advocating the use of "performance standards," a term used as a synonym for goal, accompanied by feedback and possibly praise and/or money, but describing these procedures at the theoretical level in behavioristic language (Locke, 1977). Thus performance standards or goals become "controlling stimuli" or "discriminative stimuli," and feedback, praise, and money become "reinforcers" or "conditioned reinforcers" (Fellener & Sulzer-Azaroff, 1984; Luthans & Krietner, 1975).

These labels add nothing to our understanding of how or why goal setting works. Worse, they are misleading and, in many cases, incorrect. Consider first the claim that the goal is a stimulus or discriminative stimulus. Even if the stimulus referred to here is an assigned goal, such a stimulus only affects action if the individual commits himself or herself to that goal. *Thus the efficient cause of goal-directed action is internal, not external.* A goal is an idea. Furthermore, some goals are set by the individual without any external prod (Brief & Hollenbeck, 1985).

Bandura (1986) has shown that even the behaviorist emphasis on consequents is misleading at best and mistaken at worst. Reinforcement does not affect behavior unless individuals believe that they can make the requisite response. Furthermore, making such a response presupposes that the individual knows what response to make (Levine, 1971) and wants the rewards that it brings (Dulany, 1968). Finally, goals can affect behavior in a single trial *before* any behavior has been reinforced (Locke, 1982b).

Similarly, consider the claim that feedback is a reinforcer for goal-directed activity. First, feedback is simply information. How one responds to information depends on if and how it is understood and appraised (Arnold, 1960). Feedback may lead to a negative appraisal, an appraisal of indifference, or a positive appraisal depending on the individual's values and the circumstances. In turn such appraisals can lead to many different responses, including no change in effort, greater effort, reduced effort, modified strategies, change of tasks, leaving the situation, aggression, or various defensive maneuvers. Calling feedback a reinforcer simply obscures the decision process that follows it and discourages the search for the actual mechanisms by which it does affect subsequent action (Locke, 1977, 1980a, 1980c). In Chapter 8 we present a detailed analysis of studies showing the relationship between goals and feedback.

Behavior modification advocates argue that feedback effects vary with the circumstances due to differences in individuals' "reinforcement history." Such a claim, like the concept of instinct, can "explain" everything and therefore nothing.

Other OBM advocates have claimed that since goal setting theory refers to internal mental states, it is untestable and therefore unscientific unless rephrased in terms of "objective," that is, external concepts. Since numerous studies show that goals and goal commitment can be measured (see the following chapters) and can be related to actual performance, their claim is invalid.

As noted earlier, all the sciences, including physics, chemistry, and biology, depend on inferences that go beyond what can be observed directly. Trying to pretend otherwise simply leads to the distortion of scientific concepts (Locke, 1969b, 1972); this is especially true in psychology where all the key concepts refer to mental states. Mental states and processes, as noted earlier, can be directly observed in oneself. They need only be inferred in other people. The emergence of cognitive psychology as the dominant paradigm in the field over the past ten to fifteen years, and the simultaneous decline of the influence of behaviorism in all subfields of psychology, testify to an overwhelming consensus, supported by introspection, logic, and empirical findings (e.g., see Bandura, 1986) in favor of the use of such inference.

As the influence of behaviorism has declined, a neo-behaviorist theory is emerging to take its place. It is called control theory and can be viewed as a combination or integration of behaviorism, machine-computer theory (cybernetics), goal setting theory, and, by implication, drive-reduction theory. It is derived most directly from Miller, Galanter, and Pribram's TOTE model (1960). The major concepts of control theory have been presented by Campion and Lord (1982), Carver and Scheier (1982), Hyland (1988), Lord and Hanges (1987), Powers (1973), and others. In brief, the theory asserts that there is *input* (a stimulus), which is detected by a *sensor*. This is fed into a *comparator*, which compares the input with a *reference standard*. If there is a deviation (also called a "disturbance"), a *signal* is sent to an *effector*, which generates modified *output* (a response). This output becomes the input for the next cycle. In goal theory language, the input is feedback from previous performance, the reference signal is the goal, the comparator is the individual's conscious judgment, and the effector or response is his or her subsequent action which works to reduce the discrepancy between goal and performance.

While control theory acknowledges the importance of goal setting, there are serious, if not irredeemable, flaws in the model. First, observe that the major "motive" for action under control theory is to remove disturbances or discrepancies between the goal and the input (feedback). The natural state of the organism is seen to be one of motionlessness or rest. This is true of machines, but not of living organisms which are naturally active. It is, in effect, a mechanistic version of long discredited drive-reduction theory (Cofer & Appley, 1967). Nuttin (1984) has observed that in this aspect, control theory fundamentally misstates the actual source of motivation: "The behavioral process . . . does not begin with a 'test' of the discrepancy between the standard and the actual states of affairs. Instead, it begins with a preliminary and fundamental operation, namely the construction of the standard itself, which, as a goal, is at the origin of the action and directs its further course" (p. 145). Similarly, Bandura (in press) noted that *goal setting is first and foremost a discrepancy creating process.* Control theory begins in the middle rather than at the beginning of the motivational sequence. To quote Bandura (in press):

Human self-motivation relies on both *discrepancy production* and *discrepancy reduction*. It requires *feedforward* control as well as *feedback* control. People initially motivate themselves through feedforward control by setting themselves valued challenging standards that create a state of disequilibrium and then mobilizing their effort on the basis of anticipatory estimation of what it would take to reach them. After people attain the standard they have been pursuing, they generally set a higher standard for themselves. The adoption of further challenges creates new motivating discrepancies to be mastered. Similarly, surpassing a standard is more likely to raise aspiration than to lower subsequent performance to conform to the surpassed standard. Self-motivation thus involves a dual cyclic process of disequilibrating discrepancy production followed by equilibrating discrepancy reduction. (p. 23 of preprint)

Figure 1–3 illustrates how little of the motivational process control theory, in its "core" version, incorporates.

The above is important because if discrepancy reduction is the major motive, as implied by control theory, then the most logical thing for an individual to do would simply be to adapt his or her goal to the input. This would guarantee that there would be no disturbance or discrepancy. Machines, of course, cannot do this because the standard has been fixed by people at a certain level (as in setting a thermostat). But people can and do change standards that diverge from present performance. If the individual's major motive were to remove disturbances, people would never do this. Control theorists argue that lower-level goals are actually caused by goals at a higher level in the individual's goal hierarchy (Carver & Scheier, 1982). But this only pushes the problem back a step. Why should people set higher-level goals if they only want to reduce tension? But in reality, people do set goals and then act to attain them; they do not focus primarily on eliminating disturbances. Removal of discrepancies and any associated tension is a *correlate* of goal-directed action, not its cause. The causal sequence begins with setting the goal, not with removing deviations from it.

At a fundamental level, discrepancy reduction theories such as control theory are inadequate because if people consistently acted in accordance with them by trying to eliminate all disturbances, they would all commit suicide— because it would be the only way to totally eliminate tension. If people chose instead to stay alive but set no goals, they would soon die anyway. By the time they were forced into action by desperate, unremitting hunger pangs, it would be too late to grow and process the food they would need to survive.

In their major work, Carver and Scheier (1981) denied that discrepancy reduction is motivated by a desire to reduce a drive or state of tension. But their own explanation as to why people act to reduce discrepancies is quite puzzling. "The shift [of action in the direction of the goal or standard] is a natural consequence of the engagement of a discrepancy-reducing feedback loop" (p. 145). This statement, of course, explains nothing. Why is discrepancy reduction a "natural consequence"? According to goal theory, *both* discrepancy creation *and* discrepancy reduction occur for the same reason: because people need and desire to attain goals. Such actions are required for their survival, happiness, and well-being.

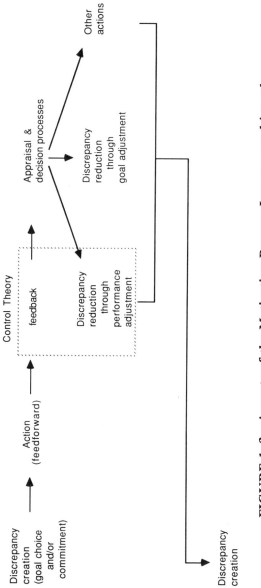

FIGURE 1–3 **Aspects of the Motivation Process Incorporated into the "Core Version" of Control Theory**

A second problem with control theory is its very use of a machine as a metaphor. The problem with such a metaphor is that it cannot be taken too literally or it becomes highly misleading (e.g., see Sandelands, Glynn, & Larson, 1988). For example, people do not operate within the deterministic, closed-loop system that control theory suggests. In response to negative feedback, for example, people can try harder or less hard. They can focus on the cause and perhaps change their strategy. They can also lower the goal to match their performance; in some cases they may raise their goal. Furthermore, they can reinterpret the discrepancy as unimportant and ignore it or can even totally deny it. They can also question the accuracy of the feedback. They can go outside the system (by leaving the situation). They can attack the person they hold responsible for the discrepancy. They can become paralyzed by self-doubt and fear and do nothing. They can drink liquor to blot out the pain. In short, they can do any number of things other than respond in machinelike fashion. Furthermore, people can feel varying degrees of satisfaction and dissatisfaction, develop varying degrees of commitment to goals, and assess their confidence in being able to reach them (Bandura, 1986). These emotions, decisions, and estimates affect what new goals they will set and how they will respond to feedback indicative of deviations from the goal (Bandura, 1988). Control theory, insofar as it stresses a mechanistic model, simply has no place for these alternatives, which basically means that it has no place for consciousness. Insofar as this is the case, the theory must fail for the same reason behaviorism failed. Without studying and measuring psychological processes, one cannot explain human action.

One might ask why control theory could not be expanded so as to accommodate the ideas and processes noted above. Attempts have been made to do this, but when it is done, the machine language may be still retained. Hyland (1988), for example, described the effects of goal importance or commitment in terms of "error sensitivity," which is represented diagrammatically by a box called an "amplifier." Expectations and memory are represented as "symbolic control loops." Decision making is done not by a person but by a "selector." What is the benefit of translating relatively clear and well-accepted concepts that apply to human beings into computer language that is virtually incomprehensible when used to describe human cognition? The greater the number of concepts referring to states or actions of consciousness that are relabeled in terms of machine language, the more implausible and incomprehensible the whole enterprise becomes. Nuttin (1984, p. 148) wrote on this: "When behavioral phenomena are translated into cybernetic and computer language, their motivational aspect is lost in the process. This occurs because motivation is foreign to all machines."

On the other hand, if additional concepts are brought into control theory and not all relabeled in machine language (e.g., Lord & Hanges, 1987), then control theory loses its distinctive character as a machine metaphor and becomes superfluous—that is, a conglomeration of ideas borrowed from *other* theories. And if control theory does not make the needed changes and expansions, it is inadequate to account for human action. Control theory, therefore, seems to be caught in a triple bind from which there is no escape. If it stays strictly mechanistic, it does not work. If it uses mechanistic language to relabel concepts referring to consciousness, it is incomprehensible. And if it uses nonmechanistic concepts, it is unoriginal. It has been argued that control theory is useful because it provides a general model into which numerous other theories can be integrated (Hyland, 1988). However, a general model that is inadequate in itself cannot successfully provide an account of the phenomena of other theories.

In their book, Carver and Scheier (1981) examined the effect of individual differences in degree of internal focus versus external focus in action. While this presentation is more plausible than the mechanistic versions of control theory, most of it actually has little to do with control theory as it relates to goal setting. For example, they discuss how expectancies and self-focus affect performance but do not examine the goal-expectancy literature (as we do in Chapter 3). And some of their conclusions (such as that self-efficacy does not affect performance directly) contradict actual research findings. Only one actual goal setting study (not in Carver and Scheier's book) has used the self-focus measure. Hollenbeck and Williams (1987) found that self-focus only affected performance as part of a triple interaction in which ability was not controlled. Thus it remains to be seen how useful the measure is, either as a moderator or as a mediator of goal setting effectiveness.

There is also a conceptual problem with the prediction that the relation between goals and performance will be higher among those high in self-focus than those low in self-focus. Goal attainment requires, over and above any internal focus, an *external* focus; most goals refer to something one wants to achieve in the external world. Thus the individual must monitor external feedback that shows progress in relation to the goal in order to make progress toward it. Individuals might focus internally as well (a) to remind themselves of what the goal is—though this can also be done externally, as on a feedback chart; (b) to retain commitment by reminding themselves of why the goal is important; and (c) to assess self-efficacy. Furthermore, depending on what is focused on, (e.g., self-encouraging thoughts or self-doubt), an internal focus could either raise or lower goal-relevant effort. In sum, the relation between where one is focused and goal-relevant performance seems intuitively far more complex than is recognized by the cognitive version of control theory.

Finally, some have argued that control theory is original because it deals with the issue of goal change (e.g., Campion & Lord, 1982). However, goal change was actually studied first by level-of-aspiration researchers in the 1930s and 1940s, so control theory can make no claim of originality here. Nor can a mechanistic model hope to deal adequately with issues involving human choice as noted above.

In sum, the present authors do not see what control theory has added to our understanding of the process of goal setting; all it has done is to restate a very limited aspect of goal theory in another language, just as was done by behavior mod advocates. Worse, control theory, in its purest form, actually obscures understanding by ignoring or inappropriately relabeling crucial psychological processes that are involved in goal-directed action (these will be discussed in subsequent chapters).

In contrast to behavior modification and control theory, Bandura's (1986) social-cognitive theory is highly compatible with goal setting theory. It not only includes goal setting as part of its content but adds two important dimensions to goal theory. The first is role modeling, which Bandura has shown to be an important social influence on action. Studies have shown that modeling has significant effects on goal choice and goal commitment (see Chapters 5 and 6).

The second added dimension is self-efficacy. Though related in meaning to expectancy (from valence-instrumentality-expectancy theory), self-efficacy has a wider meaning (see Chapter 3) and is measured somewhat differently from the way expectancy is usually measured. Self-efficacy has been found to play multiple roles in goal setting theory. It affects goal choice, goal commitment, and response to feedback, and it also has a direct effect on performance. Social-cognitive theory is also highly compatible with the metatheoretical approach of goal setting theory; both stress the importance of cognitive self-regulation.

Some mention should be made of two related theories having some similarity to goal setting literature in the area of social psychology. These are the theories of "reasoned action" and of "planned behavior" put forth by Ajzen (1987), Ajzen and Fishbein (1980), and Fishbein and Ajzen (1975). These models are mainly concerned with predicting behaviors such as purchasing coffee or using birth-control pills from measured intentions to take those actions. Intentions in turn are predicted by attitudes toward the action and subjective norms. Ajzen (1987) added perceived behavioral control to his model.

There are clearly strong parallels between such theories and goal setting theory. As we noted earlier, intentions are similar in meaning to goals. Attitudes, in the form of valences, and norms are integrated into goal setting theory in several places (see Chapters 5 and 6). And perceived control is similar in meaning to self-efficacy and plays a similar role in both theories. Reviews of the literature on these models show them to have substantial validity (Ajzen, 1987; Sheppard, Hartwick, & Warshaw, 1988).

The term *goal* is distinguished from that of intention by Sheppard, Hartwick, and Warshaw (1988) by using *goal* to refer to the desire to attain outcomes that require overcoming obstacles (such as getting enough money to implement the desire to buy a car). The term *intention* is used if there are no substantial obstacles, such as in the case of the intention to buy coffee. Our use of the term *goal*, however, is different. We use it to refer to desired outcomes in terms of level of performance to be attained on a task rather than to the desire to take a specific action. The two types of theories are therefore complementary in that they pertain to different domains but use similar approaches. Goal setting theory, as we shall see, is also more elaborated and is based on a more extensive research base than the intention theories.

Another modern movement focused on the understanding of volitional and goal-directed action is centered in West Germany; this interest is perhaps not a coincidence, since, as already noted, the academic roots of goal setting trace back to Wurzburg (Figure 1–2). Researchers such as U. Kleinbeck, H. Heckausen, J. Kuhl, and P. Gollwitzer have all written about and done research on goal-directed activity (e.g., see Halisch & Kuhl, 1987). W. Meyer (1987) has studied perceived ability, which is similar in meaning to self-efficacy. C. Antoni and J. Beckman (1987) have specifically looked at the individual difference variables of attentional focus and persistence as a moderator of goal setting effects. Kleinbeck (1986) has studied the effects of the goals when individuals are performing two tasks at once. Gollwitzer, Heckausen, and Ratajczak (1987) looked at the effects of what we in Chapter 6 call goal intensity on commitment. Frese and Sabini (1985) call this West German movement, along with its American counterparts, *action theory*, which, they argue, "begins with a conception of human behavior: that it is directed toward the accomplishment of goals, that it is directed by plans, that those plans are hierarchically arranged, and that feedback from the environment articulates with plans in the guidance of action" (p. xxiii). Action theory, in terms of its basic assumptions, is clearly compatible with goal setting theory.

Finally, in Belgium, Nuttin (1984) published a book entitled *Motivation, Planning and Action*. In addition to his incisive critiques (cited earlier) of tension-reduction and cybernetic (control) theories, he made many astute observations about the relationship between goals and needs, goals and feedback, and goals and planning, which are quite compatible with goal theory (see also Nuttin, 1985).

DIMENSIONS OF GOALS

Goals, like other mental processes (Rand, 1969), have two main attributes: content and intensity. *Goal content* refers to the object or result being sought—e.g., buying a house, getting a raise, winning a tennis match, getting a score of 26 or better on a task. Usually the content will refer to some aspect of the external world, although it is also possible for people to have psychological goals such as happiness, higher self-esteem or less anxiety and self-doubt. The content of different goals may differ qualitatively. An individual may have a career goal, a job goal, a financial goal, or a goal in sports or hobbies or in his or her social life. Goal content may vary quantitatively. The individual may have few or many goals, short-term or long-term goals (close or distant deadlines), or easy or difficult goals. Goals may also vary in degree of specificity or clarity, the clearest or most specific goals usually being quantitative (e.g., try for a 5% productivity improvement) and the least clear being more verbal (e.g., do the best you can, do a good job). An individual's goals may also be consistent or conflicting.

Most research on goal content to date has focused on the effects, alone and in various combinations, of degree of goal specificity and degree of goal difficulty. Multiple goals and goals differing in time span have been studied to some degree. Goal setting has been studied with scores of different tasks and in many different settings (see Chapter 2).

It is worth making the distinction here between goal difficulty and task difficulty, since there has been some confusion in the literature over the meanings of these two terms (see Locke, Shaw, Saari, & Latham, 1981). A *task* is a piece of work to be accomplished. A *difficult task* is one that is hard to do. A task can be hard because it is complex, that is, requires a high level of skill and knowledge. For example, writing a book on physics is a harder task than writing a thank-you note. A task can also be hard because it requires a great deal of effort: digging the foundation for a swimming pool takes more effort than digging a hole in which to plant a flower seed. The only goal setting study to have explicitly separated goal and task difficulty is that by Campbell and Ilgen (1976). Using chess problems, they found that both goal and task difficulty affected performance. Harder goals led to better performance than easier goals, and initial assignment of more-difficult problems led to better subsequent performance than initial assignment of less-difficult problems. The authors attributed the latter effect to increased task knowledge fostered by working on the more-difficult problems.

Since a goal is the object or aim of an action, it is possible for the completion of a task to be a goal. In most goal setting studies, however, the term *goal* refers to attaining a specific standard of proficiency on a given task, usually within a specified time limit. For example, two individuals are given the same task (e.g., simple addition), but one is asked to complete a large number of problems within thirty minutes and the other, a small number. The harder goal would be achieved by expending greater effort and attention than would be expended to achieve the easy goal. Harder goals, like harder tasks, can also require more knowledge and skill than easier goals (e.g., winning a chess tournament vs. coming in next to last). Harder tasks usually lead to more effort but lower performance scores than easier tasks. For example, the average person's score would be lower on a calculus test than on a test of simple addition (though as Campbell and Ilgen found, working on a harder task may lead to better subsequent performance than working on an easier task when all subjects are subsequently given tasks of equal difficulty to work on). To summarize the distinction between the terms, *goal difficulty* specifies a certain level of task proficiency measured against a standard, whereas *task difficulty* refers simply to the nature of the work to be accomplished.

The second dimension of goals, *intensity*, refers to such factors as the scope and integration of the goal setting process, the effort required to form the goals, the place of the goal in the individual's goal hierarchy, the degree to which the individual is committed to the goal, and the importance of the goal. Most research on goal intensity has focused on the determinants and effects of goal commitment, although there have been a few studies on the intensity of the goal setting process.

It should be noted that goal content and intensity are not always easy to separate. For example, a more-intense psychological process could be involved in setting clear, specific goals than vague goals in a situation where a great deal of information had to be analyzed and integrated before the goals could be clearly formulated. In such a case, clearer goals would be more intense than vague goals. In other situations, however, there might be no difference, as in a laboratory experiment in which different people were assigned specific and general goals. The different goals might lead to different degrees of effort, even though they would not necessarily differ in intensity.

In the next chapter, we present the core findings of goal setting theory.

CHAPTER

2

CORE FINDINGS

The core premise of goal setting theory is that goals are immediate, though not sole, regulators of human action. The category of actions that the theory is concerned with is performance on work tasks. In this chapter we present and summarize the core findings and degree of generality of goal setting theory. There are many additional aspects to goal theory, including goal choice and a number of specified mechanisms and moderators of goal setting effects. These will be examined in later chapters. If goals are immediate regulators of task performance, it follows that there should be a substantial and consistent relationship between goal content and task performance.

The main focus of the chapter will be on the effects of goal difficulty on performance and on the effects of specific, difficult goals vs. do best goals. We will also report findings regarding the effects of nonquantitative goals, the effects of goals "in general," the effects of goal specificity on performance variance, the effects of multiple goals and goal prioritization, the effects of goals on intrinsic motivation, and the effects of proximal vs. distal goals.

GOAL DIFFICULTY AND PERFORMANCE

Goal setting theory asserts that there is a linear relationship between degree of goal difficulty and performance. This relationship, termed the *goal difficulty function,* is shown in Figure 2–1. Empirical findings demonstrating this function can be found in Locke (1966d), Locke (1967c), Locke (1982b), Locke & Bryan (1968b), Locke, Mento, & Katcher (1978), Locke, Frederick, Buckner, & Bobko (1984), Locke, Chah, Harrison, & Lustgarten (1989), and in other sources. Locke (1968b) derived an empirical function based on the results of twelve separate studies (including some of those listed above). In all cases the functions are linear except when subjects reach the limits of their ability at high goal difficulty levels; in such cases the function levels off (e.g., see Locke 1982b).

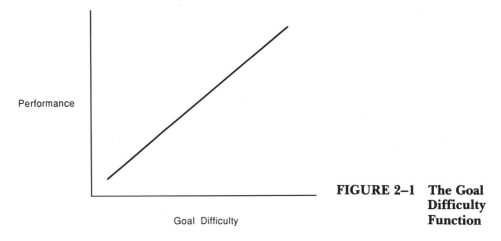

FIGURE 2–1   **The Goal Difficulty Function**

Goal Difficulty (x-axis label)

Performance (y-axis label)

There have been four separate meta-analyses of the goal difficulty–performance relationship, although the studies included in them are overlapping. The results of these meta-analyses are shown in Table 2–1. All of these studies involved designs in which goal difficulty varied quantitatively. The number of studies included in these analyses ranged from 12 to 72, and the number of subjects from 1,770 to 7,548. The mean effect size (*d*) of the Tubbs (1986) study is larger than the *d*'s in the other meta-analyses, especially those of Mento, Steel, & Karren (1987) and Wood, Mento, and Locke (1987). This is because in the latter analyses, studies using within-subjects design were deleted. Mento et al. (1987) believed that within-S studies would bias the results, although such an assertion is arguable. Within-S studies, for example, probably control individual differences better than between-S studies. Effect size also depends, of course, on the total range of goal difficulty used in the study in question. In Locke (1967c), for example, the performance of the subjects with the hardest goals was over 250% higher than the performance of subjects with the easiest goals (*d* = 12.5). In most studies the range of goal levels was not nearly this great; furthermore, subjects with easy goals, unless told to stop when they reach their goals, often set new goals when they reach their assigned goals, thus making the goal difficulty manipulation less than perfect. This issue is addressed further in Chapters 5 and 6. Within the range of the typical goal setting study, and ignoring the possibility that easy goal subjects set new goals, the mean effect sizes in Table 2–1 ranged from .52 to .82. In percentage terms these represent effects on performance of 10.4% to 16.4%.[1]

Enumerative reviews of the literature have been conducted by Latham and Yukl (1975a), Locke (1968b), Locke, Shaw, Saari, and Latham (1981), and Steers and Porter (1974). Locke et al. (1981) found that 48 out of 57, or 84%, of the studies of goal difficulty showed significant or contingently significant effects. The total number of studies of goal difficulty is now more than three times the number reviewed by Locke et al. (1981) and well more than twice the number

[1]We are indebted to Dr. Frank Schmidt for explaining how to derive percentages from *d*-scores.

Table 2–1 Results of Meta-Analyses of Goal Difficulty Effects on Performance

STUDY	NO. OF STUDIES	N	EFFECT SIZE (d)	COMMENTS
Chidester & Grigsby (1984)	12	1,770	.52	Remaining nine studies were correlational
Mento, Steel, & Karren (1987)	70	7,407	.55	Excluded within-S designs
Tubbs (1986)	56	4,732	.82	Included within-S designs
Wood, Mento, & Locke (1987)	72	7,548	.58	Corrected *d*; same studies as Mento et al., plus two

reviewed in the most recent meta-analysis by Wood, Mento, & Locke (1987). There are 175 studies showing positive (140 studies) or contingently positive (35 studies, i.e., positive for one subgroup or condition) associations between goal difficulty and performance, and 17 that show no effect or effects in the opposite direction. This represents a success rate (including contingent successes) of 91%. The positive and contingently positive studies are listed in Appendix A. An analysis of the contingently positive studies and the failures will be made below.

The explanation for the goal difficulty effect is that hard goals lead to greater effort and persistence than easy goals, assuming the goals are accepted. Related to this is the fact that hard goals make self-satisfaction contingent on a higher level of performance than easy goals. (These issues are addressed at greater length in the following two chapters.)

SPECIFIC, DIFFICULT GOALS VS. DO BEST OR NO ASSIGNED GOALS

A second core aspect of goal theory is that goals that are specific and difficult lead to a higher level of performance than vague, nonquantitative goals such as "do your best," "work at a moderate pace," or no assigned goals. The comparison of the effects of specific, hard goals and do your best goals represents the most nonobvious comparison, since "do your best" goals, despite being nonquantitative, imply a high level of motivation. When no goals are assigned, this often represents an implicit do best condition, especially in a laboratory setting, since most people try to do well in such situations (Orne, 1962). If subjects literally had no goal at all, they would do nothing and the comparison with other goal conditions would be of little or no theoretical interest. Similarly, it would be relatively trivial to compare the effects of specific, difficult goals with nonquantitative goals implying a moderate to low level of motivation such as "work at a moderate pace" or "work at a slow pace," although such comparisons have been made on occasion (Locke, Mento, & Katcher, 1978). Thus virtually all the studies reported in this section compare specific, hard with do best goals or implicit do best goals (no assigned goals).

The results of five meta-analyses of studies that made these comparisons are shown in Table 2–2. Four of the meta-analyses are from the same articles that

Table 2–2   Results of Meta-Analyses of Specific, Difficult Goals vs. Do Best or No Goal Effects on Performance

STUDY	NO. OF STUDIES	N	EFFECT SIZE (d)	COMMENTS
Chidester & Grigsby (1984)	17	2,400	.51	Remaining five studies were correlational
Hunter & Schmidt (1983)	17	1,278	.80	Based on Locke et al., 1980, mean %; N is an underestimate, since some studies used groups and did not report N for individuals
Mento, Steel, & Karren (1987)	49	5,844	.42	Excluded within-S designs
Tubbs (1986)	48	4,960	.50	Included within-S designs
Wood, Mento, & Locke (1987)	53	6,635	.43	Corrected d; same studies as Mento et al., plus four

reported the goal difficulty results summarized in Table 2–1. The fifth (Hunter & Schmidt, 1983) is simply a translation into a *d*-score of Locke, Feren, McCaleb, Shaw, & Denny's (1980) mean reported improvement of 16% for 17 field studies. The number of studies in the meta-analyses ranges from 17 to 53 and the N for subjects from 1,278 to 6,635. The mean effect sizes range from .42 to .80, a range similar to that for the goal difficulty studies. In percentage terms the *d*-scores represent performance effects of 8.4% to 16%.

A final meta-analysis (not shown) was conducted by Guzzo, Jette, and Katzell (1985) using only field studies. However, their results are difficult to interpret because, although the number of effect sizes calculated was reported, the number of separate studies and the number of subjects involved were not. Furthermore, no distinction was made between studies of goal difficulty and studies comparing specific, hard goals with do best goals. The mean effect size for performance in Guzzo et al.'s analysis was .65. This figure falls within the range of the *d*-scores reported in Tables 2–1 and 2–2.

Enumerative reviews of the specific, hard vs. do best studies were provided in the same articles that reviewed the goal difficulty studies (Latham & Yukl, 1975a; Locke, 1968b; Locke et al., 1981; Steers & Porter, 1974; plus Latham & Lee, 1986). Locke et al. (1981) found that 51 of 53 studies, or 96%, showed significant or contingently significant effects in favor of specific, hard goals. The number of studies of the specific, hard goal vs. do best effect is now almost four times that included in the largest meta-analysis and in the most recent enumerative review. There have been a total of 201 studies of this effect, with 183, or 91%, of them showing significant (152 studies) or contingently significant (31 studies) effects. Eighteen studies showed no significant effect or a reverse effect. The successful and contingently successful studies are listed in Appendix B.

Since the goal to do one's best is a hard goal, it is necessary to explain why it leads to better performance than trying for a specific, hard goal. Our explanation is that the ambiguity of difficult goals allows people to give themselves the benefit of the doubt in evaluating their performance; thus a wide range of performance levels may be interpreted as being compatible with doing one's best. In contrast, in the case of a specific, hard goal only beating a single, high score is compatible with success. In support of this interpretation, Kernan and Lord (in press) found that individuals with no specific goals generally evaluated their performance more positively than those with specific, hard goals in response to varying degrees of negative feedback. Mossholder (1980) obtained a similar finding. Similarly, Mento and Locke (1989) found that subjects with do best goals anticipated more satisfaction from every level of anticipated performance than subjects with specific, hard goals (see Chapter 3 for details). The less-stringent standards used by do best subjects to evaluate themselves may explain Locke and Bryan's (1966a) finding that subjects with specific, hard goals were significantly less likely than do best subjects to fall below their previous best performance on a learning task.

ANALYSIS OF CONTINGENT RESULTS AND FAILURES

In assessing the validity of a theory it is important to understand failures as well as successes in prediction. A theoretical prediction can be wrong for at least two reasons: (1) The theory was not tested correctly; that is, the study or experiment, as conducted, did not fall within the theoretical domain of the theory. Usually such errors involve design or measurement problems; in addition, limitations in the data analysis may also be involved. (Guidelines for conducting successful goal setting experiments in laboratory and field settings are given in Appendixes C and D.) (2) The theory is wrong in some respect; that is, in some situations it does not apply, or it does not take account of some variables that affect or limit the operation of key relationships.

Table 2–3 lists the studies that showed a contingent or negative result. They are classified as to the hypothesized cause of the failure. We have done this separately for the goal difficulty studies and the specific, hard goal vs. do best studies. In addition, we have rated each study, on a scale of 1 to 3, in terms of our degree of confidence in being able to account for the negative result; 3 means we were quite confident in our attribution, 2 that we were somewhat confident and 1 that we were not very confident. Some studies are listed more than once because they fall into more than one causal category. The causal categories are based either on known moderators of goal setting (commitment, feedback, task complexity), all of which are discussed in later chapters, or on issues of experimental design. There is also a miscellaneous category.

Category (A) lists studies in which lack of goal commitment is the probable cause of the negative result. A rating of 3 indicates that direct evidence for this was given in the study (e.g., because commitment was directly manipulated; Erez & Zidon, 1984). In other cases there was indirect evidence. For example, public commitment has been found to induce stronger goal commitment than private commitment (Hollenbeck, Williams & Klein, 1989). Similarly having subjects set their own goals before being assigned goals has been found to lead to lower commitment than not setting personal goals first (Erez, Earley, & Hulin, 1985). We extrapolated these findings to the studies by Hayes et al. (1985), Lyman

Table 2–3   Studies Showing Null or Contingent Results for Goal Setting: Categorized by Hypothesized Cause

A. COMMITMENT

Goal Difficulty

(3)[a] Baron & Watters (1982)—44% goal rejection rate (see also Sections C & D below)
(3) Bayton (1943)—no effect for low ego-involvement task
(2) Dossett, Latham, & Saari (1980)—no effect if surveys unsigned or returned to experimenter rather than signed and returned to supervisor
(3) Erez & Zidon (1984)—no effect for low-commitment Ss
(2) Kausler (1959)—no effect for goals measured as "hopes"
(3) Miller & Steele (1984)—no apparent effect for hard, assigned goals with bonus incentives; effect mediated by self-set goals
(1) Mowen, Middlemist, & Luther (1981)—similar to Miller & Steele
(2) Organ (1977)—second study; lower commitment to hard goals than to others
(2) Stedry (1962)—no effect for Ss who set own goals after being assigned goals; probable goal conflict
(1) Stedry & Kay (1966)—no effect for goals seen as impossible
(1) Steers (1975)—no effect for Ss low in need (desire) for achievement

Specific, Hard Goal vs. Do Best or No Goal

(1) Bandura & Simon (1977)—no effect of distal goals
(3) Brickner & Bukatko (1987)—second study; hard goal Ss reported lower subjective effort than do best Ss ($p < .10$)
(3) Erez & Zidon (1984)—same as above
(2) (2) Hayes et al. (1985)—two studies; no effect for private goal setting conditions
(3) Ivancevich (1974)—no effect for low organizational commitment plant
(2) Latham & Yukl (1975b)—second study; goal setting probably not implemented
(2) Lyman (1984)—no effect in private goal setting condition
(2) Mahoney (1974)—in goal-without-rewards condition, Ss were less motivated to begin with
(2) Stedry (1962)—same as above

[a]The number in parentheses next to each study represents a rating of 3, 2, or 1 to indicate our degree of confidence in being able to account for the contingent or negative result. **Note:** Some studies appear in more than one category.

3: A rating of 3 represents high confidence in our explanation, usually because the reason was given in the study itself (e.g., goal setting failed to work because feedback was withheld from some groups, the goal manipulation failed, commitment was manipulated or measured, the specific goal was easy, there was no training on a complex task, etc.).

2: A rating of 2 indicates that there is a reasonably plausible explanation for the result (e.g., the goal manipulation was private, feedback was limited or false, the task was seemingly complex, the design was suspect, etc.).

1: A rating of 1 means that the explanation is speculative. There are a number of reasons why the goal effect might have failed, but little direct evidence for any of them. In a few cases there is no obvious explanation for the result.

*Indicates study was noted previously within the same (goal difficulty or hard goal–do best) subsection of a previous main section (A, B, C, etc.).

Table 2–3 (cont.)

B. COMPLEX TASK OR COMPLEX TASK WITH NO TRAINING (OR FALSE TRAINING)

Goal Difficulty

(3) Huber (1985b)—complex computer maze (see also Section G regarding artifact)

Specific, Hard Goal vs. Do Best or No Goal

(2) Earley, Connolly, & Ekegren (1989)—multiple cue probability learning, no training provided (two additional studies added later to original manuscript)
(2) Earley, Lee, & Lituchy (1989)—no training condition
(2) Earley, Connolly, & Lee (1988)—first study; same as above
(3) Earley & Perry (1987)—for subjects primed with unsuitable strategy
(3) Huber (1985b)—same as above (see also Section G)
(3) Wood, Bandura, & Bailey (in press)—most complex version of Wood management simulation game

---

C. CRITERION DID NOT MATCH GOAL

Goal Difficulty

(3) Baron & Watters (1981)—goals were for calorie intake, but criterion was weight loss; caloric intake means paralleled goals but not tested for significance
(3)* Baron & Watters (1982)—same as 1981 study above; see also Section A regarding goal rejection

---

Specific, Hard Goal vs. Do Best or No Goal

(3) Baumler (1971)—goals were for each section manager's job (task), but criterion was for combined performance that depended on interaction between section managers in interdependent condition

---

D. DESIGN, MANIPULATION, AND/OR MEASUREMENT PROBLEMS

Goal Difficulty

(3)* Baron & Watters (1982)—see Section A above
(3) Campbell (1984)—easy-hard goal manipulation failed (all goals were two S.D.'s above actual performance); see also Section F
(3) Taylor (1981)—before setting goal, Ss only had fake feedback on related tasks

---

Specific, Hard Goal vs. Do Best or No Goal

(2) Adler & Goleman (1975)—T-group Ss had 28 hours of "practice" and feedback, while non-T-group Ss probably had little or none
(2) Mitchell, Rothman, & Liden (1985)—unclear goal measure (see also Section E below)
(3) Rust, Strang, & Bridgeman (1977)—goal manipulation failed (all were do best Ss)
(3) Weinberg, Bruya, & Jackson (1985)—second study-goal manipulation failed (83% of do best Ss set specific goals)

Table 2–3   (cont.)

Goal Difficulty

(3) Becker (1978)—goals had no effect when feedback withheld
(3) Das (1982a)—standard and hard goal groups (4 and 5) were given no feedback
(3) Erez (1977)—no goal effect for Ss not given feedback
(2) Forward & Zander (1971)—feedback was false (see also Section G below)
(3) Hom and Arbuckle (1986)—goals were set without feedback regarding prior performance
(2) Oldham (1975)—Ss had no formal feedback during performance period
(3) Strang, Lawrence, & Fowler (1978)—goals had no effect when feedback withheld

---

Specific, Hard Goal vs. Do Best or No Goal

(3) Becker (1978)—same as above
(2) Ivancevich & McMahon (1982)—goals plus self-feedback Ss (who were the ones to get frequent or continuous feedback) performed better than others
(2)* Mitchell, Rothman, & Liden (1985)—Ss had no formal feedback during performance period
(2) Motowidlo, Loehr, & Dunnette (1978)—Ss had no formal feedback during performance period
(3) Strang, Lawrence, & Fowler (1978)—same as above

Goal Difficulty

(3)* Campbell (1984)—easy-hard goal manipulation failed (all goals were two S.D.'s above actual performance)
(3) Crawford, White, & Magnusson (1983)—the goals of high previous performers were lower than their own previous performance
(3) Hall, Weinberg, & Jackson (1987)—difficulty level of two goals was similar (success rates 46% and 68%)
(3) Klockmann (1985)—narrow range of goal difficulty (success rates 2%, 9%, and 30%).

Specific, Hard Goal vs. Do Best or No Goal

(3) Amabile, DeJong, & Lepper (1976)—specific goal was very easy (100% success rate)
(3) Crawford, White, & Magnusson (1983)—same as above
(3) Hinsz (1984)—specific goal was very easy (90% success rate)
(3) Hollingsworth (1975)—specific goal was moderate (44% success rate)
(3) Latham & Yukl (1975b)—Ss setting goals participatively set harder goals than Ss with assigned goals
(3) Manderlink & Harackiewicz (1984)—specific goals were very easy (88% success rate)
(3) Organ (1977)—first study; goal was relatively easy (most Ss scored 1 S.D. above the goal)
(3) Siegfried, Piemont, McCarter, & Dellinger (1981)—goal was very easy (mean performance of 10 was way above assigned goal level of 6)
(3) Weinberg, Bruya, & Jackson (1985)—first study; goal was moderately easy (57% success rate)

Table 2–3 **(cont.)**

G. MISCELLANEOUS

Goal Difficulty

(2) Barry, Locke, & Smith (1988)— goals not effective in firms lacking competence
(1) Bigoness, Keef, & DuBose (1983)—correlational study, Ss high in Internal Locus may have had higher self-efficacy than those low on this trait; validity of supervisor and goal difficulty ratings unknown
(1) Campbell & Ilgen (1976)—goal effect significant about half the time (random variation?)
(1) Carroll & Tosi (1970)—high self-assurance Ss may have had higher self-efficacy
(1) Dachler & Mobley (1973)—extraneous factors may have affected performance; also in plant 1
(1) lack of effect for short-tenure Ss may have been random variation with a small N (40)—plant 2 correlation was the same for long-and short-tenure Ss; lack of significance was due to smaller N for latter
(1) Dossett, Latham, & Mitchell (1979)—two studies; lack of effect within assigned conditions may
(1) have been due to poorer matching of goals with ability in study 1; no explanation for study 2
(1)* Forward & Zander (1971)—in addition to false feedback (see Section E above), high pressure for performance may have distorted goal estimates
(1) Frost & Mahoney (1976)—puzzle task; visual aspect of task may have provided feedback for all Ss and affected personal goals
(3) Garland (1985)—goal effect was not significant in path analysis after controlling for valence but was significant otherwise (see also Chapter 3)
(3)* Huber (1985b)—penalty for "peeking" at maze was artifactual, since it eliminated operation of two key goal mechanisms: effort and attention (direction)
(1) Ivancevich & McMahon (1977a)—high-growth need strength Ss may have been more committed to goals than low-growth need strength Ss—no explanation for lack of significance for remaining measures
(1) Ivancevich & McMahon (1977b)—lack of relationship for blacks may have reflected lower commitment and/or self-efficacy
(1) Ivancevich & McMahon (1977c)—lack of relationship for low-education Ss may have reflected lower commitment and/or self-efficacy
(1) Jackson & Zedeck (1982)—two tasks; no ability controls; easy goal Ss may have set higher
(1) personal goals
(1) Lichtman & Lane (1983)—study difficult to understand; feedback lacking
(2) Matherly (1986)—prior success and failure may have affected self-efficacy
(1) McCaul, Hinsz, & McCaul (1987)—first study; effect significant for persistence, not performance, but persistence was associated with performance
(1) Neale, Northcraft, & Earley (1987)—lack of profit effect could have been due to easy goal Ss setting higher goals; personal goals not measured
(1) Nebeker (1987)—no measures of personal goals, commitment, self-efficacy, or valance reported
(3) Peters, Chassie, Lindholm, O'Connor, & Klein (1982)—goal setting not effective with situational constraints (manipulated variable)
(1) Roberson-Bennett (1983)—significant effect for two of three tasks (random variation?)
(1) Shalley, Oldham, & Porac (1987)—opposite finding of Dossett et al. (1979); no explanation
(1) Vance & Colella (1988)—assigned goal constantly increased (conflict with personal goal?)
(3) Wood & Bandura (in press, a) and Wood, Bandura, & Bailey (in press)—correlations for third
(3) block in these studies and in Bandura & Wood (in press) are substantial (mean $r = .62$; see Chapter 4), but high covariation between goals and self-efficacy results in low path coefficient, but which is significant for the three studies combined
(1) Zander & Newcomb (1967)—lack of goal effect for funds with a history of failure may be due to low self-efficacy or the distortion of goal choice process due to desire to improve

---

Table 2–3   (cont.)

Specific, Hard Goal vs. Do Best or No Goal

(1) Antoni & Beckmann (1987)—no goal effect for Ss high in trait of persistence and attention (goal substitute?)
(1) Brickner & Bukatko (1987)—no goal effect for Ss high in identifiability (goal substitute?)
(1) Buller & Bell (1986)—no goal effect for quality, but marginal effect for quality-relevant behaviors; many uncontrolled variables
(1) Buller (1988)—follow-up on above; many uncontrolled variables
(3)* Huber (1985b)—subjects penalized for seeking information about maze (see above)
(1) Hyams and Graham (1984)—no goal effect for Ss high in Initiative (goal substitute?)
(1) Jackson & Zedeck (1982)—manual task, ability not controlled
(1) Kanfer & Ackerman (1988)—studies 1 and 3, feedback diverted attention; criteria did not
(1) match goal; personal goals not measured, etc.
(1) Latham & Saari (1979a)—no effect for assigned goals, but ability not controlled
(2) Locke & Bryan (1967)—two pilot studies; mean difference in correct direction but small N's
(2) (8 & 9)
(1) Pritchard et al. (1981)—no effect for high performers (already near asymptote?)
(1) Schunk (1983)—assigned goals were only suggestive; actual, personal goals were not measured
(1) Shaw (1984)—effect for high-ability Ss may reflect goal-ability interaction described in Chapter 9; second half effect may reflect time lag for goals in somewhat complex task
(2) Weed & Mitchell (1980)—specific, hard goal Ss did show greater gain scores than do best Ss, but difference not tested directly; poor ability matching; personal goals not measured; possible time lag effect

---

(1984), and Stedry (1962). In other cases our explanations were more speculative; for example, the lack of effect of distal goals by Bandura and Simon (1977) was attributed to a possible commitment effect, although no direct evidence was provided by them for such a conclusion.

Category (B) includes studies in which the negative results may have been due to the use of complex tasks without suitable task strategies. In the case of the studies by Earley and his colleagues with the multiple cue probability learning task, we were somewhat cautious (in giving them confidence ratings of 2), since we believe the task is less complex than the management simulation game used by Wood. In the Wood, Bandura, and Bailey (in press) study, task complexity was actually manipulated. The Earley and Perry (1987) study included a condition where subjects were primed with an unsuitable strategy. The confidence rating of 3 for the Huber (1985b) study was as much due to the artifact of penalizing subjects for seeking knowledge about the layout of the maze as for the task being complex. (Thus this study is also listed in category G.)

Category (C) includes studies in which the goal did not match the criterion measure used. The most frequently cited of these, and the one that is most frequently misinterpreted, is the chemical plant simulation study by Baumler (1971). He found that relative to the do best goals, the specific, challenging goals facilitated organizational performance when the tasks were independent but hurt performance when the tasks were interdependent. In the independent condition, the performance of the two section managers was additive so that, if each did well, total organizational performance was high. In the interdependent condition, the relation between the jobs of the two managers was interactive so that, if each of them focused only on doing his own job well, performance of the organization as a whole was undermined. What has been overlooked, however, is that *the section managers were not given goals for the performance of the organization as a whole, but only for their own jobs.* This was beneficial in the independent condition but harmful in the interdependent condition. Since the goals were not matched to the criterion and were actually antagonistic to the overall criterion in the interdependent condition, it is not surprising that they worked poorly in that situation.

The other two studies in this category (Barron & Watters, 1981, 1982) had goals for caloric intake, but the criterion was weight loss. Since weight loss depends on factors other than caloric intake, such as exercise, the matching of goal and criterion was inexact. The 1981 study, incidentally, reported means for caloric intake that typically matched the difficult levels of the goals, but these means were not tested for significance. It should be noted that other weight loss studies have used similar goals and criterion measures and yet obtained positive results (e.g., Bandura & Simon, 1977). We have no explanation for the discrepancy in results.

Category (D) in Table 2–3 involves various design, manipulation, and measurement problems (e.g., the goal manipulations failed). A number of these studies in this section are also classified elsewhere.

Category (E) involves studies where there was inadequate feedback. Ratings of 3 were given mainly to studies that actually manipulated feedback (Becker, 1978; Das, 1982a; Erez, 1977; Strang, Lawrence, & Fowler, 1978). In other studies it appeared as though subjects had little explicit feedback concerning goal progress; however, experimental reports do not always provide enough detail to make unequivocal inferences. False feedback has been used upon occasion in successful studies (Bandura & Cervone, 1983), but it is clearly a questionable procedure because it raises the possibility of a conflict between the feedback the subjects get from the task and that which they get from external sources. Such conflicts can be processed in many different ways and can have variable effects on self-efficacy.

Category (F) lists studies in which the range of goal difficulty was very low or in which do best goals were compared with specific but easy or moderate rather than hard goals. While goal theory is somewhat vague about how big a range is needed to produce a significant difference, it seems clear that the smaller the range, the lower the chances of getting a significant difference. Furthermore, the difficulty effect will depend on how committed the subjects are to their goals. For example, if moderate goal subjects attain their goals and then try to do more, they are not really consistent moderate goal subjects. If subjects are committed only to their goals, and thus stop working when they reach them, then a small range of goal difficulty can produce significant effects (e.g., see Locke, 1982b, though individual t-tests are not reported). The goal difficulty effect also assumes that subjects have sufficient ability to attain or at least approach the goal. Goal theory does not predict any differential effect of two or more goals if they are way beyond everyone's ability (e.g., as in Campbell, 1984). In some cases moderate goals may lead to better performance than do best goals (e.g., Frost & Mahoney, 1976), perhaps because the moderate goal subjects set themselves harder goals than they were assigned or because the do best subjects were not trying their hardest. Nevertheless, do best subjects should only be consistently exceeded by subjects with specific, difficult goals.

Section (G) of Table 2–3 lists a miscellaneous group of studies. Our explanation of the failures is in most instances speculative. For example, in some studies the goal effect is significant only part of the time, e.g., on some trials and not others (Campbell & Ilgen, 1976). This could involve random variation. In other studies the N's were small (Locke & Bryan, 1967). The results of Dachler and Mobley (1973) may have been caused by extraneous factors such as workload, additional task assignments, or organization of work which overrode the effects of personal goals. The shorter-tenure groups were also much smaller than the longer-tenure groups, which clearly affected the significance of the *r*'s in plant 2. The results of the three Ivancevich and McMahon studies (1977a, b, c) could have been due to commitment or self-efficacy differences. The commitment measures used showed no direct relationship to performance, but goal commitment could have differed between subgroups. This was ruled out in Ivancevich and McMahon (1977a); however, the growth need strength moderator itself could have been an implicit and more accurate measure of commitment. In some studies there are many possible explanations for the lack of goal effects; for example, Nebeker (1987) reported no measures of personal goals, commitment, or self-efficacy.

An intriguing suggestion from three of the studies (Antoni & Beckmann, 1987; Brickner & Bukatko, 1987; Hyams & Graham, 1984) is that *there may be certain personal traits or experimental conditions that act as goal substitutes or goal equivalents.* In those three studies subjects who were high on the traits of persistence and attention, or initiative, or whose work could be identified by others, performed just as well with do best goals as with specific, hard goals. It is possible that incentives (e.g., money, competition) may also affect performance independently of their effects on goals, goal commitment, or self-efficacy, possibly through a subconscious process. This remains to be seen and suggests provocative avenues for further research. (The issue of incentives is examined in Chapter 6.) A summarized, enumerative classification of the goal setting studies is shown in Table 2–4. The contingent and unsuccessful studies are classified as to our degree of confidence in accounting for the failures using the 3-point scale noted earlier. Failures classified as 3 or 2 are explainable with some degree of confidence, and these explanations are consistent with the tenets of goal setting theory. For the studies classified as 1 the explanations must remain speculative; it is not clear if these studies would require a revision of goal setting theory or not, since the results could have been caused by a variety of unmeasured factors. The number of studies classified as 1 is only 37. This represents fewer than 10% of the 393 findings on the relation of goal difficulty–specificity and performance conducted to date.[2] (It should be noted that these are not 393 different studies, since some studies provided data relevant to both the goal difficulty and the specific, hard vs. do best aspects of the theory.)

[2]We received reports of additional unpublished or submitted goal setting studies as this chapter was being written and revised. Thus the actual number of these studies is above 400. However, after a certain point in writing this chapter, we had to say "enough."

Table 2–4 Classification of Results of Studies and Confidence in Explanation of Reasons for Contingent Results or Failures

GOAL DIFFICULTY	NUMBER		CLASSIFICATION OF CAUSES OF CONTINGENT RESULTS OR FAILURE[a]
Successful	140		3:20
Contingent	35	52	2:8
Unsuccessful	17		1:24
	192		52
SPECIFIC, HARD GOALS VS. DO BEST			
Successful	152		3:20
Contingent	31	49	2:16
Unsuccessful	18		1:13
	201		49
COMBINED			
Successful	292		3:40
Contingent	66	101	2:24
Unsuccessful	35		1:37
Total	393		101

[a]3-point scale is explained in the Table 2–3 footnote—3: strong confidence in explanation; 2: some confidence; 1: speculative.

There is no convincing evidence that there is any study in the literature that failed to find a significant effect for goals and that (1) measured and/or controlled for ability, personal goals (regardless of assigned goals), goal commitment, and self-efficacy or expectancy; (2) provided feedback showing progress in relation to goals; (3) used a reasonable degree or range of goal difficulty; (4) showed successful manipulation checks; (5) used a simple task or a complex task with trained, suitable task strategies; (6) did not have artifacts such as nonmatching goal and criterion measures or external blocks to performance. This is not to say that no such studies exist, but only that it is doubtful if any studies have been conducted to date.

On the negative side, goal theory is vague as to how hard a hard goal should be, how great the range of goal difficulty must be so that it is "enough," and when a task is to be classified as simple or complex. All of this makes it easy, perhaps too easy, to explain away negative results after the fact. Even without attempts at post hoc explanations, however, goal theory shows a remarkable consistency of results—a consistency that has held up for a period of many years.

GENERALITY OF RESULTS

The replicability of a set of experimental findings, while desirable, is not sufficient in itself to show that the results are generalizable. The replicated results could conceivably be based on a single task, setting, measure, and/or type of subject. The results of goal setting studies, however, have been replicated across a wide variety of tasks, settings, measures, subjects, time spans, criterion measures, and research designs. In a narrative review Latham and Lee (1986) found that the results of goal setting studies generalize across laboratory and field settings, quantity and quality criteria, soft and hard criteria, individual and group goals, and goals that were assigned or set participatively. Here we will extend their analysis.

Tasks

Goal setting experiments have been conducted with 88 different tasks. These are listed in alphabetical order in Table 2–5. The number of studies using each task is specified for goal difficulty studies, for specific, hard vs. do best goal studies, and for both combined.

Table 2–5   Type and Frequency of Tasks Used in Goal Setting Studies

	LAB, FIELD, OR SIMULATION	GOAL DIFFICULTY	HARD GOAL VS. DO BEST	TOTAL
Achievement test performance	L		1	1
Air traffic control	S		3	3
Anagrams, boggle, word games	L	10	4	14
Archery	F		1	1
Arithmetic/computation	L	16	16	32
Assembly (toys, etc.)	L	8	7	15
Bargaining	S	5	5	10
Beverage consumption	F	2		2
Body checking (hockey)	F		1	1
Can collecting	F		1	1
Checking soft-drink machines	F	1	1	2
Chess	L/F	1		1
Choosing geometrical figures	L	2		2
Classroom behavior	F		1	1
Clerical (miscellaneous)	L/F	18	11	29
Coding/code learning	L	2		2
Color discrimination	L	2		2
Complex coordination	S		1	1
Computer game	L	1		1
Container use	F		1	1
Course work hr/performance	F	9	2	11
Customer callback	F		1	1
Diecasting	F		1	1
Drilling holes	S	1	1	2
Driving (car, truck)	F	1	1	2
Dynamometer performance	L	2	2	4
Elbow flexion	L	1	1	2
Energy conservation	F	1	1	2

Table 2–5   **(cont.)**

	LAB, FIELD, OR SIMULATION	GOAL DIFFICULTY	HARD GOAL VS. DO BEST	TOTAL
Engine overhaul	F	1	1	2
Ergometer	L	2	1	3
Exercise (general)	F	1	4	5
Faculty research	F	1		1
Finding objects in pictures	L		2	2
Handball	F	1		1
Health-promoting behaviors	F		2	2
Injury rate	F	1		1
Juggling	F		1	1
Jumping	L		1	1
Key punching	F		1	1
Labeling	L		1	1
Lego construction	L	1	1	2
Listing nouns, objects, uses	L	23	11	34
Listing job behaviors	F		1	1
Logging	F	1	6	7
Luchins water jar problems	L	1	1	2
Manual manipulation	L		1	1
Maintenance & technical work	F	3	2	5
Making class schedules	L		2	2
Managing, supervision, management simulations	F/S	9	5	14
Management training	F	1		1
Marine recruit performance	F	1		1
Maze learning	L	1	3	4
Mental health services	F		1	1
Mining	F		2	2
Multiple cue probability learning	L	1	3	4
Nursing	F	1		1
Pain tolerance	L		1	1
Perceptual speed	L	11	4	15
Performance appraisal behaviors or scores	F	3		3
Personality change	F		2	2
Praising	F		1	1
Proofreading	L/F	1	3	4
Production/manufacturing/factory work	F	3	8	11
Puzzles	L	2	2	4
Reaction time	L	10	4	14
Reading, prose learning	L/F	8	15	23
Returning questionnaire surveys	F	1	1	2
Safety behaviors	F		5	5
Sales/selling	F	4	4	8
Scientific, engineering, & R&D work	F	3	3	6
Service work	F		1	1
Sewing	F	1	3	4
Ship unloading	F		1	1
Sit-ups	L		2	2

Table 2–5   (cont.)

	LAB, FIELD, OR SIMULATION	GOAL DIFFICULTY	HARD GOAL VS. DO BEST	TOTAL
Spelling	L	1	2	3
Sports (field hockey)	F	1		1
Study behaviors & skills	F		2	2
Teller activities	F		1	1
Tracking	L	3	1	4
Truck maintenance	F		1	1
Typing, computer data entry	F	3	1	4
United Fund performance	F	2		2
Video game performance	L	1		1
Weight lifting	F	1		1
Weight loss, eating behaviors, food intake	F	2	8	10
Welding	F		1	1
Wheel turning	L		3	3
Writing sentences	L		4	4
	Total	194*	201	395

*This total is higher than the 192 total in Table 2–4 because some reports counted as one study, such as Mace (1935), used more than one task.

The twelve most frequently used tasks are listed in Table 2–6. The distribution of task used is clearly not random, with a large percentage of the studies using fairly simple laboratory tasks (listing nouns, arithmetic/computation, etc.). However, there are an encouraging number of frequently used tasks that are more complex (reading, prose learning, managing and management simulations, bargaining, production).

Table 2–6   Most Frequently Used Tasks in Goal Setting Research

TASK	FREQUENCY OF USE
Listing nouns, objects, uses	34
Arithmetic/computation	32
Clerical	29
Reading, prose learning	23
Perceptual speed	15
Assembly (toys, etc.)	15
Managing/management simulations	14
Anagrams	14
Course work	11
Production, manufacturing	11
Bargaining	10
Weight loss, eating behaviors	10

Settings

Table 2–5 also indicates whether each task or type of task used was in a laboratory or a field setting, or whether it was a simulation. Some tasks were used in both types of settings (e.g., clerical tasks) and thus are designated as both. Table 2–7 shows the number of tasks and number of studies designated as laboratory or lab/field, and field or simulation. A greater variety of tasks have been used in field settings than in laboratory settings (53 vs. 35), even though more total studies have been done in laboratory than in field settings (239 vs. 156). These data make it unmistakably clear that goal setting findings generalize beyond the laboratory (see also Locke, 1986a).

Table 2–7   Frequency Distribution of Task Types and Studies

TASK TYPE	NUMBER OF TASKS OF THIS TYPE	TOTAL NUMBER OF STUDIES
Laboratory or Lab/Field	35	239
Field or Simulation	53	156
Total	88	395

Subjects

While a clear majority of subjects used in goal setting studies have been white male and female college students, many other types of subjects have included children (Earbaugh & Barnett, 1986; Masters, Furman, & Barden, 1977), retardates (Kliebhan, 1967; Principato, 1983), blacks (Bayton, 1943; Ivancevich & McMahon, 1977b; Latham & Yukl, 1975b), loggers (Latham & Kinne, 1974), factory workers (Koch, 1979), managers (Berlew & Hall, 1965), Marine recruits (Ashworth & Mobley, 1978), engineers and scientists (Latham, Mitchell, & Dossett, 1978), and college professors (Taylor, Locke, Lee, & Gist, 1984). Clearly the theory is not limited to any one subject population. The total number of subjects used in the goal setting studies reviewed in Table 2–4 is nearly forty thousand!

Countries

While the overwhelming majority of goal setting studies have been done in the United States, such studies have also been conducted in at least seven other countries: Australia (Wood, Bandura, & Bailey, in press), Canada (Bavelas & Lee, 1978; Latham & Marshall, 1982), the Caribbean (Punnett, 1986), England (Earley, 1986c; Mace, 1935), West Germany (Antoni & Beckman, 1987; Kleinbeck, 1986), Israel (Erez & Zidon, 1984), and Japan (Matsui, Kakuyama, & Onglatco, 1987; Matsui, Okada, & Mizuguchi, 1981; Matsui, Okada, & Kakuyama, 1982). This is strong evidence that the theory applies across cultures.

Criteria

Since the effect of goals depends on the content of the goal, there should be no limit to the types of measures used as performance criteria. Criteria used to date have included measures of physical effort (Bandura & Cervone, 1986), speed of reaction (Locke, Cartledge, & Knerr, 1970), quantity of output without regard to quality (Locke, 1966d), output with quality controlled (Pritchard & Curtis, 1973), number of correct responses (Locke, Mento, & Katcher, 1978), production efficiency (Crawford, White, & Magnusson, 1983), performance quality (Koch, 1979), time spent on the task (LaPorte & Nath, 1976), profit (Huber & Neale,

1987), costs (Klein, 1973), job behavior (Latham, Mitchell, & Dossett, 1978), perfomance appraisal ratings (Peters et al., 1984), and survey returns (Dossett, Latham & Saari, 1980).

Virtually any type of action that can be measured and controlled can be used as a dependent variable. As noted earlier, to be effective the goal must match the performance measure used. This does not preclude, of course, setting goals for actions (such as job behaviors) that have a direct causal effect on the outcome or criterion measure (such as sales or customer satisfaction). However, the effect of goals on such an outcome measure will depend on the strength of the causal relation between behavior and outcome. Usually the criteria used have been measured objectively, but there have been studies using more subjective criteria. For example, some studies of behavior on the job have employed trained, external observers as raters (Komaki, Barwick, & Scott, 1978), and others have used supervisor estimates (Latham, Mitchell, & Dossett, 1978).

Time Spans

Successful goal setting studies have covered time spans ranging from one minute to several years. The shortest goal setting study to date (1 minute) was conducted by Locke (1982b), and the longest (36 months) by Ivancevich (1974). There have been many time intervals as well—e.g., 5 minutes (Bandura & Cervone, 1986), 10 minutes (Garland & Adkinson, 1987), 20 minutes (Earley, 1985a), 30 minutes (Locke & Bryan, 1969b), 1 hour (Das, 1982a), 2 hours (Locke & Bryan, 1966a), 3 to 4 hours (Bassett, 1979), 3 weeks (Becker, 1978), 3 months (Alexy, 1985), 9 months (Latham & Baldes, 1975), and 12 months (Ivancevich, 1976). Clearly the effect of goal setting is not simply a short-term phenomenon. As Ivancevich (1972) pointed out, sustaining an organizational goal setting program across time requires an ongoing commitment on the part of higher management to the program. With such commitment, the Latham and Baldes (1975) intervention endured for nine additional years (according to company spokespeople).

Individual, Group, and Organizational Goals

The majority of goal setting studies have used the individual as the unit of analysis, but at least 41 of them appeared to have used group goals insofar as this could be inferred from the reports[3] (Barry, Locke, & Smith, 1988; Baumler, 1971; Becker, 1978; Botterill, 1977; Buller & Bell, 1986; Buller, 1988; Fellner & Sulzer-Azaroff, 1985; Forward & Zander, 1971; French, 1950; Gowen, 1986; Haberstroh, 1960; Hinsz, 1984; Klein, 1973; Klein & Mulvey, 1988; Komaki et al., 1978, 1980, 1982; Lawrence & Smith, 1955; Latham & Kinne, 1976; Latham & Locke, 1975; Latham & Yukl, 1975b, two studies; Lichtman & Lane, 1983; Matsui, Kakuyama, & Onglatco, 1987, two studies; McCarthy, 1978; McCuddy & Griggs, 1984; Migliore, 1977, two studies; O'Connell, 1980; Pritchard et al., 1988; Ronan, Latham, & Kinne, 1973; Smith, Locke, & Barry, in press; Sorcher, 1967; Stedry & Kay, 1966; Watson, 1983; Weingart & Weldon, 1988, two studies; Zajonc & Taylor, 1963;

[3]Not all of these studies were included in our previous listing because some involved simply the setting of goals without information as to their difficulty or specificity. Others were received too late to be integrated with any but this subsection.

Zander, Foward, & Albert, 1969; Zander & Newcomb, 1967). The Smith et al. study was actually an organizational simulation. Thirty-eight of these 41 studies, or 93%, yielded positive or contingently positive results, virtually the same success rate as for the total group of studies. It is clear that group goals, in addition to or instead of individual goals, are necessary or at least facilitative when the task is a group rather than an individual one (Klein & Mulvey, 1988; Matsui, Kakuyama, & Onglatco, 1987; Mitchell & Silver, 1989).

Goal setting at the organizational level is the essence of the well-known technique of Management by Objectives, or MBO (e.g., see Carroll & Tosi, 1973). Separate reviews of the MBO literature are not included in this book; however, several reviews of this literature have been completed in recent years. Kondrasuk (1981) reviewed 185 studies of MBO. It should be noted that not all of these studies actually involved the organization as a whole. Most often they included one or more units of an organization; we calculated (from Kondrasuk's tables) that 91% of the 185 studies showed positive or contingently positive results. Kondrasuk argued, however, that the better-designed studies included in his review showed poorer results than the more poorly designed studies. Of the five studies in his best-controlled category (controlled experiments), one was successful, another was successful in the plant in which there was top management commitment, another was successful for nine out of the twelve months of the study, and two were failures. In one of the failures no data were reported. Using a conservative procedure of taking reports rather than studies as the unit of analysis (thus counting each report as one study, regardless of how many studies were reported in it), we found, through inspection of Kandrasuk's tables, that 91% of the reports that provided data claimed positive or contingently positive results. In contrast, 86% of the studies that did not provide data claimed positive results.[4] By every reasonable method of counting, the overall MBO success rate (including contingent successes) hovers around the same 90% success rate obtained for the micro-and group-level studies noted earlier.

More recently Rodgers and Hunter (1989) conducted a meta-analysis of data from 68 MBO studies. Sixty-six, or 97%, of them showed positive results. The mean productivity increase for the 28 studies with ratio scale measures was 44%, a figure even larger than the previously reported 8% to 16% found for the micro-level studies. The mean percent increase in the MBO studies that were conducted with high management commitment was even higher. (These results will be discussed in Chapter 6.) Finally, a third review of the MBO literature by Carroll (1986) was as favorable as the reviews of Kondrasuk and Rodgers and Hunter. (For a narrative review of goal setting and MBO in the public sector, see Greiner, Hatry, Koss, Millar, & Woodward, 1981.) In a unique study of large companies, Welch and Pantalone (1985) found that companies that held stock price maximization as their ultimate financial goal showed a 34% greater increase in share growth over a ten-year period than companies that had other financial goals, such as maximizing earnings per share or return on equity.

Given all of the above, there is strong reason to conclude that goal setting works at the group and organizational (or unit) level as well as at the individual

---

[4]In our recount, we counted reports of multiple studies as single studies, whereas Kondrasuk counted them as multiple studies to get his count of 185.

level. Naturally one would expect more contingencies and complexities at the organizational level than at the individual level, but, except for commitment, these have not as yet been thoroughly studied. (These issues are examined in Chapter 14.)

Goal Source

Goals can be set by the individual (self-set); they can be assigned by others, such as the experimenter or supervisor; or they can be set jointly (participatively). The issue of the relative effectiveness of these different ways of setting the goal is so controversial that we have devoted an entire chapter to it (Chapter 7) and part of another (Chapter 6). Suffice it to say for now that, on the whole, all three methods of setting goals are equally effective.

Conclusions Concerning Generality of Results

The evidence is overwhelming that goal setting effects generalize across a wide range of tasks, settings, subjects, countries, criteria, and time spans. The results hold at both the individual and group levels and across different methods of setting the goal. Furthermore, while concurrent-correlation designs have been used, the great majority of goal setting studies have used experimental designs, thus leaving little doubt as to the causal role of goals. Few if any theories in the fields of industrial-organizational psychology, human resource management, and organizational behavior, or even psychology as a whole, can claim such consistent and wide-ranging support.

OVERALL COMPARATIVE ASSESSMENT OF GOAL SETTING THEORY

There have been four overall comparative assessments of goal setting theory in relation to other theories of work motivation. For now, we will discount the one by Locke and Henne (1986), since it was made by one of the present authors. Miner (1984) evaluated 32 theories in organizational science, including some that were not motivation theories. Goal setting theory was one of only four theories that he rated "high" on both the criterion of validity and that of usefulness in application (see also Miner, 1980).

In another assessment, Pinder (1984) reviewed all the major theories of work motivation and concluded that "goal setting theory has demonstrated more scientific validity to date than any other theory or approach to work motivation. . . . Moreover, the evidence thus far indicates that it probably holds more promise as an applied motivational tool for managers than does any other approach" (p. 169). Finally, Lee and Earley (1988) asked 127 leading scholars in the fields of organizational behavior and industrial-organizational psychology to rate 15 major work motivation theories on the criteria of scientific validity and practical usefulness. Goal setting theory was rated first in validity, a close second in practical usefulness, and a close second overall among the full sample of raters. Among the raters who were high in research productivity, it ranked first on the combined criteria.

The rank order correlations (rho's) between the overall ratings obtained by Lee and Earley (1988) and those reported by or provided by Miner, Pinder, and Locke and Henne (1986) were .74, .74, and .87, respectively (all p's < .01). The latter rho indicates that the ratings given by Locke and Henne (1986) were not biased. They rated goal theory and Bandura's (1986) social cognitive theory as the most valid of eleven motivation theories.

In summary, the evidence suggests that goal setting is one of the most valid theories, if not the most valid theory, of work motivation. It should be added that all the above assessments were made before this book was published and thus were not based on the full theory as presented here.

ADDITIONAL FINDINGS

There are a number of additional findings, exclusive of moderator effects, regarding goal setting and performance. These additional findings fall into the following categories: more effects of nonquantitative goals differing in difficulty; effects of goals in general and goal clarity; effects of goal specificity and difficulty on performance variance; performance with multiple goals; effects of goal importance and prioritization; effects of goals on "intrinsic" motivation; and the effects of proximal vs. distal goals. In most cases, however, these findings are less well established and/or less conclusive than those discussed previously.

Effects of Nonquantitative Goals Differing in Difficulty

Nearly all studies of goal difficulty have compared goals differing quantitatively—e.g., trying to list 4, 8, 10, 12, or 13 objects that could be called "heavy" in one minute (Locke, 1967c). Only a few studies have looked at goals differing in difficulty in which difficulty level was expressed verbally.

Bryan and Locke (1967b) found that, given generous time limits to complete an additional task, subjects trying to work "as fast as possible" worked faster than those trying to work "quickly," who in turn worked faster than those working at a "relaxed pace." Such differences did not emerge among subjects given very tight time limits, especially since the range of goals was smaller. For example, there were no subjects in this condition with the goal to work at a "relaxed pace." It was also found, however, that the goal to work "quickly" led to a significantly faster pace of work in the tight than in the loose time-limit condition. The inherent ambiguity of verbal goals allows them to be interpreted differently in different contexts; this is much less likely with quantitative goals. Telling a person to try to complete a task in 5.2 minutes means the same thing in any context (although the context could affect commitment to the goal).

Locke, Mento, and Katcher (1978) found that subjects told to do their best on a perceptual speed task and those told to work at 70% of capacity worked faster than subjects told to work at 30% of capacity. While the 70% and 30% goals were superficially quantitative, the percentages were not translated into actual numbers of problems to be completed and thus functioned more like vague than specific goals. Locke and Bryan (1968a) found that subjects trying to "do their best" or work at a "reasonably fast pace" on a complex computation task worked significantly faster than subjects trying to "work with no effort."

Finally, Locke, Chah, Harrison, & Lustgarten (1989) found that subjects trying to respond "as fast as possible" responded faster on a reaction time task than those trying to respond "moderately fast," who in turn responded faster than those trying to respond "slowly." Similarly, in their second study which used a "listing improvements" task, they found that subjects trying to list a "large" number of improvements listed more than those trying to list a "medium" or "low" number. Subjects trying to list a low number of improvements actually listed slightly more than those listing a medium number, revealing again the greater ambiguity of verbal goals. For subjects with very specific goals, the relationship between goal level and performance level was clearly linear.

In conclusion, nonquantitative goals varying in difficulty are related to performance in the same way as quantitative goals: the higher the goal, the higher the performance. These findings call into question Naylor and Ilgen's (1984) claim that goals such as do your best, because of their vagueness, do not constitute a legitimate goal intervention. However, there is evidence that the goal-performance relationship is less reliable for verbal than for quantitative goals because of the greater ambiguity of the former relative to the latter.

Effects of Goals "in General" and Goal Clarity

A number of studies have looked at the effects on performance of goal setting in general—by in general we mean that the attributes of the goals in question either were not specified or were so multidimensional that the goal setting effects could not be attributed to any one or two attributes. Almost all these studies were correlational. Anderson and Schneier (1979), for example, found that football coaches who used goal setting and other positive techniques more often with their players had better won-lost records than those who used such techniques less often. Bottger and Woods (1988) found that sales representatives who used goal setting more often perceived themselves as putting forth more effort than those who used it less often. Goal emphasis was found by Bowers and Seashore (1966) to be associated with several performance dimensions among a sample of life insurance agencies. Formen's use of goal setting in an in-basket test was found to be significantly associated with on-the-job performance in a study by Brass and Oldham (1976). Burke and Wilcox (1969) found that the use of goal setting in performance appraisal interviews was associated with performance improvement among public utility employees. Burton (1984) reported that a goal setting training program significantly improved the performance of swimmers in comparison with swimmers not given such training. Earley, Lee, and Hanson (1989) found that scores on a multidimensional goal setting questionnaire were positively associated with performance ratings for a sample of employees from 18 different companies. This was replicated by Lee, Bobko, Earley, and Locke (1988) with a large employee sample from one organization. Hall and Foster (1977) found that goal setting, defined as the desire to perform well, was significantly associated with self-rated effort but not performance on an executive game. Hall and Hall (1976) found that a similar measure was related to school performance of second to fourth graders in high-support but not low-support schools. The use of goal setting was associated with rated work effectiveness among a sample of middle managers by Oldham (1976). White and Locke (1981) found that managers, clerical workers, and professionals at a multinational company reported that goal setting was most frequently associated with high performance periods and goal blockage with low performance periods. A negative result was obtained by Barnett (1977), who found that goal setting did not improve performance on a juggling task among ninth and tenth graders. Despite the typically unclear specification of how clear and difficult the goals were in these studies, the success rate more than matches the 90% rate obtained for the core findings reported earlier.

A handful of studies have looked only at the attribute of goal clarity or specificity. Gould (1979) found that employees who developed clear career goals and plans were more successful in their careers than those who did not. Lee and Niedzwiedz (1983) found that measures of goal specificity and clarity were significantly associated with performance for a sample of service employees. Onglatco (1988) found that the clarity of individual and group goals was significantly associated with the effectiveness of quality circles in a Japanese company. Steers (1975) found that goal specificity was significantly related to rated performance for supervisors high in need for achievement (measured by a self-report questionnaire).

Goal clarity or specificity measures, of course, do not specify the difficulty of the goals in question, but making goals specific may still be more effective than making them vague if subjects with vague or no goals do not address the performance dimensions specified by the clear goals. The issue of specificity effect is discussed further in the next section.

Effects of Goal Specificity and Difficulty on Performance Variance

There has been considerable confusion in the literature regarding the effects of goal specificity as such on performance. It is often asserted that specific goals will lead to better performance than nonspecific goals, even though it is obvious from our previous discussion that this is not necessarily the case. Specific, easy goals, for example, typically lead to *lower* performance than vague, hard goals such as "do your best" (Locke, Chah, et al., 1989). Specific goals would lead to higher performance than no goals *if* no goals meant that the person would not work on the task et al. Typically, however, a "no goal" manipulation means that individuals are asked to work on the task but are not given any explicit performance goals. By default, such a condition becomes roughly equivalent to a self-set goal condition with the difficulty level unspecified, although, as noted earlier, it may often be equivalent to a do best goal.

The only direct effect of goal specificity, divorced from goal difficulty, or goal level on performance is to reduce performance variance. This is because goal specificity reduces interpretive leeway as to the exact meaning of the goal. The only two studies that have fully separated the effects of goal specificity from those of goal difficulty or goal level are those of Locke, Chah, et al. (1989). In the first study using a reaction time task, subjects who were given vague goals were asked to respond as fast as possible, moderately fast, or slowly in the hard, medium, and easy goal conditions, respectively. In the second study, using a "listing improvements" task, subjects in the vague conditions were asked to list a large, medium, and small number of ways to improve an undergraduate business program, respectively. In both studies subjects in the moderately specific goal conditions were asked to perform within a quantitative range, while subjects in the very specific goal conditions were asked to attain an exact quantitative score. In both studies it was found that the more specific the goal, the lower the performance variance. The results are shown in Figure 2–2.

It can be seen that the major difference in variance was between the vague goal conditions and the moderately specific and specific goal conditions (nonquantitative vs. verbal). However, the allowable ranges for the moderately specific conditions were narrow (e.g., list between two and four improvements), which

**FIGURE 2–2   Effect of Goal Specificity on Standard Deviation
of Performance**
From Locke, Chah, et al., 1989.

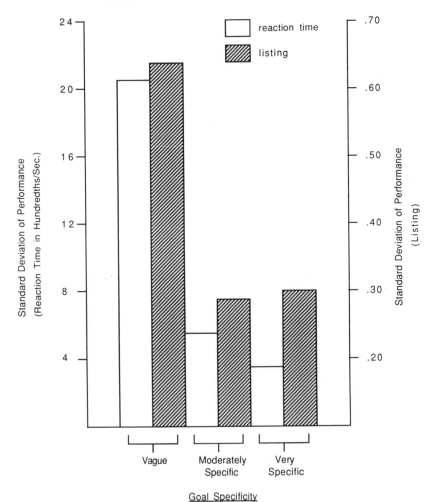

may have restricted performance more than would have been the case with a wide range.

In both studies, goal difficulty or level, regardless of specificity, was positively associated with performance level, a finding consistent with the literature. It was also found, however, that factors other than specificity could affect performance variability. One was a "ceiling" effect. Subjects who were trying to react as fast as they could showed less performance variance than those who were trying to respond moderately fast or slowly. Those with do best goals could only "err" in one direction, by responding slower than their best, whereas those with moderate or slow goals could "err" in either direction. Variance can also be affected by "floor" effects. Subjects listing improvements who were told to give a low number of uses could not list fewer than 0, whereas there was no limit for those with higher goals. Finally, controllability can affect variance. When goals are easily within their reach, individuals can perform exactly in line with their goals regardless of their level of ability; but when goals are beyond their reach, the expression of ability is not restricted and each person tries to perform to the maximum. The more challenging the goals are, the more free rein the individuals have to perform in line with their capabilities, and thus the higher the association between ability and performance (Locke, 1982b; see also Chapter 9). This necessarily makes the variance in performance higher at the higher goal levels. Sample data from three studies (taken from Locke, Chah, et al., 1989), are shown in Figure 2–3. In this context controllability in being able to reach the goal is perfectly and negatively associated with the opportunity and encouragement to perform at one's maximum ability level. Erez and Zidon (1984) also found goal difficulty to be positively associated with performance variance.

FIGURE 2–3   Relation between Performance S.D. and Goal Level

Reprinted from E. A. Locke, D. O. Chah, S. Harrison, and N. Lustgarten (in 1989), "Separating the Effects of Goal Specificity from Goal Difficulty," *Organizational Behavior and Human Decision Processes, 43,* 283. Reprinted by permission of Academic Press.

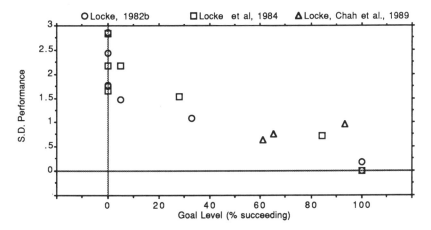

The Locke, Chah, et al. (1989) results for specificity were replicated in part by Klein, Whitener, and Ilgen (1988) using a correlational design. Difficulty was related to performance when specificity was partialed out; high specificity was associated with small goal-performance discrepancies. They also found an independent effect of goal specificity on performance. However, there are a number of potential weaknesses and ambiguities in the study, most resulting from the fact that difficulty and specificity were not experimentally manipulated. For example, difficulty and specificity were highly and negatively correlated. Moreover, there could have been error in the measurement of goal specificity and difficulty, especially since the goal measure consisted of a single self-report item. Finally, it is not clear if individuals with the most specific goals were trying for exactly that number or more than that number (see Chapter 6 for a further discussion of this issue).

Wofford (1982, study 3) also claimed to have found a specificity effect on level of performance. Three types of performance goals were assigned on a paper moon construction task: very specific (20), moderate range (18–22) and wide range (15–25). Only the very specific group attained a score of more than 18 (18.3), indicating that the goal of 20 was a hard goal. It is probable, therefore, that the operative (personal) goals for the moderate-range subjects were closer to 18 than 22, and that the personal goal for the wide-range subjects was closer to 15 than 25. In fact, neither of these two groups attained an average of 15. If 20, 18, and 15 are taken to be the actual goals of the three groups, then the mean performance ranking is identical to that of the goals. This means that the goal specificity manipulation was probably a disguised goal difficulty manipulation. Quite different results might have been obtained if all three groups had been given goals within a fully controllable performance range.

Performance with Multiple Goals

Nearly all goal setting studies have used single goals, i.e., goals for performance on one task. In most jobs, of course, individuals pursue goals on more than one task. Furthermore, these goals frequently differ in priority or importance. In many goal setting studies subjects were told to try for a certain number of *correct* answers, which implies both quantity and quality, but both dimensions were for a single task and separate goals were not assigned for each outcome.

A few goal setting studies, however, have involved goals on more than one task. Some of these involved simultaneous, dual-task experiments. Erez, Gopher, and Arazi (1987) had subjects work simultaneously on a typing and a classification task. The level of goal difficulty for each was systematically varied. As the difficulty level of the goal for one task was raised, the difficulty level of the goal for the other task was lowered. Performance was proportional to goal difficulty in all cases.

In another dual-task study (Schmidt, Kleinbeck, & Brockman, 1984), subjects simultaneously worked on a tracking task and an auditory reaction time task. When subjects were given a goal to improve their tracking performance, reaction time slowed even when subjects were trying to maintain it. Similarly, when subjects were given a goal to improve their reaction time, tracking error increased even when subjects were trying to maintain it. Kleinbeck (1986) reported several experiments, in addition to the above, with the same tasks which yielded similar results. He also reported that tracking error increased, not only during the time the subject was actually reacting to the auditory stimulus but also just before the signal was expected.

These studies illustrate the well-known fact that people have limited cognitive capacity. When cognitive resources (e.g., attention) are allocated to one task, they must, in part, be withdrawn from the other tasks and may be withdrawn even in anticipation of performing another task.

In most real-life situations goals do not have to be pursued simultaneously in the literal sense of the term, as was required in the experiments by Erez and Kleinbeck and their colleagues. Goals normally extend over a period of weeks, months, or years, and the individual can pursue the goals sequentially and/or cyclically. For example, a factory supervisor could focus one day on product quality, the next few days on quantity, and then on staffing, and then repeat the cycle the next week. A supervisor could also focus on each goal at different times during a single day. In addition, goals are often causally interrelated in a positive way so that actions taken to attain one goal help rather than hinder the attainment of other goals. For example, staffing a department with top-quality people could facilitate both quality and quantity of performance.

Ivancevich and his colleagues are the only goal setting researchers to have done extensive work with multiple goals in field settings. For example, in one study of first-line supervisors in the production and marketing departments of two plants, goals were assigned for quantity, quality, grievances, and absenteeism. All the goals led to improved performance in the plant with high top management commitment to the program (Ivancevich, 1974). In another study goals were assigned to or set participatively with salespeople for customer calls, costs, and sales. Performance of those with goals, regardless of how they were set, improved significantly more than for a control group (Ivancevich, 1976). In a subsequent study technicians were assigned or participatively set goals for absences, service complaints, costs, and lost time due to accidents. Technicians with goals improved significantly more than those without goals on three of the four measures (Ivancevich, 1977).

In yet another experimental study Ivancevich and Smith (1981) found that training in goal setting for sales managers affected both their rated behavior toward their salespeople and the sales performance of these salespeople. Ivancevich and McMahon (1982) found that, for engineers, goals setting plus self-feedback had significantly greater effects on measures of cost, quality, and unexcused overtime (a measure of efficient time use) than no goals. They had no effect on supervisory ratings of performance.

Ivancevich and McMahon (1977a, b, c) have conducted a number of correlational studies of technicians using the same four goals as in the Ivancevich (1977) study plus some additional subjective measures (supervisor ratings of effort). The results were variable, with the relation of goal attributes to performance being a function of growth need strength, race, and education.

The largest number of different goals given in any study to date was twelve. Nemeroff and Cosentino (1979) assigned management trainees goals to improve twelve different behaviors during a training program. Significant improvement was shown on all twelve behaviors as compared with subjects without goals.

Pritchard et al. (1988) reported the result of a large-scale goal setting program involving five organizational units of an Air Force base. Multiple indicators of performance were derived for each unit and translated into a common quantitative scale. The scale scores on the different indices of performance were summed to form an overall score. The number of separate indicators used was between 5 and 13 in each unit (R. Pritchard, personal communication). Providing the units with feedback and goals led to dramatic increases in overall performance.

Both productivity and rework goals were assigned to manufacturing supervisors in a study conducted by Stedry and Kay (1966). The results were somewhat confusing, but generally the overall performance improved most when the total challenge of the two goals was highest, but not so high as to be viewed as impossible.

The above studies indicate quite clearly that individuals can successfully pursue multiple goals. This might lead one to ask, "How many different goals can an individual manage or regulate?" No meaningful answer can be given to this question if posed in this form, because there are simply too many contingencies that could affect the answer. These include the following:

1. The individual's cognitive capacity or ability
2. The total amount of time available for goal completion
3. The complexity of the goals and tasks
4. The difficulty of the goals and tasks
5. The degree to which attainment of a given goal affects the attainment of other goals
6. The degree to which responsibility for goal-related performance can be delegated
7. The degree to which the goals must be attained sequentially or simultaneously
8. The quality or suitability of the individual's task strategies

Obviously this is a topic rich with research possibilities.

Effects of Goal Importance or Prioritization

In the studies by Ivancevich there was no evidence that the various goals given to the employees differed as to priority or importance. By implication they were all of equal priority. One would expect, however, that if people regulate their actions by means of goals, they would act in accordance with the relative importance of the different goals. The studies by Erez and Kleinbeck and their colleagues discussed earlier clearly indicate that manipulating the difficulty of the goal on a task in a simultaneous, dual-task situation has the effect of giving more priority to the task with the harder goal at the expense of the task with the easier goal. Similarly, Terborg and Miller (1978) found that subjects given quantity goals on a toy-assembly task produced a higher quantity of output than those assigned quality goals. The opposite outcome occurred for those given quality goals.

The only study to have looked at the effect of quantitative variations in degree of goal importance is the bank loan simulation study by Edmister and Locke (1987). Three-person loan teams set their own weights for each of four goals: loan portfolio yield, net income, charge-offs, and credit file deficiencies. Goal weights were significantly associated with performance for three of the four goals; that is, subjects performed better with respect to a given goal when its weight or importance was higher than when it was lower.

The above studies suggest that subjects can effectively prioritize goals and act in accordance with those priorities. As in the case of multiple goals, we do not know how many goals people can successfully prioritize in action. This presumably depends on many factors, including the individual's ability, the number of different goals, the degree to which clear measurement of performance is provided, and the ease with which different priorities can clearly be tied to different outcomes.

Effects of Goals on "Intrinsic" Motivation

The concept of intrinsic motivation has long puzzled many industrial-organizational psychologists. Some have argued that intrinsic motivation is that which comes from the task itself, whereas extrinsic motivation comes from sources outside the task. However, this distinction is not valid because motivation is not something inside or outside the task but rather something inside the person. The issue has been further confused by Deci and his colleagues. In a convoluted and constantly changing analysis of the concept, Deci and Ryan (1985) argued that intrinsic motivation was based on a need for self-determination (choice) and competence. It was allegedly aroused or maximized when the individual was free from external constraints and from internal doubts and compulsions, felt a strong internal locus of causality, undertook challenging tasks, and received positive but non-controlling feedback regarding performance. Ideally, intrinsic motivation is measured, according to Deci and Ryan, by allowing the individual a free choice of activities, and observing how much time he or she chooses to spend on them.

Deci is most well known, of course, for the finding that, under some circumstances, giving individuals extrinsic rewards such as money for performing a task leads to lower intrinsic motivation after the rewards are withdrawn than would have existed had the rewards not been offered at all. Deci has argued that money, if its controlling rather than its competency aspect is emphasized, lowers intrinsic motivation because it undermines the individual's sense of choice and self-determination.

There are a number of serious problems with Deci's conceptualization of intrinsic motivation and its application to the effects of rewards. First, virtually no studies (using a behavioral criterion) have verified his interpretation of the reward effect by actually measuring the hypothesized mediating variables and showing that the reward effect works through these variables (e.g., feelings of competence and self-determination). Most studies have been interpreted by making inferences from the experimental design and manipulations rather than from how the subjects actually experience them.

Second, Deci's conceptualization fails to distinguish between liking an activity for its own sake and liking it because it makes one feel competent. A logically defensible classification of types of motivation might be as follows: *intrinsic motivation* is involved when the pleasure derives from the task activity itself; *achievement motivation* is operative when the pleasure comes from performing well in relation to a standard or goal; and *extrinsic motivation* is aroused when the pleasure comes from outcomes to which task performance leads. Since the first two are clearly different phenomena, it is doubtful whether their causes are the same. Deci's measure of intrinsic motivation—namely, time spent on an activity in the absence of pressure or external constraints—seems to be more relevant to intrinsic motivation, as we have defined it, than to achievement motivation. The latter would logically be revealed more clearly when performance is undertaken in the presence of standards. Bandura (1986), incidentally, has pointed out that the so-called free choice behavior measure itself is probably not an adequate measure of intrinsic interest or motivation because time can be spent on an activity for many reasons besides interest.

Third, if intrinsic motivation is largely wiped out as Deci has claimed (Deci & Ryan, 1985) by such factors as salient incentives and rewards; competition; imposed goals, standards, and deadlines; pressure; anxiety; self-doubt; conflict; instrumental task consequences; feelings of obligation to others; appraisals of performance by others; negative feedback; surveillance; ego involvement, and the like, then it is doubtful that it has much application to real life. It seems incongruous that the need for self-determination and competence are considered to be, on the other hand, the wellsprings of all human motivation and at the same time so fragile that their effects can be negated by the most common of life's exigencies.

Deci and Ryan have stated explicitly that choice is more important than controllability in arousing intinsic motivation. If controllability is viewed as being roughly equivalent in meaning to self-efficacy as conceptualized by Bandura (1986), i.e., task-specific self-confidence, then we believe that Deci and Ryan are making a serious error in downgrading its importance. An extensive literature shows that self-efficacy has extremely powerful effects on motivation; it affects goal choice, commitment, persistence, task strategies coping with stress, and, most important, it affects performance directly (Bandura, 1977, 1986). We shall have much more to say about self-efficacy in later chapters.

Deci's theory has been discussed critically and at some length by Bandura (1986) and Locke and Henne (1986), who made several of the points noted above and more. Given the confused state of the theory itself, it would be surprising if any consistent findings emerged from studies of goals and intrinsic motivation. If we consider mainly the studies that used a behavioral criterion of intrinsic motivation, we find that the results are, in fact, very inconsistent. Of course, part of the problem is making clear theoretical predictions.

One can assume that, according to Deci, assigned goals would be considered to be controlling and would thus be expected to undermine intrinsic motivation, as compared, for example, with participatively set goals, self-set goals, or no goals. However, this conclusion would have to be tempered according to whether the goal presented a challenge or conveyed competency information. It could be argued that easy goals would be less detrimental than hard goals, since the former would result in more positive feedback; on the other hand, hard goals provide greater challenge. Finally, initial task interest could interact with the above, since there is more leeway for undermining interesting tasks than boring tasks.

Let us consider the studies that examined the effects of imposed or assigned deadlines or goals first. Amabile, DeJong, and Lepper (1976) found that setting task deadlines led to lower intrinsic motivation in word games than not setting deadlines. If deadlines are viewed as analogous to assigned goals, this study could be seen as supporting Deci's theory. Consistent with the results of Amabile et al., Cellar and Barrett (1987) found that perceived degree of influence in goal setting was related to intrinsic motivation. However, this perception was apparently not related to the actual goal manipulation (assigned vs. self-set).

In contradition to the above findings, Chang and Lorenzi (1983) found that *both* participatively set and assigned goals enhanced intrinsic motivation on an interesting task in comparison with a boring task. On the boring task, assigned goals led to greater intrinsic motivation than participatively set goals ($p < .10$). In partial contradiction to these results, Mossholder (1980) found that assigned goals reduced intrinsic motivation on an interesting task as compared with no goals, but increased it on a boring task. To confuse matters further, on a task that they described as "moderately interesting," Shalley, Oldham, and Porac (1987) found that assigned goals led to greater intrinsic motivation than participatively set goals. Hirst (1988) claimed to have obtained a finding parallel to Mossholder's in that goal setting undermined intrinsic motivation when the task was more complex and enhanced it when the task was simpler. However, Hirst used an attitudinal rather than behavioral measure of intrinsic motivation.

It appears that there are complex interactions between task interest and degree of participation in goal setting, but even these interactions show no consistent pattern. Cellar and Barrett's (1987) finding for perceived influence is congruent with Deci's theory, but their results suggest that his perception may not be closely tied to the *actual* origin of the goals. If this is the case, it may be that assigned goals and incentives will *not* undermine intrinsic motivation as long as they are not perceived as controlling. However, we do not know what factors determine how goals and incentives will be perceived.

In a study of self-set goals, Hom (1985) found that such goals slightly increased intrinsic interest as compared with no goals when there was no reward for performance. The same finding emerged even more strongly when there were rewards for performance for subjects high in achievement motivation. In contrast, self-set goals lowered intrinsic motivation for subjects low in achievement motivation in the reward condition. The existence of complex three-way interactions like this one make it clear that the phenomenon of intrinsic motivation is far from being understood.

The results are no more consistent when degree of success in attaining the goals is taken into account. Shalley and Oldham (1985) found complex interaction effects when they manipulated goal difficulty and expectation of evaluation, but examination of their Figure 1 suggests that intrinsic motivation was considerably higher following success in attaining goals than failure. In contrast, Garland (1983) found no effect of easy vs. hard goals on the decision to work additional trials on an object-listing task after the formal experiment was over, although subjects were not actually given the chance to do the extra work. Finally, Cellar and Barrett (1987) found that perceived (rather than objective) goal difficulty was positively related to intrinsic motivation (time spent on a computer task). The difficulty effect could be related to Deci's concept of challenge, but just where challenge leaves off and failure and negative feedback begin is not made clear in the theory. In Garland's (1983) study the subjects with hard goals never succeeded and those with easy goals often succeeded, but there were no differential effects of the goals. Greater challenge, of course, implies less positive feedback than lesser challenge. Since challenge and positive feedback may be negatively associated and yet are both asserted to increase intrinsic motivation, this adds confusion to the theory.

To cap the confusion are two studies comparing the effects of proximal and distal goals on intrinsic motivation. Bandura and Schunk (1981) found that proximal goals produced higher intrinsic motivation than distal goals on an arithmetic task. However, Manderlink and Harackiewicz (1984) found the opposite with a word game and an attitudinal measure of motivation. It should be recognized, however, that the former study compared daily with weekly goals while the latter compared two-minute with twenty-two-minute goals.

In conclusion, little can be concluded about the effects of goals on intrinsic motivation. The extant research raises more questions than it answers. Part of the problem is that Deci's theory is simply not well enough developed and articulated to make clear predictions possible. Furthermore, studies of intrinsic motivation typically fail to measure the mediating variables asserted to be responsible for its effects. Finally, intrinsic motivation as Deci defines it (time spent during a free work period) is probably not very significant in the world of work. Work life tends to be governed more strongly by achievement motivation (involving imposed standards) and extrinsic motivation (pay, recognition, promotion) than by intrinsic motivation. This is not to deny that liking the work one does for its own sake is important for personal happiness; it clearly is. But in real work settings such motivation rarely operates in isolation from other types of motivation. When goals and incentives are in force (as opposed to when they are withdrawn), they are highly effective (Locke et al., 1980).

Effects of Proximal Goals, Distal Goals, and Subgoals

A number of goal setting studies have compared the effects of proximal or short-term goals with those of distal or long-term goals, or what is equivalent, the effects of subgoals (or end-goals accompanied by subgoals) with the effects of end-goals alone (Bandura, 1986). Goal setting theory makes no predictions about the relative effectiveness of each type of goal. Favoring proximal goals and subgoals is the argument that such goals might entail more frequent feedback regarding progress in relation to end-goals than would end-goals alone (Bandura, 1986). Furthermore, proximal goals and subgoals might be more psychologically "real" to individuals than distant goals and thus might prevent procrastination and premature discouragement (Bandura, 1986). Favoring distal goals and end-goals is the argument that they are more flexible and can more readily be adjusted to short-term circumstances and contingencies. Favoring equality between the two types of goals is the fact that tracking of end-goals is still possible in the absence of subgoals; in such a case there would be no feedback advantage to proximal goals. Adding to the uncertainty is the fact that we have little knowledge about the ideal time span for a goal. It is likely that goals that are too proximal or frequent will be viewed as intrusive, distracting, and annoying and thus will be rejected. In contrast goals that are too distal will be seen as unreal and unworthy of serious or immediate attention. The ideal time span, of course, could differ with different tasks and situations and with different types of people.

Given the above, it will not be surprising to learn that the research findings on this matter fail to reveal consistent findings. Three experiments favor proximal goals. Bandura and Schunk (1981) and Bandura and Simon (1977) found that daily goals were more effective than weekly (seven-day) goals in improving performance in arithmetic and in facilitating weight loss, respectively. Bandura and Simon (1977) also found that some subjects given distal goals actually set proximal goals; this manipulation check has rarely been made in other studies on this topic. It was subjects who actually used proximal goals, regardless of experimental condition, who lost more weight than those who used distal goals or had no goals. Morgan (1985) found that students who set multiple subgoals for each study session in a course did better in the course than students who set only a single, broad goal for each study session. This manipulation, however, seems to have confounded distal-proximal with number of goals and goal specificity.

Contextual results were obtained by Dubbert and Wilson (1984), who found that daily calorie goals were not superior to weekly goals initially. However, in a three-month follow-up, only those using proximal goal setting continued to lose weight. Yet another weight loss study was conducted by Kincey (1983), who assigned daily and weekly goals for eating. There was no difference in weight loss for the two goal groups for those high in internal locus of control, whereas the distal goal setting was more effective for those high in external locus of control. The authors hypothesized that weekly goals give externals more flexibility and that this meshes well with their allegedly more erratic goal setting and work patterns. This study did not use manipulation checks to determine the actual frequency of goal setting by subjects in the two conditions.

A final weight loss study (Zegman & Baker, 1983) claimed that distal calorie goals worked better than proximal goals in reducing calorie intake and weight loss, although both were actually effective. However, in this study proximal and distal goal subjects actually had the same daily calorie goals. The proximal goal subjects recorded food intake and added up their calories after each meal or snack, whereas distal subjects recorded food intake but did not add up their calories until the end of the day. The real difference, then, was one of feedback frequency and flexibility rather than goal proximity.

Several studies found no difference in the effects of proximal and distal goals. Hall and Byrne (1988) found that subjects in an exercise class did not differ significantly in number of sit-ups when given goals for each weekly session plus a three-week end-goal vs. just an end-goal. On an absolute basis, the end-goal subjects performed slightly below the level of the subgoal subjects. Martin et al. (1984) found no difference in the effects of one-week and five-week goals for exercise on physical fitness. Locke and Bryan (1967) also found no significant difference between an end-goal condition and an end-goal plus subgoal condition using an addition task. The time span for subgoals was fifteen minutes, while that for the end-goal was two hours. In absolute terms the end-goal subjects performed somewhat better than the subgoal subjects. Locke and Bryan suggested that subgoal subjects in this study may have used the subgoals as performance limits rather than as minimums. It should be noted that the end-goal or distal goal time span of two hours in this experiment was shorter in time span than any of the proximal goals used in other studies.

Manderlink and Harackiewicz (1984) found no difference in the effects of distal and proximal goals for a word-puzzle game. Like the Locke and Bryan study, both the proximal and distal goals were very short term. The proximal goals were, in effect, two-minute goals (one for each two-minute trial), while the distal goals were twenty-two-minute goals (one for all trials combined).

A final study that measured both proximal and distal goals was that by Brief and Hollenbeck (1985). In a study of goals set spontaneously by insurance salespeople, they found that some salespersons set proximal goals for sales behaviors such as customer calls and some set distal goals for outcomes such as sales commissions. Only the distal sales commission goals were significantly related to commissions earned. However, the causal relationship between the proximal goal of making calls and sales commissions may be slight or nonexistent. A more logical comparison would have been between proximal sales goals (e.g., weekly, monthly) and distal sales goals (yearly). Such a comparison would only be possible if the salespeople had actually set proximal sales goals, which does not seem to have been the case.

A number of studies have looked at the effects of proximal and distal planning rather than of goal setting. The results here are no more consistent but, on the surface, have seemed more likely to favor distal than proximal planning. Kirschenbaum, Humphrey, and Malett (1981) found that elaborate daily study plans, which must have been highly burdensome, led to fewer hours spent in study than less elaborate and burdensome monthly plans. However, there were no effects of planning condition on grades. Furthermore, there is a certain confusion in this study regarding what type of planning was actually done in the various experimental conditions. For example, all subjects did daily study monitoring, which could easily have led distal subjects to set some type of daily goal. Furthermore, the distal-planning subjects actually handed in more plan sheets to the experimenter than the proximal-planning subjects. In a one-year follow-up to this study, Kirschenbaum, Malett, Humphrey and Tomarken (1982) found that for those with higher GPA's, subjects in the distal-planning condition got better grades than those in the proximal-planning condition. However, this effect did not occur for those with lower GPA's. In another study Kirschenbaum, Tomarken, and Ordman (1982) found no difference in the grades of daily and monthly planners; furthermore, the daily planners spent somewhat more time studying than the monthly planners. Again there was possible confounding because both the daily and monthly planners had to hand in weekly reports regarding their activities. Also, in this study, having the choice of being in the daily or monthly planning condition had a much stronger effect on grades than being in the daily or monthly condition as such.

In conclusion, no definite conclusions can be drawn from the studies of proximal and distal goals, although we can formulate some tentative hypotheses. There is some suggestion that, at least for weight loss, daily goals are both effective (as compared with no goals) and typically more effective than weekly goals. There is little evidence of any differential effectiveness of proximal and distal goals within a typical experimental work period of two hours or less. In a separate review of goal setting studies (in which the studies used in each comparison were not listed), Balcazar, Hopkins, and Suarez (1986) concluded that the effects of daily and weekly goals showed equal consistency of results across studies but that both showed more consistent results than studies of monthly goals. The study by Martin et al. (1984) noted above, however, did not agree with this conclusion. The studies of distal vs. proximal planning cannot really be evaluated, since there is reason to believe that the monthly planners in these studies also had daily plans.

Kirschenbaum (1985) has reviewed the proximal-distal literature on goal setting and planning and has concluded that there is "overall consistency of the findings" (p. 503), especially with respect to the alleged superiority of distal over proximal planning. We cannot agree with his conclusions, especially since they were based in part on misinterpretations of a number of the studies. For example, he denied that Bandura and Simon's (1977) study showed that proximal goals were superior to distal goals even though that is exactly what it showed. In addition, he used the method of "criterion-switching" to evaluate the results of studies, so that, for example, if the performance data did not come out, he emphasized attitudinal or attendance outcomes (e.g., pp. 500–501).

We believe that much more research needs to be done before firm conclusions can be drawn about the relative efficacy of proximal and distal goal setting. These studies need to

1. Perform manipulation checks to determine what goals people in the various goal conditions *actually* set or tried for, regardless of the experimental condition they were placed in.
2. Determine whether proximal and distal goal groups had equivalent amounts of feedback regarding progress in relation to goals. Feedback given to distal goal subjects, of course, can function as a proxy for proximal goals, thus making the treatments difficult to separate in practice.
3. Encompass a wide range of time spans—from minutes, to hours, to days, to weeks.
4. Determine whether goal commitment is different for proximal and distal goal subjects.
5. Measure and control for possible confounding and/or mediating factors, such as burdensome record keeping, degree of choice over type of goal, degree of flexibility in applying goals, and degree of perceived success and failure in goal pursuit.
6. Consider the possible effects of the nature of the task and individual differences among subjects with respect to personality, cognitive style, and the like.

Goals as Mediators of the Effects of External Incentives

In his 1968 article, Locke argued that goals or goal commitment might mediate the performance effects of incentives such as money, feedback, and participation (Locke, 1968b). There is strong evidence for the mediating effects of goals in feedback; this issue is examined in Chapter 8. There is some evidence for the mediation hypothesis with respect to participation in goal setting, but as we shall see in Chapter 7, it is hard to test the hypothesis because participation in goal setting does not have very reliable effects. With respect to monetary incentives the jury is still out, since the evidence is conflicting. These results are discussed in Chapter 6. (For a discussion of the early studies of mediation, see Tolchinksy & King, 1980.)

CONCLUSION

Goal setting theory is based on the results of some 393 findings on the goal difficulty and difficulty vs. do best aspects of the theory alone. The success rate or partial success rate of these studies, regardless of study quality, is over 90%. The core findings of the theory are based on data from close to forty thousand subjects in eight countries; eighty-eight different tasks; numerous types of performance measures; laboratory, and field settings; experimental and correlational designs; time spans ranging from one minute to three years; studies of assigned, self-set, and participatively set goals; and data from the group and organizational as well as the individual level of analysis. The overall validity and usefulness of the theory is attested to by meta-analyses, enumerative reviews, peer evaluations, and comparative assessments of goal setting against other theories. Goals also affect action: when they are nonquantitative, when they are general, when there are multiple goals, and when they are prioritized. (These results answer most of the criticisms concerning the limitations of goal theory made by Austin & Bobko, 1985.)

Thus far, however, we have presented only the core findings. In subsequent chapters the theory is further developed to encompass such issues as self-efficacy, valence, goal mechanisms, goal choice moderators such as commitment and feedback, and affect.

GOALS, EXPECTANCIES, SELF-EFFICACY, VALENCES, AND PERFORMANCE

The goal difficulty function that we described in the preceding chapter has led to a number of theoretical controversies and questions that are addressed in this chapter. One concerns the relationship between goals, expectancies, and performance. Another concerns the relationship between goals, valences, and performance. Expectancy and valence are two of the concepts that form the core of expectancy (valence-instrumentality-expectancy) theory. This theory was introduced to industrial-organizational psychology and organizational behavior by Vroom (1964) and has stimulated a massive amount of research as well as additional theoretical developments (Porter & Lawler, 1968). A final source of controversy concerns the relationship between goal theory and Atkinson's (1958) motivation theory, which also has an expectancy component.

At first glance there appear to be three conflicting theories regarding the relationship of expectancies to performance. Goal theory shows convincingly that there is a positive linear relationship between goal level or difficulty and performance level (Chapter 2). Since harder goals are more difficult to reach than easier goals, this means that expectancy of success, across goal levels, will show a negative linear relationship to performance (for illustrative data, see Locke, 1968b, Figure 1; and Locke, 1967c, Figure 1). In contrast, expectancy theory (Vroom, 1964), in all of its versions, asserts that, holding other factors constant, there is a positive linear relationship between expectancy of success (effort-performance expectancy) and performance. Again there is clear evidence supporting this assertion (Campbell & Pritchard, 1976; Mitchell, 1974).

In contrast to both of these theories, Atkinson (1958) has proposed that the relationship between probability of success and performance is curvilinear,

Portions of this chapter, including Figures 3–2 and 3–3, have been taken from E. A. Locke, S. J. Motowidlo, and P. Bobko (1986). "Using Self-Efficacy Theory to Resolve the Conflict between Goal Setting Theory and Expectancy Theory in Organizational Behavior and Industrial/Organizational Psychology." *Journal of Social and Clinical Psychology, 4*, 328–38. Reprinted by permission of Guilford Press.

with the highest level of performance occurring at moderate levels of probability or expectancy. Atkinson's theory is based on the assumption that in the absence of extraneous factors, and given that the motive to succeed exceeds the motive to avoid failure, motivation is a function of the product of the probability of success (PS) and the incentive value of success (I), which he claims is an inverse function of PS, thus $I = 1 - PS$. Clearly, the product of PS and I, or $PS \times 1 - PS$, will be at a maximum when $PS = .50$. The evidence for this theory, as shown later in this chapter, is not consistent. The prediction of these three theories is shown graphically in Figure 3–1. Let us consider goal theory vs. expectancy theory first.

GOAL THEORY VS. EXPECTANCY THEORY

Early attempts at reconciliation (Locke et al., 1981; Mento et al., 1980) suggested that expectancy (as well as valence and instrumentality) should be considered a determinant of goal choice rather than of performance as such. Goals, in turn, would mediate between expectancy theory variables and performance and be the most direct determinant of performance. Certainly this viewpoint is plausible in that both expectancy and instrumentality affect both goal choice (e.g., Klein, 1988; see also Chapter 5) and goal commitment (Chapter 6). However, the mediating hypothesis is not fully viable because, as we shall see, expectancy affects performance even controlling for the effect of goals (Klein, 1988; Locke, Frederick, Lee, & Bobko, 1984; Wood & Locke, 1987).

It has also been suggested that many of the findings of expectancy studies in which goal setting has been included as a variable have not been valid due to

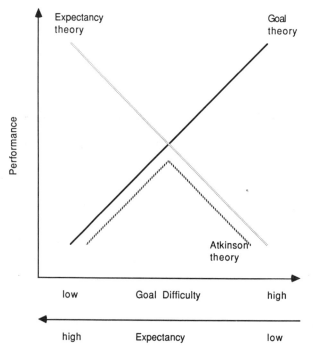

FIGURE 3–1 Predicted Expectancy-Performance Relationships for Atkinson Theory, Expectancy Theory, and Goal Theory

methodological artifacts. For example, both Mento et al. (1980) and Locke and Shaw (1984) have suggested that expectancy of success may be correlated with ability, thus making the expectancy-performance correlation artifactual. Locke and Shaw (1984), for example, found that partialing out ability vitiated a significant first-order expectancy-performance correlation. However, as noted above, expectancy has been found to be significantly related to performance even with ability controlled (e.g., Arvey, 1972). The need to control for ability, of course, is not confined to the expectancy studies since ability can be a confounding factor in many contexts.

Mento et al. (1980) also noted that goal measurements in studies that have looked at the effects of expectancies on performance have been less than adequate. Arvey (1972) and Janz (1982), for example, did not measure goals at all. Motowidlo, Loehr, and Dunnette (1978) offered their specific goal subjects a bonus for beating a specified score, but they never actually measured what goals the subjects were trying to attain. Similarly, goal acceptance and valence were seldom measured or were inadequately measured. Furthermore, feedback was not always provided to show progress in relation to the goals. Finally, the expectancy measures did not always specify that such ratings should be made on the assumption that the subject would try his or her hardest to win or reach the goal. When all of these artifacts were eliminated, Mento et al. (1980) found no main effect of expectancy on performance. When feedforward was used instead of feedback, Locke and Shaw (1984) found no expectancy effect, but they did obtain a main effect for valence on performance. However, since expectancy effects on performance have been found even with the above artifacts eliminated, there is still a need to reconcile the apparent conflict with goal theory.

There are actually two ways to resolve the goal theory–expectancy theory conflict. One is based on distinguishing between within-group and between-group levels of analysis, and the other is based on measuring expectancy in a different manner than is usually done. Bandura's (1986) social-cognitive theory, specifically his concept of self-efficacy, is the basis for the second solution.

The first solution to the conflict was suggested by Garland (1984), who identified the importance of distinguishing between within-group and between-group correlations of expectancy and performance. However, Garland's basic insight requires further explication, development, and clarification. The negative relationships found previously between expectancy and performance in goal setting research were artifacts of data analyses that confounded levels of analysis. In the usual goal setting design, different groups of subjects are assigned different goals and rate their expectancies of reaching them. Each subject reports his or her expectancy of attaining only one performance level, namely, the one that corresponds to the goal assigned to that individual. Because different groups of subjects are assigned different goals, their expectancy reports pertain to different levels of performance. As a result, although every subject is rating the expectancy of "goal attainment," it means different things in different groups. In short, the subjects are actually rating expectancies of different performance outcomes.

This confounding of levels of analysis is shown in Table 3–1, which gives the hypothetical expectancy ratings of four groups of students with grade goals of A, B, C, and D for each possible level of grade outcome (A, B, C, and D). In the

Table 3–1   Expectancy Ratings Obtained When Confounding and Not Confounding Levels of Analysis, Using Grade Goals as an Example (Hypothetical Data)

Grade Outcome	Rated Expectancy of Attaining Each Grade Outcome by Students with Goals of:			
	<u>A</u>	<u>B</u>	<u>C</u>	<u>D</u>
A	.60 *	.40	.20	.00
B	.90	.70	.50	.30
C	1.00	.90	.80	.70
D	1.00	1.00	1.00	.90
Total	3.50	3.00	2.50	1.90
Obtained Grade($\overline{x}$)	3.20	2.80	2.40	1.90

* Only expectancy estimates in boxes were obtained
  in traditional (confounded) studies.

typical or traditional goal setting study, *only the ratings within the solid boxes were obtained.* Observe that the students with the highest (A) grade goals have the lowest expectancy ratings but the highest grade achievement. The opposite is the case for students with the lowest (D) grade goals.

The overall results using this confounded procedure are shown in Figure 3–2 (from Locke, Motowidlo, & Bobko, 1986). The figure shows the relationships between expectancy of goal attainment and performance for three groups of subjects. One group has a high performance goal, one has a medium goal, and one has a low goal. Each subject rates the probability of attaining only the assigned goal (as in the Table 3–1 boxes).

First note that, on the abscissa, goal level and expectancy are negatively correlated, since, on the average, subjects who are assigned harder goals have less chance of reaching them than subjects who are assigned easier goals. Second, observe that the between-group correlation (shown by the dashed oval) between expectancy and performance is negative. Higher-performing (higher-goal) groups will have lower expectancies than lower-performing (lower-goal) groups. This part of the analysis, then, focuses on group-level data (i.e., the three group means).

Third, if one shifts to an individual, within-group level of analysis, a fundamentally different perspective emerges. That is, the within-group correlation between expectancy and performance (solid ovals) will tend to be positive. This was Garland's (1984) key insight. His finding has been replicated by Locke,

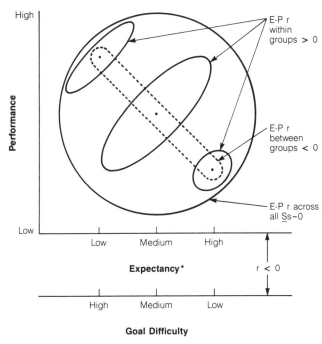

FIGURE 3–2 Expectancy-Performance Relationships When Expectancy Is Measured with Respect to Assigned or Chosen Goal Level Only

Reprinted by Permission of Guilford Press.

*Expectancy measured in terms of reaching assigned goal.

Frederick, Lee, and Bobko (1984). Note that within-group expectancy ratings are all made with respect to the same goal level. (In the same way, expectations have been found to predict intentions when the intention is for the same target behavior; Prothero & Beach, 1984.)

This within-group relationship may show up as a main effect for expectancy in a hierarchical regression analysis after entering ability and goals first (Garland, 1984; Huber & Neale, 1986, $p < .10$). However, there may also be an interaction effect (expectancy × goals) if the various within-group correlations are sufficiently different from each other in magnitude. Mento et al. (1980, study 1) found that the goal-performance relationship was stronger for those with high rather than low expectancies of success. Both Garland (1984) and Locke, Frederick, Lee, and Bobko (1984) found that the correlations are higher in the medium- and hard-goal groups than in the easy-goal group, where virtually all subjects can reach their goal (thus eliminating nearly all variance in expectancy). This finding is shown in Figure 3–2 by the within-group ovals' being larger in scope (i.e., less range-restricted) for the medium- and hard-goal groups than for the easy-goal group.

Fourth, observe that the overall correlation using all subjects (solid circle) will tend to be relatively small in magnitude, because the between-group and within-group correlations are opposite in sign and thus tend to cancel each other out. This claim is supported by the fact that expectancy-performance correlations across all subjects in goal setting studies are typically small and/or nonsignificant (Mento et al., 1980).

As an aside, note that as the range of goal difficulty becomes increasingly wide, the solid circle will become more elliptical in a negative direction, since the between-group differences will increasingly outweigh the within-group relationships. Conversely, as the range of goal difficulty becomes increasingly narrow, the solid circle will become more elliptical in the positive direction, since the within-group relationships will increasingly outweigh the between-group differences. Figure 3–2 represents the case in which there is a moderate range of goal difficulty.

A second solution to the conflict between goal setting theory and expectancy theory is based on the way in which expectancy is measured. To explain this solution, it is first necessary to introduce the concept of self-efficacy and explain its relationship to that of expectancy. Self-efficacy (SE) is a key concept in Bandura's social learning or social-cognitive theory (Bandura, 1977, 1986). *Self-efficacy* is defined as one's judgment of "how well one can execute courses of action required to deal with prospective situations" (Bandura, 1982, p. 122). Self-efficacy is influenced by past performance, modeling, persuasion, autonomic arousal, and the individual's cognitive processing of all of these and of other information relevant to beliefs about performance capability. Bandura has asserted that self-efficacy is significantly and positively related to future performance, even more so in some cases than to past performance. Furthermore, extensive research strongly supports this claim (e.g., Bandura, 1982, 1986). In this respect, the prediction is the same as for expectancy theory.

The concept of self-efficacy is related in meaning to that of effort-performance expectancy in expectancy theory but is much broader in scope. Self-efficacy is based on one's assessment of all personal factors that could affect one's performance—e.g., past performance, ability, adaptability, capacity to coordinate skilled sequences of actions, resourcefulness, etc. (Bandura, 1986, pp. 231–32). In practice, many expectancy measures are probably equivalent to self-efficacy measures or at least partially so. When people are asked to indicate their chances of succeeding at some task, their rating may include, by implication, not only their estimates of the degree to which effort will pay off in performance but their belief in their total capability of performing at a certain level.

However, in contrast to the procedure used in the typical goal setting or expectancy study, self-efficacy is not measured in relation to a single goal or performance level, but in relation to a range of performance levels (e.g., see Appendix C, #5). In addition, Bandura typically measures two aspects of self-efficacy, which he calls "magnitude" and "strength." Magnitude involves "yes" or "no" answers to each designated performance level, while strength involves a rating of the degree of certainty of reaching each level. We use the total number of " yes" answers and the mean certainty rating across all performance levels or a range of levels as predictors (Locke, Frederick, Lee, & Bobko, 1984)—a procedure that is also followed by Bandura upon occasion (e.g., Wood & Bandura, in press, a).

Expectancy ratings (which would be most nearly equivalent to the strength measure) *can* be made in exactly the same way. Suppose, for example, that the task involves solving arithmetic problems within a ten-minute period. The performance range can be defined to include levels from "relatively poor" to "superior" performance. Five specific levels can be selected to represent this range: 20 problems solved correctly within ten minutes; 30 problems; 40 problems; 50 problems; and 60 problems. For each one, we can ask all subjects, regardless of their goal levels, to rate their subjective likelihood of reaching at least that level, so that five expectancies are obtained from each subject. Then the variable of performance expectancy can be computed as the sum or average of the five expectancy estimates from each person. This procedure is shown in Table 3–1 also. If the students rate not just the probability of attaining their chosen grade goal but also the probability of attaining all other levels of grade outcomes, the matrix is filled, that is, *every* student makes an expectancy rating for *every* outcome. Table 3–1 shows that if we then sum the columns, we have the overall expectancy ratings by students in each goal group across the same outcomes. Observe that in this case the goal-expectancy correlation *reverses* as compared with the traditional case. The high-goal subjects now have the highest overall expectancy ratings. Both goals and expectancies relate positively to performance.

This will hold true whether goals are self-set or assigned. As is shown below, if goals are self-set, those with higher self-efficacy will set higher goals as a result. If goals are assigned, people will have higher self-efficacy as a result of goal assignment (and of subsequent performance).

The relationship of goals and self-efficacy to performance within and between groups using the self-efficacy measurement procedure is shown graphically in Figure 3–3 (from Locke, Motowidlo, & Bobko, 1986). Note that (on the abscissa) goal difficulty and SE or expectancy are correlated positively instead of negatively. It follows that the between-group relation of *both* goal level and

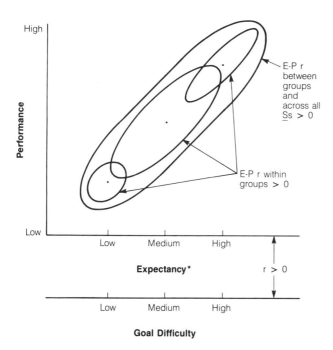

**FIGURE 3–3
Expectancy-Performance Relationships When Expectancy or Self-Efficacy Is Measured with Respect to Multiple Goal or Performance Levels**

Reprinted by permission of Guilford Press.

*Expectancy measured in terms of attaining all goal or performance levels.

expectancy to performance will be positive. And the within-group relationships between expectancy and performance will continue to be positive, as in Figure 3–2 (and in Table 3–1 as well). As a result, the overall relationship of expectancy to performance across subjects will be positive, since the between- and within-group correlations are in the same direction. Ilgen, Nebeker, and Pritchard (1981), incidentally, found that effort-performance expectancies measured across the full performance range yielded better predictions of performance than expectancies measured in other ways.

A study by Locke, Frederick, Lee, & Bobko (1984) supports the above analyses. Locke et al. measured self-efficacy by asking subjects to indicate whether they could reach each of eight objectively defined levels of performance and what their degree of confidence in reaching them was. Self-efficacy magnitude was computed as the number of "yes" answers. Self-efficacy strength was computed as the sum of the confidence judgments made for the various performance levels. Both measures were positively related to performance for all subjects combined. Wood and Locke (1987) obtained similar results in three studies of student grade performance.

GOALS, SELF-EFFICACY (EXPECTANCY), AND PERFORMANCE

The link from assigned and/or self-set goals to performance is at the core of goal setting theory and was documented in Chapter 2. In the preceding section self-efficacy was shown to be related positively to performance. It now remains to identify the full set of causal links between goals, self-efficacy, and performance.

We begin with self-set, or personal, goals. The three-way relationship is shown in Figure 3–4. Self-efficacy or expectancy affects the level of the personal goal chosen but is also independently related to performance. There is also a main effect of self-set goals on performance. The weighted mean r's shown in Figure 3–4 are based on the results of thirteen studies with a total N of 2,285, which measured each of the three relationships (Bandura & Cervone, 1986; Dachler & Mobley, 1973, 2 studies; Garland, 1985; Garland & Adkinson, 1987; Hollenbeck & Brief, 1987; Locke et al., 1984; Meyer & Gellatly, 1988, 2 studies; Meyer et al., 1988; Podsakoff & Farh, 1989; Taylor, Locke, Lee, & Gist, 1984; and Wood & Locke, 1987). All these studies used self-efficacy measures or the equivalent. The actual data are shown in Table 3–2. (To minimize the effect of differences between studies, Table 3–2 only includes studies that reported data on at least three of the

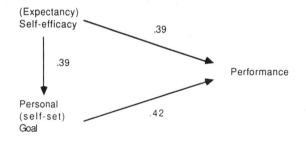

FIGURE 3–4 **Relationship between Self-Efficacy, Self-Set Goals, and Performance**

five possible relationships shown later in Figure 3–5. Klockmann's, 1985, study was omitted because she used a very narrow range of goal difficulty.)

The mean of .39 for the relationship between self-efficacy and performance is reasonably consistent with data presented by Feltz (1988). She reviewed all the studies reporting relationships between self-efficacy and performance in sports or physical activities. The mean weighted r was .46 (calculated from the data presented in her Table 1). A higher correlation might be expected in physical than in cognitive tasks because the former tasks are usually less complex and the meaning of feedback less equivocal, thus making it easier to form a clear picture of one's capabilities.

Table 3–2   Correlations Between Assigned Goals, Personal Goals, Self-Efficacy, and Performance

AUTHORS	N	AG–PG	AG–SE	SE–PG	SE–P	PG–P	NOTES
Bandura & Cervone (1986)	88			.43[a]	.50[a]	.69[a]	[a] average of four discrepancy conditions
Dachler & Mobley—1 (1973)	184			.31[b,c]	.30[c]	.42[b]	[b] average of current and future goals
—2	412			.30[b,c]	.12[c,d]	.16[b]	[c] SE = maximum expected utility [d] all jobs
Garland (1985)	176	.54[e]	.25[e]	.58	.74	.55	[e] not in article; personal communication
Garland & Adkinson (1987)	127	.70	.20	.39	.62	.45	
Hollenbeck & Brief (1987)	102		.29[f,g]	.49[g,h]	.47[f,g]	.31[f]	[f] all Ss [g] SE = task–specific ability [h] PG = self-set Ss only
Locke, Frederick, Lee, & Bobko (1984)	181			.54[i]	.61[i]	.57[i]	[i] combined SE measures, trials 5 and 6
Meyer & Gellatly—1 (1988)	56	.59	.33	.62	.73	.83	
—2	60	.29	.13	.48	.71	.62	
Meyer et al. (1988)	69	.67	.48	.60[j]	.54	.56[j]	[j] desired performance used as goal measure
Podsakoff & Farh (1989)	90			.69	.63	.73	
Taylor et al. (1984)	223[k]			.20	.38	.25	[k] average of high and low N of Ss
Wood & Locke (1987)	517			.32[l]	.22[l]	.42[l]	[l] avg. for three samples and both SE measures
Total	= 2,285						
Weighted	$\bar{r}$	.58	.27	.39	.39	.42	

AG = Assigned Goals; PG = Personal Goals; SE = Self-Efficacy; P = Performance

The result of adding assigned goals to the model in Figure 3–4 is shown in Figure 3–5. The weighted mean correlations for self-efficacy, personal goals, and performance are the same as those in Figure 3–4. The interesting finding here is that assigned goals can affect not only personal goals (a well-established finding in that assigned goals are usually accepted; see Chapter 6) *but also can affect self-efficacy even before any performance has taken place.* This is basically Eden's (1988) Pygmalion effect. Meyer and Gellatly (1988) have indicated one mechanism by which this occurs. Assigned goals appear to convey *normative information* to the individual by suggesting or specifying what level of performance the individual could be expected to attain. In Meyer and Gellatly's first study, assigned goals affected norms that in turn affected self-efficacy, and thereby personal goals and performance. In their second study, they manipulated goals and norms independently and found that perceived norms affected both self-efficacy and personal goals. The effect of normative information on motivation is well established (Mitchell, Rothman, & Liden, 1985), so this aspect of the findings is not surprising. What was not known before the Meyer studies, however, was that assigned goals were a viable, if indirect, means of conveying normative information. Meyer and Gellatly (1988) still found, moreover, that assigned goals affected personal goals independently of norms, indicating that there may be other factors involved in the assigning of goals that makes them effective (e.g., authority as such). Norms conveyed simply in terms of the alleged probability of attaining a goal, as compared with conveying an expected level of performance, do not have a consistent effect (Garland, 1983), since such information can lower as well as raise self-efficacy.

A recent study by Earley and Lituchy (1989) supports the validity of the model in Figure 3–5, except that they also found a direct path from assigned goals to performance. This could be because the two mediating variables are measured subjectively and are therefore subject to measurement error. Earley and Lituchy found no support, nor have we found any support, for Garland's (1985) claim that personal goals affect performance only through their effects on expectancy or self-efficacy.

In summary, both assigned goals and self-efficacy affect performance in two different ways. Assigned goals affect self-efficacy and personal goals, while self-efficacy affects personal goals and performance. The joint effect of self-efficacy and goals on performance indicates that performance is affected not only by what one is trying to do but by how confident one is of being able to do it.

FIGURE 3–5   Relationship between Assigned Goals, Personal Goals, Self-Efficacy, and Performance

Factors Affecting Self-Efficacy

As noted earlier, Bandura (1986) has posited four categories of determinants of self-efficacy. In order of importance or potency, they are: enactive mastery (actual performance or beliefs about performance), modeling, persuasion, and physiological feedback. There is corroborating evidence for each of the first three categories in the goal setting literature. Starting with *enactive mastery,* Bandura and Schunk (1981) found that proximal goal setting showed a greater positive effect on schoolchildren's self-efficacy, persistence, and performance on arithmetic performance than did distal goal setting or no goals. Earley (1986a) found that bogus, positive feedback regarding performance led to higher self-efficacy than bogus, negative feedback. Locke, Frederick, Lee, & Bobko (1984) also found self-efficacy to be significantly associated with past performance on a brainstorming task. Earley (1986c) found the same for tire-tread layers. Hollenbeck and Brief (1987) found that the highest association with a rating of task-specific ability was actual ability based on a pretest. Podsakoff and Farh (1989) also found self-efficacy to be related to ability.

Another form of enactive mastery is *success* in attaining goals. Mossholder (1980) found that among the subjects given specific, challenging goals on an assembly task, those who succeeded in reaching the goal rated themselves as more competent at the task than those who failed to reach the goal. Of course, those who succeeded actually did perform better than those who failed. It does not follow from this that subjects with low goals will have higher self-efficacy than those with high goals. Actually the reverse is true; the low-goal subjects will succeed more but they will feel less able to attain higher levels of performance than those with challenging goals. Interestingly, Mossholder (1980) found that subjects with specific goals, most of whom did not reach their goals, thought they performed more poorly when asked to rate themselves than did subjects with do best goals. This suggests, as noted previously, that people with vague goals find it easier to give themselves the benefit of the doubt, since the standard of success by its very nature is "loose," than do those with specific goals (see Figure 3–7).

The level of performance of a videotaped *role model* was found to affect self-efficacy as well as performance for subjects working at a card-sorting task in the study by Weiss and Rakestraw (1988). The effect, however, dissipated over time in deference to information based on the subjects' own task performance. Bandura and Wood (in press) and Wood and Bandura (in press, a) found that self-efficacy, stemming from subjects' evaluations of their own task performance, played an increasingly important role in performance with increasing task experience. Gist, Schwoerer, and Rosen (in press) found that the use of role modeling to teach neophytes how to use a computer software program was more effective in raising self-efficacy than standard instruction, although goal setting was not involved in this study. Their data indicated that self-efficacy is an important mediating variable between training and the development of skilled performance.

Persuasion, in the form of a statement before each of ten trials of an object-listing task to the effect that "you can do it," was found to increase self-efficacy (Garland & Adkinson, 1987). Providing individuals with normative information showing what other similar people can do can be considered another form of persuasive input. It was found to affect self-efficacy (Meyer & Gellatly, 1988 study 2), with higher norms leading to higher efficacy. In Meyer and Gellatly's first study, normative information conveyed simply by instructions to try for a high goal led to higher self-efficacy than instructions to try for a low goal.

Another means of influencing self-efficacy through persuasion is to convince subjects that performance on the task they are to work on is or is not controllable. Bandura and Wood (in press) found that subjects who were told that performance on a complex managment simulation task was highly controllable had higher self-efficacy, set higher goals, used more suitable problem-solving strategies, and performed better than those who were told that performance on the task was not easily controllable.

A number of other findings regarding the determinants of self-efficacy do not fall clearly into any one of the above categories. Earley (1986c) found that giving tire-tread layers information about how to perform their work more efficiently had a positive effect on their self-efficacy. Assigning a performance goal accompanied by *task-strategy information* was significantly more effective than assigning the goals with only a rationale as to why the goal was appropriate. Klockmann (1985) found that giving individuals strategy training in a brainstorming task produced higher self-efficacy than not giving such training, thus replicating a similar finding obtained by Locke, Frederick, Lee, & Bobko (1984). If the effects of strategy information or training on self-efficacy are a result of the fact that the strategies led to better performance, then these studies would fall within the enactive mastery category. If, on the other hand, they occur before performance has improved, they might be considered to be another form of persuasive input.

The relationship between self-efficacy and task strategies is undoubtedly reciprocal. Bandura and Wood (in press), Wood and Bandura (in press, a), and Wood, Bandura, and Bailey (in press) found that individuals with high self-efficacy chose better analytic task strategies than those with low self-efficacy on a complex management simulation. While the explanation for why task strategy information raises self-efficacy is obvious, the explanation for the reciprocal causal relationship is not clear. Possibly high self-efficacy people believe that they are using better *methods* of discovering viable strategies than individuals with low self-efficacy; those with low confidence may be doing more guessing or random trial and error. Thus when they perform poorly, they feel they are going about it the wrong way; and when they do well, they feel they are lucky but not really in control of the situation. This whole issue poses many fascinating research questions.

Earley (1988) found that employees had higher self-efficacy when their performance feedback came directly to them on their computer terminal than when it came from their supervisor, although this was not found in Earley (1986a). In both studies, getting feedback from the computer was associated with higher levels of *trust* in the feedback than getting it from the supervisor. Schunk (1984) found that the combination of *goals and incentives* led to higher self-efficacy, even before performance, than either one alone in a division task performed by schoolchildren.

A novel approach was taken by Kavanagh and Bower (1985), who induced happy or sad *mood states* through hypnotism. The task involved was competence in social, romantic, academic, and other activities. Subjects in whom a happy mood had been induced reported higher overall self-efficacy than those in whom no mood had been induced, who in turn showed higher self-efficacy than those in the sad mood condition. Undoubtedly, the relationship of mood and self-efficacy is reciprocal (Bandura, 1988).

THE CONCEPT OF SUBJECTIVE DIFFICULTY

Occasionally researchers will include a measure of subjective (as opposed to objective) goal difficulty in their studies (e.g., Mento et al., 1980). Generally, as found by Yukl and Latham (1978), such measures are less satisfactory than objective measures of goal difficulty. Subjective difficulty typically correlates lower with performance than does objective difficulty. This may be because subjective goal difficulty is a confounded measure; it can reflect at least two different types of estimates: how hard the goal is objectively and the individual's self-efficacy. It is evident from Figure 3–6 that these two estimates will be related to subjective difficulty in opposite directions. Objective goal difficulty or level will tend to be positively associated, and self-efficacy negatively associated, with subjective goal difficulty. The positive relationship with objective goal difficulty reflects the fact that the higher goal is in fact higher (harder to reach). The negative relationship with self-efficacy reflects that fact that the more confident the individual is of being able to perform well, the less difficult (easier) any given goal will appear to

FIGURE 3–6 Relationship between Objective Goal Difficulty, Self-Efficacy, and Subjective Goal Difficulty Ratings

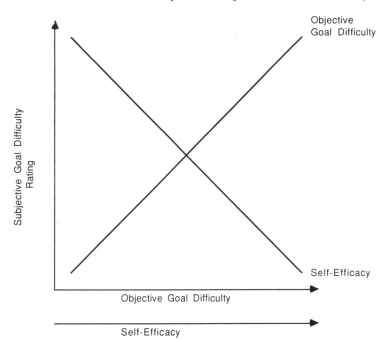

that individual. Thus the overall rating of subjective goal difficulty reflects a compromise between the objective goal level rating (how high is it?) and a self-efficacy rating (can I do it?).

Since, as noted earlier, assigned goal level shows a low, positive association with self-efficacy, this could serve to skew the subjective goal difficulty ratings in the direction of objective goal difficulty. Actually, since the subjective question can be interpreted in different ways by different people, the meaning of such a rating is indeterminate. In view of this, the use of such measures is not recommended. This caveat poses the most serious problem in correlational field studies in which goal difficulty is typically measured with a subjective question (a procedure that is necessary if multiple jobs are included in the sample). Perhaps this could be resolved by phrasing the question in a way that would clearly eliminate one of the confounds (e.g., "Ignoring your own personal capability, how challenging would you say that your work goal or goals are for the average person on this job?"). Thus far our attempts to design such items so as to be free of contamination by self-efficacy have failed (see Appendix C).

VALENCES, GOALS, AND PERFORMANCE

The findings for the relation between valences, goals, and performance, though less extensively researched, have been as puzzling as those for expectancy and self-efficacy. Locke and Shaw (1984), Matsui et al. (1981), and Arvey (1972) found positive effects of valence on performance, though Arvey's result was not significant in a regression analysis. In contrast, Garland (1985) found a *negative* correlation between valence and goal level and performance. Meyer and Gellatly (1988) found the same. None of the authors explained the reason for their results. These findings prompted Mento and Locke (1989) to examine the role of valence in more detail. In a series of five studies using a listing uses task, they assigned subjects three levels of goals (easy = 4, medium = 7, and hard = 12 uses in one minute) and then asked them to rate the expected satisfaction of attaining each of twelve levels of performance (from 2 to 13 uses). In every case, using both between- and within-subject designs, they found a strong negative relationship between assigned goal level and mean valence (expected satisfaction) across all performance levels. As a result, valence also related negatively to performance. This meant that subjects with high goals expected to get less satisfaction from virtually every level of performance than did those with medium goals, who in turn expected less satisfaction than those with easy goals. Representative "valence functions" for each of the three goal levels are shown in Figure 3–7.

Figure 3–7 also shows anticipated satisfaction ratings for subjects told to do their best. Observe that their ratings are very similar to those of the easy goal subjects, indicating that subjects trying to do their best do not have a very stringent criterion of what their best is. This is further evidence for the point made in Chapter 2 that a vague goal is compatible with a wide range of performance levels. (Typically, do best subjects perform better than those with easy goals; however, these ratings were made before any experimental trials had taken place. It is likely that the valence function of do best subjects would eventually be more stringent than that of subjects who were firmly committed to easy goals.)

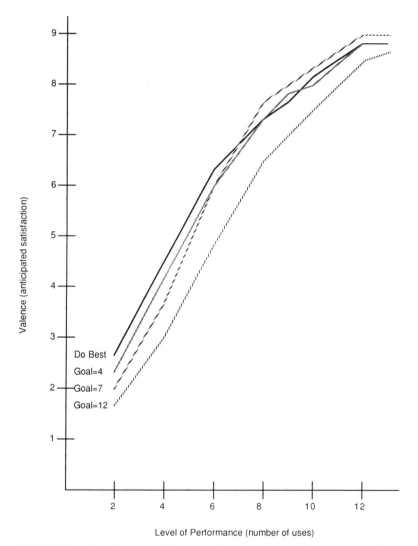

FIGURE 3–7   Obtained Valence Functions for Four Goal Groups
From Mento & Locke, 1989.

These valence functions (which are in agreement with the results of Garland and Meyer & Gellatly, noted earlier) at first seemed inexplicable, especially since previous theory and research had suggested that valence related positively to goal choice, commitment, and performance. However, the finding makes perfect sense if one grasps that *a goal is at the same time a target to aim for and a standard by which to evaluate the adequacy of one's performance.* (This is discussed in detail in Chapter 10.) Bandura (1988) has noted that "goals specify the conditional requirements for positive self-evaluation. By making self-satisfaction conditional on matching adopted goals, people give direction to their actions and create self incentives to persist in their efforts until their performances match their goals" (p.

41). Let us apply this principle to the case in which three individuals have goals of 4, 7, and 12, respectively, on the uses task. If each fully accepts the assigned goal, the subject with a goal of 4 will be minimally satisfied with a performance attainment of 4, will be increasingly more satisfied with attainments above this level, and will be increasingly less satisfied with attainments below this level. In contrast, the person with a goal of 12 will only be minimally satisfied with an attainment of 12 and will be increasingly dissatisfied with everything below that. Thus if this person attains only 4 she will be extremely dissatisfied, in contrast to the individual with the goal of 4 who will be minimally satisfied with the same level of attainment. In contrast, if the low-goal person attains a score of 12 she will be ecstatic, since it will be far above the minimum, whereas the individual with a goal of 12 will be only minimally satisfied with that level. The evaluations of the person with the moderate goal of 7 will fall between those of the other two. This reasoning is shown in idealized form in Figure 3–8. This figure illustrates the same idea as Figure 3–7 but assumes that the people totally accepted their assigned goals and had no other personal goals. (In reality, of course, people only partially accept such goals, as Figure 3–7 implies.)

What all this means is that subjects with hard goals have to perform at a higher level to be satisfied than do subjects with easy goals. Having high standards means not being satisfied with less than high performance. In sum, *having a goal means to use it as a standard for evaluating one's performance.* If one does not use a goal in this way, it is not a real goal or one is not really committed to it. To illustrate this point further, Mento and Locke (1989) developed another goal measure which

FIGURE 3–8   Idealized Valence Functions for Subjects at Three Goal Levels

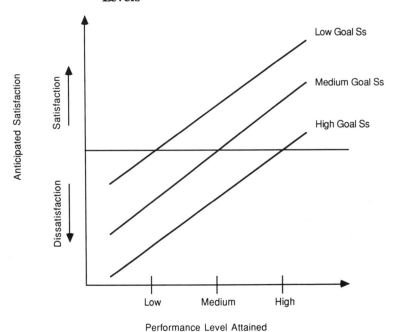

they called Minimum Goal, which was the lowest performance level on the valence function that each subject reported would bring some (slight) satisfaction. The relationship between this measure, personal goal level (measured directly), valence, and performance is shown in Table 3–3. Observe that all three measures predict performance about equally well and are highly related to one another. The valence measure, as noted above, is negatively related rather than positively related to performance, because it represents the other side of the goal coin. For high goals higher performance is required to produce satisfaction than for low goals. These results and the rationale behind them reveal why Garland (1985) found that partialing out valences vitiated the personal goal-performance relationship. In partialing out valences Garland was, in effect, partialing out the goals themselves!

The type of valence function we have been discussing so far, that measured in terms of expected satisfaction when no extrinsic incentives are offered for performance, may be called the *achievement valence function*. Note that the achievement valence function *within* any given goal level is positive; the higher the peformance in relation to the goal, the more favorable the appraisal. Thus individuals prefer to exceed rather than fall short of their goals. Raising the goal level simply shifts the valence function to a higher plane; the individual must do more for less.

Valence functions may reflect the value of different levels of performance to a department or organization as well as their value to single individuals in a laboratory setting. In an important and innovative study, Pritchard et al. (1988) helped five Air Force units to develop valence functions for 5 to 13 performance indicators each. The functions were developed by asking unit members to estimate the value or "effectiveness" to the unit and the unit's mission of different levels of performance on each indicator. This was done before any formal goals were set. Some representative valence functions are shown in Figure 3–9. Note that the functions are not all linear, and they do not all have the same slope. Valence functions with other shapes are no doubt possible. While Pritchard et al. (1988) did not introduce formal goal setting until the later stages of their study, the valence functions themselves would inevitably suggest suitable goals to the members. For example, they would not be likely to choose goals at the low end of the valence function.

Table 3–3   Relationship of Goals, Valences, and Performance
From Mento & Locke, 1989.

	PG	V	P
Minimum Goal[*]	73	−93	50
Personal Goal (PG)	–	−74	51
Valence (V)		–	−51
Performance (P)			–

N = 156 for observations; within subject design with three goal levels, so N for subjects was 52. Significance levels are not shown due to multiple use of same subjects, but all *r*'s would be significant for an N of 52.

[*]The lowest performance level for which the subject indicated he or she would get some satisfaction (i.e., which was rated 5 on the 7-point expected satisfaction scale).

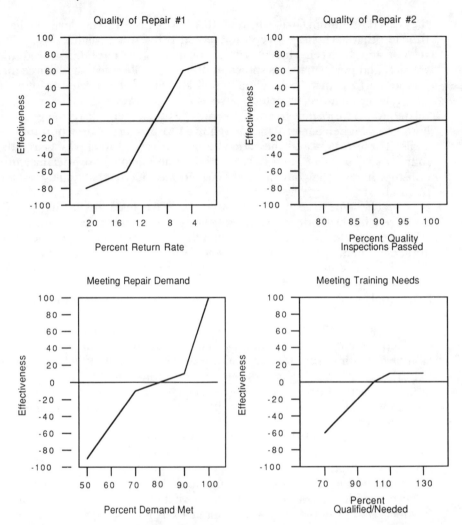

FIGURE 3–9   Sample Valence Functions
From Pritchard et al., 1988.

Observe that either the valence function can be developed first or the performance goals can be developed first; whichever is done first necessarily affects the other because they are actually two methods of doing the same thing. If minimum goals are assigned, they define at least the crossover point (between satisfaction and dissatisfaction) of the function. The slope would depend on the importance of success and the value of various performance outcomes. If the valence function is defined first, it defines what goals will be considered more or less acceptable and the attractiveness of goal deviations in either direction.

The studies that have shown *positive* relationships between goal level, valence, and performance have been either measures of the attractiveness of a single outcome (Locke & Shaw, 1984) or measures of the *instrumentality* of different levels of performance in attaining various personal outcomes (Matsui et al., 1981). Following Matsui et al.'s approach, Mento and Locke (1989) asked subjects in some of their studies why they accepted or agreed to try for the assigned goals. Four types of answers emerged. They agreed to try for the goals (1) because they were told to do so; (2) so that they could improve their skills, such as their ability to concentrate; (3) because trying for the goals gave them a sense of achievement; and (4) so that they could "prove" themselves (prove they were competent, not quitters, etc.).

In one of their studies Mento and Locke asked the subjects to rate the valence of each of these outcomes. A factor analysis of the responses to the valence rating scale yielded four factors corresponding exactly to each of the four types of items noted above. The factors can be called *obedience, skill development, achievement, and prove self.* (A two-factor solution revealed that the obedience items formed one factor and the remaining three scales a second factor.)

The subjects also rated the degree to which each goal level was instrumental in attaining each of the outcomes. Locke and Mento looked at the instrumentality ratings as a function of goal level, grouping the items into the four factors noted above. The results using item or factor means revealed that all four factors were endorsed as reasons why people accepted the three goal levels. This simply confirmed what we had learned in the interviews that had been the source for developing the scales in the first place. That is, people worked for the goals because they were told to do so, because they wanted to develop their skills, because it gave them a sense of achievement, and in order to prove their competence.

Of more interest, however, was the finding that some of the factors were endorsed *differentially* as a function of goal level. Goal level was positively correlated with instrumentality ratings for the skill, achievement, and prove self factors, but not for the obedience factor. Thus, whereas the achievement valence function correlated *negatively* with goal level, the *instrumentality functions* for three of the four factors were *positively* associated with goal level. Note that these relationships were obtained in the absence of any extrinsic incentives. In the real world, of course, high performance attainments are typically associated with better outcomes of all types (e.g., pay, promotions, opportunities, job security, recognition) than low performance attainments. Thus the goal level–instrumentality relationship should be quite strong in organizations that reward employees on merit (performance).

We can see, then, that two kinds of forces can lead people to work harder for hard goals than easier goals. Hard goals, on the one hand, require people to accomplish more in order to attain self-satisfaction and, on the other hand, are associated with more beneficial outcomes than easier goals.

GOAL THEORY VS. ATKINSON'S THEORY

The resolution of the conflict between goal theory and Atkinson's (1958) theory is somewhat difficult simply because Atkinson's original inverse–U function has not been that easy to replicate. Janz (1982) and Motowidlo et al. (1978), using objective probability of success but not subjective probability, found support for it, but

Arvey (1972), Garland (1983), Locke and Shaw (1984), Mento et al. (1980), and McClelland (1961) did not. One problem with Atkinson's model is that there are too many unspecified intervening variables. For example, in Atkinson's original (1958) study, subjects in the various probability of success conditions were not asked whether they were really trying to win.

In an attempted replication study, Locke (1969a) found in his first experiment that for subjects who were trying to win, the relationship between subjective probability and effort was negative and linear ($p < .10$), which is in line with the goal setting literature. When all subjects were included in the analysis, including those who were not trying their hardest to win, a significant quadratic trend was found, with the shape of the curve conforming to Atkinson's prediction. These results are shown in Figure 3–10. In a second experiment, in which subjects were given much more information about how hard they would have to work to win, only linear trends were found, again in line with goal setting theory. While personal goals were not measured, it can be inferred that, on the average, those with lower probabilities set higher goals in order to be in the winning group. A further attempted replication by Locke and Shaw (1984) compared three levels of information given to the subjects: no information (like Atkinson), normative information, and normative information translated into a percentage score indicating how much harder or less hard they would have to work compared with the practice trial in order to win. This was crossed with three levels of objective probability of success. In this case, there was no linear or curvilinear effect of any of the experimental conditions on performance. However, there were main effects of commitment to winning and personal goal level (as well as valence of winning) on performance, with commitment showing the strongest effect.

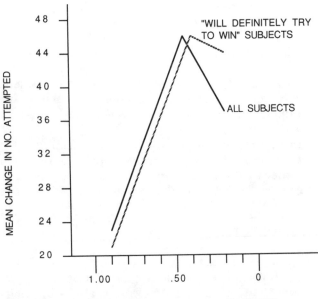

FIGURE 3–10
Relation of Subjective Probability of Success to Performance for All Subjects and Those Trying to Win
From Locke, 1969a.

Similarly, Mento et al. (1980) found no consistent effect of subjective or objective probability of success on performance, whereas there was a significant effect for personal goals. Studies that have supported Atkinson either have not measured goals or have not measured them carefully; the most plausible interpretation of the supportive studies is that there were a greater number of people in the low probability of success group who were not trying to win than in the medium and high probability groups (as in Locke, 1969a).

Furthermore, no studies of Atkinson's model have had subjects rate either self-efficacy or their expectancy of reaching the personal goal that they set in response to the announced probabilities. Even the goal of winning is somewhat vague in that it does not specify what the subject thinks it will take, in the way of effort or pace of work, to win. All of this leads to the conclusion that the effects of objective and subjective probability of success on effort are not consistently predictable unless one knows, in addition, what the individual is actually trying to do (what his or her goals are) and what the individual thinks is needed to achieve the goal being sought (Locke & Shaw, 1984).

As noted previously, the Yerkes-Dodson "law" asserts that there is a curvilinear relationship between level of motivation or arousal and performance, but this is usually interpreted to mean stressful arousal such as anxiety. The relationship between anxiety and performance, however, is by no means a simple one and depends on a host of additional factors such as task difficulty and complexity, degree of prior learning, and self-efficacy (Bandura, 1986). Furthermore, anxiety is not the only type of arousal. Motivation by goals (assuming commitment), as we have seen, does not lead to a curvilinear relationship with performance other than the one caused by limitations imposed by ability.

In achievement motivation studies, even when the curvilinear relationship between so-called "motivation" and performance does come out, it appears to be a highly complex and contingent relationship, depending on such factors as the degree of difference in the motivation to approach success and the motivation to avoid failure, the perceived difficulty of the task, the degree to which task performance affects the attainment of a future goal, and the degree to which there are multiple incentives to perform well (e.g., see Feather, 1982). In sum, neither the curvilinear relationship between probability of success and performance, nor that between "motivation" (as measured by trait or stress measures) and performance, is a very robust or replicable phenomenon. The probable reason for the latter is that trait measures, especially projective trait or motive measures, are so far removed from action and so much in the periphery of consciousness that their influence is easily swamped by situationally specific, conscious factors such as goals and self-efficacy (Locke & Henne, 1986).

It is probably no accident that achievement motivation studies have to be reanalyzed so frequently (e.g., by regrouping the subjects or by various contingencies) and reinterpreted after the fact. Our strategy, in contrast, has been to start with the specific, conscious factors and see how well they account for action. This strategy has yielded far more dependable results than strategies based on subconscious motives.

We propose a tentative decision model for the Atkinson-type experiment in Figure 3–11. After being given the objective probability information, the

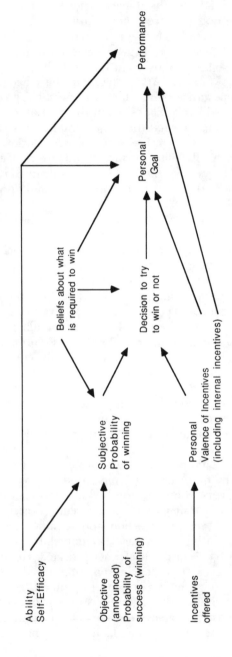

FIGURE 3–11 Model Showing Hypothesized Cognitive Processes Occurring between Providing Objective Probability of Success Information and Performance

subject translates this into a subjective probability estimate based both on the objective odds and on his or her self-efficacy for the task in question. Based on this estimate and any further information, such as information about what is required to win or succeed, feedback, normative data, and incentives, the subjects decide if they can win and if they want to win. If the decision is to try to win, the individual sets a personal goal in line with what is required to win. If the individual decides not to try to win, he or she sets some other goal that could be harder than the goal of winning (e.g., be in the top 10% of my group even though the top 90% will win) or lower (e.g., be in the top half even though only the top 10% will win) than what it takes to win, or he or she may set a more qualitative goal (e.g., do my best, have fun, just work to get done). The use of such a model (which will undoubtedly have to be revised) should eventually enable researchers to make more consistent predictions about the effects of objective probability. The model reemphasizes our main point: that it is virtually hopeless to make consistently correct predictions about motivation just from knowing probability of success alone. Observe also that self-efficacy plays an important role in the model. It affects subjective probability estimates, goals, and performance.

CONCLUSION

This chapter resolves several longstanding puzzles and conflicts in the motivation literature. Goal setting theory is in full agreement, rather than in conflict, with expectancy theory regarding the relationship of expectancy to performance. Expectancy is positively related to performance within any given goal group; self-efficacy and/or overall expectancy of performing well across the full range of possible performance levels is positively associated with goal level and performance, both within and across goal groups. Assigned goals facilitate performance because they influence both self-efficacy and personal goals. Self-efficacy affects goal choice, and both self-efficacy and personal goals affect performance. Subjective measures of goal difficulty work less well than objective measures because they are confounded. Achievement valence is negatively associated with goal level and performance because harder goals require better performance in order to attain self-satisfaction. However, harder goals are often seen as more instrumental in attaining valued outcomes than easier goals. We have argued that Atkinson's curvilinear model does not predict experimental results reliably because it does not take account of the numerous factors that intervene between the announcement of an objective probability of winning and actual performance (e.g., self-efficacy, beliefs about what is required to win, goals, etc.).

CHAPTER

4

GOAL MECHANISMS

To understand and explain the effect of goals on action, it is necessary to understand the mechanisms by which goals produce their results. A complete explanation of these mechanisms would include a detailed account of the structure and functioning of the brain and the nervous system, a topic that is beyond the scope of this book. Rather, this chapter discusses the cognitive and overt actions to which goal setting leads and which, in turn, produce effects on task performance. In other words, our thesis is that having a goal affects task performance because it leads people to do things that produce this performance.

The three most direct goal mechanisms are primarily motivational. They correspond to the three attributes of motivated action: arousal or intensity, choice or direction, and duration (Blau, Blank, & Katerberg, 1987; Katerberg & Blau, 1983). Goals affect arousal by regulating the intensity of effort the individual expends on the task, and they affect its duration by leading people to persist in their actions until the goal is reached. They affect choice by leading people to direct attention to and take action with respect to goal-relevant activities while ignoring nongoal relevant activities

The assertion that these are motivational mechanisms should not be taken to mean that no cognitive elements are present when these mechanisms operate. As noted in Chapter 1, in reality, cognition and motivation are virtually never independent. When we assert that these are motivational mechanisms, we mean that requisite cognitive elements are present but that such elements do not in themselves explain the resulting action. For example, the idea of completing 10 problems in five minutes has a different cognitive content than the idea of completing 20 problems in five minutes, but cognitive awareness of these two possible levels of performance alone does not explain the resulting performance differences. Only when such ideas become goals, based on beliefs about what is *important* or what one *wants* to attain or believes one *should* attain, do they affect action. Cognitive awareness of different possible levels of performance is a necessary element in goal setting, but it is not sufficient to motivate action in the absence of some appraisal.

As Locke, Cartledge, and Koeppel (1968, p. 475) noted, "knowledge by itself does not have the power to initiate action." The mere fact that an idea is in one's conscious or subconscious mind does not compel one to act on it. Everyone possesses millions of bits of knowledge that are not expressed in behavior at any given time. People are selective in their use of information and in the actions they take regarding it. This is necessarily so, since people's capacity to act is limited. To predict an individual's actions one must be aware not only of what he or she knows but how he or she evaluates or appraises that knowledge (Arnold, 1960). One must know the perceived significance of the information one has in a given situation. A person's knowledge and evaluations are reflected in the goals he or she sets on a particular task.

It was shown in Chapter 3 that goals *define* for the individual what an acceptable level of performance or direction of action is. Actions that fall short of desired ends are appraised as unsatisfactory (Bandura, 1988) and lead to negative performance evaluations and/or self-evaluations. Such negative appraisals ordinarily lead to actions aimed at eliminating the source of the dissatisfaction, such as improving subsequent performance. Actions that attain or exceed desired ends lead to positive appraisals. If a positive appraisal is followed by the anticipation that attaining the same performance level again will lead to a neutral or negative appraisal, the individual may set a higher goal for the future (Bandura & Cervone, 1986). As noted in Chapter 1, such an action cannot be explained by control theory (Bandura, in press).

Once the individual has a goal and once he or she chooses to act on it, the three direct mechanisms—effort, persistence, and direction—are brought into play more or less automatically. Individuals learn from an early age that, to achieve a goal, they must exert effort, persist over time (Duda, 1986), and pay attention to what they are doing and what they want to achieve.

Sometimes, however, these automatized mechanisms are not sufficient to attain the goal; the individual also has to engage in a process of problem solving in order to discover how the goal can be reached. This process involves discovering suitable task strategies. Task strategies are conscious or deliberate action plans motivated by goals. Thus, qua strategies, they are a cognitive mechanism but also constitute an indirect goal mechanism. Given some motivation to use them, they can have an independent effect on task performance. The relation between goals, task strategies, and performance, as we shall see, is a highly complex one that is only beginning to be understood.

EFFORT

Kahneman (1973) observed that effort and arousal vary with the demands made upon the person, assuming that the demands are accepted. Under high demand conditions, people have to use more of their total capacity than under low demand conditions; more attention is allocated to the task at hand and less is available for other tasks. One would expect, then, that more effort would be expended when goals are difficult than when goals are easy—or more precisely, effort should be mobilized or expended in proportion to the difficulty of the goal (Locke, 1968b). Most people assume that greater effort will pay off in greater performance (Yates & Kulick, 1977); thus they would assume that more effort will be needed to attain hard goals than easy goals. While it is not assumed that effort-performance relationships are necessarily or consistently linear (Kanfer, 1987; Yates & Kulick, 1977), more effort typically gets better results than less effort, given that ability is adequate. This section examines intensity rather than duration of effort.

Numerous sources of evidence support the view that goals regulate effort expenditure. First, some studies used tasks that, holding ability or capacity constant, *directly reflect physical effort.* The tasks used include the arm ergometer (Bandura & Cervone, 1983, 1986); the hand dynamometer (Botterill, 1977); jumping (Erbaugh & Barnett, 1986); elbow flexion (Nelson, 1978); weight lifting (Ness & Patton, 1979), and the bike ergometer (Roberts & Hall, 1987). In all these studies subjects with specific hard goals (or tasks in the case of Ness and Patton) exerted more effort (performed better) than those with less-difficult goals, do best goals, or no goals. Sales (1970), in a study using anagrams, found that heart rate was positively associated with degree of work overload, overload being a proxy for goal difficulty.

Second, scores of studies have found that *rate of work* or *rate of performance* is a linear function of goal difficulty. Since ability was controlled or randomized in these studies, the inference that the results were caused by differences in effort (in cases where the tasks were simple enough to preclude major differences in task strategies) seems justified. Such studies typically used cognitive tasks such as addition (Bryan & Locke, 1967a; Locke & Bryan, 1969a), brainstorming (Garland, 1982; Locke 1967c), anagrams (Sales, 1970), and reaction time (Locke et al., 1970). Cannon-Bowers and Levine (1988) found that the self-set goal levels of subjects listing uses for objects were significantly associated with the number listed during the first minute of the work period. Effort differences can also be inferred from studies that compared specific, hard goals with do best goals. Bryan and Locke (1967a) found that subjects with specific, hard goals on an addition task worked at a faster rate than those with do best goals. Bandura and Schunk (1981) obtained the same finding using a subtraction task. Locke and Bryan (1966a) found that specific, hard goals were more likely to keep subjects from dropping below their best previous performance on a complex coordination task than do best goals, This phenomenon was first observed by C. A. Mace (1935). Mace also found that specific, challenging goals were more likely than do best goals to intensify effort toward the latter part of long work periods. Several studies have found that effort, as inferred from rate of work, intensifies after failure, assuming commitment to the original goal. Campion and Lord (1982) found this with students working for test grades, while Matsui, Okada, and Inoshita (1983) found it with students working on a simple addition task.

A third group of studies have obtained *subjective effort ratings* from people in different goal conditions. Brickner and Bukatko (1987—study 1) found that subjects whose task was to find various objects in complex pictures reported exerting more effort when goals were specific and difficult than under do best goals. Bryan and Locke (1967a) found that subjects with specific, hard goals, in addition to actually performing better, reported exerting more effort than those with do best goals. Bryan and Locke (1967b) found that subjects with harder qualitative goals (e.g., work quickly) fostered by short time limits on a task had higher self-rated concentration than subjects with easier qualitative goals fostered by long time limits on the same task. In a correlational study, Carroll and Tosi (1970) found that goal clarity was related to subjective effort for subjects high in maturity and low in perceived job interest and supervisory support. Goal difficulty was related positively to effort for subjects high in self-assurance but negatively for those low in self-assurance. Self-assurance, as a proxy for self-efficacy, may have affected goal commitment. In the Cannon-Bowers and Levine (1988) study noted earlier, subjects with harder goals rated themselves as putting far more subjective effort than those with easier goals. Hall and Foster (1977) in another correlational study found that goal difficulty (defined as the degree of desire to perform well) was associated with subjective effort in an executive simulation game. In a business simulation study, Earley, Wojnaroski, and Prest (1987) found that specific, hard goals led to higher ratings of subjective effort than do best goals. This result was replicated in a correlational field study of two organizations. Earley, Northcraft, Lee, and Lituchy (in press) obtained the same result using a simulated stock investment task. In both the Earley reports, effort partly mediated the effect of goals on performance. Sales (1970) found the same results for subjective effort as for actual work rate and heart rate; all were higher under a work overload condition. Shapira (1977) found that *task* difficulty was positively associated with subjective effort. Terborg and Miller (1978) did not find a significant overall effect of goals on subjective effort using a tinker-toy assembly task, but the effort mean for those with quantity goals was clearly higher than the mean for those with no goals or quality goals. Unfortunately, the relevant t-test was not computed for this comparison.

In a fourth type of study, *effort inferences were made by third parties*. Meyer, Konar, and Schacht (1983) had subjects read work scenarios that specified the subjects' goal level and then make ratings of the degree of effort they thought the jobholders should exert. Recommended effort ratings were linearly related to goal difficulty. Terborg and Miller (1978), in the study cited above, obtained the same pattern of results for supervisors' ratings as for self-ratings of effort. Again the relevant t-test was not computed; effort ratings made from videotapes of the subjects actually working showed no relation to goals or performance.

Only the study by Sales (1970) used an actual *physiological indicator* of effort. However, the convergence of evidence among these five different types of studies makes the inescapable conclusion that goals affect performance, in part, through their effects on intensity of effort.

To date, only Bavelas and Lee (1978) have denied that goals affect effort. They drew this conclusion because in their first study subjects with easy goals worked at the same rate *while they were working* as did the subjects with hard goals, even though subjects with harder goals worked for a longer period than did those with easier goals. This similarity in rate of work is not surprising in that (a) subjects were denied feedback about the difficulty of their goal in relation to their practice trial performance; (b) they were apparently denied feedback during the experimental trial; and (c) they only worked at the task for one trial. Due to (a) and (b) and due to the fact that the subjects were told to work "quickly," it is logical that all would work at about the same pace. In relation to (c), if there had been a second or third trial with the same goals, it is very likely that subjects with easy goals, who finished their tasks before the time limit was up, would have slowed their pace of work, while hard goal subjects, if they had not finished previously, would have accelerated their pace. This is what Bryan and Locke (1967b) found in a laboratory study of Parkinson's law, namely, that work pace slowed to fill the time available and accelerated to get done in the time allowed. Latham and Locke (1975) found the same thing in a field study involving logging crews.

Furthermore, Bavelas and Lee ignored their more relevant finding of a linear relationship between goal level and the total number of problems completed. They asserted that it was "spurious" because the hard goal subjects worked longer than the easy goal subjects. What their results show, of course, is that goals prolong effort until the goals are attained. This is exactly what goal setting theory predicts they should do! Goals affect the duration as well as the intensity of effort. This brings us to the next goal mechanism, persistence.

PERSISTENCE

Persistence is effort maintained over time. Typically it is measured in the form of time spent at an activity or the equivalent, such as number of attempts to solve a problem. Relevant studies, therefore, must be those where the subjects can choose how much time to spend or how many trials to attempt. Duration of effort should not be confused with intensity of effort, the first goal mechanism discussed. Duration of effort, as such, does not say anything about intensity. People can spend a long time at a task while sustaining a high rate of effort (Cannon-Bowers & Levine, 1988), or they can spend a long time working at a moderate or low rate of effort. When people plan to work for a long period, such as a ten-hour day, they usually pace themselves so they will not become too fatigued (Ryan, 1947). Intensity and duration are best considered two alternative but not mutually exclusive ways of exerting effort.

A number of studies have shown that specific, challenging goals lead people to work longer at a task than other types of goals. Bavelas and Lee (1978) found, as noted above, that subjects with easier goals stopped working sooner than those with hard goals. This, of course, was because they had reached their goals and therefore had nothing more to do. While this result may seem trivial, it does illustrate that more-challenging goals keep people going longer than less-challenging goals even when all are working at the same pace. In their third study, Bavelas and Lee also found that those with harder goals worked for a longer amount of time (although their report of the result is overly brief). Using a listing-uses task, Cannon-Bowers and Levine (1988) found that subjects with harder self-set goals spent more time on the task than subjects with easier goals. Huber (1985b) found that subjects with hard goals on a computer maze task worked longer to complete the maze than subjects given moderate, easy, or do best goals; however, they did not perform better.

A number of studies of prose learning measured time spent on the task. They found that subjects with specific goals spent more time studying the text, or that part of the text relevant to their goals, than subjects without specific goals

(Kaplan & Rothkopf, 1974; Reynolds, Standiford, & Anderson, 1979; Reynolds & Anderson, 1982; Rothkopf & Billington, 1979). McCaul, Hinsz, and McCaul (1987) found a similar effect in their first study. In their second study public commitment rather than goal level affected persistence. The one exception to the usual findings was a study by Rothkopf and Billington (1975), which failed to find a goal effect on persistence.

A prose learning study conducted by LaPorte and Nath (1976) found that subjects with hard performance goals (expressed in terms of scores to be attained on a posttest) and unlimited time spent more time studying the passages in question than those with do best goals, who in turn spent more time than those with easy goals. This finding illustrates the point made in Chapter 2, that specific goals as such do not necessarily lead to better performance than general goals. In the above study the do best goal was harder than the specific, easy goal.

Locke and Bryan (1969a) found that subjects with hard goals on an addition task worked at a faster rate than those with easy goals—clearly an effort phenomenon. An interesting finding of this study, however, was that this difference in rate appeared during the longer work intervals (intervals were separated by feedback being given to the subjects); this suggests that the hard goals were *prolonging* effort within a fixed work period, even though there was no actual persistence measure. Mace had obtained a similar finding back in 1935.

Using an anagram task, Sales (1970) discovered that subjects with task overload (e.g., hard goals) spent more time working and less time resting than those with task underload (e.g., easy goals). Of course, resting or its equivalent can also be accomplished by slowing one's work rate, as Bryan and Locke (1967b) found.

Singer, Korienek, Jarvis, McCloskey, and Candeletti (1981) let subjects choose the number of trials they wanted to take to learn a complex mirror maze. Subjects given both short- and long-term goals worked for more than twice as many trials as subjects not given any goals.

While goals are usually expressed in terms of performance, they can be expressed directly in terms of time spent on tasks. Kirsch (1978), for example, found that students who set goals for how much time they would spend exercising actually spent more time exercising than when they did not set goals.

Another way that persistence can be expressed is through endurance and tenacity. Hall, Weinberg, and Jackson (1987), for example, found that male students compressed a hand dynamometer longer if they had specific, hard endurance goals than if told to do their best. Pain tolerance (immersing one's hand in cold water) was increased by giving subjects endurance goals in a study by Stevenson, Kanfer, and Higgins (1984).

Tenacity can be psychological as well as physical. Huber and Neale (1987) found that subjects given hard goals in a bargaining task were less willing to compromise and thus held out for a better deal than subjects told to do their best or given easy goals. Neale and Bazerman's (1985) results suggest that one reason that hard goal subjects made better deals than those with other goals is that they took a longer time to come to agreement—a probable concomitant of refusing to compromise until they obtained the best deal possible. Neale, Northcraft, and Earley (1987) also found that subjects with hard goals spent more time completing each contract and as a result actually completed fewer total contracts. Finally, Siegal and Fouraker (1960) found that bargaining sessions where subjects had goals tended to run longer than sessions where subjects were not trying for specific goals.

DIRECTION

Effort, regardless of its intensity and/or duration, must be directed toward some activity. Thus the third goal mechanism and third attribute of motivated activity is direction. Goals have two directional effects that are relatively automatic. First, they *orient* the individual toward goal-relevant activities and materials and away from goal-irrelevant ones. Second, they *activate* stored knowledge and skills that the individual possesses that are perceived as relevant to the task.

The principle that goals direct attention and action did not originate with goal setting theory. The idea can be traced back to at least the intentional vs. incidental learning literature. Numerous experiments have shown that people learn material better when they have an explicit intent to learn it than when they do not (i.e., when learning is incidental to whatever they are doing with the material). For example, if individuals are given a list of words, they will recall them better if they are told to memorize them than if they are told to read the list for typographical errors.

Ryan (1970), in a detailed review of this literature, concluded that one reason why intentional learning works better than incidental learning is that intentions focus attention more clearly and explicitly on the task to be accomplished than is the case without an intention. Ryan also noted that the intent to learn may lead the individual to carry out certain cognitive operations on the material, such as rehearsal and integration.

While the difficulty of the goal should be most logically related to effort and arousal, the specificity of the goal should have the most effect on direction of attention and direction of effort. As noted in Chapter 2, when performance is fully controllable, specific goals lead to less interindividual variation in performance than general or vague goals (Locke, Chah, et al., 1989). Goal specificity should also raise performance level on a task as compared with no goal at all, since if there is literally no goal, the task will not be performed. As noted earlier, specific goals will not necessarily lead to better performance than vague goals, however, since vagueness as such does not reveal anything about difficulty. For example, specific, easy goals typically lead to poorer performance than do best goals (Locke, Mento, & Katcher, 1978).

Most studies that illustrate the directive effects of goals (other than those in the classic intentional learning literature) come from studies of prose learning. For example, Rothkopf and Billington (1975) and Rothkopf and Kaplan (1972) found that students who were given specific objectives concerning what was to be learned from a prose passage learned more about the goal relevant material than did those who were given more general objectives or no objectives. Presumably the specific objectives gave the students a clearer picture of what they were to learn than did the general objectives. Rothkopf and Kaplan's (1972) finding was replicated in two additional studies by Kaplan and Rothkopf (1974). Both studies also found that students learned material that they were told to learn better than material that was incidental to their goals, thus replicating the classical intention vs. incidental learning results. Reynolds, Standiford, and Anderson (1979) obtained results similar to Kaplan and Rothkopf's, but they prompted student learning in a more indirect way. Some subjects were given questions to answer following various segments of text. Those given such questions learned later material relevant to the topic of the questions and related topics better than students not given such questions. Evidently the questions called attention to the kinds of material they were expected to learn. This basic finding was replicated by Reynolds and Anderson (1982), who suggested that the text questions cue the individual as to what is important.

In three additional studies, Rothkopf and Billington (1979) again found that specific learning objectives led to more learning than no objectives. An interesting innovation in one of these studies was the measurement of the students' eye movements and fixations. There were more frequent eye fixations and longer eye fixations on text material relevant to the learning goals than on material not relevant to the goals. This is as clear proof as one could hope for that goals actually influence direction of attention.

Rothkopf and Billington (1979) also found that students with specific learning goals learned material that was not relevant to their goals less well than students who were not given learning goals. This supports Kahneman's idea that making cognitive demands on the individual to perform a particular activity can draw attention away from other activities. In short, attention paid to X may be at the expense of Y. Wyer, Srull, Gordon, and Hartwick (1982) similarly found that prereading goals helped learning on goal-relevant material and inhibited it on non-goal-relevant material as compared with general goals. (Interestingly, post-reading goals aided the recall of all the material.) Organ (1977) also found that subjects doing proofreading under a proofreading goal learned less about the content of the passage than subjects with no such goal.

In a study that also involved the learning of text material, Terborg (1976) found that setting specific goals led subjects to pay more attention to the task, as measured by observing videotapes of the subjects working, than setting less specific goals. Terborg labeled this measure "effort," but it may more accurately be called direction, or effort plus direction. The measure was significantly associated with having a goal on the posttest.

There have been a number of studies of the directional effects of goals using nonprose learning tasks. Locke and Bryan (1969b) gave subjects objective feedback regarding five aspects of their driving performance (e.g., steering reversals, accelerator reversals, brake applications, trip time) after having them drive around a standard course. Next they were assigned goals to reduce their scores on a single aspect of their performance for the next trip. On a third trip they were assigned a goal to reduce their scores on a different performance dimension. They found that driving scores changed only on the dimension for which a goal was set. This study makes it clear that performance goals single out for action those aspects of performance that are relevant to the goal, just as learning goals single out for learning the relevant parts of a prose passage.

This same principle was illustrated in a study by Nemeroff and Cosentino (1979) of a management training program. Managers were given feedback regarding subordinate perceptions of forty-three different manager behaviors, but they were only assigned goals for twelve of them. Significant change occurred during training only for those twelve behaviors. It is obvious that the limits of the individual's cognitive capacity would preclude improvement on forty-three separate behaviors except over a considerable time span. Setting goals for a limited number of behaviors reduces cognitive confusion and overload by singling out the ones requiring immediate attention.

Kolb and Boyatzis (1970) found that the same result holds when goals are self-set. Students in sensitivity (t-group) training changed more on dimensions of their own behavior for which they had set goals than on dimensions for which they had not set goals. Adler and Goleman (1975) obtained a similar finding. Students who set goals for personal change and had feedback from t-groups showed more change on the personal trait that they had made their top priority goal than on traits that were not top priority. Similarly, Morgan (1985) found that students with time goals regarding studying actually spent more time studying than students who did not have time goals.

Terborg and Miller (1978) found that subjects with quality goals on a tinker-toy assembly task made more quality checks on their completed models than subjects with quantity goals or no goals. Similarly, Locke and Bryan (1969b), in a pilot study using an addition task conducted prior to their driving study, found that subjects with quality goals made fewer errors than those with quantity goals. This finding indicated that they had paid greater attention to quality.

Cohen and Ebbesen (1979) showed that the directional effects of goals are not confined to attention and action. They also influence the way in which people process information. They told some subjects to view actors on videotapes in order to form an impression of the taped person's personality. Other subjects were told to view them in order to learn what tasks the actor was performing. Viewers not only learned more information relevant to their goal than subjects who did not have that goal, but by pressing a button, they actually broke up the tapes they were viewing into different types and sizes of units. For example, they used larger chunks when trying to observe personality than when trying to observe the tasks being performed. Hoffman, Mischel, and Mazze (1981) also found that goals affected cognitive processing. Like Cohen and Ebbesen (1979) they assigned subjects different purposes, such as to recall the information or form a personality impression, and then had each read a series of behavioral episodes before classifying them. These purposes had a strong effect on how the subjects classified the episodes, and on how well they remembered them.

SUMMARY OF DIRECT GOAL MECHANISMS

It is clear that goals affect task performance in at least three ways. First, they energize performance by motivating people to exert effort in line with the difficulty of or demands of the goal or task. It should be stressed that it is not just physiological arousal as such (e.g., in the form of anxiety or the like; see Organ, 1977) that produces high performance, but rather goal-relevant effort. The Yerkes-Dodson "law" predicts that very high arousal will lead to poor performance, especially on nonautomatized tasks; but it is not clear just what is meant by arousal. Effort and anxiety are not the same thing. It remains to be seen whether trying too hard will disrupt goal-relevant performance, and if so, by what mechanisms such disruption will occur. Thus far the findings clearly show that the harder the goal the better the performance, given that the individual has the requisite ability and knowledge.

Second, goals motivate individuals to persist in their activities through time. Hard goals ensure that the individual will keep working for a longer period of time than would be the case with vague or easy goals. Hard or challenging goals inspire the individual to be tenacious in not settling for less than could be achieved.

Third, goals, especially if they are clear and specific, direct the individual's attention to relevant behaviors or outcomes and even affect how information is processed. This leads to less variable performance and to better performance in relation to such behaviors or outcomes than if goals are nonexistent. Specific goals may also lead to poorer performance on aspects of the task that are not relevant to the goals. Goals, in effect, give the individual "tunnel vision." This can be advantageous if one wants to stay in the tunnel, but it may not be if other outcomes are desired as well.

Our theory predicts that, holding strategies constant, if all the goal mechanisms are controlled or partialed out, then goals will not affect task performance. Unfortunately there has been no complete test of this aspect of theory, because it is difficult to measure all the mechanisms accurately. Terborg (1976) is the only one to have tried it; he partialed out measures of what he called effort and direction and found that there was no residual effect of goals on performance. His test was somewhat flawed, however, because the direction measure was actually a measure of learning strategies, and the effort measure was mainly a measure of direction of attention. But his results are at least consistent with the view that if the means by which goals affect performance are controlled, there is no longer a goal setting effect.

TASK STRATEGIES

The mechanisms of effort, persistence, and direction of attention operate virtually automatically once there is commitment to the goal and the individual decides to act to achieve it. As noted, however, these three mechanisms are not always sufficient to attain a goal. If an individual finds or anticipates that they will not be sufficient, she may then attempt to discover better methods or strategies for performing the task. Task strategies may also be developed as a means of saving effort (e.g., work "smarter rather than harder").

Task strategies are actually a directional mechanism, but of a less automatic, and therefore less direct, type than was discussed above. As noted earlier, goals can have a near-automatic directional effect. For example, if an individual accepts the goal to "get the groceries," he will almost unthinkingly get his checkbook and the grocery list, get into the car, and drive to the store. Such actions are routinized through frequent repetition. While there is conscious awareness of the goal, no conscious planning or problem solving is required. Only if his car breaks down or the grocery store is closed does he have to consciously develop a plan to attain the goal. The same is true if he is confronted by a task that he has not performed before or a goal that he has not pursued previously. Thus task strategies, as referred to in this section, entail methods of performing a task that involve more than just executing learned habits; rather they imply conscious problem solving and creative innovation. They are an indirect goal mechanism because the discovery of new task strategies—especially new, correct strategies—is not automatic. Of course, new task strategies may become automatized with repeated use. The direct and indirect goal mechanisms are summarized in Figure 4–1.

Theoretical discussions of the relationship of goals and task strategies can be found in Tatum and Nebeker (1986) and in Chapter 14. The remainder of this chapter focuses on the results of empirical research on goals and strategies.

Goals as Stimulants to Strategy Development

Numerous studies have found that when given a goal, individuals develop task strategies on their own. This is not surprising in that one of the first questions people ask themselves when confronted by a goal is, "How can it be achieved?" Often the question is readily answered, either because the task is fairly simple or because they have a repertoire of knowledge and experience from which to develop a suitable plan. Looking first at field studies of nonsupervisory employees, Adam (1975) implied that diecasting workers ran their machines at a faster speed as a means of increasing both quantity and quality of performance after goal assignment. Buller & Bell (1986) found that miners were more likely to engage in quality-improving behaviors after being given quality goals. In a laboratory simulation of a factory task, Das (1982a) found that subjects with goals and feedback on a hole-drilling task used several strategies to facilitate performance, such as prearranging the holes to be drilled and combining hand motions. Latham and Baldes (1975) observed that logging truck drivers, with goals to increase the total weight of the logs they were carrying, made minor modifications to their trucks so that they could judge the truck weight accurately. In another study of truck drivers, Latham and Saari (1982) found that drivers given goals for a number of trips to the mill per day used their radios to coordinate with each other so that there was always a truck available when timber was ready to be loaded. Kim (1984) reported that salespersons with behavioral or performance goals increased their communication with supervisors, such as noting low stock. McCuddy and

Direct

   Effort (physical effort, rate of work, subjective effort, physiological arousal)

   Persistence (duration of effort, tenacity)

   Direction (orientation toward goal-relevant activities, attention, activation of stored knowledge and skills)

Indirect

   Direction (development of new task strategies, problem-solving, creative insight)

FIGURE 4–1   Direct and Indirect Goal Mechanisms

Griggs (1984) observed that engineers constructed and publicly displayed project schedule boards in order to keep track of the projects they were working on as a means of eliminating missed deadlines.

Supervisory job activities such as training, which could be viewed as strategies for managing subordinates, were found by Blau, Blank, and Katerberg (1987) to be related to the performance of newspaper circulation supervisors (all of whom had yearly goals). Campbell and Gingrich (1986) found that having goals on a complex task led computer programmers to seek information from their supervisors during participative discussions as to how to go about writing the programs. In a management simulation game, Chesney and Locke (1988) found that manager-subjects developed various market strategies (such as increasing sales) in order to reach their performance goals. In a study by Lombardo, Hull, and Singer (1983) psychotherapists with goals for time spent servicing patients rejected an assigned strategy that they did not like (reminder calls to patients) and developed other strategies that they preferred, such as more thorough billing procedures. Stedry and Kay (1964) found that some factory foremen who were assigned difficult performance goals for their work group developed strategies such as looking for the causes of unproductive time and eliminating its causes; other foremen simply exhorted their subordinates to do better. Finally, in a field study, Bandura and Simon (1977) found that subjects who were trying to lose weight and set daily goals used such eating strategies as consuming low calorie foods, eliminating second helpings, and reducing intake before big eating occasions.

In a laboratory experiment requiring subjects to list uses for common objects, Earley and Perry (1987) found that those who were given specific, challenging goals were more likely to develop plans for thinking up uses (such as thinking up all possible uses within each of a number of categories) than subjects with do best goals. In an experiment involving complex arithmetic computation, Locke and Bryan (1966b) found that subjects with specific, hard goals committed the computation formula to memory sooner than subjects with other goals. Klein, Whitener, and Ilgen (1988) found that subjects with the most specific and difficult goals developed the most effective task strategies in a study using a computer game. In a study using a multistep clerical task, Shaw (1984) found that subjects with specific, hard goals but no assigned strategy were more likely to develop a strategy different from the one taught before the practice trial as compared with subjects with do best goals. Students learning the content of a series of programs were studied by Terborg (1976). He found that those with specific test score goals were most likely to use beneficial learning strategies such as writing notes in the margins. Terborg and Miller (1978) found that goals were not related to the number of different assembly strategies used on a tinker-toy task, but no analysis was made of the use of specific types of strategies.

Lowered Quality as an Implicit Strategy

One means by which individuals with quantity goals can attempt to attain their goals is by reducing the quality of their output (Fitts, 1966). While this can be done as a conscious decision, it can also occur simply as a by-product of increasing one's speed of work. Thus quality reduction can be an implicit strategy in that it is allowed to suffer in order to maximize quantity. Erez (in press) found, using a subtraction task, that this trade-off was most likely to occur when subjects believed that their chance of doing well in relation to their performance goal was only average. It was least likely to occur when they believed that their chance of doing well was high. In the latter case the subjects were less likely to rush and thus made fuller use of the time available to them.

Bavelas and Lee (1978; experiment 2) found that, under the pressure of high goals, subjects who were told to list objects that were hard, white, and edible were increasingly likely to list objects that were hard and white but not very edible, or hard and edible but not very white and so on. The mean quality ratings of the listed objects were inversely related to goal level. Locke and Bryan (1969a) found that subjects with hard goals made more errors while attempting more problems as an additional task than those with easy goals. Miller and Steele (1984) obtained the same finding on a typing task. Rosswork (1977) found that schoolchildren, given the task of making up sentences, made up significantly shorter sentences on the second of two experimental trials when trying for specific, hard goals.

It is important to note that, contrary to the implication of Bavelas and Lee (1978), the results of "brainstorming"-type studies come out even when quality is controlled. Garland (1982), for example, rescored protocols from an object-listing experiment after eliminating inappropriate or overlapping responses. Even though harder goals did produce more such responses than easy goals, goal difficulty was linearly related to performance even with low-quality responses removed.

Miller (1960) manipulated task difficulty by varying the amount of information input that subjects had to process. He found that the most common response to overload was simply not to respond to all the information. Thus errors of omission as well as errors of commission can occur as tasks or goals become increasingly difficult.

As noted in Chapter 2, goal setting studies have used performance criteria that entail both quantity and quality; the results were equally successful (see also Latham & Lee, 1986). Goal effects, as previously noted, are specific to the targeted goal. Thus if quality is an important outcome, quality goals, in place of or in addition to quantity goals, should be set.

Edwards Deming, the quality guru who is given much of the credit for the industrial resurgence of Japan after World War II, especially for the high quality of its products, has railed against the use of quantity goals for production. However, this seems unrealistic and contradicts what we have heard about the actual practices of Japanese firms, which are highly goal oriented. Deming actually qualifies his attack on quantity goals by arguing that they should not be given to workers who do not have the knowledge of how to reach them, implying that such goals would be all right if workers do have such knowledge. Deming does not seem to be opposed to the use of very high quality goals (do it right the first time) and constant quality improvement. Setting goals to constantly improve *all* aspects of organizational performance is the theme of Imai's (1986) book, *Kaizen*. Juran (1988), a "competitor" of Deming and who also was instrumental in teaching the Japanese about quality control, discusses effective goal setting for quality at some length in his book.

Goals as Stimulants of Amount or Quality of Planning

A number of studies, rather than looking at the effect of goals on the development of specific strategies, have examined the relationship between goal setting and amount of planning or specific planning attributes. Earley (1986a), in a study of subscription processors, found that goals plus specific feedback in the form of their actual performance led to more reported planning ("I will use a careful series of steps") than goals plus general feedback (in the form of "Your performance was 'good' or 'poor'"). General feedback probably had the effect of making the goals themselves somewhat general. Earley (1988) replicated this finding in a second study of subscription processors.

In a correlational study, Earley, Lee, and Hanson (1989, based on Earley, Hanson, & Lee, 1986), using people from a variety of jobs and organizations, found that a conglomerate goal setting measure (including the attributes of goal specificity and challenge) was significantly related to a conglomerate planning measure (including the attributes of long time perspective, contingency planning, breadth, and resource use). Earley and Perry (1987) found that subjects given specific, hard goals reported engaging in more planning on a listing-uses task than those with do best goals. Earley, Wojnaroski, and Prest (1987) found in two studies, one laboratory-experimental and one field-correlational, that specific, challenging goals stimulated more planning than do best goals.

Smith, Locke, and Barry (in press) used an organizational simulation game to examine the effect of assigned goals on planning quality and performance. Quality was defined in terms of the planning attributes as rated by the subjects (e.g., comprehensiveness, communication, future orientation). Having specific, challenging goals led to significantly higher planning quality than do best goals. Chesney and Locke (1988) found that goal difficulty level was significantly associated with the use of the most effective business strategy in another management simulation. In a correlational field study, Barry, Locke, and Smith (1988) found significant associations between firm goals and planning.

A strategy that has received little attention in the goal setting literature is to request or acquire resources as a means of attaining goals (Haberstroh, 1960). For business managers and executives, obtaining resources is often a prerequisite to even trying to attain a goal. Goals are used to identify needed resources and to justify getting them. Separate strategies may be required to get the resources and to utilize them effectively.

Several studies have shown that the effect of goals on the performance of complex tasks is lagged in time, probably because it takes time for the individuals to develop suitable strategies and plans, and for these to pay off in performance. Earley, Lee, and Hanson (1989), in the correlational study noted earlier, found that the goal-performance relationship held for all subgroups except individuals with low experience on complex jobs. Presumably people in this subgroup were still learning how to do their jobs and thus goals could not be translated into results. Shaw (1984) found that the performance superiority of individuals with specific, hard goals, or assigned strategies, or both did not appear until the second half of a fifty-minute work period. Using a more complex task (a management game), and using groups as the unit of analysis, Smith, Locke, and Barry (in press) found that significant goal setting and planning effects were not manifested until about the third hour of the total six-hour work period.

The Interaction of Goals with Assigned, Chosen, or Primed Strategies

In a number of goal setting studies, task strategies have been provided directly or by implication or assigned independently of goals, and their joint or interactive effect has been examined. Earley (1985a) conducted two studies, one laboratory and one field, in which information about how to perform the task effectively was provided for some subjects. All subjects were assigned the same specific, challenging goal. Subjects who were given strategy information had higher commitment and performance than those not given this information. In neither experiment, unfortunately, was there a group without specific, hard goals; thus a test for an interaction effect was not possible.

In a study where the task was assembling booklets (Earley, 1985b), subjects who were given both information about strategies that could be used to perform the task and an assigned goal performed better than subjects given an assigned goal only when the goals were impossible, but not when the goal was easier than this. Both groups did better than subjects with a do best goal and no information, but there was no do best information condition to allow an interaction test.

Earley and Kanfer (1985) found that subjects given a choice of both strategy and goal performed better than subjects given only goal choice or neither choice. Strategy choice increased goal commitment but also may have led to a better match between strategy and ability in the choice condition, although some attempt was made to control for this.

Locke, Frederick, Lee, and Bobko (1984) found that strategy training on a listing-uses task affected the strategies actually used and hence self-efficacy, goals, and performance. The two experiments by Earley, Wojnaroski, and Prest (1987), cited earlier, found that goals and strategy information had an independent effect on performance. Earley et al. (1987) showed specifically that goals and strategy information affected effort and planning, respectively. There was no evidence of an interaction effect. However, in Shaw's (1984) study noted previously, the subjects given both specific, hard goals and an effective task strategy out-performed all the other groups (hard goal–no strategy given, and do best with and without strategy), indicating an ordinal interaction effect. More recent studies have also found interaction effects.

In two experiments by Earley and Perry (1987), strategy information was provided more indirectly than in the preceding studies. Subjects listed uses for objects under specific, hard and do best goal conditions. Subjects were trained or "primed" with a cognitive strategy to use, either openly, by telling them to use the strategy provided, or unobtrusively, by giving them a "cover" task that would induce them to use the same strategy the other group was told to use. They were then given one of three tasks to perform: one on which the primed strategy would facilitate performance, one on which it would hurt performance, and one for which it was irrelevant. Earley and Perry found that hard goal subjects did better than do best subjects when the primed strategy was suitable and when it was irrelevant to the task. However, when the primed strategy was not suitable to the task, do best subjects did better than hard goal subjects. It appeared, then, that *the effect of specific, hard goals was to enhance the use of the primed strategy:* such enhancement could either help or hurt the performance of subjects with goals, depending on the match between the strategy and the task.

In a second experiment, Earley and Perry (1987) followed the same basic design as the first study but added a no-priming condition. They replicated the results of the first study. In addition, they found that priming was more effective than no priming when the primed strategy was suitable. The opposite was true when the strategy was unsuitable. This pattern was significant only for the specific, hard goal conditions.

The effect of goals in enhancing the use of strategies was also found in a study by Earley, Lee, and Lituchy (1989), which required subjects to predict stock prices from three pieces of information about a fictitious company across multiple trials. In their design, one-third of the subjects had specific, hard goals, one-third had a "learning" goal, and one-third had do best goals. Additionally, half were told how to go about discovering the correct prediction formula (which involved weighting the three pieces of information), whereas half were not told how to do this. It was found that the effect of strategy training was significant only for subjects with a hard goal or a learning goal. For those with strategy training, hard and learning goals worked better than do best goals. Only hard goal and learning goal subjects used specific numerical criteria or benchmarks to decide when to adjust their strategies. Without strategy training, hard goals worked less well than the other two goals; this was because hard goal subjects picked poorer strategies than the subjects with learning or do best goals.

In two follow-up studies using the same task, Earley, Connolly, and Lee (1988) replicated the latter finding. In the first study, they used specific, hard vs. do best goals and three types of training: none, content (subjects could try out a list of formulas), and process (subjects were trained how to discover the correct formula). The training only benefited the performance of the specific, hard goal subjects. Similarly, hard goals only benefited performance if there was training. In the second study, in which all subjects had a specific, hard goal, they found that both content and process training facilitated performance when the formula was correct; however, process training was superior to content training when subjects were required to discover a new prediction formula.

Consistent with the above results, Neale, Northcraft, and Earley (1987) found that hard goal subjects completed more integrative contracts than easy or do best goal subjects at a bargaining task only after the subjects received training in bargaining strategies. The hard goal subjects, in effect, benefited more from training than subjects with other goals. Locke and Bryan's (1966b) previously cited finding that subjects with specific, hard goals were more likely to memorize the computation formula needed to perform the computation task also suggests that hard goals stimulate people to make use of information relevant to task performance.

Finally, in a simulated stock investment study, Earley, Northcraft, Lee, and Lituchy (in press) found that specific, hard goals increased the probability that subjects would request useful information from a data base and that they would develop a high-quality investment strategy as compared with do best goals. These effects were enhanced if subjects were given outcome feedback and information as to the potential usefulness of the various items of information in the data base.

Goals, Strategies, and Performance
on Complex Tasks

Many of the studies discussed thus far have involved fairly straightforward tasks, such as listing uses or loading trucks. Furthermore, the strategies developed to reach the goals have been relatively straightforward (e.g., using radios to coordinate truck loading). As tasks become more complex, however, requisite strategies not only become more complex but also become more important in regulating task performance (a topic we examine in Chapter 13; see also Wood & Bailey, 1985). This was implicitly revealed in the studies by Earley and his colleagues described above.

Three studies by Wood and Bandura (Bandura & Wood, in press; Wood & Bandura, in press a; Wood, Bandura, & Bailey, in press) illustrate this further. (For an integrated overview of the three studies, see Wood & Bandura, in press b.) All three studies used a complex, computerized, management simulation developed by Wood. It involves attaining production in a furniture factory and requires the manager to allocate workers to tasks and to make decisions about what goals, feedback, and rewards to give each worker. The simulation can be run for up to eighteen trials; the manager must make four decisions (job allocation, goal, feedback, and reward) per employee per trial. The game can be played using between three and eight employees; the former would require 3 × 4, or 12, decisions per trial, while the latter would require 8 × 4, or 32, decisions per trial. The number of employees, therefore, determines the complexity of the task. The effects of each decision are determined by complex formulas (some of which are time-lagged) governing each type of decision. These decisions determine the productivity index for each trial, for each worker, and for the factory as a whole.

All the studies included measures of personal goals, self-efficacy, analytic strategies, and performance. The best analytic strategy for discovering the cause-effect relationships between decisions and outcomes is to change only one variable (job allocation, goal, etc.) for a given employee on a given trial. Only in this way can the "manager" isolate the effects of that variable (ignoring time-lagged effects). Thus the analytic strategy index was the number of times the subject (manager) changed a single variable for a given employee across the trials in question.

The relationship between personal goals, self-efficacy, strategies, and performance combined across the three studies is shown in Figure 4–2.[1] The weighted mean *r*'s for trial blocks 2 and 3 or the simulation are shown for each path. All three independent variables are related to performance. Personal goals and self-efficacy are related to each other, especially on block 3, and both are

---

[1]The authors are grateful to Dr. Robert E. Wood for supplying these data. It should be noted that past performance was not included as a variable in Figure 4–2 (in contrast to Wood and Bandura, in press b) because past performance is a result of goals, self-efficacy, and strategies and thus would lead to underestimating the independent effects of those variables.

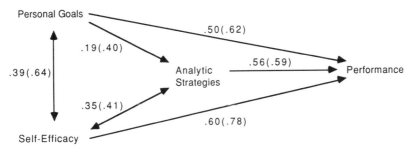

FIGURE 4–2   **Relationship (mean r̄'s) between Personal Goals, Self-Efficacy, Strategies, and Performance on Complex Tasks** [a] **(three experiments using Wood's management simulation)**
[a]*The r̄'s outside parentheses are for trial block 2; those inside parentheses are for trial block 3. All path coefficients (not shown) except goals-strategies for trial block 2 were significant.*

related to strategies. The relation between self-efficacy and strategies is bi-directional, with the strategy → efficacy link being stronger than the efficacy → strategy link (relevant data not shown). The goal-performance link in Figure 4–2 implies that the direct goal mechanisms (effort, persistence, direction) do affect performance on complex tasks, but the path coefficients (not shown) reveal that the strategy-performance link is stronger. The path coefficients are .39 and .29 for strategy for blocks 2 and 3, respectively. These coefficients are substantially higher than the corresponding path coefficients for goals (.29 and .14). Chesney and Locke (1988) also found that strategies were more highly related than goals to performance on a (different) complex, computerized management simulation.

Figure 4–3 summarizes the sources of task strategy information discussed to date. Information about task strategies can come from past experience with the task, direct instruction and strategy training, priming, modeling (which has not been studied in relation to goal strategies but whose relevance is obvious), and exploratory rule-learning as studied by Wood et al. There are undoubtedly other sources of task strategy information (e.g., experts, formal experiments, group discussion), but these have not been studied as yet in the goal setting literature.

Another series of studies of goal setting using a complex task was conducted by Kanfer and Ackerman (1988). They used a simulated air traffic control setting. However, methodological problems, make these studies difficult to interpret. These problems included the failure to measure personal goals; the

Past Experience with Task

Instruction and Training

Priming

Modeling

Exploratory Problem Solving, Rule Learning

FIGURE 4–3   **Sources of Task Strategy Information**

failure to fully match the goal and the criterion measures; the failure to use a proper measure of self-efficacy, the presentation of performance feedback in such a way that it could disrupt performance; and the failure to measure task strategies. These problems aside, Kanfer and Ackerman found that (a) goals given at an early stage of learning improved the performance of high-ability subjects but only on later trials when goals were no longer assigned; (b) goals given at the middle stage of learning improved performance generally; (c) goals improved the performance of subjects trained to memorize key task rules (thus reducing the cognitive load while performing the task); and (d) goals hurt the performance of subjects who did not get such training. These findings are consistent with the notion that goals may not help, and may even harm, performance at the early stages of learning a complex task on which there has been no prior training or inappropriate training.

It should not be assumed that performance on complex tasks is simply a matter of knowledge of appropriate strategies. Different people can use or implement the same strategy with markedly differing degrees of effectiveness due to differences in skill and self-efficacy (Bandura, 1982). A complete theory of strategy effects would have to include these and other factors.

When Do Goals Lead to Good vs. Poor Task Strategies?

If task strategies are a crucial link between goals and performance on complex tasks (and even a relevant link on simple tasks), then it is important to determine the factors that will determine whether good or poor strategies are developed in response to goals. No definitive answer to this question can be given based on present knowledge, but some clues are suggested by studies that found that specific, hard goals led to no better or to poorer performance than do best goals.

One obvious cause of using poor strategies is that the individuals are experimentally trained or deliberately cued to use strategies that hurt rather than help performance (e.g., see the Earley & Perry, 1987, studies described earlier). However, it is obvious that poor strategy choice can occur in the absence of any training. On the other side of the same coin, training in appropriate strategies can facilitate performance; similarly, individuals can develop good strategies without training.

Several studies show, however, that the nature of the goals themselves can affect the quality of the strategy chosen. Earley, Connolly, and Ekegren (1989), using the same stock price prediction task used by Earley, Lee, and Lituchy (1989) found in three separate studies that untrained subjects with do best goals performed better than those with specific, hard goals. Earley, Lee, and Lituchy (1989) found the same for their untrained subjects. Questionnaire responses as well as statistical estimates of consistency from the former study indicated that subjects with hard goals were more likely than those with do best goals to constantly switch prediction strategies, whereas those with do best goals tried fewer strategies and did less switching.

Only the studies by Earley and his colleagues noted above and one study by Kanfer and Ackerman (1988), to be noted below, found that specific, hard goals led to poorer performance than do best goals. Wood, Bandura, and Bailey (in press) found no difference in the effects of the two goals when their simulation was run at the high end of the complexity continuum, i.e., with eight employees. Do best subjects did not use better analytic strategies than the hard goal subjects. In Bandura and Wood's (in press) study, subjects who were assigned easy goals and who had high self-efficacy used better strategies than those assigned hard goals; both goal groups performed equally well. (Perhaps the goal difficulty differences canceled out the strategy differences.) Wood and Bandura (in press, a) found that subjects who were told to approach the game from a learning standpoint used better analytic strategies and performed better than those told to approach the game in order to see how good a manager they were.

Thus it appears that specific, hard goals may push individuals with hard goals into a less than systematic "scramble" to find a strategy that will get immediate results, whereas those with easy goals, do best goals, or learning goals are more likely, or at least equally likely, to take the time to use a more careful, systematic approach. Campbell (1984) also found that subjects with specific, hard goals used poor strategies in yet another management simulation. (Campbell intended to have an easy and a hard goal condition, but both the easy and hard goals turned out to be two to three S.D.'s above the attained level of performance.)

Huber (1985b) found that in a computerized maze-learning task, subjects with specific, hard goals, expressed as number of moves to complete the maze, did more poorly than subjects with moderate, easy, or do best goals. However, this result was due to the fact that subjects were penalized if they pushed a button that gave them a short "peek" at the whole maze, and hard goal subjects did more peeking. With the peeking penalty removed, there were no differences in performance between any of the goal groups.

If we consider the Campbell, Earley et al., Huber, Kanfer and Ackerman, and Wood and Bandura studies that found negative results as a group, three interrelated factors can be hypothesized to explain why the usual goal setting findings did not emerge or emerged in reverse:

1. The tasks were *complex and heuristic;* thus the direct goal mechanisms of effort, persistence, and choice were not sufficient to ensure high performance. Subjects had to learn the best strategy to use.
2. The subjects had *no prior experience or training* at the task; thus they had no proven strategies or even problem-solving processes to fall back on.
3. The subjects with specific, hard goals *felt pressure to perform well immediately;* there was no announced opportunity to learn or experiment. Hard goal subjects may therefore have had tunnel vision, focusing more on the desire to get immediate results than on learning the best way of performing the task.

There is direct evidence for the relevance of the first attribute in the Wood, Bandura, and Bailey (in press) study. Specific, hard goals led to better performance than do best goals on the low-complexity version of the game (three employees) but did not do so on the high-complexity version (eight employees). The significance of the second attribute is attested to by the finding that trained subjects (e.g., in the Earley, and Kanfer and Ackerman experiments) with specific, hard goals performed better than trained, do best subjects, whereas the results were reversed for untrained subjects.

There is indirect support for the third attribute. Christensen-Szalanski (1980) found that time pressure led to less than optimal strategy choices. Wood and Bandura (in press, a) found that subjects who approached the game from a learning perspective chose better strategies than those trying to prove how good they were. The latter is probably similar psychologically to a specific, hard goal. Similarly, Earley, Lee, and Lituchy (1989) found that untrained subjects with a learning goal performed better than those with a specific, hard goal. While Kanfer and Ackerman (1988) did not measure task strategies, their results are consistent with the view that goals and intrusive feedback do not facilitate the acquisition of needed strategies at the early stages of learning. Malone (1981) has suggested that the early learning of complex tasks or skills be undertaken with minimal outside pressures in order to ensure efficient learning. This prescription is consistent with the extensive literature on anxiety and performance. Anxiety typically disrupts performance on complex, unautomated tasks while it facilitates performance on simple or routinized tasks.

We would hypothesize, then, that the usual goal setting findings and relationships will occur to the degree that one or more of the disrupting features are absent. However, future studies would do well to separate the effects of each of these factors using different versions of the same task. Wood's factory simulation task is especially suitable for this, since the complexity level can be varied by varying the number of employees involved. The third attribute should probably be separated into two factors: pressure and time.

On the issue of time, it may be that on complex tasks in which the individual is not unduly pressured and has the capacity to discover suitable plans or task strategies, there will be a time-lagged effect of goals. The goals may not help performance until subjects are able to formulate and implement workable plans. A case in point is the study of sixteen simulated organizations by Smith, Locke, and Barry (in press) discussed earlier. Eight of sixteen organizations were given specific, hard goals and the other eight were given no goals. The trials were forty to sixty minutes long and the organizations consisted of eighteen to twenty people. It can be seen from Figure 4–4 that the goal effect did not begin to emerge until the second trial; it was not actually significant until trial 4. Some but not all of Wood and Bandura's data suggest a time-lagged effect of goals. Obviously the conditions under which this will occur are not yet fully understood. More studies of time-lagged effects on goals are clearly in order. The strategy effects on goals are summarized in Figure 4–5.

GOAL MECHANISMS FOR GROUP AND ORGANIZATIONAL GOALS

All the mechanisms discussed so far should apply to group and organizational goals as well as to individual goals. However, additional mechanisms may apply at the macro level. In a theoretical discussion of group goals, Weldon and Weingart (1988), for example, argued that group cooperation and information exchange will play a role in determining the degree to which group goal setting enhances performance. Earley and Northcraft (1989) argued that goals can be used to

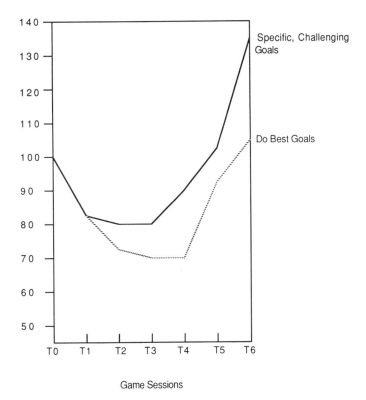

Game Sessions

FIGURE 4–4 **Plot of Performance Scores for Specific, Challenging, and Do Best Goals**
From K. G. Smith, E. A. Locke, and D. Barry, "Goal Setting, Planning and Organizational Performance: An Experimental Simulation," Organizational Behavior and Human Decision Processes *(in press). Reprinted by permission of Academic Press.*

- Stimulate Strategy Development (and resource acquisition)

- Influence Amount and Quality of Planning

- Enhance Utilization of Strategies Taught, Provided, or Primed

- Lead to Good (Effective) Task Strategies exept when:
     a. Complex, heuristic task
     b. No prior training or experience
     c. Pressure to perform well immediately

FIGURE 4–5 **Summary of Strategy Effects of Goals**

reduce conflict on interdependent tasks. At the organizational level, many factors can affect the success of goal setting; these are examined in Chapter 14.

The relationship between goals, task strategies, and performance is clearly in need of additional studies. There is a solid base of research findings, but there are many questions yet unanswered. Future research will probably take goal setting theory into the realm of decision theory and problem solving, since both are involved when people try to attain goals on complex tasks. Future research will also take us into the realm of macro-organizational behavior, because the most complex forms of goal setting are probably those done at the organizational level (see Chapter 14).

CONCLUSION

If we now combine the findings reported in this chapter and the preceding chapter, we can explain clearly *how* and *why* specific, challenging goals lead to higher performance than other types of goals. They do so because, as compared with other types of goals, specific, hard goals

1. Are associated with higher self-efficacy (whether the goals are assigned or self-set)
2. Require higher performace in order for the individual to feel a sense of self-satisfaction
3. Entail less ambiguity about what constitutes high or good performance
4. Are typically more instrumental in bringing about valued outcomes
5. Lead individuals to expend more effort
6. Stimulate individuals to persist longer
7. Direct attention and action better, and activate previously automatized skills
8. Motivate individuals to search for suitable task strategies, to plan, and to utilize strategies that they have been taught.

Therefore, what might at first seem to be a fairly simple idea turns out, on close examination, to involve multiple cognitive and motivational mechanisms and complex causal interrelationships. In 1984 Naylor and Ilgen criticized goal "theory" in its primitive, earlier versions for failing to provide a clear explanation of why goal setting works. Since then, it has become obvious that substantial progress has been made in understanding what makes it work.

The remaining aspects of goal setting theory provide the answers to two further questions, What determines which goals people will choose? and When or under what conditions do goals affect performance? The latter issue concerns the boundary conditions or moderators of goal setting effects.

CHAPTER
5

DETERMINANTS OF GOAL CHOICE

The process of choosing a goal is conceptually and introspectively separable from that of committing oneself to a goal, although the processes are obviously related. For example, many of the factors that influence goal choice also influence goal commitment. Furthermore, one way of defining commitment (when goals are assigned) is the degree of discrepancy between an assigned goal and the personal goal that the person chooses (see Chapter 6).

The conceptual distinction between choice and commitment is logically presupposed by attempts to look at causal connections between these two processes. For example, it is often asserted that allowing individuals to choose their own goals leads consistently to higher levels of commitment than assigning them a goal. Although it is shown in Chapter 7 that this assertion is incorrect, keeping the concepts separate at least allows the choice-commitment hypothesis to be tested. It also allows the opposite causal relationship to be tested. For example, Locke and Shaw (1984) found that degree of commitment to winning in a competitive situation affected the difficulty of the goal level chosen.

It may appear that concern with goal choice is unnecessary, since most goal setting studies have examined the relationship between assigned goals and performance. However, even when goals are assigned, the relationship between the assigned goal level and the individual's personal goal level is far from perfect (as we shall see below). Thus even under assigned goals, there is an individual choice process involved. And, of course, goals do not have to be and are not always assigned in goal setting experiments. Thus it is important to discover the factors that determine what goals the individual will choose when allowed free choice.

The goal choice literature has been previously reviewed by Campbell (1982). This chapter updates and expands that review. As Campbell noted, the study of the determinants of goal choice did not actually begin with contemporary goal setting research, but rather with the level-of-aspiration studies conducted mainly in the 1930s and 1940s.

LEVEL OF ASPIRATION

In the early 1930s the term *level of aspiration* (LA) was coined by Dembo, popularized by Kurt Lewin, and first studied experimentally by Hoppe (Lewin, Dembo, Festinger, and Sears, 1944). Hoppe's original definition was not entirely clear:

> The subject . . . always undertakes the task with certain demands . . . which can change in the course of the activity. The totality of these constantly shifting, now indefinite, now precise, expectations, goal settings or demands in connection with one's own future performance, we shall term the level of aspiration of the subject (cited in Gardner, 1958, p. 230).

However, Frank later gave a more succinct definition:

> The term *level of aspiration . . . is defined as the level of future performance in a familiar task which an individual, knowing his level of past performance in that task, explicitly undertakes to reach* (Frank, 1935, p. 119).

Lewin (1958) and others stressed that feelings of success and failure on a task were not determined by absolute performance, but by performance in relation to the level of performance one was aspiring to, that is, one's LA. In addition to serving as a standard of appraisal (see Chapter 10), LA was also said to act as an incentive for future performance, to be the expression of a wish, and possibly a method of defending against failure. The last was allegedly accomplished by refusing to lower the LA after failure (Frank, 1941).

Lewin et al. (1944) as well as Gould (1939) suggested that the individual did not actually have a single goal on a task but a whole "goal structure" that included multiple levels of goals. The highest level that the person hoped to reach was called the *ideal* or *hoped for goal* (see also Irwin & Mintzer, 1942). Such a goal might be based more on wish than reality, or it might represent what the individual could get if everything went right and he or she was lucky. The level the individual was actually trying to reach, Lewin et al. called the *action goal,* or actually try for goal. This goal, he thought, would be more realistic than the ideal goal and would be closely tied to what the individual *expected to get* in the way of a score on the task. An expectation, of course, is not in itself a goal but would be closely related to the individual's action goal because the latter is typically based on a realistic assessment of what the individual can actually accomplish based on past experience. The low end of the goal structure was said to be anchored by the individual's *minimum goal,* or *the minimum level of performance that the individual would be satisfied with.*

Locke and Bryan (1968b) measured "hope," "expect," "try for," and "minimum" grade goals for various courses (a common history course, the student's easiest course, hardest course, and overall GPA) among a sample of college students and found that the four types of goals were highly intercorrelated. This finding was replicated by Wood and Locke (1987). However, the expect and minimum goals in the Locke and Bryan (1968b) study had the highest relative validity for predicting future performance. This is because both the hope and try for goals had very high means and low variances. On an absolute scale the minimum goal measure corresponded most closely to the actual grade attained, while the hope and try for goals were farthest above the level of actual attainment. Evidently the *real* "action goal," the one that most closely regulates performance, is the minimum goal rather than, as Lewin claimed, the action or actually try for goal. Locke and Bryan's results are shown in Figure 5–1.

Unlike current goal setting researchers, LA researchers had almost no interest in LA as an independent variable. As noted above, they claimed that the individual's performance in relation to the LA determined the degree to which the individual would experience success or failure on the task (an issue dealt with at greater length in Chapter 10). LA research was focused mainly on the factors that determined LA and the generality of LA across tasks. Gould (1939) and Frank (1935) found, for example, that LA's were significantly correlated across tasks. Two basic categories of determinants (other than personality, which will be discussed in Chapter 9) were identified. These were the same two that affect goal commitment, namely, expectancy of success and the valence (or value) or success (e.g., Festinger, 1942). Subsequent research on the determinants of goals has remained within this broad framework but has identified a number of factors given little attention by the LA investigators. The remainder of this chapter is organized in terms of the factors that affect perceived capability of reaching and perceived desirability of attaining a given goal level.

FIGURE 5–1   Mean Deviation of Four Types of LA Rating from Obtained Grades for Four Criteria
From Locke & Bryan, 1968b.

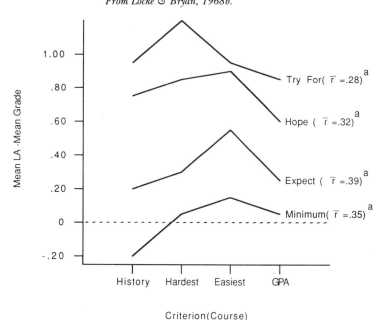

Criterion(Course)

a: Mean Validity Coefficient

FACTORS AFFECTING PERCEIVED PERFORMANCE CAPABILITY

Previous performance

A logical starting point for setting one's goal on a task is one's own past performance on that task. This, of course, does not explain why one chose the goal in question, since attributing every goal to previous performance leads to an infinite regress and does not explain how the first goal was set. However, once one has had some experience at a task, one's past performance does indicate what one is capable of achieving and thus is relevant to consider when deciding what to try for next. Numerous studies have shown that past performance or the perception of past performance is a factor in goal choice (Ashworth & Mobley, 1978; Bandura & Wood, in press; Bavelas, 1975, 1978; Campion & Lord, 1982; Cummings, Schwab, & Rosen, 1971; Hollenbeck & Williams, 1987; Locke, Frederick, Buckner, & Bobko, 1984; Locke, Frederick, Lee, & Bobko, 1984; Wilstead & Hand, 1974; Wood & Bandura, in press, a; Yukl & Latham, 1978).

Ability

Closely related to the issue of past performance is that of ability. Ability, after all, is judged to a great extent on how well one has done on the same or a similar task in the past. In fact, ability is most easily measured by giving the individual an introductory trial period to work at the task in question (i.e., a work sample). In most goal setting studies, the ability measure is simply one's score on a work sample taken at the beginning of the study, although in some cases aptitude test scores may be used (Campion & Lord, 1982). Again, many studies have found significant associations between ability or perceived ability and goal choice (Campion & Lord, 1982; Dossett, Latham & Mitchell, 1979; Garland 1983; Garland & Adkinson, 1987; Hannan, 1975; Hollenbeck & Brief, 1987; Klein, 1988; Locke, Frederick, Buckner, & Bobko, 1984; Locke, Frederick, Lee, & Bobko, 1984; Matsui, Kakuyama, & Onglatco, 1987; Mento, Cartledge, & Locke, 1980; Podsakof & Farh, 1989; Roberson-Bennett, 1983; Vance & Colella, 1988; Wood & Locke, 1987).

Success and Failure

LA researchers did extensive studies of the effects of success and failure in relation to the individual's previous goal on the level of his or her future goal. Most commonly, LA was raised after failure and lowered after success (Lewin et al., 1944). Lopes (1976) found that the immediately previous trial had the greatest effect on choice, as compared with the second or third previous trials. LA researchers found that the effect of failure was less uniform than that of success (Frank, 1941; Hilgard, 1958). Failure could lead not only to lowering the goal but to maintaining it at the same level or to raising it, and single failures within a string of successes were less likely to lead to a lowering of the goal than a series of failures (Gould, 1939, based on Hoppe).

Frank (1941) suggested that raising one's goal after failure was a defensive maneuver designed to protect self-esteem by denying the failure. Similarly,

Greenberg (1985) argued that setting one's goal at a high level when success is unlikely is a "self-handicapping" strategy, a term that he used as a synonym for defensiveness, in that failure under a hard goal excuses poor performance. However, there is a seeming contradiction in this argument. If, as LA theory asserts, one's LA is the standard for judging success and failure, then setting a goal that is too high to reach should enhance rather than dilute one's sense of failure.[1] If failure avoidance is the primary goal, then lowering the goal would be more logical. If, however, the goal is raised, this suggests that there is an *additional motive* at work, namely, a strong desire to do better next time. Bayton (1943), based on an article published in German by Hoppe, observed that three conflicting motives can affect the choice or expression of level of aspiration: the desire to appear ambitious, the desire to accurately predict how well one will do, and the desire not to fail. None of these motives suggests self-handicapping, at least not by conscious design.

Goal setting theory, in contrast to self-handicapping theory, argues that people will raise their goals after failure as a *compensation* strategy; the motive is the desire to make up for past failure by dramatically increasing future performance. This motive for raising goals was also noted frequently by LA researchers (e.g., Gould, 1939). The desire to do better *may* lead the individual to choose a future goal that is based more on wish than capability. This, in effect, detaches the goal from reality, but the conscious motive remains the desire to improve. Greenberg (1985) found that subjects were most likely to set high goals, following a work trial on which success was seemingly random rather than controlled, when they judged success to be important, even though they saw little probability of actually succeeding. The high goal clearly represented a wish, albeit one that would probably not come true. Greenberg (1985) attempted to rebut the compensation argument by noting that subjects who did not think success was important lowered rather than raised their goals following the trial on which success was random. However, this finding actually supports our point. When good performance is not important, there is no strong desire to do well and thus no incentive to raise the goal. (High performance on unimportant tasks can be achieved, of course, by assigning high goals to people, but the act of assigning the goal itself makes performance important.)

If assigned goals become so high that they are totally unrealistic, commitment could drop (see Chapter 6); then such goals could become progressively less effective in regulating action. Vance and Colella (1988) found that subjects faced with progressively larger negative discrepancies between assigned goals and performance, due to the fact that assigned goals were continually raised on a task that did not have a learning curve, increasingly rejected the assigned goals. Instead, they set personal goals that were increasingly deviant from the assigned goals. The personal goals, naturally, were far lower and more realistic than the assigned goals, especially in the later trials.

In sum, rather than being self-handicapping, most subjects are self-enhancing. They will either set a hard improvement goal following poor

---

[1]If such a goal is set so high that the individual does not even use it in judging success and failure, then for all practical purposes it is not a goal at all but an out-of-context wish or fantasy.

performance because they want to compensate for it or they will reject the hard goal and set a lower goal because they want to succeed. This is not to say that self-handicapping cannot occur, but it should not be inferred just because an individual sets a high goal. As demonstrated in Chapter 2, hard goals lead to high performance even when the goals are not reached. Partial success on a hard goal can lead to much higher performance than full success on an easy goal. In support of our compensation hypothesis, Campion and Lord (1982) found that below-goal performance on an exam often led students to raise their goal and to increase their efforts for the next exam because they needed a higher exam average in order to attain the course grade they wanted. Only after consecutive or repeated below-goal outcomes were future goals lowered. Similarly, Matsui, Okada, and Inoshita (1983) found that feedback indicative of failure in relation to a goal led to greater subsequent effort than feedback indicating success. Forward and Zander (1971) found that large goal increases after feedback indicating failure led to poor performance. But since the feedback in this study was false, subjects may have had largely random effort-performance expectancies.

Zander, Forward, and Albert (1969) found that community United Fund organizations that failed to reach their previous goals increased their future goals by a greater percentage than organizations that succeeded in reaching their goals. This did not appear to be a self-handicapping strategy, however, in that the goal levels of the failing funds, in relation to the per capita wealth available, were actually lower than those of the successful funds. Furthermore, board members of failing funds actually worked harder than those of successful funds.

Greenberg's (1985) experiment is more complex than those above because the subjects were confronted with confusing and even contradictory information. Half the subjects were persuaded that good performance was important and half that it was not important. Furthermore, half were led to believe that their past performance on the task was attained in considerable part by luck, while the other half were led to believe that their performance was the result of ability. However, all the subjects were told they had done very well on the task in comparison with previous norms. As noted, under these conditions, subjects who succeeded by luck and for whom success was important set much harder subsequent goals than those who succeeded by luck but for whom success was not important. The latter actually lowered their goals. Setting hard goals can hardly be called self-handicapping here, since performance was perceived as determined by luck rather than skill; thus goal level is almost irrelevant. It is more plausible to assume that subjects to whom good performance was important based their (higher) goals on their *desire* to do better, while subjects to whom good performance was not important based their (lower) goals on the actual *probability* of doing better. Evidence for the self-handicapping thesis would require that both goal commitment and actual subsequent effort be measured. Furthermore, there is little ecological validity in using task situations in which outcomes are determined mainly by luck. In Greenberg's study, it is revealing that there was no "self-handicapping" effect (i.e., goal-level difference) when task performance was perceived to be based on skill.

Expectancy and Self-Efficacy

The concepts of expectancy and self-efficacy are fundamental to explaining goal choice in causal terms. Expectancy in this context refers to effort-performance beliefs from expectancy theory (Vroom, 1964), and self-efficacy refers to one's beliefs about how well one can perform a task. As noted in Chapter 3, self-efficacy is a key concept in Bandura's (1986) social-cognitive theory. It is wider in meaning than effort-performance expectancy in that it refers to the individual's *overall* or total judgment of performance capability, considering all relevant information (e.g., self-assessment of ability, planned effort, attributions, beliefs about one's capacity to coordinate skills, find ingenious solutions, cope with stress, etc.). Thus self-efficacy should reflect the individual's ability, past performance, prior successes, and failures and, most importantly, the conclusions the individual has reached about total capability based on such information. If the individual concludes, for example, that he or she was not really in control of the situation or does not really understand the task or attained the previous outcome by luck, self-efficacy may be low, leading to lower future goals and performance. If self-efficacy is assessed as high, future goals and performance will be high (see Figure 3–4). Past performance, although it correlates highly with future performance, does not explain such performance. Both past and future performance reflect the causal influence of self-efficacy. Of course, ability is also a cause of performance, but it sometimes predicts it less well than self-efficacy (Bandura, 1986).

Numerous studies have measured relationships between expectancy, self-efficacy or related measures, and goal choice. The results of these studies are summarized in Table 5–1.

Consider first only the studies that used traditional expectancy measures. These are noted by an (E) next to the correlation. In these studies the expectancies had different referents for different people, since the expectancy rating was made only with respect to *their* personal or assigned goal. The mean correlation for these studies was only .04; in some studies the correlation was actually negative, since high goals with low expectancies led to higher performance than low goals with high expectancies (see Chapter 3, Table 3–1 and bottom of Figure 3–2).

Most of the remaining studies used actual self-efficacy measures; these asked the individual to rate his or her confidence in being able to attain each of the number of specific performance levels. Thus the referents for all expectancy ratings were the same. In two studies, more general self-efficacy scales were used (Hollenbeck & Brief, 1987; Silver & Greenhaus, 1983), but in both cases they were task specific. In Ashworth and Mobley's (1978) study, there was one common outcome or referent: being an outstanding Marine. The Ajzen and Madden (1986) study used a rating of perceived ability to control the behavior in question, which is equivalent to a general, but still task-specific, self-efficacy measure. The mean correlation between self-efficacy or its equivalent and the level of the goal chosen for all these remaining studies was .38. This mean correlation of .38 is slightly lower than the figure of .39 given in Chapter 3 (Table 3–2) for the same relationship, because the two means are not based on exactly the same studies. Table 5–1 presents all the known self-efficacy goal relationships (including those

Table 5–1   Relation of Expectancy and Self-Efficacy to Goal Choice

STUDY	N	r	COMMENTS
Ajzen & Madden (1986)—1	169	.57	Perceived behavioral control
—2	90	.44	
Ashworth & Mobley (1978)	1,506–1,520	.31	E of being outstanding
Bandura & Cervone (1986)	88	.43	SE; average of four conditions
Battle (1966)	250–500	.30(E)	Mean of two courses—goal certainty
Garland (1985)		.58	
Garland & Adkinson (1987)	127	.39	
Hollenbeck & Brief (1987)	47	.49	Self-perceived ability
Locke and Shaw (1984)	212	-.24(E)	
Locke, Frederick, Lee, & Bobko (1984)	181	.54	Composite SE measure
Mento et al. (1980)—1	196	-.32(E)	
—2	406	.12(E)	
Meyer & Gellatly (1988)—1	56	.62	
—2	60	.48	
Meyer et al. (1988)	69	.60	Goal measure = desired performance
Podsakoff Farh (1989)	90	.69	
Silver & Greenhaus (1983)	56	.29	Task-specific self-esteem
Taylor et al. (1984)	223	.20	
Weiss & Rakestraw (1988)	80	.60	Mean across three trials
Wood & Locke (1987)	517	.32	Mean of three samples

Weighted $\bar{r}$ for (E) studies using traditional expectancy measures = *.04*.

Weighted $\bar{r}$ for remaining studies = *.38*.

using task-specific but not precisely measured self-efficacy), whereas Table 3–2 includes only studies that showed additional relationships. Furthermore, we added the Dachler and Mobley (1973) study to Table 3–2 (but not 5–1) even though the self-efficacy "score" was a measure of maximum expected utility. Despite these differences, the two mean *r*'s are virtually identical.

It might be assumed that factors such as ability, past performance, and success or failure would work only through self-efficacy, so that partialing out self-efficacy would vitiate their effects. However, this does not necessarily happen. Locke, Frederick, Lee, & Bobko (1984), for example, found that ability, past performance, and self-efficacy each made independent contributions to the prediction of goal choice. Meyer & Gellatly (1988) also found an independent effect for ability in one of two studies where self-efficacy was measured. These results could, of course, be due to measurement error. Measures of ability and past performance, because they refer to objective accomplishment, are probably more reliable and valid than self-efficacy measures that require introspection.

Causal attributions may also affect goal levels possibly through their effects on self-efficacy. In a role-playing study, Chacko and McElroy (1983) found that after failure, subjects who attributed their failure to unstable causes such as effort or luck set higher subsequent goals than those who attributed failure to stable causes such as task difficulty or lack of ability. Unstable causes imply that the individual is capable of performing better, whereas stable causes imply that better performance is not possible. Unfortunately, Chacko and McElroy did not include a measure of self-efficacy in their study. A significant first-order correlation between internal attributions for prior performance and future goal level was obtained by Silver and Greenhaus (1983). Baron (1988) found that destructive criticism given for performance on one task lowered self-efficacy and self-set goals on a subsequent task. This could have been caused by low-ability attributions that were included in the criticism.

FACTORS AFFECTING PERCEIVED DESIRABILITY OR APPROPRIATENESS OF PERFORMANCE GOALS

In social-psychological theories designed to predict behavior, such as those of Fishbein and Ajzen (1975) and Ajzen (1987), the nonexpectancy antecedents of the intention to act are divided into two separate concepts. The first is attitude toward the object, which is roughly similar in meaning to valence (evaluation, anticipated satisfaction); the second is subjective norm, which refers to social pressures to perform or not perform the action (and perhaps to internalized norms). It remains to be seen whether these two types of antecedents can be combined into a single integrating principle. While we have no objection to the distinction, we have not made separate categories for the two concepts in our model. However, we have implicitly recognized the distinction in our heading to this section.

Group Norms and Normative Information

Level-of-aspiration researchers observed repeatedly that social-normative factors played an important role in goal choice (Frank, 1941; Gardner, 1958; Hilgard, 1958; Lewin et al., 1944). Lewin et al. (1944) specifically mentioned the norms of one's own group, the norms of other groups, and one's own standing in the group. For example, subjects who performed way above the average level of their group tended to set subsequent goals below their previous attainment levels, whereas those who performed way below average tended to set their goals far above previous attainments. This result suggests that there was an underlying desire among all the group members to perform at about the same level. However, the results could also have been obtained because the high performers found it much harder to improve or even maintain their performance than the lower performers; alternatively, the high performers, being confident in their superior performance, may have chosen not to try as hard as the low performers.

Feedback about the performance of others can affect goal choice by conveying normative information. Normative information indicates what performance level is appropriate and/or possible. Of course, role models convey such information, but it can also be conveyed in the absence of role models. Festinger (1942) found that subjects raised their LA levels in proportion to how they stood in relation to three (fictitious) outside reference groups. Subjects who thought they had done more poorly than a low status group were most likely to subsequently raise their LA, while those who thought they had done more poorly than a higher status reference group were most likely to lower their LA.

Intermediate LA changes occurred when the subjects were compared with a similar status reference group. The underlying value here was apparently the desire to be adequate in performance to similar status groups and better than the lower status groups; there was little desire to equal higher status groups.

Garland (1983) obtained an interesting interaction effect between assigned goals and norms on personal goals. Overall, those assigned low goals set lower personal goals than those assigned high goals. However, subjects assigned low goals set increasingly high personal goals in response to increasingly high normative standard information (indicating that few people could reach the goals), while those assigned high goals did the opposite. Since most subjects with low goals were able to beat these goals, the higher standard information may have been perceived as providing a challenge; thus personal goals were raised. In contrast, since almost all subjects with high goals were unable to reach them, the high normative information may have convinced them that their goals were indeed too high; thus personal goals were lowered.

A different method of conveying normative information was used by Meyer and Gellatly (1988). Rather than telling subjects the *odds* of their reaching the goal, a procedure that has unreliable effects due to differing personal assessments of the objective odds (see Locke & Shaw, 1984; Mento et al., 1980, and Chapter 3), Meyer and Gellatly told their subjects what the normal score of a college student was on the task and varied this information independently of the assigned goal level (experiment 2). The normative information, via the mechanism of the subjects' perceived norm, had a significant impact on personal goals independently of the effects of assigned goals and self-efficacy. Perceived norms also affected self-efficacy.

A somewhat different approach to the same phenomenon was taken by Podsakoff and Farh (1989). They gave subjects feedback indicating that they were above or below a normative performance standard. Negative feedback led the subjects to set high goals for future performance most reliably if they were given highly credible performance norms.

Role Modeling

The effect of role modeling on goals has been documented in several studies. Rakestraw and Weiss (1981) found that observing a high-performing role model led subjects to set higher personal goals for task performance than observing a low-performing model. If the individual had previous experience at the task, however, that direct experience (i.e., past performance) took precedence over the model's performance. In a subsequent study, Weiss and Rakestraw (1988) replicated the modeling effect and, consistent with the first study, found that the modeling effect dissipated as the individual gained experience at the task. They also found that observing the high-performing model led to higher self-efficacy than observing the low-performing model. Again the effect disappeared after the subjects gained task experience. Self-efficacy had an effect on performance as well as on goal choice. Earley and Kanfer (1985) found that observing a high-performing role model led to higher commitment to difficult goals than observing a low-performing model. Self-efficacy was not measured but probably played a role, as in the Weiss and Rakestraw study. In an interesting field study, Anderson

(1983) found that subjects who drew cartoons of themselves donating blood formed stronger intentions to give blood than was the case if they drew cartoons of other people donating blood. Thus *self-modeling* had a more powerful effect than modeling by others. Dowrick and Hood (1981) found that self-modeling had a substantial impact on performance on an assembly task—in fact, the modeling effect was greater than the effect of a monetary incentive.

Competition

Competition is another factor that can influence goals. Mueller (1983) found that competition led to higher goals under a self-set condition (but not higher goal commitment) than no competition on a brainstorming task. House (1974) found that competition led to higher goals than no competition for men when they were competing with women but not when they were competing with men. In contrast, women set their goals highest when they worked alone. Wilstead and Hand (1974) found that goal choice was affected by the performance of other teams in a simulated business game.

Group Goals

Matsui, Kakuyama, and Onglatco (1987) found that having group goals in addition to individual goals in two-person groups led to higher commitment to the individual goals than having individual goals only. The group goals may have engendered a feeling of obligation to the partner to "come through." Interestingly the group goals, on the average, were higher than the sum of the two individual goals, indicating that actual, personal goals of the members were higher than their official, individual goals. Hinsz (1984) obtained a similar finding.

Pressure and Encouragement

Social influence in the form of direct pressure (expressed as a desire or need for higher performance by the individual's team or school) was found to raise the goal levels of high school students working on a clerical task (Forward & Zander, 1971). Perceived pressure was found by Zander, Forward, and Albert (1969) to motivate United Fund campaign workers to raise their future goals even after failure to meet their preceding year's goals. Andrews and Farris (1972) and Hall and Lawler (1971) found that pressure perceived as reasonable improved the performance of scientists and engineers. Garland and Adkinson (1987) showed that both goal level and self-efficacy could be increased through persuasion and encouragement, in line with Bandura's (1986) theory.

Goal Assignment

Another "social" factor is the assignment of a goal by an authority figure, typically an experimenter or a supervisor. As noted in Chapter 3, numerous studies have obtained significant associations between assigned goals and personal goals, e.g., Garland (1983), Garland (1985), Garland and Adkinson (1987), Hannan (1975), Likert (1967, p. 60), Mento et al. (1980), Meyer and Gellatly (1988), Meyer et al.

(1988), and Terborg and Miller (1978). The mean weighted correlation in these studies (not including Likert, and Terborg and Miller, who did not provide correlations) was .52. This mean is somewhat lower than the mean of .58 given in Chapter 3. Table 3–2 includes fewer studies than was the case here because of the different criteria for inclusion noted earlier. The correlation of .52 means that only about 25% of the variance in personal goals is explained by assigned goals. To return to a point made earlier, this indicates that even with assigned goals individuals show considerable variability in their personal goals. Thus, despite the powerful influence of assigned goals, personal choices are still made in response to them.

More intriguing than the immediate effect of assigned goals on personal goals is the finding that assigned goals can affect the individual's personal goals even when the assigned goals are no longer in force. Thus when subjects are assigned goals on one or more trials and are then allowed to set their own goals on later trials, the assigned goals still influence the self-set goals (e.g., Locke, Frederick, Lee, & Bobko, 1984; Huber & Neale, 1986; Silver & Greenhaus, 1983). Goals arouse normative expectations in subjects (Meyer & Gellatly, 1988), and these expectations evidently carry over onto at least one subsequent trial. This suggests that the normative information conveyed by one assigned goal is incorporated by the subject into his or her personal conception of what performance level is appropriate. However, like the effects of modeling, the carry-over effect of assigned goals dissipates rapidly after the first trial (Locke, Frederick, Lee, & Bobko, 1984). Results obtained by Taylor (1981) suggest that task challenge has the same effect as goal challenge. Subjects initially given more-challenging tasks to perform subsequently set higher goals on later tasks of the same general type than do subjects who were initially given less-challenging tasks.

Critics of goal setting research have often claimed that assigning individuals goals in order to influence their personal goals and thereby their performance is an "artifact" in that the subjects are just trying to please the experimenter. But if assigning people goals is an artifact, then life itself is an artifact. Life is filled with demands, which take both direct and indirect forms, made on people by other people to pursue certain goals. The demands come from one's spouse, children, parents, subordinates, boss, co-workers, teachers, and friends, as well as from institutions such as charities, clubs, government bodies, professional associations, and political parties. Much of one's life is spent assessing such demands and integrating them with one's own goals and aspirations. (If one is assertive, one will also make demands on others in order to attain one's own goals.)

It would be incorrect to say that people are helpless or passive victims of their social environment, because people have free will and can think about the validity of the demands made on them. They can then choose which, if any, actions to take with respect to these demands. But people do not exist in a social vacuum; they are not controlled by others, but they do behave with respect to others. Often demands come in the form of a proposed trade; for example, the boss says, "Here is what I would like you to do on this job . . ."; in return, the employee is given recognition, raises, promotions, and/or continued employment. The individual is free to reject the terms by renegotiating with the boss, asking for a transfer, complaining to management, or seeking a job elsewhere. On the next job, however, new demands will be made. Unless one is a hermit, life is never free of social demands or requests. What we need to understand are the conditions under which such requests will influence personal goals (e.g., see Chapter 6).

Valence

The valence or value of achievement, which may have been implicit in all the previous social influence categories, has been looked at explicitly in several studies. As noted in Chapter 3, Locke and Shaw (1984) found ratings of the valence of winning on a competitive task to be significantly related to the level of the personal goal chosen by the subjects. Mento, Cartledge, and Locke (1980) found valence to be significantly related to the personal goal level in one of their two studies. Sugalski and Greenhaus (1986) found career goal choice to be significantly related to the importance of the individual work role. Weiss and Rakestraw (1988) found that the performance levels of the high-performing role models were more attractive than the performance levels of the low-performing models. Valence measures were significantly related to goal choice in two out of three trials. Matsui, Okada, and Mizuguchi (1981) found that higher goals were associated with higher instrumentalities than lower goals. Mento and Locke (1989) found the same.

As noted in Chapter 3, when valence is measured by asking subjects to rate their expected satisfaction with various performance levels, the valence ratings are lower for people with high goals than for those with easy and do best goals. It might be asked, then, why subjects would ever choose a hard goal. The answer is that in the absence of any outside factors, they usually would not; more typically they would choose moderate goals (Locke, 1965a; 1966d, experiment II). They might even choose easy goals except that the lower instrumentality of such goals (e.g., less challenge) might make them less attractive than moderate goals. Consider two real-life examples to illustrate the above. If high school students found that teachers, parents, employers, and colleges were totally indifferent to their grades, it is doubtful if many of them would try to get A's and B's instead of C's and D's. Similarly, few businesses would spend extraordinary efforts to make innovative, high-quality products at a competitive cost without the possibility of profit and loss. While high goals may be harder to reach than easy goals, in life they are usually associated with better outcomes. This does not mean that the external factors totally control the individual's choice, but only that they are taken into account when making goal choices.

An external factor that commonly influences valence is *money*, since money is a commodity valued by most people. As will be seen in Chapter 6, money can affect goal commitment if the amount is sufficiently large. Money can also affect the level at which individuals choose to set their goals, although self-set goal levels have rarely been looked at as a function of different incentive conditions. Locke, Bryan, and Kendall (1968) looked for such an effect in the first two of their five studies but did not find one. Locke and Shaw (1984) offered small payments in return for being in the winning group on a clerical task; valence was significantly related to goal level. Miller and Steele (1984), however, in a partial replication of Mowen et al. (1981), found that subjects with hard goals paid on a piece-rate basis and subjects with moderate goals paid a bonus for attaining the goal set higher goals than did hard goal subjects paid a bonus and moderate goal subjects paid on a piece rate. The valence of high goals would presumably be higher for the hard goal subjects on a piece rate than for those on bonus because the former would be paid for performance while the latter would be paid only for achieving the hard goal, an unlikely prospect. In contrast, the moderate goal subjects offered a bonus could only attain their goal if they worked hard, so it would pay them to try for a somewhat high goal. In contrast, the moderate goal subjects on a piece rate would make money regardless of whether they attained their goal. In a sophisticated design, Riedel, Nebeker, and Cooper (1988) found that subjects offered performance incentives set significantly higher goals than those not offered incentives. Both Riedel et al. and Saari and Latham (1981) found that incentives increased individuals' propensity to set goals.

Feedback

Giving subjects performance feedback can lead to the setting of higher goals than is the case without feedback by (Erez, 1977; Locke & Bryan, 1968a). Knowledge of one's previous attainment gives the individual a standard to shoot for (to beat) and thus could increase the valence of high or improved performance. We show in Chapter 8 that giving subjects feedback in a way that suggests that their score is significant almost always leads to spontaneous goal setting.

Dissatisfaction

Dissatisfaction with previous performance following feedback is clearly an impetus to change one's goal level in that the dissatisfaction indicates that one does not want to remain at the level of performance one has attained. The direction of goal change will depend, in part, on what future performance level will be most likely to attain one's overall goal on the task or provide future satisfaction (Bandura & Cervone, 1986; Locke, Cartledge, and Knerr, 1970). The relationship between goal-relevant feedback, dissatisfaction, self-efficacy, and performance is examined in Chapter 8.

Mood

Mood was found to affect goal choice by Hom and Arbuckle (1986). A positive mood induction led to the setting of higher goals than did a negative mood induction. It was not determined in that study whether mood affects self-efficacy or the valence of high performance, or some combination of the two.

CONCLUSION

The factors affecting goal choice are summarized in Figure 5–2. (Personality factors will be discussed in a separate chapter.) One can summarize the two major categories by saying that goal choice is a function of what the individual thinks *can be* achieved and what he or she *would like to* achieve or thinks *should be* achieved. As

Factors Affecting Perceived Performance Capability

Previous performance
Ability
Previous success and failure
Expectancy
Self-efficacy
Causal attributions

Factors Affecting Perceived Desirability
or Appropriateness of Performance

Group norms
Normative information
Role modeling (self-modeling)
Competition
Group goals
Pressure and encouragement
Goal Assignment
Valence (e.g., money incentives)
Feedback
Dissatisfaction with previous performance
Mood

**FIGURE 5–2   Summary of Factors
Affecting Goal Choice**

Frank (1941) put it over forty years ago, the goal a person chooses is a compromise between (actually an integration of) what the person desires, all things considered, and what he or she judges to be possible. (Lewin et al., 1944, expressed the same idea a few years later.)

Statistical attempts to measure the expectancy and valence inputs into the choice process have been made by Dachler and Mobley (1973), Klein (1988), and Riedel et al. (1988). In all cases the researchers were able to successfully predict goal choice. (Locke, 1965a, was able to predict choice of task difficulty.) Actually Riedel et al. developed goal measures that were *defined* in terms of various combinations of expectancy and valence measures. The validity of this procedure was supported by the finding that such measures correlated significantly with performance and with direct self-reports of goals. The measure that worked best was what they called "return on effort," defined as the performance level (goal) that showed the largest increase in attractiveness over the previous level. This worked better than a goal based on a maximization formula (the highest $E \times V$ product) which Dachler and Mobley (1973) had used successfully.

We noted at the beginning of this chapter that the concepts of goal choice and goal commitment are related in that they share common determinants. Thus we now turn to the topic of goal commitment.

CHAPTER

6

GOAL COMMITMENT I

It is virtually axiomatic that a goal that a person is not *really* trying for is not *really* a goal and therefore cannot have much effect on subsequent action. Only an individual who is genuinely trying for a goal can be described as being committed to that goal.

A practical demonstration of the importance of goal commitment was given by Erez and Zidon (1984, phase 2) in a laboratory experiment. They found a significant drop-off in performance as goal commitment declined in response to increasingly difficult goals. In field settings, noncommitment to organizational goals is a well-known phenomenon. It usually manifests itself in restriction of output or "soldiering," or in resistance to change (Mathewson, 1931; Roethlisberger & Dickson, 1956; Taylor, 1967). For example, in the famous bank-wiring observation room study at Hawthorne, the workers' personal goals (despite some inconsistencies in their reports) were clearly lower than the officially assigned goals or bogies (Roethlisberger & Dickson, pp. 412–13). Thus they were less than fully committed to management's goals. Coch and French's (1948) classic study of participation was specifically designed to overcome resistance by factory workers to changes in work standards or goals accompanying product changes (see also Cadwell, 1970; Goodman, 1979; Perkins, Nieva, & Lawler, 1983; and Tushman, 1974).

It is generally accepted that organizational change (driven by rapid changes in technology and the world economy) is even more a fact of life today than in the past. Understanding the factors that inhibit and promote goal commitment is therefore of practical as well as theoretical importance.

This chapter and the one following are based on an expansion and extensive revision of "The Determinants of Goal Commitment" by E. A. Locke, G. P. Latham, and M. Erez, *Academy of Management Review*, 1988, *13*, 23–89. Sections reprinted by permission of the Academy of Management.

   The terms *goal acceptance* and *goal commitment* are similar and are often used interchangeably by researchers. The confusion that may exist in the use of these two terms derives from Locke (1968b). In that article Locke implied that goal acceptance referred to initial agreement with the goal, whereas commitment referred to resistance to changing the goal at a later point in time. Our current view, however, is that both can vary over time. Commitment is now viewed as the more inclusive concept in that it refers to one's attachment to or determination to reach a goal, regardless of where the goal came from. Thus it can apply to any goal, whether self-set, participatively set, or assigned. Acceptance is a subtype of commitment and refers specifically to commitment to a goal that is assigned (Locke et al, 1981).

   One might argue that mere "acceptance" of an assigned goal represents or implies only a moderate *degree* of commitment, as in "OK, I accept the goal." To describe higher degrees of commitment, such as enthusiasm for the goal, one might prefer a term other than acceptance—for example, embracement. However, these are subtle distinctions, and it may be that our psychological measurement capabilities are not yet sophisticated enough to make such distinctions of any practical import. On the other hand, it may be that the distinctions are practically important, but that nobody has yet tried to make them.

   Thus it is possible that subsequent research will demonstrate the utility of a more marked separation of the concepts of acceptance and commitment. However, such a distinction has not as yet been shown to be empirically useful. For example, Earley and Kanfer (1985) included both commitment and acceptance measures in their study (see their Table 1, p. 382) and found that they formed one highly homogeneous index (alpha = .95). Leifer and McGannon (1986) found that a variety of commitment and acceptance measures formed four separate factors; however, only one factor, which related to commitment, was associated with performance in a regression analysis. Thus the generic term *commitment* is used throughout this chapter and book. The purpose of this chapter and the next is to summarize and integrate research findings on the determinants of goal commitment. The research on self-set and participatively set goals is discussed in a separate chapter, because the literature on these subtopics is both voluminous and controversial.

THE MEASUREMENT OF COMMITMENT

A precondition for discovering the factors that affect goal commitment is the ability to measure it or, more specifically, to measure it in a way that will show systematic relationships between it and (a) prior causal factors and (b) subsequent action (performance). While it has been suggested that goal commitment, or goal acceptance-rejection, is a dichotomous decision, the evidence indicates that commitment is a continuous variable (Erez & Zidon (1984).[1] Commitment has been measured both directly and indirectly. The use of direct questions assumes

[1]It is conceivable that certain types of tasks and incentive conditions could make commitment more of a dichotomous function than it normally is—e.g., tasks on which success is all or none rather than partial and an incentive system that offers a bonus only for reaching a virtually impossible goal (e.g., Mowen et al., 1981).

that subjects can introspect well enough to detect varying degrees of commitment, and that the scales used allow people to indicate those degrees. Examples of direct questions are, "How committed are you to attaining the goal assigned to you . . . ?" and "To what degree did you adopt the goal given to you . . . ?" (Earley, 1985a; Latham & Steele, 1983). Hollenbeck, Klein, O'Leary, and Wright (1988) and Hollenbeck, Williams, and Klein (1989) have used items such as "I am strongly committed to achieving this goal"; "Quite frankly, I don't care if I achieve this goal or not"; "It is quite likely that this. . . goal may need to be revised depending on how things go. . ."; "It wouldn't take much for me to abandon this . . . goal"; ". . . It's hard to take this goal seriously"; "I think this . . . goal is a good goal to shoot for." These items plus one more (which was more of an expectancy item) formed one factor with an alpha of .88. Such questions seem preferable to the more ambiguous questions used by Motowidlo et al. (1978), such as "I cooperated fully on this task"; "I worked on this task exactly as I was told to do"; and "I exerted much effort on this task."

In a paper combining the results of three studies including Hollenbeck et al. (1989), Hollenbeck et al. (1988) found that a subset of the Hollenbeck items was significantly associated with (a) the discrepancy between assigned and personal goals, (b) goal change, and (c) performance when goals were difficult.

An interesting variant on the direct approach was taken by Leifer and McGannon (1986) in the study noted earlier. The commitment factor that was significantly related to performance in the regression was one that asked subjects how enthusiastic they were about trying for their goal. This emotion-focused factor not only was more valid but showed higher variance than the more cognitively focused factor which simply asked subjects if they were committed.[2]

An indirect measure of commitment is the discrepancy between the assigned goal level and the personal goal the subject claims to be trying to attain (Hannan, 1975). This procedure rests on the assumption that lesser commitment to a given goal level implies greater commitment to another. Earley (1985a, 1985b) found that the direct and indirect types of measures were highly correlated (range .71 to .86 in three studies). Hollenbeck et al. (1988) found a correlation of .59 between similar measures. The direct method, of course, can only be used to measure commitment to assigned or participatively set goals, since asking subjects to set their own goals and then to indicate their personal goals is redundant. However, it is not necessarily the case that all subjects are equally committed to their personal goals. Thus even when personal goals are measured, direct questions regarding degree of commitment to them may be useful (see below). Locke and Shaw (1984) found that commitment affected performance even when personal goal level was controlled.

Furthermore, measuring personal goals is advisable even when direct commitment (to assigned goal) questions are used. Direct commitment questions, even if they accurately reveal degree of commitment, do not indicate what new goals the individual may have set after an assigned or participatively set goal has been partly or wholly rejected. Personal goals may be higher or lower than those originally assigned. Also, an individual assigned an easy goal could interpret an

[2]These details of the study were not given in Leifer and McGannon's (1986) brief Academy of Management paper but were related through a personal communication.

acceptance item to mean that he or she was trying for *at least* goal X when the subject was actually trying to perform well beyond the level of goal X.

A third way to measure commitment is by inference from performance. While performance cannot be a catchall measure of commitment, since performance can be caused by other factors such as ability, judicious use of inference from performance seems both theoretically and empirically justified. For example, Salancik (1977) argued that behavior or action is the ultimate *proof* of commitment and thus, by implication, the most accurate measure of it. Commitment, he claimed, quoting from others (e.g., see Kiesler, 1971), is "the binding of the individual to behavioral acts." He asserted that "action is a necessary ingredient of commitment" (p. 4). Thus "a person who is committed to a goal will try harder to achieve it than if he is not" (p. 27).

We think that this emphasis on action is valid because, as noted in Chapter 1, we believe that there is a volitional element to goal commitment. *Believing* that a goal is desirable and reachable does not automatically force an individual to act. The individual must *choose* to put his or her judgment into action. Individuals who simply wait for their conscious and subconscious estimates of a situation to "turn them on," more often than not find themselves doing nothing or drifting without any sustained purpose. To give a personal example, the authors perceived the writing of this book to be both desirable and possible; but these assessments did not compel them to sit down at the typewriter every day and start reading, integrating, and/or writing. Every day for about one and one-half years they had to make a conscious choice whether to allocate or not to allocate time and effort to this book, not to mention other activities. (Anyone who writes knows how difficult this choice can be.)

Empirically, commitment inferences from performance level would seem to be justified if goal level, ability, and so on, were or could be assumed to have been controlled or randomized. Furthermore, commitment would seem to be inferable from goal choice, whereas lack of commitment would be inferable from goal rejection; that is, at the time of choice it seems virtually axiomatic that people will choose the goal to which they are most or at least more committed (all forces and influences considered). Similarly, individuals who resist change, that is, resist changing from a current to a new goal, would seem axiomatically to be uncommitted or at least less committed to the new goal. (The causes of such commitment or lack thereof, of course, still need to be explained.)

It should be stressed that the fact that individuals will choose the goal to which they are most committed in a given context does not mean that assigning them a different goal will lower their commitment. Assigning goals brings *new causal influences* into the situation, as is shown later in this chapter (see also Chapter 3).

It should be noted that the process of inference is not confined to the use of behavioral measures. Inference is also involved when "direct," self-report measures of commitment are made. One is inferring that the verbal report corresponds to an actual psychological state. The inference in the case of behavior is simply more indirect and therefore risky due to possible confounding variables.

A potential problem in the measurement of commitment is that commitment may affect performance without the person's being able to report it accurately. This could be a result of poor introspection (see Bandura, 1986, and Schweiger, Anderson, & Locke, 1985, for a discussion of the validity of introspection). For example, Latham, Mitchell, and Dossett (1978) found that offering a monetary incentive affected the performance of engineers and scientists even though this difference was not mediated by differences in reported goal commitment or goal difficulty. One possible explanation of these results is that actual commitment differences existed but could not be accurately reported by the subjects.

A possible solution to the introspection problem is to use within-subject designs (e.g., Erez & Zidon, 1984). These should be more sensitive to commitment differences than between-subject designs, since different subjects may interpret the same commitment items differently. Another possibility would be to use projective measures. Although projective measures have been widely criticized by psychologists over the years, Cornelius (1983) has shown that such measures are more valid than is generally recognized.

An issue to consider in goal commitment studies is when to administer commitment questions to subjects, that is, before, during, and/or after performance. Measuring "before" prevents post hoc rationalization; measuring "after" reveals if subjects changed their goals during performance. However, the results of research on the effects of learning without awareness found that it did not really matter when such psychological variables were measured; the same results were obtained in both cases (Spielberger, 1965). In agreement with the above, Earley and Kanfer (1985) found no difference in the results when goal commitment was measured both before and after performance. However, if a before-only procedure is used, there is some risk that changes that occur during the performance period will go undetected. (See Locke & Shaw, 1984, for evidence on the effects of within-study changes in goal content.)

THE COMMITMENT-PERFORMANCE RELATIONSHIP

It has been surprisingly difficult for researchers to demonstrate the effect of goal commitment on performance, because in the majority of studies, goal commitment has easily been achieved (Locke & Latham, 1984a; Locke et al., 1981). The small amount of variability that has been found was often unrelated to performance (e.g., Crawford, White, & Magnusson, 1983; DuMont & Grimes, 1982; Frost & Mahoney, 1976; Huber & Neale, 1986; Ivancevich & McMahon, 1977b, 1977c, 1982; Locke, 1982b; Locke, Frederick, Lee, & Bobko, 1984; London & Oldham, 1976; McCaul, Hinsz, & McCaul, 1987, study 1; Mento, Cartledge, & Locke, 1980; Oldham, 1975; Pritchard & Curtis, 1973; Yukl & Latham, 1978). However, when steps are taken to deliberately increase variability, the importance of goal commitment can be demonstrated empirically. Erez and Zidon's (1984; phase 2) results are shown graphically in Figure 6–1. When goal commitment dropped markedly in response to increasingly difficult goals, as a result of instructions implying the desirability of rejecting such goals, performance dropped accordingly. The largest drop in performance occurred when commitment went, on Erez and Zidon's bipolar scale, from the positive side of the scale (presumably indicating acceptance) to the negative side (presumably indicating

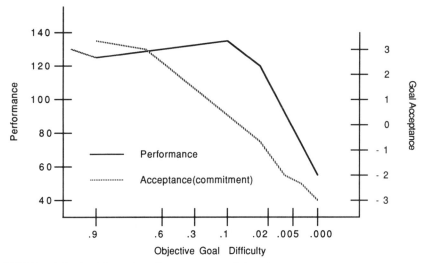

FIGURE 6–1   Mean Performance and Goal Acceptance Scores for Different Levels of Objective Goal Difficulty in Phase 2
Based on Erez & Zidon, 1984.

rejection). This finding is in accordance with the prediction of DuMont and Grimes (1982).

A number of additional studies have generated sufficient variability in goal commitment to yield significant relationships between commitment and performance [Earley 1985a, 1985b, 1986c; Earley & Kanfer, 1985; Erez, 1986; Erez & Arad, 1986; Erez, Earley, & Hulin, 1985; Hannan, 1975; Hollenbeck et al., 1988; Hollenbeck et al., 1989; Ivancevich & McMahon (1977a—acceptance measure); Kernan & Lord (in press); Klein, 1988; Kolb, Winter, & Berlew, 1968; Latham, Erez, & Locke, 1988, studies 3 & 4; Locke & Shaw, 1984; Locke, Frederick, Buckner, & Bobko, 1984, note 1; Riedel, Nebeker, & Cooper, 1988; Oliver & Brief, 1983; Silver & Greenhaus, 1983; Wofford, 1982; Wright, 1989; Wright, in press]. Ivancevich and McMahon (1977a), McCaul, Hinsz, and McCaul (in press, study 2, personal communication), and Organ (1977) obtained mixed results. Das (1982a) reported a commitment effect within one goal group but performed no statistical test. Hollenbeck and Williams (1987) found that goal importance affected performance in combination with "self-focus," an individual difference measure.

In the behavioral intention literature, researchers sometimes use "investment" as a moderator of the intention-behavior relationship. However, if one examines the items used to measure investment (e.g., How much have you invested in this activity?), it can be viewed as the equivalent of or a surrogate for commitment to the action in question (e.g., see Koslowsky, Kluger, & Yinon, 1988).

In looking for commitment effects, it is important to control for and/or measure goal level, since variations in commitment may entail variations in goal level. It bears repeating that even easy goals are not always fully accepted. However, goal "rejection" by subjects in an easy goal condition may not mean the same thing as goal rejection by subjects in a hard goal condition (Wofford, 1982). Rejection in the former case may entail setting a harder, alternative goal (Botterill, 1977; Locke, Mento, & Katcher, 1978; Peters et al., 1982), whereas rejection in the latter case may entail setting an easier goal (Vance & Colella, 1988). As noted above, one way to determine this is to measure the subjects' personal goals after the official goals have been assigned.

It is also important to recognize that when multiple goal levels are employed in a study, the overall correlation of commitment and performance across goal levels can be negative (Locke, Frederick, Buckner, & Bobko, 1984). This is because very hard goals, which lead to high performance, are generally accepted to a lesser degree than easy goals, which lead to low performance.

Theoretically, commitment should be related to performance in two ways. First, if goal level were held constant statistically or if all individuals within a given sample were given the same challenging goal, commitment could have a direct, positive effect on performance. Erez and Zidon (1984) found that within each of their difficult goal levels, there was a positive effect of commitment on performance. Wright (1989) found the same within his difficult goal condition. Locke and Shaw (1984) found a significant relationship between commitment to winning a small monetary prize, awarded competitively, on a perceptual speed task and performance even when level of personal goal was controlled. When assigned goals are easy, however, high commitment could lead to poorer performance than low commitment to the same goals, since, as noted, in the latter case individuals could set themselves higher goals.

Second, commitment could moderate the effect of goals on performance when goal level varied among individuals. Goal level should be more highly and positively related to performance among individuals with high commitment than among those with low commitment to the goals. The study by Erez and Zidon (1984) is a case in point. During phase 1, when commitment to all goal levels was high, goal level and performance were positively related. In phase 2, when commitment was artificially decreased as the goals became more difficult, goal level and performance were negatively related. Wofford (1982) found that there was a smaller goal-performance discrepancy among subjects with medium and high goals in a high commitment than in a low-commitment condition.

The above relationships are illustrated hypothetically in Table 6–1. These data show fictitious performance levels under seven levels of assigned goal difficulty and high and low commitment to each goal level. The direct effects are shown in the far-right column. Within easy goal levels, more-committed individuals perform *less well* than less-committed individuals, since the former are more wedded to *low* goals. For low to moderate goal levels, low-commitment individuals may set higher or lower goals than high-commitment people; thus there may be little or no direct effect. At each of the higher goal levels, people with high commitment perform better than those with low commitment.

The moderator effect is revealed by the difference in correlations between performance and goal level under the high- and low-commitment conditions. With these fictitious data, the correlation is shown as 1.0 under high commitment and 0 under low commitment. In an ANOVA (Analysis of Variance), Table 6–1 would probably reveal a main effect for commitment, a main effect for goal level, and a goal level–commitment interaction. All the above effects are shown in the graphic plot in Figure 6–2. If there were more easy and fewer hard goal levels, the main effect for commitment would disappear. Recently, Wright (1989) obtained an empirical function almost identical to that in Figure 6–2.

The actual research literature on goal commitment to date (with the exception of Wright, 1989) includes almost no studies that show separate direct

Table 6–1   Main and Moderator Effects of Commitment on Performance (Hypothetical Data)

Assigned Goal Level	PERFORMANCE UNDER: High Commitment[a]	Low Commitment[b]	Performance Difference
1	1	3	H < L
2	2	3	H < L
3	3	3	H = L
4	4	3	H > L
5	5	3	H > L
6	6	3	H > L
7	7	3	H > L

r between Assigned Goal Level and Performance =   1.0 ◄——————► 0   ↑
                                                      Moderator Effect   Main Effect(s) and Interaction

[a]Personal goal levels and performance correspond to assigned goal levels.

[b]Personal goal and performance = 3 for all assigned goal levels.

FIGURE 6–2   Graphic Plot of Table 6–1 Showing Main and Interaction Effect of Goals and Commitment

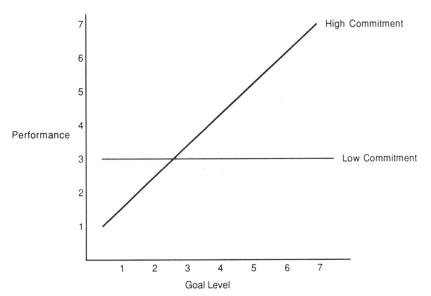

and moderator effects. Even Erez and Zidon (1984) described their data only in terms of the moderating effect of commitment, although it actually showed both effects. Most studies show only direct effects. However, such studies should not be difficult to design in a laboratory setting. Hollenbeck, Williams, and Klein (1989) looked for a moderator effect, but their highly restricted range of goal levels precluded finding one.

Observe that the commitment effects shown in Table 6–1 all reduce to goal-level effects. For the high-commitment subjects, assigned and personal goals correspond exactly, whereas for the low-commitment subjects they do not (see footnotes a and b in the table). At the same time, with these fictitious data, personal goals and performance correspond in all cases.

This raises the question as to whether, if personal goals are taken routinely as the measure of the individual's *real* goal, the direct measurement of commitment can be dispensed with entirely. This is an intriguing question, but one that cannot be answered from the experiments done so far. Based on introspection and logic, however, we are inclined to answer *no* to this question. We think that the intensity aspect of goals is logically separable from the content aspect; thus it is easy to conceive of two individuals with the same personal goals who are not attached to them to the same degree. These differences in degree of attachment *could* manifest themselves in the propensity of each to change goal content (goal level), but they could also be manifested in other ways. For example, the person with the less intensely held goal might be less likely to notice deviations from the intended goal level, or might be less likely to evaluate such deviations as important, and/or might be less likely to search for ways to reduce the discrepancy—even while still claiming to be trying for the goal. Studies of these phenomena would be most illuminating.

In summary, theory as well as empirical research suggest that there is indeed a relationship between goal commitment and performance. Thus there is a need to understand the factors that affect goal commitment. In the remainder of this chapter we review the literature with regard to the determinants of goal commitment. We will also review studies relevant to the issue of goal intensity and note some miscellaneous studies. As mentioned earlier, participation and choice as independent variables affecting goal commitment are discussed in the next chapter.

DETERMINANTS OF GOAL COMMITMENT

We will organize the factors promoting goal commitment in terms of the same broad categories as those affecting goal choice, although as we shall see, some of these factors affect both categories.

Factors Affecting Perceived Desirability or Appropriateness of Trying for a Given Goal or Goal Level

The integrating principle behind the factors discussed in this section is that they lead the individual to believe that trying for or attaining the goal is *important* and do so without arousing conflict between the goal in question and other goals, or do so by eliminating such conflict.

Authority.   Most goal setting studies have focused on the effects of assigned goals. The subjects or employees were simply asked to try for a specific level of performance on a task. Overwhelmingly, people tried to do what was asked of them (Latham & Lee, 1986). The studies reported in Chapter 5 that measured personal goals after the goals were assigned show that the two are highly correlated (r = .52). Likert (1967) found a strong association between the sales goals of salesmen and the sales goals of their managers (p. 60). Oldham (1975) found supervisory legitimacy to be significantly related to the intent to work hard for an assigned goal in a laboratory study. As noted earlier, instructions by an experimenter to try for a certain goal even affect the goals people subsequently choose for themselves.

This is not to say that instructions from an authority figure will inevitably be obeyed; they will not (Bandura, 1986; Locke, Bryan, & Kendall, 1968). Our point is rather that people usually choose to obey authority figures. This should come as no surprise to those familiar with social psychologist Stanley Milgram's (1974) studies of obedience to authority. Milgram's experiments showed that subjects would administer what they thought were painful and even life-threatening electric shocks to an alleged subject simply because the experimenter demanded it.

Commitment to assigned goals reflects compliance with legitimate authority or power (French & Raven, 1959); reward and punishment power no doubt play a background role. Legitimate authority certainly exists in both laboratory and field settings. It may account for the high degree of generalization of results found between the two settings (Latham & Lee, 1986). In the laboratory, the experimenter is typically seen as an authority figure. An experiment, by its very nature, is a "demand situation" (Orne, 1962). Subjects, who are almost always volunteers (and may get extra course credit), come to the experimental situation with the mental set: "Here I am; tell me what to do." Similarly, in industry most employees consider it the supervisor's or manager's legitimate right to tell them what to do, since doing what one is told is inherent in the employment contract (and refusing to do what one is asked could lead to termination).

The relationship between goal commitment and authority was discussed many years ago by Barnard (1938), who proposed that the source of authority does not reside in the authority figure alone but requires acceptance of authority by subordinates. According to Barnard, individuals must assent to authority and will do so if they understand the communicated order, they believe that the order is consistent with the organizational objectives and with their personal interests, and they are mentally and physically able to comply with the order. Barnard coined the concept "zone of indifference" within which orders will be accepted by a person without question. However, when the pros and cons of obeying the order result in a negative balance, the person will no longer comply with authority. In most goal setting studies, the instructions appear to have remained in the zone of indifference. In fact, Bassett (1979) viewed goal acceptance as so routine that he argued that we should develop a theory of goal rejection rather than one of goal commitment or acceptance.

Salancik (1977) argued that assigned goals lead to commitment because (a) listening to the assignment without objection is itself a form of consent, and (b) assigning the goal implies that the recipient is capable of reaching the goal. Salancik thus suggested (quite correctly, see Chapter 3) that assigned goals may affect the individual's self-efficacy or confidence. Also, as noted in Chapters 3 and 5, assigned goals convey normative information to the subordinate. They suggest what level of performance is possible and appropriate. Furthermore, as noted in Chapter 3, Mento and Locke (1989) found that assigned goals allowed the subjects to get a sense of achievement, implied that working for the goal could lead to self-improvement (such as concentrating better; see also Matsui et al., 1981), and challenged the subjects to prove themselves.

A number of studies have suggested specific aspects or actions of authority figures that may enhance their effectiveness. Although not all of these studies directly measured goal commitment, the results indicate that further exploration of these factors is worthwhile. For example, Ronan, Latham, and Kinne (1973) found that supervisors of logging crews who stayed on the job after assigning goals obtained higher productivity from their crews than those who assigned goals to their crews but did not remain on the job with them. One explanation for this finding is that the supervisor's *physical presence* enhanced goal commitment.

Latham and Saari (1979a) and Dossett, Cella, Greenberg, and Adrian (1983) explored the effects of supervisory *supportiveness* (based on Likert, 1961) on goal commitment and performance. Generally, correlations between supportiveness and commitment have not been significant due to commitment being uniformly high across treatments. But, consistent with Likert's theory, supportiveness did lead to higher goals being set and/or higher performance (e.g., Likert, 1967, pp. 53ff.). Latham and Yukl (1975b) found no effect for goal setting when management was perceived as indifferent to the goals that were set either by or for logging crews. Consistent with this result, Anderson and O'Reilly (1981) found that perceived top management support of the company goal setting system was significantly related to the performance of manufacturing managers. Based on these suggestive findings, additional studies of supportiveness would seem warranted.

Trust in authority is another dimension that has long been stressed as being important to employee motivation by OD practitioners. In a study by Earley (1986c), tire-tread layers in England and the United States were assigned goals by both union stewards and supervisors. In the U.S. sample there was no differential effect of these two sources on goal commitment, but in the English sample there was more commitment when the rationale for the goals was explained by the union steward than when it was explained by the supervisors. Earley argued that in England there was more trust of union stewards as compared with supervisors. These results support Oldham (1975), who found perceptions of trust to be significantly related to the intent to work hard for an assigned goal. Podsakoff and Farh (1989) found that normative information about performance had the greatest impact when the source was trusted.

Trust may be particularly important when the authority figure tries to provide a *rationale* or justification for an assigned goal. Latham, Erez, and Locke (1988) found that assigning goals by the "tell and sell" method was more effective in generating commitment than curtly telling subjects what to do. Selling the goal, in part, involves convincing subordinates that they can reach it and, in part, giving them a plausible reason for why it exists or is important. Latham et al. found that tell and sell instructions raised self-efficacy, but they did not separately manipulate the self-efficacy and rationale parts of the instructions. Kirsch (1978) found credibility to be significantly associated with behavior change among students given exercise goals, but it was not manipulated experimentally. Earley's (1986c) study found that giving subjects a rationale for an assigned goal was less effective than giving them a strategy for reaching it, but even information about the rationale led to significant performance improvement over baseline.

The exertion of *pressure* on subordinates by authority figures may also affect goal commitment. Both Andrews and Farris (1972) and Hall and Lawler (1971) found that pressure from superiors (and other sources) was positively related to performance among scientists and engineers. Excessive pressure, however, was found to be dysfunctional (Andrews & Farris, 1972; Forward & Zander, 1971; Likert, 1967, p. 55). Goal commitment, however, was not actually measured in these studies.

Other attributes or actions of authority figures may also affect goal commitment. These include the likability of authority figures, which may be enhanced by their doing favors for or complimenting the target (Cialdini, 1984), and the (presumed) expertise of authority figures, which may be enhanced by their title and demonstrated knowledge. These attributes, of course, are related to French and Raven's concepts of referent and expert power, respectively. Podsakoff and Schriesheim's (1985) review of this literature reveals substantial evidence for the effectiveness of legitimate, referent, expert, and reward power, especially when Likert scales rather than ranking procedures are used.

Goals assigned by an authority figure have generally been viewed by social scientists as almost axiomatically ineffective. Furthermore, the assignment of a goal has been viewed as a simple, univariate phenomenon. Both these assumptions are unfounded. Assigned goals are highly effective, as we have seen. In the next chapter, we will see that they are just as effective as participatively set or self-set goals.

A more productive and scientific approach to the subject of assigned goals than simply writing them off as ineffective, if not immoral, would be to determine the conditions under which they are effective in generating commitment on the part of subordinates. We believe that assigned goals will be most effective when

1. The authority figure is seen as legitimate
2. The assigned goals imply associated rewards and punishments
3. Goal assignment conveys (positive) self-efficacy information
4. Goal assignment conveys (high) normative information
5. Goal assignment fosters a sense of achievement

6. The assigned goals imply opportunities for self-improvement
7. The assigned goals challenge people to prove themselves
8. The authority figure
   a. Is physically present
   b. Is supportive
   c. Is trustworthy
   d. Provides a convincing rationale for the goal
   e. Exerts reasonable pressure
   f. Is knowledgeable and likable

Implicit in (f) is that the authority figure be an attractive role model, although modeling has only been studied in the goal setting literature with reference to peer models (see below).

Peer (Group) Influence.   The effect of *peer pressure* on performance is well documented in industry. Historically, the focus has been on documenting how peer pressure and past instances of rate cutting undermine commitment to the goals management assigned to workers and enhance commitment to worker-originated group goals set at a lower level. As noted earlier, Taylor (1967) called this phenomenon "systematic soldiering." Later it became known as "restriction of output" and was documented in such classics as Mathewson (1931) and Roethlisberger and Dickson (1956). Commitment to uniform production standards is determined to a great extent by the level of group cohesion. In a quantitative study, Seashore (1954) found that high cohesion led to more uniform productivity within groups than low cohesion, clearly implying a commitment effect. Group commitment to norms of high performance is facilitated by management support (Seashore, 1954), by the congruence between standards urged on the group by others and the members' own desires (Zander & Ulberg, 1971), and by the attachment of high importance to group goals and group success (Forward & Zander, 1971; Schacter, Ellertson, McBride, & Gregory, 1951; Zander & Ulberg, 1971).

Matsui, Kakuyama, and Onglatco (1987) found that commitment to individual goals was higher for subjects working in two-person groups who were assigned both group and individual goals rather than just individual goals for their segment of the group task. Weingart and Weldon (1988) found a similar, although borderline, effect for subjects given goals plus individual and group feedback vs. subjects given individual goals and feedback only. On the other side of the coin, howaever, they found in a second experiment group that group goals with group and individual feedback led to higher commitment than group goals and feedback alone. This suggests that individual and group goals together induce higher commitment than either one alone. Commitments that carry responsibility to others can generate social pressure to follow through (Bandura, 1986); at the same time, having one's own contribution pinpointed can encourage individual group members to do their share (Brickner & Bukatko, 1987).

Two studies (Rakestraw & Weiss, 1981; Weiss & Rakestraw, 1988) found that observing videotapes of high-performing *role models* on a card-sorting task led subjects with little task experience to set higher goals than observing low-performing role models. Commitment was not measured. Earley and

Kanfer (1985) had subjects observe a film of a high- or low-performing subject on a class-scheduling task. Following this, all subjects either were encouraged to set or were assigned hard goals. Commitment to these hard goals was significantly higher for those who observed the high than the low role model. Possibly modeling the high performers led subjects to have higher self-efficacy than modeling the low performers. A modeling study by Gist, Schwoerer, and Rosen (in press) involving training in using computers verified that self-efficacy was a key mediating variable between modeling training and rate of learning. Other studies, which did not measure goals, commitment, or self-efficacy, have found that positive self-modeling, involving seeing edited tapes of oneself performing a task competently, has powerful effects on performance (Dowrick & Hood, 1981; Gonzalez & Dowrick, 1982). These results as a group strongly support Bandura's (1986) claim that role modeling is a powerful motivational technique (see also Gist, Rosen, & Schwoerer, 1988; and Kliebhan, 1967).

Another peer-related factor is *competition*. Competition can be promoted directly or promoted indirectly. It can be done by telling subjects that their performance is being evaluated, by giving them feedback in relation to group norms, by posting performance scores so that they can compare themselves with each other, and so on. A number of studies have found that such procedures improve performance as compared with a no competition condition (see Chapter 8). Chung and Vickery (1976), for example, gave feedback on a clerical task in relation to the average performance of other group members. Mitchell, Rothman, and Liden (1985) gave subjects salient group norms on a labeling task. Shalley, Oldham, and Porac (1987) told some of their subjects that their performance on a toy-assembly task would be compared with that of others. White, Mitchell, and Bell (1977) used similar instructions on a sorting task. In all the above cases, the competitive groups performed better than those in the non-competitive condition.

Roberts and Hall (1987) found that overt competition on an ergometer task led to better performance than no competition unless the noncompetitive groups also had hard goals or specific normative standards, thus supporting our view that goals and competition are two sides of the same coin. Both Latham and Baldes (1975) and Komaki, Barwick, and Scott (1978) found that when employees were given objective feedback concerning specific aspects of their job performance, spontaneous competition developed among them.

Of course, we do not know whether competition in the above studies affected goal commitment. The effects obtained by Mitchell et al. (1985) and White et al. (1977) were independent of goal content. Only Mueller (1983) specifically tested Locke's (1968b) hypothesis that competition can increase performance if it leads to the setting of and/or commitment to high goals. The hypothesis with regard to goal difficulty was supported. Subjects in the competitive condition set significantly higher goals and performed significantly better than those who were not in the competitive condition. However, competition did not affect the commitment of subjects in either the assigned or self-set goal conditions. It remains to be seen whether subsequent studies will show commitment as well as goal-level effects of competition. Locke and Shaw (1984) found that commitment to being in the winning group (which yielded a monetary prize) had a significant relationship to performance on a perceptual speed task even with goal level controlled. This suggests that exploring the effects of competition on commitment is worthy of further study (see also Somers, Locke, & Tuttle, 1985-86). It would be useful to know whether goal level and commitment are the sole mechanisms by which competition affects performance.

Publicness.   Lewin (1952) introduced the idea of public commitment in his famous studies of how to change eating habits. Lewin, however, did not isolate the effects of public commitment from his other experimental manipulations (see Locke & Schweiger, 1979, for details). Salancik (1977) argued that making a public commitment to a course of action binds one more strongly to the action than making it in private. Presumably this is because one does not want to project a lack of integrity or stability or to submit oneself to later embarrassment (Bandura, 1986; Janis & Mann, 1977). Several studies in the goal setting literature suggest that public commitment to goals has a greater effect than private commitment.

Hayes, Rosenfarb, Wulfert, Munt, Korn, and Zettle (1985) conducted two such experiments. In the first, students read and answered questions on passages from the graduate record examination. Goals were phrased in terms of number of correct answers. Students in the public condition handed their written goals to the experimenter, who then read them aloud. Students in the private condition placed their written goals anonymously in a box with the goals of others. In this study all the students were run individually. The goal levels of the public and private groups were not significantly different, but the public goal group performed significantly better than the private goal group.

In the second study the students were asked to read a series of modules on how to improve their study skills. They set goals in terms of how many modules they would read and how they would score on a posttest. The students in this study were run in groups. Those in the public condition wrote down their goals, signed them, and then read them aloud to the group, whereas those in the private condition wrote down their goals and placed them anonymously in a sealed box. Again, although the two groups did not differ in the goals they set, the public commitment subjects far outperformed the private commitment subjects. Commitment was not measured directly in either study but may be inferred from performance, since goal level and initial ability were controlled. The authors concluded from these studies and from their social-behaviorist perspective that goals *only* affect action when they are public. This is clearly an arbitrary claim; people set themselves private goals in real life all the time (Bandura, 1986). The authors make much of the finding that the private goal subjects did not improve any more than the control subjects who were not asked to set goals. However, the control group subjects could have set goals on their own. It is significant in this regard that, in both studies, the control and private goal setting groups *both* improved over their pretest performance. In the second study the control subjects read almost the same number of modules as the public group, even though they did not learn as much from them.

In support of our claim that private goal setting *can* be effective, Ferris and Porac (1984) found that goals on a video game were significantly related to performance under an "alone" condition. In fact, that relationship was higher ($p < .10$) than in a condition where the subjects were observed and evaluated by an experimenter. On the average, subjects set higher goals in the "observed" condition, but they did not perform better than subjects in the alone condition.

McCaul and Kopp (1982) found no effect of a somewhat weak public-private manipulation on a task that involved collecting aluminum cans. The public aspect consisted of having one's name put in the campus paper; the private condition did not but was not totally private, since the cans were collected from each participant by the experimenter. Fryer (1964) found no difference between the effects of public vs. private expression of goals in a training study. However, in the private condition, while subjects did not tell their peers what their goal was, they did write their goal in their work booklet and these booklets were later seen by the experimenter.

Another public commitment study was conducted by McCaul, Hinsz, & McCaul (1987) using a task similar to that used in the first Hayes et al. (1985) study, namely, paragraph comprehension. After a pretest, public goal subjects were assigned a hard or an easy goal for the next part. The experimenter computed this goal publicly, and then the subjects wrote their goals on a sheet, signed it, and had the goals posted for all to see. Private goal subjects computed their goal on their own and did not sign their goal sheets or post them. Public goal subjects showed significantly higher rated goal commitment than private goal subjects only if the goals were hard. A regression analysis (McCaul et al., 1987, personal communication) revealed a borderline effect ($p < .10$) of rated commitment on performance with goal level controlled. Lyman (1984) found that public goal setting but not private goal setting was effective in changing the class conduct of 11- to 13-year-olds with conduct disorders, even though neither group seems to have been given much feedback.

Finally, Hollenbeck et al. (1989; see also Hollenbeck et al., 1988) studied the effect of public versus private commitment to self-set or assigned grade goals (GPA for one quarter). Subjects in the public condition gave their name and goal to other subjects within their condition and also mailed their goal to one self-chosen, significant other, while those in the private condition did not do this. There was a significant effect of publicness on commitment and, in addition, a significant effect of commitment on performance independent of goal level.

Incentives and Rewards.   Expectancy, operant, and social learning theories would all agree, at least by implication, that commitment to action alternatives is affected by incentives and rewards.

A number of studies have examined the effect of monetary incentives on performance when various goals were also assigned. Overall the use of incentives added increments to performance about as often as not. On the positive side, Campbell (1984) found significant effects of contingent pay on a management simulation task in which all subjects had assigned, specific goals. Huber (1985a) found that contingent pay was more effective than noncontingent pay when no goals were set. When goals were set, assigned goals plus goal-contingent pay was more effective than any other combination. London and Oldham (1976) found that piece rate or no incentives worked better than hourly pay when all subjects had goals on a clerical task. The reason for the no incentive finding is not clear.

In a weight loss study, Mahoney (1974) found that adding self-administered monetary rewards to a self-monitoring and goal setting condition led to significantly greater weight loss than monitoring and goals alone. Pritchard and Curtis (1973) found that goals plus a small money incentive led to no better performance than goals alone, but goals plus a large money incentive led to better performance than either of the first two conditions. Schunk (1984), in a study of long division, found that goals plus rewards led to better performance by 9- to 11-year-olds than either one alone.

Terborg (1976) found an effect of contingent incentives independent of goal setting using a learning (programmed text) task. Terborg and Miller (1978) replicated this finding on a tinker-toy assembly task. Winett, Kagel, Battalio, and Winkler (1978) found that feedback plus incentives worked better than feedback alone in reducing electricity consumption, although it is not clear what type of spontaneous goal setting the feedback produced. In a correlational study, Carroll and Tosi (1973) found that high-perceived rewards strengthened the association between goal difficulty and effort.

Balancing the positive findings are an almost equal number of negative results. Das (1982a), using a hole-drilling task, found that a goal-feedback-incentive condition led to no higher performance than goals and feedback alone. Erez, Gopher, and Arazi (1987) found that monetary incentives sometimes led to worse performance than not giving incentives in a highly complex, computerized dual-task experiment involving simultaneous performance of both letter typing and digit classification. Kleinbeck (1986) found that monetary incentives added nothing to what was achieved through the use of goals and feedback alone in another dual-task study. In the first two studies conducted by Locke, Bryan, and Kendall (1968), small monetary incentives added nothing to the goal effect on a brainstorming or toy-assembly task. There were incentive effects in the next three experiments by Locke et al. (1968), but these were choice rather than level-of-performance studies.

Monetary incentives plus self-monitoring and goals were no more effective than the latter two alone in an experiment on student study-time by Mercier and LaDouceur (1983). Phillips and Freedman (1988) found that goals plus bonuses for goal attainment led to better performance than no goals or bonuses, whereas goals only did not. However, since the goal only condition was not significantly different from the goal plus bonus conditions, the effect of the bonus as such must be considered nonsignificant. Finally, Rosswork (1977) found no performance effect for small monetary incentives on a sentence-writing task with schoolchildren.

A number of negative findings have also been reported in studies where nonmonetary rewards were used. Hayes et al. (1985) found that self-administered candy or snack food rewards had no effect on reading task performance in which goals were also assigned. Kirsch (1978) found no self-reward effects in two experiments and a borderline effect on a third where the task was to engage in daily exercise. Finally, Siegfried et al. (1981) found that a reward consisting of extra credit for participation had no effect on performance on a pencil-and-paper maze task that also involved goal setting.

The reason or reasons why some of these studies found that money led to higher performance than goals alone whereas others did not cannot be determined definitively from the reports available. However, two possibilities, which are not mutually exclusive, suggest themselves. One concerns the *total amount* of the incentive. Consider first the studies with positive results (omitting London & Oldham, 1976, whose results were not consistent). Subjects in Campbell's (1984) study could earn up to $30 over a period of six weeks, while Huber's (1985a) subjects could earn about the same amount in five days. In Mahoney's study (1974), the total possible earnings were evidently about $35 over six weeks. In Terborg's (1976) study, subjects could earn up to $50 in five days, and in Winett et al.'s (1978) study, $15 a week for ten weeks plus possible additional bonuses. In Terborg and Miller's (1978) study, the maximum was $5 for one hour's work. The Pritchard and Curtis (1973) study was the lowest-paying successful study: the maximum was $3 but was paid for only ten minutes' work.

Now consider the negative studies. In Locke et al. (1968) the maximum was about $3, in Das (1982a) about $3.50, and in Rosswork (1977) about $1, each for less than an hour's work. In Pritchard and Curtis's (1973) low-incentive condition, the bonus was 50 cents. The bonus in the Phillips and Freedman (1988) study was $3 for fifteen minutes' work. The major exception was Mercier and LaDouceur (1983), where subjects could earn up to $20, but the goals were self-set and at a very low level. (The amount of the incentive could not be determined in the remaining studies.)

A second possibility is that incentives interact with goal difficulty to influence performance. (The following two studies were also discussed in Chapter 5.) Mowen et al. (1981) obtained an interesting interaction between money and goals. Under a piece-rate system (the rewards were tokens that could be redeemed for school supplies), high goals resulted in higher performance than medium or easy goals. But when subjects were paid a bonus *only* if they attained their goal, performance was lower when the goal was hard than when it was moderately difficult or easy. This interaction is shown in Figure 6–3. A plausible explanation for these results is that under the hard goal plus bonus system, subjects were not committed to their assigned goals, since they believed that they had no chance of earning the bonus. Under a goal plus bonus system, partial success, in the sense of coming close to the goal, is not rewarded. In contrast, the piece-rate payment system did reward partial success, since payment was based on performance rather than on goal attainment. Even when hard goals are assigned without the offer of tangible rewards, people can feel some sense of accomplishment even if they do not fully attain the goals. Under such conditions one might expect that commitment to hard goals would be higher than under a task-and-bonus system.

In partial replication of this study using self-set goals on a typing task, Miller and Steele (1984) found that subjects given hard goals plus piece-rate pay, or given medium goals plus bonus pay, set higher personal goals than subjects given hard goals and bonus pay or medium goals and piece-rate pay. Goals, in turn, were significantly related to performance. This is further evidence that all the subjects in Mowen et al.'s study may not have been committed to their assigned goals to the same degree. Consistent with these results, Wright (in press) found that subjects with hard goals set higher personal goals in a piece-rate condition than in a bonus condition on a card-sorting task. However,

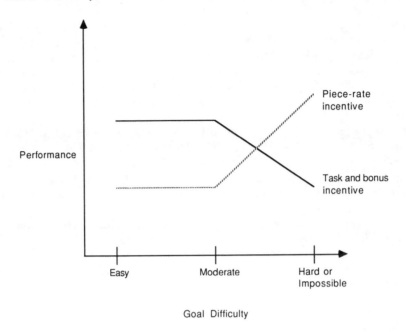

FIGURE 6–3   The Interaction of Goal Difficulty and Incentive Type
Based on Mowen et al, 1981.

degree of reported commitment to assigned goals was nonsignificantly higher in the bonus than in the piece-rate condition. This suggests that the personal goal and commitment effects were working in *opposite* directions, possibly canceling each other out. This would explain why there was no main incentive effect on performance.[3] In a subsequent study by Wright (1989), the piece-rate and bonus conditions showed equally high commitment and higher commitment than subjects paid by the hour or given no pay. For subjects given very difficult goals, those under piece-rate pay showed higher performance than those on bonus, and this effect was partly mediated by commitment differences. Unfortunately, personal goals were not measured in this study. Using a computerized clerical task, Nebeker (1987) found that larger contingent bonuses reduced the performance of subjects with hard goals as compared with those with easy goals. Again some goal rejection by the hard goal subjects may have occurred. Huber (1985a), as noted earlier, found that the combination of moderate assigned goals and bonus pay led to higher performance on a proofreading task than moderate goals or no goals with piece-rate or non-contingent pay. Clearly, more studies are needed before we can fully understand the goal-incentive interaction. No single study to date, for example, has used multiple-goal levels, obtained a significant incentive effect, and measured commitment to both assigned goals and personal goals. Nor have any of these studies measured self-efficacy.

[3]These results suggest the advisability of measuring commitment to both assigned goals and personal goals, since in this case their relationship was opposite to that of incentive conditions.

In sum, most studies suggest that bonus pay for moderate goals is effective. But when goals are hard to reach or unreachable, pay for performance rather than pay for goal success should be used to prevent the goals from being rejected. It is worth reiterating that such rejection of hard goals does not seem to occur if subjects are given very hard goals in the absence of incentives. Perhaps the offering of a monetary bonus changes the subjects' mental set regarding the task from "get as close as you can" under no bonus to "succeed or nothing" under a bonus scheme. Research on how incentives affect the way in which people perceive these situations would be helpful. Despite a large literature on the effect of extrinsic incentives on intrinsic motivation (Deci & Ryan, 1985), a subject not directly pertinent to goal setting as such (but see Chapter 2), almost none of those studies have examined how subjects actually view the task or task situation under various incentive conditions.

An apparent contradiction to the above interpretation is found in the Campbell (1984) study. He found a significant bonus pay effect compared with hourly pay (there was no piece-rate condition), even though the goals (despite being labeled hard and easy) were all, in fact, impossible. However, the subjects actually rated these goals as moderate in difficulty even in the last of five work sessions. Perhaps the high incentive had biased their estimates.

Very few of the goal and incentive studies reviewed above actually measured goal commitment, so we could only infer that a commitment effect was involved. Latham et al. (1978) did measure commitment and found that it was not related to various incentive conditions among R&D professions; however, those offered a monetary bonus for high performance in relation to a reachable goal performed significantly better than those offered just recognition or no incentive, even with goal difficulty and commitment controlled. In a simulation study of clerical work, Riedel, Nebeker, and Cooper (1988) found that bonus pay for surpassing a reachable assigned standard led to three significant effects. Incentive pay had a significant influence on the propensity of subjects to set personal goals, the level of difficulty of the goals set, and goal commitment. Surprisingly, but in agreement with Latham et al. (1978) and with Pritchard and Curtis (1973), incentives had a significant effect on performance over and above that attributable to goal commitment and goal difficulty.

These results suggest that incentives may have effects on performance through a variety of different mechanisms, of which commitment is only one. Money may also affect personal goal difficulty level when goals are chosen, as well as the propensity to set specific personal goals regardless of whether goals are assigned. The latter effect was found by Saari and Latham (1981), as well as by Riedel et al. (1988). However, the additional effect of incentives, with commitment and other aspects controlled, found by Latham et al. (1978), Pritchard and Curtis (1973), and Riedel et al. (1988), remains a mystery. One possibility is that self-reports across subjects are not accurate enough to reveal actual commitment effects; this possibility could be tested by the use of a within-subjects design. Another possibility is that a different type of commitment measure might work better, such as questions asking subjects to indicate their degree of enthusiasm for the goal. A third possibility is that the effect is subconscious. Only additional research will enable us to choose between these possibilities.

Self-Administered or Internal Rewards.   Masters, Furman, and Barden (1977) found that self-administered rewards in the form of statements such as "I did very good [sic]" led to such dramatic improvements among 5- and 6-year-old children that subjects in all goal conditions reached asymptote. This did not occur when the children were given tangible prizes for goal attainment. Possibly the effect of the self-reward was to increase the children's self-efficacy (Bandura, 1986) and thus commitment.

Ivancevich and McMahon (1982) found no relationship between goal commitment and performance for engineers. However, goal setting plus self-generated feedback led to higher organizational commitment and performance than goal setting plus feedback given by the supervisor. The reason for this is not clear, but perhaps the self-generated feedback was more accepted or seen as more meaningful than feedback provided by others. There may be a parallel here with the Masters et al. study (1977) in which self-reward had a greater effect on motivation than rewards given by others.

In an experiment that involved getting students to engage in daily exercise, Kirsch (1978) found that goal setting plus (unspecified) self-reward was more effective than goal setting without self-reward, but generally no more effective than asking subjects to commit themselves to the goal.

Punishment.   Latham and Saari (1982) found that unionized truck drivers committed themselves to a goal setting program under four conditions: that it would not lead to layoffs; that monetary incentives (which they viewed as potentially punitive) would not be used; that the goals would be voluntary; and that supervisors would be supportive of attempts to reach the goals and not punish them for failure. The program was successful only as long as the employees believed that these terms would be met. When the members concluded that these conditions would not be met, they interpreted the program as punitive and rejected it in the form of a wildcat strike—an extreme form of goal rejection.

Emurian and Brady (1981) also found that a punitive approach to the use of incentives undermined commitment to goals. In a simulated skylab experiment, team members in the punitive condition were told that they had to meet certain group performance goals on various tasks or bonus money would be subtracted from their group bonus account. This condition led to much lower performance (plus more intragroup conflict and lower morale) than a positive condition in which they earned money for positive accomplishments.

In contrast to the above results, Miller (1965) found that judicious use of punishment can be effective. Machinists given only feedback concerning work quality soon became indifferent to it despite the urging of management to improve. Quality only improved permanently when the workers were threatened with formal verbal and written warnings. Surprisingly, the operators did not react negatively to this. In three additional studies, operators lost incentive pay when they did poor-quality work by being compelled to stop their regular work and rework the poor-quality items. Again performance improved dramatically.

It appears that the effects of punishment depend on how it is used and perceived (Arvey & Ivancevich, 1980). Employees in the Miller studies may have seen the punishment as objective and fair while seeing those in the Latham and Emurian studies as arbitrary and unfair.

General Valence and Instrumentality. Valence and instrumentality ratings indicate how individuals process and respond to incentives. Thus they should be more precisely and reliably related to various response and action measures than the amount of the incentive as such. Yukl and Latham (1978) found an overall measure of goal instrumentality to be significantly related to goal commitment for female typists. Oliver and Brief (1983) found the same for sales managers. Mento et al. (1980) found significant relationships between the overall valence of winning and commitment to winning a monetary prize in a competitive setting. Oldham (1975) found, with a clerical task, that the stronger the belief that the supervisor in a lab study had the power to reward performance, the stronger the intention to reach the assigned goal.

Matsui, Okada, and Mizuguchi (1981) found that the overall instrumentality of attaining hard goals was higher than that of attaining easy goals in a within-subject design using a number comparison task. Goal commitment was not measured, but degree of performance change across goal conditions was highly correlated with the difference in valence ratings across goal conditions. This suggests more commitment to high performance in the high goal (and thus high instrumentality) condition than in the low goal condition. Saari and Latham (1981) found that instrumentality ratings were higher for a variable ratio than for a regular piece-rate schedule.

Dachler and Mobley (1973) found that complex measures of general expected utility (based on combined expectancy, valence, and instrumentality ratings) were significantly related to both current and future production goals of blue-collar employees in two plants. The self-chosen goal can be inferred to be the one to which the employees were most committed. These findings show that perceived rewards can increase the level of goal commitment and thereby, in many cases, performance. Klein (1988) found that a similar utility measure was significantly related to measured commitment, although the relationship was weak.

A number of internal, *personal* factors can affect the valence of a goal independently of the external incentives offered. Bayton (1943) found that under high *ego involvement,* defined as a task on which the subjects wanted to excel, goal level was related to performance, whereas under low ego involvement, defined as a task on which doing well was less important, goal level was not related to performance. This, incidentally, is the only moderator study of commitment that we found other than that of Erez and Zidon (1984). We can infer that ego involvement, defined as the belief that performance on that task was important, was associated with commitment even though the latter was not measured. In a theoretical discussion of level of aspiration, Hilgard (1958) suggested that ego involvement and commitment were closely related.

Another internal factor of relevance to commitment is that of goal *conflict.* One can assume that there is less commitment to goals that involve conflict than to goals that entail no conflict. An example would be a goal to lose weight (Bandura, 1986). Most overweight people are in conflict about losing weight, not just because they like fattening foods but because they may have a psychological vested interest in being overweight (e.g., it may remove an anxiety about being rejected in a romantic context). Frequently, people who claim they want to lose weight do not actually want to do so. Baron and Watters (1982), for example, found that 44% of the subjects in one weight loss program rejected the behavioral goals assigned to them. Chapman and Jeffrey (1979) found in another study that weight loss was directly related to the degree of attention paid to setting goals, a behavior that was probably indicative of the degree of commitment to the overall idea of weight loss.

On this issue, a personal anecdote is worth reporting. The first author has a professional acquaintance who had been about seventy-five pounds overweight for many years. One day, after not having seen him for several months, I went to a meeting with him and hardly recognized him because he had lost the extra seventy-five pounds. I asked him how he did it, knowing how hard it was for most people to lose so much weight. He said, "Actually, it was quite simple. I simply decided that I *really wanted* to do it." Schacter (1982) has argued that most people who break bad personal habits such as smoking and overeating do so on their own, simply as a result of deciding that they really want to do so. People who enter formal treatment programs, on the other hand, may be those who are most conflicted and thus need help getting and remaining committed to change goals.

One indicator of conflict, then, may be the degree to which people *really want* to pursue the goal they are asked to pursue. Lombardo, Hull, and Singer (1983) found that mental health service providers did not want to make reminder calls to prevent no shows and therefore did not do so; in contrast, they were willing to increase their number of direct service hours even to the point of competing on this measure. As a result, performance on the latter measure increased.

One means of inducing conflict in a goal setting study is to have the individual *set a personal goal and then assign him or her a goal that is discrepant from the personal goal.* Stedry (1962) found that when the assigned goals were difficult, this procedure led to much lower performance than when personal goals were set *after* goals had been assigned. Commitment was not measured in this study but may be inferred.

Commitment under two similar conditions was directly measured by Erez, Earley, and Hulin(1985) using a simulated class-scheduling task. Goal commitment was consistently and significantly higher when subjects did not set personal goals before being assigned goals or setting them participatively. This finding was replicated by Latham, Erez, and Locke (1988), but only for low-ability subjects. A related way to induce conflict is to arbitrarily assign subjects constantly increasing goals on a task where there is no natural improve-ment due to learning. Thus every time the subject accepts a goal or sets a personal goal, it is contradicted by a new assigned goal for the next trial. Vance and Colella (1988) found that such a procedure leads to steadily decreasing commitment to the assigned goals.

An additional internal factor to consider is *satisfaction*. Numerous studies show substantial relationships between organizational commitment and job satisfaction. These studies are reviewed in Chapter 10. None, however, have looked at the relationship between *goal* commitment and job satisfaction except for Anderson & O'Reilly (1981), who found a significant correlation between them among a group of manufacturing managers. In a laboratory setting, it is not clear what the relevant sources of satisfaction might be—e.g., the task, the goal, the experimenter, one's own past performance, etc. Studies will have to be designed to explore this issue.

Finally, *personality* factors undoubtedly affect goal commitment, although they have received almost no attention in the literature. (What little is known about this in relation to personality in goal setting will be discussed in Chapter 9.)

Factors Affecting Perceived Capability of Attaining a Given Goal or Goal Level

The integrating principle behind the factors discussed in this section is that they lead the individual to believe that reaching to goal or making progress toward it is *possible* or (preferably) *probable*.

Expectancy of Success and Self-Efficacy.   The objective difficulty of the goal or task can affect commitment (Erez & Zidon, 1984; Hannan, 1975), especially, as noted above, when the goals are arbitrarily increased in difficulty (Vance & Colella, 1988), but presumably these factors operate via their effect on expectancy and self-efficacy. Expectancy theory (Dachler & Mobley, 1973; Vroom, 1964) argues that one's choices are affected by one's perceived chances of performing well on a task. A number of studies have found that commitment declines as the goal becomes more difficult and/or as the person's perceived chances of reaching it declines. A dramatic, if artifactual, effect of commitment was obtained in the experiment noted earlier by Erez and Zidon (1984). In the second phase of a two-part experiment, technicians were shown bogus goal acceptance norms allegedly based on the responses of high-level professionals. These norms suggested the appropriateness of low commitment to more difficult goals. The result was a high level of goal rejection and low performance in response to the more difficult goals; the same effect was present to a much smaller degree in phase 1 where commitment was not discouraged.

Many additional studies found that the mean degree of goal commitment was lower for more objectively difficult goals (presumably associated with lower expectancies) than less objectively difficult goals (e.g., DuMont & Grimes, 1982; Earley, 1985b; Erez, Earley, & Hulin, 1985; Hanges, Alexander, & Herbert, 1987; Hannan, 1975; Locke, 1982b; Locke, Frederick, Buckner, & Bobko, 1984; Organ, 1977; Vance & Colella, 1988). However, Huber (1985b), Oldham (1975), and Shalley and Oldham (1985) found no such effect. Locke (1982b) and Garland (1983) found that even impossible goals could motivate high performance in the short term. Significant effects of rated subjective expectancy of success on commitment were found by Huber and Neale (1986), in two studies by Mento et al. (1980), and by Oliver & Brief (1983).

Related to the concept of expectancy of success is that of self-efficacy. As noted earlier, Bandura defines self-efficacy as a judgment of "how well one can execute courses of action required to deal with prospective situations" (1982, p. 122; see also 1986). This concept is broader in scope than expectancy in that it includes a judgment of one's total capability of performing a task (Gist, 1987). Since self-efficacy ratings are always performance-based, they do not apply to goals as such. However, one could predict that the chances of committing oneself to a hard goal would be higher when self-efficacy for a task is high as opposed to low. Bandura (1986, 1988) has demonstrated that self-efficacy plays a major role in keeping people committed to a course of action, especially when pursuing that course of action involves overcoming setbacks, failures, and obstacles. Bandura and Cervone (1983, 1986) found that when subjects were given feedback indicating performance below the level of the assigned goal, subsequent effort was higher for those with high than for those with low self-efficacy. Locke, Frederick, Lee, & Bobko (1984) found that self-efficacy was significantly related to commitment to self-set goals but not to assigned goals. This finding is consistent with previous comments regarding the effects of restriction of range, since it was found that the variance in commitment was significantly higher for self-set than for assigned goals.

Earley (1985a, two studies) found that information about how to perform the task increased goal commitment. In a subsequent study, Earley (1986a) found that information affected commitment and performance directly and also through its effects on self-efficacy. Earley (1985b) also found an effect of self-efficacy on goal commitment.

If easier goals yield greater acceptance than difficult goals, what about the effect of succeeding in reaching a goal? Hall and Foster (1977) found that success increased commitment to goals, but his finding must be tempered by the findings of the level-of-aspiration studies (Chapter 5), which showed that individuals are very likely to raise their goals after success. This suggests that goal commitment decreases after success *if* one means that commitment indicates attachment to *exactly* the same goal. One could support Hall and Foster's finding, however, by arguing that after success the individual becomes more committed to the previous goal *or* a higher goal. Furthermore, one might expect that individuals with a history of success would be more committed to new challenging goals than those with a history of failure (Zander et al., 1969). This may be because the successful individuals would have high self-efficacy.

While few studies of *attributions* have been made in relation to goal setting, it is likely that they affect self-efficacy. Silver and Greenhaus (1983) found that individuals who made internal attributions about previous performance on a clerical task were most committed to subsequent goals especially if the goals were difficult, probably because they felt more confident of achieving them.

It is possible that breaking a large or complex task or a hard goal down into subtasks or subgoals could affect commitment by making the task or goal seem more attainable; but to the author's knowledge, this hypothesis has never been tested.

GOAL INTENSITY

A phenomenon that has not been studied very much but seems to hold promise of being a powerful causal factor in commitment is that of goal intensity. *Goal intensity* refers to the amount of thought or mental effort that goes into formulating or conceptualizing the goal or a plan of action to realize it. (It should be noted that the following studies did not unequivocally control for goal content when looking at intensity effects.)

The earliest study relevant to goal intensity was that by Henderson (1963). In a study of fifth graders, he found that those who formulated a greater number of reading purposes, and more detailed and carefully thought out reading purposes, attained their purposes to a greater extent than subjects with superficial and meager reading purposes. Those who set more and better purposes had been identified by teachers as better readers than those who set fewer and poorer purposes. This occurred despite the fact that the two groups did not differ in IQ. The better readers also achieved reading purposes assigned to them more successfully than did the poorer readers.

In the second of two studies of personality change within a t-group setting by Kolb, Winter, and Berlew (1968), the subjects had to write two papers, one on their ideal self and one on their real self. They then discussed possible goals for personal change during two class periods before actually deciding on their goals for the t-group sessions to follow. Subjects in this study were considerably more committed to their goals and changed more than the subjects in the first study who did not do this preparatory work. In a later study of t-group change, Kolb and Boyatzis (1970) again had students write papers describing their major strengths and weaknesses, their goal choices for traits they wanted to change, and the factors that might help or hinder the change process. Those subjects who subsequently; changed the most showed significantly greater awareness of the forces in themselves or outside themselves that facilitated or inhibited personal change.

In a totally different type of study, Anderson (1983) tried to encourage students to donate blood or discourage them from doing so by having them draw one, two, or three imaginative cartoons of themselves donating or not donating blood. The greater the number of cartoons drawn, the greater the effect on the intention to donate or not donate blood. In a second study, drawing three cartoons also had a significant effect on the intent to donate blood and the intent to join a political group. This effect was still present three days after the experiment.

Finally, Gollwitzer, Heckhausen, and Ratajczak (1987) devised various cognitive strategies for subjects to use in thinking about how to solve two personal problems. This included thinking of all the consequences; thinking of only one realistic, positive consequence; thinking of one "fantasy" consequence; or imagining a complete implementation plan with all the steps included. After practicing one of those strategies on an assigned decision problem (studying abroad for a year), each subject was instructed to use the same strategy on his or her two personal problems. Generally the most intensive and comprehensive exercises were most likely to produce progress toward a resolution of the personal problems, a commitment to a resolution, and an actual resolution of the problems.

It remains to explain why goal intensity might affect commitment. One reason could be that intense cognitive processing makes people more aware of the different values that are implicated in the choice to pursue a goal and of what those values mean to them. Another reason could be that such processing makes people more aware of how the goal might be attained and thus leads to the formation of better plans and higher self-efficacy.

QUALITATIVE FACTORS IN COMMITMENT

Terborg (1978) has suggested that there may be different qualitative types of commitment. Drawing from the social psychology literature, he distinguished between *compliance* (going along with the authority figure despite private disagreement), *identification* (going along because one likes the authority figure), and *internalization* (going along because one personally agrees with the goal). Terborg suggested that these different forms of commitment have different causes and consequences. Thus far, however, there has been no research relevant to this in the goal setting literature.

COMMITMENT AT THE MACRO LEVEL

While goal commitment has most often been studied at the level of the individual, nearly all organizational change consultants claim that top management support is needed if organizationwide change programs are to succeed. A case in point is Management by Objectives (MBO). In a review of MBO research, Rodgers and Hunter (1989) found that the key factor in the success of MBO programs, measured in terms of objective change indices such as productivity and cost reduction, was organizational (which, in effect, meant top management) commitment to MBO. High-commitment programs showed a mean improvement of 56%, while low-commitment programs showed a mean improvement of only 6% (see Anderson & O'Reilly, 1981, for additional confirmation).

Ivancevich (1972, 1974) suggested several management procedures that foster and/or reveal commitment. These include involvement of a top-level management committee in the MBO process, frequent meetings with managers who are involved in the program, and rewards for good performance under the program. Top management involvement seems related to the concept of legitimate authority at the micro level. What is new at the macro level are the group meetings. While such meetings may involve feedback, a topic whose importance we acknowledge in Chapter 8, such meetings may also involve communication in a more general sense (two-way, upward, downward, horizontal, etc.). Adequate communication can be taken for granted in a simple laboratory experiment where all that is necessary is to tell the individual what the goal is and to provide feedback regarding progress, but it cannot be assumed to occur when an entire division or organization adopts MBO. Under MBO, communication has to include frequent feedback to be successful (Carroll & Tosi, 1973). Thus it has to involve much more than a single announcement, and it has to extend over a much longer period of time than in a laboratory study. (We also discuss this issue in Chapter 14). Latham and Yukl (1975b) found that organizational commitment to a goal setting intervention was critical even to the success of a micro-level field study.

CONCLUSION

We have reviewed a wide variety of factors that can affect goal commitment. These are summarized in Figure 6–4. Undoubtedly there are others that have not yet been studied. It should be repeated that all of those factors could affect, and in many cases (e.g., money incentives) have been shown to affect, goal choice in addition to goal commitment.

We have organized the factors that affect commitment in a way similar to Hollenbeck and Klein (1987), i.e., using expectancy theory categories. However, we did not make their distinction between external and internal determinants, because we assume that all external factors such as authority are cognitively processed and therefore have an internal aspect. The particular factors we listed as determinants of commitment under each category do not correspond exactly to those listed by Hollenbeck and Klein, because we have listed only factors for which we had some research evidence or at least inferential evidence, and because we include a number of studies not available at the time of their review.

FIGURE 6–4 Factors Affecting Goal Commitment

FACTORS AFFECTING PERCEIVED DESIRABILITY OR APPROPRIATENESS OF TRYING FOR A GIVEN GOAL OR GOAL LEVEL

Authority	—communicates legitimacy
	—implies rewards and punishments
	—conveys self-efficiency information
	—conveys normative information
	—fosters sense of achievement
	—implies opportunities for self-development
	—poses challenge to prove self
	—maintains physical presence
	—furnishes support
	—exhibits trustworthiness
	—provides rationale
	—exerts pressure
	—is knowledgeable and likable
Peer Group	—exerts pressure
	—provides role modeling
	—presents competition

Publicness
Incentives and Rewards
Self-rewards
Punishments
Valence and Instrumentality
Ego involvement
Conflict
Satisfaction
Personality
Goal Intensity

FACTORS AFFECTING PERCEIVED ABILITY OF ATTAINING A GIVEN GOAL OR GOAL LEVEL

Expectancy, Self-Efficacy, Task Difficulty
Authority—self-efficacy information, trust
Rcle Models—(same as authority)
Competition
Attributions
Goal Intensity

In some cases the same factor is listed under both the valence and the expectancy headings. For example, trust can influence valence in that it can affect the degree to which one cares about the supervisor's opinion. It can also influence expectancy in that it can affect one's confidence in the ability of the leader to assign a task or goal that is attainable. Similarly, role models can affect how attractive it is to take a certain course of action (try for a goal) and also one's view of the degree to which the goal is attainable (Bandura, 1986). Competition can affect the desirability of performing at a high level and, depending on who is competing and how well he or she is doing, the expectancy of winning. Extensive cognitive processing (goal intensity) could affect the experienced importance of attaining the goal and also the judged feasibility of doing so.

Most of the factors discussed in this chapter are ones for which there is reasonable evidence of their effectiveness in fostering goal commitment. In the next chapter we address two potential determinants of goal commitment that, though viewed as very powerful by most behavioral scientists, have much less consistent effects on commitment.

7

GOAL COMMITMENT II:
Assignment, Participation, and Choice

There are at least three ways by which goals can be set. They can be assigned, they can be set participatively, or the person can choose the goal. In this chapter the relative effectiveness of these three methods of setting goals will be discussed in terms of their impact on goal commitment and performance.

In reading this chapter it is important to note that goal setting theory makes no a priori assumptions regarding the relative effectiveness of different ways by which a goal can be set. However, the most appropriate manner of setting a goal is an important practical question. In addition, the answer to this question is of theoretical importance. According to classical management theories (e.g., Massie, 1965; Taylor, 1967), it is the leader's responsibility to assign goals and to ensure that people commit to them. Humanistic organization theories (e.g., Likert, 1961, 1967; McGregor, 1960) advocate the subordinate's participation in decision making, because participation is said to increase an employee's commitment to implement decisions after they have been made relative to that which could be achieved without participation. Job redesign advocates (Hackman & Oldham, 1980) favor high subordinate autonomy, a stance that would appear to favor self-set goals.

Essays and reviews of the literature on participation by scholars are fraught with ideology (e.g., Dachler & Wilpert, 1978) and emotionalism. With regard to the latter, Sashkin (1984, 1986) has argued that participative management is an ethical imperative (but see Locke, Schweiger, & Latham, 1986, for a rebuttal). The ideology of North American behavioral scientists may stem in part from the political basis on which Canada and the United States is founded, namely

A portion of this chapter has been taken from G. P. Latham, M. Erez, and E. A. Locke (1988), "Resolving Scientific Disputes by the Joint Design of Crucial Experiments by the Antagonists: Application to the Erez-Latham Dispute Regarding Participation in Goal Setting," *Journal of Applied Psychology* (Monograph), *73*, 753–72. Copyright 1988 by the American Psychological Association. Adapted by permission of the publisher.

constitutional democracy, and the antipathy of most behavioral scientists toward totalitarian governments in Europe during the 1930s and in some Central and South American countries today. This chapter does not focus on ideology and politics. Instead, it examines the empirical data that have compared assigned versus participative goal setting methodologies. This is followed by a review of the studies on goal choice as it affects commitment and performance. (As Locke & Schweiger, 1979, and Locke, 1981, have shown, ideology can even bias the interpretation of experiments. We have assiduously tried to avoid this in our analysis. We should note that both authors came out of graduate school strongly believing that participation was a very robust phenomenon in terms of its effects.)

ASSIGNED VS. PARTICIPATIVE GOALS

Early Studies

Among the first investigations of the effectiveness of assigned versus participatively set goals was a study conducted at the General Electric Company (French, Kay, & Meyer, 1966; Kay, French, & Meyer, 1962; Meyer, Kay, & French, 1965). In addition to the experimental manipulation of participation, the perceived participation of the subordinates and observer judgments of the amount of participation during performance appraisal interviews were measured, as well as the subordinates' perception of the usual amount of participation they had previously been allowed. Perception of the usual amount of participation, which was measured prior to the appraisal interview, was positively related to acceptance of job goals, but not to subsequent performance. Nor was actual participation consistently related to performance.

A number of limitations of this study make it difficult to reach any clear conclusions. The participation manipulation was not always successful, the participation treatment was somewhat confounded with the usual level of participation that occurred between the supervisor and his subordinates, and no objective performance measures were obtained. Ultimately, the authors concluded that it is not so important how a goal is set as it is that a specific goal in fact be set. This is based on their finding that "the setting of specific goals results in over twice as much improvement in performance as the making of criticisms without goal setting" (French, Kay, & Meyer, 1966, p. 11).

Carroll and Tosi (1969, 1970) included a measure of perceived influence in establishing goals in their questionnaire survey of managers in an MBO program. The results showed that participation in goal setting was not significantly correlated with the amount of goal attainment or effort increase.

In a study by Duttagupta (1975), R&D managers in an MBO program were interviewed and answered a brief questionnaire. No relationship was found between self-reported motivation and perceived influence in the goal setting process. Similarly, Greller (1975) found that participation in the setting of a goal did not correlate significantly with perceptions of appraisal helpfulness and satisfaction. Hannan (1975) found that participation in goal setting only affected a measure of commitment; it had no effect on performance.

Latham Studies

Although aware of the above studies, Latham was influenced by the work of Likert (1967) and a contingency theory articulated by Morse and Lorsch (1970). Work conducted with the American Pulpwood Association had already shown the positive effects of an assigned goal on an objective measure of productivity, namely, cords per employee hour (Latham & Kinne, 1974; Ronan, Latham, & Kinne, 1973). The Weyerhaeuser Company was now interested in finding ways to increase the effectiveness of the goal setting process. Hired as their first staff psychologist, Latham did his doctoral dissertation on the effects of assigned versus participative goal setting in the rural south and in Oklahoma. Consistent with contingency theory, two studies were conducted. It was hypothesized that assigned goals would be more effective than participative goals with uneducated woods workers in North Carolina (mean education = 7.2 years; range = 0–9), and that the reverse would be true with regard to educated woods workers in Oklahoma (mean education = 12.9 years; range = 12–16). This hypothesis, based on Juster's (1975) finding that education enhances decision making by increasing information-processing skills, was not supported (Latham & Yukl, 1975b).

The educationally disadvantaged logging crews in the participative goal setting condition had higher productivity and attained their goals significantly more often than either the crews with assigned goals or the crews in the "do your best" condition. No significant differences were found among the goal setting conditions for the educationally advantaged groups. The management team responsible for the educationally advantaged crews basically had ignored the goal setting program because the director was in the process of being transferred to another region.

Two conclusions were drawn from this research. First, an analysis of the difficulty level of the goals set showed that the educationally disadvantaged crews in the participative condition set significantly higher goals than the crews with assigned goals. Consistent with goal setting theory, high goals led to high performance. Second, as was discussed in Chapter 6, goal setting does not work unless there is management support for the process. This latter finding has a theoretical basis in Likert's system 4, namely, the principle of supportive relation-ships. It also has an empirical basis.

Unfortunately, goal commitment in the above research was not measured because many of the job incumbents were illiterate. Subsequently, a second study was conducted with Weyerhaeuser's word-processing employees (Latham & Yukl, 1976). No significant differences were found with regard to goal attainment or performance between the typists with assigned versus participatively set goals. Unlike the study conducted with the educationally disadvantaged logging crews, the goal difficulty level was not significantly different between the two conditions. Thus participation does not necessarily lead to the setting of goals that are higher than those that are assigned, because goals can be set at any level. Moreover, the authors found that the supervisors in the assigned conditions were highly supportive. Specifically, they lowered the goal when a person had trouble meeting it, and then gradually increased it so that the person would continually experience a sense of accomplishment.

A measure of goal commitment per se was not included in this study either. Instead the authors measured job satisfaction, which was shown to decrease equally in both conditions. This is because the study was conducted at a time when there was a hiring freeze, and the employees were worried about possible layoffs. Thus there was fear that systematic evaluation of their performance would be detrimental to them. In short, goal setting, regardless of whether assigned or set participatively, introduced evaluation apprehension (see Chapter 10 for a detailed discussion of goal setting and affect).

The fear of layoffs was not limited to the word processors. The forest products industry was experiencing an economic recession. A task force within Weyerhaeuser was formed to find ways to motivate engineers and scientists in R&D to achieve excellence. The first step in the process was to define excellence. This was done behaviorally, using a systematic job analysis, namely, the critical incident technique (Latham & Mitchell, 1976). The second step was to train observers to recognize excellence free of such rating errors as halo, similar-to-me effect, contrast effects, leniency, and so on. This was done using a training program developed by Latham, Wexley, and Pursell (1975). The third step was to motivate people to improve their performance.

One R&D director argued in favor of assigned goals because they had proved to be so effective in other areas of the company. Another director disagreed vehemently, arguing that assigned goals are inappropriate in an R&D organization; they must be set participatively or the scientists will not accept them. Still a third director rejected the concept of goal setting altogether as unnecessary because most of the R&D personnel had graduate degrees and were, he said, intrinsically motivated. Goal setting would be viewed, he argued, as a gimmick. People already come to work with the strong desire to do their best. He stated that ways to recognize or reward them so that they would remain with the company during these hard times needed to be implemented. A survey (Latham & Mitchell, 1976) had revealed that the engineers/scientists wanted praise, public recognition, and money as rewards for their efforts.

Because consensus among the directors could not be achieved, Latham proposed that each director's recommendation be advanced as a hypothesis to be tested within a 3 × 3 factorial design over a six-month period (Latham, Mitchell, & Dossett, 1978). The design is shown in Figure 7–1.

Each engineer/scientist was aware of who was in what condition. Nevertheless, the people in cells 7, 8, and 9 who were urged to do their best after

FIGURE 7–1   Design of Reward (Incentive) by Goal Setting Method

	ASSIGNED GOALS	PARTICIPATIVELY SET GOALS	DO YOUR BEST
Praise	1	4	7
Public Recognition	2	5	8
Monetary Bonus	3	6	9
	CONTROL GROUP 10		

receiving a performance appraisal, and who were informed that they would receive either praise, public recognition, or a monetary reward, did not perform significantly better than the people in the control group who were given neither goals nor feedback (Latham, Mitchell, & Dossett, 1978).

This was the first field experiment to show that, consistent with the prediction of goal setting theory, knowledge of results or feedback does not affect commitment or behavior if it is not associated with the setting of a specific, hard goal (see Chapter 8). With regard to goal commitment and performance, participation in setting the goal was found to be no more effecctive than an assigned goal. Participation, however, led to the setting of more difficult goals than supervisors assigned unilaterally for those receiving praise. This is of theoretical as well as of practical importance, since goal setting theory and empirical studies, including the present one, show that the higher the goal, the higher the performance.

It was clear from this study that subsequent comparisons of assigned versus participatively set goals needed to avoid confounding the method by which the goal is set with the difficulty level of the goal. Thus the decision was made to enter the laboratory where rigorous research could be conducted without concern for the consequences to employees in their day-to-day functioning in a company. People in a participatively set goal condition were evaluated relative to those in an assigned and a do best condition.

A brainstorming task was used because of the high degree of commonality between the way brainstorming could be run in a laboratory setting and the way it is actually conducted in an organization. The assigned goal in this study was identical to the one agreed upon by a student in the corresponding participative condition. This yoked design revealed that there was no significant difference in goal commitment between those people in the assigned and in the participative goal setting conditions. Nor was there any significant difference between these two groups in performance. And the number of ideas generated in both the assigned and the participative goal setting conditions was significantly higher than in the do best group (Latham & Saari, 1979b). Goal attainment was literally the same in the two goal setting groups. Judges who were not aware of the purpose of the experiment nor of the three groups from whom the brainstorming ideas were collected rated the quality of the ideas. This was done as a check on the possible demand characteristics of goal setting that could have resulted in a mechanical listing of redundant uses. Again, no significant differences in quality were found among the three conditions. Latham and Saari (1979b) concluded that when goal difficulty is held constant, participation does not lead to greater goal commitment or higher performance than is the case when the goals are assigned.

An opportunity in Weyerhaeuser Company allowed two follow-up studies in a field setting involving word-processing operators (Dossett, Latham, & Mitchell, 1979). A 3 × 2 design involving participative, assigned, and do best goals crossed with feedback was used. With goal difficulty held constant, there was no significant difference between the assigned and participative conditions on performance on a clerical task or goal commitment. Goal attainment, however, was significantly higher in the assigned condition than it was in the participative condition. And only those with assigned goals had higher performance than the employees in the do best condition. This task, however, was only six minutes in duration, as it involved performance on a selection test. Thus a follow-up study reported in the same paper was done using performance appraisals of the word-processing operators as the dependent variable.

A performance premeasure was obtained to control for any differences in effort or ability. After four months the people with assigned goals performed significantly better than those with participatively set goals, even though goal difficulty was controlled through yoking. In addition, goal commitment was significantly higher in the assigned than in the participative condition. Four months later there was no significant difference in goal commitment or performance between the two conditions. Dossett et al. (1979) concluded that when goal difficulty is held constant, an assigned goal is indeed as effective as one that is set participatively.

In a personal conversation, Likert suggested, after reviewing the preceding studies, that from a motivational standpoint participation in itself may not be critical for high performance per se. Its importance, he suggested, may lie in high goals being viewed as attainable. In addition, Likert noted that in each of the preceding studies the supervisor/experimenter had behaved in a supportive manner. This latter observation led to another laboratory experiment.

In this experiment (Latham & Saari, 1979a), college students were randomly assigned to a 2 × 3 study where the experimenter was either very supportive or nonsupportive (e.g., rude, abrupt) in assigning goals, allowing people to participate in setting goals or urging them to do their best. Nevertheless, there was no significant main or interaction effect for goal commitment. But the people in the supportive condition set significantly higher goals than the people in the nonsupportive condition, and the correlation between goal difficulty and performance was significant. Supportiveness appears to be important primarily because it gives people the confidence to pursue high goals.

Contrary to the Dossett et al. (1979) studies, Latham and Saari (1979a) found that participatively set goals led to significantly higher performance than either assigned goals or instructions to "do your best." The debriefing of the experimenter, who was blind as to the hypotheses of the study, revealed that the number of questions asked by college students in the participative condition exceeded those asked in the assigned condition. Thus these performance-related questions may have increased their understanding of what was required of them. This indicated a cognitive rather than a motivational effect of participation in goal setting. As is discussed subsequently in this chapter, the cognitive effects of participation in goal setting have been largely ignored by researchers.

It was time to return to the field (Latham & Marshall, 1982). A Canadian government agency wanted to define effective supervisory behavior. Seventy-six government employees participated in a job analysis. The employees were randomly assigned to one of three goal setting conditions: self-set, participatively set, or assigned goals. The task required each individual to brainstorm job behaviors that had been seen to make the difference between effective and ineffective job behavior as a supervisor. Goals were set in terms of the number of behaviors to be listed within twenty minutes. The results revealed no significant difference in goal difficulty between those with participatively set goals and those with self-set goals. Goal difficulty was held constant between the participative and assigned goal conditions by imposing a goal agreed upon by an employee in the participative condition upon an employee in an assigned condition. There was no significant difference among the three goal setting conditions regarding goal commitment or actual performance. This was true regardless of employee age, education, position level, years as a supervisor, or time employed in the public sector.

Two additional studies were conducted in the laboratory to correct a limitation of previous research designs. A problem with the experimental design used in each of the three laboratory studies reviewed here is that comparisons between assigned and participatively set goals were essentially a test of the null hypothesis. That is, goal difficulty was held constant between participative and assigned goal setting conditions rather than being systematically manipulated. The purpose of the study described below was to replicate the findings of the three previous studies with an experimental design where the difficulty level of assigned goals was varied rather than only being held equal. A secondary purpose was to correct a potential flaw in the design of the two laboratory studies by Latham and Saari (1979a, 1979b) and the field study by Latham and Marshall (1982). In those three studies, goals were assigned to individuals in the assigned yoked condition regardless of their ability. Thus some people in the yoked condition may have received goals that were above or below their ability to attain. This limitation was overcome in the second field study by Dossett et al. (1979) by matching each person with a person of similar ability on a performance appraisal premeasure score before being randomly assigned to a participative or an assigned goal condition. In the Latham and Saari studies it was not practical to collect premeasures on college students, match them on ability, randomly assign them to conditions, and then request them to return at a later date to perform the task. Similarly, it was difficult in the Latham and Marshall (1982) study to collect premeasures from government employees in a nonresearch setting.

The hypotheses of the next study (Latham, Steele, & Saari, 1982) were that college students with very hard assigned goals would have higher performance than peers with lower goals that were either assigned or set participatively; and that with goal difficulty held constant, individuals with participatively set goals would have higher performance than peers with assigned goals. The first hypothesis was supported. The second was not, a result consistent with the previous finding that the difficulty of the goal is far more important than how the goal is set.

None of the preceding ten studies conducted by Latham and his colleagues addressed the issue of participation in decision making independent of goal setting. As Tolchinsky and King (1980) correctly pointed out, these ten studies only tested the effectiveness of setting goals in a participatory versus a nonparticipatory manner. Thus one could not conclude that participation as a variable by itself affects performance only through its effects on goals.

The purpose of the eleventh and final study in this series was to manipulate independently, for the first time, the effects on performance of participative decision making (PDM) in work strategy versus goal setting (Latham & Steele, 1983). This was done in the context of an assessment center exercise. A

3 (participative, assigned, do best goals) × 2 (participation versus no participation in decisions) analysis of covariance was conducted using the performance pre-measure (ability) as the covariate. The analysis revealed a significant main effect for goal setting, but no main effects for PDM or for the interaction of PDM and goal setting.

The experimental design used by Latham and Steele (1983) was an improvement over previous investigations in that both PDM in task strategy and in goal setting were manipulated independently. Yet, the conclusions were the same. The motivational effect of participation in itself was small or nonexistent. Only when PDM led to higher goals than those that were assigned did PDM lead to performance that was higher with assigned goals. When assigned goals were higher, the opposite occurred (Latham, Steele, & Saari, 1982). In all the studies there was a positive linear relationship between an objective measure of goal difficulty and performance.

In summary, of the eleven studies in a series of investigations examining the effects of participation in goal setting on performance, four studies were conducted in the laboratory and seven studies were conducted in the field. The samples included loggers, typists, engineers/scientists, governmental workers, and college students. The tasks included felling trees, typing, test scores in a selection battery, performance appraisals, brainstorming, basic arithmetic, and performance in a business game. The duration of the studies ranged from six minutes to six months. It is clear that it is the specificity and difficulty of the goal that affects performance rather than whether it is assigned or set participatively.

Corroborating Research.   Despite the convergence of findings from the eleven laboratory and field experiments, they were conducted under the supervision of one person. Thus it could be argued that the possibility of experimenter bias existed. For this reason it was imperative that the results be replicated by other investigators. This was done in both laboratory and field settings.

Ivancevich (1976) found that in a nine-month study of salespeople, both the participative and assigned goals were more effective in improving task performance than the do best comparison group. Participative goal setting, however, was not superior to assigned goal setting. Satisfaction, however, was higher in the assigned goal treatment than in the participative one.

Ivancevich (1977) replicated these findings with skilled technicians. Again, both goal setting methods were superior to the do best condition on such performance variables as service complaints, cost, safety, and job satisfaction. However, the differences between the two goal setting conditions were not appreciably different. For two criteria, the assigned goal condition showed the most improvement, and on one criterion the participative condition showed the most improvement. Goal difficulty levels in the two goal setting conditions were not reported.

In a replication of Latham and Saari's (1979a) study regarding supervisory supportiveness, Dossett, Cella, Greenberg, and Adrian (1983) found that goal difficulty and acceptance were the same for people working on a reference search task with assigned and participatively set goals. They concluded that "participation seems to be unimportant for purely motivational purposes provided that difficult goals are set and accepted" (p. 9).

In a replication of Latham and Steele's (1983) study, Leifer and McGannon (1986) found that performance in the assigned and participatively set goal conditions was greater for subjects working on a toy-assembly task than that in the do best condition. Goal commitment (measured with items reflecting enthusiasm for the goal) was higher in the participative condition. However, a separate, more cognitively focused measure of goal commitment showed no such difference. Most importantly, the two goal setting conditions did not differ significantly in performance.

Vanderslice, Rice, and Julian (1987) controlled goal difficulty level through yoking. They too found that performance on a simulated task was the same regardless of whether the goal was assigned or set participatively. Satisfaction was higher in the participatively set condition. Similarly, in a laboratory experiment involving an assembly task, Chang and Lorenzi (1983) found that participative and assigned goal setting did not bring about significantly different effects on performance when goal difficulty level was held constant. In a field experiment on occupational safety, Fellner and Sulzer-Azaroff (1985) also found no significant difference on overall performance between the assigned and participative goal setting conditions. This finding is in agreement with those of Shalley, Oldham, and Porac (1987), who, in a laboratory experiment involving an assembly task, found that within a given goal difficulty level there were no significant differences in goal commitment or performance between individuals who were assigned goals and those who set them participatively.

Both Chacko, Stone, and Brief (1979) and Dossett and Greenberg (1981) have argued that when goals are participatively set, individuals may attribute their performance to an external or nonpersonal cause. On the other hand, when the goals are assigned to them, individuals may attribute their performance to such internal factors as ability and effort. This interpretation is consistent with Luginbuhl's (1972) experiment with college students who were working on achievement tests. Those who has a choice on a task felt less personally responsible than those who had no choice. Thus subjects who are allowed to participate may perceive that they had the opportunity to influence the nature of the task. They may therefore be more likely to ascribe the tasks, rather than ability or effort, as a causal variable. These attribution differences may offset other, potential motivational benefits that participation may have.

In a field experiment, Wexley and Baldwin (1986) found that relative to the control condition, both assigned and participatively set goals were equally effective in bringing about the transfer of training as measured two months after a training program. The task involved the mastery of time-management skills. In a well-controlled laboratory experiment, Kernan and Lord (1988) yoked the goals of the subjects in the assigned condition to those of the participative condition. The task was clerical and involved adding daily work hours for payroll time sheets. The authors' conclusions are quoted below because of their candid bias in favor of participation:

> Results from the study concerning assigned vs participative goal setting were contrary to our initial expectations as well as preferences for more participative approaches (Heilman, Hornstein, Cage, & Herschlag, 1984). Assigned rather than participative goal setting led to significantly higher commitment levels at all

time periods. Despite improved measurement of goal acceptance, the use of a multitrial task, and clear feedback, no differences were found for initial goal acceptance, effort, or performance. Although these findings are not supportive of the prevailing ideology of many behavioral scientists, they are consistent with most prior research that has compared assigned and participative goal setting. (Kernan & Lord, 1988, p. 84)

Erez Studies

The view that participation in goal setting is crucial to goal commitment and hence to performance is articulated mainly by scholars who worked with Erez when she was on a sabbatical at Illinois, namely Earley, Hulin, F. Kanfer, and R. Kanfer. Their orientation has its scientific roots in seminal research by Lewin (1943, 1947, 1951, 1952) and Coch and French (1948). The primary purpose of those early studies was to show how participation could be used to overcome resistance to change. Lewin conceived of participation as a group discussion leading to a decision (Lewin, 1943). He hypothesized that the motivational mechanisms underlying group participation are (1) involvement in goal setting, (2) an active approach to making decision, (3) the achievement of consensus, and (4) public commitment to the final decision.

Resistance to goals has seldom been an issue in goal setting studies (Locke & Latham, 1984a). Nevertheless, the primary thesis of Erez and her colleagues was that "a goal is more likely to be accepted when it is not perceived as externally imposed" (Erez & Kanfer, 1983, p. 455). Empirical support for this assertion has been obtained by Earley (1985b), Earley and Kanfer (1985), Erez (1986), Erez, Earley, and Hulin (1985), and Erez and Arad (1986). In addition, these studies found significant relationships between goal commitment and performance. It is noteworthy that Erez's procedures, as a package, produced a much wider range of goal commitment among various experimental groups than did those of Latham et al. For example, in Erez, Earley, and Hulin (1985), the range in goal acceptance among subgroups ranged from 1.70 to 6.75 on a 7-point scale in the first study and 4.20 to 6.50 in the second. In Erez and Arad (1986) the range was 3.58 to 5.79. In Erez (1986) it was 4.24 to 5.91. In contrast the largest range reported by Latham within one study (on a 5-point scale) was 3.63 to 4.08 (Latham & Steele, 1982).

Earley and Kanfer (1985) cited the procedural justice literature to argue that opportunity for input provides the individual with perceived mastery or control over the situation. This in turn results in the enhancement of perceived fairness. Moreover, they claimed that individuals may experience a release of frustration during their "day in court" because of an increase in control over the process through which the outcome is generated. These two factors, they argued, explain why participation in setting a goal should affect goal commitment and performance.

In summary, based on Lewin's (1951) early work, studies of overcoming resistance to change (e.g., Goodman, 1979; Perkins, Nieva, & Lawler, 1983), and her own experiments, Erez argued that when there are reasons to suspect that goal commitment may not be high, a goal is more likely to be accepted when people have a voice in setting it rather than having it assigned to them.

Corroborating Research. Only two studies conducted independently of her colleagues could be found that supported Erez's work regarding the beneficial effects of participatively set goals relative to those that are assigned. A case study by Raia (1965, 1966) suggested that productivity was highest with self-set goals followed, respectively, by participative and assigned goals. Because experimental controls were lacking, no firm conclusions could be drawn from such a claim.

Searfoss and Monczka (1973) examined employee participation in the budgeting process. The results indicated that the greater the involvement in the decision-making and goal setting processes, the higher the perceived levels of motivation by the person's subordinates to achieve the budget. However, neither actual performance nor goal attainment was measured.

Resolution

Typically, when there are disagreements regarding a certain finding or relationship in science, the disputants attack one another in the literature. Each may claim that the other used a flawed procedure, an invalid design, or inappropriate analyses or that the findings were valid but misinterpreted. The rest of the scientific community then lines up on either side (or in the middle).

At this point several things can happen. The disputants may each conduct further experiments until one side wears the other down or persuades the scientific community that his or her view is correct. This occurred in the controversy surrounding motivator-hygiene theory, with its critics winning the day. Sometimes a controversy continues because of strong convictions that may in part be ideologically based. A case in point is the heritability of intelligence dispute, which continues to this day. In other instances the scientific community may simply lose interest in the issue on the grounds that it is not worth pursuing. An example is the controversy over intrinsic motivation; industrial-organizational psychologists have, in recent years, basically ignored it.

What has rarely been done in scientific disputes is for the disputants themselves to work together to try to design one or more "crucial experiments" to resolve the differences in their findings. It is not difficult to understand why one rarely if ever sees this method used. It can be ego-threatening to work with an antagonist after each has made opposing scientific claims in print; the antagonists face the risk that their work may be shown to be wrong. That Erez and Latham agreed to jointly design four experiments, using a third party, namely Locke, as a mediator, in order to discover why the two camps obtained such contradictory findings, may have been unique in the history of psychology (Latham, Erez, & Locke, 1988).

Face-to-face discussions were followed by extensive telephone calls and written correspondence. Thus every experimental condition, including the choice of tasks, the experimental manipulations (including verbatim instructions), and all questionnaire measures (most of which were common to all the experiments), was agreed on by the three researchers prior to the experiments. In addition, the experiments were conducted, not by the protagonists themselves, but by research assistants who were blind to the hypotheses of the studies. The experimenters were truthfully told that the researchers did not know how the studies would come out.

With Locke acting as mediator, the first two studies were conducted under the direction of Latham, and the last two under the direction of Erez (Latham, Erez, & Locke, 1988). The first step in this process involved a meeting during which Erez and Latham, with Locke present, "brainstormed" differences in the two sets of experiments that might account for the differences in their results. Five hypotheses were generated initially.

1. Task Importance. Latham's experiments, unlike Erez's, stressed to the subjects in laboratory experiments that the experimental tasks were important ones. On the other hand, Erez believed that the tasks she used (e.g., simulated scheduling, evaluating job descriptions) were judged as less important than those typically used by Latham (e.g., brainstorming, real-life jobs). Participation may have had a greater motivational effect in the Erez experiments, she argued, because there was little motivation provided by perceived task importance.

2. Group Discussion. Latham's participative goal setting conditions usually involved a dyad (e.g., a supervisor or experimenter and a subordinate or student). In contrast, Erez's participative conditions always involved group discussion. The experimenter discussed the goal to be set with groups of five or six people. In one study, Erez and Arad (1986) experimentally separated the effects of participation in setting the goal from those of group discussion about the goal (i.e., in the participation/no group discussion condition, the goal was set through secret ballots given to the experimenter). They found that both participation in setting the goal and group discussion of the goal had significant effects on both goal commitment and performance. Furthermore, the combination of the two produced a significant increment (interaction) over and above the additive effect. Consistent with these results, Matsui, Kakuyama, and Onglatco (1987) found that group goal setting (within groups of two) led to higher goal commitment and performance than did self-set goals.

3. Instructions. Everything that an experimenter does in an experiment does not always appear in the published article. In discussions between Erez and Latham concerning possible reasons for the differences in their results, they discovered that the instructions the two of them typically used in the assigned goal condition were quite different. Typical instructions used in laboratory experiments by Latham (e.g., Latham, Steele, & Saari, 1982) were as follows:

> Thank you for agreeing to participate in this study. Weyerhaeuser Company has employed us to [rationale given] . . . You are now familiar with the task. I would like you to do the following. . . . This goal is difficult but attainable.

These instructions were always given in a polite, friendly manner so that the experimenter would be seen as supportive.

Contrast this with the terse instructions typically given by Erez:

> Now that you have already had a practice session to get familiar with the task, you are asked to next attain a score of _____ . You will have _____ minutes.

Three differences between these two sets of instructions may be significant: (a) Latham provided a rationale for why the task was an important one, thus utilizing a "tell and sell" rather than only a "tell" approach; (b) Latham told all his subjects that the goal was reachable; and (c) Latham stressed a warm and friendly rather than an abrupt tone, i.e., high supportiveness. Supportiveness was not measured in any of the Erez studies. Thus it is possible that the differences in the results obtained by Erez and Latham are due to Erez's assigned condition working less well than Latham's rather than Erez's participative condition working better than Latham's.

4. Setting Self-Set Goals Prior to the Experimental Manipulations. Erez, Earley, and Hulin (1985) had half their subjects set their own goals before the assigned or participative manipulation took place. They found that commitment to subsequent goals was higher in all cases when prior goals had not been set. This commitment difference did not affect performance, however, except among subjects in the participative condition (where the commitment differences tended to be greatest). Subjects who initially set their own goals may have been upset about being misled, especially when the new goals were very high.

5. Value Differences. Some, though not all, of Erez's studies have been conducted in Israel, a more collectivistic society than North America (Hofstede, 1980). Thus one might expect that participation in goal setting would be relatively more effective than assigned goals, as compared with the United States and Canada where all of Latham's studies were conducted.

Direct evidence for cultural differences was provided by Erez and Earley (1987), who tested the effects of participative goal setting strategies on goal commitment and performance for American and Israeli students. They found that for the Israeli sample, assigned goals led to a significantly lower level of performance than did participatively set goals. The difference between the assigned and participative goals was not significant for the American sample.

Value differences can also occur within cultures. Indirect evidence for this hypothesis was also provided by Erez (1986). She found significant differences in the effects of degree of participation within Israel among subjects drawn from the private, Histradrut (trade union) and kibbutz (commune) sectors. Assigned goals produced greater goal commitment and performance in the private sector (which is relatively less collectivistic as measured by Hofstede's items) than in the other two sectors. Participative goal setting was relatively more effective in the more collectivistic Histradrut and kibbutz sectors. It may be noteworthy that, with one exception (Latham & Marshall, 1982), all of Latham's field experiments were conducted in the private sector.

In the course of conducting the four experiments, Latham, Erez, and Locke (1988) discovered three additional factors that might have affected the results obtained in Erez's earlier work: (6) Erez used a two-phase design that included a drastic increase in goal difficulty in the second phase. Latham emphasized the use of goals that were difficult but attainable. (7) Self-efficacy instructions were given by Erez only to the subjects in the participative condition. Latham told all his subjects that the goals were difficult but attainable. (8)

Instructions that were given by Erez to the subjects told them to reject goals with which they did not agree. This was never done in the Latham experiments.

The primary purpose of the first two studies, conducted under the supervision of Latham, was to determine the effect of task importance and group set goals on goal commitment and performance. As noted above, Erez argued that the tasks she typically used may have been seen as less important by the subjects than were those typically used by Latham. Moreover, Latham's previous research assistants had conveyed verbally and through tone of voice to the subjects that the task activity was an important one regardless of goal setting condition.

The results from these two experiments showed that perceived task importance and goals set within a group setting did not explain the differences in findings obtained by Erez versus others. With goal difficulty held constant, and with the supportiveness of the experimenter both constant and high, performance was the same in both conditions. In the second study, goal commitment was lowest in the assigned goal condition where the task was perceived as unimportant. However, this difference did not affect performance.

The third experiment, conducted under the supervision of Erez, compared participatively set goals with assigned goals where an explanation was provided for the goal (tell and sell) versus assigned goals where no rationale was provided (tell). In addition, the effect of setting a personal goal before the formal establishment of one was examined.

There were no significant differences in goal commitment or performance between those with "tell and sell" versus participatively set goals, but both conditions were superior to the "tell" condition in goal commitment (for all subjects) and performance (for low-ability subjects). The results indicated that the difference in findings between the Latham and Erez studies was not due to the methods by which the participative goals were set, but rather to the methods by which the assigned goals were set. In short, this third experiment not only replicated the Latham studies but made it clear that the difference between Latham's and Erez's findings was due mainly to the curtness of the Erez "tell" instructions. The setting versus nonsetting of a personal goal prior to the establishing of the formal goal (which did lower commitment to assigned goals) did not explain these differences.

The fourth and final experiment replicated the "tell" vs. the "tell and sell" difference and confirmed the biasing effect of giving self-efficacy instructions to only one condition. That is, self-efficacy instructions given to some PDM subjects gave them a clear edge over other PDM subjects who were not given instructions. Finally, this and the second experiment suggested a borderline effect of goal difficulty, with difficult assigned goals producing somewhat lower commitment but not lower performance than participatively set goals.

In brief, the four experiments conducted jointly by Latham, Erez, and Locke (1988) showed that when goal difficulty is held constant, when attempts to enhance self-efficacy are held constant, when there is not undue brevity, and when artifacts such as telling subjects to reject goals are eliminated, the motivational effects of assigned goals are as powerful as participatively set goals in generating high goal commitment and subsequent performance.

SELF-SET GOALS

Empirical studies have shown the effectiveness of self-set goals. For example, Kliebhan (1967) found that educable male retardates who were enrolled in a job training center, and who set a specific personal goal with regard to affixing samples of tapes to unbound pages of a salesperson's advertising booklet, had significantly higher production than those who did not set a specific goal.

Drawing upon the level-of-aspiration literature (e.g., Festinger, 1942), Kausler (1959) showed in a laboratory experiment that performance on an arithmetic test was higher when subjects were asked to state how many problems they hoped to answer correctly within six minutes than was the performance of those who had been randomly assigned to a control group.

Not surprisingly, Erez has argued that allowing a person a choice in the goal that is set provides individuals with feelings of control over their actions. These feelings, she argued, affect goal commitment positively (Erez & Kanfer, 1983). Empirical support for this assertion has been obtained by her colleagues.

In a laboratory experiment where the task involved scheduling classes, Earley and Kanfer (1985) found that goal acceptance and subsequent performance were highest for individuals who were given both a choice over their goal and the strategy to attain it. In another laboratory experiment, Earley (1985a) examined the effects of choice of the strategy to attain the goal and choice of when to schedule a work break. Goal commitment was higher in the high choice than in the low choice condition, but the variance accounted for by choice was relatively small. Moreover, choice only affected performance when Earley provided information to the subjects on how to perform the task.

Although the hypotheses of other investigators have been consistent with those of Erez, few of them have obtained supporting data. In an early laboratory experiment by Helmstadter and Ellis (1952), self-set goals were compared with those that were assigned by an experimenter. The task used was a modified form of the block-turning portion of the Minnesota Rate of Manipulation Test. There was no significant difference in performance between those with an assigned or a self-set goal.

In a laboratory experiment involving brainstorming, Locke (1966d) found that hard, assigned goals resulted in performance that was significantly higher than self-set goals. This was because the students in the latter condition set goals that were only moderately difficult. Locke's findings were not replicated by Siegfried, Piemont, McCarter, and Dellinger (1981); however, in that study the goals were very easy in both goal setting conditions. Thus neither condition proved superior to the control group.

Two laboratory experiments by Schuldt and his colleagues support Erez. The task involved cranking a wheel for four minutes (Schuldt & Bonge, 1979; Mizes & Schuldt, 1981). With goal difficulty held constant, subjects who selected their goals responded with significantly higher performance than those who had goals that had been assigned by an experimenter. Schuldt, however, was unable to replicate this finding in a third experiment (Alexander, Schuldt, & Hansen, 1983).

Botterill (1977) studied the number of hand contractions that one can make using a dynamometer. Self-set goals were compared with goals that were set within a group setting. In addition, two assigned goal conditions were yoked in terms of goal difficulty to either the group or the self-set goal conditions. Only the group-set goal and its assigned goal counterpart had performance that was significantly higher than that of a control group. This may have been due to the fact that the goal level in these two conditions was far higher than the goal in the self-set condition and its assigned goal counterpart.

Lichtman and Lane (1983) found that subjects who were assigned the average of the self-set goals coded significantly more data than subjects who set their own goals. However, neither of these means differed significantly from that generated by subjects who had been assigned a specific hard goal by the experimenter.

In two subsequent laboratory experiments (McCaul, Hinsz, & McCaul, 1987) involving memorization tasks, the means for the goal commitment measure showed no significant difference between those in a high versus a low choice condition. Subjects who were permitted choice over their goals, however, spent more time studying than subjects who were not permitted choice. But neither an analysis of variance on the change scores nor an analysis of covariance revealed any reliable effects with regard to actual performance.

Shapira (in press) on the basis of a laboratory experiment, found that assigning a difficult goal to an intrinsically motivated person who has chosen his or her optimal level of task difficulty has a negative effect on that person's performance. Statistical and methodological flaws in the execution of the experiment prevent any conclusions from being drawn (e.g., no regression was done to control for ability, less than adequate ability measures were used, means and standard deviations were not reported, some samples were combined inappropriately, self-efficacy was not measured, and choice and difficulty level may have been confounded).

Bassett (1979) argued that in field settings where pressure is brought to bear in support of an assigned goal, acceptance by the worker depends largely on the perceived legitimacy of the authority of the goal setter. This argument is in alignment with Dember (1975), who, after examining the literature on the cognitive aspects of motivation, concluded that in the right setting, being told to do something is tantamount to being motivated to do it. This is because instructions, once implanted, take on the formation of powerful internally generated drives.

To test these hypotheses, Bassett simulated an organizational setting. Actual employees were hired from a temporary employment agency to perform a clerical task. Quantity of performance was measured in terms of the number of documents checked per two minutes of scheduled working time. Choice, however, failed to enhance performance. Workers who were assigned a goal/ schedule/pace that was harder than that which they preferred performed better than those who were given their choice. The results of this simulation and Dember's review of the cognitive literature suggest that research is needed to identify those conditions that lead to goal rejection rather than goal commitment as evidenced by performance.

Taken as a group, these laboratory experiments show that it is not the method by which a goal is set that is important, but rather it is the difficulty level of the goal that affects performance positively. Specific, easy goals can reduce the variance in performance, but they are unlikely to increase performance levels over those of a control group.

In a field setting, Dickerson and Creedon (1981) examined the effects of self-selected versus teacher-selected standards on the performance of students in the second and third grades. The pupil-selected standards condition resulted in a significantly greater number of correct responses in a writing and mathematics task than did the condition where the teacher set the standard. However, Barling (1980) found no such difference in a similar study.

In a field study involving government employees, Latham and Marshall (1982) found that goal difficulty, goal acceptance, goal attainment, and performance (defined as the number of ideas generated in a job analysis) were the same regardless of whether the goals were assigned, self-set, or set in a participatory manner. Hollenbeck, Williams, and Klein (1989) found that commitment to difficult goals with regard to grade in a college class was not significantly higher in a self-set goal condition than it was in an assigned goal condition.

In sum, it would appear that the findings obtained in the laboratory experiments generalize to the field. Self-set goals are not consistently more effective in bringing about goal commitment or an increase in performance than other methods of setting a goal.

NARRATIVE REVIEWS AND META-ANALYTIC FINDINGS

The conclusion that the motivational effects of participation on performance are negligible is supported by both narrative reviews of the literature and meta-analyses. For example, the narrative review on goal setting by Latham and Lee (1986) found that assigned goals were as effective as participatively set goals. A meta-analysis of the goal setting literature by Mento, Steel, and Karren (1987) focused on effect size rather than direction. A borderline effect of about 4% was obtained in favor of participation. Such a finding is considered trivial (Fowler, 1985). In another meta-analysis, Tubbs (1986) too found a negligible participation effect even when goal difficulty was not held constant.

At least six additional articles have been published on the motivational effects of participation in general. Among the first comprehensive reviews was Dachler and Wilpert's (1978) paper. They argued that participation can and does affect both performance and satisfaction. Other, more painstaking narrative reviews (e.g., Locke & Schweiger, 1979; Schweiger & Leana, 1986) concluded that participation can affect satisfaction positively but has, at best, a marginal effect on performance.

A meta-analysis supported their conclusion (Miller & Monge, 1986). However, Wagner and Gooding (1987), in another meta-analysis, showed that even the above conclusions were overstated. After removing the influence of percept-percept research methods, they found no noteworthy relationship between participation and satisfaction, or participation and performance. (Their analysis did not include the Erez studies).

In a subsequent narrative review, Cotton, Vollrath, Froggatt, Lengnick-Hall, and Jennings (1988) claimed to find support for the original thesis advanced ten years earlier by Dachler and Wilpert (1978). They argued that participation as a variable or concept is multidimensional, with some forms being more effective than others with regard to subsequent performance and satisfaction.

To test this hypothesis, Wagner (1988) conducted a meta-analysis to reexamine the studies reviewed by Cotton et al. Again, percept-percept artifacts were controlled. The studies were categorized into the six nonindependent dimensions defined by Cotton et al., namely, participation in decisions, consultative participation, short-term participation, informal participation, employee ownership, and representative participation. The results showed that there were no noteworthy differences in outcome effects among the six forms of participation. Leana, Locke and Schweiger (in press) further criticized Cotton et al. for using an invalid classification scheme, for misreporting the results of some of the studies, and for using an inappropriate sample of studies.

COGNITIVE EFFECTS OF PARTICIPATION IN GOAL SETTING

The studies reviewed thus far in this chapter have examined only the motivational mechanism (commitment) by which PDM in setting goals has been hypothesized to affect performance. Locke and Schweiger (1979) and Tjosvold (1987), have argued that a second major mechanism by which both PDM and goal setting may affect performance is cognitive in nature (e.g., generating ideas for improving a method or product).

Campbell, Dunnette, Lawler, and Weick (1970) were among the first to argue the possible cognitive benefits of goal setting as such. Specifically, they stated that goals should help clarify the task to be performed to the extent that they give employees explicit knowledge of where to direct their effort. Similar arguments have been made with regard to the effects of participation. For example, Mitchell (1973) forcefully pointed out that including people in decision making should have the cognitive effect of clarifying expectations. In addition, Latham and Steele (1983) argued that participation in decision making can lead to the development of strategies to accomplish the task. Their conclusion was based in part on the laboratory experiment described earlier in this chapter (Latham & Saari, 1979a). In that experiment, the numerous questions asked by college students in the participative condition resulted in performance that was higher than that of the assigned condition. This suggested a cognitive effect of participation in goal setting.

To date only four laboratory experiments have considered the cognitive effects of participation in goal setting. The first experiment, cited earlier, was done by Erez and Arad (1986). An increase in performance quality was found to be due to a cognitive factor, namely, information, which the authors claimed was an element of participation. High information subjects were given a demonstration on how to perform the task, guidance on performance strategies, and methods for improving performance. In short, the people who were given the knowledge of what to do performed better than the people who were denied this knowledge.

A second experiment (Campbell & Gingrich, 1986) found that computer programmers given goals to complete complex programs performed better when they had participative discussions with their supervisors than when they did not. No such difference emerged when the programs were simple. The first finding was shown to be a result of the information exchange that occurred rather than an increase in goal commitment relative to the assigned goal condition. The authors posited that the discrepancy between their findings and previous goal setting participation studies was due to the cognitive complexity of the task. Cognitive abilities are less important on relatively straightforward tasks. Thus goal setting is effective on a straightforward task where the person already has the requisite ability to perform it, to the extent that the goal affects choice, effort, and persistence. A goal may be effective on a complex task, or a task where an increase in ability is needed, to the extent that, in addition to the above, it brings about effective planning and strategy choice (Chapter 4). This conclusion is supported by a meta-analysis. Wood, Mento, and Locke (1987) found that goal setting effects were strongest for straightforward tasks and weakest (though still significant—see Chapter 9) for cognitively complex tasks.

In a study involving a ten-hour, five-day proofreading task, Huber (1985a) found that participation in choosing between one of three levels of goal difficulty did not result in greater mastery than that achieved when the subjects were assigned a goal. She concluded that participation may be useful only to the extent that it provides people with information concerning task goals and the behaviors to achieve them. "Participation might have been ineffective because subjects acquired no additional or useful information through their participation" (p. 233).

Finally, Latham and Winters (1989) experimentally separated the cognitive and motivational effects of participation by manipulating participation in goal setting independently from participation in developing task strategies. Participation in setting the goal had some effect on commitment but no effect on performance. However, subjects who jointly developed suitable strategies to use when performing the task developed significantly better task strategies and performed significantly better (as measured by number of error-free responses) than those who did not participate in developing strategies. A mediator analysis showed that, rather than goal commitment, it was the quality of the task strategies used, combined with the heightened self-efficacy fostered by the use of such strategies, that was responsible for the higher performance of the high-participation subjects.

CONCLUSION

The primary focus of this chapter has been on the motivational effects of different methods of setting goals. We have long believed that the cognitive benefits of participation are far more powerful than the motivational effects. The field is currently in need of research on this former topic. Further research on the motivational effects of different goal setting methods would appear to have limited value. This conclusion is based on both the number of meta-analyses of goal setting studies and the participation literature, which have found a negligible participation effect on either satisfaction or performance.

Contrary to the conventional wisdom (e.g., Kiesler, 1971) that letting people have a say or make choices leads to greater feelings of self-control or commitment, and thereby better performance, it may be that telling people what goals to try for is in itself an indirect means of inducing self-efficacy, especially when the goals are high (see Chapters 3 and 6). This argument (cited previously) has been made by Salancik, who asserted that "the assignment of a specific goal . . . implies that the person is capable of achieving the goal" (1977, p. 30). Psychologists have perhaps been overly influenced by the cliché that self-control or choice is good; therefore any procedure that increases choice automatically increases commitment and performance. Social-cognitive theory (Bandura, 1986) would argue that choice in the absence of self-efficacy would not lead to high performance and could even lead to increased stress in that people will be faced with the need to cope with situations that they cannot handle. Thus procedures that increase a person's choice should be most successful when combined with additional procedures that promote self-efficacy with respect to the task in question.

As indicated at the outset, the findings reported in this chapter may run counter to the prevailing ideology of many behavioral scientists, but they do not run counter to the empirical evidence. As Locke and Schweiger (1979) pointed out, the issue of participative decision making should be regarded as a pragmatic rather than a moral one. Too frequently a false dichotomy is presented to management: an authoritative approach or a participative one. Goal setting, supportiveness, and job or task understanding are not necessarily precluded by a leadership style that does not always emphasize participative decision making.

It would appear that these conclusions will not be reviewed as particularly new or controversial by many European or Latin American readers. In the *Annual Review of Psychology*, Faucheux, Amado, and Laurent (1982) reported that (a) the industrial democracy movement in Scandinavia has lost much of its initial thrust of the 1960s; (b) the assumptions of Theory Y are contradictory to the social reality of Latin America as well as the Catholic work ethic in Latin Europe; and (c) in many areas of France and Italy the human relations movement is viewed as naive. Thus behavioral scientists should not use ideological deductions to draw conclusions about the nature of specific causal relationships in the realm of science. In North America the error that many behavioral scientists made was not in overestimating the power of choice and participation in decision making in fostering commitment and subsequent performance, but rather in underestimating the power of a supportive leadership style and authority on these same two outcomes.

This chapter completes our discussion of goal commitment as a moderator of the effects of goal setting. In the next two chapters we discuss additional moderators.

CHAPTER

8

GOALS AND FEEDBACK
(Knowledge of Results)

It has been claimed that the positive effect of knowledge of the results of one's performance (KR) or feedback upon subsequent performance is a well-established if not one of the best-established findings in the psychological literature (e.g., Ammons, 1956; Annett, 1969; Bilodeau & Bilodeau, 1961; Kopelman, 1982, 1986). As previous chapters have indicated, goal setting is also one of the most well established and robust findings in psychology.

This chapter will show that unqualified claims for the effectiveness of either one alone are misleading in that neither is very effective in the absence of the other. The relationship between goals and feedback is a complex one in that, with respect to feedback, goals are a *mediator;* they are one of the key mechanisms by which feedback gets translated into action (Locke, Cartledge, & Koeppel, 1968). With respect to goals, feedback is a *moderator;* goals regulate performance far more reliably when feedback is present than when it is absent (Locke et al., 1981). The two major sections of this chapter focus on goals as a mediator of feedback, and feedback as a moderator of goals.

It should be noted at the outset that meta-analyses of the goal setting literature have not shown strong, consistent evidence for the interdependence of goals and feedback (Mento et al., 1987; Tubbs, 1986). There are at least two reasons for this. First, the meta-analyses did not include the large number of studies reviewed in this chapter. Second, some of the key goal–KR studies could not be included because they did not contain the information needed for meta-analysis treatment (e.g., S.D.'s). Despite these limitations, both meta-analyses found some evidence for the moderating effects of feedback.

Portions of this chapter have been taken from "Latham vs. Komaki: A Tale of Two Paradigms" by E. A. Locke, *Journal of Applied Psychology*, 1980, 65, 16–23; and from "Motivational Effects of Knowledge of Results: A Goal Setting Phenomenon?" by E. A. Locke, N. Cartledge, and J. Koeppel, *Psychological Bulletin*, 1968, 70, 474–85. Both excerpts are reprinted by permission of the American Psychological Association.

GOAL SETTING AS A MEDIATOR OF FEEDBACK

A mediator is a causal mechanism that accounts, in whole or in part, for the effects of another variable (e.g., effort is a mediator of the goal difficulty effect on performance). A mediator differs from a moderator in that the latter is a variable that may or may not have any direct causal effect but affects the relationship between two other variables. For example, commitment is a moderator of the goal-performance relationship (Chapter 6). As we shall see later, feedback is also a moderator of this relationship.

The need to look at mediators of the effect of feedback on performance is twofold. First, there is a need to understand the mechanisms by which any external factor affects human action. Since a person is not a mindless machine, some of these mechanisms must be psychological. Second, feedback, despite the claims of some (e.g., Kopelman, 1982), does not always improve performance (e.g., Balcazar, Hopkins, & Suarez, 1986; Ilgen, Fisher, & Taylor, 1979). This indicates that more knowledge is required before the effects of feedback can be fully understood and, therefore, predicted and managed.

Feedback, given some motivation to perform, can of course improve performance for strictly cognitive reasons. For example, if an individual is told that his or her footwork is wrong in tennis or that he or she is misspelling certain words in English class, such information can be used to improve subsequent performance. This chapter, however, is concerned with the motivational effects of feedback.

Such motivational effects are usually studied by providing individuals with summary knowledge of their performance or previous actions. This is often called knowledge of score or knowledge of results (KR). The term *feedback* will be used interchangeably with KR, although, as we shall see below, these terms are not synonymous.

To see what must be involved in determining the effects of feedback on performance, let us begin with an introspective analysis. A tentative model summarizing the following discussion is shown in Figure 8–1. A classroom example is used because it is common to everyone's experience. Let us assume that you are a student in a mathematics class and you have just been given your score on a test. The presentation of this score to you by the teacher constitutes feedback. Before this feedback can affect you, you first must detect it, that is, you must see the numbers written on your test paper. The psychological process involved is perception. If you do not see the score (perhaps because you left your glasses at home and are too shy to ask anyone else to read the score to you), the score cannot, for now, affect you. Assuming you do see the score, you will also try to understand what it means; thus the feedback, an external event, will be translated into knowledge of results, i.e., conceptual understanding. For example, does 72.5 on this test mean A, B, C, D, or F? Is there a curve? If so, what is it? The psychological process involved here is *cognitive appraisal*. There may be further cognitive appraisals involved. For example, does this information have implications for my course grade, or for getting into graduate school, and so on?

Almost simultaneous with this cognitive appraisal, and based on it, will come a *value appraisal* in the form of an emotional response (see Locke, 1976,

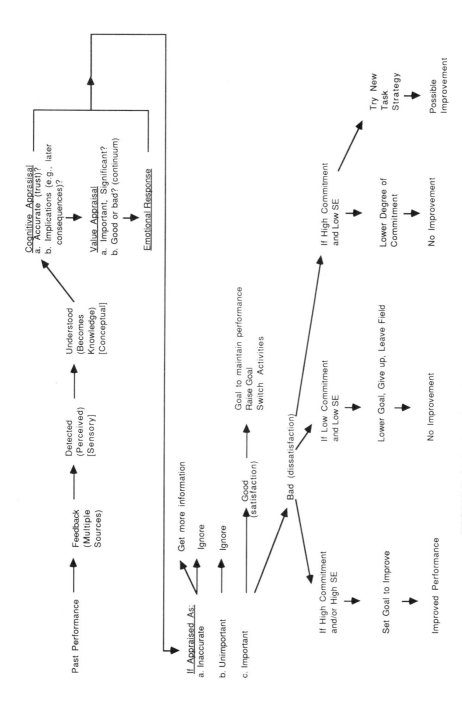

FIGURE 8–1 Model of How Feedback Leads to Action

1984; and Packer, 1985a, 1985b, for a detailed discussion of emotions: see also Chapter 10 of this book). This value appraisal involves an automatic, subconscious evaluation of the test score as you understand it in relation to your value standards. For example, at the simplest level, if you wanted to get a B and instead got a C, you would experience conscious dissatisfaction. If you wanted a B and got a B, you would experience satisfaction. If you wanted a B and received an A, you might experience ecstasy. And if you got a D, you would feel very dissatisfied and perhaps even disgusted and angry. You might also conclude (along with an emotion of indifference) that the grade you got simply did not matter; maybe you are a last-semester senior with job in hand and graduation all but assured. The strength of the emotion would depend on the degree of discrepancy between your goal and your score and the importance of the value to you (Mobley & Locke, 1970; Locke, 1976, 1984).

As a result of your cognitive and value appraisals, which include your projections of the future, many conclusions would be possible. And these would have different implications for action. For example, you might suddenly realize that the teacher calculated your score incorrectly. You would then ask the teacher to change the grade. You might conclude that your grade was quite satisfactory and seek to maintain it on the next test. Or you might decide that the work was easier than you thought and decide to spend less time on this course in the future relative to other activities.

If, in contrast, you thought your score was important, but you did poorly on the test and were therefore dissatisfied with your grade, several possible courses of action might be considered. If you remained committed to your original goal and thought you could improve, you might set a goal to do better on the next test. If you used suitable study strategies, your subsequent score then would improve. You could, however, reduce commitment to your previous goal, perhaps because you did not think you were capable of reaching it. You would then lower your goal or level of aspiration for the next test. This would probably lead to a decrease in subsequent performance. Or you might not bother to formally change your goal but just feel less committed to it and try less hard to attain it. This would also lead to lower performance, other things being equal. You might also remain committed to your goal but conclude that effort alone would not enable you to reach it and then resolve to try a different strategy in order to prepare for the next test, beginning with a conference with the teacher.

The model in Figure 8–1 is not meant to be complete. Rather it is designed to illustrate that the effects of feedback depend on the psychological processes that follow it, and that one of these processes is the goal the individual sets in response to the feedback. Other processes mentioned directly or by implication are the degree of satisfaction or dissatisfaction, commitment, and expectancy of success (or self-efficacy). As is shown later, all of these additional processes are involved in the response to feedback. But let us consider goal setting first.

To demonstrate that goal setting acts as at least a partial mediator of feedback, two things must be shown. First, if goal setting in response to feedback is prevented, then feedback should have no effect on performance or a much smaller effect than when it is not prevented. Second, when feedback does lead to improved performance, it must be shown that this effect is vitiated or reduced when differential goal setting among subjects is statistically or experimentally controlled.

Few studies have actually tested these propositions. Those that did, obtained results that are consistent with the mediation hypothesis. Only two studies have absolutely prevented goal setting by subjects given feedback or prevented differential goal setting by subjects in feedback and no feedback conditions.

Locke (1967b) used an addition task and 2 × 2 design: feedback (KR) vs. no KR; and specific, hard goals vs. do best goals. (The goal subjects did have some additional feedback regarding progress in relation to goals—an issue discussed below.) Goal setting was prevented in response to the KR by giving subjects knowledge of their scores at the end of each of the five trials but making the trials of alternating length. Thus scores on consecutive trials were not directly comparable. The results showed a significant goal effect in favor of the specific, hard goal subjects, but no significant KR effect and no interaction.

This finding was replicated by Locke and Bryan (1969a) with the same task and a similar 2 × 2 design. The do best condition, however, was replaced by an easy goal condition. The trial lengths were made even more irregular than in the previous study, and feedback cues from the task materials themselves that could have been present in the previous study were eliminated. The results were the same: there was a significant goal effect but no significant KR or interaction effect.

It is significant that these two studies obtained no KR effect because *they are the only studies in the literature to have unequivocally prevented goal setting by KR subjects.*

Only three studies have carefully measured the various goals that were set in response to different degrees or types of KR. In the first, Locke and Bryan (1966b) used six trials on a complex computation task and three experimental conditions: a specific, hard goal plus KR, KR only, and no KR, both the latter groups being told to do their best. There was no significant effect of the experimental conditions on performance; however, the subjects were regrouped according to the goals they actually reported trying for, which were quite varied within each condition. The goals were then coded as to the level of motivation implied by the goals (specific, hard = 3, do best = 2, improvement—an easy goal—and other low goals = 1). There was a significant correlation between the goal scores and performance. Thus the results indicated that varying degrees of KR alone did not affect performance but varying degrees of goal difficulty did. However, the results are not conclusive, since there was no initial KR effect.

In the second study, Locke and Bryan (1968a) refined the procedure used in the previous study while using the same task. There were only two initial experimental conditions, KR and no KR. There were sixteen trials, and all the subjects filled out a questionnaire asking them to indicate what goals they had after the eighth and sixteenth trials. In this experiment there was a significant KR effect on the last eight trials in favor of the KR group. However, when the goals of subjects in the two groups were examined, it was found that more subjects in the KR group had higher goals such as "trying to do my best" or "go reasonably fast," while fewer had lower goals such as "worked with little or no effort" as compared with subjects in the no-KR group. A post hoc 2×2 ANOVA showed a significant effect of goals on performance and no effect (or an interaction effect—depending on which goal questionnaire was used) for KR. A correlational analysis of the data showed significant goal and KR effects (by initial condition). However, when goal setting was partialed out, the KR effect became nonsignificant, whereas the goal effect remained significant when KR was partialed out.

The third study, by Locke (1968a), used a reaction time (RT) task. Subjects in three of the groups were given dichotomous KR in the form of signal lights that indicated whether their previous response was better than their previous worst, previous best, or immediately previous RT. Another group was given full KR consisting of their actual RT scores. Another had no KR at all. Among these five groups, the more KR, the better the performance. Later, two additional full KR groups were added, one being assigned a high (fast), specific RT goal and another being assigned a low (slow), specific RT goal. These seven groups were then coded according to the amount of KR they had (full KR = 2, dichotomous KR = 1, no KR = 0) and the difficulty level of the goals they were trying for (based on interviews) or were assigned (specific, high goal or trying to beat best previous score = 4, trying to beat immediately previous RT = 3, trying to beat worst previous RT = 2, do best or low qualitative goal = 1, and specific, low goal = 0).

If the data for the specific, low goal group are initially excluded from the analysis, the correlations between goals, KR, and performance are all very high (range .84 to .95). The KR-performance correlation is high because for these remaining groups there is an artificially high correlation between KR and goal level. For example, the full KR, specific goal group was assigned high goals; the no KR group tended to have low goals. When the full KR, low goal group is included, this has the effect of partialing out the artificial correlation between goal level and degree of KR. The correlation is artificial because a high goal level is not necessitated by a high level of KR. With the inclusion of the low goal group, the correlations between KR and goals and KR and performance become nonsignificant (r's = .25, .12), despite the fact that the correlation between goal level and performance remains significant (.94). This result indicates that it is not the KR as such that controls performance, but the goals that are associated with the varying degrees of KR.

It is worth reiterating that virtually no other studies in the literature have actually measured the goals that the subjects in various KR and no KR conditions actually set. A minor exception to this statement is a study by Morgan (1984). In a complex, time series design clerical workers were given various types of feedback. There was one questionnaire item about goal setting ("To what extent do you set goals for yourself?"). This item did not specify the types of goals set or their degree of difficulty. Nevertheless, the item significantly mediated the effect of feedback on rate of encoding.

That the effectiveness of goal setting in response to feedback depends on the nature of the goals that are set was also shown by Locke (1966a) in a reanalysis of data gathered by Fryer (1964). Fryer had argued that having subjects set goals in a code-learning task after being given KR enhanced performance as compared with subjects who did not set goals. Locke (1966a), however, found that in three out of four comparisons, only subjects who set high goals outperformed those given KR alone.

The laboratory experiments on feedback and goal setting described above may be unrepresentative of the real world in one important respect. In non-laboratory, including organizational, settings, most people are bombarded with information about their actions. An example is the receipt of information about one's previous spending. Recently the authors received from American Express a summary of their yearly card charges in seventeen different categories for each of twelve months. Counting subtotals and eliminating blank spaces, this resulted in a total of about seventy different pieces of information about past spending. Would anyone assert that all seventy of these items would more or less automatically affect their subsequent actions? If not, under what conditions might they affect such actions?

The most obvious answer is that they would not affect them at all unless they used the information to develop a budget (i.e., spending goals). *One could view goals then as singling out feedback (and other information) for action* as a result of appraising the feedback as important. As shown in Chapter 4, goals focus attention on information that is considered to be significant and direct subsequent action with respect to it. Information that is not so isolated by the formation or application of goals should, therefore, not lead to action. Dossett, Latham, and Mitchell (1979, study 1) and Latham, Mitchell, and Dossett (1978), for example, found that giving clerks knowledge of their score on a clerical test, or giving scientists and engineers their scores on a Behavioral Observation Scale, did not affect their performance in the absence of specific goals to be attained. In fact, the engineers/scientists who received no goals but explicit feedback and the promise of praise, public recognition, or a monetary bonus performed no better than their colleagues in a control group.

Several studies in the literature have provided the individual with feedback on multiple dimensions of performance but with goals for only certain of these dimensions. The results are in full agreement with the mediation hypothesis.

The first was by Locke and Bryan (1969b), who gave subjects quantitative information on five aspects of their driving performance after one drive around a prescribed course (e.g., trip time, number of accelerator reversals, number of brake applications, number of steering reversals). However, on the second trip they were given goals to improve only one of these five scores (e.g., steering reversals). And on the third and last trip they were again given feedback on all five scores but were asked to improve on a different dimension (e.g., accelerator reversals). A different group of subjects were given the same two goals on trips 2 and 3, but in reverse order. Performance improved only for those dimensions for which goals had been set (some minor and uninterpretable interaction aside). The results for steering reversals are shown in Figure 8–2.

In a totally different type of situation, Kolb and Boyatzis (1970) studied self-directed behavior or personality changes by subjects in t-groups. Change was significantly higher on those dimensions for which subjects set goals than for those for which they did not set goals. They were presumably receiving feedback for many different behaviors and traits.

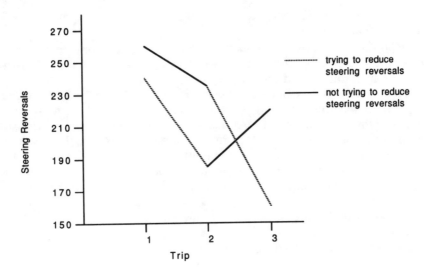

FIGURE 8–2   Effects of the Goal to Reduce Steering Reversals for Subjects Given Feedback Regarding Multiple Dimensions of Driving Performance
Based on Locke & Bryan, 1969b.

Weinberg and Schulman (1974) performed two relevant studies with computer programmers. In the first study they found that those told to complete a computer program rapidly, regardless of the amount of computer time used, finished it faster than those told to use a small amount of computer time. Conversely, those told to use less computer time actually used less time than those told to finish the program rapidly. Presumably all the programmers had information on both outcomes. In a second, more elaborate study six different programming groups were given one of six goals (such as to minimize time, maximize readability of the output). Each group ranked first or second on its goal, even though all the groups presumably had information relevant to each of the goals.

In a study of training in performance appraisal procedures or behaviors, Nemeroff and Cosentino (1979) gave some managers only feedback and gave other managers feedback plus goals. Managers given goals improved their behaviors toward subordinates only on the twelve categories for which goals were set, out of the forty-three on which they were given feedback. Managers who were only given feedback did not show a significant change in their performance.

Kleinbeck (1986) and Schmidt, Kleinbeck, & Brockmann (1984) reported the results of several dual-task studies in which subjects had to perform a tracking task and a reaction time task simultaneously. When subjects were given a goal to improve their performance on one task by a specific amount while maintaining their performance on the other, performance on the task with the improvement goal improved while performance for the other task deteriorated; however, the same results occurred if feedback was given instead of goals. Presumably, the feedback led to spontaneous goal setting. But in a subsequent experiment, goals and feedback were placed in opposition by giving goals for one task (degree of feedback being unspecified but subjects must have had some knowledge of how they were doing) and feedback (without goals) for the other. Performance improved for the task with goals and declined for the task with feedback only.

This last set of studies indicates, again, that when information, including feedback, is available regarding performance on more than one dimension or task, goals determine which information will be acted on so as to improve performance.

These findings suggest an explanation for studies that did not find any effect for feedback or KR alone on performance (e.g., Bandura & Simon, 1977; Baron & Watters, 1981; Chapanis, 1964; Das, 1982a; Dockstader, 1977; Dossett, Latham, & Mitchell, 1979; Latham & Baldes, 1975, before intervention; Latham, Mitchell, & Dossett, 1978; Locke & Shaw, 1984; Mercier & LaDouceur, 1983; Nemeroff & Consentino, 1979; Miller, 1965; Schuldt & Bonge, 1979; Sloat, Tharp, & Gallimore, 1977; Winett, Kagel, Battalio, & Winkler, 1978). In such cases one can presume that no goals to improve performance had been set or accepted in response to or along with the feedback.

On the other side of the same coin, studies that have allegedly found significant effects of KR "alone" have probably done so because the KR has inspired people to set goals to improve their performance. In some cases the confounding of goals and feedback was explicit. In one of the earliest experimental studies of KR, Wright (1906), using a Cattell Ergograph, required subjects to press the carriage downward with their thumbs once each second. For two "incentive" conditions, KR was provided by having subjects watch and count their strokes. In one condition, goals for each response were furnished by lines of varying lengths drawn on the recording sheet; subjects were supposed to press enough so that the recording needle reached these lines. Goals were set for another incentive condition by requiring subjects to press down the blocks of varying thicknesses that were placed under the carriage of the ergograph. Both groups were urged to reach their goals as often as possible. All incentive condition subjects were also run in a no-incentive condition in which they received no KR and were told to work as long and hard as they could. The KR-specific goal condition showed an average superiority in performance of 22.6% over the no-KR–no specific goal condition.

Book and Norvell (1922) gave each of 124 subjects four different tasks to perform, including crossing out specified letters in lists of words and multiplying digits. An "interest in improvement" (II) group was told to count and record their scores, to try to reach or surpass their "best previous score," and to improve more than they had previously. A "no interest in improvement" (NII) group was not given KR and was told to work "as rapidly . . . as possible." On the average the II group showed 26% greater improvement than the NII group.

Crawley (1926) required four subjects to lift weights with their arms and legs in time to a metronome each day for seventy-two days. On half of the days subjects were simply told to work until exhaustion; no specific goals were provided and no KR was given. On the other half of the days, subjects were told how much work had been done in the no-goal–no-KR condition and were told to try to surpass this score (or a goal based on this score). They were also allowed to view the drum on which their performance was recorded. The subjects performed 13% to 16% more work under the specific goal-KR condition than under the no-goal–no-KR condition.

Mackworth (1950, pp. 119–31), dissatisfied with Crawley's method of presenting KR because of the subjects' difficulty in determining their progress in relation to their goals, repeated his basic test procedure. He replaced the "graphic record" with a display that accumulated the amount of work done. A sixty-inch tape measure was calibrated so that each pull moved the tape reading two inches and gave subjects an accurate measure of the amount of work done and the amount needed to beat a goal assigned by the experimenter. The goal was set 25% above the person's best previous score. In addition to the visual knowledge, subjects were provided with words of encouragement, a running commentary on their progress, and their progress relative to other subjects. In the no-KR condition the tape measure was concealed, no specific goals were given, and the experimenter made no comments on the amount of work subjects had done. Half the subjects were run under a KR–no-KR sequence, and the other half performed under the reverse sequence. Performance was significantly better in the KR than in the no-KR condition.

In a study of psychomotor performance, Locke and Bryan (1966a) had two groups of fourteen students each work for 12 ten-minute trials. One group was given KR after each trial and assigned specific quantitative goals by adding a fixed increment to the individual's best previous score. The other group was told to "do their best" and given no knowledge of their trial scores. The specific goal–KR group performed significantly better than the do best–no-KR group during all segments of each trial and on the task as a whole.

A number of other KR studies did not explicitly confound KR and goal setting effects by directly assigning KR and no-KR subjects different goals. However, the KR was given in these studies in such a way that goal setting on their part was almost inevitable. In one group of studies the KR was always given in relation to a standard; KR was based on the subject's performance in relation to his or her own previous performance or to that of others. Given the "demand characteristics" of the typical experimental situation (Orne, 1962), it is highly likely that the KR subjects used this knowledge to appraise their effort on the task and, specifically, to set improvement goals if the feedback showed them to be doing "poorly."

Adams and Humes (1963), in a study of visual monitoring (vigilance), used two no-KR control groups, and a KR group that was told the amount and degree of deviation of each response, in terms of latency, from their shortest previous latency. The KR group showed shorter latencies over four three-hour work sessions than the no-KR groups. Montague and Webber (1965) performed a related experiment in which subjects worked for six consecutive hours on a visual monitoring task. Feedback was given to two KR groups by means of a set of lights indicating their latency in relation to the performance of subjects in a previous study. The light signaling "superior" performance indicated that the subject had surpassed the 95th percentile of the latency distribution. The "adequate" feedback light indicated the response was between the 50th and 95th percentiles, and the "poor" light indicated a response below the 50th percentile of the latency distribution. Points were awarded based on the type and frequency of feedback achieved. The KR group given only the lights and points did not surpass the no-KR group, but a second group given KR plus monetary rewards and penalties based on their point scores surpassed both groups. If it can be assumed that the addition of the monetary incentives motivated Ss to try harder for "superior" feedback, this would be consistent with our thesis regarding the importance of goal setting. Locke, Bryan, & Kendall (1968), in a series of studies, found support for the theory that monetary incentives affect performance by affecting the intentions Ss develop on a task.

In a different type of experiment, Ross (1927) had subjects tally sets of four vertical lines crossed by a fifth for one minute a day for twelve days. The subjects in one group were told each day whether they were above or below the average of all Ss in the study, but not by how much. The no-KR group was in the same experimental room as the other subjects (and could hear all that went on) but were not given any KR. The two groups did not differ in performance. Since the no-KR group might well have set covert goals of their own in such a context, it is unclear to what extent the goals of the two groups actually differed.

Payne and Hauty (1955) explored the effect of KR on performance on a multidimensional pursuit test requiring psychomotor coordination. Subjects worked for four hours at the task; trials were one minute long. After each "cycle" of eight trials, one KR group of subjects were told their performance on that cycle in relation to a normative group. However, the standards were "fudged" so that each subject's score was always represented as being one standard deviation lower than it actually was (which meant that an average person would be expected to beat the group mean only 16% of the time). Thus the subjects always thought they were doing worse than they actually were. Under these conditions, the KR group performed significantly better than the no-KR group. Chung and Vickery (1976) gave KR subjects their own (quantity) scores as well as those of another group to serve as a comparison standard in a study using a clerical task. The KR treatment had a far greater impact on work quantity than did the no-KR treatment.

Visual reaction time (RT) studies were carried out by Church and Camp (1965), McCormack, Binding, and Chylinski (1962), and McCormack, Binding, and McEhleran (1963). In these studies the subjects were given dichotomous (green light or red light) feedback indicating their latency in relation to a standard based on their previous performance. For Church and Camp, the standard each day was a score representative of the 33rd percentile of the previous day's latency distribution. In the McCormack studies, the standard was the subject's immediately previous RT. In all these studies the KR groups showed significantly faster RT's or showed less RT decrement than the no-KR groups. Three conditions in the Locke (1968a) study, discussed earlier, were similar: those given green-light feedback if they beat the best previous RT score outperformed those given the same feedback for beating their immmediately previous score, who in turn beat those given the same feedback for beating their worst previous RT score. All three groups outperformed the no-KR subjects.

In another group of KR studies, rather than being given KR in relation to a standard, the KR subjects were given their raw scores and were allowed to see (or told to plot) a record of their performance as they went along. Again the likely effect of such information was to encourage KR subjects to keep improving and to imply that they should beat their previous scores.

Arps (1920) performed a series of ergographic experiments in which subjects lifted weights with their middle finger. Half the time they received knowledge of their performance both during and after the work periods and were also shown their scores from previous work periods. They performed approximately 10% more work with KR than without KR. Statistical tests, however, were not made.

Brown (1932) had 138 schoolchildren work on arithmetic problems ten minutes a day for twenty days using counterbalanced control and experimental conditions. In the KR condition subjects scored their own papers and then drew a bar graph representing their score. The no-KR subjects did not score their papers, nor did they draw any bar graph. The KR condition produced a higher mean number correct than the no-KR condition. Again, no statistical tests were conducted.

Sacket (1947) had two groups of ten subjects each work at a simulated aircraft target-tracking task. The KR subjects received their mean time-on-target scores after each trial and at the end of each day, and their daily scores were plotted on a graph to give each person a record of his progress. This group did not differ from the no-KR group for the first five days of the study, but when the conditions were reversed on the sixth day, the new KR group significantly reduced its errors while the new no-KR group did not.

A variety of variables were confounded by Chapman and Feder (1917), who gave subjects three different tasks (addition, cancellation, and symbol substitution) to work on each day for ten days. One group received their raw scores for the previous day, a graph showing the progress of the class as a whole, stars for improvement and/or performance in the top half of the group, and an offer of a prize for those gaining the most stars. The group given all these incentives significantly surpassed a group given no KR (or other incentives) on two of the three tasks.

In the line-tallying experiment by Ross (1927) described earlier, the members of another KR group were given their raw scores each day in addition to the score distribution of the whole section; each subject was also told to make a learning curve and to "watch" his progress from day to day. This group outperformed the dichotomous KR group by 6.2% and the no-KR group by 8%.

There was also another KR group in the Payne and Hauty (1955) study of multidimensional pursuit performance described above. The members of this group were given the same "fudged" norms as the other KR group, and in addition were shown all their previous scores by means of a board in which pegs were inserted. This group performed significantly better than the no-KR group, but not better than the KR group given only fudged norms.

Finally Gibbs and Brown (1955) had two groups of subjects operate a document copying machine four hours a day for eight days. On the first four days, half the subjects were given KR by means of a counter that recorded their output; they also had to record the counter readings in a log book at ten-minute intervals. The other half received no KR. On the last four days, the conditions were reversed. Subjects showed significantly higher output under the KR condition.

Let us now summarize what we have established thus far: (1) There is a very extensive literature on KR with most, though not all, of the studies showing positive effects for it. (2) A key mechanism by which KR motivates improved performance is goal setting. This is attested to by the fact that (a) many successful KR studies explicitly or implicitly confounded KR and goal setting by telling or encouraging KR subjects to set goals while not doing the same for no-KR subjects; (b) when differential goal setting among KR and no-KR subjects is either prevented or measured and partialed out, KR has no residual effect on performance; and (c) when KR is given or is available with respect to multiple aspects of performance, the performance dimensions that show the most improvement (and often the only ones that show improvement) are those dimensions for which goals have been set.

The mediating of feedback effects by goal setting has seldom been acknowledged in the literature for three reasons. First, literature reviews have often been incomplete; thus studies that have clearly separated feedback and goal setting effects have not been reported. Second, in studies where goal setting was manipulated along with feedback, the feedback aspect has been stressed in the write-up and interpretation of the studies. Third, in studies where only feedback was explicitly manipulated, it was assumed that only what was formally manipulated was a cause of the results. The latter two biases are legacies of behaviorism. Behaviorists always assumed that external factors such as feedback constituted legitimate causal explanations of behavior while internal factors like conscious goals were neither legitimate nor necessary (Bandura, 1986; Locke, 1969b, 1971, 1972). This issue is now discussed in more detail.

Feedback as a Reinforcer

Behaviorists have repeatedly asserted that feedback affects performance because it acts as an external reinforcer. Parsons (1974), in a frequently cited paper, asserted that the results of the Hawthorne studies could be explained by the reinforcing effects of feedback, even though this claim is refuted by information provided by one of those very studies. In the Bank Wiring observation room, "each man seemed to know just where he stood at any time [during the day]" (Roethlisberger & Dickson, 1956, p. 428). Despite this, output did not increase among this group of workers because they were deliberately restricting their output—that is, they had goals to limit output to a certain level.

Similarly, Komaki has attributed the results of several of her studies solely to the reinforcing effects of feedback (Komaki, Barwick, & Scott, 1978; Komaki, Collins, & Penn, 1982; Komaki, Heinzmann, & Lawson, 1980). Despite the fact that goal setting was manipulated along with feedback in all three studies, explicitly in Komaki et al. (1978) and Komaki et al. (1980) and implicitly in Komaki et al. (1982, see p. 336), the causal role of goal setting was barely acknowledged except in the 1980 study. In that study Komaki et al. argued that "no studies have adequately addressed the question of whether feedback alone would improve performance in the absence of goal setting" (Komaki et al., 1980, p. 269). As the above review of the literature shows, this statement is incorrect. Such studies have indeed been done, and they do not show any feedback effect when it is divorced from goal setting.

The claim that feedback is a reinforcer has been discussed at length by Locke (1980c). In commenting on the Komaki et al. (1978) study, he made the following points:

1. The feedback in her study was not contingent; it was not provided only for "good" performance but simply for performance. According to operant principles, reinforcement is supposed to work only if it follows desired responses and does not follow undesired responses. However, if people are simply reinforced by feedback for whatever they do, they should be most likely to repeat whatever they last did. This should lead to static performance rather than to the steady improvement found by Komaki et al. It could be argued in rebuttal that Komaki et al.'s subjects were reinforced both for their immediately preceding performance and simultaneously for performance improvement (since they typically did improve, even though they should not have according to operant principles). Since the reinforcement interpretation allows for two possible responses (i.e., maintain or further improve performance), how are we to predict or explain which they will choose? Presumably their choice will be determined by what they decide to do about feedback, that is, by their goals.

2. Reinforcement theory asserts that each reinforcement makes the reinforced response class more likely to occur in the future. Thus one would expect (and in animal studies one usually obtains) a learning or performance curve showing gradual improvement in the form of an increase in response frequency over time. Response frequency increases in small increments as a function of the number of reinforcements and, of course, the reinforcement schedule. The performance curves shown in Komaki et al.'s (1978) Figure 1, however, show no such gradual improvement. Rather, a dramatic improvement in performance immediately follows the treatment, namely, the introduction of the goals plus feedback. It remains at the level specified by the standard for the duration of the treatment. When the feedback is terminated so that performance cannot be tracked against the goals, performance immediately returns to the pretreatment level. Thus, rather than conditioning, more likely what occurred was a conscious redefinition of the job resulting from the new standards and the more accurate feedback regarding performance in relation to those standards (Locke, 1977). This parsimonious interpretation seems to make the concept of reinforcement superfluous in this content.

3. As noted above, Komaki et al.'s performance curves show an immediate improvement in performance during the first observation session for each group. Thus performance must have improved *before* there was any feedback to reinforce improvement. How would reinforcement theory account for this initial improvement in advance of the reinforcer? A behaviorist might claim that the initial improvement was due to some form of verbal conditioning; however, the nature and mechanisms of such a process were not specified by Komaki et al.

4. If we ignore the above issues, it might be argued that feedback that was "closer" to the standard was more positive than feedback that was "farther" from the standard (i.e., below it); thus higher performance (positive feedback) would be more reinforcing than lower performance (negative feedback). This could very well be true, but consider the implications: (a) it would mean that

feedback, by itself, was *not* the reinforcer; (b) it would mean that the reinforcer was not an event or an object but a relationship (between feedback and the standard); and (c) this type of so-called reinforcement would require mental calculations or at least an awareness, by employees, of where they stood in relation to their goal. Such an explanation is hardly consistent with the concept of conditioning, which is supposed to regulate action independently of the mind.

Fellner and Sulzer-Azaroff (1984) have argued that when feedback is given, for example, indicating the number of safe behaviors a worker takes, then "feedback has served as a reinforcer for safe behaviors . . . and a punisher for unsafe behaviors" (p. 42). But how can the *same* reinforcer do both unless it is *interpreted* differently by the workers depending on how good the score is? These authors acknowledge that "cognition plays a role in performance" (p. 43) but argue that there is no way to measure cognitive processes objectively. This last claim ignores thousands of findings from almost every field of psychology. Fellner and Sulzer-Azaroff asserted that their explanation of goal setting is "parsimonious," but parsimony divorced from reality is hardly beneficial to the progress of science. The behaviorist might argue that goals increase the salience of feedback and thus make it more reinforcing. However, the term *salience* is clearly a euphemism for the act of communicating to the subject that "it is important to improve your score on this measure." In other words, increasing salience affects performance *because* it affects the way the individual appraises the feedback.

The probable reason why goal setting has been de-emphasized and feedback emphasized in the behavior modification literature is that goal setting is frankly an embarrassment to behavior modification theory. Behaviorism asserts that the key events controlling human action are *consequents*, things that occur after behavior. However, goals are things that occur before behavior; thus they are antecedents. Perhaps recognizing this problem, Komaki, Collins, and Penn (1982) made an attempt to compare the power of "antecedents" and "consequents" in one of their studies of safety behaviors. However, the study was clearly biased in that the antecedents consisted of a very weak intervention (a discussion of safety rules) while the consequents consisted of direct and frequent observations of the workers, quantitative feedback charts, and implicit goal manipulations—all of which undoubtedly became antecedents for subsequent work periods! Ignoring the relative meaninglessness of the antecedent condition, the key fallacy here is the failure to recognize that *a consequent cannot affect action unless it becomes an antecedent.* How else can the past affect the future? Feedback does not result in anything unless the recipients do something with it, such as decide that they will try to improve their performance the next time they act. If consequent information is incorrectly interpreted or cannot be interpreted, it does not lead to any increase in the desired actions (Bandura, 1968; Dulany, 1968; Levine, 1971). Nuttin (1984) identifies the fundamental behaviorist error as follows: "Human behavior does not consist of [automatically] repeating previously reinforced responses; it involves setting immediate or distant goals, elaborating behavioral projects or plans, and working toward their realization by means of learned and readapted behavioral techniques and experiences" (p. 41.)

It should be noted that the very act of *introducing* a work measurement and feedback system into an experimental setting or work group, a process that is often accompanied by special meetings, outside observers, public posting of scores, and explicit statements to the effect that "measure X is important," is enough to almost guarantee "spontaneous" goal setting. To take a typical example from the behavior modification literature, J. Saari (1987) conducted a study aimed at improving housekeeping (tidiness) in a factory. Employees were given a written list of correct work practices, shown slides illustrating correct and incorrect practices, given a one-hour training seminar, shown posters indicating correct practices, observed on the factory floor, and presented with posted boards showing their performance on a quantitative index. (The scores were updated weekly.) It is inconceivable that employees would not set some type of an improvement goal in response to a barrage of interventions that unequivocally communicate the message "Improve your tidiness." Despite this, the success of the intervention was attributed entirely to feedback. Similarly, McCarthy (1978) used both feedback and goal setting interventions in a factory setting, but only the term *feedback* was deemed significant enough to appear in the title of the article.

Pritchard, Jones, Roth, Stuebing, and Ekeberg (1988), who were not working within a behavior modification framework, openly attributed the effectiveness to a very successful feedback program developed by the Air Force to three factors. It allowed for the identification and diagnosis of problems (defined as scores that "started to slip"); it promoted competition across units (a form of goal setting); and it got everyone focusing on the same goals or objectives.

There is an interesting historical example of how competitive feedback promotes goal setting. During the digging of the Panama Canal, George Goethals, Chief of the Canal Commission, started a weekly newspaper, the *Canal Record,* in which the productivity of every steam shovel and dredge was published daily. The result was an immediate increase in output. One of the operators revealed why: "It wasn't so hard before they began printing the *Canal Record.* We were going along, doing what we thought was a fair day's work . . . [but then] away we went like a pack of idiots trying to get records for ourselves" (McCullough, 1977, p. 537).

Ultimately, the claim that feedback acts as a reinforcer simply discourages the search for a genuine causal explanation of its effects. By focusing solely on external events, the behaviorist approach blinds itself to the exploration of cognitive processes that determine if and how external events lead to subsequent action. As shown in Figure 8–1, there are cognitive processes other than goal setting that determine how feedback affects action.

All of this is not to deny that rewards (both external and internal) play a role in getting people to accept goals and motivating them to maintain goal-relevant behavior over the long term; but the key reward in organizational settings is probably not feedback but rather the consequences to which feedback leads, such as recognition, self-praise, raises, and promotions (or their opposite). Furthermore, the effect of rewards themselves is mediated by cognitive factors (Bandura, 1986).

1. Did you consider some scores to be good scores and other scores to be bad scores on this measure, or didn't it matter what you got?
2. What would be a good score? A bad score? A borderline score?
3. Were you trying to get a good score? What?
4. What was the lowest score that you would consider satisfactory?
5. Were you trying for a specific score? If so, what score?
6. If not, were you trying to: Do your best? Work at a reasonable pace? Work at an easy pace? Just do enough to get by? Do below the minimum?
7. What score were you hoping to get if everything went smoothly?
8. Were you trying to improve over your previous score? By how much?
9. Did you know the scores of other people or units?
10. Were you trying to beat their scores (to compete)? Whose scores were you trying to beat?
11. Did your supervisor, manager, or boss know your scores?
12. Did he or she care how you did?
13. What was the lowest score that was acceptable to him or her?
14. Were you pressured to get at least a certain score? What?
15. Did this affect your priorities or what you were trying to do? How?
16. Were there rewards for high scores? Penalties for low scores? In the short term? The long term?
17. Did these affect what you tried to do?
18. Did your co-workers stress trying to get certain scores?
19. Did this affect what you tried to do?
20. In sum, what would you say your goal was after you started getting feedback?
(X) Did any of the above change over time?
(Y) If there were scores on multiple-performance dimensions, repeat for each (or at least indicate which scores were more and which were less important).

FIGURE 8–3 Goal Setting Questions for Subjects Given Performance Feedback

Those who remain skeptical about whether feedback affects action through its effects on goal setting are asked to administer a goal questionnaire similar to the one outlined in Figure 8–3 to subjects during and after the administration of feedback. The questions can be elaborated and scaled so that they can be related quantitatively to degree of improvement shown in response to feedback. The authors predict that these items, in some combination, will significantly mediate the relationship between feedback and performance (assuming there is reasonable variation between subjects).

Now consider the second major question, Does feedback moderate the effect of goals on performance?

FEEDBACK AS A MODERATOR OF GOAL SETTING

The studies by Locke and others reviewed earlier did not answer the question of whether feedback moderates goal setting effects because all the subjects with goals, even those in the no-KR conditions, had other feedback signaling them as to whether they were progressing in line with the pace required to attain their goals. In the Locke and Bryan (1969a) study, the signals were in the form of colored lights. The Locke (1968a) study also used signal lights for some subjects. In the Locke (1967b) study, subjects with specific goals could observe their progress by seeing how many 3×5 problem cards with addition problems on them remained to be done before reaching a colored vertical marker. To determine whether goal setting works in the absence of feedback, subjects with goals would need to be deprived of *any* knowledge of how they were doing.

Erez (1977) was the first investigator to fully separate goal setting and feedback and show the moderator effect statistically. Using a number comparison task, she gave half her subjects knowledge of their actual scores in one work period before setting goals for a second work period. The other half set goals in the absence of such feedback. In the second work period, there was a significant goal-performance relationship only for the subjects with KR.

Some years earlier, studies with less complete separation had also supported the role of feedback as a moderator. Kolb, Winter, and Berlew (1968) had t-group participants choose personal change goals at the beginning of a five-week and a ten-week study. In both experiments, subjects who had more feedback from the group showed greater change toward their goals than those who had less feedback. In a case study, Feeney (At Emery Air Freight, 1973) reported that the benefits of performance standards given to air freight employees for customer callbacks and container use disappeared when feedback was not provided. No data were present to verify this conclusion, however.

Frost and Mahoney (1976) used a reading task (picking out a wrong word) and a jigsaw puzzle task to test the effects of various types of goals and feedback frequency on performance. On the reading task, subjects with high and moderately high goals performed far better when they had feedback (tied to seven subgoals, one every seven minutes of a forty-two-minute work period) than when they had only a forty-two-minute goal with no feedback during performance. Examination of their Table 1 indicates that goal difficulty was only related to performance for subjects with feedback (though the significance of this effect was not tested). This same effect did not come out in the jigsaw puzzle task; however, in that task feedback was probably built in, since subjects could see how many pieces they had completed.

Kim and Hamner (1976) conducted a complex study of telephone service workers that supported the role of feedback. On two of four performance measures (cost and safety), workers only given goals performed more poorly than workers given goals plus various types of feedback. Only the goal-without-feedback groups failed to reach their cost and safety goals. Inexplicably, this pattern of results was exactly reversed for the service measure. The goal-only group showed the best average performance, although one of the goal-plus-feedback groups showed the highest improvement during the course of the study. There was no treatment effect on a fourth measure, absenteeism, because the base rate was extremely low.

Komaki et al. (1978) found that when feedback in the form of direct observations of safety behaviors was posted on a chart along with a line indicating the goal, safety performance improved dramatically. When the feedback was interrupted during a reversal phase, performance reverted to baseline levels even though the workers were supposed to be trying for the goal.

In a well-designed study of energy (electricity) conservation, Becker (1978) used a 2 × 2 design with high vs. low goals and feedback vs. no feedback plus a control group. Families without feedback could not easily know how much electricity they were using, whereas this information was provided to the KR groups in quantitative form three times per week. Only the families with hard goals plus feedback conserved more electricity than the control group. They also outperformed all the other groups which did not differ from each other. Hard goals without feedback, therefore, did not improve performance.

Strang, Lawrence, and Fowler (1978) obtained the same basic results as Becker in a laboratory setting using an arithmetic task. The subjects with high goals plus feedback outperformed all the others; the remaining groups did not differ among themselves. Furthermore, the hard goal group with KR was the only group not to increase its error rate over the baseline rate.

An exception to the above pattern is a study by Strang (1981) in which one group of subjects set difficult goals on a reaction time task while another group tried to do their best. Even though neither group received KR and the hard goal group failed to correctly estimate their actual performance, the hard goal group significantly outperformed the do-best group. Possibly on simple tasks there is a proactive, energizing effect of goals that does not require accurate tracking of performance to yield some beneficial effect.

Bandura (1988) has noted that goals can have an anticipatory, feedforward effect by energizing action at the beginning (e.g., on the first trial) of a task or work period. Such an effect was found by Bandura and Cervone (1983) in the first period of their experiment. Thus goals can sometimes influence action before any formal feedback is provided. Subsequent feedback allows people to adjust their efforts in accordance with new information.

It should be emphasized that just as one should not assume that no goal setting has taken place when feedback is provided and goals are not assigned, one should not assume that feedback is unavailable when goals are assigned and no formal feedback is provided. Subjects can use many cues to get an idea of how well they are doing on a task. For example, they can see how many spaces they completed on their answer sheets or how many problem sheets they completed; they can sometimes keep track of progress in their head. They can even use internal cues such as how fast they feel they are working or how much effort they are exerting. Internal cues are often quite inaccurate, as in the Strang (1981) study, but may still play a role at the initial stage of goal-directed activity. For example, individuals just assigned a hard goal may say to themselves, in effect, "I am going to try really hard since the goal is very hard" and initially use internal cues to make sure effort is being exerted. Such cues, however, would probably not yield very accurate information about progress in relation to the goal after ten to twenty minutes' work. At this point external feedback would be needed to ensure goal attainment.

One issue that needs more research concerns when feedback should be given. In Erez's study, the feedback was given to the KR subjects before choosing their goals. Presumably this ensured that the goals were tied to their actual capabilities. In the other studies, however, the goals were assigned and feedback was provided during performance so that individuals could regulate their effort as required by the goal. Ideally it seems preferable to supply KR both before performance (here is how you did on the practice or warm-up trials) and during performance such as between trials (here is how you are doing thus far). The fact that feedback can play an important role both before goals are set and after goal-related effort has taken place is more evidence of the futility of viewing feedback only as a consequent.

In summary, when KR is withheld from individuals with goals, goal setting seems to have little effect on performance. If it is the case, then, that feedback without goal setting is ineffective, and goal setting without feedback is ineffective, then it follows that the combination of goal setting plus feedback should be more effective than either one of these alone. The evidence relevant to this deduction is given next.

GOALS AND FEEDBACK TOGETHER
VS. EITHER ONE ALONE

There have been at least 33 studies comparing the effectiveness of goals plus feedback with either goals alone or feedback alone. These are summarized in Figure 8–4 (some of these have already been discussed). Seventeen out of 18 studies found the combination of goals and feedback to be better than goals alone, and 21 out of 22 studies (counting two studies with contingent results each as half-successful) found it to be better than feedback alone. (Seven of the above studies compared the combination with both goals alone and feedback alone.)

FIGURE 8–4   Comparison of Goals and Feedback Combined vs. Either Alone

	Goals Plus KR Together vs:		TIME SERIES DESIGN		Reversals	
	Goals only	Feedback/ KR only	Goal 1st	Feedback 1st	Goal Removed	Feedback Removed
Anderson et al. (1988)		X		X		
At Emery Air Freight (1973)	X					X
Bandura & Cervone (1983)	X	X				
Bandura & Simon (1977)		X				
Baron & Watters (1981)		X				
Becker (1978)	X					
Chhokar & Wallin (1984)	X		X			X
Das (1982a)	X	X				
Dockstader (1977)		X				
Erez (1977)[a]	X	X				
Fellner & Sulzer-Azaroff (1985)[b]		X(=)		X		

FIGURE 8–4 (cont.)

| | Goals Plus KR Together vs: | | TIME SERIES DESIGN | | | |
| | | | | | Reversals | |
	Goals only	Feedback/ KR only	Goal 1st	Feedback 1st	Goal Removed	Feedback Removed
Frost & Mahoney (1976)[c]	X					
Ilgen & Moore (1982)	X	X				
Ivancevich & McMahon (1982)		X				
Kazdin (1974)[d]	X	X				
Kim & Hamner (1976)[e]	X					
Komaki et al. (1978)	X					X
Latham et al. (1978)		X				
Locke (1966a)		X				
Locke (1968a)[f]		X				
Locke & Bryan (1966b)[g]	X					
Locke & Bryan (1969b)		X				
McCarthy (1978)	X					X
Morgan (1984)		X				
Nemeroff & Cosentino (1979)		X				
Pritchard et al. (1988)		X		X		
Ralis & O'Brien (1986)	X		X			
Reber & Wallin (1984)	X		X			
Sagotsky, Patterson, & Lepper (1978)[h]	X	X(=)				
Sloat et al. (1977)		X		X		
Stevenson et al. (1984)[i]	=	X				
Strang et al. (1978)	X					
Warner & Mills (1980)		X		X	X	

[a]In a simultaneous regression analysis, Erez found that only the goal-feedback interaction term accounted for a significant portion of the variance.

[b]Significant only for assigned goals for some groups.

[c]Their Table 1 shows that the high (feedback) Ss with goals performed better than the low (no feedback) Ss with goals (no statistical test done).

[d]Main effects for goals and feedback were found, even though the goal–KR means were highest. It is doubtful if the goal and KR factors were fully separated.

[e]This finding held for two of four measures.

[f]All KR–goal groups were better than the no-KR group.

[g]Though it was not tested in the article, the goal groups with KR performed better than the same goal groups without KR (Table 1).

[h]Combined group had highest mean, though all relevant statistical comparisons were not made and combined-feedback-only difference was not significant.

[i]A condition with goals only performed as well as the groups with goals plus feedback; however, the subjects could get some feedback by estimating the passage of time in their heads.

Twenty-two of the studies used standard (non-time series) experimental designs. Twelve of these we have not discussed previously in this chapter or, in one case, not from the same viewpoint.

Bandura and Cervone (1983) compared a goal plus feedback condition with goals alone, feedback alone, and no goals or feedback using an ergometer task. They found the combined condition to be better than the other three, which did not differ among themselves.

In a weight loss study, Baron and Watters (1981) found that monitoring plus setting goals for caloric intake worked better than monitoring alone. In another study of the same phenomenon, Bandura and Simon (1977) found that dieters with proximal goals and feedback lost more weight than those who only monitored their weight. The latter did not do much spontaneous goal setting. Das (1982a) compared seven combinations of feedback regarding (quantity and quality), goals, and incentives. Basically, conditions that combined goals and feedback led to higher output on a hole-drilling task than either one alone. Dockstader (1977) found that key punchers given feedback alone did not improve their work rate, but those given both goals and feedback showed significant improvement.

Ilgen and Moore (1982) used a 2 × 2 design with KR and no-KR and easy vs. hard goals on a proofreading task. The goals were set in terms of time to complete the task. KR subjects were given information on both errors and amount of time that had passed. A standard ANOVA showed two main effects on completion time and no interaction, but both main effects were solely due to the superiority of the hard goal–KR cell to the other three which differed little from each other.

One confusion that has surrounded the testing of the goal-feedback interaction is what test to use. The interaction hypothesis clearly predicts that the specific, hard goal KR cell will show higher performance than the other three. Thus a conventional ANOVA test is inappropriate, since it will typically reveal two main effects and no interaction (as in the Ilgen and Moore, 1982, study). The proper test to use here is the Bobko (1986) ordinal interaction test, which involves a t-test between the goal KR cell and the other three combined, followed by a 1 × 3 ANOVA among the other three cells. Only the first test should be significant.

Ivancevich and McMahon (1982) found that goal setting and self-feedback (which appeared to be more frequent than feedback given to their other experimental groups) led to better performance by engineers on several objective performance measures than feedback without goals. Kazdin (1974) had subjects construct sentences starting with various pronouns, with "I" and "We" sentences being the target pronouns. In experiments 2 and 3, the monitoring of the number of sentences (feedback) and goal setting were manipulated separately. Independent effects for both goals and feedback were found in each case, but the largest effect was obtained for the combination of the two. It was not determined whether goal subjects counted sentences on their own or whether the monitoring subjects set goals; both could easily have occurred.

Latham, Mitchell, and Dossett (1978) found that engineers and scientists with assigned or participatively set goals on a Behavioral Observation Scale (BOS) got better appraisal scores than subjects told to do their best but who had the same feedback on the BOS as those with goals.

In the study by Locke and Bryan (1966b) described earlier using a complex computation task, their Table 1 showed that the subjects with goals and KR performed at a higher level than subjects who reported having the same goals but had no KR. These differences were not tested statistically.

Sagotsky, Patterson, and Lepper (1978), in a somewhat questionable study, examined the effects of monitoring study behavior and having fifth and sixth graders estimate the number of math problems they could solve. The KR was therefore not matched to the goals, and the goal treatment was very weak. The design was a 2 × 2, monitoring vs. none, goal setting vs. none. The most relevant criterion used, number of problems correctly completed, was highest for the combined goal and monitoring condition and substantially lower for the other three cells, which probably did not differ significantly from each other.

Stevenson, Kanfer, and Higgins (1984) studied pain tolerance when immersing a hand in cold water. The six conditions were goal only (expressed only in terms of immersion time), goal plus "time left" KR, goals plus "time elapsed" KR, time left KR only, time elapsed KR only, and no goal or KR. Overall the first three groups outperformed the last three in tolerance. The only anomaly is that the first group which had a goal and no KR performed as well as the KR plus goal groups. However, since subjects can estimate elapsed time with some degree of accuracy on their own, this was probably not a true goal–no-KR condition.

Excluded from Figure 8–4 is a study of goals and feedback by Schuldt and Bonge (1979). This is because their feedback-only condition seems to have involved goals. Subjects with self-set goals plus feedback performed better on a wheel-turning task than those in the feedback-only condition, but those with assigned goals did not.

There were 11 time series designs in which either feedback or goal setting was introduced after a baseline period. The other element was added later, or both were introduced together and one element was subtracted. Some designs both added and subtracted elements. Anderson, Crowell, Doman, and Howard (1988) used feedback charts to record body checks for a college hockey team. Later the team captain assigned goals to each team member. In each of two years, the addition of each element not only increased overall body checking but led to a greater number of games won. Feeney (At Emery Air Freight, 1973), as noted earlier, introduced both goals and feedback together for tasks involving customer callbacks and container use but noted that performance dropped off markedly when the feedback was stopped.

Chhokar and Wallin (1984) used a six-stage time series design for machine shop workers: baseline, training plus goal setting, weekly feedback added, monthly feedback added, training and goal setting only, and bimonthly feedback added. Training and goal setting led to improved performance. Introducing feedback led to a further improvement, removing it led to lower performance, and introducing it once again led to higher performance.

Fellner and Sulzer-Azaroff (1985) introduced feedback on safe behaviors to foremen and workers in a paper mill and then added goal setting. Goal setting improved performance in some units if goals were assigned, but not if they were set by the workers. The safety study by Komaki et al. (1978) was discussed above and involved introducing goals and feedback together and then removing the feedback which led to a return to baseline performance. McCarthy (1978) used a time series design to reduce the number of "high bobbins" in a textile mill (bobbins are spindles of thread which, if not pushed down far enough, cause tangles). Introducing goals of increasing difficulty plus feedback led to a steady decrease in the number of high bobbins. When feedback was removed, the number of high bobbins increased and then decreased again when feedback was reintroduced.

Pritchard et al. (1988) developed elaborate performance measures for Air Force personnel and presented unit scores on feedback charts. Later, goal setting was added. Both interventions, especially feedback that also involved competition between work units, increased performance. Reber and Wallin (1984) studied safety behaviors among farm machine manufacturing workerss. The intervention sequence was: baseline, training, training plus goal setting, and the addition of feedback. Each stage led to better performance than the previous one. Ralis and O'Brien (1986) introduced goal setting for waiters and waitresses pertaining to suggestions that the customer order red or white wine. Subsequently, feedback charts were added. Both interventions led to increased suggestions to customers and an increase in wine sales.

Sloat, Tharp, and Gallimore (1977) trained teachers to use praise with their students using the following sequence: training, modeling, video feedback, coaching, graphed feedback, and graphed feedback plus goals. Only the last stage and modeling worked for all five teachers. Graphed feedback alone added nothing to the prior stages.

Finally, Warner and Mills (1980) used the following four-stage design with retarded adolescents who were assembling flashlights and other objects: baseline, feedback, feedback plus goals, then feedback alone. The combined condition led to better performance than either of the feedback-only conditions.

These results are remarkably consistent in view of the many potential flaws in these time series studies. For example, learning effects could lead to false conclusions about the effects of the interventions if there were no reversal phase, since treatment effects could be confounded with learning effects. However, in most cases the baseline performance had been fairly stable, thus making it unlikely that substantial learning was taking place. Furthermore, the results of these studies are in full agreement with those that did not use time series designs. More serious, however, is the very strong probability that the feedback interventions actually involved formal feedback plus informal (spontaneous) goal setting, and that the goal setting interventions involved formal goal setting plus informal (self-generated) feedback.

It is not at all unreasonable to assume that there was a spontaneous goal setting when formal feedback was introduced. As noted earlier, feedback is typically introduced as relating to something very important. New measures are developed, workers are directly observed by experimenters, charts are posted for all to see, and special meetings are held. The unmistakable message of such interventions must be, Here is something on which you should improve! Under these conditions it would be highly unlikely that the subjects would fail to set, in some form, goals to improve their scores.

We can also assume that there was informal feedback when goal setting was introduced, because when people are given goals, they naturally want to know how they are doing in relation to the goals, and if they are committed to the goals, they try to track their progress in relation to them. In view of all this potential confounding, the consistency of the results is indeed striking.

On the average, the feedback "only" stage, especially when it was introduced first, led to a greater percentage improvement than did goal setting when it was added later (e.g., see Pritchard et al., 1988, Fellner & Sulzer-Azaroff, 1985). This does not mean, however, that feedback is the more powerful force. As we have seen, neither is really effective without the other. There are four further factors to consider about the feedback-goal designs. First, as just noted, it is almost certain that the subjects given feedback were setting goals. (Pritchard et al., 1988, p. 353, openly acknowledged this in their study.) Second, since the feedback plus spontaneous goal setting phase was quite successful, a ceiling effect could easily make further improvements more difficult, as several of the authors themselves mention. Third, there is a certain asymmetry between goals and feedback in that anyone who has feedback can set goals and track progress accordingly; but anyone who has goals does not necessarily have enough information to judge performance in relation to goals accurately. Fourth, feedback in a number of the studies was accompanied or followed by praise, which adds another confounding element to the equation.

The overall results of our analysis are in agreement with a separate but probably overlapping view of the literature by Balcazar, Hopkins, and Suarez (1986). They found that the results of feedback plus goal studies were much more consistently positive than those of feedback-only studies. (These authors did not list the studies used in each calculation.)

The most useful way to conceive of the relation between goals and feedback is as follows: Feedback tells people what is; goals tell them what is desirable. Feedback involves information; goals involve evaluation. Goals inform individuals as to what type or level of performance is to be attained so that they can direct and evaluate their actions and efforts accordingly. Feedback allows them to set reasonable goals and to track their performance in relation to their goals, so that adjustments in effort, direction, and even strategy can be made as needed. Goals and feedback can be considered a paradigm case of the joint effect of motivation and cognition controlling action.

To correct an old but not quite accurate aphorism: What gets measured *in relation to goals* gets done.

MECHANICS OF THE GOAL-FEEDBACK INTERACTION

We have established that goals and feedback work most effectively together to improve performance, but we have yet to show precisely how this occurs. Research by Matsui, Bandura, and others has provided valuable insights into this process.

Matsui, Okada, and Inoshita (1983) conducted two experiments using a simple addition task. In the first experiment, all subjects were given the same specific, challenging goal and were then interrupted after working for five of the ten-minute total work period and given feedback regarding their progress to that point. The subjects were then divided, for purposes of analysis, into a low progress group consisting of that half of the sample showing the lowest performance in relation to the pace needed to reach the goal (i.e., basically the lower-ability half) and the high progress group consisting of that half of the sample showing the highest performance in relation to the assigned goal (basically the higher-ability half). During the second five-minute work period, only the low progress group significantly improved their performance. This group also had a lower expectancy of reaching the goal and greater dissatisfaction with performance than did the high progress group.

This finding was replicated in their second experiment using the same task. In this study, a control group was added which was given goals but no feedback at the end of the first five-minute work period. The results are shown in Figure 8–5. (The ordinates have been superimposed to control for ability differences between the high and low progress groups.) Only the goal-feedback group subjects who were making low progress toward the goal improved during the second five-minute work period. This improvement was mediated by the degree to which they intended to work fast in the second period; statistically controlling for intent to work fast vitiated the improvement.

The finding that low progress subjects increased their efforts in the second work period more than high progress subjects was also observed by Matsui, Okada, and Kakuyama (1982). Second-half improvement was also associated with high achievement motivation (using a self-report measure developed by Steers). These results were also partially replicated in an unpublished study by Matsui, Okada, and Kakuyama (1983) using a perceptual speed task. In this study the

FIGURE 8–5   Improvement of High and Low Progress Groups
Based on Matsui, Okada, & Inoshita, 1983.

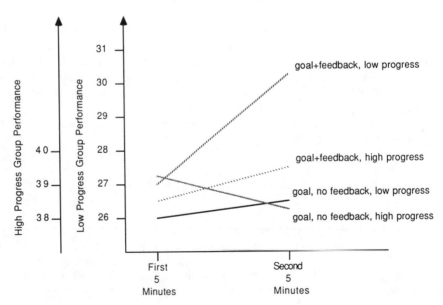

subjects were divided into *three* equal subgroups: high, medium, and low progress. In this case, only the subjects in the medium progress group improved in the second work period, and only if they were high in achievement motivation (using Steers's measure again). The expectancy ratings of the low progress group (the lowest one-third of the subjects) were the lowest of any group and perhaps too low to spur them to greater effort.

Podsakoff and Farh (1989) further replicated the Matsui et al. findings using a different task (object listing) and a slightly different procedure. After seven trials, subjects were told either that they had performed well, and above the level of a normative group, or that they had performed poorly, and below the level of a normative group. They then worked on the task for another seven trials. Subjects given negative feedback set harder personal goals and improved more than did subjects given positive feedback.

The above studies show that *degree and direction of discrepancy from the initial goal*, mediated by subsequent personal goals or intentions, affect the response to feedback given in relation to initial goals. However, this is not the whole story. Dissatisfaction and self-efficacy also play a role. Matsui, Okada, and Inoshita (1983) and Podsakoff and Farh (1989) also found that low progress or negative feedback subjects were more dissatisfied with their initial task performance than high progress or positive feedback subjects. These results were consistent with the results of five studies conducted by Locke, Cartledge, and Knerr (1970). They found that feedback indicative of a large goal-performance discrepancy produced high performance dissatisfaction and led the individual to set goals to make major changes in performance. Feedback indicating low goal-performance discrepancies led to performance satisfaction and goals to maintain the present level of performance. Future goals were based on anticipated as well as past satisfaction with various levels of performance.

In addition, Matsui, Okada, and Kakuyama (1983) implied, and Podsakoff and Farh (1989) actually found, that expectancy or self-efficacy affected the individual's response to goal-relevant feedback. In Matsui, Okada, and Kakuyama's (1983) study the lowest progress group, the group with the lowest expectancy of reaching the goal, did not improve. In Podsakoff's study the subjects with higher self-efficacy (regardless of other factors) showed greater improvement than subjects with lower self-efficacy.

The self-efficacy variable was first brought into the feedback picture by Bandura and Cervone (1983), who used, as noted earlier, an ergometer task in a 2 × 2 goal-feedback design. Within their goal plus feedback condition, performance improvement was positively associated with degree of self-efficacy and with degree of dissatisfaction with past performance, and even more strongly with anticipated dissatisfaction with future (low) performance. The subgroups showing the greatest performance improvement were those consisting of subjects with high dissatisfaction and high self-efficacy. Various other combinations showed proportionately lower performance.

In a follow-up experiment with a more complex design, Bandura and Cervone (1986) again used the ergometer task. Four artificial levels of goal-performance discrepancy were created through false feedback: large negative, moderately negative, small negative, and small positive. Subsequently, self-set goals, satisfaction, and self-efficacy were all measured. Performance (effort expenditure) was positively and significantly correlated with self-set goals within all four groups, with self-efficacy within three of the four groups, and with dissatisfaction within two of the four groups. Self-efficacy and dissatisfaction were significantly associated with goal choice within three and two of the groups, respectively. Regression analyses showed significant goal effects on performance in three of four cases. In the fourth case, high covariation among the variables reduced the highly significant first-order goal effect. In addition the regression analyses showed significant self-efficacy effects on performance in all four groups, and dissatisfaction effects in two groups. Thus, while the relative weights of the various mediating variables were somewhat different within each of the original discrepancy groups, the combination of dissatisfaction, high self-efficacy, and high goals had a very marked effect on motivation and performance.

Figure 8–6 shows the results of this study for subjects divided into three groups: (1) low self-efficacy, low goals, and high anticipated satisfaction for performing at the same level on the next trial; (2) mixed combinations of the three

**FIGURE 8–6   The Joint Effects on Performance Improvement
of Self-Efficacy, Goals, and Anticipated Satisfaction**
From Bandura & Cervone, 1986; data supplied by Bandura.

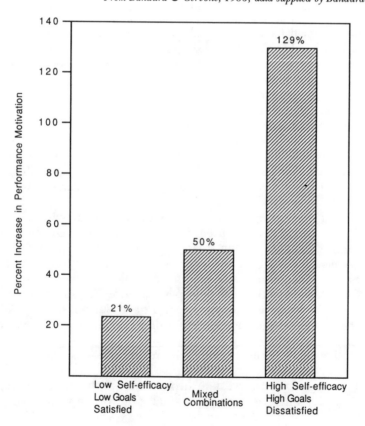

variables; and (3) high self-efficacy, high goals, and low anticipated satisfaction for performing at the same level on the next trial. The differences in subsequent improvement among the three groups are striking. The group with high self-efficacy and goals plus low satisfaction showed a mean improvement of 129%, whereas the group with low self-efficacy and goals plus high satisfaction showed an increase of only 21%, with the mixed combination group showing an intermediate effect. (These results did not appear in Bandura & Cervone, 1986, but were supplied to the authors by Bandura.)

The overall picture of what we have found thus far with respect to goals and feedback is shown in Figure 8–7 (which elaborates on certain segments of Figure 8–1). Goals are shown to have an initial proactive effect on performance. Once feedback has been provided, however, then performance depends on the appraisal and decision sequence that follows. If there is a low goal-performance discrepancy, the individual will usually be satisfied and will maintain the same level of performance providing he or she does not change goals. Goals may, of course, be raised after success (see Chapter 5), because attaining previously mastered levels of performance becomes less satisfying.

If there is a high goal-performance discrepancy, but the individual is not dissatisfied or will not be dissatisfied with the same performance in the future (e.g., due to viewing the goals as unimportant), performance will again tend to stay the same. If the individual is dissatisfied with the past and anticipates dissatisfaction if future performance is at the same level, the results will depend on further appraisals. If the person has high self-efficacy and sets high goals (with the former influencing the latter), this will lead to substantial motivation and performance increases (assuming ability and opportunity). If the individual has low self-efficacy and sets low goals, performance will not improve much and may even decline.

The foregoing model illustrates the inadequacy of both behaviorist theory and control theory (see Chapter 1) in accounting for the way in which goals and feedback interact to regulate performance. The sequence is not a mechanical one. Rather it involves numerous, complex cognitive processes. *Such processes, as the studies have shown, are both measurable and lawfully related to task performance. They are the means by which feedback effects can be understood.*

Figure 8–7 shows clearly that goal setting is not the only mediator of feedback effects. Actually, all the factors noted in Figures 8–1 and 8–7 are mediators of feedback. The evidence in this chapter, however, indicates that goal setting, along with self-efficacy and dissatisfaction, is an important mediator. With one partial exception, goal setting appears to reflect the cognitive processing done at the earlier stages. The partial exception is self-efficacy. Feedback could have an independent motivational effect through its effect on self-efficacy. Self-efficacy can affect performance in several ways. In Chapter 3 we saw that it can affect performance directly. Chapters 3 and 5 showed that it can affect goal choice and Chapter 6 that it can affect goal commitment. Feedback may also lead people to infer that performance will be followed by rewards or punishments. It remains to be seen, however, whether incentives or the anticipation of rewards or punishment can affect performance independently of goals. It was noted in Chapter 6 that several studies suggest that incentives can have independent effects on performance (Latham, Mitchell, & Dossett, 1978; Pritchard & Curtis, 1973;

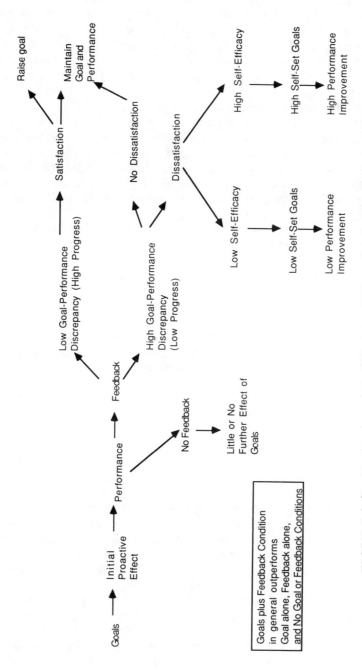

FIGURE 8–7   Mechanics of Performance Effects for Subjects Given Both Goals and Feedback

Riedel, Nebeker, & Cooper, 1988), but possible methodological weaknesses of those studies make any firm conclusion premature.

As noted earlier, feedback can have strictly cognitive effects on performance. Feedback can reveal to people what they are doing wrong (e.g., you misspelled "psychology") or can indicate that certain task strategies are not working and need to be changed.

The model in Figure 8–7 of course is not complete. To prevent clutter, neither ability nor situational constraints are included. Furthermore, other variables belong in the model. One of the most important of these is the *credibility* or degree of *trust* in the feedback. Podsakoff and Farh (1989) found that the effect of negative feedback was enhanced if the feedback had high rather than low credibility. Earley (1986c) found that U.S. tire workers were more likely to accept goals assigned by a supervisor in the United States and by a shop steward in England. Trust can be inferred as a moderator variable here. Earley (1986d) found that a direct measure of trust (and a measure of the importance of the feedback) moderated the effect of feedback on performance in two studies, although measures of goal setting were not included. In a study of subscription processing, Earley (1988) found that employees who got their own goal-relevant performance feedback from the computer trusted the information more and performed better than employees who got such feedback from their supervisors. This study replicated the findings of a nearly identical, earlier study (Earley, 1986a). Ivancevich and McMahon (1982) found that engineers performed best when goal setting was accompanied by self-feedback, although feedback sources could have been confounded with feedback frequency. Bartlem and Locke (1981) even suggested that trust (in addition to other, not widely recognized, factors) might have played a major role in the initial rejection of company goals and standards by workers in the famous Coch and French (1948) study.

Earley (1986a, 1988) found that degree of *specificity* of feedback affected performance either directly or through its effects on planning. Specific feedback clearly provides more information about how one is doing than vague or general feedback, and it thus allows one to better regulate one's effort level. It also may be more useful in providing individuals with information about the correctness of the direction of activity, including the task strategies they are using. Specific feedback does not, of course, guarantee that the best strategies will be chosen, but it does provide the individual with better information on which to base task strategies. Feedback *specificity* was found to facilitate performance directly or indirectly by Carroll and Tosi (1973) and Pritchard, Montagno, and Moore (1978). They also found that *delayed* was better than immediate feedback and *impersonal* (factual) feedback better than personal (more evaluative) feedback.

Another factor of possible importance with respect to feedback is the *type* or *types of feedback* that are given. Ilgen and Moore (1987) used a computerized proofreading task in which all subjects had the same goal, involving both quantity and quality. The goal was to be achieved within a fixed time limit. Those provided with both time and quality feedback performed better and faster than those provided with one or the other or neither. Time feedback alone led to the fastest completion time; quality feedback alone led to the most learning. These results suggest clearly that feedback will be most effective when it matches the performance dimensions for which goals are set. In a unique study, Earley, Northcraft, Lee, and Lituchy (in press) gave subjects performing a simulated stock investment task varying degrees of both process and outcome feedback. The outcome feedback pertained to knowledge of overall performance of the type used in the other experiments reviewed in this chapter. The process feedback included mainly information as to the practical usefulness (to the subjects) of the information (which they were allowed to query from a data base) about the past success of five brokerage houses in buying and selling each of five stocks. Such information obviously would help the subjects in developing correct investment strategies. The highest level of investment performance was achieved by subjects with specific, hard goals, specific outcome feedback, and specific process feedback. Subjects in this condition were most likely to search for useful (as opposed to useless) information and to develop correct strategies. More studies that provide the subjects with different types of feedback are clearly warranted.

Feedback *frequency* has rarely been studied as a separate variable in goal setting research, since it is typically given after each trial. Frost and Mahoney (1976) found frequent feedback to be better than infrequent feedback on one of their tasks. But infrequent in this case meant no feedback until the work period was over. Feedback in general was found to be beneficial along with goal setting in correlational studies by Anderson and O'Reilly (1981) and Steers (1975).

A thorough discussion of the consequences of feedback that summarizes much of the literature through the late 1970s can be found in Ilgen, Fisher, and Taylor (1979). Clearly there are many dimensions of feedback yet to be studied.

FEEDBACK AND NONSPECIFIC GOALS

This chapter has focused on the relationship between specific goals, specific feedback, and performance. Neither we nor previous researchers have addressed the issue of what happens when one gets specific feedback in relation to vague or general goals, or when one gets vague or general feedback in relation to specific goals. In the first case, it is our stong impression that giving subjects specific feedback when they have general goals, such as do your best, encourages them to set specific goals as a way of making explicit what it means to do their best, and because the challenge of improvement is exciting. Once this occurs, our previous analysis applies.

In the second case, a person who gets vague feedback while working toward a specific goal will probably first attempt to make the feedback more explicit. For example, a manager who has a goal of increasing sales by 15% and received a computer printout from the information systems department saying "sales are doing well" would undoubtedly demand to know just what "well" means. If the feedback were quantified, again the previous analysis applies. We might hypothesize that if the feedback remained vague, the individual would be likely to maintain his or her existing performance level if the sign of the feedback were positive and would try to change it if the sign were negative. In actuality, however, performance might be highly variable, since people would really not know exactly how well they were doing.

In everyday life we often have both vague goals and vague feedback. For example, Ms. X may have as a goal to "make a good impression" on her boss, and the boss may tell her that she is "doing fine" or "doing OK." This would encourage her to conclude that she was on the right track, but it would also leave open numerous possible future actions that might seem to her to be equally consistent with her goal and feedback.

People with vague goals can, of course, choose to make them specific; if they do not choose to do this, we would predict that such people would accomplish very little as compared with people with specific goals, assuming of course that such goals were reasonably challenging.

CONCLUSION

The relationships between goals and commitment and goals and feedback are relatively well understood. In the next chapter we discuss some additional moderators that have been less systematically researched or are less fully understood, namely, task complexity, ability, situational constraints, personality, and demographic factors.

CHAPTER

9

OTHER MODERATORS:
Ability, Demographic Variables, Personality, Task Complexity, and Situational Constraints

In this chapter, studies are examined with regard to the moderating effects of ability, demographic variables, personality, task complexity, and situational constraints on goals.

ABILITY

It is axiomatic that people cannot perform in accordance with their goals if they do not have the ability to reach them. Locke (1982b) found that when subjects were assigned goals across a wide range of difficulty levels, including levels far beyond their capacity, the relation of goal level to performance level was curvilinear (see Figure 9–1), with performance leveling off at the higher goal levels. Similar relationships have been reported by Bavelas and Lee (1978) and Locke, Frederick, Buckner, and Bobko (1984). In Locke (1982b), for example, the relationship between goal level and performance level was .82 (p <.001) for goals within the easy to very difficult range, and .11 (ns) for goals within the impossible range. Similar findings were obtained by Locke, Frederick, Buckner, and Bobko (1984).

The opposite pattern occurred for the ability-performance relationship. In Locke's (1982b) study, ability and performance were correlated .13 (ns) for goals within the easy to difficult range, and .55 (p <.001) for goals within the difficult to impossible range. The former relationship was low because individ-

Portions of this chapter have been taken from R. E. Wood, A. J. Mento, and E. A. Locke (1987), "Task Complexity as a Moderator of Goal Effects: A Meta-Analysis," *Journal of Applied Psychology*, 72, 416–25; and E. A. Locke, K. M. Shaw, L. M. Saari, and G. P. Latham (1981), "Goal Setting and Task Performance: 1969–1980," *Psychological Bulletin*, 90, 125–52. Copyright 1987 by the American Psychological Association. Reprinted by permission of the publisher.

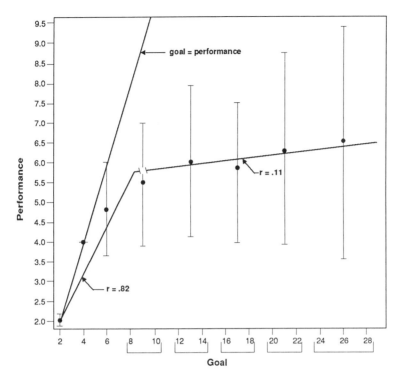

FIGURE 9-1 **Performance and Standard Deviation of Performance as a Function of Goal Level. (Vertical lines mark one standard deviation above and below the mean.)**
Reprinted from Locke (1982b) by permission of the American Psychological Association.

uals were told to stop working when they attained their goals; thus people with easy goals could not work in accordance with their ability. No such constraints, however, limited those with hard or impossible goals. Again, Locke, Frederick, Buckner, and Bobko (1984) replicated this finding. Thus, in sum, goals and ability are moderators of each other. Locke, Mento, and Katcher (1978) found that ability-performance correlations were higher for subjects with hard and moderate goals than for those with easy goals. The correlation was still substantial for easy goal subjects, however, because they were *not* told to stop when they reached their goals.

Having subjects stop working when they attain their goals has often been described as an artifact in the literature. This description is misleading. If subjects who are asked to try to attain an easy goal upon reaching it choose to continue working, this no longer constitutes an easy goal setting condition. It is an easy-goal-plus condition (see Chapter 6). If the experimenter is interested in the effect of the goal that the person is assigned, then telling the person to stop when the goal is reached is justified.

While there is a strong goal-ability interaction when a wide range of goal levels is involved, there is weaker but still tenable evidence for such an interaction when the range of goal difficulty is restricted. Battle (1966) found that the combination of high self-set goals and high academic ability added a significant increment to performance over and above the additive effects of these two variables. Locke (1965b) looked for the same interaction effects using data from four goal setting studies. Only one interaction actually reached significance, but on the average, goal setting had a bigger effect on high than on low ability subjects, while ability had a greater effect on subjects with difficult goals than on those with easier goals. Nevertheless, significant ability effects occurred for subjects with low goals in those studies because subjects were not told to stop when they reached their goals.

All the above relationships are summarized in Figure 9–2. First, the general shape of both curves is curvilinear because performance levels off when goal difficulty exceeds the person's ability; thus the goal difficulty effect holds only for goals within the low to high range. Second, the effect of ability is greater at high and impossible than at low levels of goal difficulty, as shown by the increasing separation of the ability curves as difficulty increases. (This assumes that subjects with reachable goals stop working when they reach them.) Third, the goal difficulty effect is stronger for those with high ability than for those with low ability within the moderate to high goal range, as shown by the difference in the slope of the two ability curves in that range.

FIGURE 9–2   The Goal Difficulty-Ability Interaction

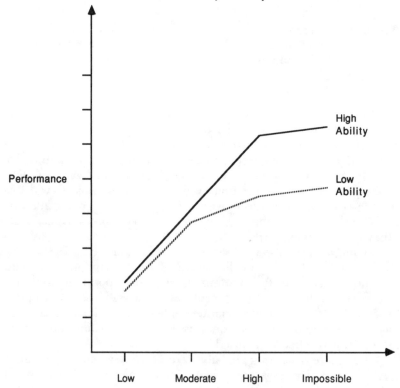

In possible contradiction to the third point above is the finding in two studies that subjects who were initially low performers improved more after goals had been assigned to them than did those with high ability. Crawford, White, and Magnusson (1983) found this in a study of engine overhaulers; Pritchard, Bigby, Beiting, Coverdale, and Morgan (1981) obtained the same results in a study of data processors. However, it is not clear whether the low performers were truly of low ability relative to the high performers or whether they were simply less motivated. Bryan and Locke (1967a) found that low-performing subjects can readily be motivated by challenging goals. Furthermore, in Crawford et al.'s (1983) study, the goals of the previously low-performing subjects were actually harder in relation to their prior performance than the goals of the high-performing subjects. Finally, subjects who are already performing at a high level, due presumably to high motivation and ability, may be limited in their ability to improve further because they are already close to their maximum performance (ceiling effect).

Another factor that affects the correlation between ability and performance is the degree of homogeneity in motivation with a given group. Locke et al. (1978) found that the more similar the subjects within a given group are with respect to goal specificity and/or goal difficulty, the stronger the relationship of ability to performance. Eliminating individual differences in motivation within a group has the effect of removing "random" error, i.e., error produced by within-group differences due to another causal factor.

Wood and Bandura (in press, a) have shown that one's conception of intellectual ability affects performance. In a management simulation exercise, those who viewed ability as an acquirable skill that could be enhanced through practice set challenging goals, which was followed by good problem-solving strategies and subsequent high performance. Those who viewed intellectual ability as a more or less fixed capacity regarded errors and mistakes as indicative that they indeed were not intelligent; thus they set low goals. Their problem solving deteriorated, as did their subsequent performance.

DEMOGRAPHIC VARIABLES

Of the few goal setting studies that have investigated demographic variables, most have dealt with the effects of education, race, and job tenure.

Education

In a study involving electronics technicians, Ivancevich and McMahon (1977c) found that perceived goal challenge was significantly related to performance only for educated technicians (twelve years or more of education). In contrast, perceived goal clarity and goal feedback were significantly related to performance only for less-educated technicians (fewer than twelve years of education).

Level of education did not moderate the effects of either participative or assigned goal setting in Latham and Yukl's field experiments involving loggers (Latham & Yukl, 1975b) and female typists (Latham & Yukl, 1976). Similarly, Steers (1975) found no moderating effect of education on goal setting in a study of 113 female supervisors.

Although Latham et al. (1978) did not examine education as a moderator variable, the study is cited here because of the education level of the subjects. Goal setting had a significant effect on the performance of engineers and scientists with master's and doctoral degrees.

In short, there is no consistent evidence for the effect of education as a moderator of goal setting, nor is there any convincing theoretical reason why there should be one. Goal setting appears to be effective for individuals of all educational levels, ranging from elementary school children (Masters et al., 1977) to loggers with a mean education of 7.2 years (Latham & Yukl, 1975b) to engineers and scientists (Latham et al., 1978) with advanced degrees (see Chapter 2).

Race

Latham and Yukl (1975b) found that educationally disadvantaged black loggers who participated in setting their goals were more productive and attained their goals more frequently than crews who were assigned goals by their supervisors or told to do their best. But goal difficulty was not held constant between the two conditions. Those in the participation condition set higher goals than those who had goals assigned to them.

Ivancevich and McMahon (1977b), in a study of technicians, supported these findings. Perceived participation in goal setting was related to several measures of performance for black technicians, but not for whites. Goal clarity and feedback were also related to performance for the blacks only, whereas goal challenge was related to performance for the whites only. Perhaps goal clarity, feedback, and participation affected the performance of blacks because, as Ivancevich and McMahon (1977b) stated:

> It has been found that blacks have a higher need for security in performing their jobs. . . . One way to derive more security in a goal setting program is to have goal clarity, receive feedback, and participate in the process (p. 298).

Additional studies are needed to verify this interpretation. If it is valid, then the racial factor would be reducible to a personality attribute that would undoubtedly cut across racial lines.

Job Tenure

At least seven studies have examined tenure as a moderator variable in the goal setting process. Three of them (Ivancevich & McMahon, 1977a; Latham & Yukl, 1976; Steers, 1975) found no moderating effect. Two studies conducted by Dachler and Mobley (1973) found no significant relation between stated goals and productivity for short-tenure employees (less than 1–2 years), but a significant relation between these measures for long-tenure employees (1–2 or more years). Their explanation for this difference was that longer tenure employees have more accurate perceptions of their chances of reaching various levels of performance and of performance-outcome contingencies. It is not clear, however, why it should take one or more years to obtain accurate perceptions. In their study of government employees, Latham and Marshall (1982) found no main or interaction effect for number of years in a supervisory position or time employed in the public sector. In short, the extant evidence shows little promise regarding job tenure as a moderator.

The only exception to the above pattern is the correlational field study by Earley, Lee, and Hanson (1989) which found a three-way interaction involving job tenure. Goal setting did not enhance the performance of employees who had complex jobs and little job experience but did enhance it for all other combinations. Our theory would suggest that the inexperienced employees with complex jobs had not yet developed appropriate task strategies and thus could not implement their goals.

Age

In the Ivancevich and McMahon (1977a) study of technicians, age was not related to goal setting or performance. The same was true in the study by Latham and Marshall (1982). To our knowledge, no other studies have investigated the moderating effects of age. However, as previously noted, goal setting has been shown to be effective for children (e.g., Masters et al., 1977; Rosswork, 1977) as well as adults.

Sex

An early series of experiments by Himmelweit (1947) showed that the behavior of women differed from that of men in three respects on a pursuit meter task. Women had (a) a lower average goal discrepancy score as defined by estimates of future performance, (b) a lower average judgment discrepancy score as defined by estimates of past performance, and (c) a higher index of flexibility as defined by responsiveness in setting goals to changes in performance. One four-minute experiment assessed whether subsequent performance would vary as a function of the experimenter's sex. The results showed that subjects who had assigned goals turned a wheel more when the experimenter was male rather than female. (Alexander, Schuldt, & Hansen, 1983). The practical significance of these findings is unclear. What is clear is that goal setting has been shown to significantly increase the performance of both males (e.g., Latham & Yukl, 1975b) and females (Latham & Yukl, 1976; Steers, 1975) using both assigned and participatively set goals. In the area of sports, however, Duda (1985) found that females were more oriented toward mastery goals than they were toward social comparison goals.

Cultural Values

In a work simulation conducted in Israel requiring the evaluation of job descriptions, Erez (1986) found that goal commitment was highest in the assigned and participative goal condition for supervisors who worked in the private sector; it was highest in the representative and group participation conditions for supervisors from the public sector. However, these conclusions are based on an overall F test. An *a posteriori* test was not conducted to test which differences were significant.

With regard to performance, no main effect was obtained. However, a significant interaction effect followed by an *a posteriori* test revealed that in the no participation (i.e., assigned goal) condition, performance scores of people from the private sector were significantly higher than those from the public sector and the kibbutz. In the representative participative condition, performance scores of the public sector were significantly higher than those of the private sector and the kibbutz. But in the group participation condition, the performance of the kibbutz members was not significantly higher than that of the other two sectors. No controls were implemented to ensure that goal difficulty and the supportiveness of the experimenter were held constant across conditions. Nonetheless, the significant interaction effect was interpreted by Erez as suggesting that effectiveness of group participation in goal setting over assigned goals is amplified among people with collectivistic-participative values.

In a second experiment, Erez and Early (1987) compared the goal commitment and performance of three groups of students. One group consisted of U.S. students at a midwestern university, a second came from a kibbutz system in Israel, and the third from a non-kibbutz urban area. The task involved scheduling classes. Again, a significant interaction was obtained. Participative and representative goal setting had stronger effects on performance for individuals low in power distance, as in Israel, than high in power distance, as in the United States. No significant interaction effect on goal commitment was obtained. In short, the method by which the goal was set had no effect on the performance of the American students; it did have an effect on the Israelis. There, the assigned goals were least effective. But the meaning of the significant interactions in both studies must be tempered by the fact that experimenter supportiveness was not held constant; furthermore, the authors used the "tell" rather than the "tell and sell" technique in assigning goals. Thus they increased the probability that commitment to the goal would be low in the assigned condition (see Chapter 7). Moreover, attempts were made to increase the self-efficacy of subjects in only the participative condition in order to increase their "willingness to set difficult goals" (p. 660). Thus no final conclusions on culture as a moderator can be reached until these other variables are controlled. As we noted in Chapter 7, these three variables, namely tell (i.e., abrupt, curt) instructions, self-efficacy enhancement, and supportiveness of the experimenter have been shown to have marked effects on commitment and/or performance (Latham, Erez & Locke, 1988).

In their four laboratory experiments designed to explain the discrepancies in results obtained in the Erez versus Latham studies, Latham, Erez, and Locke (1988) used a value-for-participation questionnaire developed by Erez. This questionnaire was used because of the hypothesis that collectivistic values, existing in many cultures, moderate the effects of the two goal setting methods.

The questionnaire was comprised of three independent scales. The first scale, which focused on preference for a "tell" vs. a "tell and sell" style, contained two items (e.g., "I prefer a manager who usually makes decisions promptly, communicates them to subordinates, and expects them to carry out the decisions loyally. . . ."). The alpha was .76.

The second scale, containing five items, focused on a preference for participation (e.g., "Employees should be extensively involved in the decisions made about their jobs"). The alpha was .64.

The third scale, containing three items, focused on authoritarianism (e.g., "Obedience and respect for authority are the most important virtues employees should have"). The alpha was .75. None of the scales correlated significantly with goal commitment or performance in any of the four experiments. Given these findings and the lack of experimental controls in the two studies conducted on culture, it is far from clear whether value for participation or the more molar concept, culture, is a moderator of goal setting effects.

Possibly a more promising approach is that of Earley (1986b), who measured how "comfortable" English and American workers were with participation and how "legitimate" they viewed it to be. These ratings were significantly related to degree of satisfaction with experienced participation.

PERSONALITY VARIABLES

Need and Value for Achievement

Steers (1975), in a study of female supervisors, found that performance was related to feedback and goal specificity only for high-need-achievement individuals. Participation in goal setting, on the other hand, was related to performance only among low-need-achievement supervisors. These findings indicate that high-need achievers perform best when they are assigned specific goals and receive feedback on their progress toward these goals. Conversely, low-need achievers (who are perhaps less confident) perform best when they are allowed to participate in the setting of their goals.

In his study using anagrams, Sales (1970) varied the workload given to subjects. Overall, productivity for subjects high in need for achievement was not higher than that for subjects who were low in need for achievement. However, there was a significant interaction between workload and need for achievement. Sales reported a positive linear relation between need for achievement and productivity in the underload condition, and a curvilinear (inverted–U) relation between need for achievement and productivity in the overload condition. Since high-need achievers prefer goals of moderate difficulty, they presumably considered the overload condition too challenging for their liking.

In a laboratory experiment, Singh (1972) found that students with high need for achievement set higher goals for themselves over repeated trials of a mathematical clerical task than did low-need achievers. Yukl and Latham (1978) obtained comparable results in their study involving typists. High-need achievers who were allowed to participate in the goal setting process set more difficult goals than did low-need-achievement typists. Nevertheless, they did not perform any better than low-need achievers.

Matsui, Okada, and Kakuyama (1982) found that the need achievement scores of subjects working on a perceptual speed test correlated significantly with the goals set and the total number attempted. Specifically, the achievement need affected performance through its effect of goal difficulty. Subjects with a high need for achievement set harder goals than did those who were lower in need for achievement.

When goal difficulty was held constant in two experiments involving word-processing operators, Dossett et al. (1979) found no moderating effects of need for achievement on performance apppraisal measures, or on performance on a selection test measuring mathematical ability. Goal difficulty level was also held constant in the Latham and Marshall (1982) study of government workers. No main or interaction effect was obtained for need for achievement. But Kernan and Lord (1988) obtained a moderating effect for need for achievement such that high-need achievers were more committed to the goal and performed better with participative goal setting than were low-need achievers. This occurred despite the fact that goal difficulty level was held constant.

In a study of handball contests (Ostrow, 1976), athletes scoring high on need for achievement set more realistic goals and performed better under competitive conditions than those who scored low. But this was only true in the first tournament.

With regard to goal commitment, Hollenbeck, Klein, O'Leary, and Wright (1988) obtained low but significant correlations of .17 and .23 with a measure of need for achievement. And Hollenbeck, Williams, and Klein (1989) found that students high in need for achievement with regard to a course grade demonstrated higher goal commitment than low need for achievement subjects. This was specially true when the goals were self-set.

It is ironic that none of the above studies measured need for achievement using the TAT. McClelland (McClelland et al., 1953; McClelland & Winter, 1969) has argued that only the TAT should be used because it measures the need for achievement at the subconscious motive level; the self-report measures used in the above studies only measure a person's conscious value for achievement. The irony is that the only study that could be found that used the TAT obtained negative results. In a series of laboratory experiments, Roberson-Bennett (1983) found that N-ach had little or no impact on goal choice or performance. Excluding Bennett, of the twelve studies reviewed, only three showed no effect of value for achievement on goal setting or performance. It would appear that this concept, specifically value for achievement, is worthy of further study.

Type A Behavior

Research has shown that Type A's initiate more tasks for themselves and attend to more tasks simultaneously than do Type B's (Kirmeyer, 1987). Freedman and Phillips (1988) examined the affective reactions of Type A and Type B under-graduate students to assigned goals in a laboratory experiment. Their results showed that Type B's were interested in a goal only to the extent that it was instrumental in attaining other incentives. Types A's, however, perceived the value of goals primarily as a source of information about competence. In a field study investigating faculty research productivity, Taylor, Locke, Lee, and Gist (1984) found that Type A's were higher performers in part because they set higher performance goals than did Type B's. Consistent with this finding, Lee, Earley, and Hanson (1988) observed that Type A employees on high-variety (complex?) jobs outperformed Type B's.

In a field experiment, Dean, Phillips, and Ivancevich (1988) found that Type A's performed significantly better under an assigned goal in comparison with one that was set participatively. Most interestingly, Type A's reported higher levels of uncertainty with assigned goals. The researchers concluded that the employees responded to this heightened uncertainty by increasing their efforts to achieve it. "The A's under the participative goal setting condition apparently did not feel this uncertainty and thus did not have to search for additional information. Not only did this result in lower performance than the Type A's under assigned goals, it also resulted in lower performance than the Type B's" (p. 14).

With regard to self-set goals, Ward and Eisler (1987a,b) found that in two general information tests Type A's, compared with Type B's, set significantly higher performance goals, but performed no differently. However, the use of a knowledge test as a criterion for a goal setting study is highly inappropriate, since scores on such tests have very little to do with motivation.

Self-esteem and Depression

Bandura (1988) has observed that people who become easily depressed set high standards for themselves—well above their perceived capabilities. High aspirations, he noted, are self-motivating rather than self-discouraging, if one's accomplishments are measured against attainable subgoals rather than distant aspirations.

These conclusions are reminiscent of the early literature on level of aspiration. For example, in a study involving children, Sears (1941) found that a low-positive discrepancy reaction (i.e., level of aspiration slightly above one's performance) was found in individuals

> who feel a confident security in their own achievement. The high positive discrepancy reaction is found in individuals who feel insecure about their own achievement, and who, in addition, by reason of the structuring of their personalities, are able to admit failure without too serious damage to self-esteem. The negative-discrepancy response (i.e., level of aspiration below one's previous performance) is found in children who probably feel some insecurity with respect to their achievement but who show much more markedly a general self-protective, defensive reaction to situations in which they may fail in the sight of other people. (pp. 334–35)

In contrast to Bandura's result, a study by Ahrens, Zeiss, and Kanfer (1988) found that dysphoric or depressed subjects set significantly lower goals than did nondepressed people. Deficits in performance associated with depression were said to be a function of a depressive person's tendencies to maintain low personal standards relative to nondepressed individuals. Low goals do not energize people. Simon (1988), however, found that depressed people do not adjust their proximal goals to appropriately reflect their rate of improvement. Thus, as performance gains become smaller, they set higher goals relative to nondepressed persons. In contrast, under large performance gains, they set relatively low goals. Bandura (1988) argued that people who become easily depressed set goals that are beyond their ability and then belittle their accomplishments. In his book titled *Rejection*, John White (discussed in Bandura, in press) found that the striking characteristic of people who have achieved eminence in their field was an inextinguishable sense of high self-esteem that enabled them to overcome repeated rejections of their early work. For example, Gertrude Stein submitted poems to editors for twenty years before one was finally accepted (Bandura, in press).

In the study involving typists (Latham & Yukl, 1976), self-esteem did not moderate the effects of participative and assigned goal setting on performance. However, it was found that self-esteem and goal instrumentality interacted in their effects on performance (Yukl & Latham, 1978). *Instrumentality* was defined as "the extent to which desirable outcomes (e.g., job security, pay promotion) are perceived to be contingent upon goal attainment" (Yukl & Latham, 1978, p. 312). Specifically, when goal instrumentality was low (goal attainment not perceived as linked to important outcomes), typists with high self-esteem showed greater performance improvement than individuals with low self-esteem. There was no self-esteem effect when instrumentality was high. When self-esteem was low, typists who perceived high goal instrumentality showed greater performance improvement than those with low goal instrumentality; when self-esteem was high, there was no instrumentality effect. The integrating principle here may be that self-esteem and instrumentality are alternative but not additive motivators.

Carroll and Tosi (1970) found in a correlational study that individuals with high self-assurance increased their effort in the face of increasingly difficult goals, whereas those with low self-assurance worked less hard as the goals became harder. It is likely that different self-perceptions regarding ability underlie the self-assurance measure.

Dossett et al. (1979) found that work-processing operators with high self-esteem who were given performance feedback attained their goals significantly more often than individuals with low self-esteem. These results are consistent with those of Shrauger and Rosenberg (1970). They found that shifts in performance following feedback depended on the self-esteem of the individual. Specifically, high self-esteem people improved their performance more than low self-esteem people following positive feedback; the performance of low self-esteem individuals decreased more than high self-esteem individuals following negative feedback. Thus, high self-esteem individuals are influenced more by positives, whereas low self-esteem people are influenced more by negatives.

These results are supportive of Korman's (1976) thesis that individuals are motivated to behave in a manner that is congruent with their self-concept. Thus people respond more to feedback that agrees with their self-concept, whether it is positive or negative, than they do to feedback that is inconsistent with their self-concept.

With regard to self-set goals, Silver and Greenhaus (1983) had undergraduate students set their own goals after completing a clerical task. Self-esteem and goal difficulty were positively correlated. Hollenbeck and Brief (1987) found a three-way interaction between goal origin, goal difficulty, and self-esteem on performance. Specifically, a strong negative correlation was found between difficulty and performance for low self-esteem subjects under assigned goal conditions. In a subsequent study, the correlation between self-esteem and goal commitment was not significant (Hollenbeck et al., 1988).

It would appear that self-esteem and related measures such as self-efficacy should be studied further in terms of their effect on goals. In doing so, Weiss (1982) would argue for aggregating measures of goal setting behaviors across repeated observations on a particular task, and across diverse tasks. He found that this increased the correlation between self-esteem, goals, and performance. When criterion measures were aggregated across tasks—specifically, over the two tasks that the subjects appeared to find most self-involving, namely, a creativity and an anagram task—self-esteem correlated .46 with aggregated goal difficulty and .50 with aggregated perfromance.

Need for Independence

French, Kay, and Meyer (1966) found that employees with a high need for independence had greater goal commitment when participation in goal setting was increased than when participation was reduced or not changed. Goal commitment was not affected by changes in participation for employees with a low need for independence.

The moderating effect of need for independence has not been found by most researchers. For example, Searfoss and Monczka (1973) found no moderating effect of need for independence on the relationship between perceived participation on the part of managers in setting specific budgetary goals and subsequent motivation to achieve those goals. Similarly, in their study with typists, Latham and Yukl (1976) found that need for independence did not moderate the effects of either participative or assigned goal setting on performance. Dossett et al. (1979) also found no moderating effects of need for independence on the performance of word-processing operators. In a subsequent laboratory experiment (Latham, Steele, & Saari, 1982), no moderating effects were obtained. Arvey and Dewhirst (1976) studied the goal setting practices of 271 engineers at a nuclear research center. They found that need for autonomy did not significantly moderate the goal setting–job satisfaction relationships.

In the study by Ivancevich and McMahon (1977a) involving technicians, initial analyses revealed no consistent relationships between various goal attributes and performance measures. However, when higher-order-need strength (e.g., desire for autonomy) was used as a moderator, goal clarity, feedback, and challenge were related to effort (toward quantity and quality) and attendance for technicians with high higher-order-need strength. Conversely, for technicians with low higher-order-need strength, goal commitment was related to effort (toward quality) and attendance. No obvious interpretation can be made of these findings.

Internal vs. External Control

Bigoness, Keef, and DuBose (1983) found that there was a positive significant relationship between personal goal difficulty and performance for those people with an internal orientation; for those with an external orientation, there was an inverse relationship between perceived goal difficulty and performance. Unfortunately, the performance measure was based on self-ratings. Thus the results could have been biased by the use of percept-percept measures. In their study of typists (Latham & Yukl, 1976), belief in internal versus external control was found to have no moderating effect on performance. Dossett et al. (1979) also failed to find a moderating effect for locus of control on job performance appraisal measures or on test performance for word processors. Similarly, Latham and

Marshall (1982) found no moderating effect in their field study, nor did Latham et al. (1982) in their laboratory experiments. However, Latham and Yukl (1976) found that typists with participatively set goals who were "internals" set more difficult goals than "externals." It is likely that anything useful obtained from locus of control measures can be subsumed under the self-efficacy concept (Chapter 3). The latter measure is task specific and will probably work better than more general measures.

Other personality traits that have not been studied very much and yet show promise with respect to their relationship to goal setting include attention-persistence (Antoni & Beckman, 1967), ambition (Howard & Bray, 1988), initiative (Hyams & Graham, 1984), and future time perspective (Lens, 1986; Nuttin, 1985). Hollenbeck and Williams (1987) found a triple interaction involving a cognitive-personality measured, called "self-focus"; but, as noted in Chapter 1, it is not clear that goals work better when a person is self-focused, since goals also require one to be externally focused.

TASK COMPLEXITY

As noted in Chapter 4, the direct relationship between goals and performance should be lower on complex than on simple tasks; conversely, the relationship between task strategies and performance should be higher on complex than on simple tasks (see also Chaper 13). While there have been only a limited number of studies relevant to the second proposition, there have been a considerable number relevant to the first.

The data presented here are from the meta-analysis performed on 125 goal setting studies by Wood, Mento, and Locke (1987). Seventy-two of the studies involved comparisons among goals of varying degrees of difficulty, and 53 involved comparisons between specific, difficult goals and do-best goals.

The tasks used in these studies were independently rated on a 10-point scale as to task complexity, using Wood's (1986) criteria of complexity. On a 10-point scale Figure 9–3 gives a representative picture of the mean complexity rating of tasks at various difficulty levels.

Tasks that have been used in goal-setting studies show a strong bias toward more simple tasks such as brainstorming, perceptual speed, and toy-assembly tasks. The frequency distribution of goal-setting studies as a function of task complexity, shown in Figure 9–4, is clearly skewed to the right, with most

FIGURE 9–3   Representative Tasks for Various Complexity Levels

1	2	3	4	5	6	7	10
Reaction Time	Brainstorming	Toy Assembly	Sewing machine work	School or college course work	Supervision	Science and engineering	
	Simple arithmetic	Anagrams	Production work		Middle management		
	Perceptual speed	Typing	Floor plan analysis		Technician work		

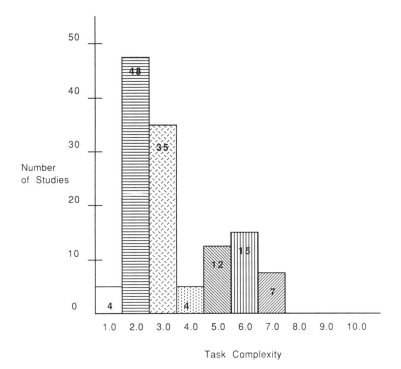

FIGURE 9–4 Frequency Distribution of Goal-Setting Studies by Task Complexity ($n = 125$).

being at the less complex end of the scale. However, among the large number of studies that have been conducted, significant numbers of studies have used more complex tasks. It was felt that there were enough studies at different levels across the range of task complexity to provide an adequate test of the moderator hypotheses.

For the 72 studies of goal difficulty ($N = 7,548$), the mean effect size, corrected for measurement error, was $d = .5770$, and the variance corrected for measurement error was $s_c^2 = .1487$. The unexplained variance after correcting for sampling error was .1014; therefore only 32% of the variance in results across the studies was attributable to sampling error. In the subset of 37 studies with experimental designs, ($n = 3,377$) the corrected d was .6171. The associated variance, corrected for measurement error, was $s_c^2 = .2118$, and 26% of this was attributable to sampling error.

Across the 53 studies of goal specificity/difficulty ($N = 6,635$), the mean corrected effect size was $d = .4315$, and the variance corrected for measurement error was $s_c^2 = .0626$. The variance due to sampling error was .0374, or 60% of the corrected variance. For the subset of 44 experimental studies ($n = 4,772$), the mean corrected d was .4669 and the associated $s_c^2 = .0732$, 60% of which was attributable to sampling error.

Clearly, both goal difficulty and goal specificity have significant relationships with performance, and there is sufficient unexplained variance in the strength of these relationships across studies to warrant investigation of potential moderators.

The results of the regression analyses (Table 9–1) support both hypotheses. Task complexity was a significant moderator of the size of the performance relationship for goal difficulty and goal specificity/difficulty. Both betas were negative, indicating that the magnitude of goal-to-performance effects *decreased* as task complexity increased.

Table 9–2 shows the average corrected effect-size *d*s for a subgrouping of studies. The magnitude of effects for both goal specificity/difficulty and goal difficulty are more pronounced on simple tasks than on complex tasks. This result was consistent across many different subgroupings of studies (not shown), indicating that the result was not an artifact of the groupings used. The finer the distinctions between subgroupings on the task complexity scale, the greater the differences between the simplest and most complex tasks for both goal difficulty and goal specificity/difficulty. Figure 9–5 shows the plot of the mean corrected *d*s for the different levels of task complexity. The moderating effects of complexity were more pronounced for the goal-difficulty-performance relationship than for the goal-specificity/difficulty-performance relationship.

It is interesting that across the full range of studies included in the regression analyses, the effects were stronger for goal specificity/difficulty ($R^2 = .0926$) than for goal difficulty ($R^2 = .0579$). This is the opposite of what would be expected after an inspection of Table 9–2 and Figure 9–5, and can be attributed to the difference in consistency of results in each type of study. The range of effect sizes was much greater in the goal-difficulty studies.

Table 9–1 Multiple Regression Analysis Using Task Complexity as a Potential Moderator to Predict Goal Difficulty and Goal Specificity/Difficulty Performance Effects

VARIABLE	NO. OF STUDIES	B	R^2
Goal difficulty	72	−.240	.0579[*]
Goal specificity/difficulty	53	−.304	.0926[*]

[*]$p < .05$.

Table 9–2 Meta-Analysis *d*s for Task Complexity Subgroupings for Goal Difficulty and Goal Specificity/Difficulty

Task Complexity Rating	GOAL DIFFICULTY			GOAL SPECIFICITY/DIFFICULTY		
	n	No. of Studies	*d*s[a]	*n*	No. of Studies	*d*s
1.0–2.75	3,297	33	.6941	2,115	19	.4727
3.0–4.75	1,615	18	.4991	3,138	21	.4338
5.0–7.25	2,636	21	.4781	1,382	13	.3583

[a]*d*s are meta-Analytic corrected for measurement error.

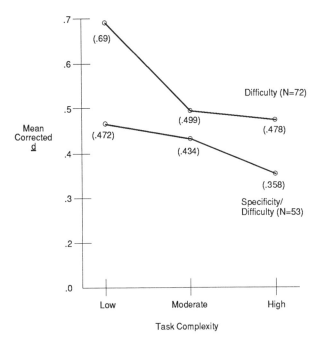

FIGURE 9–5 Goal Effect as a Function of Task Complexity (separately by each set).

In Table 9–3, the *d*s for all studies combined, subgrouped into quintiles by numbers of studies, are shown. The plot of these results (Figure 9–6) shows that, overall, the moderating effects on the relationship between specific, difficult goals and performance are most pronounced at the lowest levels of complexity. For studies in the middle range of the task-complexity scale (2.25–5.00), there was little difference in the goal-performance relationship.

One possible explanation for our results is that performance measures for complex tasks, because they often involve less-standardized outputs, are less reliable than performance measures for simple tasks. Therefore it could be argued that the differences in goal effects between complex and simple tasks are an artifact of the differences in criterion reliabilities. This argument does not apply to the current results because the size of effects for each study was adjusted for the reported reliability of the criterion used.

Table 9–3 Meta-Analysis *d*s for Task Complexity Subgroups, by Quintiles, for All Studies Combined[a]

TASK COMPLEXITY RATING	*n*	NO. OF STUDIES	*d* [b]
1.0–2.0	2,702	27	.7672
2.25–2.75	2,710	25	.4485
3.0–3.25	2,082	20	.4370
3.5–5.0	4,234	28	.4697
5.25–7.0	2,455	25	.4173

[a]Effects of goal specificity/difficulty and goal difficulty are combined.

[b]*d*s are meta-analytic corrected for measurement error.

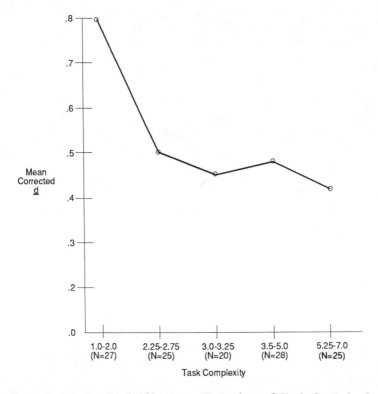

FIGURE 9–6   **Goal Effect as a Function of Task Complexity (combined studies) by Quintiles.**

However, to further test the potential validity of the argument, sensitivity analyses were conducted to see how great the differences in criterion reliabilities had to be in order to remove the observed effects. The 125 studies were split into two groups representing simple and complex tasks. The subgroup analyses were then rerun, assigning all studies in the simple group a reliability of 1 and all studies in the complex group a range of differing reliabilities (.8, .7, .6, .5, etc.). The results of these analyses showed that the differences between the two groups disappeared when the criterion reliability for the complex group was dropped to just below .6. Therefore it appears that the observed differences in goal effects are sensitive to differences in the reliabilities of performance measures of .4 and above. However, for the current set of studies, differences in the criterion reliabilities between complex and simple tasks were not the cause of the differences in the size of the goal effects.

SITUATIONAL CONSTRAINTS

It is self-evident that constraints in the environment or task situation can limit the degree to which goals are translated into action. This was verified in a laboratory experiment by Peters, Chassie, Lindholm, O'Connor, and Kline (1982), who found that goal level was significantly correlated with performance when situational constraints were low ($r = .63$, $p < .001$) and not significantly related to performance when such constraints were high ($r = .19$). The constraints involved three factors: completeness of task information, ease of use of materials and supplies, and similarity of the work environment to the training environment. However, the relative contribution of each of these factors was not assessed.

While one cannot argue with the assertion that situational factors can prevent goals from being attained (e.g., see White & Locke, 1981), it should not be assumed that individuals always react passively when performance is in some way blocked or hindered. If there is commitment to high goals, individuals should be more motivated to find ways to overcome or remove obstacles than when goals are moderate or easy or vague (Chapter 4). This is to be expected if goals function to mobilize effort and persistence. The effect of goals on reaction to obstacles could be tested in experiments like that of Peters et al. (1982) by allowing subjects to seek more tasks information, rearrange the materials and supplies, and restructure the work environment. To date the authors know of no studies that have examined the effect of goals on reactions to obstacles. The only studies that *imply* an effect of goals on overcoming obstacles are those that found hard goal subjects were more tenacious in getting what they wanted than easy or do best goal subjects in a bargaining situation (e.g., Huber & Neale, 1987). If the bargaining opponent's refusal to give the subject what he or she wanted right away can be considered an obstacle, then such studies (reviewed in Chapter 4) could be viewed as supporting our thesis.

Another factor that should affect persistence and effort in the face of frustration and obstacles is self-efficacy (Bandura, 1986; Bandura, in press). It was observed in Chapter 8 that self-efficacy affects the reactions of subjects to one type of "obstacle," namely, failure (Bundura & Cervone, 1986). High goals combined with high self-efficacy lead to greater efforts to overcome obstacles than any other combination.

CONCLUSION

The findings regarding ability and situational constraints are straightforward. Goal setting is a theory of motivation. If the goals set are not within the ability of the person to attain, they will not be attained. Similarly, if situational constraints block goal attainment, the person is less likely to attain the goal. This will be true regardless of demographic variables (e.g., race, age, or sex). However, personality variables such as need (value) for achievement, Type A, and self-esteem appear to affect the extent to which one will take steps to increase one's ability, find ways to overcome situational constraints, or deal successfully with complex tasks.

The history of personality variables as moderators has been a cloudy one. Gardner (1940) was among the first to show that level of aspiration is "a surprisingly stable experimental variable" (p. 204) and that it "shows a considerable degree of generality in unrelated tasks" (p. 204). He did not believe that level of aspiration would be explained in terms of personality traits. Nearly forty years later in his *Annual Review of Psychology* chapter, Mitchell (1979) concluded that personality variables in the field of organizational behavior control little of the variation in behavior. He pointed out that the few empirical results that are statistically significant often lack practical significance.

Longitudinal research may be needed before the effects of personality as a moderator of goal setting can be revealed. Weitz (1966) and Helmreich, Sawin, and Carsrud (1986) have argued that the effects of personality may not become evident until there is prolonged experience with the task. This is because the influence of personality on performance increases as the influence of ability and situational factors decrease with continued task experience. This theme has been emphasized by Eden (1988). He found that the cumulative effects of positive experiences over time are required to elevate trait expectancies and hence higher motivation and better performance. This cannot be demonstrated in goal setting experiments in the laboratory that last a few minutes or even a few hours.

In a different vein, Adler (1986) has advanced the argument that goal setting research is typically conducted in the context of what Mischel (1977) termed "strong situations"; such situations are relatively structured and unambiguous. They offer clear cues to guide behavior, thus leaving little room for personality-based individual variation." Consequently, Adler urged the use of complex, ambiguous tasks in goal setting studies to study personality variables.

Epstein and O'Brien (1985) concluded that personality "traits have received an undeservedly low reputation as predictors because they were expected to do the impossible" (p. 532). The major use for traits, they argued, lies not in their usefulness in predicting specific behaviors, but in their value as predictors of aggregated behavior, that is, of behavior in the long haul averaged over many situations, occasions, and responses. But Bandura (1986) responded that the averaging approach addresses the wrong issue because it leaves unanswered the question of whether that form of behavior will be expressed uniformly or selectively in different social situations: "Indeed, averaging behavior across social conditions not only obscures the analysis of causal processes, but it also reduces their predictability, because an average index is less indicative of how people are likely to behave in dissimilar situations than is the knowledge of how they typically behave in each different situation" (p. 11).

Resolving this debate is beyond the scope of this chapter. To be useful, personality variables must either account for variance in performance unaccounted for by situationally specific factors (e.g., ability, goals, commitment) or be shown to be causes of those situationally specific factors. In addition, personality variables can be used as dependent variables in their own right (e.g., self-esteem). Adler (1987) has suggested one dependent variable that may prove to be particularly sensitive to personality effects, namely, the very propensity to set goals. Also personality measures themselves can be situationally specific. For example, Howard and Bray's (1988) twenty-year study of managers found that ambition, as defined by setting goals to "get ahead," was the best motivational predictor of career progress in AT&T.

The findings regarding task complexity do not contradict our earlier conclusion that the performance effects of goal difficulty/specificity are highly generalizable. However, task complexity affects productivity gains resulting from goal setting. The average effect-size of goals for all of the studies combined is $d = .521$, equivalent to a 10.39% increase in productivity (Mento et al., 1987). For tasks coded at the low, moderate, and high levels of complexity, the equivalent productivity increases are 12.15%, 9.12%, and 7.79%, respectively. In Chapter 13 we speculate at some length about how goals and strategies affect performance on complex tasks. But before we turn to that issue, we must complete our presentation of goal setting theory. Our last major topic is the relationship between goals and affect.

CHAPTER

10

GOALS AND AFFECT

Few issues in the goal setting literature have been more misunderstood than that of the relationship between goal setting and affect. Blanket statements, for example, are often made to the effect that "goal setting enhances satisfaction"—a claim that is incorrect as stated. There are several reasons for this misunderstanding. First, the goal setting literature has focused mainly on the effects of goals on performance, so that affective reactions have not been examined in the majority of studies. Second, researchers who have looked at affective reactions have seldom read the literature that does exist. Some of it has appeared in journals not typically read by I/O psychologists or management researchers, such as *Psychological Reports* and *Journal of Personality and Social Psychology* (e.g., Locke, 1966c, 1966e, 1967a, 1967d). Third, researchers have not attempted to connect goal setting concepts with the theoretical literature on job satisfaction that has appeared in the major I/O psychology and management journals. This literature constitutes the theoretical base needed to understand the relationship of goals to affect (e.g., satisfaction). This chapter begins, therefore, with a presentation of this theoretical base (see Locke, 1969c, 1976, 1984 for more-detailed discussions).

AFFECT (EMOTION) AND APPRAISAL

Arnold (1960) was perhaps the first psychologist to identify the fact that emotional responses were the result of a process of appraisal. She observed that such appraisals were intuitive or subconscious. Objects that were seen as favorable to one's well-being were appraised positively, while those seen as inimical to one's well-being were appraised negatively. This appraisal view of emotional response,

A portion of this chapter has been taken from "Job Satisfaction" by E. A. Locke, in M. Gruneberg and T. Wall (Eds.), *Social Psychology and Organizational Behaviour*, 1984 (Chichester, England: Wiley Ltd.). Reprinted by permission of J. Wiley & Sons Ltd.

which can be validated by introspection and inference, is now well accepted. For example, it forms the foundation of Lazarus's theory of stress and coping (Lazarus & Folkman, 1984) as well as that of Locke and Taylor (in press). For detailed discussions of emotions and appraisal, see Packer (1985a, 1985b).

Arnold and Lazarus, however, did not make it explicit that (a) appraisal is a form of psychological measurement (a measure of the relationship of things to oneself) and (b) that measurement requires a standard or unit. Rand (1964) identified that, in the case of emotions, the standards of appraisal were the individual's values. A "value is that which one acts to gain and/or keep" (Rand, 1964, p. 25). It is that which one considers good or beneficial to one's life or well-being. The appraisal process consists, in fact, of an automatic, subconscious value judgment—an estimate of the degree to which an object or situation furthers or threatens one's well-being as measured by the standard of one's values. The sequence of events leading to an emotion is: object → cognition → appraisal (value judgment) → emotion. We will now consider each of these stages in turn.

Object

Every emotion is about something—an object, an action, an attribute, a situation, an idea, a person—including oneself or even a prior emotion. Anything that can be perceived or conceived can be the object of an emotion. This is not to say that an individual can always identify the actual object of an emotion. The individual may not be skilled at introspection. Sometimes there is more than one object involved (e.g., a sequence of actions or consequences) or the situation or object is highly complex (e.g., another person), making the identification of the object difficult. The true object is sometimes displaced for defensive reasons (e.g., people who are angry at their boss may kick their dog). Nevertheless all emotions are about something.

Cognition

This stage actually involves two processes (although they are not experienced as separate): sensory perception and conceptual identification. For example, if during a hike in the wilderness one meets a large bear on the trail, one automatically perceives the bear, and this perception is automatically associated with one's conceptual knowledge about bears (e.g., "this is a grizzly bear, grizzly bears are very strong and can run fast; they have been known to attack human beings"), as well as one's knowledge of the total context in which the object is perceived (e.g., "the bear is quite close to me; I have no weapons; there is no place to hide; maybe there are cubs nearby which will make her especially dangerous; somebody was attacked last week in this park").

Value Appraisal

This stage involves an automatic, subconscious estimate of the relation between what was perceived and conceived and one's value standards. If the situation is appraised as furthering or facilitating the attainment of one's values, then a positive emotion is experienced. If the situation is perceived as threatening, blocking, or destroying one's values, then a negative emotion is experienced. For example, if you get a letter in the mail announcing that you have won the state lottery, you immediately experience joy and even relief if you have a number of debts. In contrast, if the letter announces that your neighbor is suing you for $100,000 because he slipped on your path, you may experience anything from anxiety to depression to anger, or perhaps all three.

The intensity of an emotion will depend on the place in one's *value hierarchy* of the values implicated in the emotion. If the values involved are not important, then attaining or not attaining the values will produce less intense emotion than in the case where the values are important. The relationship between value importance and emotional intensity is shown in Figure 10–1.

The more important the value, the wider the possible range of affect; the actual amount of affect will depend both on value importance and on the degree of value fulfillment (see Figure 10–2; for further details and illustrative data, see Mobley & Locke, 1970; Locke, Fitzpatrick, & White, 1983; and Locke, 1969c, 1976). Value importance, when applied to goals, can be viewed as a determinant of goal commitment; people are more committed to goals that they deem important than to those that they view as unimportant.

It is sometimes asserted that affect depends on the relationship between actual performance and expected performance (e.g., Ilgen & Hamstra, 1972; McClelland, Atkinson, Clark, & Lowell, 1953). However, as Locke (1969c, 1976) has pointed out, a deviation from expectation produces only a *cognitive* evaluation: surprise, i.e., "this is not what I expected to occur." The emotional coloring of the surprise will depend on whether the deviation is in a direction one values or a direction one disvalues. Expecting to go bankrupt and being saved at the last minute gives rise to a highly positive emotion, whereas expecting to survive and

FIGURE 10–1   Effect of Value Importance on Satisfaction

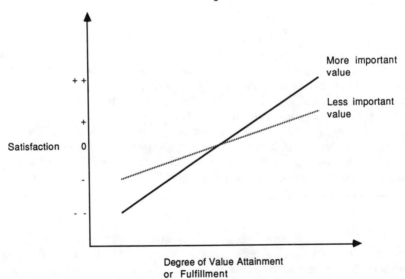

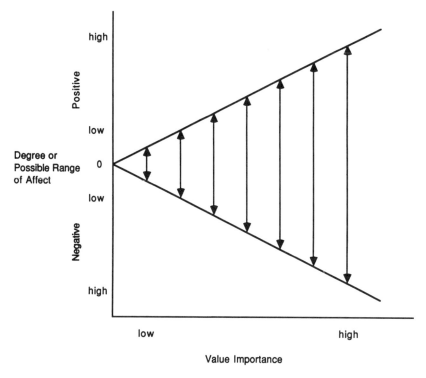

FIGURE 10–2   **Effect of Value Importance on Possible Range of Affect**

then going bankrupt produces a highly negative emotion, even though the degree of surprise is equal in both cases. Only two studies have clearly separated the effects of success in relation to expectation from success in relation to aspiration. Locke (1967d) found that success was equally valued regardless of whether or not it was expected, whereas failure was equally disvalued regardless whether or not it was expected.

In seeming contradiction to Locke's study, Rakestraw and Flanagan (1984) found that success produced more satisfaction when it was unexpected than when it was expected. However, rather than having the subjects rate their expectancy, Rakestraw and Flanagan told half their subjects that there was a small chance of attaining their goal, while the other half were told that there was a high chance of success. Such predictions by an authority figure could well have influenced the importance or valence of success; for example, succeeding against the odds (which is called an "upset" in competitive situations) is usually considered a greater achievement (i.e., more important or significant) than succeeding when it is expected. In sum, it may be that value importance was indirectly manipulated as a consequence of the expectancy manipulation.

Expectations may affect value appraisals indirectly in other ways (Locke, 1976). If an individual succeeded unexpectedly and concluded that a future value that he or she thought was unobtainable was now within reach, the contrast effect might temporarily yield more pleasure than would be experienced by the person who expected success all along. Similarly, if an individual unexpectedly failed, it might cause more disappointment than if he or she had been prepared for it and had therefore erected coping or defensive mechanisms. In these cases, however, expectations would still have their effect by influencing the operation of the value appraisal mechanism.

Emotion

Emotions are the result of value appraisals. They are the form in which one experiences the attainment or negation of one's values (Packer, 1985a). Emotions involve both psychological and physiological reactions. In daily life there are few "pure" emotions, i.e., emotions that involve only one object and one simple value appraisal. Most emotions are more complex. For example, consider an individual who has just been fired from his job. He might feel: *anger* at his boss or the company for treating him unjustly; *fear* and *anxiety* because he does not know whether he will have enough money to live on or whether he will find another job; *despair* because years of work seem to have gone down the drain; *self-doubt* or *self-condemnation* because maybe it was, in some respects, his fault; and *guilt* because he should have seen it coming and done something about it and/or because he is letting his family down.

   Analyzing complex emotions can be a very difficult task, especially because when having an emotion one does *not* consciously experience the full sequence described above. For example, if one meets a grizzly bear in the wilderness, one does *not* consciously make an assessment of the entire situation and then reach a conscious conclusion which then produces an emotion. What one actually experiences in this situation is: bear → fear.

   The intervening steps occur automatically and subconsciously. The individual's stored knowledge and values are automatically activated as soon as the object is perceived. We discover their existence through retrospective introspection and inference, by working backward from the emotion and looking for the values and premises behind it. The survival value of the automaticity of emotions is obvious; in emergencies one needs an immediate estimate of the fact that there is danger and an immediate impetus to take some action in regard to it. The emotion provides both.

   As Arnold (1960) has observed, every emotion contains, as part of the emotional experience, a felt impetus to action. If an object is appraised as beneficial, the action tendency is to approach, keep, or protect the object. If an object is appraised as harmful, there is a felt tendency to avoid, remove, or destroy the object.

   Emotions, of course, also *result* from actions and their outcomes. If an action is successful, one experiences satisfaction or joy; if it is unsuccessful, one experiences dissatisfaction or suffering. Thus emotions are at the same time a payment or penalty for past actions and, because people can anticipate the future based on past experience and reason, an incentive (positive or negative) for future actions. Emotions provide the psychological fuel for action. If people experienced no emotions (for example, if they experienced their values only as abstract principles or cognitive abstractions), they would have no motivation to act. Their values would not be experienced as personally real, significant, or important. A creature like Mr. Spock in the TV and movie series *Star Trek* is a psychological impossibility.

It should be clear from the above model that one cannot make blanket statements about the effect of goal setting on affect without knowing how the goals or goal setting program and their outcomes are appraised by the individual. As we shall see below, goal setting can lead to negative as well as positive appraisals.

THE MEASUREMENT OF APPRAISAL

In addition to confusion about the relation of goals to affect, including satisfaction, there has been confusion about how to measure the appraisal process. For example, researchers often attempt to compare different "models" of satisfaction such as "is now" (asking people to describe the attributes of their job) and "discrepancy" models (asking people to indicate how much of some attribute they want, how much they have, and calculating the difference between the two). Still others measure "fulfillment" (asking to what degree people get the attribute they want) or "instrumentality" (the degree to which the job provides a valued attribute).

What has not been generally recognized is that *if the attribute in question is something that most people value, then all the above approaches to measurement are conceptually (even if not psychometrically) equivalent.* All of them measure value fulfillment, either directly or indirectly. This is illustrated in Table 10–1.

If the "is now" item were something disvalued (e.g., unfairness), then it would of course be negatively rather than positively related to dissatisfaction (see Locke, 1984, Table 2, for illustrative data). Similarly, if the "is now" item were something to which the person was indifferent, the response would be unrelated to satisfaction. For valued attributes the choice among measures is really more of a psychometric than a conceptual issue. For example, difference scores are less reliable than direct or single measures.

Let us now apply the appraisal model specifically to the issue of satisfaction with performance.

Table 10–1 Conceptually Equivalent Variations in Ways to Measure Job Appraisals (Using Autonomy as an Example)

METHOD	SAMPLE ITEM
Is Now	How much autonomy do you have on this job? (Assumes autonomy is valued.)
Discrepancy (two items)	How much autonomy do you have? How much do you want? (Difference score.)
Discrepancy (alternative measure, one item)	How big a discrepancy is there between the amount of autonomy your job offers and the amount you want?
Fulfillment	To what degree does this job fulfill your desire for autonomy?
Instrumentality	To what degree is this job instrumental in providing you with autonomy (or with the autonomy that you want)?

PERFORMANCE, SUCCESS, AND SATISFACTION

As noted in Chapter 5, Lewin (1958) pointed out many years ago that the experiences of success and failure do not depend on the absolute level of performance attained, but on performance in relation to one's personal standard. He called this standard (based on Hoppe) the individual's *level of aspiration.* In our terminology, the level of aspiration or performance goal is the value standard used to appraise performance. If the standard is exceeded, the individual experiences success and feels pleasure and satisfaction; if the individual does not meet the standard, failure, displeasure, and dissatisfaction are experienced. This observation has been made by many others (e.g., Bayton, 1943; Gardner, 1958; Hilgard, 1958; Mace, 1935).

In Chapter 5 it was shown that the level of aspiration, even for a given individual and task, may be multidimensional. Individuals may have a "minimum" goal: a score below which they would not like to fall and would consider their performance to be poor. They may also have a "hope for" or maximum goal, which involves the highest score they could hope to get. Or they might have a "try for" goal, the actual score they will aim for. This goal will typically be in between the minimum and maximum goals.

The most straightforward prediction, then, about the relationship of goals to satisfaction is this: the greater the success experienced, the greater the degree of satisfaction experienced. Similarly, dissatisfaction will be experienced when there is goal blockage or failure (Locke, 1976; Peters et al., 1982). These conclusions follow from the principle that goals are used as the value standard for appraising performance. It should not be surprising, then, that the relation between success and satisfaction is an extremely reliable one. The results of studies that have examined this relationship are summarized in Table 10–2.

Table 10–2   Relation of Success to Satisfaction

STUDY	N	r(F,t)	COMMENTS
Bandura & Cervone (1986)	88	(1.00)	r based on group mean satisfaction as a function of four goal-performance discrepancy levels.
Bottger & Woods (1985)	130	.41	Self-reported success and growth satisfaction.
Das (1982b)	56	(t = 5.16, p <.001)	Hard standards produced less work satisfaction than normal standards (JDI measure only).
Garland (1982)	86	(1.00)	r based on group mean task enjoyment and JDI as a function of goal difficulty level.
Garland (1983)	58	(F = 13.18, p <.001)	Ss in hard goal group less satisfied with their performance than those in easy goal group.

Table 10–2   (cont.)

STUDY	N	r(F,t)	COMMENTS
Gebhard (1948)	80	—	Ratings of liking for task, personal interest in task, and satisfaction greater after success than after failure.
Hall, Weinberg, & Jackson (1987)	94	—	Self-rated success higher for easier than harder goal.
Hamner & Harnett (1974)	160	.33	Goal-performance discrepancy (reversed) and performance satisfaction.
Jackson & Zedeck (1982)	236	.36/.39	Number of successes and satisfaction for manual and cognitive task, respectively.
Locke (1965c)	1—85	.49	Number of successes and task liking.
	2—71	.41/.43	Task liking/JDI.
	3—112	.29/.41	Task liking/JDI. (Original Table 6 liking results were misreported.)
Locke (1966c)	46	.57	Number of successes and personal satisfaction.
Locke (1966e)	1—19	.39	Number of successes and task liking.
	2—21	.45	Number of successes and task liking.
Locke (1967a)	45	.67/.63	Number of successes and personal satisfaction/task liking.
Locke (1967d)	1—105	.72	Satisfaction with success vs. failure
	2—46	.98	(r_{cos-pi} estimates).
Locke (1969c, p. 324)	1—83	.70	Goal-performance discrepancy (reversed) and grade satisfaction.
	2—157	.69	
Locke, Cartledge, & Knerr (1970)	1—20	.92a	Goal-performance discrepancy (reversed) and satisfaction with performance.
	2—20	.61/.72a	Same as study 1/instrumentality of performance.
	3—20	.60/.72a	Same as study 2.
	4—15	.75/.64a	Same as study 2.
	5—69	.84/.89	Same as study 2; a-within-subject relationships.
Matsui, Okada, & Inoshita (1983)	87	(F = 5.93 p <.01)	High progress Ss in relation to goals more satisfied than low progress Ss.
Meyer, Schact-Cole, & Gellatly (1988)	69	(1.00)	r based on group mean satisfaction as a function of goal difficulty level.

Table 10–2   (cont.)

STUDY	N	r(F,t)	COMMENTS
Podsakoff & Farh (1989)	90	(F = 36.86 p <.001)	Ss given feedback indicating successful performance in relation to goals more satisfied than those given negative feedback.
Rakestraw & Flanagan (1984)	223	.45	Satisfaction and goal success vs. failure.
Rakestraw & Weiss (1981)	174	.27/.42	Satisfaction and goal-performance discrepancy (reversed); discrepancy between own and model's performance (reversed).
Sales (1970)	73	(F = 2.75 p <.10)	Ss enjoyed work underload more than work overload.
Schwartz (1974)	40	.56	Goal-performance discrepancy + r with depression.
Stedry (1962)	108	(.32)	Raw performance vs. satisfaction.
Zander & Medow (1963)	225	(t = 6.38 p <.01)	Success led to more satisfaction with team performance than failure.
Zander, Forward, & Albert (1969)	255	—	Success led to higher evaluation of performance than failure.

$\bar{r}$ (excluding those in parentheses and taking median where there is more than one r) = .51.

The mean weighted correlation between success and satisfaction is .51. This mean is based on those studies in which correlational data are reported or could be calculated, and eliminating results based on between-*group* correlations (shown in parentheses in Table 10–2). Success was typically defined in terms of number of successes attained or degree of discrepancy between the goal and the performance. When subjects perform well, they not only feel satisfied with their performance but also generalize this positive affect to the task, i.e., they like the task more than they did previously.

It may be asked why the relationship between success and satisfaction was not 1.0 if the goal was in each case the value standard used to appraise performance. There are at least six reasons. First, and most obvious, is *measurement error*. This is especially likely in *between-subject designs*, since different subjects may define the meaning of the scale points differently. Such error can be reduced by the use of *within-subject designs*. Four studies in Table 10–2 (Locke et al., 1970, studies 1–4) used within-subject designs. The mean weighted correlation between success and satisfaction in these studies was .74. The two studies from Locke (1967d) involved a combination of within- and between-subject data; the two *r*'s were .72 and .98, respectively.

A second type of measurement error (which could be called *measurement omission*) may also be involved in goal setting and satisfaction studies. While it is assumed that the only standard that individuals use to appraise performance consists of the goals they claim to be trying for, they often use more than one standard to evaluate their performance. Rakestraw and Weiss (1981), for example, found that when subjects were given role models to watch, subjects used the performance levels of the role models as well as their own goals to appraise their performance. Similarly, Hamner and Harnett (1974) found that subjects used the performance of their opponent in a bargaining task as well as their own goal to appraise their performance. In each study satisfaction was affected by both appraisals. If subjects are using multiple standards and only one of them is measured, obviously there will be measurement error. No one, for example, has yet tested whether performance in relation to hope, minimum, and try for goals has additive effects on satisfaction.

Not only can subjects use more than one present goal or standard, they can also use both a *present* and a *future* goal to assess performance. Locke et al. (1970), for example, found that satisfaction with performance over repeated trials in which subjects had an end goal (a total score to attain by the last trial) was a function not only of the goal-performance discrepancy for that trial but also of the degree of perceived instrumentality of that trial's performance for attaining the end goal. The combination of goal-performance discrepancy and perceived instrumentality predicted satisfaction significantly better than either one alone. The multiple r's for studies 2, 3, 4, and 5 in Locke et al. (1970) were, respectively, .82, .83, .80, and .91 (weighted $\bar{r}$ = .87 vs. $\bar{r}$'s of .75 and .77 for discrepancy and instrumentality alone, respectively).

If a person chronically believes that he or she cannot attain values or standards, the result can be depression. Kanfer and Zeiss (1983) found that depressed students had performance standards for home, social, and work activities similar to those of nondepressed students but felt much less capable of attaining those standards. Depression results not just from past failure but from the expectation of future failure to attain values and the conclusions one draws from this about oneself and the world (Beck, Rush, Shaw, & Emery, 1979). Depressed persons may set unrealistically high standards for themselves and thus doom themselves to disappointment (Bandura, 1986, 1988). Often these standards are adopted uncritically from peers without considering the individual's personal context and abilities. When the arbitrary standards are not met, the individual may engage in self-belittlement and self-condemnation. This may in turn be followed by setting even higher goals leading to further disappointment, or to apathy leading to no action and therefore no sense of achievement. However, it should be noted that the findings of studies comparing goal setting among depressed and nondepressed people are not entirely consistent (Ahrens, 1987; see also Chapter 9).

A third factor affecting the success-satisfaction relationship is change of standards over time. The relation between performance and satisfaction is *dynamic*, not static. For example, it is not only the amount or degree of success that determines satisfaction but also *when it occurs*. In study 3 of Locke at al. (1970), the multiple r between discrepancy and instrumentality with satisfaction was .89 for the last ten of the twenty experimental trials as compared with .83 for all twenty trials. Similarly, in study 2, deviating from the goal was more disvalued during the later trials than during the earlier trails. In both cases goal deviations were viewed as more serious toward the later trials because such deviations were a greater threat to attaining the end goal than were earlier deviations. The latter could be compensated for or corrected more easily than the former. Recent research by Simon (1988) suggests that changes in rate of improvement or learning can affect satisfaction with performance. Subjects who were given (false) feedback indicating a decelerated rate of learning on a task were significantly less satisfied than those given feedback indicating an accelerated rate of learning. Subjects evidently used their past rate as a standard by which to judge the adequacy of their future performance.

Fourth, the relation of success and satisfaction may be affected by the *significance* or *importance* of success to the individual (see Figure 10–1). The value of succeeding at a given task may be tied to deeper values held by the individual. For example, if the individual bases his or her self-esteem or self-concept on task performance, success on that task will be much more important to that person than to a person who does not base self-esteem on success. High ego involvement implies high value importance, and thus stronger effects of the goal (Bayton, 1943). The wider principle is that an individual's reactions to specific situations may be colored by deeper, metaphysical value judgments, i.e., basic assumptions about the individual's own self and/or the world. Packer (1985b) calls these "core evaluations." People who believe subconsciously, for example, that they are fundamentally incompetent will tend to view success as less significant and failure as more significant than those who believe that they are fundamentally efficacious (Korman, 1976). Goal importance can also be affected by external means. Phillips and Freedman (1988), for example, gave some subjects goals with no explanation or rationale, while others were told that their performance in relation to the goals would indicate how well they were performing in relation to other students. Students given this information generally felt more task and goal satisfaction from working at the task than those not given this information.

A fifth factor that affects the success-satisfaction relationship pertains to the issue of *degree of success*. On tasks where performance is a continuous function as opposed to all or none (e.g., unscrambling words), satisfaction may be a function not only of whether the goal was attained but also of the degree to which the goal was missed or surpassed. Typically, individuals are less dissatisfied when they miss the goal by a little than when they miss it by a lot (Bandura & Cervone, 1986; Locke, 1967d, study 1.) Similarly, they are more satisfied when they surpass the goal by a large margin than when they just attain it. The underlying value standard is: "the more the better." In Chapter 3, Figures 3–7 and 3–8 illustrate this principle within each goal level. (Of course, if the individual is trying for a point goal—an exact amount, or score—then deviations in either direction will be disvalued.) A number of the studies in Table 10–2 involved relating satisfaction to degree of performance-goal discrepancy. Studies that take into account the degree of discrepancy should show stronger relationships than those that look only at success or failure as such. The mean weighted r in the latter type of studies in Table 10–2 was .43—as compared with the discrepancy studies where the mean r was over .54. (Of course, many of the latter studies were also within-subject designs, thus somewhat confounding the results.) A further complication is that in the discrepancy studies, different people may evaluate the same actual discrepancy in different ways. Hamner and Harnett (1974), for example, found that discrepancy was highly correlated with degree of satisfaction (or dissatisfaction) when performance was below standard but not when it was above standard. Evidently, negative deviations were appraised similarly by most subjects, but positive deviations were not.

A sixth factor that can affect the appraisals individuals make of performance in relation to goals pertains to their *causal attributions.* People tend to take credit for successful actions and to blame others or the task for unsuccessful actions (Locke, 1965c; Weiner, 1986). This may be partly valid (Locke, 1976) and a partly defensive maneuver to protect self-esteem. Such attributions can affect the individual's degree of satisfaction. For example, satisfaction is enhanced when individuals credit themselves for successful action and diminished when they attribute success to luck or the easiness of the task (Weiner, 1986). Attributions can also affect subsequent expectations of success.

Figure 10–3 summarizes the factors that can affect the degree of satisfaction and dissatisfaction experienced in response to goal success and failure. Observe that all of these factors fit within the appraisal framework that was outlined earlier. They show that the appraisal process can indeed be a highly complex phenomenon.

AFFECT AND ACHIEVEMENT

The wider and more general value underlying the desire for success is that of achievement, namely the desire to accomplish something or do well (see, for example, Gould, 1939). At the deepest level this represents the individual's need to deal with the world effectively in order to achieve his or her survival and happiness. White (1959) called this effectance motivation.

Many studies have found that a sense of achievement is an important source of work and job satisfaction (e.g., Herzberg, Mausner, & Snyderman, 1959;

FIGURE 10–3 Factors Affecting Satisfaction with Success

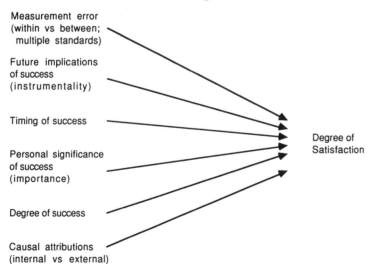

Harris & Locke, 1974; Locke, 1973, 1976; Locke & Whiting, 1974), especially for white-collar and skilled employees. Locke, Fitzpatrick, and White (1983) found that a work achievement factor, which included items pertaining to work signifi-cance, work interest, responsibility, opportunity to learn, use of skills and abilities, feelings of accomplishment, sense of completion, and success, was strongly related to three criterion factors among college professors: overall job satisfaction, intended tenure, and job involvement. Observe that the achievement factor did not involve success alone but success in relation to significant, interesting, and mentally challenging work. This is clearly in line with Hackman and Oldham's (1980) job characteristics theory. In broadest terms, achievement could be viewed as growing and meeting life's challenges by successfully pursuing goals or activities that are personally important and meaningful.

Aside from its leading to a sense of achievement, there is another reason why goal success could lead to positive affective reactions. Success, because it is positively valued by others (including one's supervisor or manager) as well as oneself, can lead one to anticipate that it will lead to external rewards such as recognition, a raise or bonus, and/or a promotion. Insofar as an organization rewards merit, people come to anticipate that successful performance will lead to valued outcomes and that unsuccessful performance will lead to disvalued outcomes (Porter & Lawler, 1968).

BOREDOM AND INTEREST

The use of goal setting by factory workers to generate interest in the work or reduce boredom was reported as early as 1934 by Wyatt, Frost, and Stock:

> One of the most frequent devices adopted by the operatives for the purpose of relieving boredom was the creation of definite aims. From time to time they attempted to complete a certain number of units in a given period; arranged the material in the form of pleasing designs; or competed against each other during short outbursts of great activity. (p. 54)

Roy (in Whyte, 1955, pp. 28ff.) also observed that goal setting activity among workers on piece-rate payment systems was quite prevalent as a means of increasing task interest.

Four controlled, experimental studies conducted with students in a laboratory setting by Locke and Bryan (1967) corroborated these anecdotal accounts. Using three different tasks (perceptual speed, simple addition, and complex psychomotor coordination), Locke and Bryan found consistently that giving subjects specific, quantitative goals to aim for produced a higher degree of task interest (less boredom) than a general goal of "do your best." Furthermore, the effect seemed more reliable as the trial length or duration of the experiment increased. This set of findings was replicated in a fifth study by Bryan and Locke (1967a). Mossholder (1980) replicated these findings, but only for a task that subjects found intrinsically boring. Manderlink and Harackiewicz (1984) also partially replicated Locke and Bryan's findings using the game of "Boggle." Distal goals, expressed as scores to try for based on eleven games, significantly increased task interest, whereas proximal goals, expressed as goals for each game, did not do so. Locke and Bryan (1967) used distal and proximal goals in their experiment 2 on an addition task and found no difference in their effects. It may be significant that Manderlink and Harackiewicz's proximal goals were 2-minute goals, whereas their distal goals were for 22 minutes. In contrast, Locke and Bryan's proximal goals were 15-minute goals, whereas their distal goals were for 120 minutes. This suggests that very short term goals may not enhance task interest, although the reason is not clear. White, Mitchell, and Bell (1977) found no effect of goals on boredom on a sorting task; this may be because they only used a single, postexperimental item as their measure. Since boredom is highly variable over time, it is preferable to measure it repeatedly during performance.

In an intriguing study, Malone (1981) asked sixty-five schoolchildren to rate how much they liked twenty-five different computer games. (Liking ratings in this context are roughly equivalent to interest ratings.) Game attributes were then correlated with the ratings. The two most important attributes associated with liked games were that the game include a goal (i.e., a challenge) and that it provide feedback about performance. A subsequent study in the same article revealed that games designed to give the feedback in a visually compelling form (as in a brick wall being broken down brick by brick) were especially attractive.

The reasons for the above results must now be identified. Boredom and interest are somewhat different from other emotions in one respect. Most emotions entail a particular type of value appraisal (Packer, 1985a, 1985b). For example, guilt is the result of concluding subconsciously that one has violated one's moral standards; satisfaction is the result of concluding that a value is possessed or has been achieved. Interest stems from the subconscious judgment that the activity one is engaged in has *some* personal value significance, that there is some meaningful purpose involved. However, no particular *type* of value judgment is implied. Similarly, boredom results from the implicit appraisal that there is no value significance to the activity, that it lacks any meaningful purpose. Interest is experienced as a positive emotion because the appraisal is: "there is something in this for me." Boredom is experienced as negative because it is appraised as "there is nothing in this for me."

Goal setting has a positive effect on interest (or as a reliever of boredom) because goal setting provides the individual with a sense of purpose on the task. Subjects in the Locke and Bryan (1967) pilot studies specifically mentioned goal setting more than any other factor as the source of their interest. In a laboratory setting, this purpose may be only short-term ("achieve this goal in the next hour"), but it does engage people's values temporarily by challenging them to see how well they can do. Goals in this respect are mechanisms for engaging values, especially the value of achievement. Engaging values is enough to promote interest; satisfaction, as noted earlier, is determined by degree of success in attaining the value (goal).

Interest and boredom may also be affected by the degree of mental attention required by an activity. Bryan and Locke (1967a) found that specific, challenging goals led not only to increases in interest but to increases in the self-reported degree of mental focus and the intensity of focus on the task. Because the interest and focus correlation was concurrent, it does not prove that the focus changes resulting from the goals actually caused the interest changes. However, it does suggest that such a relationship is plausible.

It remains to explain why focusing attention as such would produce a positive appraisal. One possibility is that by becoming absorbed by the task, the individual will discover aspects of it that produce pleasure. A second possibility is that one will attain a sense of efficacy by coping in some form with a task that requires mental effort. A third explanation could be that one gets pleasure simply from being purposeful. A fourth is that in paying attention to the task, one forgets about the passage of time. These explanations, of course, are not mutually exclusive.

It must be made clear that goal setting is not the only source of task interest. Although the ultimate causes of people's interests are not well understood, it is clear that people enjoy and find interesting certain tasks and activities, and that they dislike and find boring other activities independently of (or over and above) the existence of goal setting. One person renovating a cabana, for example, may find it a lot more interesting than another person performing the same task, even when both have the same goals.

Mossholder (1980) found that the nature of the task had a powerful effect on task interest during his experiment, regardless of the goal setting manipulations. Furthermore, on the intrinsically interesting task, goal setting actually *decreased* task interest. This finding is contrary to the other findings in the literature (see also Locke, 1966b). Since it was obtained using what was probably a more interesting task (complex assembly) than those used in the other studies, this result is clearly worthy of further study.

Pure "intrinsic" interest might be defined as liking an activity for its own sake (see Chapter 2). In practice, however, it is difficult to separate the pleasure derived from an activity as such from that derived from doing well at it (attaining goals) and/or from that derived from anticipating valued outcomes to which the activity might lead. However, when intrinsic interest is high, goals might conceivably divert attention away from the pleasure derived from the task activity.

ROLE CLARITY AND HARMONY

Role clarity and harmony, the opposites of role ambiguity and conflict, as such are cognitive rather than value appraisals. However, there is evidence that because they are generally valued, they are associated with job satisfaction (Jackson & Schuler, 1985). The setting of clear and specific goals, in turn, is assumed to enhance role clarity and harmony. While this belief is plausible, we know of no experimental studies that have tested for a positive effect of goal setting through the mechanisms of enhanced role clarity and harmony, or reduced role ambiguity and conflict. (Correlational studies are discussed below.)

FAILURE, CONFLICT, ANXIETY, AND STRESS

Thus far we have discussed goal setting solely in terms of its affective benefits. However, goal setting can have negative consequences as well. It is possible that a poorly designed goal setting program could increase role conflict. For example, the individual could be confronted by incompatible demands from different authority figures or contradictory demands from the same manager. Similarly, an individual could be asked to attain a goal or follow a plan that went against his or her moral values or violated his or her best judgment. The introduction of goal setting confronts individuals with a potential threat. The existence of goals means the existence of standards by which their performance will be evaluated. Consequently, it means the possibility of failure. Failure can lead to lowered self-esteem (depending on how it is interpreted) and self-confidence, and to disvalued practical consequences such as criticism from the authority figure, negative performance appraisals, lower raises, slower or nonexistent promotions, and, ultimately, career setbacks. The very existence of goals implies pressure on the individual to perform, especially time pressure. Thus far only White, Mitchell, and Bell (1977) have measured perceived pressure in a goal setting experiment. They found that specific, challenging goals led to significantly more pressure than no goals. The harder the goal, the greater the pressure and the greater the chances for failure. The clearer the goal, the more clear-cut success and failure will be. Under a vague goal such as "do your best," the individual has room to maneuver; "do your best" can be interpreted in many different ways, including ways favorable to the person. But when goals are explicit, success and failure are unambiguous.

Anxiety is the emotional response to perceived (future) threat, threat to one's self-esteem, or threat to one's physical well-being or safety (Locke & Taylor, in press). Threat that is present, concrete, and known is called fear. Anxiety is the emotional core of stress. It should not be surprising if goal setting, at least in some circumstances, led to greater anxiety and stress. Few studies have actually looked for stress reactions, but where they have been looked for, they have usually been found. P. Smith (personal communication) found in one study that time pressure was the variable most strongly related to the experience of work stress. Time pressure may be associated with both work overload and the likelihood of failure.

Ivancevich (1982) trained sixty leaders of R&D professionals to use various combinations of goal setting and feedback techniques in conducting performance appraisals. Subordinates' subjective reactions to the performance appraisals were assessed two months after their leaders had been trained, and after they had used their training to conduct appraisal interviews. Ivancevich found that the use of assigned goal setting in the appraisal process was associated with higher anxiety.

In a work simulation experiment, Nebeker (1987) gave computer operators various types of goals and incentives in a nine-week study involving seventy-two hours of working time. Generally, those assigned hard standards experienced greater stress than those assigned easier standards. This was especially the case when the incentives were small. It also held true regardless of whether the subjects attained their standards.

In a laboratory experiment, Sales (1970) assigned some subjects more than they could complete in a given time period (overload condition), and others an amount of work that could be completed in less than the time allowed (underload condition). He found that subjects in the overload condition experienced more tension and anger and had a higher heart rate than those in the underload condition.

Sloat, Tharp, and Gallimore (1977) found that teachers who were trained to use praise felt pressure when given goals to use praise a certain number of times. They also felt annoyed that the praise goals distracted them from aspects of their teaching.

The degree of anxiety and stress experienced under a goal setting program will undoubtedly be influenced by the total context in which the goal setting process occurs. For example, goal setting accompanied by threats will undoubtedly lead to higher stress reactions than goal setting introduced in a more benign manner. Similarly, goal setting accompanied by lack of training or self-efficacy enhancement (Bandura, 1986) will be more anxiety-producing than setting goals after confidence has been developed. Supervisory supportiveness, including help in developing action plans and clarifying goal priorities, should also mitigate the effects of stress. Similarly, the method of setting the goals (i.e., assigned, self-set, participatively set) might affect stress even though it does not seem to affect goal commitment or performance (Chapter 7). Latham and Yukl (1976) found that job satisfaction decreased regardless of whether the goals were assigned or set participatively because of fear of layoffs. The goals were undoubtedly perceived as enabling management to identify the ineffective performers. Thus it may not be the method by which a goal is set but rather beliefs about its consequences that produce anxiety and stress.

INEQUITY

Although few studies have looked at the effects of goal setting on feelings of equity (see below), it is an outcome that needs to be seriously considered, especially to the degree that the goal setting program is effective. If individuals do significantly better quality work or produce a greater quantity of work as a result of trying for challenging goals, they may come to expect more extrinsic rewards in return for their better work. Thus they may become dissatisfied if such rewards are not forthcoming. The work of Adams (1965) has made it clear that employees judge the fairness of their pay partly in terms of output/input ratios.

FIGURE 10–4   Possible Positive and Negative Affective Outcomes of Goal Setting

ASPECTS OF GOAL SETTING PROCESS LEADING TO POSITIVE APPRAISALS WHEN PRESENT (SATISFACTION, INTEREST)	ASPECTS OF GOAL SETTING PROCESS LEADING TO NEGATIVE APPRAISALS WHEN PRESENT (DISSATISFACTION, STRESS, ANXIETY)
Success	Failure
Anticipation of success	Anticipation of failure
Anticipation of positive consequences of success	Anticipation of negative consequences of failure
Value engagement (achievement, challenge)	Feelings of pressure, threat
Cognitive focus, absorption, sense of purpose	Role conflict
Visually compelling feedback	Feelings of inequity
Role clarity	
Role harmony	

Figure 10–4 summarizes the possible positive and negative affective consequences of goal setting. Since there are multiple positive and negative outcomes that might occur in response to goal setting, it is difficult to predict the net affective outcome of a goal setting intervention. Conceivably the positive and negative effects could offset one another leading to no net change. In the next section the results of goal setting interventions in field settings are examined.

RESULTS OF EXPERIMENTAL FIELD STUDIES

The results of experimental field studies have been highly variable. Two showed negative outcomes. Koch (1979), for example, found that the work satisfaction of sewing machine operators given quality goals and feedback decreased as compared with a control group who were not given goals. This occurred even though the goal setting intervention increased performance quality dramatically. Pay satisfaction did not change in this group but increased significantly in the control group as a result of the 10% pay raise given to all employees. Koch speculated that feelings of inequity may have mitigated the pay satisfaction effects in the experimental group but had no plausible explanation for the work satisfaction effects.

Latham and Yukl (1976), as noted earlier, found that job satisfaction decreased significantly for typists who participated in setting goals as well as for those who did not despite a significant increase in productivity for both groups. Latham and Yukl, based on discussions with the typists, concluded that the satisfaction effect was due to the typists' feeling pressured by the joint imposition of quality as well as quantity standards and the fear of subsequent layoffs.

The single most frequent outcome among the experimental field studies was: no change in affect as a result of the goal setting intervention. Seven studies yielded null results: Adam (1975) in a study of diecasting workers; Crawford, White, and Magnusson (1983) with engine overhaulers; Gaa (1973) with first and second graders trying to improve their reading skills; Kim (1984) in a study of salespersons; Latham, Mitchell, and Dossett (1978) with scientists and engineers; Pritchard, Bigby, Beiting, Coverdale, and Morgan (1981) with data processors; and Umstot, Bell, and Mitchell (1976) using a simulated coding task. It should be noted that in all of these studies there were significant performance effects for the goal setting interventions.

Mixed affective results were obtained in three studies. Carroll and Tosi (1970) evaluated an MBO program conducted in a manufacturing firm. The majority of respondents liked the program "in some ways but not others." Attitudes toward the program were more positive when the goals were perceived as difficult, clear, and focused on self-improvement than when they were not. Ivancevich, Donnelly, and Lyon (1970) found that reactions to a similar program were positive if there was top management commitment to and ongoing interest in the program but were not positive if top management was not actively involved. This study appears to be based on the same data set as that by Ivancevich (1972); thus we do not discuss the latter study separately. Kim and Hamner (1976), in a study of telephone service employees, found that satisfaction with supervision and co-workers increased in response to a goal setting intervention, whereas satisfaction with pay decreased. They interpreted the pay finding as an equity effect, paralleling the Koch study in this respect. Kim and Hamner found no change in work satisfaction.

In contrast to the mixed or negative results described above, a series of four studies by Ivancevich and his colleagues (Ivancevich, 1976, 1977; Ivancevich & McMahon, 1982; Ivancevich & Smith, 1981) found consistently positive effects of goal setting programs. Specifically, Ivancevich (1976) and (1977) found significant increases in satisfaction with work and supervision for salespeople and technicians, respectively. Ivancevich and McMahon (1982) found that goal setting increased the intrinsic satisfaction of engineers. Ivancevich and Smith (1981) obtained the same results for sales representatives. Neither study found any effects on extrinsic satisfaction. Finally, Quick (1979) found that a goal setting program significantly reduced role conflict and ambiguity among a group of life insurance managers and staff.

Rodgers, Hunter, and Rodgers (1987) conducted a meta-analysis of twenty-one MBO studies that looked at affective reactions. This review included some, if not all, of the studies discussed above and also some additional studies, some of which reported very incomplete data. Rodgers et al. report a mean effect size (d) of .11, which although significantly greater than 0, is almost twenty times smaller than their estimated mean effect size of MBO on productivity ($d = 2.00$; also reported in Rodgers, Hunter, and Rodgers 1987). At most these data suggest a very modest impact of MBO on satisfaction.

Finally there are a number of positive anecdotal reports regarding the effects of goal setting and feedback programs on satisfaction (e.g., Komaki, Barwick, & Scott, 1978; Komaki, Heinzmann, & Lawson, 1980; Migliore, 1977, Chaps. 5 and 7; Pritchard, Jones, Roth, Stuebing, & Ekeberg, 1988; Raia, 1965). But in the absence of objective data, no firm conclusions can be drawn from these studies.

What, then, can be concluded from the experimental field studies? Only that the results of goal setting interventions on satisfaction were small and/or inconsistent. We must assume that the cause of the inconsistency was that different programs were conducted differently and that different attributes of the programs were introduced or emphasized in the different studies. It is almost impossible to tell from reading the research reports just what was emphasized. Undoubtedly the style of the supervisor or manager plays an important role in the affective outcome. For example, it was clear from the description by Ivancevich and Smith (1981) that there was very extensive training of the sales managers who introduced the goal setting process to the sales representatives. Measurement on relevant process variables in that study revealed that the trained managers were rated very high on such actions as openness, supportiveness, information giving, and clarifying. Future studies would do well to measure such process variables when conducting studies of affective reactions to goal setting, and to relate these process measures to the degree of satisfaction experienced (Carroll & Tosi, 1970). It can also be suggested that in future studies multiple affective outcomes be measured (e.g., satisfaction with supervision, pay, co-workers, the work itself), since reactions can be positive on some dimensions and negative or neutral on others.

Laboratory and/or well-controlled simulations or field studies should be designed to isolate particular aspects of goal setting programs that influence affective reactions. Raven and Rietsema (1957), for example, found that degree of goal and plan clarity affected task liking, although their clarity manipulation was extreme. Wexley and Nemeroff (1975) found that managers trained to do goal setting interviews with subordinates while being telecoached via an earphone produced significantly less subordinate work satisfaction than those not telecoached, possibly because the telecoaching disrupted their interviews. Laboratory research by Latham and Saari (1979a) suggested that supervisory supportiveness may have positive consequences. Locke and Schweiger (1979) concluded that participation was more likely to influence satisfaction than performance, although Wagner and Gooding's (1987) meta-analytic results throw some doubt on this conclusion. They found that the mean correlation between satisfaction and participation was .10 for studies that did not employ *r-r* designs.

RESULTS OF CORRELATIONAL FIELD STUDIES

The correlational field studies reveal a different picture than the experimental studies in that the results are far more consistent. The simplest way to summarize the correlational studies is to say that practically every, seemingly positive, attribute of goal setting that these studies have measured has been found to be correlated with satisfaction with the job or some aspect of it. These aspects include *goal specificity* or *clarity* (or nonambiguity, Carroll & Tosi, 1973; Anderson & O'Reilly, 1981; Arvey, Dewhirst, & Brown, 1978; Arvey & Dewhirst, 1976; Lee & Niedzwiedz, 1983; Steers, 1976; Zultowski, Arvey, & Dewhirst, 1978); *participation* and *flexibility* (Anderson & O'Reilly, 1981; Arvey et al., 1978; Arvey & Dewhirst, 1976; Steers, 1976; Zultowski et al., 1978); *support* and *helpfulness* (Anderson & O'Reilly, 1981; Burke & Wilcox, 1969); *feedback* (Anderson & O'Reilly, 1981; Arvey et al., 1978; Arvey & Dewhirst, 1976; Carroll & Tosi, 1973; Steers, 1976; Zultowski et al., 1978); *rewards* for goal-relevant performance (Anderson & O'Reilly, 1981); and *communication,* or opportunity to state feelings and opinions (Burke & Wilcox, 1969; Greller, 1975).

The most comprehensive correlational study to date has been that by Lee, Bobko, Earley, and Locke (1988; see also Lee, Locke, Earley, 1988), who used a questionnaire adapted from Locke and Latham's (1984a, appendix) 53-item goal setting measure (reprinted in our Appendix E). The questionnaire was completed by 441 employees (all job levels) in one organization. While the factor analytic solution to the questionnaire was complex, the positive factors were all associated with satisfaction, and the negative factors with dissatisfaction. The positive factors were *goal clarity; supervisory support; rewards* for goal achievement; *constructive use of goal setting in performance appraisal; goal efficacy* (I feel proud when I . . . reach my goals); *goal rationale* (my boss explains the reasons . . .); and *organizational facilitation of goal achievement* (work teams . . . work together). The negative factors were *stress and failure* (goals are too difficult); *dysfunctional uses of goals* (overload, goals used to punish): and *goal conflict.* The positive factors formed a higher-order factor that correlated .52 with overall job satisfaction. The negative factors formed a separate higher-order factor that correlated −.49 with satisfaction. The positive higher-order factor also correlated negatively with somatic complaints and anxiety, whereas the negative factor correlated positively with these measures.

The integrating principle behind these correlational results is this: Goal setting enhances satisfaction when it leads to or is associated with attributes or conditions of the job that are generally valued, and it undermines satisfaction when it leads to or is associated with the absence of these factors or the presence of disvalued job attributes.

The correlational studies do not contradict the experimental studies, since the latter studies did not relate individual differences in job perceptions to affective outcomes. As a group, the studies suggest that it is not goal setting as such that affects job satisfaction but the way in which goal setting is perceived and the consequences to which it leads. This principle can be applied to an issue that is not yet resolved in the goal setting literature, How hard should goals be?

RESOLVING THE PERFORMANCE VS. SUCCESS DILEMMA IN GOAL SETTING

The results with respect to goals and performance are quite clear: given goal commitment, feedback, self-efficacy, suitable strategies, and so on, the higher, harder, or more difficult the goal, the better the performance. However, the more difficult the goal, the less likely it is to be attained and thus the less likely it is to produce satisfaction. In Chapter 3, Figures 3–7 and 3–8 show that satisfaction for people with hard goals is contingent on a higher level of achievement than is satisfaction for people with easy goals. Precisely for this reason, failure is more likely for people with hard goals. Failure not only is disvalued in itself but also can produce stress and lack of rewards. This dilemma is shown graphically in Figure 10–5. Maximizing one outcome (e.g., performance) minimizes the other (e.g., satisfaction).

FIGURE 10–5   Relation of Goal Difficulty to Performance and Satisfaction

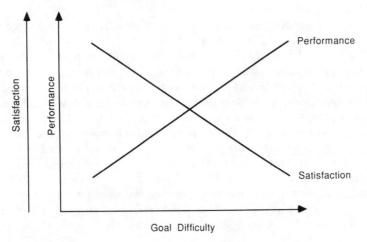

Obviously one solution to this is to make goals moderately difficult, that is, challenging but ultimately reachable. When difficult goals are used to pressure, overwhelm, and punish the individual, satisfaction is decreased. The moderate goal or compromise solution would not maximize either outcome but would maximize the combination of the two.

The major disadvantage of any approach that emphasizes that goals must be reached or surpassed is that it motivates the individual not to take risks. This may be especially dysfunctional for managers. MBO, for example, has frequently been criticized on the grounds that it is easy for managers to "play games" by gathering data to convince the boss that their goals are difficult when they are, in fact, relatively easy. Such gaming is hard to resist when rewards such as bonuses are based on goal attainment.

A goal setting procedure that avoids this problem is to use goals for motivational purposes, but to reward performance rather than goal attainment. An illustrative example is shown in Figure 10–6. The figure shows the goal difficulty level, degree of success or attainment, and overall performance of two managers (goal importance is held constant in this example). Manager A has relatively easy goals and achieves them fully, while Manager B has very difficult goals and only partly attains them. The question is, Who is the better manager? According to the MBO philosophy, Manager A is the more successful of the two and should be the more highly rewarded. However, Manager B, who has been less successful, is actually a greater asset to the organization in terms of what she has accomplished (see last column of the figure) because her total contribution (225) is substantially more than that of A (150). Under a traditional MBO system, B would get low rewards and would quickly learn to lower her goals the next year to ensure success. She would also probably accomplish substantially less in the following year. Under our system, on the other hand, B would get the greater rewards, and the next year, A would be highly motivated to increase the difficulty of his goals so as to achieve more.

This system, of course, means that top management must make difficult judgment calls when evaluating their subordinates. They would have to judge, for example, the difficulty level of their subordinates' goals. But top manage-

FIGURE 10–6 Goal Success and Performance of Two Hypothetical Managers

Manager A

		Difficulty x	Importance X	Degree of Success =	Total Performance
Goal	A	5	10	1.0	50
	B	5	10	1.0	50
	C	5	10	1.0	50
				$\bar{X}$(Success)=100%	Total=150

Manager B

Goal	D	10	10	.75	75
	E	10	10	.75	75
	F	10	10	.75	75
				$\bar{X}$(Success)= 75%	Total=225

ment must make similar judgments even under a traditional MBO system; for example, if A does not attain his goals, is it due to uncontrollable circumstances such as a change in the external environment, or is it due to lack of effort or competence? The advantage of our system is that managers would be rewarded for undertaking very challenging goals even if they did not completely reach them. At the same time they would not be rewarded simply for *setting* high goals; rewards would be based on their net contribution to the organization's mission.

Another solution to the performance-satisfaction dilemma is to employ a broader definition of goal difficulty (i.e., probability of success) than has been done traditionally. Goal difficulty can be viewed more widely as including such factors as the absolute level of performance; the degree of thought, effort, and skill, needed to attain the goal; the number of steps in the process; the number of tasks that have to be integrated; the relationships among the tasks; the time required; the number of people involved; and so on. Goals can be difficult and yet reachable but may require considerable planning, preparation, and time to attain.

A variation on this theme is the Japanese principle of *Kaizen* (Imai, 1986), which means "constant improvement." Consider, for example, a computer chip with a defect rate of 1 per 100. This goal might be readily attainable. But the Japanese, driven by an underlying meta-goal or vision of high quality, would then set a goal to improve the defect rate to 1 in 1,000. When this goal was achieved, they would try for 1 in 10,000, then 1 in 100,000. Each goal would be, in time, fully achievable, but as each one was reached, a new, harder goal would be set. This same principle is used by the Japanese to reduce costs and develop product innovations. The ultimate goal might be impossible and demoralizing if taken on at the outset, but it becomes quite achievable if attacked in small steps.

THE ACTION CONSEQUENCES OF AFFECT

The final task of this chapter is to identify the consequences of job satisfaction and dissatisfaction. As noted earlier, Arnold (1960) observed years ago that emotions contain, as part of the total experience, action tendencies. These tendencies are basically to approach objects appraised positively and to avoid objects appraised negatively (Locke, 1970a, 1976). However, action tendencies (felt urges to action) are only tendencies, not determinants of action. A given action tendency may be opposed by a countervailing urge and, more importantly, may be evaluated by a process of thought (Henne & Locke, 1985). Individuals have the capacity to decide whether they want to act on a given desire, and, more fundamentally, they have the power to choose among multiple action alternatives in response to a given feeling, including the power to take no action at all. Given the fact that people do not have to act on their feelings and that there are many different actions they can take, it should not be surprising to find that the association between satisfaction and task or job performance is quite modest.

It has been known for at least seven decades that individuals can be improving their performance at the same time as their degree of boredom or dissatisfaction is increasing (Poffenberger, 1928; Thorndike, 1917). It was once thought that the shape of the output curve could reveal the factory worker's degree of boredom (discussed in Ryan, 1947), but Patricia Cain (Smith) discovered that the output curve was regulated mainly by the operator's production goal rather than by feelings alone (see Ryan, 1947, pp. 199ff.; Smith, 1953). Locke, Cartledge, and Knerr (1970) found that satisfaction related to productivity *if* the satisfaction were a function of the degree of goal-performance discrepancy. In that case, large discrepancies produced dissatisfaction and a subsequent goal aimed at removing the discrepancy, whereas small discrepancies produced satisfaction and a subsequent goal aimed at maintaining performance at the same level (see also Bandura & Cervone, 1986). Similarly, White and Locke (1981) found in a critical incident study that it was not satisfaction alone that led to high productivity but satisfaction in combination with other factors such as goals and deadlines. The converse held for dissatisfaction and low productivity.

Satisfaction by itself, then, does not enable one to predict subsequent performance. Reviews of the literature have consistently found that job satisfaction and productivity have a very weak relationship (e.g., the mean r was .18 in Podsakoff & Williams, 1986; see also Iaffaldano & Muchinsky, 1985). There is more support for the notion that satisfaction is the result of productivity when productivity is rewarded (Podsakoff & Williams, 1986; Henne & Locke, 1985), but this finding does not answer the question, After satisfaction, then what?

Recent developments in job satisfaction research are now documenting that job satisfaction and dissatisfaction can have multiple consequences in action (Fisher, 1980; Locke, 1986b). On the positive side, Organ (1987) found that satisfied employees are more likely than dissatisfied employees to engage in "citizenship" activities such as helping co-workers, helping customers, and so on. On the negative side, Fisher and Locke (1987), based on Henne (1986) and others, found that dissatisfied employees are more likely than satisfied employees to report engaging in such actions as job avoidance and withdrawal, aggression, defiance, work avoidance, constructive protest, and psychological defensiveness.

The most common action resulting from dissatisfaction, perhaps because it is the most direct or natural effect of the associated action tendency, is withdrawal from the job (quitting), as documented in the work of Mobley (1982) and others (see Henne & Locke, 1985, and Locke & Henne, 1986, for summaries). But Mobley (1982) has shown that even here the individual goes through a thought process before actually quitting. Dissatisfaction leads to actual quitting only when the individual, based on his or her thinking, forms a specific intent to quit and then follows through on it.

These findings suggest that dissatisfaction with the job reduces the individual's commitment to the organization. Lack of commitment to the organization implies and necessitates, if the individual actually leaves, lack of commitment to its goals and therefore to the individual's own job goals. Mowday, Porter, and Steers (1982) *defined* commitment as entailing acceptance of the goals and values of the organization; willingness to exert effort on behalf of the organization; and a desire to stay with the organization.

A number of studies have looked at the correlation between commitment and satisfaction. In every case the correlation is substantial. The results of these studies are summarized in Table 10–3. The mean, weighted correlation between satisfaction and commitment is .64.

Table 10–3   Correlations between Commitment and Satisfaction

	N	r
Abelson (1983)	107	.76
Arnold & Feldman (1982)	654	.69
Bateman & Strasser (1984)	time 1—129	.55 ⎱
	time 2—129	.63 ⎰ .59
Brooke, Russell, & Price (1988)	577	.55
Curry, Wakefield, Price & Mueller (1986)	time 1—508	.50 ⎱
	time 2—508	.53 ⎰ .52
Farrell & Rusbult (1981)	study 2—107	.67
Griffin (1988)	experimental group—73	.38
	comparison group—73	.38
Lee & Mowday (1987)	1,621	.70
Oliver & Brief (1983)	114	.62
Porter, Steers, Mowday, & Boulian (1974)	33–60 (46)	.46
Williams & Hazer (1986)	sample 1—106	.68[a]
	sample 2—154	.75[a]
	(weighted) $\bar{r}$ =	**.64**

[a]Not in published report; personal communication from authors.

There is some controversy over the causal interpretation of these concurrent, correlational data, however. Bateman and Strasser (1984) claimed that their data support a reverse-causal interpretation, with commitment causing satisfaction. Curry, Wakefield, Price, and Mueller (1986) reported no support for a causal interpretation in either direction. Williams and Hazer (1986), using data from previous studies conducted by others, support a model in which job conditions cause satisfaction, which in turn causes commitment, which in turn affects the intent to leave or remain and then actual turnover. We prefer the last model, although since all the above studies were correlational, no particular causal interpretation can be proved. It seems logical that satisfaction would affect organizational commitment, although satisfaction is certainly not its only determinant. (The failure of longitudinal studies to support the satisfaction causes turnover interpretation may be due to the fact that there is no causal lag or that the lag is very short.)

It is conceivable that commitment could play a causal role in satisfaction as well. For example, an individual who for various reasons could not leave an organization (e.g., age, family attachments to the area) might look harder for things to like about the job or adjust his or her values to match what the job offers.

Thus the relationship between satisfaction and commitment may very well be reciprocal, but we believe that the stronger causal relationship goes from satisfaction to commitment (with additional personal and job factors affecting each reaction as well). If this is true, it is an important breakthrough in the satisfaction-performance controversy in that it allows one to get, at last, from affect to performance. The relation, however, is indirect rather than direct. Satisfaction keeps the individual attached to the organization and makes him or her willing to accept new goals. A recent, unpublished study by Mayer (1989) was the first to develop separate measures of commitment to remain with the organization and commitment to its goals and values. Job satisfaction was significantly related to *both* types of commitment. *If* these goals to which the individual is committed are challenging (and the other requisite conditions are present), *then* high performance will be the result. Of course, if the goals are *too* challenging, they may cause increased stress, dissatisfaction, and turnover.

Looking at the same issue from a more macro perspective, satisfaction will encourage citizenship behaviors that would probably not show up in any one individual's performance record, but would facilitate overall organizational functioning. On the other side of the same coin, dissatisfaction, by promoting defiant, aggressive, work avoidant, and defensive behaviors, would make it less likely that organizational goals and policies would be taken seriously. Fisher and Locke (1987) have summarized the results of a number of studies that have found that job satisfaction and dissatisfaction correlate substantially with conglomerate measures of pro- and anti-organizational actions.

CONCLUSION

We have now presented goal setting theory in its entirety. We next integrate this chapter and the nine preceding chapters into a coherent formulation of the theory. This formulation also provides an integration of goal setting theory with relevant aspects of other work motivation theories.

11

INTEGRATION: THE HIGH PERFORMANCE CYCLE

The purpose of this chapter is twofold. First, it represents a condensed summary and integration of the previous chapters. (Since we wanted to make the chapter stand alone, it is deliberately repetitious of previous material.) Second, it integrates our theory, insofar as possible, with other theories of work motivation.

Industrial-organizational psychologists have been studying motivation and satisfaction in the workplace for some five decades. For at least three reasons, however, progress in understanding these phenomena has been slow. First, it turned out that the motivation to work (exert effort) and satisfaction are relatively independent outcomes; thus somewhat different theoretical perspectives are required to understand them (Locke, 1970a, 1970b). Connecting the two types of theories has proven to be especially difficult (Henne & Locke, 1985). Second, theories within each domain, especially motivation-performance theories, have focused on only a very limited aspect of the domain such as needs (Maslow, 1954), perceived fairness (Adams, 1965), or managerial motives (Miner, 1977). Third, the phenomena themselves are highly complex, thus extensive research has been required to understand them regardless of any attempts to connect them.

It is now possible, however, to piece several of these theories together into a coherent whole using goal setting theory as the core. This integrated model can not only explain, in terms of broad fundamentals, both the motivation to work and job satisfaction, it can specify certain interrelationships between them. For purposes of simplicity we will describe this model in terms of a single, interrelated sequence of events. We call this sequence the high performance cycle. It is outlined in Figure 11–1. This model is restricted primarily to the individual level of

This chapter has been adapted from E. A. Locke and G. P. Latham (in press), "Work Motivation: The High Performance Cycle," in U. Kleinbeck, H. Thierry, H. Haecker, and H. Quast (Eds.), *Work Motivation* (Hillsdale, NJ: Lawrence Erlbaum Associates). Reprinted by permission of L. Erlbaum.

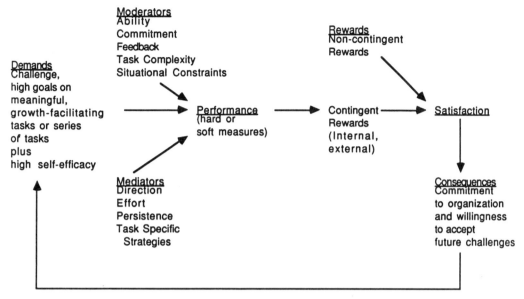

FIGURE 11-1   The High Performance Cycle

analysis, though there is evidence that the same principles apply to groups and organizations (Locke & Latham, 1984a; Latham & Lee, 1986; Smith, Locke, & Barry, in press). For purposes of simplicity, the model omits some causal paths including bidirectional causal relationships.

DEMANDS (CHALLENGE)

The model starts with demands being made of or challenges provided for the individual employee or manager. The theoretical base for this part of the model is goal setting theory (Lee, Locke, & Latham, 1989; Locke, 1968b; Locke, 1978; Locke & Latham, 1984a; Locke, Shaw, Saari, & Latham, 1981). This theory (based on earlier work by Ryan, 1970) asserts that performance goals are immediate regulators or causes of task or work performance.

Goal setting theory approaches the explanation of performance quite differently from that of motive or need theories such as those of McClelland and Maslow. While needs and (subconscious) motives are no doubt crucial to a full understanding of human action, they are several steps removed from action itself (Locke & Henne, 1986). Goal setting theory was developed by starting with the situationally specific, conscious motivational factors closest to action: goals and intentions. It then worked backward from these to determine what causes goals and what makes them effective. In contrast, need and motive theories started with more remote and general (often subconscious) regulators and tried to work forward to action, usually ignoring situationally specific and conscious factors. Generally, the specific, close-to-action approaches (including goal setting theory;

social-cognitive theory, Bandura, 1986; and turnover intentions theory, Mobley, 1982) have been much more successful in explaining action than the general, far-from-action approaches that stress general, subconscious needs, motives, and values (Locke & Henne, 1986; Miner, 1980; Pinder, 1984).[1] The interrelationship between the two types of theories and sets of concepts is highly complex and not yet fully understood. For example, need for achievement (measured as a subconscious motive using the TAT) has been found to be unrelated to goal choice (Roberson-Bennett, 1983). But the value for achievement, a conscious motive that is not correlated with N-ach, has been found to be significantly related to goal choice (Matsui, Okada, & Kakuyama, 1982). We could hypothesize that one way that general needs, motives, and subconscious values influence behavior is through their effects on situationally specific, conscious goals and intentions in conjunction with perceived situational demands.

Goal setting research has shown repeatedly that people who try to attain specific and challenging (difficult) goals perform better on a task than people who try for specific but moderate or easy goals, vague goals such as "do your best," or no goals at all. This finding, replicated in close to four hundred studies involving forty thousand subjects, has been verified by both narrative and enumerative reviews (Latham & Lee, 1986; Locke at al., 1981) and meta-analyses (Mento, Steel, & Karren, 1987; Tubbs, 1986). These findings have shown external validity across a wide variety of tasks ($n = 88$) from simple reaction time to scientific and engineering work, as well as across laboratory and field settings, short and long time spans, hard and soft performance criteria, quantity and quality measures, and individual and group situations (Latham & Lee, 1986). The findings also generalize outside North America (Earley, 1986c; Erez, 1986; Punnett, 1986; Schmidt, Kleinbeck, & Brockman, 1984; Wood, Bandura, & Bailey, in press).

The finding of goal setting theory—that performance is a positive function of goal difficulty (assuming adequate ability)—is at odds with achievement motivation theory. Achievement motivation theory (Atkinson, 1958) asserts that maximum motivation will occur at moderate levels of difficulty where the product of probability of success (PS) and the incentive value of success (assumed to be 1-PS) is highest (assuming the motivation to succeed is stronger than the motivation to avoid failure). However, the curvilinear, inverse–U function originally obtained by Atkinson (1958) has proven difficult to replicate (Arvey, 1972; Locke & Shaw, 1984; McClelland, 1961; Mento, Cartledge, & Locke, 1980). Two problems with that model are the failure to include an explicit goal setting stage and the failure to measure commitment to succeeding. These factors are crucial to predicting the individual's response to subjective probability estimates (Locke & Shaw, 1984).

Challenging goals are usually implemented in terms of specific levels of output to be attained (e.g., 50 assemblies completed in eight hours; 10% improvement in sales in six months). However, work challenges can be provided

---

[1] It is worth noting that attitude theory has recently gone through the same metamorphosis as work motivation theory in that theories that predict behavior from generalized attitudes have been supplanted by far more successful theories that focus on situationally specific attitudes and intentions to act (e.g., see Fishbein & Ajzen, 1975).

in many forms—e.g., a performance quality goal to be achieved (Koch, 1979); the frequency with which specific job behaviors are to be engaged in (Latham, Mitchell, & Dossett, 1978); a deadline to be met (Bryan & Locke, 1967b); a high degree of responsibility (Bray, Campbell, & Grant, 1974); or a cost goal (Klein, 1973).

There are several different sources of job demands or challenges. They may come from authority figures such as supervisors, managers, or the CEO (Bray et al., 1974). They may come through a joint decision on the part of the boss and a subordinate (participation). Demands may also come from peers either as direct pressure to perform at a certain level or in the form of role models (Earley & Kanfer, 1985; Rakestraw & Weiss, 1981). Direct peer pressure to restrict output has been observed frequently, including in the famous Hawthorne studies (Roethlisberger & Dickson, 1956). However, there can also be peer pressure to not produce below a certain minimum or to produce at a high level (Seashore, 1954). Goals, deadlines, and high workloads can also be chosen by the individual employee in the form of self-set goals. Research on "level of aspiration" in the 1930s and 1940s found that self-set goals were affected by past successes and failures and by personality factors (Lewin, 1958). More recently it has been argued that in addition to those who value achievement, Type A personalities (specifically those high in job involvement) are especially likely to put high demand on themselves (Kirmeyer, 1987; Taylor, Locke, Lee, & Gist, 1984). Finally, demands can stem from forces external or partly external to the organization, such as unions, bankers, stockholders, competitors, or customers.

In summary, the precursor of a high level of work motivation will be present when the individual is confronted by a high degree of challenge in the form of a specific, difficult goal or its equivalent. Challenge both affects and is affected by the expectancies and valences that are associated with goals.

EXPECTANCY, SELF-EFFICACY, AND VALENCE

Expectancy and self-efficacy play a ubiquitous role in the high performance cycle. As we shall see below, high expectancy and self-efficacy lead to high levels of goal commitment. They also lead to high goal levels when goals are self-chosen (Locke, Frederick, Lee, & Bobko, 1984). Furthermore, they affect the individual's response to feedback concerning progress in relation to goals and may even affect the efficiency of their task strategies (Wood & Bandura, in press b). Finally, they have a direct effect on performance independently of goals.

At first glance there may seem to be a contradiction between goal theory and expectancy theory, a subjective expected utility model first introduced into industrial-organizational psychology by Vroom (1964). Expectancy theory states that the force toward a given choice or action will be a product of the individual's belief that exerting effort will produce a certain level of performance (expectancy), the belief that such performance will lead to valued outcomes (instrumentality) and the value (valence) of those outcomes. Expectancy theory, therefore, posits a positive relationship between expectancy and performance (holding instrumentality and valence constant). Goal theory asserts that hard goals, which have a low probability of being reached, lead to better performance than easy goals, which have a high probability of being reached. Thus probability of success is negatively related to performance.

The apparent contradiction between expectancy theory and goal setting theory regarding performance has been resolved in two different ways by Locke, Motowidlo, and Bobko (1986) based on the ideas of Garland (1984) and Bandura (1982). Garland (1984) found that *within* any given goal group where the expectancy measure has the same referent for all subjects, there was a positive association between expectancy and performance (see Locke, Frederick, Lee, & Bobko, 1984); only *between* groups did high goals with low mean expectancies lead to higher performance than low goals with high mean expectancies—the opposite of the within-group pattern. The between-group finding was an artifact of the different reference points for measuring expectancy of success.

Another resolution by Locke et al. (1986) is based on Bandura's self-efficacy concept. Self-efficacy is a key concept in Bandura's (1986) social-cognitive theory and is defined as one's judgment of "how well one can execute courses of action required to deal with prospective situations" (Bandura, 1982, p. 122). Self-efficacy is broader in meaning than expectancy in that it includes one's estimate of one's capacity to perform at a certain level all factors considered (e.g., ability, effort, adaptability, attributions, situational factors, etc.). Self-efficacy is measured by having individuals rate their confidence in attaining each of a number of different performance levels; it is not measured in relation to goal levels. Thus the measures are directly comparable between and within groups. Locke, Frederick, Lee, and Bobko (1984) found that self-efficacy was related positively to performance both within and between groups; subjects with higher goals have higher self-efficacy on the average than those with lower goals. The higher the efficacy, the higher the performance.

The relationship between goals and valences is also a provocative one. If individuals are asked to indicate their expected satisfaction with attaining each of a number of different performance levels after being given specific performance goals, it is found that the mean valence rating is related *inversely* to goal level. That is, subjects with low or easy goals anticipate greater satisfaction with virtually *every* level of performance than high or hard goals.

This finding becomes intelligible once it is realized that goals (and values) are the standard by which one judges the adequacy or successfulness of one's performance (Bandura, in press; Locke, 1976). Since satisfaction is contingent on attaining one's goal, it follows that people with low goals will be minimally satisfied with a low performance attainment and will be progressively more satisfied with every level of attainment above their goal. The principle is the same for people with high goals except that to be minimally satisfied, they must achieve more than people with low goals. Thus they use a higher standard in judging the adequacy of *every* level of performance. In short, people with high standards have to achieve more to be satisfied than people with low standards. *Goal level is inversely related to valence because they are opposite sides of the same coin.* At the same time, instrumentality is typically higher for higher than for lower goals because high performance attainments in life are typically associated with greater rewards (jobs, promotions, raises, recognition) than low attainments.

MODERATORS

There are five known factors that moderate the strength of the relationship between goals and action. (Personality and demographic factors are less reliable moderators and are not discussed here—but see Chapter 9.)

Ability

It is obvious that ability limits the individual's capacity to respond to a challenge. Goal setting research has found that the relation of goal difficulty to performance is curvilinear in that performance levels off after the limit of ability has been reached (Locke, 1982b; Locke, Frederick, Buckner, & Bobko, 1984). Furthermore, there is some evidence that goal setting has stronger effects among high than among low ability individuals, and that ability has stronger effects among high goal than among low goal individuals (Locke, 1965b, 1982b). One reason for the latter finding is that when goals are low and people are committed to them, output is limited to levels below what is possible.

Commitment

Challenging goals lead to high performance only if the individual is committed to them. The effect of variation in goal commitment on performance is shown in phase II of Erez and Zidon's experiment (1984); they found that as commitment declined in response to increasing goal difficulty, performance declined rather than increased.

     Many factors have been found to affect goal commitment (Locke, Latham, & Erez, 1988). Most of these can be interpreted within the framework of expectancy theory in that they involve either the individual's expectancy or instrumentality-valence (value) of performing well or reaching the goal. Expectancy theory concepts have been found to be significant predictors of goal commitment (Klein, 1988; Mento et al., 1980). A partial exception may be authority that has normative as well as instrumental components. One of the most powerful determinants of goal commitment, in fact, is what French and Raven (1959) termed legitimate power or authority. Authority in the form of the experimenter in the laboratory or the manager at the workplace has been sufficient to guarantee high goal commitment in the overwhelming majority of goal setting studies. The "demand" aspect of the experimental settting has been documented by Orne (1962). In short, goals that are assigned by authority figures typically affect the individual's personal goal. Instructions to try for a certain goal even carry over to later trials in which the individual is free to choose his or her own goal (Locke, Frederick, Buckner, & Bobko, 1984; Locke, Frederick, Lee, & Bobko, 1984). The power of authority to produce commitment has surprised many people, but it should not shock those familiar with the potent demand effects obtained in the controversial Milgram experiments (Milgram, 1974). In those studies, experimenter-authority figures were able to convince some people to take actions that were far more extreme than simply trying for a goal. Field studies have shown that direct pressure for performance is effective in raising performance as long as it is not viewed as excessive (Andrews & Farris, 1972; Hall & Lawler, 1971). (In addition to its normative aspects, authority, of course, may enhance expectancy and is typically associated with rewards and punishments such as praise, raises, promotions, criticisms, and firing.)

Related to the above is the finding that setting goals participatively does not lead to greater goal commitment or productivity than having the authority figure simply assign the goals (Latham & Lee, 1986; Tubbs, 1986; Schweiger & Leana, 1986; Wagner & Gooding, 1987). An apparent exception to these conclusions is found in several experiments by Erez and her colleagues (Erez, 1986; Erez & Arad, 1986; Erez, Earley, & Hulin, 1985). They found that participative goal setting led to higher commitment and performance than did assigned goals. Latham, Erez, and Locke (1988) conducted four jointly designed experiments to resolve this apparent contradiction. While a number of factors were found to have contributed to the difference in results, the most important was that Erez and her colleagues used very brief, curt "tell" instructions in the assigned goal setting conditions, whereas Latham and his colleagues, who had obtained null results, used somewhat more lengthy "tell and sell" instructions. In the jointly conducted experiments, no difference was found between the tell and sell and participative styles, but both were more effective than the tell style. Thus assigned goal setting is as effective as participative goal setting providing the goals are accompanied by a reasonable explanation and the experimenter or manager is supportive.[2]

A second factor affecting goal commitment is peer influence, specifically peer pressure and modeling. As noted earlier, peer pressure has long been known to induce commitment to low goals in the form of restriction of output (Mathewson, 1931; Roethlisberger & Dickson, 1956; Taylor, 1967). Strong group norms also may produce commitment in the form of low variance in production among group members (Seashore, 1954). Commitment to high goals will occur when the group norms are high (Seashore, 1954) and when there are peer models performing at a high level (Bandura, 1986; Earley & Kanfer, 1985). Assigning both individual and group goals for a group task produces higher commitment to the individual goals than assigning individual goals alone (Matsui, Kakuyama, & Onglatco, 1987).

A third factor known to affect commitment is the use of rewards or incentives. Numerous work motivation theories predict this either directly or by implication, including expectancy theory (rewards promote high valences), behavior modification (rewards act as reinforcers), and social-cognitive theory (rewards are information cues). Goal commitment is high when working to attain the goals is perceived as instrumental in gaining other valued outcomes (Mento et al., 1980; Yukl & Latham, 1978). Specific outcomes that have been studied include winning in a competitive situation (Locke & Shaw, 1984) and money (Oldham, 1975). In another study verbal self-congratulations were especially powerful in motivating children working toward goals (Masters, Furman, & Barden, 1977). The commit-

---

[2] There may be important cognitive benefits of participation in terms of getting better ideas of how to perform a task by asking for subordinate input (Campbell & Gingrich, 1986; Latham & Winters, 1989), but this issue is not directly pertinent to the motivational (commitment) effect of participation.

ment concept may also explain why incentives sometimes fail to work. For example, Mowen, Middlemist, and Luther (1981) found that offering a bonus only for reaching a very difficult to impossible goal led to lower performance than assigning the same goal but paying people for performance (on a piece-rate basis) rather than for goal success as such. Although commitment was not actually measured in this study, it was presumably higher when there was a reward for partial success (difficult goals with piece rate) than when only full success was rewarded (difficult goals with bonus); the instrumentality of effort was presumably higher in the former case.

A fourth factor affecting commitment, as noted earlier, is the individual's expectancy of being able to reach the goal or perform at a high level. In general, goals that are or are perceived as difficult are less likely to be accepted than goals that are moderate or easy, although in laboratory setting a high degree of commitment can be obtained for a short time to goals that are impossible to reach (Locke, 1982b). Individuals usually *prefer* goals in the moderate range of difficulty, but their choices can be influenced by previously assigned goals (Locke, Frederick, Buckner, & Bobko, 1984). Like expectancy, self-efficacy is related to goal commitment and to choice of goal difficulty level (Locke, Frederick, Lee, & Bobko, 1984).

Other factors that have been found to affect goal commitment include the publicness of the goal (Hollenbeck, Williams, & Klein, 1989); the subjects' degree of ego involvement (Bayton, 1943); and attributions regarding previous performance (Silver & Greenhaus, 1983).

Feedback

Both laboratory and field research have shown that knowledge of one's overall score on a task (knowledge of results or KR) does not lead to improved performance when differential goal setting by KR and no-KR groups is controlled (Locke, Cartledge, & Koeppel, 1968). Thus KR by itself is not a sufficient condition for improved performance (Latham et al., 1978).[3] Frequent positive findings reported for the effects of KR (Ammons, 1956; Annett, 1969; Kopelman, 1982, 1986) probably stem from the deliberate or inadvertent confounding or combining of KR with other factors such as goal setting, information regarding better task strategies, recognition, and reward (e.g., see Locke, 1980c).

Other research, however, has shown that goal setting in the absence of feedback is also ineffective (Erez, 1977; Locke et al., 1981). Goals and feedback together lead to higher performance than either one alone (Becker, 1978; Reber & Wallin, 1984; Strang, Lawrence, & Fowler, 1978). The joint benefit of goals and feedback is attributable to their fulfilling different but crucial functions: goals direct and energize action, while KR allows the tracking of progress in relation to the goal.

Matsui, Okada, and Inoshita (1983) found that when individuals working toward a goal were told that they were behind the pace required to attain their

---

[3] Knowledge of performance can affect subsequent performance if it promotes learning (e.g., of better techniques). The present discussion is confined to the motivational effects of feedback.

goal, they subsequently improved their performance, while those told they were "on target" did not. Bandura and Cervone (1983, 1986) found that self-efficacy moderates the individual's response to feedback indicative of below target performance. Maximum performance following feedback is attained when individuals anticipate low satisfaction for performance at the same level again, have high self-efficacy, and set high goals for future performance (Bandura, 1988).

Task Complexity

Wood (1986) defined *task complexity* in terms of three dimensions: component complexity (number of elements in task), coordinative complexity (the number and nature of the relationships between the elements), and dynamic complexity (the number and types of elements and the relationships between them over time). Wood, Mento, and Locke (1987) rated the tasks used in 125 goal setting studies on the basis of these dimensions and related these complexity ratings to the size of the goal setting effect obtained. The meta-analysis results confirmed a significant moderating role for task complexity. The average effect size was significantly larger on the simpler than on the more complex tasks, although the effects were significant on both types.

An explanation for this finding is that on simple tasks, the effort induced by the goals leads relatively directly to task performance. In more complex tasks, however, effort does not necessarily pay off so directly. One must decide where and how to allocate effort. For example, setting a goal for high grades may not actually lead to higher grades unless the student uses proper study habits and an appropriate course strategy based on knowledge of what the professor is looking for. Thus in more complex tasks, the plans, tactics, and strategies used by the individual play a larger role in task performance than they do in simpler tasks where the number of different strategies is more limited and are generally known to all performers (Chesney & Locke, 1988).

There is some evidence that on complex, heuristic tasks where the individual has had no previous experience with the task and is pressured to perform well immediately, specific, hard goals may not lead to better performance than "do best" goals and may even lead to poorer performance (Earley, Connolly, & Ekegren, 1989; Huber, 1985b). Under these conditions hard goal subjects seem to choose less than optimal strategies. We will have more to say about task strategies in a later section.

Situational Constraints

Goals are less likely to be accomplished if there are situational constraints blocking performance than if there are no such blocks (Peters, Chassie, Lindholm, O'Connor, & Kline, 1982; White & Locke, 1981). On the other hand, one of the consequences of hard goals (especially if accompanied by high commitment and self-efficacy) is to motivate people to overcome obstacles through tenacity and perseverance (Huber & Neale, 1987).

In summary, a specific, challenging goal has maximum effect when the individual has high self-efficacy and ability, there is commitment to the goal, there is feedback showing progress in relation to the goal, the task is simple, and there are no blocks to performance. Let us now consider the mechanisms by which goals affect performance.

MEDIATING MECHANISMS

Given that the individual has a challenging goal and the moderating variables facilitate goal attainment, what are the mediators or mechanisms by which goals actually affect performance? There are three relatively direct mechanisms, which Wood and Locke (see Chapter 13) call *Universal Task Strategies* (UTS's). These are direction of attention, effort, and persistence. They correspond to the three attributes of motivated action: direction (choice), intensity, and duration. We call them UTS's because virtually all individuals learn at an early age that they perform better on a task if they pay attention to it, exert effort on it, and persist at it over time than if they do not.

When acted on, goals direct attention to the activity specified by the goal and simultaneously away from goal-irrelevant activities. Locke and Bryan (1969b), for example, gave individuals six types of feedback on car driving performance but goals for only one of them. Performance improved only on the performance dimensions for which a goal was set. Similarly, if an individual reads a prose passage and is told to look for information about man-eating sharks in an article about sea creatures, he or she will (given goal commitment) focus on content relevant to sharks and pay less attention to information not related to sharks (e.g., see Rothkopf & Billington, 1979). Goals will direct attention most effectively when they are specific (e.g., look for three facts about sharks) rather than vague or general (e.g., look for information about sea creatures). More specific goals regulate action more closely than more general goals (Locke, Chah, Harrison, & Lustgarten, 1989).

The effort aroused and expended in response to a goal depends on the difficulty of the goal (Locke, 1968b); the greater the demands, the greater the expended effort (Locke, 1967c), assuming the goal is accepted. For example, the individual who tries to do forty push-ups will expend more energy than the one who tries to do only four, other things (e.g., ability), being equal. Effort effects of goals have been found using both objective (Bandura & Cervone, 1986) and subjective (Earley, Wojnaroski, & Prest, 1987) measures of effort.

Third, goals affect task persistence in that, given goal commitment, people will continue working at the task until the goal is reached. Persistence is really directed effort extended over time. Thus, if there are no time limits, people will work longer and more tenaciously for a harder goal than for an easier goal (Cannon-Bowers & Levine, 1988; Huber & Neale, 1987; Laporte & Nath, 1976). There can be a trade-off between speed and time, so that people with low demands and a long time limit or no time limit may work more slowly than those with high demands in order to fill the time available (Bryan & Locke, 1967b; Latham & Locke, 1975). The excess time in such a case, however, is the result of a slower pace rather than of greater persistence.

Finally, goals can affect performance indirectly by motivating the individual to develop task specific strategies or plans. Wood and Locke (see Chapter 13) have suggested that there are, broadly speaking, two types of task-specific strategies: Stored Task Specific Strategies (STSS's) and New Task Specific Strategies (NTSS's). Stored strategies are learned through practice and instruction on the task (e.g., how to hit the basic strokes in tennis) and become automatized in the form of skills. Such strategies will be brought into play automatically when the individual works on the relevant task. If STSS's fail to work either because the task is actually new or because certain aspects of the task situation are different (e.g., a businessperson faced with changing market or new competitors), the individual may develop NTSS's in order to cope with the new circumstances. Creative thinking and problem solving will come into play. There is no guarantee that individual will always discover or choose appropriate task-specific strategies when confronted with a goal on a task, but goals may promote the search for and adoption of strategies.

Research on goals and strategies indicates that (1) goals naturally lead to the development and execution of task-specific strategies (Latham & Baldes, 1975); (2) one of these strategies, when the goal is for quantity of output only, can be to lower quality (Erez, in press); (3) specific, hard goals stimulate planning in general and often high-quality planning (Smith, Locke, & Barry, in press); (4) specific, hard goals increase the probability that primed or trained strategies will actually be used (Earley & Perry, 1987; Earley, Connolly, & Lee, 1988); (5) task strategies and self-efficacy are reciprocally related and both affect performance independently (Wood & Bandura, in press, b); (6) task strategies are more strongly related than goals to performance on complex tasks (Chesney & Locke, 1988); and (7) specific, hard goals are most likely to lead to the development of poor task strategies when (a) the task is complex and heuristic; (b) the subjects have had no prior experience with the task, and (c) the subjects are pressured to perform at a high level immediately.

PERFORMANCE

To the degree that the demands are challenging, the facilitating moderators are present, and the mediators are operative, task performance will be high on whatever dimensions the goal specifies as important (quantity, quality, etc.). In work settings, three basic types of "hard" or objective outcome measures can be used to index performance (Locke & Latham, 1984a): units of production or quality (amount produced, number of errors); dollars (profits, costs, income, sales); and time (job attendance, lateness in meeting deadlines).

When objective outcome measures are unavailable or inappropriate, various behavioral measures are recommended (Latham, 1986). An example would be the frequency with which various suitable or critical behaviors are performed by employees or supervisors. For example, does the supervisor explain to his or her subordinates the reasons for a pending organizational change? Does the salesclerk smile when approaching a customer? The frequency of such behaviors can be measured by an observer, thus making it a more objective measure, or it can be estimated by supervisors, subordinates, customers, or others, thus making it a more subjective measure. If critical behaviors, derived from a job analysis, are demonstrated frequently, they will lead to or help lead to desirable outcome measures such as productivity, sales, and profits (Latham & Wexley, 1981).

REWARDS

Rewards are placed toward the end rather than at the beginning of our model in contrast to behaviorist theory which would put them, at least in terms of causal importance, at the beginning—in the form of past reinforcements. The instrumental response in behaviorist theory is assumed to be emitted at the initial stages more or less randomly; when the response is regularly reinforced, the reinforcement schedule becomes controlling.

Bandura (1986) has identified many flaws in this theory. For example, responses are made not just on the basis of past outcomes but also on the basis of anticipated future outcomes, observations of models, internal standards, and self-efficacy. Past rewards can be an incentive to act under certain conditions, but they are not controlling. Furthermore, rewards will not necessarily encourage high performance in the future unless such performance is first emitted—which may never happen in the absence of high demands.

Once high performance has been demonstrated, rewards can become important as inducements to continue, but not all rewards are external. Internal, self-administered rewards that can occur following high performance include a sense of achievement based on attaining a certain level of excellence, pride in accomplishment, and feelings of success and efficacy. The experience of success will depend on reaching one's goal or level of aspiration (Lewin, 1958) or making progress toward the goal. Satisfaction will also depend on the perceived instrumentality of performance in attaining longer-term goals (Locke, Cartledge, & Knerr, 1970). The self rather than others is typically given credit for successful actions (Locke, 1976). Higher satisfaction is experienced if the success is attributed to the self rather than to external factors such as luck (Weiner, 1986).

High goals may lead to less-experienced satisfaction than low goals, since they are attained, by definition, less frequently. Satisfaction with performance is positively associated with the number of successes experienced (Locke, 1965c). Thus some compromise on goal difficulty may be necessary in order to maximize both satisfaction and performance. However, there are sources of satisfaction associated with simply trying for hard goals, such as the satisfaction of complying with a respected authority figure, the satisfaction of responding to a challenge, the satisfaction of making some progress toward the goals, and the belief that future benefits may accrue in terms of skill development (Matsui, Okada, & Mizuguchi, 1981). Furthermore, it is possible to reward partial success.

Success and failure (depending on how they are appraised) can affect subsequent self-efficacy. Bandura (1988) has noted that high self-efficacy itself can produce positive affect just as low self-efficacy can lead to negative affect, including anxiety and depression.

Another issue to consider with respect to the effects of goal attainment is the nature of the task. Hackman and Oldham's (1980) job characteristics theory states that the degree to which the work is seen as rewarding is dependent on the degree to which the task possesses four core attributes: (personal) significance; feedback; responsibility/autonomy; and identity (as a whole piece of work). In general, empirical studies support this theory with regard to work satisfaction (Locke & Henne, 1986). These core attributes are growth-producing, and they may fulfill important needs. An extensive review of the literature on the relation of job scope to satisfaction also supports the Hackman-Oldham theory (Stone, 1986).

The external rewards that are most likely to be tied to performance in relation to goals are pay, promotion, and recognition. Expectancy theory (Vroom, 1964; Dachler & Mobley, 1973) states that the motivational power of pay in producing high performance will be a function of the belief that high performance can be attained, the belief that high performance will lead to outcomes, and the degree to which those outcomes are valued.

Equity theory (Adams, 1963, 1965) asserts that pay will bring satisfaction to the degree that it is seen as fair or equitable. Equity judgments will be based on the judged ratio of the individual's outputs and inputs in comparison with the output/input ratio of people with whom the individual compares himself or herself. If pay is seen as inequitable, thus producing dissatisfaction, people will take steps to restore equity by, for example, modifying the quantity or quality of their output (Locke & Henne, 1986).

Perceptions of equity will depend on who the comparison person is. Consider, for example, Park Jin Kean (Halberstam, 1986), who works twelve hours a day, six days a week, as a foreman in an auto factory and makes $9,600 a year. Park is very proud of his job and his salary. Park is Korean, and in Korea the average wage is $2,000; furthermore, he grew up on a farm where he worked even harder for less return. Clearly, Park's adaptation level (Helson, 1964) is radically different from that of most Americans and even of most Japanese workers.

An important reward for most employees is that of recognition (Herzberg, Mausner, & Snyderman, 1959; Locke, 1976). A recent survey of public sector employees who performed staff work for a state legislature (Locke, 1987) found that the most important forms of recognition were personal thanks and credit from the recipients of the work; being given responsibility for a new project; being sent to a professional meeting as an expert representative on a topic; and seeing one's work have an impact (in this case an impact on actual legislation). Peters and Waterman (1982) have noted that the most effective American organizations make heavy use of recognition not only in the forms previously mentioned but also in the form of badges, pins, plaques, buttons, notices on the bulletin board, and membership in high performance "clubs."

In addition to contingent rewards, virtually all employees receive various noncontingent rewards based simply on the fact they hold the job. These may include, for example, fringe benefits, base pay, seniority awards, job security, flexible hours, good equipment, considerate supervision, congenial co-workers, and association with a prestigious or reputable organization. While such rewards may not serve directly to motivate high performance, they do encourage the employee to remain with the organization rather than leaving.

SATISFACTION

If internal and external rewards provide the individual with what he or she wants or values or considers appropriate or beneficial, the individual experiences satisfaction with the job (Locke, 1969c, 1976, 1984). Job satisfaction can be viewed as the result of a positive appraisal of the job against one's value standards. This appraisal model is based on Arnold (1960) and is congruent with Lazarus and Folkman's (1984) appraisal approach to stress. Job satisfaction is not a result of the person alone or of the job alone but of the person in relation to the job—the job as appraised by the person. Thus, if the job is appraised as fulfilling or facilitating attainment of values, satisfaction is experienced; if the job is appraised as blocking or negating one's values, dissatisfaction is experienced.

More important values have a greater impact on affective reactions than less important values (Locke, 1976; Locke, Fitzpatrick, & White, 1983; Mobley & Locke, 1970). The work itself is usually a more important aspect of the job for professional and skilled people than for others. Thus, as a category, the work itself is usually the job aspect most strongly related to overall job satisfaction for people at the higher job levels (Locke et al., 1983). As noted earlier, having meaningful work leads to high work satisfaction, and if rewarded by the organization, to high satisfaction with rewards as well.

CONSEQUENCES OF SATISFACTION
AND DISSATISFACTION

The most difficult problem for industrial-organizational psychology researchers has been to determine what happens after the individual employee becomes satisfied or dissatisfied. It was originally assumed that high satisfaction would lead to high productivity out of gratitude to the employer (Locke, 1986b), but this association has consistently failed to be supported in the literature (Iaffaldano & Muchinsky, 1985; Podsakoff & Williams, 1986). At best, when the reward system is clearly tied to performance, satisfaction results from productivity (Henne & Locke, 1985; Podsakoff & Williams, 1986)—the opposite of the original assumption. However, even this relationship does not hold if the tie between rewards and performance is loose. Nor does the reverse model specify what satisfaction *does* lead to.

Recent theoretical and empirical work has suggested two important modifications of the simplistic assumption that satisfaction causes high performance. First, it has been recognized that satisfaction and dissatisfaction can have many different consequences (Fisher, 1980) depending on subsequent choices that the individual makes. Second, it has been found that a number of processes intervene between the experiencing of satisfaction and the taking of action.

Henne (1986, based on Henne & Locke, 1985) found through asking people to list their responses to dissatisfaction that there were at least six possible categories of responses. More recent work by Fisher and Locke (1987) and others has led to a refinement of these categories. The six current categories are (1) job avoidance (quitting); (2) work avoidance; (3) psychological defenses (e.g., drug abuse); (4) constructive protest (e.g., complaining); (5) defiance (refusing to do what is asked); and (6) aggression (theft, assault). The most reliable effect of dissatisfaction is with the first category, quitting.

Mobley (1982) developed a turnover model which starts with dissatisfaction but posits a number of intervening steps before the individual actually quits, such as thinking of quitting, considering alternative jobs, and searching for a job. The key step before actually leaving, however, is the formation of the intention to quit. The latter is the best predictor of actual turnover. It intervenes between the experience of dissatisfaction and quitting (Mobley, 1982; Steel & Ovalle, 1984).

The other side of the coin of the intent to leave is organizational commitment. Williams and Hazer (1986), in a reanalysis of data collected by others, found that job satisfaction affected organizational commitment, which in turn affected the intent to stay. Lee and Mowday (1987) obtained similar findings. O'Reilly and Chatman (1986) found significant correlations between commitment and the intent to stay. Curry, Wakefield, Price, and Mueller (1986) found strong associations between satisfaction and commitment but claimed these were due to both variables being associated with exogenous variables such as the nature of the work.

Mowday, Porter, and Steers (1982) reported consistent evidence for an association between commitment and turnover across a number of studies. Furthermore, they found that work experiences of the type that would lead to satisfaction (job scope or challenge, considerate supervision, compatible work groups) were associated with commitment.

Mowday et al. (1982) actually *defined* commitment as entailing three aspects: (1) the acceptance of the goals and values of the organization; (2) willingness to exert effort on behalf of the organization; and (3) a desire to stay with the organization. We have found eleven studies that calculated correlations between organizational commitment and job satisfaction, the mean weighted r in these studies was .64 (see Chapter 10). While there is still some controversy about the precise causal relationship betweeen these two variables, we believe that satisfaction is at least one causal factor in commitment. Only one study has looked for a relationship betweeen *goal* commitment and job satisfaction, and it was found to be significant (Anderson & O'Reilly, 1981).

If we assume, in line with at least some research evidence, that positive job experiences conducive to satisfaction are a crucial factor in bringing commitment about, and that commitment is a key factor in getting people to stay with the organization and cooperate with its members, then presumably committed employees will be prone to accept organizational goals or demands. Organ (1987) found that satisfaction is associated with "organizational citizenship" activities. In sum, individuals who are both satisfied with and thus committed to the organization should be more likely to stay with the organization and to accept the challenges that it presents to them. This link brings us back full circle to the beginning of our model (see Figure 11–1).

We have not attempted to specify the time span of the high performance cycle. Substantial aspects of it are repeated daily: the individual goes to work, is confronted by the day's challenges, takes action in response to them, experiences certain consequences as a result of that action, and increases, maintains, or decreases the degree of satisfaction and commitment experienced. The decision to quit when the individual becomes dissatisfied is not typically a decision that is made quickly but rather evolves gradually, incrementally, out of day-to-day experiences. Mowday et al. (1982) found that lowered commitment may precede actual quitting by several months. The final decision may be the sum total of accumulated experiences considered in conjunction with an estimate of the outlook for the future.

CONCLUSION

The high performance model has important implications for the management of organizations. Effective organizations must expect a lot of their employees and must try to ensure that they gain a sense of satisfaction in return for their efforts. Employee satisfaction will derive, in part, from giving employees personally meaningful work that they are capable of handling and, in part, from taking pains to reward good performance. Peters and Waterman (1982) have argued, consistent with this model, that the best American organizations in the private sector have organizational philosophies that place a high premium on excellence in performance and on respect for employees.

It is important to note that our model posits no *direct* connection between satisfaction and subsequent productivity. The lack of such connection has long puzzled researchers. The model shows two ways in which these factors are connected. First, consistent with the evidence (Henne & Locke, 1985), high satisfaction is shown to be the *result,* not the cause, of high performance when rewards are commensurate with such performance. Second, the model shows that *the subsequent effect of satisfaction on action is indirect, not direct.* Satisfaction only leads to high performance *if* it leads to organizational commitment and *if* this commitment is to specific, challenging goals, and *if* these goals, in turn, are associated with the relevant moderators and mediators. If the goals of the organization are low or other elements of the model are absent, high satisfaction will be followed by low rather than high performance. Thus it is not satisfaction alone that is the key to high performance but *satisfaction in conjunction with other factors* (White & Locke, 1981).

The model specifies the moderator variables that managers should take into account to ensure both high performance and satisfaction among the people they manage. Managers must ensure that their people are thoroughly trained before a high performance cycle can impact performance and satisfaction positively. Training is especially needed to enhance self-efficacy and hence goal commitment. If the person does not believe that goal attainment is possible, goal commitment will be low if not zero. Goal commitment will be high to the extent that the manager models the high performance cycle by making subordinates' goals clear and giving support and recognition. Feedback to subordinates regarding their progress toward goals is especially critical to the implementation of a high performance cycle. Without it, goals have little or no effect on subsequent performance. From a learning standpoint, feedback helps the employee to develop effective task strategies. From a motivational standpoint, feedback, if positive, builds self-efficacy and, if negative, pinpoints the need to improve by revealing a discrepancy between the goal and present performance.

The high performance cycle also has implications for self-management, a concept that has been studied for at least two decades in clinical settings (Kanfer, 1970) and only recently in organizations (Frayne & Latham, 1987; Latham & Frayne, 1989). Again, feedback plays a critical role. Goals are set in relation to feedback. A behavioral contract is written to oneself, specifying the strategies that one will take to attain the goal, and the rewards one will self-administer for both goal approximation and attainment. Rewards self-administered for goal approximation facilitate perceived self-efficacy and ensure ongoing goal commitment. In addition, they increase self-monitoring. The outcome is not only high performance but satisfaction derived from a sense of achievement. This has recently been demonstrated among union employees who increased their job attendance in a climate where peers encouraged absenteeism (Frayne & Latham, 1987; Latham & Frayne, 1989).

Because task complexity limits the positive effects of goals on performance and hence satisfaction, managers need to work with their people to enrich their jobs and then formulate effective task strategies. To the extent that this is ongoing, people should remain committed to the organization in which they work because of the degree of satisfaction that they continually experience. A concomitant finding of self-management in industry is that peers seek one another's input for ways of accomplishing tasks and derive pleasure from helping one another do so.

The high performance model also might be extended beyond work organizations to the field of education. For example, American education has in recent years been compared unfavorably with the educational system of the Japanese. Much more seems to be demanded of Japanese students (in terms of amount of homework, number of courses, etc.), especially in mathematics, than of American students. The result is that the average worker is very competent in math, a factor that helps Japanese organizations to use sophisticated quality control techniques very successfully. This, in turn, makes their goods highly competitive in the international marketplace.

This is not to deny that many factors have contributed to the success of the Japanese, but there seems to be little doubt that the Japanese educational system is one factor responsible for the remarkable growth of their economy over the past forty years. On the other side of the same coin, the American system with its lower demands may not bode well for our future. Perhaps the high performance cycle should be made part of our schools as well as our work organizations.

12

APPLICATIONS:

The Role of Goal Setting in Human Resource Management

> Merck knows exactly what the FDA wants and how it wants it—down to the size of the margins on the pages. It divides each task into small responsibilities, assigning a rigid deadline to each. Over the course of six months, some 75 regulatory people met 6,000 individual target dates to meet FDA approval.
>
> (*Business Week*, October 19, 1987)

In this chapter the central role of goal setting in the management of an organization's human resources is described. Human resource management includes such activities as job analysis, employee selection, performance appraisal, training, motivation, labor relations, decision making, and leadership.

In recent years management has recognized the importance of concentrating on an organization's human resources to improve productivity. This is because managing people is not totally restricted by the price of fuel, the purchase of a new facility, the discovery of a raw material, or the infusion of capital, as are other methods for improving productivity. But the problem of how to manage employees so they come to be and/or remain concerned with productivity has puzzled and frustrated managers for generations. One reason the problem has seemed difficult, if not mysterious, is that motivation ultimately comes from within the individual and therefore cannot be observed directly. Moreover, most managers are not in a position to change an employee's basic personality structure. The best they can do is to try to develop human resource systems that will increase the probability that the right people are chosen and are motivated to do the right things on the job. Such systems include a comprehensive job analysis to ensure the development of valid selection procedures for hiring and promotion purposes, valid performance appraisal systems to ensure that the person is measured on the "right" things and receives accurate feedback, effective training procedures to ensure that the person is adequately developed, and labor relations that are conducive to employee motivation.

This chapter is based in part on G. P. Latham (1983), "The Role of Goal Settting in Human Resource Management," *Research in Personnel and Human Resources Management, I*, JAI Press, 169–99. Reprinted by permission of JAI Press.

JOB ANALYSIS

A thorough job analysis is indispensable to most, if not all, human resource systems because job analysis identifies the knowledge, skill, or behavior that is critical for a person to demonstrate in performing a given set of duties. With this knowledge, the performance appraisal instrument is developed. The person is then assessed in terms of the frequency with which the person demonstrates this knowledge, skill, and/or behavior.

Similarly, the selection system is based on job analysis—the person designing the selection systems tries to make it job related. For example, job analysis indicates the type of questions the applicant should be asked in an interview and is the base from which suitable employee performance goals are derived.

In specifying the critical knowledge, skill, or behavior required of a person in a given job or position, job analysis identifies what a person must do on the job. If it is judged that the person has the aptitude to do what is required but lacks the skill, job analysis identifies the content of training programs needed to correct this deficiency. If the job is not being done despite the fact that the person has the requisite skills, job analysis makes it clear what the person has to start doing to keep the job. In this vein, a job analysis can assist in the development of effective union-management relations through the development of uniform guidelines for management's expectations of employee job behavior.

For these reasons, it is important that a job analysis yield a representative sample regarding the requisite knowledge, skills, and behavior of employees in given positions. With this in mind, Latham and Marshall (1982) conducted a job analysis of supervisors in a government agency. Employees were asked to list what they believed constituted effective job behavior, on the basis of firsthand observation. This request was in accordance with the 1978 Civil Service Reform Act (see Latham & Wexley, 1981, for an overview). In brief, this act states that each federal agency should develop appraisal systems that encourage employee participation in establishing performance standards. These standards are to be based on the critical elements of the job.

Because of the necessity for obtaining comprehensive information in a job analysis, and the emphasis in the Civil Service Reform Act on employee involvement in establishing standards, the usefulness of self-set goals was examined, in addition to assigned and participatively set goals. The goals set dealt with the number of standards or individual job behaviors that each person could list as critical for performance as a supervisor.

The importance of goal setting to job analysis is that job analysis must yield information that constitutes a representative sampling of the critical job behaviors in question. If each person contributing to the job analysis lists only one or two behaviors, the information generated from the job analysis may be incomplete. Consequently, fifty-seven supervisors in this study were randomly assigned to one of three conditions: participatively set, self-set, and assigned goals. Supervisors in the self-set goal condition were asked to specify the number of observable behaviors that they could list within twenty minutes. It was emphasized that the goal should be difficult, but attainable.

In the participative condition, the results from a pilot study were used to determine whether a goal was "difficult but attainable." If the goal set by an individual was too high or too low, the person was reminded that the goal should be truly difficult, but attainable: "Are you sure that a goal of _____ fits that description?" If the answer was no, the person was asked to set another goal.

Three supervisors, one in each condition, were processed concurrently. Thus it was possible to assign the goal agreed upon by the experimenter and the individual in the participative condition to the individual in the assigned condition. In this way, goal difficulty was held constant between the assigned and participatively set goals. This was obviously not possible in the self-set condition. However, a statistical analysis showed that the goal difficulty level in the self-set ($\bar{X}$ = 12.84) and the participative ($\bar{X}$ = 12.42) conditions were not appreciably different.

Eighty-four percent of the people in each condition attained their goals. The correlation between goal difficulty and performance was significant in all three conditions. Productivity, as defined by the actual number of items generated, did not differ among the three conditions. Thus goal setting proved to be useful as a technique in job analysis for getting people to contribute their knowledge. This was true regardless of whether the goals were assigned, participatively set, or self-set. The knowledge gained from the job analysis was of immediate use for developing valid methods for hiring people.

SITUATIONAL INTERVIEW

One of the first exhaustive literature reviews on the selection interview appeared over forty years ago (Wagner, 1949). The evidence showed that the interview lacked both reliability and validity. In the next two decades, seminal research (e.g., Webster, 1964) was conducted to investigate why this was the case. Among the findings were that applicants were not asked the same questions, and when they were asked the same questions, the questions were often not job related. When the same job-related questions were asked, the "correct" answers were usually transparent to the interviewee. When the correct answers were not obvious to the interviewees, they were usually not obvious to the interviewers either. Thus, two decades later, literature reviews of the interview showed that the reliability and validity of the interview were still low (Mayfield, 1964; Ulrich & Trumbo, 1965).

The seminal research by Webster (1964) and his colleagues was particularly helpful in identifying observation-judgmental errors that interviewers make when evaluating others. This research was seminal in that it stimulated investigations on ways to train people to increase their objectivity in evaluating others (e.g., Hedge & Kavanagh, 1988; Latham, Wexley, & Pursell, 1975; Wexley, Sanders, & Yukl, 1973). However, the results of these subsequent studies affected performance appraisal practices far more than they did the selection interview (Latham, 1986, 1988; Latham & Wexley, 1981). Thus by the end of the 1970s, there was no appreciable improvement in the reliability and validity of the interview (Arvey & Campion, 1982). In 1980 the first study on the situational interview appeared in the scientific literature (Latham, Saari, Pursell, & Campion, 1980). The method was shown to be both reliable and valid (Tenopyr & Oeltjen, 1982).

The situational interview is among the very few, if only, interview techniques that are grounded in theory. The theory, namely goal setting, states that intentions or goals are the immediate precursor of a person's behavior. The purpose of the situational interview is to identify a potential employee's intentions by presenting the person with a series of job-related incidents and asking what he or she would do in that situation (Latham, 1989). The steps for developing a situational interview are as follows:

1. Conduct a job analysis using the critical incident technique (Flanagan, 1954).
2. Develop an appraisal instrument such as behavioral observation scales (Latham & Wexley, 1981) based on the job analysis.
3. Select one or more incidents that formed the basis for the development of performance criteria (e.g., cost consciousness) that constitute that appraisal instrument.
4. Turn each critical incident into a "what would you do if . . ." question.
5. Develop a scoring guide to facilitate agreement among interviewers on what constitutes a good (5), acceptable (3), or an unacceptable (1) response to each question. If (2) and (4) anchors can also be developed, do so.
6. Review the questions for comprehensiveness in terms of covering the material identified in the job analysis and summarized on the appraisal instrument.
7. Conduct a pilot study to eliminate questions where all the interviewees give the same answers, or the interviewers cannot agree on the scoring.
8. Conduct a criterion-related validity study when feasible to do so.

As noted in step 4, critical incidents are the basis of the situational questions. An example of a critical incident is the following:

> The company was trying to bring about a culture that valued teamplaying. The manager hurt his own bottom line for the quarterly review by cooperating with a peer who badly needed some of his resources. Specifically, the manager sold the product internally to the peer for a much lower cost than would have been obtained on the external market.

Literary license is taken with an incident to turn it into a situational question where the wording is not biased against people who are unfamiliar with internal company operations. A scoring guide is developed that contains acceptable answers illustrating a 5, 3, and 1 response. The result with regard to the above incident is shown in Table 12–1. The interviewees are not shown the scoring guide, nor are they informed of the dimension that is being assessed. The interview is conducted by a panel of two or more people. One person reads the question. All members of the panel record the answers. A typical panel consists of two managers of the job for which the interviewee is applying and a person from human resources.

Reliability and Validity

In the 1980s at least eight studies examined the psychometric characteristics of the situational interview. Three studies were conducted by Latham et al. (1980), two by Latham and Saari (1984), one by Weekley and Gier (1987), one by Maurer and

Table 12–1   An Example of a Situational Question and Scoring Guide

You are in charge of truck drivers in Philadelphia. Your colleague is in charge of truck drivers 800 miles away in Atlanta. Both of you report to the same person. Your salary and bonus are affected 100% by your costs. Your colleague is in desperate need of one of your trucks and also for your help. If you say no, your costs will remain low and your group may win the Golden Flyer award for the quarter. If you say yes, the Atlanta group could win this prestigious award because they will make a significant profit for the company. Your boss is preaching not only costs but also cooperation with one's peers. Your boss has no control over the department that keeps score. Your boss is highly competitive, he or she rewards winners. You are just as competitive; you are a real winner! Explain what you would do.

Record answer:

_____

_____

_____

_____

Scoring Guide:

1. I would go for the award. I would explain the circumstances to my colleague and get his or her understanding.
3. I would get my boss's advice.
5. I would lend the truck to my colleague. I'd get recognition from my boss and my buddy that I had done what was in the best interests of the company. Then I'd explain the logic to my people.

Fay (in press), and another by Campion, Pursell, and Brown (1988). The data indicate that the method is both reliable and valid.

The criteria used in the validity studies included Behavioral Observation Scales (BOS) in both the Latham and Campion et al. studies, and hard criterion measures, namely, sales volume, in the study by Weekly and Gier. The samples included unionized hourly workers, applicants for a sales position, and first-line supervisors. The validation studies have been conducted separately for whites and nonwhites and males and females (Latham et al., 1980). Campion et al. (1988) evaluated test fairness using a moderated regression strategy, which assessed equality of intercepts and slopes. Intercept differences were tested by adding race to the equation, and the slope differences were tested by adding the race by interview interaction to the equation. A similar analysis was conducted for the applicant's sex. The results indicated a significant intercept difference for race, but a plot of the separate regression lines indicated a common line slightly over predicted (i.e., was not unfair) for minority applicants. No slope or intercept differences were obtained for sex.

Practicality

Latham and Finnegan (1987) conducted a study to identify the practicality of the unstructured (people are not asked the same questions), patterned (people are asked the same questions, and the interviewee probes responses), and situational interviews as perceived by users and applicants, and to identify the reasons for their perceptions. *Practicality* was defined as the ease or likelihood with which each group perceived that their objectives would be obtained with each interview method.

Users were defined broadly as falling into one of three categories. First, interviewers who had used each of the three interview methods were identified in two international companies. The job titles included line vice-presidents and personnel managers. A second group of interviewers were managers who had no experience with the situational interview, but who did do unstructured and patterned interviewing of applicants. Thus these people were categorized as potential users of the situational interview. These people were included in the study specifically to determine the salability (Smith, 1976) of the situational interview relative to the two alternatives.

The second category was comprised of applicants, who included college students in a senior-level management and organization class. These people were selected because they would be interviewing for jobs upon graduation. A second group of applicants consisted of people who worked for a company that uses unstructured, patterned, and situational interviews. These people were selected because they had actually experienced, as applicants, the three interview formats.

Finally, attorneys who practice Title VII related litigation were identified in the Seattle metropolitan area. Attorneys were defined as users because they are called upon by clients to defend the method that is used to make a selection decision.

The results showed that both groups of managers preferred the patterned interview to the unstructured interview, but they viewed the situational interview as significantly better than the patterned interview in meeting their needs. Specifically, both groups strongly agreed that the situational interview allowed them to appear organized and prepared to the applicant, helped them to determine whether the applicant had the ability to perform the job, enabled them to compare the applicants on an objective basis, and helped them to hire or reject the applicant for solely job-related reasons. The situational interview received the lowest rating relative to the patterned and unstructured interviews on ease of preparation. This is because the situational interview does in fact require significantly more time to develop in contrast to an unstructured interview which can be done on the spur of the moment.

The employee hires did not view one interview method as preferable to another. However, college students rated the unstructured interview as significantly more appealing than the patterned and situational interviews, especially with regard to allowing them to say everything they wanted to say. Thus they viewed the interview experience as a personal selling opportunity. Moreover, if this opportunity were not realized, they indicated that the use of an unstructured interview would most likely enable them to win a lawsuit.

Practicality for attorneys was defined in terms of ease of supporting a client's decision in court. Attorneys rated the situational interview as most easy to defend, and the unstructured interview as least easy to defend in the courtroom. They stressed the importance of being able to show that the questions are based on a job analysis, are a representative sample of the types of occurrences that the applicant would encounter on the job, that the evaluation is unaffected by the biases of the interviewers, and that all the applicants are asked the same questions.

On all items, the situational interview was rated by the attorneys as significantly better than the other two alternatives.

Campion et al. (1988) estimated the gain in utility from using the situational interview over random selection using formulas suggested by Schmidt, Hunter, McKenzie, and Muldrow (1979). The conclusions were as follows:

> Relevant data included interviewer time and administrative costs of $30 per applicant, selection ratio of .62, average standard score on the interview of those selected of .42, and validity coefficients of .34 uncorrected and .56 corrected. The standard deviation of job performance in dollar terms was estimated at $5,000 per year by supervisors using the Schmidt et al. direct estimate technique. This value was 33% of annual mean wages, which was slightly below the 40% estimate often discussed in utility research (Schmidt & J. Hunter, 1983; Schmidt, J. Hunter, Outerbridge, & Trattner, 1986). Using these figures, the one-year utility from the 149 hires was estimated at approximately $100,000 using the uncorrected validity. Assuming a 10% annual interest rate and no separations (Boudreau & Berger, 1985), the estimated gain in 10 years would be over $1 million in net present value in the year 1980. Precise development costs were unknown, but they would be small compared with this gain in utility (e.g., $20,000 to $30,000 in salaries) (Campion et al., 1988, p. 34).

PERFORMANCE APPRAISAL

A primary purpose of the performance appraisal process is to feed back information to the employee for counseling and development purposes so that the person will start doing or continue doing the activities critical to performing effectively on the job (Latham & Wexley, 1981; Latham, 1986). However, feedback in itself is necessary, but not sufficient, for bringing about and maintaining a behavior change. The feedback, according to goal setting theory, must lead to the setting of and commitment to specific goals (see Chapter 8).

Support for this hypothesis was obtained in a study of engineers/scientists (Latham, Mitchell, & Dossett, 1978). People who received explicit feedback during their performance appraisal, and, in addition, were told to "do their best," subsequently performed no better than people who were in a control group. Only people who received feedback and set specific goals improved their performance. This finding is in accordance with a literature review (Burke, Weitzel, & Weir, 1978) which showed that goal setting is a major characteristic of appraisals that are effective in bringing about a behavior change. Specifically, the authors found that setting specific performance goals results in twice as much improvement in performance than does a discussion of general goals, or criticism without reference to specific goals.

Huber (in press) examined the appraisals made by federal government comptrollers. She found that the sex of the rater, the order of the evaluation, and the prior performance rating biased judgments when the performance standards were vague or general. This bias in appraisals was minimized when the goals were specific. In addition, positive leniency error was significantly lower when the goals were specific rather than vague.

Since 1981, Latham has been involved in two organizations in which ways of increasing the necessity for accepting and setting goals in relation to performance feedback were examined. The results of the two pilot studies have been highly encouraging.

The process studied is a variation of sensitivity training. A primary goal of sensitivity training is to teach people to become aware of or sensitive to how they are perceived by others (Wexley & Latham, 1981). The training is often ineffective, because it is conducted in a group setting where the members of the group are strangers to one another. Consequently, positive behavior changes that may take place during training are not reinforced by colleagues when the trainee returns to the job. Sensitivity training is generally ineffective even when the training takes place with people from the same work setting, because the feedback is usually not job related. Finally, specific goals for achieving and/or maintaining the behavior change in most instances are not set (a study by Kolb & Boyatzis, 1981, is an exception to this last statement).

To correct these limitations, a job analysis was conducted for a group of first-line supervisors and a vice-president and his immediate staff. Two Behavioral Observation Scales (BOS) were developed for each respective group. Each person was then evaluated anonymously on the BOS by his or her peers.

The performance problem in both instances was that the group members were not committed to attaining common goals. Instead each individual was working to impact favorably the "bottom line" statistics (e.g., costs) of the department for which he or she was accountable. Actions that one department took often had an adverse effect on other departments.

The advantage of using BOS, within the context of sensitivity training, is that the individual employee is involved in the job analysis that is the basis for developing the yardstick (BOS) on which he or she is assessed. Thus the BOS are developed by the employees for the employees. Moreover, the items are job related. They represent what the employee and colleagues have observed to be the critical behaviors a person must demonstrate on a given job or set of jobs to be successful. Finally, the items on the BOS facilitate recognition and recall for the appraiser of what a job incumbent is doing correctly/incorrectly on the job. Two open-ended questions at the end of the BOS request each appraiser to summarize what the person should (a) continue doing on the job and (b) start doing, stop doing, or do differently.

The arithmetic mean of the ratings on each item for each employee is calculated prior to the appraisal session. The appraisal process is then conducted similarly to the appraisal in interpersonal team building (Beer, 1976). The employees meet as a group. Each person's appraisal is typically given in a one- to two-hour time period. A psychologist or a person skilled in group processes facilitates the feedback by first asking the individual if he or she has any questions regarding his or her colleagues' evaluations. Colleagues are then requested to offer comments regarding the evaluations. Peers are coached by the facilitator on how to emphasize, in giving feedback, what the person is to do differently in the future. The listener is then asked to summarize what was "heard" and to set specific goals as to what he or she will do differently as a result of this feedback. Discussion then focuses on another individual in the group until every individual has received feedback and has set goals.

The results have proven to be highly beneficial in terms of inducing and sustaining behavior change. The mechanisms are straightforward. The feedback is based on job-related items; specific goals are set regarding job-related items. It is difficult for an employee to downplay the importance of these job-related items, because they were identified as important to job success by the employee and his or her peers. It is difficult for the employee to say that the BOS do not provide a comprehensive measure of what is required of him or her on the job, because everyone in the group participated in the development of the BOS. Most importantly, it is more difficult to discredit the observations of a group of people, namely, one's peers, than it is to discredit the observations of one person, namely, the boss. The employee cannot risk the condemnation of the group for failing to work toward the attainment of the goals agreed upon during the appraisal but can enjoy the reinforcement for working toward and attaining these goals on an ongoing basis on the job.

To date, this approach has been studied using an action-research model (French & Bell, 1978). Future research should involve, at a minimum, quasi-experimental designs that hopefully include a comparison group.

The potential damage in using goal setting with end result variables that ignore the behavior for attaining them has been noted repeatedly by academicians (e.g., Campbell, Dunnette, Lawler, & Weick, 1970; Latham, 1986; Latham & Wexley, 1981). An article in the *Washington Post* (Burnham, 1988) illustrates the dilemma. The IRS evaluates people on number of seizures performed, number of criminal tax matters that have been uncovered, and most importantly, number of investigations closed. Superficially, these would appear to be highly relevant criteria for appraising an IRS employee's performance. The problem is the unintended dysfunctional effects. For example, these goals can lead to arbitrary and improper harassment of taxpayers.

As an article in the *Harvard Business Review* (Chew, 1988) noted, behavioral measures are not true gauges of productivity for the economist. But they do focus managers' and employees' attention on critical aspects of the production process. Therefore they do lead to improved performance. The positive correlation between behaviors and cost-related variables in nonmanagerial jobs has been explicitly shown (e.g., Latham & Wexley, 1977). This is difficult, if not impossible, to do in middle managerial positions. Nevertheless, what people do (behavior) affects the bottom line.

TRAINING

When employees resist the goal setting process, it may be because they feel they lack the ability, knowledge, and hence the confidence to attain the goal. Motivation without knowledge is useless. This of course puts a premium on proper selection and training. It requires that the supervisor know the capabilities of subordinates when goals are assigned to them. Asking an employee to formulate an action plan for reaching the goal, as in Management by Objectives (MBO), can be very useful, as it may indicate any knowledge deficiencies.

A comprehensive review of the training literature to correct knowledge/ skill is beyond the scope of this chapter. However, it should be noted that it is not only the employee who may be in need of training on how to attain goals in order for goal setting to be effective; it may very well be the manager who needs training in setting them.

Training Managers

For example, a division of a large national manufacturer and distributor of office equipment, supplies, and electronic systems evaluated the effectiveness of two training programs (Ivancevich & Smith, 1981). The purpose of the training programs was to make sales managers more effective in assigning goals to sales representatives (reps) than they had been during the three years in which the goal setting program had been in effect.

Prior to the training, no formal instruction in goal setting procedures had been provided to the managers. The firm had relied on a standard operating manual that described the process, the sequence, and the forms used. A copy of the manual had been given to each manager. Each manager was expected to learn how to assign goals and counsel with the reps on goal setting matters.

The sales managers were randomly assigned to one of three groups: training through the use of modeling, role playing, and videotape feedback; training via lecture and role playing; or a control group. In the first group, the trainees were given a one-hour lecture on goal setting procedures, followed by three videotapes (models) of appropriate goal setting skills and styles. The trainees were then divided into dyads for role playing. Each person acted out the role of superior and subordinate in two instructional scripts. Both trainers and peers provided feedback on each role-play performance.

The results showed the two trained groups did not differ significantly from each other. However, both groups were significantly better than the no-training group on such variables as production (orders/sales presentations; new accounts) and reps' perceptions of supportiveness, challenge, clarity, feedback, and job satisfaction.

Self-Management

Goal setting is at the core of training in self-management. For example, F. Kanfer's (1970, 1975, 1980) training program teaches people to assess problems, to set specific, hard goals in relation to those problems, to monitor ways in which the environment facilitates or hinders goal attainment, and to identify and administer reinforcers for working toward, and punishers for failing to work toward, goal attainment. In essence, this training teaches people skills in self-observation, to compare their behavior with goals that they set, and to administer reinforcers and punishers to bring about and sustain goal commitment (Karoly & Kanfer, 1982). The reinforcer or punisher is made contingent on the degree to which their behavior approximates the goal. Kanfer viewed these two outcome variables in terms of informational as well as emotional feedback in order to account for cognitive as well as action and autonomic effects.

Training in self-regulation has been evaluated rigorously in both laboratory and clinical settings. Positive results have been obtained with regard to teaching oneself to stop smoking (Kanfer & Phillips, 1970), to overcome drug addiction (Kanfer, 1974), to reduce weight (Mahoney, Moura, & Wade, 1973), to improve study habits (Richards, 1976), and to enhance academic achievement (Glynn, 1970).

Few, if any, empirically based experiments have been conducted in organizational settings on the efficacy of training in self-management. A notable exception is the study by Frayne and Latham (1987), which investigated its effectiveness with regard to increasing the job attendance for unionized state government employees.

Both the control group and the experimental group in this study were exposed to ongoing organization sanctions (e.g., two or more days off per month without a medical slip, failure to call in) regarding absenteeism. These sanctions consisted of an oral warning, a written warning, being placed on three-month probation, and termination. The incentive for job attendance was that employees earned eight hours of sick leave each month. Hours that were not used by the end of the year would be applied to the next year. People were given compensation upon retirement for the total number of sick leave hours that were not used. These policies had been in existence for twelve years. Nevertheless, absenteeism was high.

The training program itself consisted of eight weekly one-hour group sessions followed by eight thirty-minute one-on-one sessions. Each training group consisted of ten people. The one-on-one sessions were conducted to tailor the training to the specific concerns of each individual and to discuss issues that the person might have been reluctant to introduce in a group setting.

In the first week, an orientation session was conducted to explain the principles of self-management. In the second week, the reasons given by the trainees for using sick leave were listed and classified into nine categories, namely, legitimate illness, medical appointments, job stress, job boredom, difficulties with co-workers, alcohol- and drug-related issues, family problems, transportation difficulties, and employee rights (i.e., "sick leave belongs to me"). Of these nine categories, family problems, incompatibility with supervisor or co-workers, and transportation problems were listed most frequently. Sick leave was the focus of discussion in this session because it accounted for 49.8% of the total recorded absenteeism in the organization.

The third week focused on goal setting. The distal goal was to increase one's attendance within a specific time frame (e.g., one month/three months). The proximal goals were the specific behaviors that each individual was to engage in to attain the distal goal.

The fourth week focused on the importance of self-monitoring one's behavior. Specifically, the trainees were taught to record (a) their own attendance, (b) the reason for missing a day of work, and (c) the steps that were followed to subsequently get to work. This was done through the use of charts and diaries. Emphasis was placed on the importance of daily feedback for motivational purposes as well as accuracy in recording.

In the fifth week, the trainees identified rewards and punishments to administer to themselves as a result of achieving or failing to achieve the proximal goals. The training emphasized that the reinforcer must be powerful and easily self-administered (e.g., self-praise, purchasing a gift). The punisher was to be a disliked activity and easily self-administered (e.g., cleaning the garage). Each individual developed specific response-reward contingencies.

In the sixth week, the trainees wrote a behavioral contract with themselves. Thus each trainee specified in writing the goals(s) to be achieved, the time frame for achieving the goal(s), the consequences for attaining or failing to attain the goal(s), and the behavior necessary for attaining the goal(s).

The seventh week emphasized maintenance. Discussion focused on issues that might result in a relapse in absenteeism, planning for such situations should they occur, and developing coping strategies for dealing with these situations.

During the final week of training, the trainer reviewed each technique presented in the program, answered questions from the trainees regarding these skills, and clarified expectations for the management of the program's effectiveness.

The assumption underlying training in self-management is that the treatment package should "include as many component procedures as seem necessary to obtain, ideally, a total treatment success" (Azrin, 1977, p. 144). Empirical support for combining goal setting, feedback (self-monitoring), and rewards into a treatment package can be found in both the organizational behavior and clinical psychology literature. For example, Erez (1977) found that goal setting in the absence of feedback has no effect on behavior (see Chapter 8). Latham, Mitchell, and Dossett (1978) found that feedback in the absence of goal setting has no effect on behavior subsequent to a performance appraisal. Similarly, Simon (1979) showed that self-monitoring in the absence of goal setting has no effect on behavior.

Analyses of variance revealed that compared with a control condition (n = 20), training in self-regulatory skills taught the employees how to manage personal and social obstacles to job attendance, and it raised their perceived self-efficacy (Bandura, 1986) in being able to exercise influence over their behavior. Consequently, employee attendance was significantly higher in the training than in the control group. The higher the perceived self-efficacy, the better the subsequent job attendance.

Latham and Frayne (1989) conducted a six-month and a nine-month follow-up to determine the long-term effects of this training in self-management. A repeated measures analysis of variance showed that the employees with training in self-management continued to have higher job attendance than those in the control group. The control group was then given the same training in self-management, but by a different trainer. Three months later, this group showed the same positive improvement in their self-efficacy with regard to coping with obstacles preventing them from coming to work, and in their actual job attendance, as the original training group.

Learning Incentives

Huber (1985a) examined the effectiveness of goal setting (participative, assigned, and no goals) and financial incentives (noncontingent, piece rate, and goal contingent) as techniques to stimulate learning. Inexperienced trainees performed a ten-hour, five-day proofreading proficiency task in a laboratory setting.

The assigned goal/goal contingent condition resulted in the highest performance. This finding with regard to goal contingent pay is consistent with Mowen et al.'s (1981) finding that when moderately difficult goals are assigned, performance is highest with goal contingent rewards; when goals are difficult, performance is highest when a piece-rate incentive is provided. The finding that assigned goals resulted in superior performance to participatively set goals is consistent with a field study that showed that nonparticipative goals are more effective than participatively set goals with new or inexperienced employees (Hillery & Wexley, 1974). Again, these findings are congruent with a cognitive interpretation of the benefits of participation in decision making discussed in Chapter 7. New employees usually lack the ability to provide more useful information through their participation than is provided by a knowledgeable superior.

LABOR RELATIONS

Although the concept of setting specific goals has been advocated since the time of Frederick Taylor and the era of time and motion studies, it is only recently that management and labor have found a process whereby they can agree on setting and working toward attaining specific goals. The label given to this process is referred to by many overlapping terms, such as quality of working life (QWL), relations by objectives (RBO), quality circles (QC), and employee involvement groups. Here we discuss specifically relations by objectives.

The present timing for establishing mutual goals between management and labor is excellent. Labor unions are confronted with a loss of jobs by their members; management is confronted with escalating costs; both management and labor are confronted with a shrinking marketplace. Thus both management and labor have a reason for joining forces to attain specific goals. RBO proceeds as follows.

Action Steps

The process for setting mutually agreed upon goals is similar, if not identical, in many respects to team building (French & Bell, 1978). Each representative of management and labor is interviewed individually by a neutral party and is ensured confidentiality. The neutral party is often an industrial psychologist or someone knowledgeable of group processes and conflict resolution. The questions Latham (Latham, 1983; Locke & Latham, 1984a) has asked are as follows:

1. *What is management/union doing right in their relationship with one another?* The purpose of this question is to allow both parties to see how far they have to go in establishing a working relationship. Generally both sides are pleased to see that, collectively, there is much that is perceived favorably by the other.
Examples of responses given to this inquiry by management regarding the union include:
   (a) They're well informed on safety.
   (b) The standing committee knows the contract; they are more knowledgeable than we are.
   (c) When the union local has a bona fide problem, they give management the opportunity to gather the facts to respond to it before getting everyone aroused.

Examples of responses given to this inquiry by the union regarding management include:

(a) If there is a difference in opinion in interpreting contract language, they are now beginning to explain their interpretation to us. It doesn't appear that they are just trying to pull a fast one on us.

(b) They really put the money into the safety program. The foremen are right there to point out and solve safety issues.

(c) The foremen know their jobs, which enables them to get us to do our work properly.

2. *What would you like to see management/union start doing, stop doing, or do differently?* It is the answers to this question that form the basis for setting specific goals. Examples of answers given to this question by management include:

(a) We need to get a workable understanding of posting with the union. A person should not be allowed to change jobs every month.

(b) We need a workable understanding of what it means to select the most senior *qualified* individual. Competency must be stressed along with seniority.

(c) We need open discussion of a potential grievance prior to writing it out. When an employee has a problem, the person should talk first to the supervisor. Saying "I'm going to file a grievance" is not talking it out. The correct procedure is to talk the issue out with the supervisor, then go to the superintendent if the issue is not resolved, and only then to file a grievance if the issue is not resolved.

Examples of answers to this question given by the union include:

(a) More needs to be done by management on record keeping: who is working, who is laid off, when laid off, when coming back, and so forth.

(b) Get cooperation among the units within a camp. The competition among units is absurd.

(c) We file grievances because your word is not worth anything. We have to document through grievances. Honor your word, improve your memory, and many grievances will be eliminated.

3. *What can you (management/union) do to improve the working relationship?* This question is asked to see to what extent the two parties from the outset are truly interested in taking the first step in working together. Representative comments from management include:

(a) We need to build trust through frankness/openness with them. We're with them. We're not devious *now,* but we don't always remember to tell them everything about bumping rights/responsibilities.

(b) We need to communicate the *why's* behind unpopular decisions.

(c) We need to meet the requirements of the contract in spirit as well as to the letter. We need to truly know and understand the contract.

The union's responses include:

(a) Stop patting ourselves on the back for "gotcha" feelings. Realize we're here to make a profit for the company.

(b) Get with the company and help them on seniority-bumping, and call backs. Stop trying to "catch them."

(c) Be truthful in dealing with supervisors; be less brassy.

After the interviews have been conducted, the neutral facilitator edits the comments and groups them together in terms of underlying themes. The first goal setting meeting is then held. This meeting is generally held off the plant site free of interrupting telephone calls and messages. The meeting typically lasts one-half to one day.

The purpose of this meeting is to review the interview notes and to modify, add, or delete items as the group sees fit. The facilitator checks the accuracy/clarity of the notes by calling upon people at random to explain the meaning of a given statement and then determining if there is consensus on the explanation.

The themes (e.g., safety, trust, job posting) are examined by the group to see if they are related to one another. Those that are interrelated are placed in the same category. The group then prioritizes the categories in the order in which they wish them to be addressed.

The group is then divided, depending on its size, into two or more subgroups. Each subgroup consists of union and management personnel. The people in the subgroups choose one of the categories that were agreed on as a priority item in the previous step. The goal of each subgroup is to brainstorm solutions to the problem. The parties are made aware of the fact that they are to develop viable proposals for solving the problem.

In recognition that participation in group brainstorming is not as effective as brainstorming alone as individuals (Taylor, Berry, & Block, 1958), each person is assigned the goal of generating a minimum of five solutions to the problem while working alone. Each person then reads the solutions to the subgroup. Discussion then follows with the objective of reaching a consensus.

After reaching consensus, the subgroups reconvene in one overall group to explain their proposals to one another and to make modifications where needed. Management and the union can then agree to implement the proposals or request time to study them. Regardless of the alternative selected, specific action steps with timetables are agreed upon at the meeting as to who will do what in making or implementing the decision(s). At the end of this meeting, a date is set for a subsequent meeting to review progress and to set new goals. Thus the team-building approach becomes a continuous, ongoing process, rather than a discrete activity with starting and stopping points.

The danger in this approach is that management and labor must recognize that it is strictly a vehicle for problem solving. It is not a vehicle for people to become "buddies" as an end in itself. However, people who solve problems common to one another generally develop respect for one another. Another danger is that problems that are not solved because of management or union reluctance or inability are perceived by employees as indicators of a lack of commitment to the problem-solving process by one or both parties. Thus, if a proposal is rejected and/or a problem fails to disappear, a premium must be placed on communication to employees as to "why."

A limitation of this work is that it has followed an action-research model. Experimental or quasi-experimental designs are needed to document the effectiveness of the process and to isolate the variables that are crucial to its effectiveness. An action-research model, at best, provides hypotheses as to the effectiveness of a process. In this regard, we believe that the present process is effective because of the cognitive benefits (ideas) derived from participation and the setting of specific goals to attain the cognitively derived strategies.

The above activity has been an ongoing process throughout the past decade. The results to date look promising. The companies with which Latham has been working are expanding their involvement in this area. The major benefits derived from these approaches have included improved communications, shorter time periods to solve problems, a large decrease in grievances, constructive standing committee meetings, and productivity/costs that were in the black in January 1982 when every other similar operation of the West Coast was in the red.

Guidelines for Obtaining Union Support for Goal Setting

A quasi-experimental design, rather than an action research approach, involving unions was used in a study by Latham and Saari (1982). The study replicated and extended the findings of Latham and Baldes (1975).

In the Latham and Baldes study, unionized drivers in the southwestern United States were not loading their trucks to maximum capacity. Instead, the trucks were being loaded to approximately 60% of what was possible. All the drivers knew this based on daily feedback. Attaching scales to the trucks was not feasible from a cost-benefit standpoint because the trucks were constantly driven over rough terrain. This resulted in the scales being broken. Exhorting the drivers for three consecutive months to try harder than they had in the past to increase the amount being hauled, without exceeding the truck's legal weight restrictions, resulted in no increase in productivity. As a last resort, the union was approached by the company with a goal setting program.

The above productivity problem was explained to the union. The company emphasized that no one would be rewarded for attaining the goal; similarly, it was stressed that no one would be punished for failing to attain the goal. With this understanding, a specific goal of 90% of maximum allowable truck weight was agreed upon by the company and the union as reasonable to assign to the drivers. Productivity improved the first week that the goal was given to each driver. The increase in productivity over a month saved the company over a quarter of a million dollars.

The purpose of the Latham and Saari (1982) study was twofold. First, the above findings were replicated with employees in a different union, in a different area of the country, using a different dependent variable, i.e., trips per truck rather than truck weight. A more stringent experimental design than the time series used by Latham and Baldes (1975) was employed by using a comparison group. Second, and more importantly, information was collected through interviews with the union that could serve as guidelines for gaining acceptance for goal setting programs in other unionized settings in the future.

The participants in this study were 74 unionized logging truck drivers. Thirty-nine drivers participated in the experimental group; 35 drivers formed the comparison group. All the truck drivers were male. Each had worked for the company four or more years.

Prior to conducting this study, the drivers were not at the logging sites when needed. The logs were stacked at the landing, ready to be transported, with no room to place additional logs. This held up the work flow. Supervision of the truck drivers was relatively lax because only one truck foreman was in charge of each group of 35 to 40 drivers. The foremen were located at a central location and were usually able to communicate with the truck drivers by radio. However, since the truck drivers spent much of their time on the road and were not always accessible by radio, they could not be directly supervised.

The drivers' explanations for their inefficiencies ranged from mild apathy to acknowledging outright violations of company rules. For example, it was not uncommon for drivers to admit that they frequently pulled off the road to talk with one another or to take an extended lunch hour. Since all the drivers had received intensive driver's training and orientation to company policy, additional training was not believed to be necessary for increasing their productivity. Economic conditions made it impossible to consider the benefits, if any, of increasing the number of supervisors. Therefore it was decided that a motivation program for the truck drivers had to be developed.

The implementation of the goal setting program was straightforward. The necessity for improving productivity was discussed with the union. Previous benefits of goal setting were explained to them. Finally, the union was interviewed on factors that had to exist for their support of entering into a goal setting program without formal negotiations. These factors were as follows:

> First, working to attain a goal must be voluntary for an employee.
>
> Second, there must be no monetary rewards for or special treatment of those people who attain the goal. The union contract prohibits the use of monetary incentives for individual efforts.
>
> Third, supportive supervisory behavior in terms of setting a goal for an employee that is difficult, but attainable, is encouraged, providing that it is clear to the employee that working to attain the goal is voluntary on his part. Giving verbal praise for goal attainment is acceptable supervisory behavior and does not constitute "special treatment" of employees. This is designated as supportive behavior that the union would like to see all supervisors engage in whenever an employee does good work.
>
> Fourth, there must be no punishment for failing to attain a goal.
>
> Finally, and most importantly, there must be sufficient long-term work that goal attainment will not lead to layoffs or a reduction in the work force through attrition (i.e., a policy not to replace an employee who leaves the company).

With the implementation of the goal setting program, the foreman of the 39 truck drivers in the experimental condition introduced a weekly goal for each driver in terms of average number of trips per day from the logging sites to the mill. The goal took into account factors such as (1) distance of the logging sites from the mill, (2) road conditions, (3) size of timber being logged, and (4) skill of the driver. The weekly goals ranged from an average of three to seven trips per day.

When explaining the program to the truck drivers, the truck foreman stated that the goals were not "production standards," nor would any negative consequences occur if they were not met; rather, the goals were merely something for the drivers to strive for if they so desired. The importance of goal setting for injecting challenge into a task was stressed. The company also stressed that the union had been informed of the program.

Subsequent to informing the drivers of the goal setting program, the weekly goal for each truck driver was written next to each driver's name and posted on a bulletin board in the room where they met each morning and evening with the truck foreman. An average weekly goal for the truck drivers as a group was also calculated and placed at the top of this sheet.

Each evening, the foreman posted the information he received from the mill regarding the number of trips made by each truck driver. This information had always been collected by the foreman, but in the past it had been used only for his own record-keeping purposes. This information had also been available to an individual driver regarding his own performance; for every load of logs taken in, each driver had received a ticket receipt, which he was free to keep for his own records.

Trips per truck data were obtained for five weeks prior to the implementation of the goal setting program and eighteen weeks after its implementation. In addition, data on trips per truck were obtained for the same time period on 35 drivers from another logging area for comparison purposes. This area was located in the same region as that where the goal setting program took place, it had a similar terrain and log mix, it had the same number of logging sites and approximately the same number of truck drivers, and it had similar production figures on trips per truck averages during the five-week premeasure period, as did the area where the goal setting program was implemented.

There was no significant difference between the experimental and comparison groups during the premeasure period. However, there was a significant difference between the two groups following the implementation of goal setting, with the goal setting group having a significantly higher weekly average number of trips per truck than the comparison group. The average increase for the experimental group was .53 trips per truck. Computed on a daily basis for the 39 drivers over the eighteen-week goal setting period, the increase in number of truck trips was approximately 1,800. Company representatives indicated that the value of the timber from one truck trip was approximately $1,500. Thus the value of the increase in trips per truck of the goal setting group could be estimated as high as $2.7 million.

Support for the validity of the interview data collected from the union can be inferred from the following incident. Latham and Saari's study lasted eighteen weeks. On the nineteenth week, the company hired a consulting firm specializing in time study to implement a formal goal setting program for all woods operations. At this point, production measures were no longer recorded in terms of trips per truck, but rather were a "percent expected miles" computation. The immediate consequence of the program was a wildcat strike. The union and the company got the employees back to work by agreeing to the five points elaborated upon earlier in this article for the truck drivers. The events leading to the agreement of these points is discussed below. The following information was obtained from interviews with union and company representatives conducted after the resolution of the wildcat strike.

When the consulting firm began its work, the union employees were not told that the goals recommended by the consultants would be voluntary. The employees observed the consultants on the job site with stopwatches. Rumor led them to believe that they would be required by the company to reach specific goals.

The employees believed that attainment of a goal would be tied to rewards and punishment. Many said that they thought they would be "browbeaten" for not attaining a goal. They also concluded that their jobs would be at stake if they did not attain the goals.

To make it clear to the union that the company would abide by the five points discussed earlier, the timberlands manager went to the union hall and explained that the goals set would be *voluntary*, as they had been in the past for the truck drivers. More importantly, he stressed that supervisors would be supportive of effective performance and goal attainment, but no negative comments or consequences would occur if goals were not met. He also emphasized that there would be no cutbacks or layoffs as a result of productivity increases.

After clarifying these issues, the manager asked the union members to give the program a two-month trial period, after which they could reject the program if they were not satisfied with the way it was being run. The union agreed to these conditions.

Following this meeting, the manager met with all logging foremen. He emphasized the importance of adhering to the above points, and he stressed that their behavior toward the employees was critical to this program's success. The program has now been in operation for seven years with no subsequent negative incidents or complaints.

This acceptance of goal setting is in contrast to the United Parcel Service (UPS). For the fourth consecutive year, *Fortune* reported in 1988 that UPS was among the top of the industry in its corporate reputation survey. Moreover, it was by far the most profitable U.S. transportation company, with net earnings of $700 million on revenues of $700 billion a year (Labich, 1988). A key to its success, according to *Fortune,* was high specific goals based on time studies. For example, sorters at the giant UPS hub outside Chicago were expected to load delivery vans at the rate of between 500 and 650 packages per hour. Drivers were meticulously timed, each regular stop on each route was studied with a stopwatch, and supervisors periodically rechecked to make sure conditions had not changed. While these techniques were obviously successful, it should not be surprising that there was ongoing tension between the Teamster membership and UPS management, especially with the latter's refusal to bargain productivity standards.

The technique of goal setting, however, is not limited to blue-collar workers. *Inc.* magazine (Mamis & Pearlstein 1988) reported how a similar technique is applied to help CEOs turn around failing companies. The

> ... whole system is actually a matter of breaking down a business into its component businesses, and setting for each of them clear and attainable goals that you can look at weekly and monthly and quarterly and see how you are doing and how much further you have to go. And if there are 35 pieces in a business, 20 of them can be winners and 15 don't win then overall you're still a winner, because you don't really expect all 35 of them to win. Whereas, if you look at it simply as one business and you're organized that way, and it goes to hell, then you really, truly have got a major problem to fix (*Inc.,* February 1988, p. 28).

EQUITY EFFECTS

Equity theory (Adams, 1963, 1965) argues that people judge the fairness of their outputs (e.g., pay) by comparing them with their inputs (e.g., effort, performance) and comparing their own input-output ratio with that of colleagues. It has been found that when inequity is perceived, people often take steps to reduce it. For example, people who feel they are overpaid on an hourly basis may work harder at a task than those who feel they are equitably paid in order to restore equity (Miner, 1980). Goodman and Friedman (1968) found such an effect using the usual overpayment induction that involved telling the subjects that their hourly pay rate was higher than their experience with the task warranted. Subjects in this condition showed significantly higher performance than those not told that they were overpaid. However, when subjects in both these conditions were given performance standards, explained as the normal performance level attained by experienced people, the equity effect disappeared. This suggests that the equity effect itself may be mediated by differences in goal level or difficulty, although this hypothesis has never been directly tested. The results also imply that equity and inequity can be induced not only by the pay but also by the performance goals that people are given. Disputes about the fairness of the relationship between performance standards and pay, of course, have a long history in industry (e.g., Roethlisberger & Dickson, 1956; see also Chapter 6). The findings of Latham and Saari (1982) described above, however, suggest that such disputes may not at root revolve around goal setting as such but around the way that goals are used by management.

MOTIVATION

Because this entire book is devoted to the topic of motivation, only a few additional comments will be made here. Among the first scientifically controlled field experiments to show the motivational technique of goal setting was a study conducted by Latham and Kinne (1974). The United States was undergoing an economic recession. The financing of equipment for woods workers in the rural south was becoming increasingly difficult to obtain. Yet, multimillion-dollar companies such as International Paper and Union Camp were dependent on these people to supply them with raw material. Aggravating the situation of these paper companies was the fact that the pulpwood producers worked independently of the companies, that is, they were independent businessmen. Thus they were free to work 2 days one week, 4 days a second week, and no days a third week. The companies often found it impossible to predict their wood inventory.

Latham and Kinne, based on correlations conducted on a survey of woods workers (Ronan, Latham, & Kinne, 1973) and Locke's (1968b) laboratory experiments, hypothesized that goal setting would be an effective way of increasing employee productivity. Pulpwood crews were matched with regard to size, equipment, terrain, and so on, and were randomly assigned to an experimental or a control group. The sawhands were given a tallymeter to keep track of the number of trees they cut down. The result was not only a significant increase in the productivity of the experimental groups relative to the control group in the very first week of the experiment but also a decrease in employee absenteeism. Interviews revealed that the setting of difficult but attainable goals resulted in the workers in the experimental group seeing their work as not only challenging but meaningful. They left work each day with a sense of accomplishment. A subsequent study (Latham & Baldes, 1975) showed that goal setting led workers to find innovative ways of loading the logging truck so as to increase their efficiency in getting wood to the woodyard. This finding has been reaffirmed by the Center for Creative Leadership. Burnside (1988) reported that a key stimulant to creating a climate for innovation is a "challenge." This is because challenge facilitates the feeling that the work one is doing is important. Thus goal setting resulted in a significant increase in the performance of engineers and scientists in a large research and development center. This increase occurred even though the people who were randomly assigned to the control group were aware that their colleagues in other conditions were setting specific, difficult goals and working to attain them (Latham, Mitchell, & Dossett, 1978). The argument that goal setting is trite because everyone, especially those in higher-level jobs, sets goals was shown to be incorrect.

A frustration of behavioral scientists (Latham, 1988) is the difficulty of transferring knowledge from scientific experiments to lay audiences. This has not been a problem regarding goal setting. Numerous business magazines repeatedly report the effectiveness of goal setting. For example, *Inc.* (Posner & Burlingham, 1988) reported what they called the "true McDonald's of hair salons" (p. 47), namely, Visible Changes. Salon managers in these stores are given goals for and are paid according to their respective salon's volume; the manager of the top-performing salons get a brand-new Nissan 300 ZX as well. The best receptionist receives an award, a company-paid trip, and a chance to move up. Even the trainees have performance goals. Each is expected to sell $135 of conditioner treatments per week to the customers whose hair she shampoos. If she doesn't, her training as a hair cutter is slowed until she can meet her goal.

According to *Inc.*, not only does the system work but the haircutters themselves contribute to its refinement. By decision of the employees, for instance, every haircutter must achieve a request rate of 25% within three months, and 50% within six months, or leave.

Business Week reported how savvy companies are making office automation pay off. "To get productivity out of office systems, they must be aimed at a clear goal. And that goal can't be as generic as better planning. It must be something as specific as getting sales representatives to spend 10% more of their time with customers" (*Business Week*, October 12, 1987).

Even *Parade Magazine* attributed a quote from Burt Lancaster as an explanation for the number of awards he has won as an actor:

> "You always strive for something that's a little beyond you and may be not attainable, but you have to work for it." (Dermaris, 1988, p. 5.)

LEADERSHIP

An increasing number of studies of leadership are finding that one of the key functions of a leader is to develop goals for the organization, which includes goals for both the leader and the subordinates. Bennis and Nanus (1985), for example, found that effective leaders formulate core visions for their organizations and then communicate these visions in a way that is clear and compelling to subordinates. Core visions can initially be general but must eventually be translated into relatively specific goals for the organization and its divisions, departments, and individuals. Bradford and Cohen (1984) recommended setting overarching goals for each work unit—goals that are clear and challenging. Kotter's (1982) study of general managers indicates that successful ones develop first general and then increasingly elaborate and specific agendas (goals and plans) for their divisions. After extensively reviewing the leadership literature and his own research, Yukl (1989) concluded that setting and clarifying goals and objectives was one of the most important leadership behaviors. Boyatzis (1982) found that skill in goal setting and planning was among the key determinants of a manager's success. The results of a twenty-year longitudinal study by Howard and Bray (1988) found that one of the most powerful determinants of managerial progress (promotion) was the manager's personal ambition. Ambition involves setting high goals for one's own career and life progress. A case study in the use of goal setting for effective leadership was reported by Locke and Somers (1987). A new staff judge advocate in the Air Force wanted to speed up processing times for court-martials in order to meet performance standards that had long been ignored. To accomplish this, the new judge advocate made direct requests to the judge advocate officers on each base to improve their performance, gave them the reasons why the goals needed to be met, provided feedback showing performance in relation to the goals, encouraged improvement and expressed confidence that the goals could be met, recognized and praised actual accomplishments, and provided suggestions for improved work strategies. The result was a significant improvement in court-martial processing time in comparison with Air Force units that were given no such goal setting treatment. While we would not go so far as to assert that goal setting and its corollaries (feedback, reward, etc.) are all there is to leadership, they may well be at the core of this phenomenon.

DECISION MAKING

Staw (1976, 1981) and Staw and Fox (1977) were among the first to systematically study the tendency for people to commit additional resources to an unsuccessful or failing course of action. This phenomenon is called the escalation effect. Staw concluded that self-justification processes explained this behavior. This is because individuals who feel personally responsible for negative consequences allocate the greatest amount of resource to the previously chosen decision. Thus the decision maker acts retrospectively in a rational manner by increasing commitment to a failing alternative in an attempt to make previous behavior appear correct.

In a laboratory experiment, Kernan and Lord (in press) found that general goals led people to commit the same amount of resources to a problem regardless of prior degree of failure. Specific goals, however, enabled people to use feedback information intelligently. They committed fewer additional resources to courses of action that had led to extreme failure. General goals allow people to give themselves the benefit of the doubt concerning the adequacy of their performance. For feedback to have a desirable effect, it must be interpreted in relation to specific goals (Kernan & Lord, in press).

IMPRESSION MANAGEMENT

Huber, Latham, and Locke (1989) showed how goal setting can affect the ability of supervisors and subordinates to affect the impressions they make on each other. For example, supervisors can create a positive impression with subordinates when they engage in the following strategies:

1. Assign clear goals so that they show that they know what they are doing.
2. Provide a rationale for the goal.
3. When needed, provide specific task information about how to attain the goal.
4. Serve as a role model setting difficult goals for themselves and attaining these goals.
5. Be physically present during goal setting.
6. Allow subordinate input as appropriate: for new employees, assign goals; for more-experienced and competent subordinates, participatively set goals; and for highly experienced and competent workers, delegate.
7. Express confidence in the subordinate's ability to attain the goal; be supportive.
8. Once the goal is set, give subordinates the opportunity to develop their own strategies to attain the goal.
9. Provide specific knowledge of results.
10. Present positive performance information before presenting negative information.
11. Give fair rewards that are perceived as equitable.

Similarly, subordinates can create a positive impression with superiors when they engage in the following strategies:

1. Take the initiative to set goals on their own or ask for supervisory assistance in goal choice and accept that advice.
2. Choose challenging goals.
3. Show commitment to goals through persistence and problem resolution.
4. Project high but not inaccurate self-efficacy.
5. Develop effective plans using all information available.
6. Succeed in attaining or approaching goals.

Equally important, the authors showed how goal setting can create a positive self-impression, namely:

1. Choose appropriate goals and plans.
2. Get input when needed.
3. Develop performance skills so that you can execute desired behaviors.
4. Ask for specific feedback.
5. Develop strategies to overcome deficiencies.
6. Shape behavior beginning with simpler tasks and goals that steadily increase in difficulty.

CONCLUSION

Science has long maintained that one test of a theory's worth is its practical utility (Campbell, 1920). More recently, Miner (1984) argued the need to evaluate a theory in terms of its usefulness in application.

In this vein, Lee and Earley (1988), in the study referred to in Chapter 2, surveyed APA Division 14 Fellows, Academy of Management Fellows, the Editorial Boards of five mainstream scientific journals, and one out of every ten names of the Academy of Management Organizational Behavior Division as to their evaluation of the following fifteen theories of motivation/leadership: achievement motivation, behavior modification, contingency theory of leadership, equity theory, expectancy theory, goal setting, intrinsic motivation, job characteristics, need hierarchy, participative leadership, path-goal, social learning theory, system 4, two-factor theory, and theory X/Y. Goal setting theory was ranked number 1 in terms of its practical utility, followed by behavior modification. Given that goal setting is at the core of most behavior modification techniques (see Chapter 1, also Kirschenbaum & Flanery, 1984; and Locke, 1977), this is a strong endorsement by the leading behavioral scientists in North America of goal setting as a technique for bringing about a positive behavior change.

The principle of goal setting can of course be applied to nonwork settings. Locke and Latham (1985) have written at length about the applications of goal setting to sports (see also Anderson et al., 1988; and Lee, 1988). In Chapter 11 it was noted that goal setting could be applied to education. It can be (and is being) applied to psychotherapy in the form of homework assignments for patients. We noted in Chapter 2 that it has been used for personal health management (Alexy, 1985). Harvey and Snyder (1987) have shown that even charities need to set goals in order to be effective. In short, goal setting can be used to regulate any controllable action or outcome.

Goal setting does not apply just to work; it applies to life!

GOAL SETTING AND STRATEGY EFFECTS ON COMPLEX TASKS

This chapter has two objectives: first, to present a more detailed and more speculative formulation than has been presented to date of the relationship between goals, plans (task strategies), and performance; and second, to apply this model to the domain of complex tasks.

An aspect of goal setting theory that requires further development is the means by which goal setting affects performance (Wood & Bailey, 1985). Previously, three direct motivational mechanisms (direction of attention, effort, and persistence) and one, indirect cognitive mechanism (strategy development) were shown to mediate goal setting effects. These mechanisms combine the effects of energy-related resources and the allocation or direction of those resources to specific acts (Humphreys & Revelle, 1984; Woodworth, 1918). In this chapter these views are revised, elaborated, and extended to consider how the impact of goals on performance is mediated through task strategies, and how this relationship varies as a function of task complexity. The two major propositions are as follows:

1. On simple tasks, goals affect performance relatively directly by activating one or more of three automatized, universal task strategies or plans (direction of attention, effort, and persistence) and one or more automatized task specific plans.
2. As tasks become more complex, universal plans and simple task-specific plans become progressively less adequate by themselves to ensure goal achievement, while problem solving and the development of task-specific plans become progressively more important. Automatized plans of all types play a less direct role as task complexity increases.

This chapter is reprinted, with minor changes, from R. E. Wood and E. A. Locke (in press), "Goal Setting and Strategy Effects on Complex Tasks." In B. Staw and L. Cummings (Eds.), *Research in Organizational Behavior,* Vol. 12. Greenwich, CT: JAI Press. Reprinted by permission of JAI Press.

THE MODEL

The model is shown in Figure 13–1 and will be discussed in some detail. The model is concerned with cognitively based, as distinct from biologically based, motivators. It assumes a cognitive perspective in which people regulate their actions through anticipation and standards (Bandura, 1986, 1988). Behavior is seen as being goal directed and regulated by plans for achieving valued future outcomes. The focus is on what happens after a person becomes committed to a goal, either through being assigned a goal or task by another person, setting it jointly (participation), or setting it on his or her own.

Step 1.   The first question one asks, explicitly or implicitly, when confronted by a task and/or goal is, What does it involve or require—that is, what thoughts, actions, strategies are needed to perform it? We suggest that the perception of the task and/or goal automatically brings to awareness a repertoire of strategies or plans stored in the subconscious based on past experience. By experience, we do not mean only firsthand experience with the task but also the experience of observing others as well as plans one has heard or read about. Thus if one sees a friend suddenly start choking on food during a meal, one might immediately think of the "Heimlich maneuver" even though one had only read about it in the *Reader's Digest*. In the case of a simple repetitive task or goal, such as driving downtown to pick up the dry cleaning, one hardly needs to think of a plan of action at all in order to perform it. In contrast, if the task is new and complex, conscious problem solving may be required.

There are two broad types of stored plans. The first we call *Stored Universal Plans* (SUP's) because they apply, at least to a considerable extent, to virtually every task. SUP's are primarily motivational in nature but contain cognitive elements. The three general types of universal plans are what we previously called direct goal mechanisms: direction, effort, and persistence. Most people learn at a fairly young age that when they are trying to accomplish something, they must at some point do three things: they must direct some attention to the task or task attributes they are trying to regulate; they must exert mental and/or physical effort; and they must persist for some amount of time. The amount of effort and attention devoted to a task will vary, in part, as a function of goals and task attributes such as difficulty and complexity. The amount of effort expended in the performance of a set of acts will also reflect the expectations and values that the individual associates with an outcome. For an adult at least, SUP's are so automatized or programmed that when confronted with a goal to perform a familiar or easy task, they do not consciously ask themselves, "What plan would work here?" They simply activate SUP's. In this respect SUP's are "built into" goals; any action to achieve a goal will automatically utilize them unless deliberately suppressed. Even on more complex tasks, people will use SUP's, but in conjunction with other types of plans.

There is no assumption that SUP's always work as intended. For example, a person may pay attention to one part of the task or type of task information and ignore others even though those others are necessary for optimal performance. Furthermore, a person may try too hard at a task, get

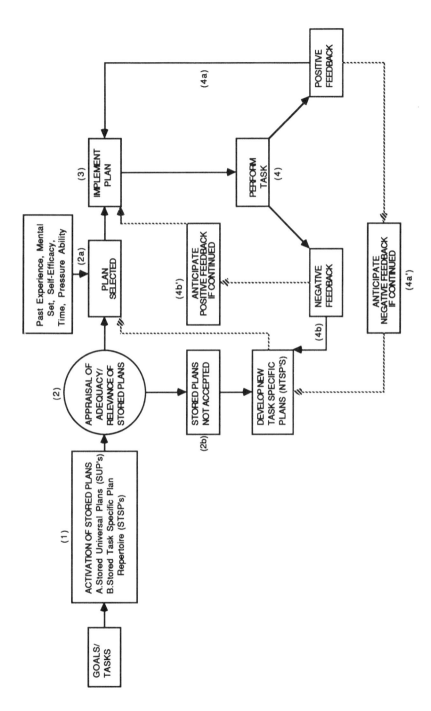

FIGURE 13–1   Relationship of Goals, Plans, and Performance

tense, and perform more poorly than if he or she had relaxed. And a person may persist too long, so that fatigue interferes with effective functioning. Nevertheless, in virtually all tasks, directed attention, effort, and persistence, when used properly, are not only functional but necessary for superior performance.

Some goal setting studies have isolated (insofar as is possible) the beneficial effects of these three types of plans on performance. For example, Locke and Bryan (1969b) found that drivers only paid attention to improving measured driving dimensions that were relevant to their goal. Specific goals have a cueing effect, by shaping the definition of tasks they direct attention and effort to acts that are seen as most instrumental to goal attainment. In the Locke and Bryan (1969b) study, subjects focused on acts that improved performance on the goal-relevant dimensions and paid less attention to acts that would have improved their performance on goal-irrelevant dimensions of the task.

Level of goal challenge primarily affects performance through the amount of effort that is mobilized for task performance. Bassett (1979) and Bryan & Locke (1967b) found that people worked faster and harder under shorter time than under longer time limits. La Porte and Nath (1976) found that students persisted longer in reading a prose message when their goal was to attain a high criterion of mastery than when it was to attain a low criterion of mastery. The more challenging the goal, the greater the attention and effort an individual will devote to a task, and the greater his or her perseverance (Locke et al., 1981). Task attributes such as complexity will also influence the level of attention and effort that an individual allocates to a task (Kahneman, 1973; Schroder, Driver, & Streufert, 1967; Scott, 1966). However, as we will discuss later, the combined effects of challenging goals and high task complexity can lead to conditions of overarousal that impede rather than enhance performance.

The second type of stored plans we call *Stored Task Specific Plans* (STSP's). Such plans have previously been learned through modeling, practice, or instruction at the task in question or at some similar or analogous task. These are more cognitive and skill-oriented than SUP's and represent the cognitive organization of response patterns for a task. STSP's are acquired on several levels. At one extreme the individual can learn specific strategies for dealing with very specific task situations—e.g., a department store salesclerk might learn that, if a customer forgets his or her store credit card, to call central billing, get the card number, and then ask the customer for some ID. Or a tennis student might learn that, if a tennis opponent hits a short ball, to use a slice approach shot down the line.

When such strategies are acquired through repeated practice and are elevated to a high level of proficiency, we call them skills. Task-specific skills become highly automatized, so that the individual uses them almost unthinkingly, even though they had to be acquired originally through full conscious awareness and concentration. Typically, the individual develops STSP's for tasks that (a) are well understood and (b) are performed repeatedly. There is no assumption that all STSP's are optimal; some habits may be inefficient (e.g., a typist who uses two fingers) or even harmful (e.g., the person who smokes to relieve stress).

At a more general level, the individual can acquire meta-strategies or heuristics that apply to a variety of related situations but must be applied in different concrete ways depending on the circumstances. For example, a salesclerk heuristic might be: When you have a problem, use common sense. The tennis player might learn: When your opponent makes an error, apply pressure or respond aggressively. At the highest level of abstraction, the individual is guided by certain implicit or explicit philosophical premises (e.g., take facts seriously; do not evade; use reason to solve problems; consider long-range consequences, etc.). Such premises have millions of particular applications in everyday life. Earley, Wojnaroski, & Prest (1987) found that meta-plans do not lead to effective performance in pursuit of goals unless the planning process produces an STSP that is suitable to the task at hand. Thus, to be successful, the most abstract-level plans must be applied appropriately to a given situation. Holland, Holyoak, Nisbett, & Thagard (1986) have observed that human performance requires the acquisition of task-relevant knowledge along with heuristic rules that apply to that task domain.

The structures and sequences in which behavioral rules are organized and applied will vary between tasks because different domains of activity have different structures. In our framework an STSP represents a mental model involving various levels of specificity which regulates the acts performed in response to task stimuli. The basic building block of STSP's is a set of expectations about the relationships between acts, events, objects, situations, and task outcomes. At the point of action, these expectations become rules for how to act (Holland et al., 1986). The STSP activated in a specific situation will be a set of rules that identify a number of discrete acts that the individual believes must be performed in order to produce the task outcomes. The organization of STSP's may be hierarchical, involving different decision points for the selection of subplans (Miller, Galanter, & Pribram, 1960; Powers, 1973). It may also include sequences where the ordering of acts is related to the expected outcome. The process of assembling the rules for a particular STSP will be a dynamic one, with later rules being modified by the feedback from the actions based on earlier rules. Experience may lead to elaboration, revision, or rejection of these models.

Step 2.   Immediately following the activation of a plan repertoire, but in some cases almost simultaneous with it, there is an appraisal of the activated plans. This appraisal actually involves two related but separable appraisals. Putting these appraisals in the form of questions, they are (1) Will the plan work? and (2) Can I implement it? The appraisal of the suitability of the plan or the probability that it will work involves an external focus: if the plan is put into action, will it get the desired result? For example, if someone breaks the bully's nose, will he stop picking on the neighborhood kids? However, it is quite possible that one could come up with a plan that would work if executed by somebody but could not be executed by oneself—e.g., since the bully outweighs me by seventy-five pounds and I am a poor boxer, I cannot break his nose. The second judgment involves an estimate of one's self-efficacy or task-specific self-confidence (Bandura, 1986). Thus the individual must not simply select a good plan or a plan that could work, but one that will work when implemented by him or her.

A number of factors may influence the plan that the individual selects (step 2a). Obviously a key factor is past success. Individuals will naturally favor plans that they believe have worked for them in the past and avoid those that they perceive to have failed. This is even true of SUP's. For example, if an individual concludes that he or she "tried working hard in math before and it did not work," he or she may reject the use of effort—a choice that will guarantee that success will never be attained in math. In the case of STSP's, individuals learn that certain types of plans are best suited to certain types of goals.

For example, a goal to improve quality will evoke different rules about correct behavior from a goal to increase performance quantity. An STSP for the former may include a rule of performing slowly and carefully in order to reduce errors, while the STSP for the latter may dictate working harder and faster. The content of the goal will cue certain STSP's through its definition of the task product. For complex tasks requiring multiple products or products with multiple attributes—e.g., both quality and quantity—STSP's may include either complex behavioral rules or, when the task can be factored into components, a series of STSP's linked to different subgoals.

Another factor is "mental set," which has been well publicized in the problem-solving literature in psychology. A mental set is an implicit expectation or belief that is usually based on past experience and affects one's approach to problems. The evoking of a mental set can often lead to a framing of the task problem that impedes rather than enhances performance. For example, the individual is given six matchsticks and told to make four equilateral triangles. The implicit mental set most people approach this problem with is that the solution must be in two dimensions, whereas the problem can only be solved by constructing a pyramid.

Sweller and Levine (1982) gave individuals mazes to solve in which they could only reach the goal box by taking a path that led away from it several times in a row. Most individuals hold the implicit premise that the fastest way to get to a specific place is to head directly or at least generally toward it, a heuristic that serves people in good stead in everyday life. Thus, when they are shown the location of the goal box which can only be reached by an indirect path, they do very poorly, since they repeatedly choose the path that heads toward the box. In contrast, people who were not shown the location of the goal box learned the maze much faster, since the incorrect mental set was presumably not aroused in them (Sweller & Levine's interpretation of this experiment did not focus on mental set, but we believe that ours is a valid interpretation). Earley and Perry (1987) found that mental set could be activated by priming experimental subjects with a task that was either suitable or not suitable to the main experimental task. The priming task led subjects with specific goals to perform either better or worse on the main task than those who were not primed, depending on the suitability of the set aroused.

A further factor that can affect the appraisal and selection of plans is time pressure. When there is pressure to perform well with minimal chances for learning, individuals must either rely on previously learned plans that may or may not be applicable to the present task or engage in trial and error activity that may be less than optimal (e.g., changing several variables at once so that the effect of changing any one variable cannot be determined; Wood & Bandura, in press, b). Time constraints can also undermine the effective appraisal and selection of plans through their negative effects on the cognitive approach to search and judgment (Janis & Mann, 1977).

We would hypothesize that people would be most likely to put stored plans into action, without carefully checking their applicability, when the task is judged to be similar to tasks on which stored plans have worked in the past and/or when there are severe time pressures for accomplishing the task and/or severe penalties for failure, as in stress situations. Such pressures may be accompanied by anxiety and impatience and an accompanying tendency to want to get results or relief right away without considering alternative courses of action (Janis & Mann, 1977). Under the pressure of time constraints, search behavior often becomes focused on the most immediate and most obvious problem cues, feedback is underutilized, and judgments are biased by the use of the simplifying heuristics such as the availability heuristic (Tversky & Kahneman, 1974). When the plans used are in fact applicable, time pressures may lead to high levels of performance (Bryan & Locke, 1967b; Latham & Locke, 1975), whereas when they are not, poor performance may result (Earley, Connolly, & Ekegren, 1989; Huber, 1985b).

The selection of STSP's will also be influenced by self-conceptions and the self-efficacy that a person feels in relation to various STSP's (Bandura, 1986). For example, a person whose self-concept includes the image of a leader and is confident about his or her ability to be a leader, will have different STSP's for group problem-solving situations than a person who lacks either the self-concept or the self-efficacy required for a leadership role. Individuals with a resilient sense of self-efficacy are better able to cope with the setbacks and short-term problems that may accompany the implementation of a plan than those who begin with self-doubts about their capabilities. The more resilient persons are able to test and revise their plans, while those with low perceived self-efficacy become more self-doubting, set themselves lower goals, and become less systematic in their appraisal and selection of plans (Bandura & Wood, in press; Wood, Bandura, & Bailey, in press; Wood & Bandura, in press, a).

For any task situation, a range of competing STSP's may be considered, and the enacted plan may be either a straight repetition of a previously used plan or some combination of STSP's. The selection and assembly of plans will be a dynamic process, with continual adjustments and changes throughout the performance of a task (Campbell, 1988; Terborg, 1976). For example, if two subordinates are in conflict, several courses of action are open to their supervisor, all of which he or she may have taken before in similar occasions. Such actions might include doing nothing and seeing if the conflict blows over, meeting with two subordinates together, meeting with them individually, talking to their co-workers, firing one of them, transferring them, giving them orders to cooperate, and so on. Testing of alternatives may be involved in deciding which plan to use on this occasion, and the plan of choice may be changed during the task in response to feedback.

If the stored plans, especially STSP's, are judged not to be applicable to the task/goal situation, then the individual will attempt to develop *New Task*

Specific Plans (NTSP's)—e.g., through study, research, creative problem solving, trial and error, etc. (step 2b). These activities are primarily cognitive in nature and can range from a recombination of stored plans to a totally new approach to the problem. The quality and comprehensiveness of the problem-solving activities will often determine the originality and/or effectiveness of the NTSP's developed. New Task Specific Plans can be used either in addition to or in place of STSP's. Obviously there is a continuum of newness or originality in NTSP's. (We believe that SUP's will *always* be used except when they are deliberately inhibited—e.g., as in meditation.)

The development of NTSP's may be motivated by the failure of STSP's or by their anticipated failure (e.g., an individual observes that the task environment is changing so that what worked to attain the goal in the past will not work in the future)—more often by the former than the latter, since people seem loath to abandon STSP's that have served them well for a long period of time. The development of NTSP's at the specific, concrete level will be guided by more abstract STSP's. For example, an automobile manufacturer may find that styling and price are no longer enough to sell cars. A higher-level heuristic, look at the facts and objectively see what's causing us to lose market share, may then be applied. The manufacturer may then discover that quality must be higher in order to compete effectively. He or she then develops specific procedures (e.g., statistical quality control) to upgrade quality. The above process, of course, may occur over a period of many years.

It must be stressed that SUP's continue to play a major role in the development of NTSP's even though they are not in themselves sufficient for effective task performance. If the individual gives up or refuses to expend the effort required to discover a new strategy, it is unlikely that a successful NTSP will be discovered. The amount of effort and attention, the focus of the attention, and the persistence in the problem-solving process will determine the quality of solutions (i.e., NTSP's) obtained.

A question arises as to whether NTSP's can become STSP's with repeated practice. To answer, a distinction must be made between complex tasks that one performs repeatedly under conditions that, though not identical, are highly similar, and complex tasks that are of such a nature as to be continually changing. An example of the first type would be that of an airline pilot. While the task is quite complex, it is repeated with only minor variations day after day, so that the key plans become fairly automated (stored). Only in rare emergencies do the automatized plans not apply, and then NTSP's take over. Similarly, there are certain general strategies that facilitate faculty research productivity—e.g., having several different projects going at the same time (Taylor, Locke, Lee, & Gist, 1984). While each research project may be different, having multiple projects going may always facilitate productivity.

In contrast, running a business in a dynamic environment may require constant change, even though there may be some elements that stay constant (e.g., need to manage people). Thus some major activities could never be automatized and the search for new strategies is continual. Such tasks could be more complex than tasks such as that of an airline pilot because of the greater degree of dynamic complexity (Wood, 1986). This presents fewer possibilities for automatizing task-specific plans and a greater need for a constant stream of new plans.

Successful performance on complex tasks may require the testing and appraisal of several different task-specific plans (TSP's), both stored and new plans. Complex tasks may also require the application of nonlinear and compound behavioral rules, which are especially difficult to learn (Brehmer, Hagafors, & Johansson, 1980). To discover them, people have to construct TSP's about the form of the rules, test their judgments against the consequences of their actions, and remember which TSP's they have tested and how effective different acts were. It requires a strong sense of self-efficacy to operate in this exploratory mode in the face of ongoing task demands and decrements in performance due to the failure of TSP's. The stronger a person's perceived self-efficacy, the more effective he or she is in the testing and appraising activities leading to rule learning and the development of NTSP's (Bandura & Wood, in press; Wood, Bandura, & Bailey, in press; Wood & Bandura, in press, a).

Step 3. The individual implements his or her stored and/or newly developed plans and actually performs the task in order to attempt to reach the goal with which he or she started. (We will not be concerned here with goal change.) It is possible at that stage for a potentially effective TSP to fail because an individual lacks the specific manual, physical, or cognitive skills needed to perform the required acts in a task. Behavior will reflect the joint influences of learning and motivation. Effective action requires learning how to organize action sequences through monitoring of behavior and outcomes, comparisons against TSP's, and the correction of incorrect behaviors. Individuals learn that in certain situations particular actions will produce some results and not others.

The implementation of TSP's follows the conception-matching process of behavior production described by Bandura (1986). Initially, the individual selects a TSP that provides a *model* for task-related behaviors and a *standard* for behavioral correction. The TSP then guides the initiation of specific acts, which are monitored for effects and compared against the TSP model. Behavior then continues through a process of matching action to plan and modifying behaviors on the basis of feedback to achieve a progressively closer correspondence between plan and action.

Flexibility and adaptiveness in behavior is possible due to the generative conceptions of the rules that guide the selection and sequencing of behaviors. If TSP's were composed solely of simple stimulus-response rules, then their implementation would not show the variability and responsiveness to situations that are characteristic of human behavior. Bandura (1986) has described generative rules as those that can produce behavior patterns that share the same basic characteristics but may differ in other respects. He gives the example of drawing triangles (Bandura, 1986, p. 111). Once a person understands the basic steps, he or she can display behavioral flexibility by drawing large or small triangles or creating triangular enclosures, even though he or she may have never produced a particular construction previously. Because of the generative conceptions of rules, an individual can also be adaptive in specific situations where constraints or obstacles require adjustment in behavior. Therefore a person given a piece of paper and no pencil may create a triangle by folding the paper into the correct shape.

Step 4.   Both during and after task performance the individual gets feedback of varying degrees and types and from various sources—the task, self-tracking, supervisor, computer, etc. (Ilgen, Fisher, & Taylor, 1979). Since the feedback regarding progress will be evaluated in terms of how far and in what direction performance deviates from the goal, it will be experienced on a continuum from positive (indicating success or high goal progress) to negative (indicating failure or poor goal progress).

   If only stored plans are used and feedback is positive, this will tend to reinforce the assumptions or conviction that the stored strategies were appropriate and they will tend to be repeated (step 4a). There are exceptions, however. The individual may become bored by previous strategies and want to try something new or, as noted earlier, may anticipate that conditions are changing so that new strategies will need to be developed for the future (step 4a'). An example of the latter would be an executive who concludes that a product that has sold in the past will not sell in the future because the market has changed and thus develops a new product.

   If either stored and/or new plans are used but the feedback is negative, there will be a tendency to develop or look for other stored or new task strategies (step 4b). Again, however, there are exceptions to this tendency (step 4b'). People may stick to old plans even after failure due to habit; the commitment to past decisions (Staw, 1976); assumption of a time lag between strategy use and positive outcome; a long period of previous success; the failure to see the connection between the plans used and failure; fear of trying something new; or a determination to try harder, thus reinvoking SUP's (e.g., see Matsui, Okada, & Inoshita, 1983). Further, persistence often *does* pay off.

Individual Variables

Throughout our discussion of the model, perceived self-efficacy has been mentioned as an important factor in the subprocesses of appraisal, selection, development, and implementation of TSP's. Self-efficacy also impacts on the levels of self-set goals which can initiate the processes described in the model. The stronger the perceived self-efficacy, the more challenging the goals people set for themselves (Taylor, Locke, Lee, & Gist, 1984; Wood, Bandura, & Bailey, in press) and the greater their commitment to them (Locke, Frederick, Lee, & Bobko, 1984).

   There is evidence that beliefs about self-efficacy are as important as ability in the self-regulation of human action (Bandura, 1986, 1988). Self-efficacy refers to a person's beliefs about his or her capacity to successfully perform some course of action. These self-beliefs are based partly on past performance but also reflect appraisals of one's current capacities and the specific circumstances that will either inhibit or enhance performance. Self-efficacy beliefs affect the attentional and thinking processes in the evoking and appraisal of STSP's—i.e., steps 1 and 2 of the model (e.g., Kent & Gibbons, 1987). Those with a strong sense of efficacy are able to maintain a task orientation when confronted with challenging goals and high task demands. Those who judge themselves to be inefficacious in coping with task demands tend to become more self-doubt focused than task-focused and thus concentrate attention more on the evaluative implications of performance than on the required actions or TSP's (M. Bandura and Dweck, 1987).

Also, the stronger the perceived self-efficacy, the more effective the analytic thinking in rule learning for NTSP's (Wood, Bandura, & Bailey, in press; Wood & Bandura, in press, a). Individuals with high self-efficacy are better able to control their self-doubts and more systematically test alternative TSP's when confronted with the failure of prior plans than subjects with low self-efficacy. Bandura (1986, 1988) has described operative self-efficacy as a generative capability in which multiple subskills are continuously improvised to manage ever-changing task demands. In the implementation of TSP's, self-efficacy beliefs will directly influence how well individuals utilize their skills, their interpretations of feedback in self-aiding or self-debilitating terms, and their perseverance. They have been shown to affect motivation directly through the mobilization and maintenance of effort (Bandura & Cervone, 1983, 1986). Self-efficacy beliefs will, therefore, exert an influence at all stages of the model.

The role of ability in the model shown in Figure 13–1 should also be noted briefly. First, STSP's, once automatized, will function, in effect, as abilities (capacities for action). Other abilities affect how rapidly and well an individual can develop stored plans. Abilities can also come into play in judging the relevance of stored plans, in implementing plans, in developing new plans, and in drawing the correct conclusions from positive and negative feedback. In short, ability too can come into play at all stages of the model. For all but the simplest of tasks, cognitive abilities will play a critical role in the selection and development of TSP's. Because of this, cognitive abilities should affect performance across a wider range of tasks than other types of abilities, as is found in validity generalization studies of selection tests (Hunter, 1980; Pearlman, 1982). During the implementation of plans (step 3), the particular abilities that are required for effective performance (i.e., manual, psychomotor, cognitive, etc.) will depend on the particular task being performed.

Plan Characteristics

Task-specific plans, whether STSP's or NTSP's, are a cognitive mechanism through which behavior is organized, enacted, and evaluated. They include conceptions of what behaviors must be enacted and how acts must be combined and sequenced in order to achieve goals. As previously mentioned, the TSP's guide behavior through a conception-matching process (Bandura, 1986). As a set of rules that guide action, TSP's have something in common with earlier conceptions of scripts, which Abelson (1976) defined as a "coherent sequence of events expected by the individual, involving him either as participant or observer." However, the conception of scripts, as it has been applied to the study of information processing, includes both declarative and procedural knowledge and can be descriptive as well as prescriptive (e.g., Hastie & Carlston, 1980; Wyer & Carlston, 1979; Wyer & Srull, 1980). Our conception of TSP's is more limited in that we are concerned with the production of goal-directed behavior and focus on the prescriptive procedural knowledge or response guidelines that are evoked during task performance. In the enactment of plans, a person may draw on his or her declarative knowledge of information relating to a task; however, the content of TSP's is limited to the prescriptive procedural rules that guide the selection and sequencing of behavior.

Task-specific plans will vary in the content of rules (i.e., acts and outcomes) and in their organization. As noted earlier, task plans and strategies have been described in terms of their generality of application, ranging from task-specific strategies which are restricted in application to a single task to global strategies which are used on a wide variety of tasks and are not restricted by the particular nature of a task (e.g., Dansereau et al., 1979; Sternberg, 1986; Tatum & Nebeker, 1986). SUP's are very general motivational strategies.

A distinction can be drawn between TSP's that specify the *content* of required acts for task performance and those that emphasize more dynamic problem-solving *processes* for learning about the appropriate acts such as hypothesis-testing or means-ends analysis (Levine, 1975; Sweller, 1983; Wood & Bandura, in press, a). TSP's that specify the required responses for a particular task or category of tasks will have less general application than process TSP's, such as hypothesis testing, which may be used to learn behavioral rules and develop NTSP's for a wide range of task types. The first type of TSP specifies the content of rules or required acts for effective task performance. The second type is a set of rules that specify the process by which the required acts can be learned.

The *content* of TSP's can be described in a manner similar to that used in the policy literature where strategy content refers to options chosen or actions taken (e.g., Frederickson, 1984). In the Chesney and Locke (1988) study, the Market Leadership strategy used by subjects (which involved increasing the sales force, entering new markets, etc.) is an example of strategy content. Another example of strategy content is provided in a study by Earley, Connolly, and Lee (1988), who trained subjects in one of their two strategy conditions in a content model TSP for predictions on a multiple-cue probability learning (MCPL) task. The prescribed acts in the TSP included steps such as calculate the mean value for the set of the predictors and use this as the predicted value of the criterion variable. The specified steps in this calculation presented subjects with a step-by-step strategy for the prediction task.

Operationalization of TSP's based on strategy content will need to allow for the fact that strategy content will be task specific in several ways. First, the formulation of TSP's will depend on the options available for a particular task: for example, Market Leadership would not be applicable as a task strategy for complex clerical tasks of the type used in the Shaw (1984) study. Therefore, predicting the choice of TSP's from goal attributes will probably require the specification of options for each particular task being studied. However, the diversity of spontaneously developed strategies in the Shaw (1984) study suggests that this may not be an easy task, either ex ante or ex post. As has been noted in descriptions of scripts (Abelson, 1981), TSP's can incorporate multiple paths to goals. This factor contributes to the flexibility and adaptability of behavior (Lord & Kernan, 1987), making it difficult to identify and measure a defined set of options in the study of TSP content. If only a limited range of options is possible, then predicting the choice of TSP's will be easier. To allow generalization of results across tasks, however, what is needed is a typology of TSP's or task-strategy options. The work by Tatum and Nebeker (1986) and the description of script properties by Lord and Kernan (1987), which can be applied to TSP's, represent a beginning to this very difficult task.

A second area in which predictions about the content of TSP's will be task specific is in the impact of different options on performance. On some tasks, for example, the pursuit of a quality strategy (e.g., minimize errors, avoid rework, etc.) may undermine performance on quantity or speed criteria (e.g., Locke and Bryan, 1969b). On other tasks, for example, sports such as swimming and baseball, quality strategies that lead to improvements in style will often produce higher performance levels on quantity criteria (e.g., number of hits). Because the contingencies between acts and products vary from task to task (Wood, 1986), the effectiveness of different types of TSP's will also vary, and the indirect effects of goals on performance will vary as a function of the task strategies chosen. Of special interest will be those situations in which the directing and energizing effects of goals lead to a choice of suboptimal task strategies (e.g., Earley & Perry, 1987; Huber, 1985b).

An alternative approach to the study of task strategies is to consider the properties of the *process* by which NTSP's are developed. The development of task strategies includes the activities of search, development, evaluation, and choice of options. The characteristics of the strategy development process apply across all tasks and can be described in terms of dimensions such as comprehensiveness, communication, negotiation, and participation (Frederickson, 1984; Smith, Locke, & Barry, in press;). Therefore it will be possible to formulate and test general hypotheses about how various goal attributes impact on the planning processes by which NTSP's are developed.

For example, goal specificity may lead to lower communication and more-focused search processes in the development of NTSP's. A post hoc analysis of communications between subjects in a study of Baumler (1971) showed that those with specific goals communicated less than those with no goals. It is possible that the individually specified performance goals gave subjects "tunnel vision" which undermined the information-sharing activities that could have helped them to improve their performance on the complex task used in that study. In contrast, Smith, Locke, and Barry (in press) found that *group* goal challenge led to comprehensive planning activities (search for alternatives, etc.) in the development of NTSP's. Further research into hypotheses about the effects of goal attributes, such as specificity and challenge, on characteristics of the strategy development process, such as communication and comprehensiveness, would be particularly useful in the design of goal interventions for complex tasks.

Two major processes employed in the performance of problem-solving tasks are means-ends analysis (Newell & Simon, 1972) and hypothesis testing (Levine, 1975). In the means-ends approach, the individual generates the full set of rules or TSP that he or she believes will move him or her from the problem state to the goal state. This is typically achieved by a process of working backward and forward between the goal state and the problem state. However, when achievement of a goal requires learning of new actions due to the novelty of the problem state, dynamic complexity, or failure of an existing TSP, a hypothesis-testing approach may need to be adopted (Bruner, Goodnow, & Austin, 1956; Sweller & Levine, 1982; Sweller, 1983). That is, the individual constructs a tentative set of rules about the relationships between acts and outcomes leading to a goal state and then assesses their validity through the feedback received. The hypothesis-testing approach requires extensive search for the composite rules of an NTSP, during performance of the task. In this process, control over the self-regulation of behavior shifts from previously set goals to feedback about performance (Sweller, 1983).

An example of a process TSP is the strategy condition in the Earley, Connolly, and Lee (1988) study in which subjects were presented with a set of steps for formulating hypotheses and testing the effects of different cues and combinations of cues on a prediction task. Subjects were able to use this process TSP to learn the appropriate content of an NTSP for combining multiple cues into a single prediction. Therefore, while the content TSP described in an earlier reference to the Earley, Connolly, and Lee study provided a direct means-ends path to the task goal of accurate predictions, the process TSP presented an indirect path in which performance depended on the development of an NTSP.

Another example of a process TSP is provided in studies by Bandura & Wood (in press), Wood and Bandura (in press, a), and Wood, Bandura, & Bailey (in press), who analyzed the stream of decisions made by subjects in a multiple trial stimulation. In the managerial decision task used in the studies, changing more than one factor at a time was a deficient analytic strategy for testing hypotheses regarding the impact of factors on performance, because it confounded the contributions of different factors to outcomes. Therefore it was possible to score the correctness of subjects' process TSP's by summing the number of decisions across trials on which subjects changed only a single factor. More correct use of analytic strategies enhanced performance on later trials suggesting that correct use of a process TSP led to the development of NTSP's. The process TSP measured in these studies, that of hypothesis testing, can be applied across a wide range of tasks in which learning and problem solving are essential components.

The approaches that have been taken to the measurement of TSP's reflect the potential variety in operationalizations of this cognitive construct. These have included weighting of cues (Earley, Connolly, & Ekegren, 1989), content analyses of self-reported strategies (Campbell, 1984; Earley & Perry, 1987), assessments of decisions taken (Wood & Bandura, in press, a; Wood, Bandura, & Bailey, in press), and global assessments of strategy (Huber, 1985b; Earley, Lee, & Hanson, 1989). Others have relied on assessments of the effort devoted to planning activities (Smith, Locke, & Barry, in press).

Many of these operationalizations rely on ex post self-reports of strategies and task plans. Such an approach has several problems (Wood, Bandura, & Bailey, in press). First, the use of self-report measures confounds needs, preferences, and self-concepts of the person with the objective characteristics of the TSP. A second potential problem relates to the recall of strategies actually used, which may vary as a function of individual memory capacity and task characteristics. Finally, the ex post nature of self-reports means that they can be confounded by the individual's knowledge of how he or she performed on the task. The ease of collecting self-reports and the difficulty of obtaining more objective measures of cognitive constructs, such as TSP's, will mean that these problems will not always be avoidable.

However, there are examples of studies where the operationalization of TSP's using self-reports has minimized the types of confounding effects mentioned above. Schweiger, Anderson, and Locke (1985) have shown that self-reports of decision-making processes, when taken under optimal conditions, can yield useful predictive information about performance on complex tasks. Ericsson and Simon (1980) have identified some of these conditions as follows: the information to be reported is in focal awareness; the task has not been highly automatized; the time interval between the occurrence of the cognitive process and the self-report is short; the self-report does not require excessive encoding; there is no cognitive overload and few distractions; and the report is oral.

Let us now consider the concept of task complexity and how it relates to the previously described model.

TASK COMPLEXITY AND GOAL EFFECTS

The effects of goal setting on task performance have been studied on a wide range of tasks of varying complexity, including brainstorming, clerical tasks, prose learning, typing, supervision, and selling (Locke, et al., 1981; Locke & Latham, 1984b). Across the range of goal setting studies using different tasks, the magnitude of goal effects on performance decreases as the complexity of the task increases (Wood, Mento, & Locke, 1987). However, the means by which task attributes such as complexity affect the relationship between goals and task performance has received little study thus far.

Recently, Wood (1986) has advanced a general definition of task complexity that can be used to standardize the different approaches to task complexity for a wide variety of task types. This includes the manual, psychomotor, and cognitive types of tasks that have been used in goal setting studies (Locke et al., 1981). The definition is built on descriptions of the acts-to-product relationships for a task and the information cues that have to be consciously processed in the performance of acts. The characteristics of tasks that contribute to task complexity are described in Figure 13–2.

The three general categories of task complexity identified in Figure 13–2 can apply to both manual (including psychomotor) and cognitive tasks (see Wood, 1986). However, variations in complexity may have different consequences for these two types of tasks because of the basic differences between them in the work processes and skill requirements.

Component Complexity

In goal setting studies, component complexity (Wood, 1986) or the number of acts required has ranged from single-act tasks such as simple reaction time (e.g., Locke, Cartledge, & Knerr, 1970), simple computation (e.g., Erez, 1977), and brainstorming (e.g., Locke, 1967c; Garland, 1982) to the more complex, multiact tasks of

1. **Component complexity:** refers to the number of distinct acts and information cues that are inputs to a task product. This can be broken down into two parts:
   a. **The number of acts required** to complete a task, where an act is a complex pattern of behavior with some identifiable purpose (e.g., lifting, reading)
   b. **The number of information cues** that must be attended to and processed in order to make the judgment needed to complete a task
2. **Coordinative complexity:** refers to the nature of relationships between task inputs (i.e., acts and information cues) and task products. Several different aspects of the relationships between task inputs will impact on coordinative complexity, including the following:
   a. **Sequencing of acts** required to complete a task: specifically the number of precedence relations between the required acts for a task.
   b. **Form of the relationships** between task inputs and task products. In manual tasks this relates to the physical coordination required in the performance of different acts, either simultaneously or in quick succession. In cognitive tasks the equivalent forms of complexity include the integration of cues in judgments and simultaneous processing of information from different sources in decision making.
   c. **Strength of association** between task inputs and task products, i.e., the predictability of the effects of acts and the predictive validity of information cues.
   d. **Time allowed** for performance of a task. This will influence the speed at which acts must be performed and information processed.
3. **Dynamic complexity:** refers to changes in the acts and information cues for a task. As such, dynamic complexity represents different levels of the various types of component and coordinative complexity for a single task at different points in time. The changes can be analyzed in terms of
   a. **Continuity** of the change over time, i.e., whether the change is a singe discontinuous event or continuous
   b. **Predictability** of the change when it is continuous

FIGURE 13–2   Task Complexity Taxonomy

college course work (e.g., Locke & Bryan, 1968b; Wood & Locke, 1987) and scientific work (Latham, Mitchell, & Dossett, 1978). For tasks with few required acts, the implications of specific, challenging goals are obvious to the task doer. He or she simply has to invest more attention and effort into the acts that lead directly to the specified product and performance should improve (i.e., he or she uses SUP's). As the number of different required acts for a task increases, the implications for performance may be less obvious and require some choice about which of many alternative actions to take—thus the need for STSP's and NTSP's. Furthermore, in some cases, the quality of this plan may be as potent a determinant of performance as the type of goal (Smith, Locke, & Barry, in press). For example, a student who studies the wrong material or studies in the wrong way may fail no matter how much studying is done. In a field study of the effects of varying component complexity for a range of different jobs, Earley, Lee, and Hanson (1989) found that plan quality mediated the relationships of goal setting to performance on more complex jobs.

The cueing effects of specific goals will vary as a function of the number of components in a task. As the required number of acts in a task increases, the performance effects of a specific goal will be weakened unless the task is well understood and the goal cues the appropriate TSP.

Coordinative Complexity

In general, the coordinative complexity resulting from the need for integration of acts or information cues will require higher levels of perceptual, physical, and motor coordination skills for manual tasks and greater information-processing and problem-solving skills for cognitive tasks.

Task complexity caused by the need to integrate information cues in goal setting studies has ranged from relatively simple cognitive tasks such as solving computational problems (e.g., Erez, 1977) up to the more complex judgment and decision tasks used by Erez and Arad (1986), Latham, Mitchell, and Dossett (1978), and Wood, Bandura, and Bailey (in press). Again, goal setting and SUP's affect performance on all types of tasks. However, a translation of goals into performance on cognitive tasks that are coordinatively complex may require that the individual discover the required integration model (e.g., Earley, Connolly, & Ekegren, 1989; Wood, Bandura, & Bailey, in press). This, in turn, will require either the application of STSP's or information processing and problem solving (i.e., development of NTSP's) in order to identify and implement an effective approach to the task.

One goal setting study in which the task required complex physical coordination was that by Locke and Bryan (1966a). Subjects were required to match patterns of lights in two dimensions using both foot pedals and a hand-arm control. Studies that have required lower levels of physical coordination are those that have used, for example, toy-assembly tasks (e.g., Jackson & Zedeck, 1982; Latham & Steele, 1983). As the coordinative complexity of a manual task increases due to physical coordination requirements or tighter time constraints, the skill requirements or need for STSP's will increase. However, as the Locke and Bryan (1966a) study shows, the SUP's activated by goals can still have direct effects on performance for tasks that require high levels of skilled physical coordination when an individual has the necessary skills. For many tasks requiring complex physical coordination, such as operating a lathe or skiing, skillful performance requires automatic execution of STSP's. The allocation of scarce attentional resources to the conscious selection, development, or implementation of TSP's during the performance of the task will limit performance, although such allocation is necessary in order to develop the skills initially.

For complex motor tasks, challenging goals that increase performance pressure may produce detrimental effects by creating a condition of overarousal (Humphreys & Revelle, 1984). Overarousal can lead to loss of direct behavioral control, resulting in lowered performance despite the effort and attention being directed to the task. Overarousal may also lead to shifting critical attentional resources from the execution of the required behavior to the outcome. When assigned a challenging goal, individuals may think in terms of the outcome and its consequences and fail to devote sufficient attention to the performance of specific behaviors. The intrusion of distracting thoughts is more likely to occur when a person judges himself or herself inefficacious in coping with the demands of the challenging goal (Bandura, 1986).

In general, coordinatively complex cognitive tasks will require the conscious application of TSP's. Studies by Earley and his colleagues employing an

MCPL task have shown that training in TSP's increases judgmental accuracy (Earley, Connolly, & Lee, 1988; Earley, Connolly, & Ekegren, 1989; Earley, Lee, & Lituchy, 1989). Subjects who had relevant TSP's available as a result of their training were better able to combine multiple cues into a predictive judgment than those who had specific, challenging goals but who did not receive the training.

Dynamic Complexity

Complexity that is due to changes in the required acts and information cues of a task will typically require problem-solving responses (i.e., NTSP's) before the motivational effects of goals are reflected in increased performance. In particular, changes in task demands will require the search for and processing of information in order to discover or develop alternative courses of action (March & Simon, 1958). The business tasks or games used in some goal setting studies (e.g., Campbell & Gingrich, 1986; Chesney & Locke, 1988; Wood, Bandura, & Bailey, in press) and the tasks included in some field studies (e.g., Latham, Mitchell, & Dossett, 1978) all contain tasks that are dynamically complex. The dynamic complexity in these studies is due to changes in the cues to be processed and the decisions to be made across different trials of the task. In the stochastic multiple cue probability learning (MCPL) task used by Earley and his colleagues (e.g., Earley, Connolly, & Ekegren, 1989), dynamic complexity was present due to variations in the predictive values of cues on a trial-by-trial basis. By comparison, many other goal setting studies have employed single-trial laboratory tasks in which the information and required acts do not change (e.g., Locke, 1982b).

Dynamically complex tasks have uncertain or varying relationships between acts and outcomes, requiring adjustments in the rules that regulate behavior during the performance of the task, i.e., the development of NTSP's. Studies on a dynamically complex decision simulation have shown that systematic use of a hypothesis-testing approach has a positive effect on performance on such tasks (Bandura & Wood, in press; Wood & Bandura, in press, a). In both studies the effects of self-set goals had a positive effect on the level of systematic hypothesis testing by subjects in later trials of the decision-making task. The systematic development of NTSP's was, in turn, positively related to level of performance. Earley, Lee, and Lituchy (1989) achieved a similar effect by training subjects in the correct hypothesis-testing procedures for the development of NTSP's on a dynamically complex MCPL task. Subjects who were assigned specific, challenging goals and received training outperformed those who were assigned goals but not trained. In both sets of studies performance was enhanced by the combination of specific, challenging goals and systematic development of NTSP's through hypothesis testing. Specific, challenging goals alone did not have the same positive effect on performance for the complex tasks used in the above studies, as has generally been found for simpler tasks (Locke et al., 1981).

GOAL PROPERTIES, PLANS, AND TASK COMPLEXITY

In the preceding section we argued that complex tasks will require greater development and dynamic selection of TSP's than simple tasks. The prior specification of complete means-ends hierarchies in the form of STSP's will be more difficult as the complexity of a task increases due to the increasing number of uncertain or unknown alternatives and consequences of action; greater uncertainty about the relationships between acts and outcomes; and the greater number of subtasks, which may not be easily handled by subgoals (March & Simon, 1958). The information-processing requirements of these consequences of complexity will quickly exceed individual knowledge and memory capacities, invalidating STSP's and creating a need for NTSP's. For component and certain types of coordinative complexity requiring the performance of several subtasks and their integration, complexity may be handled through the use of process STSP's, which specify subgoals (Ernst & Newell, 1969) or series of choices for completion of the task (Greeno, 1978). For nonsequential coordinative complexity and dynamically complex tasks, learning will be required as the task proceeds and the development of NTSP's will involve search and hypothesis testing.

We will now summarize our arguments for the relationships between goal properties and TSP's before presenting our propositions for the relationships between goals, TSP's, and performance for tasks of differing complexity.

Goals influence behavior through their effects on the level of individual resources (i.e., attention and effort) devoted to a task and through their cueing effects in the focusing of attention and allocation of effort to specific acts. The effects of these processes are mediated by TSP's whose selection is determined in part by the properties of the goals. Goal properties that have been shown to influence the level of individual resources and their allocation to specific acts are goal specificity and goal challenge or difficulty.

Goal specificity aids the selection of TSP's by focusing on certain product attributes and excluding others, thus shaping the definition of the task and constraining the set of alternative TSP's to be considered in the selection phase of the model. Specific goals also provide clearer standards against which to evaluate one's performance, further cueing the allocation of attention and effort. General or vague goals provide indefinite criteria for the evaluation and selection of TSP's. The regulatory effects of such goals are manifest through the implementation of SUP's, with less effort being spent in the evaluation and selection of TSP's (Earley, Wojnaroski, & Prest, 1987; Terborg, 1976; Smith, Locke, & Barry, in press). Specific goals also provide clearer cues and benchmarks in the development and testing of NTSP's (Earley, Connolly, & Lee, 1988). Thus specific goals aid the selection and development of TSP's by stimulating individuals to think about tasks in more-focused terms than general goals.

However, on complex tasks where there is uncertainty about the appropriate means or TSP's to be followed, highly specific statements of end goals may generate pressures for immediate performance and thus may lead to the selection of simple means-ends plans when a more complex hypothesis-testing approach may be needed to develop an NTSP (Earley, Connolly, & Ekegren, 1989; Sweller & Levine, 1982). The focusing of attention can be counterproductive when the task requires broader scanning of options and creative problem solving for goal attainment (Janis & Mann, 1977).

The level of challenge or difficulty of a goal will influence the level of resources that are allocated to a task. There is considerable evidence that the more challenging a goal, the harder people work to attain it, and the better their performance (Locke et al., 1981). This includes effort and attention that are devoted to the selection and development of TSP's (Earley, Wojnaroski, & Prest, 1987; Smith, Locke, & Barry, in press;). People plan more and work harder at tasks with challenging goals.

However, challenging goals may also create a level of arousal that interferes with the cognitive processes involved in the selection and development of TSP's (cf. Humphreys & Revelle, 1984), leading to the misdirection of attention and effort (e.g., Huber, 1985b). The negative effects of challenging goals are most likely to occur on complex tasks and will be moderated by a person's self-efficacy and experience or knowledge of the task (Earley, Lee, & Hanson, 1989). When a person is committed to the attainment of a difficult goal but doubts his or her ability to attain it, strategic thinking becomes impaired and performance suffers (Bandura & Wood, in press; Wood, Bandura, & Bailey, in press; Wood & Bandura, in press, a). Preoccupation with a challenging goal for which a person feels inefficacious may also undermine performance by diverting attention away from the selection and development of TSP's to the formidableness of the goal and the consequences of failing to achieve it. Intrusive, nonproductive thinking will be heightened when a person lacks self-efficacy for the attainment of goals that have important personal consequences, such as the social evaluations that may result from assigned goals.

When the effort spent on the search for and testing of TSP's is itself dysfunctional, specific, challenging goals may have a negative effect on performance. For example, on a complex maze task in which use of a search option was penalized, Huber (1985b) found that subjects with a specific, challenging time goal overused the search option. As a result, they accumulated more time penalties and found their way out of the maze less quickly than subjects with a general goal to find their way out the maze as quickly as possible. Earley, Connolly, and Ekegren (1989) obtained similar results in three studies, using an MCPL task. Subjects with a specific, challenging goal engaged in greater search for TSP's but made less-accurate predictions than subjects with a general goal to be as accurate as possible. Subjects with specific, challenging goals actually selected poorer strategies. For complex tasks on which performance is more a function of TSP's than SUP's, the effectiveness of strategy search may represent a boundary condition for the superiority of specific, challenging goals over more general goals (Earley, Connolly, & Ekegren, 1989).

The arousal induced by a challenging goal leads to higher levels of search for TSP's, but that search may be less systematic and not lead to efficient learning of the rules governing performance on complex tasks. On a complex, multitrial managerial decision-making simulation, Bandura and Wood (in press) found that subjects assigned a specific, challenging goal made more tests of rules but were less systematic in their tests than those assigned a specific, easy goal. The press for large performance gains under a challenging goal led subjects to change many variables simultaneously, which only confounded their effects and hindered subjects' efforts to discover the optimal decision rules for the simulation task. Subjects were better able to maintain strategically effective thinking in their testing and appraising of TSP's under achievable goals than under the more difficult ones.

The potential negative effects of challenging goals are also more likely to occur in the task performances of inexperienced and untrained individuals who lack a set of relevant STSP's for the task (Campbell, 1984; Earley, Lee, & Hanson, 1989) and feel inefficacious about their capabilities. For more experienced individuals or those who have received training in TSP's, challenging goals lead to enhanced performance on complex tasks (Earley, Lee, & Lituchy, 1989; Earley, Connolly, & Lee, 1988). Those with a stronger perceived self-efficacy will use more effective strategic thinking to develop NTSP's (Bandura & Wood, in press; Wood & Bandura, in press, a; Wood, Bandura, & Bailey, in press). On complex tasks where the allocation of attention and effort is a nontrivial problem, the energizing effects of challenging goals will only be translated into performance when the appropriate TSP's are available as a result of training, experience, or the spontaneous development of NTSP's.

Fundamentally, the complexity of the task should be most likely to affect the relative potency and adequacy of SUP's, STSP's, and NTSP's in the manner shown in Figure 13–3. First, let us consider simple tasks, that is, tasks with few acts to be performed, where little or no coordination is required and where the acts to outcome relationships do not vary. Stored Universal Plans and, to an extent, simple STSP's should show substantial relationships with performance, whereas NTSP's would be less relevant. This relationship is shown in Figure 13–3(a).

The reason for this is that the simplicity of the task precludes major individual differences in task strategies or task-strategy options. For example, consider a reaction time task. About all one can do is to pay attention and be ready to respond, and possibly tense one's muscles in anticipation of the signal. Thus, within the limits of ability to respond, and assuming simple stored plans are implemented uniformly by all participants, goals should be highly correlated with performance (e.g., see Locke, Cartledge, & Knerr, 1970, studies 1–4).

As soon as one goes beyond this simplest level of complexity, however, TSP's begin to play a role in performance, especially after explicit training (Earley, Wojnaroski, & Prest, 1987; Locke, Frederick, Lee, & Bobko, 1984).

Now consider moderately complex tasks. SUP's should still work on such tasks, but STSP's should be more important than for simple tasks. Consider, for example, reading a prose passage for understanding and recall. Paying attention to the words and trying to grasp the material relevant to the goal should still aid performance; but, in addition, various ways of integrating the concepts and rehearsal strategies to facilitate memory should have an impact on performance. This will involve utilizing previously learned study skills (STSP's) and possibly developing some new plans that apply to the material (NTSP's). This relationship is shown in Figure 13–3 (b).

On a moderately complex clerical task, Shaw (1984) found that both goals (thus by implication SUP's) and assigned strategies had significant effects on performance. Shaw also found that subjects with specific, challenging goals and no assigned strategies were significantly more likely to spontaneously develop new task strategies (NTSP's) than those told to do their best who had no assigned strategies. However, so many different strategies were used, it was not possible to grade them as to effectiveness. These results highlight the potential difficulties of linking TSP's to performance discussed in an earlier section.

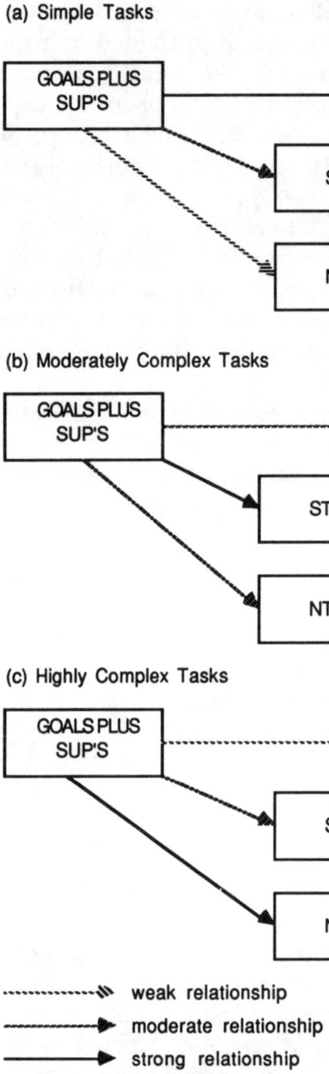

(a) Simple Tasks

(b) Moderately Complex Tasks

(c) Highly Complex Tasks

⋯⋯⋯⋯⋯⋙ weak relationship

⋯⋯⋯⋯⋯► moderate relationship

────────► strong relationship

FIGURE 13–3   Predicted Strength of Relationships between Goals, Plans, and Performance on Tasks of Differing Complexity

Finally, in highly complex tasks, such as managing a high-technology business in a volatile environment, SUP's may help but not so much directly as through their effect on the development of NTSP's. The dynamic complexity of such an environment will mean that previously learned STSP's will not work for a very long period of time and strategies for discovering NTSP's will be needed continuously. The effects of goals on performance are mediated through their effects on the development of NTSP's (Bandura & Wood, in press; Wood & Bandura, in press, a; Wood, Bandura, & Bailey, in press). This model is shown in Figure 13–3 (c). Under certain conditions, such as time constraints or other forms of pressure, goal setting may impede the learning of NTSP's. Specific goals may have a priming effect that leads to the selection of a particular STSP, even though it is inappropriate for the particular task situation. However, the persistence of such a goal-induced error would depend on the feedback received and its effects on the conception-matching process of behavioral production described earlier.

Studies using a dynamically complex management game (Earley, Wojnaroski, & Prest, 1987; Smith, Locke, & Barry, in press) show that specific, challenging goals stimulate higher levels of planning activity (i.e., development of NTSP's) than no goals, and the quality of planning activity is significantly related to performance. These results, along with Shaw (1984), support the argument that goals stimulate strategy development on more complex tasks. However, this effort will only be translated into performance effects if the strategy development includes the testing and appraising of new rules or strategies (Bandura & Wood, in press; Wood & Bandura, in press, a; Wood, Bandura, & Bailey, in press).

A meta-analysis of goal setting studies conducted between 1966 and 1985 provides strong evidence that the performance effects of specific, challenging goals are moderated by task complexity (Wood, Mento, & Locke, 1987). Across all 125 studies included in the analysis, goal effects were strongest for simple tasks, such as reaction time and brainstorming tasks, and weakest for more complex tasks, such as business game simulations and faculty research productivity. It is possible that the indirect effects of goals on complex tasks were weaker than the direct effects of SUP's on simple tasks due to greater variation in the mediating effects of TSP's on complex tasks. Therefore, although not a direct test of our model, the Wood, Mento, and Locke (1987) finding is consistent with the hypothesized direct effects of SUP's on simple tasks—i.e., Figure 13–3 (a)—and indirect effects of TSP's complex tasks—i.e., Figure 13–3 (a and b).

Time lag. On simple tasks goal setting effects are virtually immediate. Locke (1982b), for example, has found goal effects on the task of giving uses for objects in a single, one-minute trial. On complex tasks there may be a time lag in the effects of goals and/or strategies on performance. The lag in the effect of goals may be caused by the fact that effort does not pay off right away on complex tasks. Consider, for example, the effort involved in starting a new company, hiring new personnel, or spending more money for R&D. It could take a year or many years before the results show on the bottom line. The task strategies that are developed in response to the goals take time to formulate, to master, and to affect outcome measures. Thus studies of performance on moderately or extremely complex tasks should look for time lag effects. Evidence of lag effects on complex tasks has been found in several studies (Campbell, 1984; Earley, Lee, & Hanson, 1989; Shaw, 1984; Smith, Locke, & Barry, in press). In each of these studies, goals and plans only had significant effects on performance in the latter trials of tasks with multiple trials or after subjects had gained experience with their jobs.

PARTICIPATION AND FEEDBACK EFFECTS ON
COMPLEX TASKS

If, as has been argued, the performance effects of specific, challenging goals on complex tasks are mediated through their effects on information search, problem solving, and strategy development, then goal effects on complex tasks should be enhanced by other interventions that contribute to these processes. Two interventions of relevance to this issue and which have long been of interest to goal researchers are participation and feedback.

It has been argued that participative goal setting influences performance through both motivational and cognitive or information-sharing processes (Locke & Schweiger, 1979). The great majority of goal setting studies have looked only at the motivational effects of goal setting, i.e., the effects of participation on goal acceptance. Generally these effects have been minimal (Schweiger & Leana, 1986). However, there is reason to believe that the effect of participation on the development of task strategies will be far more substantial than its effect on motivation (Latham & Winters, 1989; Lord & Kernan, 1987). A case in point is the study by Campbell and Gingrich (1986), which manipulated participation regarding task knowledge and strategies among computer programmers writing either simple or complex programs. Participation did not enhance performance on the simple programs but markedly enhanced it on the complex programs. Thus one might predict that participation would facilitate the development of productive NTSP's on complex tasks when the knowledge of superior and subordinate together is greater than the knowledge of either one alone.

Hacker (1985) has also reported that workers who were given discretion in the choice of task plans reported greater job satisfaction and less fatigue. This would be less likely for simple tasks where effective strategies are known to all and performance is governed more directly by SUP's, i.e., Figure 13–3 (a). Participation could help on simple tasks if it heightened motivation or commitment (Erez, Earley, & Hulin, 1985). But as we have noted (Chapter 7), the real benefits of participation may be cognitive rather than motivational. If so, positive results would be more likely to emerge in complex than in simple tasks.

A meta-analysis of participation studies by Miller and Monge (1986) provides some support for the hypothesis that the performance effects will be stronger for complex tasks than for simple tasks. In participation studies not specifically investigating goal effects there was a moderately high positive correlation between participation and performance in field studies and either no correlation or a negative correlation in laboratory studies. A major difference between the field and laboratory studies of participation is the complexity of the tasks that have been used in each of these settings. Field studies have typically involved naturally occurring, more complex activities; laboratory studies have typically employed simpler, well defined tasks (Miller & Monge, 1986). If the differences in the effects for the two settings were due to the moderating effects of task complexity, as Miller and Monge argue, then these results are consistent with Figure 13–3 (a) for simple tasks and Figure 13–3 (b and c) for more complex tasks.

However, in another meta-analysis of participation studies, Wagner and Gooding (1987) found that the differences identified by Miller and Monge could be attributed to the methods used in different studies. Studies using percept-percept measures of participation and performance find a stronger relationship than studies in which either participation was manipulated or more objective measures of variables were used. The extent to which this is due to method variance versus task complexity is difficult to establish because of the confounding of methods and task complexity in participation studies. Field studies typically use more complex tasks, but they also use percept-percept methods. Laboratory studies have more objective measures or manipulations of variables but typically use simpler tasks. Therefore, when controlling for methods, Wagner and Gooding (1987) may have also removed variance in participation effects that was due to differences in task complexity. Because of the confounding of task complexity and study methods, neither explanation can be ruled out by meta-analysis. Whichever variable is entered into the analysis first will remove effects that may be correctly attributed to the other variable, and the choice of entering variables into the analysis is arbitrary. What the Wagner and Gooding finding does demonstrate is the need for more participation studies using complex tasks and objective measures to establish the validity of the mediating hypotheses contained in Figure 13–3 (b and c). Campbell and Gingrich (1986) is an example of such a study (see also Latham & Winters, 1989).

Feedback that indicates progress in relation to a goal has been identified as a necessary condition for goals to lead to higher performance (Locke et al., 1981). Once a goal is established, knowledge of results feedback (KR) will influence effort and persistence on a task over time, i.e., the application of SUP's. When individuals are constrained (as in a laboratory experiment) so that they can only try or not try for a goal, their degree of subsequent effort in response to failure (negative feedback) is a positive function of the degree of goal-performance discrepancy; the degree of dissatisfaction with performance; self-efficacy; and the resulting personal goal (Bandura & Cervone, 1986).

However, for effective strategy development to occur, KR feedback may have to be supplemented with other task-related information. Studies within the multiple cue probability learning (MCPL) paradigm have provided subjects with three general classes of information about their predictive judgments: *outcome feedback* on the correct criterion value, thus indicating the accuracy of their predictions; *feedforward* on the nature of the model they are competing against; and *diagnostic feedback* about their performance which can be compared with information about the model. Both the feedforward and the diagnostic feedback contain information about cue to criterion relationships that can be used to infer TSP's for the prediction task. Outcome feedback is less effective than either feedforward or diagnostic feedback for learning on MCPL tasks (Deane, Hammond, & Summers, 1972; Hammond, 1971; Hammond, Summers, & Deane, 1973), and complex tasks may not be learned at all with outcome feedback alone (Goldberg, 1968; Hammond, 1971).

Therefore we would argue that on complex tasks, the effectiveness of feedback will be dependent on its effects on strategy development, as shown for goals in Figure 13–3 (b and c; e.g., see Earley et al, in press). On dynamically complex tasks, KR alone can be ineffective for learning because of the difficulty of interpreting the effects of random error in performance data (Hammond, 1971;

Wood, 1986). When random error in performance data is interpreted as true variation, correct TSP's may be discarded due to misinterpretation of feedback and adjustments in task inputs can lead to decrements in performance.

Supplementation of KR feedback on more complex tasks is evident in some goal setting studies. In the study by Komaki, Barwick, and Scott (1978), the potentially complex choice of behaviors for obtaining a higher-level plant safety record was simplified by discussions of appropriate behaviors and by providing feedback on specific safety behaviors (i.e., TSP's). Therefore the selection or development of TSP's to obtain the goals set could have been facilitated by discussions of the task requirements and the specificity of the feedback given (see also Erez & Arad, 1986). Similarly, in the study by Becker (1978), the choice of TSP's for achieving energy conservation goals was facilitated by a list of appliances and their power usage rates, which was provided to subjects in the feedback condition at the beginning of the study. By way of contrast, in the studies by Erez (1977) and Strang, Lawrence, and Fowler (1978), goals and KR feedback alone led to higher levels of performance on relatively simple computational tasks, for which all subjects would have had highly automatized STSP's.

In summary, feedback and participation may influence performance on complex tasks by providing information that contributes to task understanding and facilitates the selection and evaluation of STSP's and the development of NTSP's. The effects of feedback on performance will be mediated by its impact on the conception-matching process of behavioral production in the implementation of TSP's. In order for feedback to contribute to strategy development, KR feedback may need to be supplemented with additional task information on complex tasks.

DISCUSSION

The model proposed in this chapter has some similarity with Miller, Galanter, and Pribram's (1960) classic model. They argue, in brief: (1) that individuals possess images of desired outcomes or valued states that they want to achieve (i.e., what we call goals); (2) that people execute plans in order to achieve such states; and (3) that plan, choice, and execution are guided by a "test-operate-test-exit," or TOTE, cycle that compares existing states of affairs with the image based on feedback. They also note that when plans are well learned, they become programmed into the subconscious and operate automatically as habits or skills.

Our model is more comprehensive than theirs, however. For example: (1) we identify three different types of plans (SUP's, STSP's and NTSP's); (2) our model includes advance appraisal of plan suitability, so it does not rely entirely on post-performance feedback; (3) we make no assumption regarding a simple or direct relationship between feedback sign and plan choice, since many different responses to both positive and negative feedback are possible; and (4) our model specifically considers how variations in the complexity of tasks can influence the processes by which goals, plans, and related activities (i.e., participation and feedback) affect performance. Furthermore, our model is more explicitly psychological and less mechanistic than Miller et al.'s.

Research Implications

The arguments in this chapter suggest several new directions for goal setting research. It is recommended that more attention be given to the effects of goals on complex tasks and the different processes by which goals influence performance on such tasks. Several of the studies by Earley and Wood and their colleagues, which were discussed in this chapter, represent a beginning.

There are many directions in which this research can proceed, and we would like to highlight one area in which further theory development and testing is required, i.e., the area of task strategies or TSP's. Figure 13–3 (b and c) raises questions of how goals activate and direct different TSP's and/or how TSP's differ as a function of goal attributes. The answers to these questions will require further conceptualization of the task-strategy concept to direct the operationalization of STSP's and NTSP's in different goal setting studies.

Examining the effects of STSP's can be done in two ways: either by selecting subjects based on prior task knowledge (e.g., Campbell & Ilgen, 1976) or by training subjects in the use of effective task-specific plans (e.g., Shaw, 1984; Earley, Lee, & Lituchy, 1989). Examining the effects of NTSP's is more difficult because the set of potential TSP's that can be developed for complex tasks is very large, making even ex post measurement very difficult. However, it is possible to measure various properties of the planning activities that are used in the development of NTSP's (e.g., Smith, Locke, & Barry, in press) and to trace hypothesis-testing activities on decision tasks (e.g., Wood, Bandura, & Bailey, in press). Further research on the effects of goal attributes, such as specificity and challenge, and on characteristics of the strategy development process, such as communication and comprehensiveness, would be particularly useful in the design of goal interventions for complex tasks.

Another area for research is the study of how goal effects vary as a function of the different types of task complexity. In the MCPL research, variations in complexity, such number of cues and functional forms of predictive models, have been shown to influence the effects of different types of feedback and feedforward on prediction accuracy and learning (Hammond, 1971). This work could be extended to consider how goals of varying specificity and difficulty affect performance and learning on MCPL tasks of differing complexity.

Research is also needed on how goals affect performance on complex psychomotor tasks of the type that are part of skilled, manual work (Wood, Mento, & Locke, 1987). In this discussion we have focused on cognitive tasks for which performance is primarily a function of search, information processing, and strategy development and not solely of effort. These cognitive processes will be less influential on those motor tasks that require programmed behavioral responses. Without a set of well-learned and effective motor programs, the attentional demands of outcome goals may undermine the execution of complex motor activities. Therefore, although goal effects on complex motor tasks would fit our moderator hypothesis (i.e., specific, challenging goals would lead to poor performance on more complex tasks unless there are suitable plans), the underlying processes by which goals and plans affect performance may be different.

CHAPTER

14

MACRO VS. MICRO GOAL SETTING RESEARCH:
A Call for Convergence

It is widely accepted that goals play a significant role in regulating human action at both the micro and macro levels. At the micro level, as noted previously, goals affect action by directing attention and effort, prolonging effort over time, and motivating individuals to develop relevant task strategies. Goals serve also as a benchmark against which performance feedback can be evaluated (Locke & Latham, 1984a). These functions have parallels at the macro level. It has been asserted that goals serve a unifying function by mobilizing and directing organization members' efforts toward a common end (Bradford & Cohen, 1984). Similarly, it is claimed that an organizations' goals direct its planning process, influencing both its mission and its strategy (Pearce & David, 1987; Richards, 1986; Schendel & Hofer, 1979), and that such goals serve as a standard by which to measure success (Richards, 1986). Organizational goals also define the very nature and purpose of the organization (Parsons, 1960; Simon, 1964), just as individual goals can define one's life purpose.

Despite this commonality, micro and macro goal setting theory and research have been very different in method, scope, and content. For example, most micro research has been conducted by organizational behavior researchers and industrial-organizational psychologists who have typically studied goal setting at the individual level (although they have conducted some studies of group goal setting). As a rule these studies have been conducted using quantitative, experimental designs in laboratory settings, although many studies have been conducted in field settings as well (Latham & Lee, 1986; Locke, Shaw, Saari, & Latham, 1981). The time span of the laboratory studies frequently does not exceed one hour, the goals are defined by the experimenter in advance, commitment to them is routinely obtained, and the tasks tend to be simple (although some relatively complex tasks have been used; Wood, Mento, & Locke, 1987). Typically (though

This chapter was written by Ken J. Smith and Edwin A. Locke especially for this volume.

not exclusively), single goals are assigned. Moreover, goal conflict has not been an issue and the external environment has been fixed or held constant. The relationship between goals and task strategies has been studied, especially in recent years, but is far from fully understood.

In contrast, macro goal setting has been the interest of researchers in strategic management and organizational theory whose focus is on the organization (or division) as a whole. Due to the obvious difficulty of using controlled experimental designs, they have used correlational and observational methods and both quantitative and qualitative approaches have been employed. This research has been done almost exclusively in field settings. Furthermore, goal commitment is not routinely obtained at the organizational level because of the existence of multiple coalitions and associated conflicts. Complexity is taken for granted at the macro level, as there are multiple goals and multiple goal alternatives. Organizations typically perform complex tasks in uncertain, unpredictable environments. Organizational goals are studied in relation to corporate or business unit strategies rather than in relation to task strategies.

We have chosen the generic terms "micro" and "macro" to classify the two goal setting approaches, even though these terms in themselves only involve a disparity in level of aggregation (Jackson & Morgan, 1978; Wolf, 1968). Figure 14–1 summarizes the patterns of micro and macro goal setting research that exist today. The thesis of this chapter is that there should be a greater rapprochement between these two approaches. Although the pattern of research and theorizing done thus far corresponds to the dichotomy summarized above and in Figure 14–1, this pattern is *not* necessary. For example, organizational behavior researchers could study multiple goals and goal conflict at both the individual and organizational levels. Moreover, strategy researchers could attempt to use at least quasi-experimental designs and more quantitative methods.

Aside from being different in content and method, macro goal setting theory and research is not nearly as advanced as micro theory and research. Beyond relatively simple models linking goal setting to strategy formulation (Richards, 1986; Schendel & Hofer, 1979), current macro goal setting theory has been widely criticized as being inadequate for describing organizational behavior. For example, Perrow (1961) emphasized the difficulty of determining the organization's real goals, whether short term or long term. He distinguished the announced or "official goals" of the organization from the organization's real or "operative goals." Michels (1962) showed that the stated (official) goals of the organization were substantially divorced from the actual functioning of the organization. Instead the stated goals were informally displaced to reflect the interests of those in power. Merton (1957) concluded that organizational goals were often subordinated to means as organizational members treated rules, policies, and strategies as ends in themselves. And Etzioni (1960) argued that the term *organizational goal* was "too singular," that organizational members were not one dimensional and they often resisted behavior formally prescribed for them. For these reasons it has been argued that formal organizational goals are "completely irrelevant to organizational behavior and [this fact] always limited very considerably the degree to which organizations could be understood through their goals" (Georgiou, 1973).

ISSUE	MICRO	MACRO
Unit of Analysis	individual (some groups)	organization or division
Academic Specialty	organizational behavior industrial-organizational psychology	strategic management organizational theory
Methodology		
Design	experimental	correlational or observational
Setting	laboratory and field set- tings	field settings
Analysis	quantitative	qualitative, some quantitative
Time Span	mostly short	long
Goals & Tasks	relatively simple, bivariate	complex, multivariate
Commitment & Conflict	routine, no conflict	problematic, high potential for conflict
Strategy Focus	task	corporate or business level

FIGURE 14–1   Micro-macro Goal Setting Patterns

These negative views of organizational goals may be the reason why there have been very few quantitative studies of macro goal setting (Molz, 1987; Murray 1979; Richards 1986), and even these studies have been based on "official" goals as opposed to the real or "operative" goals studied in micro research. We believe that organizational goals, especially operative goals, are important and deserving of further study. Gross (1969) concluded that "whatever else authors have to say on the general subject, there seems general agreement . . . that it is the dominating presence of a goal that marks off an 'organization' from all other kinds of systems" (p. 277).

The present authors could locate only eleven quantitative, macro, goal setting studies, and these were limited to three goal setting issues. First, researchers have observed the number and different types of organizational goals. For example, Dent (1959), England (1967), England and Lee, (1973), Shetty (1979), and Welch and Pantalone (1985) all found support for the existence of multiple goals in organizations. The goals most frequently identified from this research were organizational efficiency, productivity, profit, organizational growth, industrial leadership, organizational stability, employee welfare, and social welfare. Another group of researchers examined the relationship between goal consensus and performance, with one study finding no relationship (Grinyer & Norburn, 1975), two studies finding a negative relationship (Bourgeois, 1980, 1985), and one finding a positive relationship (Dess, 1987). The final group of studies explored the relationship between goal content and performance. Smith, Locke, and Barry (in press) found that specific challenging goals enhanced the quality of a simulated organization's planning activities and that goals and planning quality were positively related to performance. Barry, Locke, and Smith (1989) partially replicated Smith et al. but found that specific goals only influenced performance indirectly by way of planning in the sixty high-technology firms they studied.[1]

Macro theorists have more often studied goals using qualitative methods. For example, Peters and Waterman (1982) implied that organizations should employ specific and challenging goals based on their study of sixty-two excellent companies (for example, see pp. 57, 153, 154, 164, 171, 181, and 242). Quinn (1980), on the other hand, argued in favor of vague organizational goals based on nine case studies of effective organizations. Wrapp (1967), like Quinn, employed a qualitative methodology and argued for vague goals in order to avoid goal conflict. Perrow (1970) developed a typology of goals based on his qualitative study of two hospitals and two industrial organizations. Perrow's types included *output* goals such as productivity; *system* goals such as growth and profitability; *product* goals such as quality and innovation; and *derived* goals such as employee development.

There is a need for a great deal more research on macro-level goal setting; this research should be done by *both* micro and macro researchers. Ideally, micro researchers should become more macro, and macro researchers should become more micro—but in different respects. Specifically, micro goal setting research, though extensive within its own domain, would benefit from expanding its domain to include issues that are important at the macro level. (This does not preclude, of course, expanding micro-level research as well.) At the same time macro researchers, in addition to doing more goal setting research in general, would benefit from emulating the methodological rigor characteristic of the micro research. In sum, this chapter urges greater convergence in the content and methodology of micro and macro research on goal setting. Specific research questions that micro and macro researchers might address are discussed below.

KEY GOAL SETTING ISSUES

Multiple Goals and Goal Mix

At the micro level, subjects have typically (though not exclusively) been given one goal to try for. At the macro level, however, multiple goals are virtually the norm. Of course, individuals in real organizational settings have multiple goals, but these have rarely been examined in micro studies. Papandreou (1952) and Drucker (1958) were among the first to observe that effective organizations satisfy the demands of multiple-interest groups or stakeholders, both inside and outside the organization. Each class of stakeholder (i.e., capital suppliers, resource suppliers, etc.) has somewhat different expectations for the organization that are related to

---

[1]Management by Objectives (MBO), of course, has been the object of considerable research (Kondrasuck, 1981). However, the most well-controlled and quantitative of these studies have involved mid-levels of the organization (Richards, 1986) and have been "micro-macro" rather than macro in nature. That is, they have involved giving goals to all individuals within a given unit or department or division but have generally not examined organizational-level goals *and* outcomes.

its own goals, needs, and interests. Because these stakeholders often control critical resources necessary for organizational survival, the goals of the firm are likely to be complex and multifaceted and reflect the interests of these different groups.

One question that arises with multiple goals is, What is the relationship between the number of organizational goals and organizational effectiveness? Peters and Waterman (1982) reported that the high-performing firms they studied had multiple goals (e.g., customer service, quality, delivery, etc.) and that multiple goals were better than a single, overall goal such as profit. However, Bourgeois (1985) found no relationship between the number of goals and performance in a study of twenty corporations in seventeen industries. However, there is probably a limit to the number of goals that individuals and groups can effectively handle. Shetty (1979) concluded that the number of goals varied positively with the firm's size. He argued that larger firms could handle the information requirements of a greater number of goals (presumably by delegation). It can be expected that the optimal number of goals can vary by goal type, time horizon for goal achievement, size of the firm (and associated resources), stage of organizational development (entrepreneurial vs. professional management), and industry (e.g., firms in a stable industry may be able to pursue more goals effectively than firms in an unstable industry).

In addition to considering the number of goals, it is important to study the effects of goal content on organizational performance. Peters and Waterman (1982), for example, argued that the best-run companies place heavy emphasis on customer service and innovation goals. Furthermore, the recent macro research by Barry et al. (1989) and Smith et al. (in press) suggests that goals that are specific and challenging will produce better performance than goals that are vague and/or easy.

The existence of multiple goals also creates specific process questions. For example, how are multiple goals best integrated into the organization? Should different goals be assigned to different individuals or should all goals be given to all individuals? Goldratt and Cox (1986), March and Simon (1958), Simon (1964), and Thompson (1967) argued that multiple goals require significant information-processing requirements that are beyond the capability of most individuals. Thus different organizational goals may need to be given to different departments and organizational members.

A related process question is whether multiple goals should be pursued simultaneously or sequentially. Cyert and March (1963) favored sequential goals: "The business firm is likely to resolve conflicting pressures to 'smooth production' and 'satisfy customers' by first doing one and then the other" (p. 118). Closely allied to the issue of simultaneous versus sequential goal pursuit is that of prioritizing. Organizations have to decide not only if their goals should be prioritized but how. What should come first: customer service, quality, innovation, job security, or profits? Similarly, the pursuit of multiple goals may involve trade-offs so that one goal may have to be attained at the expense of another. Donaldson (1985) argued that priorities should be assigned to multiple goals based on the power of constituent groups represented by these goals. He claimed that managing organizational goals is a never-ending process in which "competing and conflicting priorities must be balanced" (p. 58). At any point the goal system may be unstable because of shifts in constituency power. Treating an organization's goals as a system is useful to the extent that it allows one to link multiple goals and multiple coalitions or constituents together.

Finally, there is the issue of whether goals should stress maximizing or satisficing of the activity in question. This may interact with the issue of multiple goals in that it may be impossible to maximize performance when many goals are present, whereas satisficing may be possible on all of them. Daft (1983) described how Ralston Purina Company tries to achieve satisfactory levels of profits, market share, and new products. According to Daft, Ralston "doesn't maximize any of these goals" (p. 89). On the other hand, satisficing may lead to lower performance on some goals than would be the case if goal achievement were maximized.

Time Horizon and Causal Ordering of Goals

Micro researchers have primarily focused on the short-term consequences of goal setting. Consequently, little is known about setting goals with extended time horizons. Few micro-level studies have looked at the time span issue. Bandura and Simon (1977) found that daily goals were more effective than weekly goals for weight loss. This study does not come remotely close to the typical time span of an organizational goal (e.g., one to five years). Only Ivancevich (1977) looked at goal setting over a time span of more than one year. One hypothesis is that to make long-term goals effective, it may be necessary to have short-term supporting goals or intermediate targets.

American companies, of course, have for many years been accused of focusing too much on short-range goals at the expense of the long range, as compared with Japanese companies which allegedly have a longer-range focus. However, this difference may be due to different pressures exerted on companies in the two countries, with American companies being more influenced by stock prices, short-term performance-oriented salary structures, and the fear of corporate raiders (Hayes & Abernathy, 1980). Such pressures may serve as a constraint on the time span of goals and thus on the selection of long-term goals. Recently American companies have been criticized for poor quality and service. Often these goals take considerable time to achieve.

The time issue may interact with that of multiple goals in that a long-term goal may only be achievable by giving it up, in part, in the short run. Consider the firm that has the goals of improving product quality and profitability. The short-term consequence of these goals may be improved product quality but decreased profits, as it generally costs something to improve quality. These potential goal trade-offs suggest that organizational goals need to be ordered not just as to priority "in general" but in terms of priority in time and causality. If the goals are causally related (e.g., improved quality, customer service, and innovation cause higher profits), then the goals at the beginning of the causal chain must be emphasized over those later in the causal chain. And the time span for the earlier goals needs to be shorter than the time span for the later ones. Such ordering may be beneficial in another way in that it reduces the cognitive load on top managers. An organization that has multiple goals with varying dates for achievement may be able to handle more goals than one that has multiple goals that all come "due" at the same time. Maximization of multiple goals may be possible when the time horizons of goals are ordered to fit the different goals. The above suggests that organizations will be more successful if they give high priority to short-term goals that are linked to longer-term goals than if they ignore causal priorities.

Goal Commitment

In micro studies commitment to goals is relatively easy to attain (Locke, Latham, & Erez, 1988). In fact, it is goal *rejection* that is hard to achieve in laboratory settings without using artificial procedures that suggest to volunteer subjects that goal rejection is appropriate (Erez & Zidon, 1984; Latham, Erez, & Locke, 1988). Even in micro field studies attaining commitment has posed no major obstacle except in special circumstances (Latham & Saari, 1982). However, commitment is obtained typically in one-on-one situations in which a superior simply asks a subordinate to do something. Through various means, enough variation has been generated in commitment in the micro research to discover a number of its determinants, including legitimate authority, peer pressure, role models, expectancy of success and self-efficacy, incentives and rewards, and publicness of the commitment process (Hollenbeck, Williams, & Klein, 1989; Locke et al., 1988).

In the macro setting things are very different. The stakes are greater with macro goals, and so are the risks. Signaling commitment to a goal is an acknowledgment that one is willing to be held accountable if the goal is not achieved. Failure to achieve a macro goal can result in loss of income, status, or even one's job. Quinn (1980) and Wrapp (1967) have argued that managers try not to publicly commit themselves to a set of specific goals, because they can become personally identified with and held responsible for the non-attainment of these goals. They note that managers like to keep their options open for as long as possible.

Perhaps the most serious block to goal commitment in real organizations is the existence of different personal agendas among the various top managers (Donaldson, 1985; Cyert & March, 1963; Michels, 1962). Harrison (1981) described how employees ignored assigned goals in a new start-up organization in favor of their own personal goals. These employees had a general disregard and distrust for the goal setter. Personal agendas may reflect past preferences and judgments about what is important and, in part, the pressures to which managers are subjected. Personal goals in micro studies have been found to be more highly related to task performance than assigned goals (Garland, 1983), but at the same time personal goals are significantly correlated with assigned goals (Chapter 5). To ask is to get. In the macro setting, where power differences are less severe and where coalition making is a fact of life (Cyert & March, 1963), getting a group of executives to commit to a single set of goals can be a difficult feat, sometimes requiring years of effort, negotiation, and coalition building (Kotter, 1982). An obvious hypothesis is that the greater the conflict between coalitions, the less committed each will be to the official organizational goals, and the less likely the official goals will be translated into operative goals.

A key question, of course, is how to distinguish "official goals" from "operative goals" (Perrow, 1961). Some important characteristics of "official goals" may be that they are abstract, vague, and impossible to measure as stated (March & Simon, 1958). "Operative goals," on the other hand, may have to be inferred from observing the behavior of individuals, from private interviews, and from confidential reports. Micro research suggests that operative goals, being analogous to personal goals, will be more strongly related to organizational performance than will official goals (which are analogous to assigned goals).

A related problem is coming up with valid measures of goal commitment (Locke et al., 1988). Micro researchers have traditionally asked their subjects direct questions, such as "How committed are you to the goal?" This approach may not be effective at the macro level where there are multiple goals (both "official" and "operative") and where executives may be afraid that public statements of commitment may be used for evaluation purposes. Micro researchers have also looked at the discrepancy between assigned and personal goals as a measure of commitment to assigned goals. At the macro level one could look at the discrepancy between official and operative goals as a measure of commitment to official goals. Clearly, research is needed on the importance of goal commitment at the macro level and the factors that explain why some individuals commit to goals while others do not.

Goal Conflict

Closely related to the issue of commitment is that of conflict. There is usually only one goal in micro research, so there is no issue of conflict between goals. In addition, because the micro task often involves a short time frame and goals that are not tied to career success, individuals are more likely to accept the assigned goals.

At the macro level, however, goal conflict may be the norm. The traditional view of organizational goal setting comes from classical economic theory where there was a single actor who established the goal of the firm. While strong "value-driven" leadership does seem to be crucial to organizational effectiveness (Peters & Waterman, 1982), theorists such as Barnard (1938), Blau and Scott (1963), Cyert and March (1963), Georgiou (1973), Etzioni (1960), and others have argued that organizations are political arenas where various coalitions attempt to influence the choice of organizational goals. Consequently, as noted above, it is often difficult to produce a set of organizational goals that everyone will agree with (Cyert & March, 1963).

Conflict over goals creates a number of questions that have not been of concern to micro researchers. For example, what is the influence of goal conflict on the goal formation process in organizations? Cyert and March (1963) argued that the bargaining process through which goal conflict is resolved will result in more satisficing goals and fewer maximizing goals. Similarly, Mintzberg (1983) contended that when conflict arises it will be impossible to make predictions about goal effects, since "all have arrived in the same organization to pursue what seems to be their own personal or parochial goals. . . . Anyone can end up getting some piece of the action" (pp. 426–27). Thus, one important question created by goal conflict is its result on the goal formation process; when goal conflict is great, the resultant goals may provide little direction.

Leadership.   Certainly one way to eliminate or control conflict is to provide strong leadership, at least in cases where the top executive has the power and will to do it. Donaldson (1985) argued that one of the prime responsibilities of a chief executive officer is the articulation of goals "as a tangible focus for its business mission and strategy" (p. 57). Bennis and Nanus (1985) found that effective leaders created a vision of what the organization will be and do and communicated this vision in a way that was compelling to the rest. Similarly, Kotter (1982) and Boyatzis (1982) noted that effective managers develop plans and agendas for where the organization is going and are able to convince others to go along. Locke and Somers (1987) have shown how a strong leader, through setting goals, providing feedback, giving direct and indirect communication, providing encouragement and criticism, and giving advice about strategy can get large numbers of people to pursue a common goal.

However, a leader may face important trade-offs at the macro level between defining goals clearly and specifically (which can have important motivational benefits) and defining goals more broadly in vague terms (which may result in greater individual support and less goal conflict). Vague goals may be necessary in order to build cohesion and support when the leader's power is insecure (Quinn, 1980). In contrast, specific goals may be more appropriate when power is secure and goals can be assigned without fear of conflict. At the same time, vague goals, even when necessary to build cohesion, may not be effective in generating results because their unspecified content is compatible with so many different courses of action.

Rewards and Incentives.   Another important method of reducing conflict is through rewards and incentives. Micro researchers have long recognized the importance of rewards in influencing performance. For example, Locke, Feren, McCaleb, Shaw, and Denny (1980) reported that individual monetary rewards increased worker performance by a median 30% and group rewards by 15% to 20%. One means by which rewards influence behavior is by affecting the degree of commitment to goals (Locke et al., 1988).

Macro writers such as Barnard (1938) and Cyert and March (1963) have also described how rewards reduce goal conflict and produce commitment. Barnard (1938) introduced the notion of "equilibrium theory," or the theory that individuals in the organization had to be offered inducements in return for their commitment to organizational goals. Inducements are "payments" (wages, services, etc.) to stakeholders made by the organization for their support. Similarly, Cyert and March (1963) noted that "all conflict is settled by side-payment bargaining." Side payments go beyond simple financial rewards and can be made in many forms: personal treatment, authority, and policy commitments. The key point, however, is that side payments "represent the central process of goal specification in organizations" (p. 30).

One goal setting technique that is directly related to rewards and incentives is Management by Objectives (MBO). MBO is a technique for reducing goal conflict and building goal consensus. It attempts to coordinate and align individual and organizational goals and reward performance for goal achievement (Odiorne, 1965). There has been a significant amount of research on MBO, but most of this research has been micro-macro in nature. Recently, Rodgers and Hunter (1989) conducted a meta-analysis and concluded that when accompanied by high management commitment, MBO resulted in an average increase in performance of almost 56%. It is not clear, however, exactly how MBO influences performance. That is, does MBO improve performance by increasing effort (Steers & Porter, 1974), by increasing the amount and level of organizational communication (Rodgers, Hunter, & Rodgers, 1987), by reducing goal conflict (Migliore, 1977), by rewarding goal success, or all of these?

If rewards can reduce conflict and build commitment, then one would expect to find a relationship between formal reward systems, goal setting, and performance. The hypothesis is that there will be less conflict, more commitment and higher performance when rewards are linked directly to goals.

Participation.   Participation is another approach that has been suggested as a means of building goal commitment and reducing goal conflict (Steers & Porter, 1974) and thereby increasing productivity and morale. However, consistent benefits for participation have not been demonstrated at the micro level where most of the studies have looked for motivational benefits of participation (see Chapter 7). It is possible that the micro studies have been completely on the wrong track and that participation, used properly, might work *better* at the macro level than at the micro level. Latham and Winters (1989) argued that the real benefit of participation may not be to increase commitment to goals but rather to gather and disseminate knowledge (Chapter 7). By soliciting input from many organization members in areas of their expertise, organizations may be able to set more suitable and achievable goals, and perhaps more importantly, develop better tactics and strategies for achieving those goals than could be done by the top executive without participation. In micro studies, all subjects typically know how to perform the task in question, so that the cognitive benefits of participation are less easily discernible. At the macro level, where the tasks, goals, and strategies are highly complex, cognitive input from many sources may have substantial impact. Thus one hypothesis is that organizations that allow cognitive input into the goal setting and planning process from relevant experts will be more effective than those that do not solicit such input.

The distinction between participation in setting the goals and in participation in selecting strategies for their attainment or implementation may be crucial at the macro level. Peters and Waterman (1982) argued that effective organizations do not engage in internal debates about what their culture, philosophy, and key goals are. These are taken as given, and anyone who does not accept them does not stay long. The debates, rather, seem to be about the best way to achieve the organizational goals.

Communication.   At the micro level, the experimenter informs the subject that his or her goal is to complete, for example, one hundred problems; the communication is then over and subjects go to work. At the macro level, the communication of goals is not quite so simple; goals must be communicated to many people, in many forms, and many times over a period of days, weeks, months, or years. Even then, goal communication may often be incomplete and inadequate throughout the organization (Donaldson, 1985).

Some writers have suggested that goal conflict could be reduced by limiting the communication of goals. For example, Wrapp (1967) noted that it is impossible to state goals clearly enough so that everyone in the organization will agree and understand what they mean. He suggested that managers gauge the extent of support for certain goals by sending up trial balloons. For example, managers might use the grapevine to test the resistance to a new goal. Managers then communicate goals only to those individuals who will be supportive. Supporters of goals are then used throughout the organization to build consensus.

The micro literature takes it for granted that goals must be communicated to individuals if they are to influence behavior (Locke, 1968b). MBO advocates argue for the communication of goals throughout the organization (Migliore, 1977; Odiorne, 1965). Clearly, more research is needed on the subject of goal communication. Specifically, it would seem important to determine the extent to which all members need to be informed about organizational goals and whether conflict can be reduced by initially limiting the communication of goals. One might predict that when power is centralized or that when reward systems are in place (so that there is low conflict), the goals of the organization should be communicated to all individuals at the outset.

Strategy

In the early micro studies, the strategy devised to achieve a goal was not an important issue. The tasks were relatively simple and the means to carry them out were obvious. However, micro researchers are now beginning to recognize the importance of task strategies (Earley & Perry, 1987; Earley, Wojnaroski, & Prest, 1987). Wood, Mento, and Locke (1987) found that direct goal effects on performance were smaller on complex than on simple tasks and suggested that strategy effects were correspondingly greater (see also Wood & Locke, in press). However, task strategies are much simpler than corporate or business unit strategies. At the macro level, a significant amount of research has clearly demonstrated the importance of macro strategy to performance (Hambrick, 1983; Hofer, 1975; Hofer & Schendel, 1978; Miles & Snow, 1978; Miller & Friesen, 1978; and Zeithaml & Fry, 1984).

At the micro level, it has generally been argued that goals influence performance primarily by motivating individuals to work harder, to focus on goal-relevant activities, and to persist on the task. The influence of goals at the macro level (as with complex micro-level tasks) may be more indirect, occurring via strategy formulation and implementation. That is, in order for macro goals to influence performance, it may be necessary that the goals be translated into strategies and that these be suitable to the goal and the situation. Simon (1964) has argued that organizational goals influence the process of alternative generation and testing by limiting the courses of action (strategies) available to decision makers. Smith et al. (in press) found that specific, challenging goals enhanced the quality of a simulated organization's planning activities and that planning quality was positively related to performance. They theorized that goal specificity aroused an individual's attention, providing more specific data for planning. These authors also reported that vague goals were associated with a lower-quality planning process and poorer performance. Similarly, Barry et al. (1989) found a positive association between goal specificity, and planning comprehensiveness and formality among high-technology firms.

More needs to be learned about the relationship between goal setting and strategy formulation or the planning process. At the micro level, Wood and Locke (Chapter 13) argued that specific goals may result in a means-ends planning process, whereas vague goals may lead to more of a hypothesis-testing approach. The same may be true at the macro level where the means-ends planning process has been referred to as synoptic/rational and its hypothesis-testing counterpart has been referred to as incrementalism (Andrews, 1971; Braybrooke & Lindblom, 1970; Frederickson & Mitchell, 1984). We hypothesize that specific goals would lead to a more synoptic/rational planning process resulting in strategies that are detailed and comprehensive. Such strategies would generally be well documented and would include extensive contingency plans. When goals are vague or absent, we would expect the planning process to be more incremental, leading to strategies that are vague and less comprehensive. The incremental approach will be characterized by constant testing and modification.

It is also likely that strategy influences the selection of future goals. Both Schendel and Hofer (1979) and Richards (1986) emphasized the important influence of past strategy on goal formulation. Miles and Snow (1978) found that current strategies constrained a manager's choices during future cycles of adaptation. And Braybrooke and Lindblom (1970) noted that "clearly what we establish as policy objectives we derive in large part from an inspection of our means" (p. 93). In short, the evaluation of a future goal must be made in light of the availability of means to achieve it. Availability will, in part, be a function of what has worked well in the past.[2]

Macro goal setting is also related to how strategy is implemented in organizations. Strategy implementation is largely a behavioral process (Schendel & Hofer, 1979). Consequently, all the goal setting issues raised earlier in this chapter are relevant to how strategy is implemented. For example, an organization attempting to improve profits (the goal) by implementing a "lowest-cost" production strategy must establish budgets, allocate resources, organize departments, determine incentives, and so on, in such a way that production costs are lowered. Accordingly, managers must determine the number of goals and the time horizon of these goals (e.g., budgets), manage the conflict that may result from these goals (e.g., allocation of resources), decide the extent to which employees will participate in goal setting (e.g., form of structure), and how they will be rewarded for goal achievement. All the above are relevant to strategy implementation. In fact, strategy implementation can be conceived of as a goal settting process whereby the means at one level of the organization become the ends of the next level, and so on. One hypothesis is that the task of implementing strategy will increase in difficulty as the number and variety of lower-level goals necessary to implement the strategy increase. This will be particularly true when lower-level goals are new and short term, and when employee conflict is high.

[2]Certainly, numerous other macro organizational variables, such as culture, structure, and ideology, will also affect goal setting.

Environmental Uncertainty

The micro-level research has traditionally involved relatively simple tasks where the information required to complete the task is known and available, the task is fixed, and the task environment is unchanging. The macro level is generally characterized by much greater uncertainty.

One important issue is the relationship between environmental uncertainty and the number and variety of goals. Lawrence and Lorsch (1967) found that different parts of the organization's environment can vary in uncertainty. These authors found that the degree of goal differentiation between functional departments in an organization varied with the amount of uncertainty facing these units. In the more certain and stable food industry, the goals across departments (e.g., production, research & development, etc.) were undifferentiated and focused on sales (the most uncertain function). However, in the more uncertain plastics industry, where each of the functional departments faced unstable environments, the goals were highly differentiated across function. Thus at the macro level, goal setting may be an important mechanism by which organizations reduce uncertainty. One hypothesis is that the number and variety of goals will be in accordance with the amount of uncertainty faced by the organization and its departments. As uncertainty increases, so will the number and variety of goals.

However, goal setting in a highly uncertain environment will be problematic, since the information required to set goals may be unavailable (Cohen & March, 1974). Or even when the information is available, it may be made obsolete by environmental change (Braybrooke & Lindblom, 1970). Thus one would expect that as uncertainty increases, it will become increasingly difficult to develop specific long-term goals and plans. In such cases it may be necessary to rely on shorter-term goals. We can hypothesize that as environmental uncertainty increases, the time horizon for goal achievement should decrease. A short-term time horizon for goals would mean that performance would be evaluated more frequently, allowing the organization to modify goals to fit changing environmental conditions. Locke and Latham (1984b) argued that the time span of organizational goals ranges from two years in the case of highly volatile and uncertain industries to as many as thirty years in more stable industries.

In summary, it would seem especially important to study the relationship between environmental uncertainty and goal setting. Of particular interest is the relationship between uncertainty and the number, variety, and time horizon of organizational goals.

METHODS FOR RESEARCHING MACRO GOALS

Micro and macro researchers might consider pooling their expertise to study the questions raised in this chapter. Focusing on macro issues may provide micro researchers with important ideas for extending the scope or broadening the content of their studies. Macro researchers may also benefit by trying to show quantitatively the role that macro goals play in explaining strategy formulation and implementation, and organizational performance. Table 14–1 lists the key questions identified in the above review.

Table 14–1   Key Goal Setting Issues

TOPIC	RESEARCH QUESTION
Multiple Goals and Goal Mix	a. What is the relationship between the number and content of goals and organizational performance? b. What are the contextual factors that influence the optimal number, type, and mix of organizational goals? c. How are multiple goals integrated into the organization? d. Should different goals be assigned to different individuals or should all goals be given to all individuals? e. Should multiple goals be pursued simultaneously or sequentially? f. Should multiple goals be ordered and prioritized? If so, how and in what order? g. Should multiple goals stress maximizing or satisfying the outcome in question?
Time Horizon and Causal Ordering	a. To what extent should long-term goals be supported by short-term goals or targets? b. What is the relationship between different types of goals and the time it takes for their achievement? c. Are there trade-offs between short-and long-term goals? d. To what extent is the maximization of multiple goals possible by varying the time horizon for their achievement?
Goal Commitment	a. To what extent is goal commitment more difficult to achieve with macro than with micro goals? b. What are the conditions that foster high or low commitment to macro goals—e.g., goal conflict? c. How can "operative" goals be distinguished from "official" goals? d. Are "operative" goals more closely related to organizational performance than "official" goals? e. How should goal commitment be measured at the macro level?
Goal Conflict	a. What is the influence of goal conflict on the goal formation process in organizations? How does conflict over goals get resolved? b. How can leaders use goals to reduce conflict? (1) Do vague goals lessen macro goal conflict?

Table 14–1   (cont.)

TOPIC	RESEARCH QUESTION
Goal Conflict (*cont.*)	(2) What are the leadership trade-offs of employing vague vs. specific macro level goals?
	c. To what extent can macro goal conflict be reduced by a system of rewards and incentives, and which rewards work best?
	d. To what extent does participation lessen macro goal conflict, and what are the consequences of allowing individuals to participate in macro-level goal setting?
	e. Can goal conflict be lessened by limiting the communication of macro goals?
	f. To what extent do individuals need to be informed about macro goals?
Strategy	a. How do macro goals influence strategy formulation/implementation and performance?
	b. Do specific macro goals enhance planning quality?
	c. How is macro goal setting related to the steps employed in planning?
	(1) Do specific goals lead to a more synoptic/rational planning process?
	(2) Do vague goals lead to a more incremental process?
	d. What is the relationship between goal specificity and the detail and comprehensiveness of the strategy developed to achieve it?
	e. How does past strategy impact the selection of macro goals?
	f. Can strategy implementation be enhanced by macro goal setting? If so, how and in what ways?
Environmental Uncertainty	a. What is the influence of environmental uncertainty on the number and type of organizational goals?
	b. How should organizations set goals in uncertain environments?
	c. What is the appropriate time horizon for macro goals in uncertain environments?

Despite the greater difficulty of conducting rigorous studies at the macro level of analysis, a number of steps could be taken to improve our knowledge of macro goal setting. One is to attempt to develop valid instruments for measuring macro goals and the goal attributes of interest. For example, methods need to be developed to measure the operative, as well as the official, goals of organizations. One approach to the former might be to see how many concrete policies and procedures are designed to achieve a certain end such as quality, and what priority such procedures are given in the organization. Attempts are now being made to develop valid measures of subjective goal difficulty for use in organizations. As noted in Chapter 3, direct questions about subjective goal difficulty have been found to be invalid, because they confound objective goal difficulty with self-perceptions of ability. Measures of goal conflict and commitment to macro goals are also needed.

In terms of actual studies, qualitative methods are clearly the least rigorous, but such studies are still useful, especially for hypothesis generation. Concurrent correlational studies cannot prove causality, but they can at least show whether certain causal relationships are plausible. The research on goal consensus and performance (Bourgeois, 1980, 1985; Dess, 1987; Grinyer & Norburn, 1975) and on goal content and performance (Barry et al., 1989) are examples of the few concurrent, correlational studies of goal setting at the macro level.

At the next level of rigor, longitudinal correlational studies would be useful; these would allow causal direction to be inferred with somewhat more confidence than in the case of concurrent studies. Better yet would be organizational simulations where at least some of the variables of interest could be manipulated experimentally. Smith et al. (in press) have reported the only organizational goal setting experimental simulation conducted to date. However, organizational simulations could be designed to study many additional issues—e.g., effects of official vs. operative goals, effects of conflict, effects of inventives, effects of leadership, effects of multiple goals, effects of prioritizing, effects of time horizons, etc. While simulations cannot simultaneously reflect *all* the factors that affect organizational behavior, they can isolate for intensive causal study, specific factors of interest. Moreover, there is no a priori reason to believe that the organizational processes occurring in simulations will be totally different from those occurring in actual organizations. At the micro level, laboratory results have been replicated very well in field settings (Locke, 1986a; Latham & Lee, 1987).

Finally, it would be most ideal to design experimental studies of organizational goal setting. For obvious reasons this is seldom possible, but it might be feasible in some cases, especially for small organizations headed by a willing entrepreneur. It might also be possible to conduct a goal setting experiment within a multidivisional firm. Certainly a combination of the methodologies summarized above could greatly increase our knowledge of macro goal setting.

CONCLUSION

This chapter has reviewed some of the differences that exist between micro and macro approaches to goal setting. An unnecessary dichotomy exists between these two approaches. Furthermore, we argued that micro researchers would benefit by expanding their domain to include issues that are important at the macro level. Macro researchers, in addition to doing more research on goal setting, would benefit from emulating the methodological rigor characteristic of the micro research. The ideal would be a marriage between micro and macro researchers. Each side brings a unique perspective and approach to goal setting research, which in combination can greatly advance our understanding of goal setting.

Observe, however, that in this chapter we have refrained from formulating a theory of macro goal setting; nor have we shown that the questions we have asked are the most significant ones in terms of their effects on organizational performance. These omissions were intentional. Goal setting theory at the micro level was *not* built by starting with a theory, since there was no knowledge available on which a theory could be built. Rather it started with a core hypothesis: that goals influenced action. Goal setting theory emerged gradually, based on the results of hundreds of studies. The same process should be followed in building a theory of macro goal setting or an expanded micro-macro theory. Only by scrutinizing empirical results can aspects of goal setting that are important be determined, along with the mechanisms by which they impact organizational effectiveness.

APPENDIX A

STUDIES SHOWING SIGNIFICANT OR CONTINGENTLY SIGNIFICANT RELATIONSHIPS BETWEEN GOAL DIFFICULTY AND PERFORMANCE [a]

Anderson & O'Reilly (1981)
Andrews & Farris (1972)
Ashworth & Mobley (1978)
Bandura & Cervone (1983)
Bandura & Cervone (1986)
Bandura & Wood (in press)
*Barry, Locke, & Smith (1988)—for more successful firms
Bassett (1979)
Battle (1966)
Bavelas (1978)
Bavelas & Lee (1978)—six studies; study 1 effect was for total work, not rate of work
*Bayton (1943)—high ego involvement task
*Becker (1978)—for subjects with feedback
Berlew & Hall (1965)
*Bigoness, Keef, & DuBose (1983)—for subjects high in internal locus of control
Blumenfeld & Leidy (1969)
Botterill (1977)
Bray, Campbell, & Grant (1974)—job challenge
Brief & Hollenbeck (1985)
Bryan & Locke (1967b)—two experiments combined into one result
*Campbell & Ilgen (1976)—difficulty effect significant about half the time
Cannon-Bowers & Levine (1988)

[a] These studies include those using related concepts, such as pressure or challenge; a few that measured goals in the form of expectancy questions; and a few that did not present data, but the report suggested a clear effect of goal difficulty.

* Denotes a contingently positive result (** denotes two such studies).

*Carroll & Tosi (1970)—for managers high in self-assurance, reward, and maturity

Chesney & Locke (1988)—for self-set goals

Cosier & Alpin (1980)

*Crawford, White, & Magnusson (1983)—only for initially low performers

**Dachler & Mobley (1973)—two studies; only those with longer tenure

Dey & Kaur (1965)

**Dossett, Latham, & Mitchell (1979)—two studies; for participative conditions only

*Dossett, Latham, & Saari (1980)—only for surveys signed and returned to supervisor (mean in Table 1 for "two days" should be 2.5, not 7.0)

Earley (1985b)

*Erez (1977)—for subjects with feedback

Erez & Earley (1987)

Erez, Earley, & Hulin (1985)—study 1

*Erez & Zidon (1984)—for subjects committed to high goals

Ferris & Porac (1984)

Frost & Mahoney (1976)—reading task suggested linear effect for subjects with feedback, but not tested separately

Garland (1982)

Garland (1983)

Garland (1985)—significant first-order correlation

Garland & Adkinson (1987)

Haberstroh (1960)

Hall & Lawler (1971)

Hamner & Harnett (1974)—goal measure was an expectancy

Hannan (1975)—for self-set goals

Henderson (1963)

Hollenbeck & Brief (1987)

Hollenbeck & Williams (1987)

Hollenbeck, Williams, & Klein (1989)

Howard, Curtin, & Johnson (1988)—three studies

Huber & Neale (1987)

Ilgen & Moore (1982)

*Ivancevich & McMahon (1977a)—for challenge vs. effort only

*Ivancevich & McMahon (1977b)—for challenge vs. all criteria for whites only

*Ivancevich & McMahon (1977c)—for challenge vs. all criteria for high-education subjects only

Ivancevich & Smith (1981)

*Kausler (1959)—for subjects given a minimum standard

Kernan & Lord (1988)

Kirsch, Saccone, & Vickery (1981)

Klein, Whitener, & Ilgen (1988)

Kleinbeck (1986)—three studies

LaPorte & Nath (1976)

Latham & Marshall (1982)

Latham, Mitchell, & Dossett (1978)

Latham & Saari (1979a)

Latham, Steele, & Saari (1982)

Latham & Steele (1983)

Latham & Yukl (1975b)—first study; high-participation group had more difficult goals

Lee (1988)

Likert (1967)

Locke (1966a)

Locke (1966d)—three studies

Locke (1967c)

Locke (1968a)

Locke (1982b)

Locke & Bryan (1966b)

Locke & Bryan (1967)—two pilot studies

Locke, Bryan, & Kendall (1968)—first two studies

Locke & Bryan (1968a)

Locke & Bryan (1968b)

Locke & Bryan (1969a)

Locke, Cartledge & Knerr (1970)—five studies

Locke, Chah, Harrison, & Lustgarten (1989)—two studies

Locke, Frederick, Buckner, & Bobko (1984)

Locke, Frederick, Lee, & Bobko (1984)

Locke, Mento, & Katcher (1978)

Locke & Shaw (1984)

London & Oldham (1976)

Mace (1935)—various studies; no statistical test made (counted as one study)

Mahlman, Vance, Colella, Waung, & Urban (1988)

Masters, Furman, & Barden (1977)—two studies; all subjects reached asymptote by end of second study

*Matherly (1986)—for subjects with prior success at another task

Matsui, Kakuyama, & Onglatco (1987)—two studies

Matsui, Okada, & Mizuguchi (1981)

Matsui, Okada, & Kakuyama (1982)

Matsui, Okada, & Inoshita (1983)—second study

McCarthy (1978)

*McCaul, Hinsz, & McCaul (1987)—two studies (counted as one); borderline results provided in personal communication

McLaughlin (1982)

Mento, Cartledge, & Locke (1980)—two studies

Meyer & Gellatly (1988)—two studies

Meyer, Konar & Schacht (1983)

Meyer, Schacht-Cole, & Gellatly (1988)

Miller (1960)—no data provided

*Miller & Steele (1984)—for piece-rate subjects only

Motowidlo (1977)

*Mowen, Milldemist, & Luther (1981)—for piece-rate subjects only

Mueller (1983)

Neale & Bazerman (1985)

*Neale, Northcraft, & Earley (1987)—borderline effect for number of integrative contracts; no effect for profit

Nelson (1978)

Ness & Patton (1979)—may have involved task difficulty

O'Connell (1980)

Ostrow (1976)

*Peters, Chassie, Lindholm, O'Connor, & Kline (1982)—for low-environmental constraint condition

Peters, O'Connor, Pooyan, & Quick (1984)

Podsakoff & Farh (1989)

Rakestraw & Weiss (1981)

Riedel, Nebeker, & Cooper (1988)

*Roberson-Bennett (1983)—two of three tasks (treated as one study)

Rothkopf & Billington (1975)

Rothkopf & Billington (1979)—first study

Rothkopf & Kaplan (1972)

Sales (1970)

Shalley & Oldham (1985)

*Shalley, Oldham, & Porac (1987)—for assigned goal subjects only

Siegal & Fouraker (1960)

Silver & Greenhaus (1983)

*Stedry (1962)—for subjects who set personal goals after being assigned goals

*Stedry & Kay (1966)—for goals not seen as impossible

*Steers (1975)—for subjects high in "need" for achievement

*Strang, Lawrence, & Fowler (1978)—for subjects with feedback

*Taylor (1981)—for word problems task

Taylor, Locke, Lee, & Gist (1984)

Terborg & Miller (1978)

Uhlinger & Stephens (1960)

*Vance & Colella (1988)—significant for about half the trials

Weiss (1982)

Weiss & Rakestraw (1988)

Wofford (1982)—studies 1 and 3

*Wood & Bandura (in press, a)—for second trial block

*Wood, Bandura, & Bailey (in press)—for second trial block

Wood & Locke (1987)—three studies

Wright (in press)

Yukl & Latham (1978)

Zajonc & Taylor (1963)

Zander, Forward, & Albert (1969)—successful funds had higher goals than failing funds in relation to constituent income

*Zander & Newcomb (1967)—for funds with a history of success

STUDIES SHOWING SIGNIFICANT OR CONTINGENTLY SIGNIFICANT DIFFERENCES BETWEEN SPECIFIC, HARD GOALS AND DO BEST OR NO GOALS [a]

Adam (1975)—for quality, not quantity

Alexy (1985)

*Amabile, DeJong, & Lepper (1976)—specific goal, which was easy, was better than No Goal but not Do Best Condition

Anderson, Crowell, Doman, and Howard (1988)

*Antoni & Beckmann (1987)—for those low in the "trait" of persistence and attention (our trait label)

At Emery Air Freight (1973)—two jobs; no data provided

*Bandura & Simon (1977)—for subjects with proximal goals

Barnett & Stanicek (1979)

Baron & Watters (1981)

*Baumler (1971)—for independent (as opposed to interdependent) task

Bayton (1948)

Bazerman, Magliozzi, & Neale (1985)

*Becker (1978)—for subjects with feedback

Blumenfeld & Leidy (1969)

Botterill (1977)

*Bottger & Woods (1985)

Brickner & Bukatko (1987)—first study; for subjects whose work was not personally identifiable

Bryan & Locke (1967a)

*Buller & Bell (1986)—major effect was for quantity

*Buller (1988)—follow-up on above; major effect was for quality and revenue

Chapman & Jeffrey (1978)

Chapman & Jeffrey (1979)—follow-up of previous study

[a]See note a to Appendix A.
*Denotes a contingently positive result (** denotes two such studies).

Chhokar & Wallin (1984)

*Crawford, White, and Magnusson (1983)—for low initial performers

Das (1982a)

Dickerson & Creedon (1981)

Dockstader (1977)

Dossett, Latham, & Mitchell (1979)—two studies (second study: both groups improved)

Dossett, Latham, & Saari (1980)

Dubbert & Wilson (1984)

Earley (1985b)

*Earley, Connolly, & Lee (1988)—first study; for subjects primed within suitable strategy

*Earley, Lee, & Lituchy (1989)—for subjects given strategy training

*Earley & Perry (1987)—if primed within suitable strategy

Earley, Wojnaroski, & Prest (1987)—two studies

Erbaugh & Barnett (1986)

*Erez & Zidon (1984)—for subjects committed to hard goals

Felixbrod & O'Leary (1974)

Fellner & Sulzer-Azaroff (1985)

French (1950)—goals manipulated along with social factors (but see Chapter 7)

Frost & Mahoney (1976)—two studies; study 1, for subjects with feedback (but not separately tested); study 2, borderline effect

Gaa (1973)

Gaa (1979)

Garland (1985)

Gowen (1986)

Hall & Byrne (1988)

Hall, Weinberg, & Jackson (1987)

Hannan (1975)

**Hayes et al. (1985)—two studies, for those making public commitments

Huber (1985a)—borderline effect

Huber & Neale (1987)

*Hyams & Graham (1984)—for subjects low on initiative (Ghiselli scale)

*Ivancevich (1974)—for high organizational commitment setting

Ivancevich (1976)

Ivancevich (1977)

*Ivancevich & McMahon (1982)—for subjects with self-feedback on objective criteria

Ivancevich & Smith (1981)

*Jackson & Zedeck (1982)—two studies; for manual task, SHG better than No Goals, but not Do Best Goals

Jackson & Zedek (1982)—cognitive task

**Kanfer & Ackerman (1988)—study 1 for low-ability subjects; study 3 for low cognitive demand setting

Kanfer & Ackerman (1988)—study 2

Kaplan & Rothkopf (1974)—two studies

Kausler (1959)

Kazdin (1974)—second and third studies

Kim (1984)

Kincey (1983)
Kirsch (1978)—three studies
Klein (1973)
Kliebhan (1967)
Koch (1979)
Kolb & Boyatzis (1970)
Komaki, Barwick, & Scott (1978)
Komaki, Collins, & Penn (1982)
Komaki, Heinzmann, & Lawson (1980)
Krackhardt, McKenna, Porter, & Steers (1981)

LaPorte & Nath (1976)
Latham & Baldes (1975)
Latham & Kinne (1974)
Latham & Locke (1975)—implicit goal based on delivery quota
Latham, Mitchell, & Dossett (1978)—second study
*Latham & Saari (1979a)—for participative group only
Latham & Saari (1979b)
Latham & Saari (1982)
Latham & Steele (1983)
*Latham & Yukl (1975b)—first study; significant for participative group
Latham & Yukl (1976)
Lawrence & Smith (1955)
Leifer & McGannon (1986)
Locke (1967b)
Locke (1968a)
Locke & Bryan (1966a)
Locke & Bryan (1966b)
Locke & Bryan (1967)—two studies
Locke, Bryan, & Kendall (1968)—first two studies
Locke & Bryan (1969b)
Locke, Chah, Harrison & Lustgarten (1989)—first study
Locke, Frederick, Lee, & Bobko (1984)
Locke, Mento & Katcher (1978)
Lombardo, Hull, & Singer (1983)
*Lyman (1984)—for subjects setting goals publicly

Mace (1935)—various studies; no statistical tests made (counted as one study)
*Mahoney (1974)—for goal setting with rewards
Martin et al. (1984)
McCarthy (1978)
McCaul & Kopp (1982)
McCuddy & Griggs (1984)
McLaughlin (1982)
Mercier & LaDouceur (1983)
Meyer & Gellatly (1988)—second study
Migliore (1977)—two studies

Mizes & Schuldt (1981)

Morgan (1985)

Mossholder (1980)—two tasks

Mueller (1983)

Neale & Bazerman (1985)

Neale, Northcraft, & Earley (1987)

Nelson (1978)

Nemeroff & Cosentino (1979)

Organ (1977)—second study

Phillips & Freedman (1988)—two tasks

Principato (1983)

Pritchard & Curtis (1973)

*Pritchard et al. (1981)—mainly for lower performers

Pritchard et al. (1988)

Pruitt (1983)

Punnett (1986)

Ralis & O'Brien (1986)

Reber & Wallin (1984)

Reynolds & Anderson (1982)

Reynolds, Standiford, & Anderson (1979)

Roberts & Hall (1987)

Ronan, Latham, & Kinne (1973)—two studies

Rosswork (1977)

Rothkopf & Billington (1975)

Rothkopf & Billington (1979)—three studies

Rothkopf & Kaplan (1972)

Sagotsky, Patterson, & Lepper (1978)

Schafer, Glasgow & McCaul (1982)

Schmidt, Kleinbeck, & Brockmann (1984)

Schuldt & Bonge (1979)

*Schunk (1983)—for subjects with goals plus norms

*Shaw (1984)—for subjects with high ability; second half of work period

Singer et al. (1981)

Sloat et al. (1977)

Smith, Locke, & Barry (in press)

Sorcher (1967)

*Stedry (1962)—for subjects who set personal goals after being assigned goals

Stevenson, Kanfer, & Higgins (1984)

Strang (1981)

*Strang, Lawrence, & Fowler (1978)—for subjects with feedback

Switzky & Haywood (1974)

Terborg (1976)

Terborg & Miller (1978)

Umstot, Bell, & Mitchell (1976)

Vance & Colella (1988)
Warner & DeJung (1971)
Warner & Mills (1980)
Watson (1983)
Weingart & Weldon (1988)—two studies
Wexley & Nemeroff (1975)
White, Mitchell, & Bell (1977)
*Wood, Bandura, & Bailey (in press)—for low-complexity task
Wyer, Srull, Gordon, & Hartwick (1982)
Zegman & Baker (1983)

APPENDIX C

GUIDELINES FOR CONDUCTING SUCCESSFUL GOAL SETTING STUDIES IN LABORATORY SETTINGS

These guidelines were developed as a result of having conducted over ninety goal setting studies between us, having reviewed well over one hundred such studies for journal editors, and having read and evaluated several hundred studies for inclusion in this book. These guidelines take account of the major flaws found in previous studies as well as our knowledge of the key mediators and moderators of goal setting effectiveness.

(1) *Control for ability.* If ability is "controlled" only through randomization, even if it is successful, individual differences in ability become error variance when testing for goal effects, thus making the test less powerful. Furthermore, randomization is often not successful unless the N's are very large. It is best to use a work sample test rather than a general ability test, because the latter may correlate very modestly with task performance, since there may be task-specific as well as general abilities involved. If the task is complex and requires considerable learning, a work sample may not tap all the relevant abilities, since some of those abilities may come into play later in the learning process. If these are known, of course, they may be measured at the outset. If they are not known, a work sample may still be better than using nothing. Also it may be possible to give several work sample trials or a longer practice period on complex tasks so that some of the task-relevant abilities will come into play. When ability is measured, use ANCOVA (Analysis of Covariance) or regression entering ability first when testing for goal effects.

(2) *Give feedback* (see Chapter 8). Feedback regarding one's progress toward the goal may be provided in a nondistracting manner during the trial (e.g., by a red line on the answer sheet) or at the end of each trial in a multitrial task. Multiple trials may be preferable to ensure that the individual has time to act on the feedback. Fake feedback is occasionally used with success but is not recommended, since subjects may not believe it.

(3) *Measure personal goals if goals are assigned.* The correlation between assigned and personal goals is substantial (Chapter 5), but not perfect. Personal goals will usually relate more strongly to performance than assigned goals. They will also indicate whether the experimental goal manipulation succeeded. The discrepancy between assigned and personal goals is one measure of commitment (Chapter 6). When there is low commitment to assigned goals, the personal goal reveals whether the low commitment was due to the personal goal being set higher *or* lower than the assigned goal.

(4) *Measure commitment.* If goals are assigned and personal goals measured, commitment to the assigned goals may correlate highly (and negatively) with the assigned–personal goal discrepancy (Chapter 6), as noted. However, there may be differences in degree of commitment even to personal goals, so if the effect of personal goals is the major variable of interest, commitment to them could be measured also (see Chapter 6 for sample items).

(5) *Measure self-efficacy.* Self-efficacy plays a key role in goal setting theory (Chapters 3, 5, 6, 8). It predicts goal choice, goal commitment, and performance, and response to feedback and can be affected by various experimental manipulations. The authors recommend measuring both self-efficacy magnitude (total number of *yes* answers) and strength (total of certainty ratings), since both of these seem to contribute to prediction (Locke, Frederick, Lee, & Bobko, 1984; Wood & Locke, 1987). It is important that *all subjects fill in all blanks in each scale* so that the efficacy ratings are comparable across subjects. To combine magnitude and strength scores, convert to z-scores first. A sample self-efficacy scale is shown in Table C–1.

General self-efficacy scales ("I am good at psychology") are not nearly as accurate or as precise as quantitative scales like the one in the table. Subjects should have had some feedback regarding their performance on the task before rating their degree of self-efficacy. Self-efficacy scores can be derived for just the key parts of the total performance range (e.g., grades A through C only).

Table C-1   Self-Efficacy Scale for Grade in Psychology 100

GRADE	MAGNITUDE	STRENGTH
	Yes/No	Confidence (use scale of 1 to 10 or 1 to 100; tell Ss to rate confidence in obtaining grade, not confidence of yes/no)
D− or higher	_____	_____
D or higher	_____	_____
D+ or higher	_____	_____
C− or higher	_____	_____
C or higher	_____	_____
C+ or higher	_____	_____
B− or higher	_____	_____
B or higher	_____	_____
B+ or higher	_____	_____
A− or higher	_____	_____
A or higher	_____	_____

Note: Extremes of scale can be deleted if there is no variation between subjects.

Self-efficacy ratings can also be made for task components as well as for the task as a whole (e.g., understanding the text, recall of material; see Wood & Locke, 1987).

(6) *Eliminate or check for situational constraints* (Chapter 9).

(7) *If the task is complex,* try to (a) measure task strategies to determine whether goals led to the choice of optimal task strategies and (b) consider allowing a sufficiently long time span to allow strategies to be acquired and implemented (Chapter 4). Strategy training may greatly facilitate goal effects on such tasks (also Chapter 4).

(8) *Measuring the valence and instrumentality* of various goals has not been found to be essential in the past, but recent studies suggest that this would be a productive area for further study (Chapter 3).

(9) *If the effect of goal difficulty* is being studied, make sure that there is a reasonable range of difficulty among the goals. Goals that 10%, 50%, and 90% of the subjects can reach in a three goal-level design typically result in substantial performance differences. In contrast, goals that 75% and 90% of the subjects can reach (in a two goal-level design) will probably not show reliable performance differences unless the experiment is extended for a considerable period of time and subjects do not set personal goals at variance with their assigned goals. Also be aware that when the same goals are assigned to a random group of subjects, the goals are not equally difficult for all members of that group, since the subjects will differ in ability. This can be avoided by assigning goals in relation to ability or by controlling ability (and measuring self-efficacy) when looking at goal effects. Finally, when subjects are assigned easy goals, remember that they may set their personal goals at a higher level than what they were assigned (Chapter 6). This can be prevented by telling subjects to stop when they reach their goals or can be taken account of by measuring personal goals.

(10) When comparing *do best* vs. *specific, difficult goals,* the specific goals must be difficult, not moderate or easy. A goal that only 10% of the subjects can reach is usually difficult enough to produce reliable performance differences, but a 50% level of difficulty is not. Less difficult goals may work over a long time span. Also make sure that *do best subjects do not set specific goals* when making the do best–specific, hard goal comparison. Providing do best subjects with feedback may well lead to spontaneous goal setting. This can be prevented by withholding feedback from do best subjects, by giving them feedback based on work periods of varying and unknown length (Locke & Bryan, 1969a), or by convincing them that the feedback is not important.

(11) *Measures of subjective goal difficulty* are *not* recommended because they confound objective goal difficulty with self-efficacy (Chapter 3). This poses a problem in correlational field studies when measures of goal difficulty are desired. The authors are now working with Cynthia Lee and Chris Earley to develop a relatively nonconfounded measure of subjective goal difficulty. So far this endeavor has been unsuccessful.

(12) If the study is focused on the issue of *goal and affect,* the main thing to look at is frequency and degree of success in relation to the goals. However, other factors can affect satisfaction as well. In field studies, satisfaction with the

goal setting program will depend on how it is perceived as affecting all the individual's job values (see Chapter 10).

(13) *The criterion must match the goal.* Goal effects are goal-specific, so unless the outcome variables of interest are naturally correlated, do not expect goals for criterion A to affect performance on criterion B.

(14) *Postexperimental goal measures* or goal measures derived from interviews should not just ask, Did you set goals? Without knowing the goal attributes (specificity, difficulty), little can be predicted confidently as to the performance effects of such goals. Individuals may have more than one goal or even a goal range, so that detailed questioning is required to determine exactly what they were trying to do. Furthermore, goals may change over time.

(15) *Measures of goal mechanisms* (in addition to measures of strategy that were devised above) are not necessary to get positive results but are theoretically interesting (Chapter 4). It makes little sense to use a task where the goal mechanisms cannot operate (such as scores on a knowledge test) or where one is penalized for using them (such as penalties for information search), although in real organizational settings there may be trade-offs between information acquisition and costs. In *group goal setting,* studies measuring mechanisms such as information exchange or expressions of enthusiasm for the goal might yield important theoretical and practical insights.

GUIDELINES FOR CONDUCTING SUCCESSFUL GOAL SETTING STUDIES IN FIELD SETTINGS

Guidelines applicable to laboratory experiments serve as ideals to attain when conducting studies in the field. However, the guidelines in Appendix C are usually more difficult to achieve in the field than in laboratory settings due to less ability on the part of the experimenter to exert experimental controls. Rather than duplicate Appendix C, Appendix D focuses on variables that have facilitated goal setting effects on performance in the field.

(1) *Organization support:* In organizational settings, the field experiment is likely to be conducted correctly if one or more managers are held accountable for the execution of the study.

This conclusion was reached painfully in the Latham and Yukl (1975b) experiment where the performance of uneducated loggers in North Carolina was compared with that of educated loggers in Arkansas. The manager in Oklahoma was in the process of being transferred to another region. Consequently, the goal setting study was given minimal attention and the results proved to be inconclusive.

For organization support to be effective, the one or two company people who will oversee the project must be viewed as relatively permanent to the organization and have credibility with the people who will be participating in the experiment. This is necessary in order to get adherence to or compliance with the instructions.

For researchers to get organizational support, it is advantageous for them to adopt industry rather than university-laden jargon. Thus the researcher should advocate a project rather than an experiment, documentation of project effectiveness rather than data collection, and a focus on bottom-line measures rather than dependent variables. Most importantly the project should be viewed by all participants as meeting a perceived need of the organization.

For example, goal setting was used with loggers because the member companies of the American Pulpwood Association were looking for an inexpensive means of improving the productivity of independent business people on whom they were dependent for their wood supply.

In obtaining organizational support, it is critical that the researcher (i.e., project consultant) does not promise too much. A positive change in behaviors that were previously dysfunctional will be greatly appreciated by the client. This behavior change may or may not lend itself to cost accounting or utility analysis.

(2) *A control group:* In 1974 a memo from a vice-president of human resources was sent to his colleagues describing enthusiastically the discovery by Latham of a control group. Soon memos poured in to Latham informing him that control groups had been discovered throughout the company. He was told that he was welcome to use them. The enthusiasm reflected line management's desire to measure human resource programs in terms of behavior changes. The offer was taken up in the project by Latham, Mitchell, and Dossett (1978) involving research engineers and scientists.

The potential fear in the use of a control group in the field is that they will soon learn, via the grapevine, what is occurring in the treatment conditions. This fear has not been shown to be a problem in goal setting experiments.

For example, Latham et al. (1978) found that people in the do best conditions performed no better than the people who were in a "true" control group. The "true" control group was not only in another state, but the people in it did not even know that they were participants in the experiment. The people in the do best conditions were aware of the goal setting interventions in the other conditions, but they considered goal setting trite—i.e., everyone does it, therefore it is nothing new.

Similarly, self-management experiments designed to increase employee job attendance showed that a change in behavior did not occur in the control group that was aware of the program until after that group too had been exposed to the treatment (Frayne & Latham, 1987; Latham & Frayne, 1989).

Thus with regard to goal setting experiments, awareness of goal setting among members of the control group does not appear to affect the results. We believe that this is because goal setting is considered trite until people begin making their goals specific, difficult, and attainable.

In closing, there should seldom be an excuse for failing to find a control or comparision (quasi-experimental design) group. It is our experience that not everyone can or should be exposed to the goal setting treatment simultaneously. There are too many people. By promising management that others will get the treatment once its effectiveness has been documented, getting cooperation from them for a control group has proven to be relatively easy.

(3) *Goal Meaningfulness:* The goal must be something that has meaning to the goal participants. Cords or C units per employee hour have great meaning to upper management in forest products companies but are of little significance to loggers. For them, it is number of trees cut down; for the logging truck drivers, it is weight of a truck's load as well as truck turns. A benefit of setting a goal in terms of that which the participants can relate to is that it usually

facilitates self-feedback. The employee can count the number of trees cut, weigh the truck, or count the number of times the truck was loaded and unloaded (truck turns).

(4) *Proximal versus distal goals:* Similarly, upper management is usually interested in quarterly and yearly goals. Employees usually have a shorter time horizon. This horizon should be based on the work cycle that they perform. Thus loggers are usually interested in daily or weekly goals. The art is in getting employee understanding and participation in choosing an appropriate time horizon. Goals that are too short may prove discouraging in that they fluctuate too much or too little (e.g. weighing oneself every five minutes) to motivate behavior. Goals that are too distant may facilitate procrastination. In the studies on job attendance, proximal (weekly) and distal (quarterly) goals were set (Frayne & Latham, 1987; Latham & Frayne, 1989).

(5) *Task:* The measurement of the task needs to be reliable (i.e., stable). Lack of reliability in measuring performance has been a major aspect of the criterion problem (Ronan & Prien, 1971). Sometimes the task changes in response to changes in the organization's mission. This needs to be ascertained where possible prior to conducting the experiment. In a different vein, Latham and Kinne (1974) experienced a problem where university professors and doctoral students from the Forestry School arrived unexpectedly with stop-watches to time functions being performed by people, unknown to the Forestry School, who were in our control group. The result was a tremendous one-day improvement in the control group's performance. It took us weeks to find out the cause of this temporary performance improvement.

(6) *Response shift phenomenon:* This can occur when the level of aspiration increases among people who are selected to receive the treatment relative to those who were not chosen. For this reason, it is especially critical in field experiments to show as much attention, support, and concern for those in the control group as is shown to the experimental group. Consequently, we strongly recommend that manipulation checks include a measure of supervisory/experimenter supportiveness.

(7) *Goal difficulty:* Unlike laboratory experiments, we do not recommend "game playing" or any attempt to mislead the participants. The goal set should be difficult, but attainable rather than impossible. Thus the person or group's ability should be taken into account when establishing the goal. Because goal setting is a motivational technique, the goal should represent a stated target rather than average expected performance. The latter is likely to be construed as a minimum standard rather than as a challenge.

(8) *Emphasize performance:* The emphasis should be on maximizing performance rather than attaining a goal. Emphasizing goal attainment can encourage the setting of easy goals shrouded in language that makes the goal appear more difficult than it really is. This finding is common among our clients who have MBO programs. As one CEO commented, MBO rewards creative people who make easy goals look difficult, who subsequently reach them and who then in the spirit of company loyalty continually raise them a little bit higher the subsequent year.

That goals not be viewed as standards can be critical in gaining union support for goal setting programs. It has been our experience that the union leadership readily supports goal setting programs because the goals provide meaning to repetitious work in the same sense that goals provide meaning to athletic sports such as golf or bowling. Goals provide challenge and concurrently a sense of accomplishment. But when goals are suddenly perceived as standards, a strike can occur (see Latham & Saari, 1982).

(9) *Data collection:* Either the experimenter needs to be present during data collection (which is often physically impossible where there are multiple data sites) or the experimenter needs to train the data collectors thoroughly. For example, in one goal-based study (Latham & Saari, 1984) we found that what we believed the participants were doing was by no means what they were doing. The erroneous conclusion was that the technique, in this case a situational interview, was ineffective for evaluation purposes.

(10) *Make the information public:* In the Latham and Saari (1982) study of union truck drivers, the graph showing performance was posted outside the men's room. The employees wanted it there because it was the one place where everyone would be sure to see it. This facilitated discussion and problem solving among them as to why performance was increasing or decreasing. It also allowed public recognition of those who were doing well. This procedure is not unlike posting scores in a golf club. The only grievance that occurred as a result of this program was when the results were not posted during the Christmas holidays due to the number of people who were on vacation.

(11) *Job level/complexity:* Goal setting is effective regardless of whether the employees are loggers or engineers/scientists. The issue is whether the person has the ability to attain the goal. Goal setting is a motivational technique that affects attention, effort, and persistence. If the job is so difficult that the person lacks the ability to perform it, the appropriate intervention is a training rather than a motivation technique.

(12) *Multiple goals:* A primary value of goal setting is that it focuses attention. Thus it is likely that three to five goals will do just that, while thirty-five goals are likely to cause the person to lose focus. No one to our knowledge has documented the point at which the sheer number of goals has a dysfunctional effect on performance.

GOAL SETTING QUESTIONNAIRE

This questionnaire originally appeared in our previous book (Locke & Latham, 1984, a) but has not been widely used. Cynthia Lee, Chris Earley, and Ed Locke have been trying to determine the factor structure of the questionnaire (Lee, Locke, & Earley, 1988; see also Chapter 10). Thus far the factors appear to be more strongly related to satisfaction than to performance. One reason may be that there are no suitable goal difficulty items in the scale. (Only item 3 refers to challenge, and it is worded in favor of moderate goals). In Appendix C we note the difficulties involved in trying to develop useful measures of subjective goal difficulty (see Appendix C, #11)

1. I understand exactly what I am supposed to do on my job.
   Almost Never   0   1   2   3   4   Almost Always
2. I have specific, clear goals to aim for on my job.
   Almost Never   0   1   2   3   4   Almost Always
3. The goals I have on this job are challenging but reasonable (neither too hard nor too easy).
   Almost Never   0   1   2   3   4   Almost Always
4. I understand how my performance is measured on this job.
   Almost Never   0   1   2   3   4   Almost Always
5. I have deadlines for accomplishing my goals on this job.
   Almost Never   0   1   2   3   4   Almost Always

E. A. Locke and G. P. Latham, *Goal Setting: A Motivational Technique That Works,* ©1984, pp. 173–75. Reprinted by permission of Prentice-Hall, Inc., Englewood Cliffs, New Jersey.

[a]Participation in setting goals may foster satisfaction (though not necessarily; Wagner & Gooding, 1987); there is little evidence that it fosters productivity (see Chapter 7).

For some preliminary analyses of the factor structure of this questionnaire, see Lee, Bobko, Earley, and Locke (1988) and Lee, Locke, and Earley (1988). This questionnaire does not yield a goal difficulty factor (see Chapter 10).

6. If I have more than one goal to accomplish, I know which ones are most important and which are least important.
Almost Never   0   1   2   3   4   Almost Always

7. My boss clearly explains to me what my goals are.
Almost Never   0   1   2   3   4   Almost Always

8. My boss tells me the reasons for giving me the goals I have.
Almost Never   0   1   2   3   4   Almost Always

9. My boss is supportive with respect to encouraging me to reach my goals.
Almost Never   0   1   2   3   4   Almost Always

10. My boss lets me participate in the setting of my goals.[a]
Almost Never   0   1   2   3   4   Almost Always

11. My boss lets me have some say in deciding how I will go about implementing my goals.
Almost Never   0   1   2   3   4   Almost Always

12. If I reach my goals, I know that my boss will be pleased.
Almost Never   0   1   2   3   4   Almost Always

13. I get credit and recognition when I attain my goals.
Almost Never   0   1   2   3   4   Almost Always

14. Trying for goals makes my job more fun than it would be without goals.
Almost Never   0   1   2   3   4   Almost Always

15. I feel proud when I get feedback indicating that I have reached my goals.
Almost Never   0   1   2   3   4   Almost Always

16. The other people I work with encourage me to attain my goals.
Almost Never   0   1   2   3   4   Almost Always

17. I sometimes compete with my co-workers to see who can do the best job in reaching their goals.
Almost Never   0   1   2   3   4   Almost Always

18. If I reach my goals, I feel that this will enhance my job security.
Almost Never   0   1   2   3   4   Almost Always

19. If I reach my goals, it increases my chances for a pay raise.
Almost Never   0   1   2   3   4   Almost Always

20. If I reach my goals, it increases my chances for a promotion.
Almost Never   0   1   2   3   4   Almost Always

21. I usually feel that I have a suitable or effective action plan or plans for reaching my goals.
Almost Never   0   1   2   3   4   Almost Always

22. I get regular feedback indicating how I am performing in relation to my goals.
Almost Never   0   1   2   3   4   Almost Always

23. I feel that my job training was good enough so that I am capable of reaching my job goals.
Almost Never   0   1   2   3   4   Almost Always

24. Company policies here help rather than hurt goal attainment.
Almost Never   0   1   2   3   4   Almost Always

25. Work teams in this company work together to attain goals.
Almost Never   0   1   2   3   4   Almost Always

26. This organization provides sufficient resources (e.g., time, money, equipment, co-workers) to make goal setting work.
Almost Never   0   1   2   3   4   Almost Always

27. In performance appraisal sessions with my boss, he stresses problem-solving rather than criticism.
    Almost Never   0   1   2   3   4   Almost Always

28. During performance appraisal interviews my boss:
    a. explains the purpose of the meeting to me.
       Almost Never   0   1   2   3   4   Almost Always
    b. asks me to tell him what I have done that deserves recognition.
       Almost Never   0   1   2   3   4   Almost Always
    c. asks me if there are any areas of the job on which he or she can assist me.
       Almost Never   0   1   2   3   4   Almost Always
    d. tells me what he or she thinks I have done that deserves recognition.
       Almost Never   0   1   2   3   4   Almost Always
    e. if there are problems with my performance, never brings up more than two of them at once.
       Almost Never   0   1   2   3   4   Almost Always
    f. listens openly to my explanations and concerns regarding any performance problems.
       Almost Never   0   1   2   3   4   Almost Always
    g. comes to agreement with me on steps to be taken by each of us to solve any performance problems.
       Almost Never   0   1   2   3   4   Almost Always
    h. makes sure that at the end of the interview I have a specific goal or goals in mind that I am to achieve in the future.
       Almost Never   0   1   2   3   4   Almost Always
    i. schedules a follow-up meeting so that we can discuss progress in relation to the goals.
       Almost Never   0   1   2   3   4   Almost Always

29. I find working toward my goals to be very stressful.
    Almost Always   0   1   2   3   4   Almost Never

30. My goals are much too difficult.
    Almost Always   0   1   2   3   4   Almost Never

31. I often fail to attain my goals.
    Almost Always   0   1   2   3   4   Almost Never

32. My supervisor acts nonsupportively when I fail to reach my goals.
    Almost Always   0   1   2   3   4   Almost Never

33. I have too many goals on this job (I am too overloaded).
    Almost Always   0   1   2   3   4   Almost Never

34. Some of my goals conflict with my personal values.
    Almost Always   0   1   2   3   4   Almost Never

35. I am given incompatible or conflicting goals by different people (or even by the same person).
    Almost Always   0   1   2   3   4   Almost Never

36. I have unclear goals on this job.
    Almost Always   0   1   2   3   4   Almost Never

37. My job goals lead me to take excessive risks.
    Almost Always   0   1   2   3   4   Almost Never

38. My job goals serve to limit rather than raise my performance.
    Almost Always   0   1   2   3   4   Almost Never

39. The goals I have on this job lead me to ignore other important aspects of my job.
    Almost Always   0   1   2   3   4   Almost Never

40. The goals I have on this job focus only on short-range accomplishment and ignore important long-range consequences.
    Almost Always   0   1   2   3   4   Almost Never

41. The pressure to achieve goals here leads to considerable dishonesty and cheating.
    Almost Always   0   1   2   3   4   Almost Never

42. The top people here do not set a very good example for the employees, since they are dishonest themselves.
    Almost Always   0   1   2   3   4   Almost Never

43. Goals in this organization are used more to punish you than to help you do your job well.
    Almost Always   0   1   2   3   4   Almost Never

44. My boss wants me to avoid mentioning negative information or problems regarding my goals or action plans.
    Almost Always   0   1   2   3   4   Almost Never

45. If my boss makes a mistake that affects my ability to attain my goals, he or she refuses to admit it or discuss it.
    Almost Always   0   1   2   3   4   Almost Never

NOTE: Employees who work under a successful goal setting program will tend toward the "Almost Always" side of the scales in their answers to items 1 through 28, and toward the "Almost Never" side of the scales for items 29 through 45. The scales are keyed so that "4" is always toward the "good" end of the scale while "0" is always toward the "poor" end.

LEADING GOAL SETTING RESEARCHERS
(Number of Studies)

Below we list the leading goal setting researchers based on the number of studies conducted as of late 1988. Each co-author of a study was given credit for one study regardless of the number of co-authors. Only original empirical studies were included; meta-analyses, review articles, and theoretical pieces were excluded from the count. Studies did not have to deal with goals and performance to be counted as long as they were relevant to goal setting (e.g., goal setting and affect, goal choice.) In some cases the count may be slightly exaggerated because different aspects of the same study were reported in more than one article (e.g., performance results in one study and affect results in another). However, such double counting would have only minor effects on the totals. Finally, if an article reported more than one study (e.g., five studies), it was counted as multiple studies. Researchers who published only with Locke (i.e., Bryan) or Latham (i.e., Saari) have not been listed.

E. Locke (64)	J. Bavelas (7)	D. Dossett (5)
G. Latham (28)	J. Hollenbeck (7)	H. Garland (5)
C. Earley (25)	T. Matsui (7)	T. Mitchell (5)
C. Lee (12)	E. Rothkopf (7)	R. Weinberg (5)
M. Erez (11)	H. Klein (6)	
J. Ivancevich (11)	R. Wood (6)	

While quantity is not always a valid index of impact, the above list does show a reasonable relationship to influence, with the exceptions of Bavelas and Weinberg, who have been less influential than their numbers imply.

GOAL SETTING RESEARCH QUESTIONS THAT NEED TO BE ADDRESSED

Chapter 2—CORE FINDINGS

1. What factors enhance or inhibit the successful attainment of multiple goals? How should goals be set to avoid conflict?
2. What is the ideal time span for a goal? When are proximal or distal goals more effective for task performance?
3. Is intrinsic motivation a viable psychological concept? If so, what does it mean? What is the relationship between goals and intrinsic motivation?

Chapter 3—GOALS, EXPECTANCIES, SELF-EFFICACY

1. How are concepts in expectancy theory related to self-efficacy? Can these concepts be reconciled? Do they form separate components of goal setting theory?
2. What is the reciprocal causal relationship between self-efficacy and task strategies? How are these related to attribution theory?
3. To what extent does objective probability of success affect performance on goal setting tasks? What factors mediate this relationship? (See Figure 3–11.)
4. What is the relationship between goal level and instrumentality functions under different compensation systems (e.g., merit vs. incentive)?

Chapter 4—GOAL MECHANISMS

1. How are behavioral modeling and participation related to task strategy development? Under what conditions do modeling and participation enhance or inhibit goal attainment?
2. When does goal setting result in a time-lagged effect? What contextual variable and task types affect this process?

3. How is task strategy development under goals related to concepts in the decision theory literature (e.g., anchoring, availability, prospect-theory)?
4. What conditions lead people with goals to select good or poor task strategies? (See Figure 4-5.)

Chapter 5—GOAL CHOICE

1. What factors account for the most variance in the determinants of goal choice? Are social factors (e.g., normative information, role modeling) or individual factors (e.g., previous performance, self-efficacy) better predictors of goal choice or do these work in concert?

Chapter 6—GOAL COMMITMENT I

1. Is the distinction between goal commitment and goal acceptance of theoretical or practical importance? How could a study be designed to test the differential effects of these factors?
2. How are emotional variables such as mood and enthusiasm, related to goal commitment?
3. What is the relationship between supervisory and organizational support and goal commitment? How do these factors interact to affect performance?
4. What is the relationship between competition, goal level, and goal commitment?
5. How do incentives interact with goals to affect performance? How do individual *perceptions* of incentives affect goal commitment?
6. What is the relationship between goal intensity and goal commitment? What factors moderate or mediate this relationship (e.g., self-efficacy, task strategies)?
7. What are the effects of goal conflict on commitment?

Chapter 7—COMMITMENT II

1. Under what conditions are assigned, self-set, or participatively set goals most effective? Are there contexts where one method is clearly superior to another in achieving high commitment and performance?
2. What are the cognitive (as opposed to motivational) benefits of participative goal setting (e.g., task strategy development)?

Chapter 8—FEEDBACK

1. When is feedback most likely to lead to spontaneous goal setting?
2. What type of feedback is most effective in the goal-performance relationship (e.g., process, outcome oriented)? Under what conditions are certain types most appropriate?
3. How frequently should feedback be given? What factors affect feedback frequency?
4. What are the effects of feedback, self-efficacy, dissatisfaction, and goals on responses to prior feedback?

Chapter 9—ABILITY, DEMOGRAPHIC VARIABLES, PERSONALITY

1. Are there consistent cultural, gender, and racial differences in the goal-performance relationship? How can these differences be translated into effective management techniques?
2. How do individual personality differences affect goal choice? What is the role of individual differences in response to assigned goals?

Chapter 10—AFFECT

1. How does task focus affect interest and boredom? What mechanisms underlie this relationship?
2. Under what conditions does goal setting increase stress, anxiety, and role conflict? How can such negative affective reactions be mitigated or reduced?

Chapter 11—INTEGRATION

1. Are all theories of work motivation (which have achieved some scientific validity) ultimately reducible to goal theory? Do other motivation techniques affect performance through their effects on goals or commitment? How can this be tested?
2. What role does need for achievement play in goal setting theory? Are there alternative ways to measure N-ach (other than TAT) which would correlate more highly with goal choice?
3. What leadership activities and attributes result in effective goal setting?
4. Does satisfaction help to *cause* commitment to the organization? To its goals?

Chapter 12—HRM

1. How can experimental studies be designed to test the effectiveness of the RBO model? How could one ensure the external validity of such experiments?
2. What is the relationship between pay fairness, equity, and goal setting? How can goal setting be further incorporated into compensation issues (e.g., incentives, merit pay)?

REFERENCES

ABELSON, M. A. (1983). The impact of goal change on prominent perceptions and behaviors of employees. *Journal of Management, 9,* 65–79.

ABELSON, R. P. (1976). Script processing in attitude formation and decision-making. In J. Carroll & J. Payne (Eds.), *Cognition and social behavior.* Hillsdale, NJ: L. Erlbaum.

ABELSON, R. P. (1981). Psychological status of the script concept. *American Psychologist, 36,* 715–29.

ACH, N. (1935). *Analyse des willens.* Berlin: Urban & Schwarzenberg.

ADAM, E. E. (1975). Behavior modification in quality control. *Academy of Management Journal, 18,* 662–79.

ADAMS, J. A., & HUMES, J. A. (1963). Monitoring of complex displays: IV. Training for vigilance. *Human Factors, 5,* 147–53.

ADAMS, J. S. (1963). Toward an understanding of inequity. *Journal of Abnormal and Social Psychology, 67,* 422–36.

ADAMS, J. S. (1965). Inequity in social exchange. In L. Berkowitz (Ed.), *Advances in experimental social psychology, Vol. 2.* New York: Academic Press.

ADLER, N. E., & GOLEMAN, D. (1975). Goal setting, T-group participation, and self-rated change: An experimental study. *Journal of Applied Behavioral Science, 11,* 197–208.

ADLER, S. (1986). Toward a role for personality in goal setting research. Presented at the International Congress of Applied Psychology meeting, Jerusalem, Israel.

ADLER, S. (1987). Toward a role for personality in goal setting research. Stevens Institute of Technology, unpublished manuscript.

AHRENS, A. H. (1987). Theories of depression: The role of goals and the self-evaluation process. *Cognitive Therapy and Research, 11,* 665–80.

AHRENS, A. H., ZEISS, A. M., AND KANFER, R. (1988). Dysphoric deficits in interpersonal standards, self-efficacy, and social comparison. *Cognitive Therapy and Research, 12,* 53–67.

AJZEN, I. (1987). Attitudes, traits, and actions: Dispositional prediction of behavior in personality and social psychology. *Advances in Experimental Social Psychology, 20* 1–63.

AJZEN, I., & FISHBEIN, M. (1980). *Understanding attitudes and predicting social behavior.* Englewood Cliffs, NJ: Prentice Hall.

AJZEN, I., & MADDEN, T. J. (1986). Prediction of goal-directed behavior: Attitudes, intentions and perceived behavioral control. *Journal of Experimental Social Psychology, 22,* 453–74.

ALEXANDER, C. J., SCHULDT, W. J., & HANSEN, C. K. (1983). Effects of locus of goal imposition and sex on performance. *Perceptual and Motor Skills, 56,* 518.

ALEXY, B. (1985). Goal setting and health risk reduction. *Nursing Research, 34,* 283–88.

AMABILE, T. M., DEJONG, W., & LEPPER, M. R.

(1976). Effects of externally imposed deadlines on subsequent intrinsic motivation. *Journal of Personality and Social Psychology, 34,* 92–98.

AMMONS, R. B. (1956). Effects of knowledge of performance: A survey and tentative theoretical formulation. *Journal of General Psychology, 54,* 279–99.

ANDERSON, C. A. (1983). Imagination and expectation: The effect of imaging behavioral scripts on personal intentions. *Journal of Personality and Social Psychology, 45,* 293–305.

ANDERSON, C. R., & SCHNEIER, D. B. (1979). The effects of leader motivational style on subordinate performance: The case of the collegiate football coach. College of Business & Management, University of Maryland, unpublished manuscript.

ANDERSON, D. C., CROWELL, C. R., DOMAN, M., & HOWARD, G. S. (1988). Performance posting, goal setting, and activity-contingent praise as applied to a university hockey team. *Journal of Applied Psychology, 73,* 87–95.

ANDERSON, J. C., & O'REILLY, C. A. (1981). Effects of an organizational control system on managerial satisfaction and performance. *Human Relations, 34,* 491–501.

ANDREWS, F. M., & FARRIS, G. F. (1972). Time pressure and performance of scientists and engineers: A five-year panel study. *Organizational Behavior and Human Performance, 8,* 185–200.

ANDREWS, K. R. (1971). *The concept of corporate strategy.* Homewood, IL: Dow Jones-Irwin.

ANNETT, J. (1969). *Feedback and human behavior.* Baltimore: Penguin.

ANTONI, C. H., & BECKMANN, J. (1987). An action control conceptualization of goal setting and feedback effects. University of Mannheim, W. Germany, unpublished manuscript.

ARNOLD, H. J., & FELDMAN, D. C. (1982). A multivariate analysis of the determinants of job turnover. *Journal of Applied Psychology, 67,* 350–60.

ARNOLD, M. B. (1960). *Emotion and personality: Psychological aspects, Vol. 1.* New York: Columbia University Press.

ARPS, T. F. (1920). Work with knowledge of results versus work without knowledge of results. *Psychological Review Monograph Supplement, 28,* (3 Whole No. 125).

ARVEY, R. D. (1972). Task performance as a function of perceived effort-performance and performance-reward contingencies. *Organizational Behavior and Human Performance, 8,* 423–33.

ARVEY, R. D., & CAMPION, J. E. (1982). The employment interview: A summary and a review of recent research. *Personnel Psychology, 35,* 281–322.

ARVEY, R. D., & DEWHIRST, H. D. (1976). Goal-setting attributes, personality variables, and job satisfaction. *Journal of Vocational Behavior, 9,* 179–89.

ARVEY, R. D., DEWHIRST, H. D., & BROWN, E. M. (1978). A longitudinal study of the impact of changes in goal setting on employee satisfaction. *Personnel Psychology, 31,* 595–608.

ARVEY, R. D., & IVANCEVICH, J. M. (1980). Punishment in organizations: A review, propositions and research suggestions. *Academy of Management Review, 5,* 123–32.

ASHWORTH, D. N., & MOBLEY, W. H. (1978). Relationships among organizational entry performance goals, subsequent goals, and performance in a military setting. College of Business Administration, University of South Carolina, unpublished manuscript.

AT EMERY AIR FREIGHT: Positive reinforcement boosts performance (1973). *Organizational Dynamics, 1*(3), 41–50.

ATKINSON, J. W. (1958). Towards experimental analysis of human motivation in terms of motives, expectancies, and incentives. In J. W. Atkinson (Ed.), *Motives in fantasy, action and society.* Princeton, NJ: Van Nostrand.

AUSTIN, J. T., & BOBKO, P. (1985). Goal setting theory: Unexplored areas and future research needs. *Journal of Occupational Psychology, 58,* 289–308.

AZRIN, N. H., (1977). A strategy for applied research: Learning based but outcome oriented. *American Psychologist, 32,* 140–49.

BALCAZAR, F., HOPKINS, B. L., & SUAREZ, Y. (1986). A critical, objective review of performance feedback. *Journal of Organizational Behavior Management, 7*(3/4), 65–89.

BANDURA, A. (1977). *Social learning theory.* Englewood Cliffs, NJ: Prentice Hall.

BANDURA, A. (1982). Self-efficacy mechanism in human agency. *American Psychologist, 37,* 122–47.

BANDURA, A. (1986). *Social foundations of thought and action: A social-cognitive view.* Englewood Cliffs, NJ: Prentice Hall.

BANDURA, A. (1988). Self-regulation of motivation and action through goal systems. In V. Hamilton, G. Bower, & N. Frijda (Eds.),

Cognitive perspectives on emotion and motivation. Dordrecht: Kluwer Academic Publishers.

BANDURA, A. (in press). Reflections on nonability determinants of competence. In J. Kolligan & R. Sternberg (Eds.), *Competence considered: Perceptions of competence and incompetence across the lifespan.* New Haven: Yale University Press.

BANDURA, A., & CERVONE, D. (1983). Self-evaluative and self-efficacy mechanisms governing the motivational effects of goal systems. *Journal of Personality and Social Psychology, 45,* 1017–28.

BANDURA, A., & CERVONE, D. (1986). Differential engagement of self-reactive influences in cognitive motivation. *Organizational Behavior and Human Decision Processes, 38,* 92–113.

BANDURA, A., & SCHUNK, D. H. (1981). Cultivating competence, self-efficacy, and intrinsic interest through proximal self-motivation. *Journal of Personality and Social Psychology, 41,* 586–98.

BANDURA, A., & SIMON, K. M. (1977). The role of proximal intentions in self regulation of refractory behavior. *Cognitive Therapy and Research, 1,* 177–93.

BANDURA, A., & WOOD, R. E. (in press). Effect of perceived controllability and performance standards on self-regulation of complex decision-making. *Journal of Personality and Social Psychology.*

BANDURA, M. M., & DWECK, C. S. (1987). The relationships of conceptions of intelligence and achievement goals to patterns of cognition, affect and behavior. Harvard University, unpublished manuscript.

BARLING, J. (1980). Performance standards and reinforcements effects on children's academic performance: A test of social learning theory. *Cognitive Therapy and Research, 4,* 409–18.

BARNARD, C. I. (1938). *The functions of the executive.* Cambridge, MA: Harvard University Press.

BARNETT, M. L. (1977). Effects of two methods of goal setting on learning a gross motor task. *Research Quarterly, 48,* 19–23.

BARNETT, M. L., & STANICEK, J. A. (1979). Effects of goal setting on achievement in archery. *Research Quarterly, 50,* 328–32.

BARON, P., & WATTERS, R. G. (1981). Effects of goal-setting and of goal levels on weight loss induced by self-monitoring of caloric intake. *Canadian Journal of Behavioral Science, 13,* 161–70.

BARON, P., & WATTERS, R. G. (1982). Effects of goal-setting and of goal levels on weight loss induced by self-monitoring. *International Review of Applied Psychology, 31,* 369–82.

BARON, R. A. (1988). Negative effects of destructive criticism: Impact on conflict, self-efficacy, and task performance. *Journal of Applied Psychology, 73,* 199–207.

BARRY, D., LOCKE, E. A., & SMITH, K. G. (1988). Strategic goal systems, firm planning, and firm performance. School of Management, Syracuse University, unpublished manuscript.

BARRY, D., LOCKE, E. A., & SMITH, K. G. (1989). The effects of synoptic vs. incremental goals on planning and performance. Working paper, Syracuse University (alternative version of Barry et al., 1988).

BARTLEM, C. S., & LOCKE, E. A. (1981). The Coch and French study: A critique and reinterpretation. *Human Relations, 34,* 555–66.

BASSETT, G. A. (1979). A study of the effects of task goal and schedule choice on work performance. *Organizational Behavior and Human Performance, 24,* 202–27.

BATEMAN, T. S., & STRASSER, S. (1984). A longitudinal analysis of the antecedents of organizational commitment. *Academy of Management Journal, 27,* 95–112.

BATTLE, E. S. (1966). Motivational determinants of academic competence. *Journal of Personality and Social Psychology, 4,* 634–42.

BAUMLER, J. V. (1971). Defined criteria of performance in organizational control. *Administrative Science Quarterly, 16,* 340–50.

BAVELAS, J. B. (1975). Systems analysis of dyadic interactions: The role of interpersonal judgement. *Behavioral Science, 20,* 213–22.

BAVELAS, J. B. (1978). Systems analysis of dyadic interaction: Prediction from individual parameters. *Behavioral Science, 23,* 177–86.

BAVELAS, J., & LEE, E. S. (1978). Effect of goal level on performance: A trade-off of quantity and quality. *Canadian Journal of Psychology, 32,* 219–40.

BAYTON, J. A. (1943). Interrelations between levels of aspiration, performance, and estimates of past performance. *Journal of Experimental Psychology, 33,* 1–21.

BAYTON, J. A. (1948). Performance as a function of expressed and non-expressed levels of aspiration. *American Psychologist, 3,* 274.

BAZERMAN, M. H., MAGLIOZZI, T., & NEALE, M. A. (1985). Integrative bargaining in a competitive market. *Organizational Behavior and Human Performance, 35,* 294–313.

BECK, A. T., RUSH, A. J., SHAW, B. F., & EMERY, G. (1979). *Cognitive theory of depression.* New York: Guilford Press.

BECKER, L. J. (1978). Joint effect of feedback and goal setting on performance: A field study of residential energy conservation. *Journal of Applied Psychology, 63,* 428–33.

BEER, M. (1976). The technology of organization development. In M. Dunnette (Ed.), *The handbook of industrial and organizational psychology.* Chicago: Rand McNally.

BENNIS, W., & NANUS, B. (1985). *Leaders.* New York: Harper & Row.

BERLEW, D. E., & HALL, D. T. (1965). The socialization of managers: Effects of expectations on performance. *Administrative Science Quarterly, 11,* 207–23.

BIGONESS, W. J., KEEF, K. M., & DuBOSE, P. B. (1983). Perceived goal difficulty, locus of control, and performance ratings. School of Business Administration, University of North Carolina, unpublished manuscript.

BILODEAU, E. A., & BILODEAU, I. McD. (1961). Motor-skills learning. *Annual Review of Psychology, 12,* 243–80.

BINSWANGER, H. (1986). The goal-directedness of living action. *The Objectivist Forum, 7*(4), 1–10.

BLAU, G., BLANK, W., & KATERBERG, R. (1987). Investigating the motivational determinants of job performance. Human Resources Administration Department, Temple University, unpublished manuscript.

BLAU, P. M., & SCOTT, W. R. (1963). *Formal organizations: A comparative approach.* London: Routledge & Kegan Paul.

BLUMENFELD, W. S., & LEIDY, T. R. (1969). Effectiveness of goal setting as a management device: Research note. *Psychological Reports, 24,* 752.

BOBKO, P. (1986). A solution to some dilemmas when testing hypotheses about ordinal interactions. *Journal of Applied Psychology, 71,* 323–26.

BOOK, W. F., & NORVELL, L. (1922). The will to learn: An experimental study of incentives in learning. *Pedagogical Seminary, 29,* 305–62.

BOTTERILL, C. B. (1977). Goal setting and performance on an endurance task. University of Alberta, unpublished doctoral dissertation.

BOTTGER, P. C., & WOODS, M. A. (1985). The

different determinants of short term motivation and longer term professional growth: Individual differences, goal setting and job characteristics. *Working Paper 85–020,* University of New South Wales, Australia.

BOTTGER, P. C., & WOODS, M. A. (1988). Joint effects of role stress, mastery, self-control beliefs and planning on job anxiety and task effort. *Working Paper 88–001,* University of New South Wales, Australia.

BOUDREAU, J. W., & BERGER, C. J. (1985). Decision-theoretic utility analysis applied to employee separations and acquisitions. *Journal of Applied Psychology, 70,* 581–612.

BOURGEOIS, L. J. (1980). Performance and consensus. *Strategic Management Journal, 11,* 227–48.

BOURGEOIS, L. J. (1985). Strategic goals, perceived uncertainty, and economic performance in volatile environments. *Academy of Management Journal, 28, 548–73.*

BOWERS, D. G., & SEASHORE, S. E. (1966). Predicting organizational effectiveness with a four-factor theory of leadership. *Administrative Science Quarterly, 11,* 238–63.

BOYATZIS, R. E. (1982). *The competent manager.* New York: Wiley.

BRADFORD, D. L., & COHEN, A. R. (1984). *Managing for excellence.* New York: Wiley.

BRASS, D. J., & OLDHAM, G. R. (1976). Validating an in-basket test using an alternative set of leadership scoring dimensions. *Journal of Applied Psychology, 61,* 652–57.

BRAY, D. W., CAMPBELL, R. J., & GRANT, D. L. (1974). *Formative years in business.* New York: Wiley.

BRAYBROOKE, D., & LINDBLOM, C. E. (1970). *A strategy of decision: Policy evaluations as a social process.* New York: Free Press.

BREHMER, B., HAGAFORS, R., & JOHANSSON, R. (1980). Cognitive skills in judgment: Subjects' ability to use information about weights, function forms, and organizing principles. *Organizational Behavior and Human Performance, 26,* 373–85.

BREWER, W. F. (1974). There is no convincing evidence for operant or classical conditioning in adult humans. In W. B. Weimer & D. S. Palermo (Eds.), *Cognition and the symbolic processes.* Hillsdale, NJ: L. Erlbaum.

BRICKNER, M. A., & BUKATKO, P. A. (1987). Locked into performance: Goal setting as a moderator of the social loafing effect. University of Akron, unpublished manuscript.

BRIEF, A. P., & HOLLENBECK, J. R. (1985). An

exploratory study of self-regulating activities and their effects on job performance. *Journal of Occupational Behavior, 6,* 197–208.

BROOKE, P. P., RUSSELL, D. W., & PRICE, J. L. (1988). Discriminant validation of measures of job satisfaction, job involvement, and organizational commitment. *Journal of Applied Psychology, 73,* 139–45.

BROWN, F. J. (1932). Knowledge of results as an incentive in school room practice. *Journal of Educational Psychology, 23,* 532–52.

BROWNELL, K. D., COLLETTI, G., ERSNER-HERSHFIELD, R., HERSHFIELD, S. M., & WILSON, G. T. (1977). Self-control in school children: Strigency and leniency in self-determined and externally imposed performance standards. *Behavior Therapy, 8,* 442–55.

BRUNER, J. S., GOODNOW, J., & AUSTIN, G. A. (1956). *A study of thinking.* New York: Wiley.

BRYAN, J. F., & LOCKE, E. A. (1967a). Goal setting as a means of increasing motivation. *Journal of Applied Psychology, 51,* 274–77.

BRYAN, J. F., & LOCKE, E. A. (1976b). Parkinson's law as a goal-setting phenomenon. *Organizational Behavior and Human Performance, 2,* 258–75.

BULLER, P. F. (1988). Long term performance effects of goal setting and team building interventions in an underground silver mine. *Organizational Development Journal 6(2)* 82–93.

BULLER, P. F., & BELL, C. H., JR. (1986). Effects of team building and goal setting on productivity: A field experiment. *Academy of Management Journal, 29,* 305–28.

BURKE, R. J., WEITZEL, W., & WEIR, T. (1978). Characteristics of effective employee performance review and development interviews: Replication and extension. *Personnel Psychology, 31,* 903–19.

BURKE, R. J., & WILCOX, D. S. (1969). Characteristics of effective employee performance review and development interviews. *Personnel Psychology, 22,* 291–305.

BURNHAM, D. (1988). Punish or perish at IRS. *Washington Post,* March 13, 1988, C1 & C2.

BURNSIDE, R. M. (1988). Encouragement as the elixir of innovation. *Issues and Observations, 8* (Summer), Greensboro, NC: Center for Creative Leadership.

BURTON, D. (1984). Goal setting: A secret to success. *Swimming World and Junior Swimmer,* February, 25–29.

BUSINESS WEEK, (1987). Office automation: Making it pay off, October 12, 134–36.

BUSINESS WEEK, (1987). The miracle company, October 19, 84ff.

CADWELL, R. B. (1970). *Barriers to planned change: A study of two business organizations.* Dublin, Ireland: Irish National Productivity Committee, Development Division.

CAMPBELL, D. J. (1982). Determinants of choice of goal difficulty level: A review of situational and personality influences. *Journal of Occupational Psychology, 55,* 79–95.

CAMPBELL, D. J. (1984). The effects of goal-contingent payment on the performance of a complex task. *Personnel Psychology, 37,* 23–40.

CAMPBELL, D. J. (1988). Task complexity: A review and analysis. *Academy of Management Review, 13,* 40–52.

CAMPBELL, D. J., & GINGRICH, K. F. (1986). The interactive effects of task complexity and participation on task performance: A field experiment. *Organizational Behavior and Human Decision Processes, 38,* 162–80.

CAMPBELL, D. J., & ILGEN, D. R. (1976). Additive effects of task difficulty and goal setting on subsequent task performance. *Journal of Applied Psychology, 61,* 319–24.

CAMPBELL, J. P., DUNNETTE, M. D., LAWLER, E. E., & WEICK, K. E., (1970). *Managerial behavior, performance, and effectiveness.* New York: McGraw-Hill.

CAMPBELL, J. P., & PRITCHARD, R. D. (1976). Motivation theory in industrial and organizational psychology. In M. D. Dunnette (Ed.), *Handbook of industrial and organizational psychology.* Princeton: Van Nostrand.

CAMPBELL, N. R. (1920). *The physics: The elements.* New York: Cambridge University Press.

CAMPION, M. A., & LORD, R. G. (1982). A control systems conceptualization of the goal-setting and changing process. *Organizational Behavior and Human Performance, 30,* 265–87.

CAMPION, M. A., PURSELL, E. D., & BROWN, B. K. (1988). Structured interviewing: Raising the psychometric properties of the employment interview. *Personnel Psychology, 41,* 25–42.

CANNON-BOWERS, J., & LEVINE, E. L. (1988). Psychometric and motivational properties of self-efficacy: Disentangling the complex web. University of South Florida, unpublished manuscript.

CARROLL, S. J. (1986). Management by objectives: Three decades of research and experience. In S. L. Rynes & G. T. Milkovich (Eds.), *Current issues in human resource management,* Plato, TX: Business Publications.

CARROLL, S. J., & TOSI, H. L. (1969). Relationship of goal setting characteristics as moderated by personality and situational factors to the success of the management by objectives approach. *Proceedings of the 77th annual convention,* American Psychological Association.

CARROLL, S. J., & TOSI, H. L. (1970). Goal characteristics and personality factors in a management by objectives program. *Administrative Science Quarterly, 15,* 295–305.

CARROLL, S. J., & TOSI, H. L. (1973). *Management by objectives.* New York: Macmillan.

CARVER, C. S., & SCHEIER, M. F. (1981). *Attention and self-regulation: A control-theory approach to human behavior.* New York: Springer-Verlag.

CARVER, C. S., & SCHEIER, M. F. (1982). Control theory: A useful conceptual framework for personality-social, clinical, and health psychology, *Psychological Bulletin, 92,* 111–35.

CELLAR, D. F., & BARRETT, G. V. (1987). Script processing and intrinsic motivation: The cognitive sets underlying cognitive labels. *Organizational Behavior and Human Decision Processes, 40,* 115–35.

CHACKO, T. I., & McELROY, J. C. (1983). The cognitive component in Locke's theory of goal setting: Suggestive evidence for a causal attribution interpretation. *Academy of Management Journal, 26,* 104–18.

CHACKO, T. I., STONE, T. H., & BRIEF, A. P. (1979). Participation in goal-setting programs: An attributional analysis. *Academy of Management Review, 4,* 433–38.

CHANG, G. S., & LORENZI, P. (1983). The effects of participative versus assigned goal setting on intrinsic motivation. *Journal of Management, 9,* 55–64.

CHAPANIS, A. (1964). Knowledge of performance as an incentive in repetitive, monotonous tasks. *Journal of Applied Psychology, 48,* 263–67.

CHAPMAN, J. C., & FEDER, R. B. (1917). The effect of external incentives on improvement. *Journal of Educational Psychology, 8,* 469–74.

CHAPMAN, S. L., & JEFFREY, D. B. (1978). Situational management, standard setting, and self-reward in a behavior modification weight loss program. *Journal of Consulting and Clinical Psychology, 46,* 1588–89.

CHAPMAN, S. L., & JEFFREY, D. B. (1979). Processes in the maintenance of weight loss with behavior therapy. *Behavior Therapy, 10,* 566–70.

CHESNEY, A. A., & LOCKE, E. A. (1988). An examination of the relationship among goals, strategies and performance on a complex management simulation task. College of Management, Georgia Institute of Technology, unpublished manuscript.

CHEW, W. B. (1988). No-nonsense guide to measuring productivity. *Harvard Business Review, 66,*(1), 110–18.

CHHOKAR, J. S., & WALLIN, J. A. (1984). A field study of the effect of feedback frequency on performance. *Journal of Applied Psychology, 69,* 524–30.

CHIDESTER, T. R., & GRIGSBY, W. C. (1984). A meta-analysis of the goal setting performance literature. *Academy of Management Proceedings,* 202–6.

CHRISTENSEN-SZALANSKI, J. J. J. (1980). A further examination of the selection of problem-solving strategies: The effects of deadlines and analytic aptitudes. *Organizational Behavior and Human Performance, 25,* 107–22.

CHUNG, K. H., & VICKERY, W. D. (1976). Relative effectiveness and joint effects of three selected reinforcements in a repetitive task situation. *Organizational Behavior and Human Performance, 16,* 114–42.

CHURCH, R. M., & CAMP, D. S. (1965). Change in reaction time as a function of knowledge of results. *American Journal of Psychology, 78,* 102–6.

CIALDINI, R. B. (1984). *Influence.* New York: Morrow.

COCH, L., & FRENCH, J. R. P. (1948). Overcoming resistance to change. *Human Relations, 1,* 512–32.

COFER, C. N., & APPLEY, M. H. (1967). *Motivation: Theory and research.* New York: Wiley.

COHEN, C. E., & EBBESEN, E. B. (1979). Observational goals and schema activation: A theoretical framework for behavior perception. *Journal of Experimental Social Psychology, 15,* 305–29.

COHEN, M. D., & MARCH, J. G. (1974). *Leadership and ambiguity.* Boston, MA: Harvard Business School Press.

CORNELIUS, E. T. (1983). The use of projective techniques in personnel selection. In K. Rowland and G. Ferris (Eds.), *Research in personnel and human resources management.* Greenwich, CT: JAI Press.

COSIER, R. A., & APLIN, J. C. (1980). Effects of delegated choice on performance. *Personnel Psychology, 33,* 581–93.

COTTON, J. L., VOLLRATH, D. A., FROGGATT, K. L., LENGNICK-HALL, M. L., & JENNINGS, K. R.

(1988). Employee participation: Diverse forms and different outcomes. *Academy of Management Review, 13,* 8–22.

CRAWFORD, K. S., WHITE, M. A., & MAGNUSSON, P. A. (1983). The impact of goal setting and feedback on the productivity of navy industrial workers. Navy Personnel Research and Development Center, NPRDC TR 83-4, San Diego, CA.

CRAWLEY, S. L. (1926). An experimental investigation of recovery from work. *Archives of Psychology, 13,* No. 85.

CUMMINGS, L. L., SCHWAB, D. P., & ROSEN, M. (1971). Performance and knowledge of results as determinants of goal setting. *Journal of Applied Psychology, 55,* 526–30.

CURRY, J. P., WAKEFIELD, D. S., PRICE, J. L., & MUELLER, C. W. (1986). On the casual ordering of job satisfaction and organizational commitment. *Academy of Management Journal, 29,* 847–58.

CYERT, R. M., & MARCH, J. G. (1963). *A behavioral theory of the firm.* Englewood Cliffs, NJ: Prentice Hall.

DACHLER, H. P., & MOBLEY, W. H. (1973). Construct validation of an instrumentality-expectancy-task-goal model of work motivation: Some theoretical boundary conditions. *Journal of Applied Psychology (Monograph), 58,* 397–418.

DACHLER, H. P., & WILPERT, B. (1978). Conceptual dimensions and boundaries of participation in organizations: A critical evaluation. *Administrative Science Quarterly, 23,* 1–35.

DAFT, R. L. (1983). *Organizational theory and design.* St. Paul, MN: West.

DANSEREAU, D. F., McDONALD, B. A., COLLINS, K. W., GARLAND, J., HOLLEY, C. D., DIEKHOFF, G. M., & EVANS, S. H. (1979). Evaluation of a learning strategy system. In H. O'Neil & C. Spielberger (Eds.), *Cognitive and affective learning strategies.* New York: Academic Press.

DAS, B. (1982a). Effects of productive feedback and standards on worker productivity in a repetitive production task. *AIIE Transactions,* March, 27–37.

DAS, B. (1982b). Effects of production feedback and standards on worker satisfaction and job attitudes in a repetitive production task. *AIIE Transactions,* September, 193–203.

DEAN, D. L., PHILLIPS, J. S., IVANCEVICH, J. M. (1988). Type A behavior, reactions to uncertainty, and goal setting: A field test of the self-appraisal hypothesis. Presented at Academy of Management meeting.

DEANE, D. H., HAMMOND, K. R., & SUMMERS, D. A. (1972). Acquisition and application of knowledge in complex inference tasks. *Journal of Experimental Psychology, 92,* 319–24.

DECI, E. L., & RYAN, R. M. (1985). *Intrinsic motivation and self-determination in human behavior.* New York: Plenum Press.

DEMBER, W. N. (1975). Motivation and the cognitive revolution. *American Psychologist, 30,* 161–68.

DENT, J. K. (1959). Organizational correlates of the goals of business managements. *Personnel Psychology, 12,* 365–93.

DERMARIS, O. (1988). He'd rather take a chance. *Parade,* November 6, 4–7.

DESS, G. G. (1987). Consensus on strategy formulation and organizational performance: Competitors in a fragmented industry. *Strategic Management Journal, 8,* 259–78.

DEY, M. K., & KAUR, G. (1965). Facilitation of performance by experimentally induced ego motivation. *Journal of General Psychology, 73,* 237–47.

DICKERSON, E. A., & CREEDON, C. F. (1981). Self-selection of standards by children: The relative effectiveness of pupil-selected and teacher-selected standards of performance. *Journal of Applied Behavior Analysis, 14,* 425–33.

DOCKSTADER, S. L. (1977). Performance standards and implicit goal setting: Field testing Locke's assumption. Presented at American Psychological Association meeting.

DONALDSON, G. (1985). Financial goals and strategic consequences. *Harvard Business Review, 63*(3), 57–66.

DOSSETT, D. L., CELLA, A., GREENBERG, C. I., & ADRIAN, N. (1983). Goal setting, participation and leader supportiveness effects on performance. Presented at American Psychological Association meeting.

DOSSETT, D. L., & GREENBERG, C. I. (1981). Goal setting and performance evaluation: An attributional analysis. *Academy of Management Journal, 24,* 767–79.

DOSSETT, D. L., LATHAM, G. P., & MITCHELL, T. R. (1979). Effects of assigned vs. participatively set goals, knowledge of results, and individual differences on employee behavior when goal difficulty is held constant. *Journal of Applied Psychology, 64,* 291–98.

DOSSETT, D. L., LATHAM, G. P., & SAARI, L. M. (1980). The impact of goal setting on survey returns. *Academy of Management Journal, 23,* 561–67.

DOWLING, W. F. (1975). At General Motors: System-4 builds performance and profits. *Organizational Dynamics, 3,* 23–38.

DOWRICK, P. W., & HOOD, M. (1981). Comparison of self-modeling and small cash incentives in a sheltered workshop. *Journal of Applied Psychology, 66,* 394–97.

DRUCKER, P. F. (1954). *The practice of management.* New York: Harper.

DRUCKER, P. F. (1958). Business objectives and survival needs: Notes on a discipline of business enterprise. *Journal of Business, 31,* 81–90.

DUBBERT, P. M., & WILSON, G. T. (1984). Goal setting and spouse involvement in the treatment of obesity. *Behavior Research and Therapy, 22,* 227–42.

DUDA, J. L. (1985). Sex differences in mastery vs. social comparison goal emphasis in a recreational sport setting. Presented at North American Society for the Psychology of Sport and Physical Activity.

DUDA, J. L. (1986). Toward a developmental theory of children's motivation in sport: The consideration of variations in goals. Presented at North American Society for the Psychology of Sport and Physical Activity.

DULANY, D. E., JR. (1968). Awareness, rules and propositional control: A confrontation with S–R behavior theory. In D. Horton & T. Dixon (Eds.), *Verbal behavior and general behavior theory.* New York: Prentice Hall.

DUMONT, P. F., & GRIMES, A. J. (1982). The hard-impossible threshold: A pragmatic limitation of the task goal model and a link to individual differences theories. Presented at American Institute for Decision Sciences meeting.

DUTTAGUPTA, D. (1975). An empirical evaluation of management by objectives. Baruch College, unpublished Master's thesis.

EARLEY, P. C. (1985a). Influence of information, choice and task complexity upon goal acceptance, performance, and personal goals. *Journal of Applied Psychology, 70,* 481–91.

EARLEY, P. C. (1985b). The influence of goal setting methods on performance, goal acceptance, self-efficacy expectations, and expectancies across levels of goal difficulty. Presented at American Psychological Association meeting.

EARLEY, P. C. (1986a). An examination of the mechanisms underlying the relation of feedback to performance. *Academy of Management Proceedings,* 214–18.

EARLEY, P. C. (1986b). Perceived legitimacy of worker participation: A comparison between subsidiaries of a heavy-manufacturing company in the United States and England. *Cross-Cultural Psychology Bulletin, 20,* 15–20.

EARLEY, P. C. (1986c). Supervisors and shop stewards as sources of contextual information in goal setting: A comparison of the U.S. with England. *Journal of Applied Psychology, 71,* 111–17.

EARLEY, P. C. (1986d). Trust, perceived importance of praise and criticism, and work performance: An examination of feedback in the U.S. and England. *Journal of Management, 12,* 457–73.

EARLEY, P. C. (1988). Computer-generated performance feedback in the magazine-subscription industry. *Organizational Behavior and Human Decision Processes, 41,* 50–64.

EARLEY, P. C., CONNOLLY, T., & LEE, C. (1988). Task strategy interventions in goal setting: The importance of search and strategy development. Department of Management and Policy, University of Arizona, unpublished manuscript.

EARLEY, P. C., CONNOLLY, T., & EKEGREN, G. (1989). Goals, strategy development and task performance: Some limits on the efficacy of goal setting. *Journal of Applied Psychology, 74,* 24–33.

EARLEY, P. C., HANSON, L. A., & LEE, C. (1986). Relation of task complexity, task strategies, individual differences and goals to performance. *Academy of Management Proceedings,* 184–88.

EARLEY, P. C., & KANFER, R. (1985). The influence of component participation and role models on goal acceptance, goal satisfaction and performance. *Organizational Behavior and Human Decision Processes, 36,* 378–90.

EARLEY, P. C., LEE, C., & LITUCHY, T. R. (1989). Task strategy and judgments in goal setting: The effects of a learning emphasis and training sequence on performance. Department of Management and Policy, University of Arizona, unpublished manuscript.

EARLEY, P. C., LEE, C., & HANSON, L. A. (1989). Joint moderating effects of job experience and task component complexity: Relations among goal setting, task strategies, and performance. *Journal of Organizational Behavior, 10.*

EARLEY, P. C., & LITUCHY, T. R. (1989). Delineating goals and efficacy effects: A test of three models. Department of Management and Policy, University of Arizona, unpublished manuscript.

EARLEY, P. C., NORTHCRAFT, G. B., LEE, C., & LITUCHY, T. R. (in press). Impact of process and outcome feedback on the relation of goal setting to task performance. *Academy of Management Journal.*

EARLEY, P. C., & NORTHCRAFT, G. B. (1989). Goal setting, resource interdependence, and conflict management. In M. Rahim (Ed.), *Managing conflict: An interdisciplinary approach.* Westport, CT: Praeger.

EARLEY, P. C., & PERRY, B. C. (1987). Work plan availability and performance: An assessment of task strategy priming on subsequent task completion. *Organizational Behavior and Human Decision Processes, 39,* 279–302.

EARLEY, P. C., WOJNAROSKI, P., & PREST, W. (1987). Task planning and energy expended: Exploration of how goals influence performance. *Journal of Applied Psychology, 72,* 107–14.

EDEN, D. (1988). Pygmalion, goal setting, and expectancy: Compatible ways to boost productivity. *Academy of Management Review, 13,* 639–52.

EDMISTER, R. O., & LOCKE, E. A. (1987). The effects of differential goal weights on the performance of a complex financial task. *Personnel Psychology, 40,* 505–17.

EMURIAN, H. H., & BRADY, J. V. (1981). Appetitive and aversive reinforcement schedule effects on team performance. Technical Report #2, Johns Hopkins University.

ENGLAND, G. W. (1967). Organizational goals and expected behavior of American managers. *Academy of Management Journal, 10,* 107–17.

ENGLAND, G. W., & LEE, R. (1973). Organizational size as an influence on perceived organizational goals: A comparative study among American, Japanese, and Korean managers. *Organizational Behavior and Human Performance, 9,* 48–58.

EPSTEIN, S., & O'BRIEN, E. J. (1985). The person-situation debate in historical and current perspective. *Psychological Bulletin, 98,* 513–37.

ERBAUGH, S. J., & BARNETT, M. L. (1986). Effects of modeling and goal-setting on the jumping performance of primary-grade children. Wayne State University, unpublished manuscript.

EREZ, M. (1977). Feedback: A necessary condition for the goal setting–performance relationship. *Journal of Applied Psychology, 62,* 624–27.

EREZ, M. (1986). The congruence of goal setting strategies with socio-cultural values, and its effect on performance. *Journal of Management, 12,* 585–92.

EREZ, M. (in press). Performance quality and work motivation. In U. Kleinbeck, H. Thierry, H. Haecker, & H. Quast (Eds.), *Work motivation.* Hillsdale, NJ: L. Erlbaum.

EREZ, M., & ARAD, R. (1986). Participative goal setting: Social, motivational and cognitive factors. *Journal of Applied Psychology, 71,* 591–97.

EREZ, M., EARLEY, P. C., & HULIN, C. L. (1985). The impact of participation on goal acceptance and performance: A two-step model. *Academy of Management Journal, 28,* 50–66.

EREZ, M., & EARLEY, P. C. (1987). Comparative analysis of goal-setting strategies across cultures. *Journal of Applied Psychology, 72,* 658–65.

EREZ, M., GOPHER, D., & ARAZI, N. (1987). Effects of self-set goals and monetary rewards on the performance of complex tasks under time-sharing conditions. Faculty of Management and Industrial Engineering, Technion, (Haifa, Israel), unpublished manuscript.

EREZ, M., & KANFER, F. H. (1983). The role of goal acceptance in goal setting and task performance. *Academy of Management Review, 8,* 454–63.

EREZ, M., & ZIDON, I. (1984). Effect of goal acceptance on the relationship of goal difficulty to performance. *Journal of Applied Psychology, 69,* 69–78.

ERICSSON, K. A., & SIMON, H. A. (1980). Verbal reports on data. *Psychological Review, 87,* 215–51.

ERNST, G. W., & NEWELL, A. (1969). *GPS: A case study in generality in problem solving.* New York: Academic Press.

ETZIONI, A. (1960). Two approaches to organizational analysis: A critique and a suggestion. *Administrative Science Quarterly, 5,* 257–78.

FARRELL, D., & RUSBULT, C. E. (1981). Exchange variables as predictors of job satisfaction, job commitment, and turnover: The impact of rewards, costs, alternatives and investments. *Organizational Behavior and Human Performance, 28,* 78–95.

FAUCHEUX, C., AMADO, G., & LAURENT, A. (1982).

Organizational development and change. *Annual Review of Psychology, 33,* 343–70.

FEATHER, N. T. (1982). *Expectations and actions.* Hillsdale, NJ: L. Erlbaum.

FELIXBROD, J. J., & O'LEARY, K. D. (1974). Self-determination of academic standards by children: Toward freedom from external control. *Journal of Educational Psychology, 66,* 845–50.

FELLNER, D. J., & SULZER-AZAROFF, B. (1984). A behavioral analysis of goal setting. *Journal of Organizational Behavior Management, 6,* 33–51.

FELLNER, D. J., & SULZER-AZAROFF, B. (1985). Occupational safety: Assessing the impact of adding assigned or participative goal-setting. *Journal of Organizational Behavior Management, 7,* 3–24.

FELTZ, D. (1988). Self-confidence and sports performance. In K. Pandolf (Ed.), *Exercise and sport sciences reviews.* New York: Macmillan.

FERRIS, G. R., & PORAC, J. F. (1984). Goal setting as impression management. *Journal of Psychology, 117,* 33–36.

FESTINGER, L. (1942). A theoretical interpretation of shifts in level of aspiration. *Psychological Review, 49,* 235–50.

FISHBEIN, M., & AJZEN, I. (1975). *Belief, attitude, intention and behavior: An introduction to theory and research.* Reading, MA: Addison-Wesley.

FISHER, C. D. (1980). On the dubious wisdom of expecting job satisfaction to correlate with performance. *Academy of Management Review, 5,* 607–12.

FISHER, C. D., & LOCKE, E. A. (1987). Job satisfaction and dissatisfaction: Enhancing the prediction of consequences. Presented at Bowling Green Conference on Job Satisfaction.

FITTS, P. M. (1966). Cognitive aspects of information processing: III. Set for speed versus accuracy. *Journal of Experimental Psychology, 71,* 849–57.

FLANAGAN, J. C. (1954). The critical incident technique. *Psychological Bulletin, 51,* 327–58.

FORD, R. N. (1969). *Motivation through the work itself.* New York: American Management Association.

FORWARD, J., & ZANDER, A. (1971). Choice of unattainable group goals and effects on performance. *Organizational Behavior and Human Performance, 6,* 184–99.

FOWLER, R. L. (1985). Testing for substantive significance in applied research by specifying non-zero effect null hypotheses. *Journal of Applied Psychology, 70,* 215–18.

FRANK, J. D. (1935). Individual differences in certain aspects of the level of aspiration. *American Journal of Psychology, 47,* 119–28.

FRANK, J. D. (1941). Recent studies of the level of aspiration. *Psychological Bulletin, 38,* 218–26.

FRAYNE, C. A., & LATHAM, G. P. (1987). Application of social learning theory to employee self-management of attendance. *Journal of Applied Psychology, 72,* 387–92.

FREDERICKSON, J. W. (1984). The comprehensiveness of strategic decision processes: Extension, observations and future directions. *Academy of Management Journal, 27,* 445–66.

FREDERICKSON, J. W., & MITCHELL, T. R. (1984). Strategic decision processes: Comprehensiveness and performance in an industry with an unstable environment. *Academy of Management Journal, 27,* 399–423.

FREEDMAN, S. M., & PHILLIPS, J. S. (1988). Goal utility, task satisfaction, and the self-appraisal hypothesis of type A behavior. Management Department, University of Houston, unpublished manuscript.

FRENCH, J. R. P. (1950). Field experiments: Changing group productivity. In J. G. Miller (Ed.), *Experiments in social process: A symposium on social psychology.* New York: McGraw-Hill.

FRENCH, J. R. P., KAY, E., & MEYER, H. H. (1966). Participation and the appraisal system. *Human Relations, 19,* 3–20.

FRENCH, J., & RAVEN, B. H. (1959). The bases of social power. In D. Cartwright (Ed.), *Studies in social power.* Ann Arbor, MI: Institute for Social Research.

FRENCH, W. L. & BELL, C. H. (1978). *Organization development: Behavioral science interventions for organization improvement.* Englewood Cliffs, NJ: Prentice Hall.

FRENCH, W. L., & BELL, C. H. (1984). *Organization development: Behavioral science interventions for organization improvement.* Englewood Cliffs, NJ: Prentice Hall.

FRESE, M., & SABINI, J. (1985). *Goal directed behavior: The concept of action in psychology.* Hillsdale, NJ: L. Erlbaum.

FROST, C. F., WAKELEY, J. H., & RUH, R. A. (1974). *The Scanlon plan for organizational development: Identity, participation, and equity.* East Lansing, MI: Michigan State University.

FROST, P. J., & MAHONEY, T. A. (1976). Goal setting and the task process: I. An interactive influence on individual performance. *Orga-*

nizational *Behavior and Human Performance* *17*, 328–50.

FRYER, F. W. (1964). *An evaluation of level of aspiration as a training procedure.* Englewood Cliffs, NJ: Prentice Hall.

GAA, J. P. (1973). Effects of individual goal-setting conferences on achievement, attitudes, and goal-setting behavior. *Journal of Experimental Education, 42,* 22–28.

GAA, J. P. (1979). The effect of individual goal-setting conferences on academic achievement and modification of locus of control orientation. *Psychology in the Schools, 16,* 591–97.

GARDNER, J. W. (1940). The relation of certain personality variables to level of aspiration. *Journal of Psychology, 9,* 191–206.

GARDNER, J. W. (1958). The use of the term level of aspiration. In C. Stacey & M. DeMartino (Eds.), *Understanding human motivation.* Cleveland: Howard Allen.

GARLAND, H. (1982). Goal levels and task performance: A compelling replication of some compelling results. *Journal of Applied Psychology, 67,* 245–48.

GARLAND, H. (1983). Influence of ability, assigned goals, and normative information on personal goals and performance: A challenge to the goal attainability assumption. *Journal of Applied Psychology, 68,* 20–30.

GARLAND, H. (1984). Relation of effort-performance expectancy to performance in goal-setting experiments. *Journal of Applied Psychology, 69,* 79–84.

GARLAND, H. (1985). A cognitive mediation theory of task goals and human performance. *Motivation and Emotion. 9,* 345–67.

GARLAND, H., & ADKINSON, J. H. (1987). Standards, persuasion, and performance. *Group and Organization Studies, 12,* 208–20.

GEBHARD, M. E. (1948). The effect of success and failure upon the attractiveness of activities as a function of experience, expectation, and need. *Journal of Experimental Psychology, 38,* 371–88.

GEORGIOU, P. (1973). The goal paradigm and notes toward a counter paradigm. *Administrative Science Quarterly, 18,* 291–310.

GIBBS, C. B., & BROWN, I. D. (1955). Increased production from the information incentive in a repetitive task. Medical Research Council, Applied Psychology Research Unit (Great Britain), No. 230.

GIST, M. E. (1987). Self-efficacy: Implications for organizational behavior and human resource management. *Academy of Management Review, 12,* 472–85.

GIST, M. E., ROSEN, B., & SCHWOERER, C. (1988). The influence of training methods and trainee age on the acquisition of computer skills. *Personnel Psychology, 41,* 255–65.

GIST, M. E., SCHWOERER, C., & ROSEN, B. (in press). Effects of alternative training methods on self-efficacy and performance in computer software training. *Journal of Applied Psychology.*

GLYNN, E. L. (1970). Classroom applications of self-determined reinforcement. *Journal of Applied Behavior Analysis, 3,* 123–32.

GOLDBERG, L. R. (1968). Simple models or simple processes? Some research on clinical judgments. *American Psychologists, 23,* 422–32.

GOLDRATT, E. M., & COX, J. (1986). *The goal* (2nd ed.). New York: North River Press.

GOLLWITZER, P. M., HECKHAUSEN, H., & RATAJC-ZAK, H. (1987). From weighing to willing: Approaching a change decision through pre- or postdecisional mentation. Max-Planck-Institute for Psychologische Forschung, Munich, West Germany, unpublished manuscript.

GONZALES, F. P., & DOWRICK, P. W. (1982). Mechanisms of self-modeling: An investigation of skills acquisition vs. self-belief. University of Alaska, Anchorage, unpublished manuscript.

GOODMAN, P. S. (1979). *Assessing organizational change: Rushton quality of work experiment.* New York: Wiley.

GOODMAN, P., & FRIEDMAN, A. (1968). An examination of the effect of wage inequity in the hourly condition. *Organizational Behavior and Human Performance, 3,* 340–52.

GOULD, D. (1986). Goal setting for peak performance. In J. Williams (Ed.), *Applied sport psychology: Personal growth to peak performance.* Palo Alto, CA: Mayfield.

GOULD, R. (1939). An experimental analysis of "level of aspiration." *Genetic Psychology Monographs, 21,* 3–115.

GOULD, S. (1979). Characteristics of career planners in upwardly mobile occupations. *Academy of Management Journal, 22,* 539–50.

GOWEN, C. R. (1986). Managing work group performance by individual goals and group goals for an interdependent group task. *Journal of Organizational Behavior Management, 7,* 5–27.

GREENBERG, J. (1985). Unattainable goal choice

as a self-handicapping strategy. *Journal of Applied Social Psychology, 15,* 140–52.

GREENO, J. G. (1978). Nature of problem solving abilities. In W. Estes (Ed.), *Handbook of learning and cognitive process,* Vol. 5. Hillsdale, NJ: L. Erlbaum.

GREENWOOD, R. G. (1981). Management by objectives: As developed by Peter Drucker, assisted by Harold Smiddy. *Academy of Management Review, 6,* 225–30.

GREINER, J. M., HATRY, H. P., KOSS, M. P., MILLAR, A. P., & WOODWARD, J. P. (1981). *Productivity and motivation: A review of state and local government initiatives.* Washington, D.C.: Urban Institute Press.

GRELLER, M. M. (1975). Subordinate participation and reactions to the appraisal interview. *Journal of Applied Psychology, 60,* 544–49.

GRIFFIN, R. W. (1988). Consequences of quality circles in an industrial setting: A longitudinal assessment. *Academy of Management Journal, 31,* 338–58.

GRINYER, P. H., & NORBURN, D. (1975). Planning for existing markets: Perception of chief executives and financial performance. *Journal of the Royal Statistical Society, 138* (Part 1), 70–97.

GROSS, E. (1969). The definition of organizational goals. *British Journal of Sociology, 20,* 277–94.

GUZZO, R. A., JETTE, R. D., & KATZELL, R. A. (1985). The effects of psychologically based intervention programs on worker productivity: A meta-analysis. *Personnel Psychology, 38,* 275–91.

HABERSTROH, C. J. (1960). Control as an organizational process. *Management Science, 6,* 165–71.

HACKER, W. (1985). Activity: A fruitful concept in industrial psychology. In M. Frese, & J. Sabini (Eds.), *Goal directed behavior: The concept of action in psychology.* Hillsdale, NJ: L. Erlbaum.

HACKMAN, J. R., & OLDHAM, G. R. (1980). *Work redesign.* Reading, MA: Addison-Wesley.

HALBERSTAM, D. (1986). The Korean challenge. *Parade Magazine,* November 2, 4–7.

HALISCH, F., & KUHL, J. (EDS.) (1987). *Motivation, intention, and volition.* New York: Springer-Verlag.

HALL, D. T., & FOSTER, L. W. (1977). A psychological success cycle and goal setting: Goals, performance, and attitudes. *Academy of Management Journal, 20,* 282–90.

HALL, D. T., & HALL, F. S. (1976). The relationship between goals, performance, success, self-image, and involvement under different organization climates. *Journal of Vocational Behavior, 9,* 267–78.

HALL, D. T., & LAWLER, E. E. (1971). Job pressures and research performance. *American Scientist, 59,* 64–73.

HALL, H. K., & BYRNE, A. T. J. (1988). Goal setting in sport: Clarifying recent anomalies. *Journal of Sport and Exercise Psychology, 10,* 184–98.

HALL, H. K., WEINBERG, R. S., & JACKSON, A. (1987). Effects of goal specificity, goal difficulty, and information feedback on endurance performance. *Journal of Sport Psychology, 9,* 43–54.

HAMBRICK, D. C. (1983). Some tests of the effectiveness of functional attributes of Miles and Snow's strategic types. *Academy of Management Journal, 26,* 5–26.

HAMMOND, K. R. (1971). Computer graphics as an aid to learning. *Science, 172,* 903–8.

HAMMOND, K. R., SUMMERS, D. A., & DEANE, D. H. (1973). Negative effects of outcome feedback in multiple-cue probability learning. *Organizational Behavior and Human Performance, 9,* 30–34.

HAMNER, W. C., & HARNETT, D. L. (1974). Goal-setting, performance and satisfaction in an interdependent task. *Organizational Behavior and Human Performance, 14,* 1–22.

HANGES, P. J., ALEXANDER, R. A., & HERBERT, G. R. (1987). Using regression analysis to empirically verify catastrophe models. Presented at the Society of Industrial and Organizational Psychology meeting.

HANNAN, R. L. (1975). The effects of participation in goal setting on goal acceptance and performance: A laboratory experiment. Department of Psychology, University of Maryland, unpublished doctoral dissertation.

HARRIS, T. C., & LOCKE, E. A. (1974). Replication of white-collar–blue-collar differences in sources of satisfaction and dissatisfaction. *Journal of Applied Psychology, 59,* 369–70.

HARRISON, R. (1981). Startup: The care and feeding of infant systems. *Organizational Dynamics, 10*(1), 5–29.

HASTIE, R., & CARLSTON, D. E. (1980). Theoretical issues in person memory. In R. Hastie, T. Ostrom, E. Ebbeson, R. Wyer, D. Hamilton, & D. Carlston (Eds), *Person memory: The cognitive basis of social perception,* Hillsdale, NJ: L. Erlbaum.

HARVEY, P. D., & SNYDER, J. D. (1987). Charities

need a bottom line too. *Harvard Business Review, 65,* (1), 14–22.

HAYES, R. H., & ABERNATHY, W. J. (1980). Managing your way to economic decline. *Harvard Business Review, 58*(4), 67–77.

HAYES, S. C., ROSENFARB, I., WULFERT, E., MUNT, E. D., KORN, Z., & ZETTLE, R. D. (1985). Self-reinforcement effects: An artifact of social standard setting? *Journal of Applied Behavior Analysis, 18,* 201–14.

HEDGE, J. W., & KAVANAGH, M. J. (1988). Improving the accuracy of performance evaluations: Comparison of three methods of performance appraiser training. *Journal of Applied Psychology, 73,* 68–73.

HEILMAN, M. E., HORNSTEIN, H. A., CAGE, J. H., & HERSCHLAG, J. D. (1984). Reactions to prescribed leader behavior as a function of role perspective: The case of the Vroom—Yetton model. *Journal of Applied Psychology, 69,* 50–60.

HELMREICH, R. L., SAWIN, L. L., & CARSRUD, A. L. (1986). The honeymoon effect in job performance: Temporal increases in the predictive power of achievement motivation. *Journal of Applied Psychology, 71,* 185–88.

HELMSTADTER, G. C., & ELLIS, D. S. (1957). Rate of manipulative learning as a function of goal-setting techniques. *Journal of Experimental Psychology, 43,* 125–129.

HELSON, H. (1964) *Adaption level theory.* New York: Harper & Row.

HENDERSON, E. H. (1963). A study of individually formulated purposes for reading in relation to reading achievement comprehension and purpose attainment. Department of Psychology, University of Delaware, unpublished doctoral dissertation.

HENNE, D. (1986). Thoughts and actions as consequences of job dissatisfaction. College of Business & Management, University of Maryland, unpublished doctoral dissertation.

HENNE, D., & LOCKE, E. A. (1985). Job dissatisfaction: What are the consequences? *International Journal of Psychology, 20,* 221–40.

HERZBERG, F. (1966). *Work and the nature of man.* Cleveland: World Publishing Co.

HERZBERG, F. (1975). One more time: How do you motivate employees? In R. M. Steers & L. W. Porter (Eds.), *Motivation and work behavior.* New York: McGraw-Hill.

HERZBERG, F., MAUSNER, B., & SNYDERMAN, B. B. (1959). *The motivation to work.* New York: Wiley.

HILGARD, E. R. (1958). Success in relation to level of aspiration. In C. Stacey & M. De-Martino (Eds.), *Understanding human motivation.* Cleveland: Howard Allen.

HILLERY, J. M., & WEXLEY, K. N. (1974). Participation in appraisal interviews conducted in a training situation. *Journal of Applied Psychology, 59,* 168–71.

HIMMELWEIT, H. T. (1947). A comparative study of the level of aspiration of normal and of neurotic persons. *British Journal of Psychology, 37,* Part 2, 41–59.

HINSZ, V. B. (1984). Individual and group goal setting for individual task performance. University of Illinois, unpublished manuscript.

HIRST, M. K. (1988). Intrinsic motivation as influenced by task interdependence and goal setting. *Journal of Applied Psychology, 73,* 96–101.

HOFER, C. W. (1975). Toward a contingency theory of business strategy. *Academy of Management Journal, 18,* 748–810.

HOFER, C. W., & SCHENDEL, D. E. (1978). *Strategy formulation: Analytical concepts.* St. Paul, MN: West.

HOFFMAN, C., MISCHEL, W., & MAZZE, K. (1981). The role of purpose in the organization of information about behavior: Trait-based vs. goal-based categories in person cognition. *Journal of Personality and Social Psychology, 40,* 211–25.

HOFSTEDE, G. (1980). *Culture's consequences.* Beverly Hills, CA: Sage.

HOLLAND, J. H., HOLYOAK, K. J., NISBETT, R. E., & THAGARD, P. R. (1986). *Induction: Processes of inference, learning and discovery.* Cambridge, MA: MIT Press.

HOLLENBECK, J. R., & BRIEF, A. P. (1987). The effects of individual differences and goal origin on goal setting and performance. *Organizational Behavior and Human Decision Processes, 40,* 392–414.

HOLLENBECK, J. R., & KLEIN, H. J. (1987). Goal commitment and the goal setting process: Problems, prospects and proposals for future research. *Journal of Applied Psychology, 72,* 212–220.

HOLLENBECK, J. R., KLEIN, H. J., O'LEARY, A. M., & WRIGHT, P. M. (1988). An investigation of the construct validity of a self-report measure of goal commitment. Presented at Academy of Management meeting.

HOLLENBECK, J. R., & WILLIAMS, C. R. (1987). Goal importance, self-focus, and the goal-setting process. *Journal of Applied Psychology, 72,* 204–211.

HOLLENBECK, J. R., WILLIAMS, C. R., & KLEIN, H. J. (1989). An empirical examination of the antecedents of commitment to difficult goals. *Journal of Applied Psychology, 74,* 18–23.

HOLLINGSWORTH, B. (1975). Effects of performance goals and anxiety on learning a gross motor task. *Research Quarterly, 46,* 162–68.

HOM, H. L., JR. (1985). Intrinsic interest: Self goal effects upon high/low need achievers. Paper presented at Western Psychological Association meeting.

HOM, H. L., JR., & ARBUCKLE, B. (1986). Mood induction effects upon goal setting and performance in young children. Southwest Missouri State University, unpublished manuscript.

HOUSE, W. C. (1974). Actual and perceived differences in male and female expectancies and minimal goal levels as a function of competition. *Journal of Personality, 42,* 493–509.

HOWARD, A., & BRAY, D. W. (1988). *Managerial lives in transition.* New York: Guilford Press.

HOWARD, G. S., CURTIN, T. D., & JOHNSON, A. J. (1988). The hardening of a "soft" science. Presented at American Psychological Association meeting.

HUBER, V. L. (1985a). Comparison of monetary reinforcers and goal setting as learning incentives. *Psychological Reports, 56,* 223–35.

HUBER, V. L. (1985b). Effects of task difficulty, goal setting, and strategy on performance of a heuristic task. *Journal of Applied Psychology, 70,* 492–504.

HUBER, V. L. (in press). Comparison of the effects of specific and general performance standards on performance appraisal decisions. *Decision Sciences.*

HUBER, V. L., LATHAM, G. P., & LOCKE, E. A. (1989). The management of impressions through goal setting. In R. A. Giacalone & P. Rosenfeld (Eds.), *Impresssion management in the organization.* Hillsdale, NJ: L. Erlbaum.

HUBER, V. L., & NEALE, M. A. (1986). Effects of cognitive heuristics and goals on negotiator performance and subsequent goal setting. *Organizational Behavior and Human Decision Processes 38,* 342–65.

HUBER, V. L., & NEALE, M. A. (1987). Effects of self- and competitor goals on performance in an interdependent bargaining task. *Journal of Applied Psychology, 72,* 197–203.

HUMPHREYS, M. S., & REVELLE, W. (1984). Personality, motivation and performance: A theory of the relationship between individual differences and information processing. *Psychological Review, 91,* 153–194.

HUNTER, J. E. (1980). Validity generalization for 12,000 jobs: An application of synthetic validity and validity generalization to the General Aptitude Test Battery (GATB). Washington, D.C.: U.S. Employment Service, Department of Labor.

HUNTER, J. E., & SCHMIDT, F. L. (1983). Quantifying the effects of psychological interventions on employee job performance and work force productivity. *American Psychologist, 38,* 473–78.

HYAMS, N. B., & GRAHAM, W. K. (1984). Effects of goal setting and initiative on individual brainstorming. *Journal of Social Psychology, 123,* 283–84.

HYLAND, M. E. (1988). Motivational control theory: An integrative framework. *Journal of Personality and Social Psychology, 55,* 642–51.

IAFFALDANO, M. T., & MUCHINSKY, P. M. (1985). Job satisfaction and job performance: A meta-analysis. *Psychological Bulletin, 97,* 251–73.

ILGEN, D. R., FISHER, C. D., & TAYLOR, M. S. (1979). Consequences of individual feedback on behavior in organizations. *Journal of Applied Psychology, 64,* 349–71.

ILGEN, D. R., & HAMSTRA, B. W. (1972). Performance satisfaction as a function of the difference between expected and reported performance at five levels of reported performance. *Organizational Behavior and Human Performance, 7,* 359–70.

ILGEN, D. R., & MOORE, C. F. (1982). Combined effects of goal setting and feedback. Purdue University, Technical Report No. 82–1.

ILGEN, D. R., & MOORE, C. F. (1987). Types and choices of performance feedback. *Journal of Applied Psychology, 72,* 401–06.

ILGEN, D. R., NEBEKER, D., & PRITCHARD, R. (1981). Expectancy theory measures: An empirical comparison in an experimental simulation. *Organizational Behavior and Human Performance 28,* 189–223.

IMAI, M. (1986). *Kaizen: The key to Japan's competitive success.* New York: Random House.

IRWIN, F. W., & MINTZER, M. G. (1942). Effect of differences in instructions and motivation upon measures of the level of aspiration. *American Journal of Psychology, 55,* 400–06.

IVANCEVICH, J. M. (1972). A longitudinal assessment of management by objectives. *Administrative Science Quarterly, 17,* 126–138.

IVANCEVICH, J. M. (1974). Changes in performance in a management by objectives program. *Administrative Science Quarterly, 19,* 563–74.

IVANCEVICH, J. M. (1976). Effects of goal setting on performance and job satisfaction. *Journal of Applied Psychology, 61,* 605–12.

IVANCEVICH, J. M. (1977). Different goal setting treatments and their effects on performance and job satisfaction. *Academy of Management Journal, 20,* 406–19.

IVANCEVICH, J. M. (1982). Subordinates' reactions to performance appraisal interviews: A test of feedback and goal-setting techniques. *Journal of Applied Psychology, 67,* 581–87.

IVANCEVICH, J. M., DONNELLY, J. H., & LYON, H. L. (1970). A study of the impact of management by objectives on perceived need satisfaction. *Personnel Psychology, 23,* 139–51.

IVANCEVICH, J. M., & MCMAHON, J. T. (1977a). A study of task-goal attributes, higher order need strength and performance. *Academy of Management Journal, 20,* 552–63.

IVANCEVICH, J. M., & MCMAHON, J. T. (1977b). Black-white differences in a goal-setting program. *Organizational Behavior and Human Performance, 20,* 287–300.

IVANCEVICH, J. M., & MCMAHON, J.T. (1977c). Education as a moderator of goal setting effectiveness. *Journal of Vocational Behavior, 11,* 83–94.

IVANCEVICH, J. M., & MCMAHON, J. T. (1982). The effects of goal setting, external feedback, and self-generated feedback on outcome variables: A field experiment. *Academy of Management Journal, 25,* 359–72.

IVANCEVICH, J. M., & SMITH, S. V. (1981). Goal setting interview skills training: Simulated on-the-job analyses. *Journal of Applied Psychology, 66,* 697–705.

JACKSON, J. H., & MORGAN, C. P. (1978). *Organization theory.* Englewood Cliffs, NJ: Prentice Hall.

JACKSON, S. E., & SCHULER, R. S. (1985). A meta-analysis and conceptual critique of research on role ambiguity and role conflict in work settings. *Organizational Behavior and Human Decision Processes, 36,* 16–78.

JACKSON, S. E., & ZEDECK, S. (1982). Explaining performance variability: Contributions of goal setting, task characteristics, and evaluative contexts. *Journal of Applied Psychology, 67,* 759–68.

JANIS, I. L., & MANN, L. (1977). *Decision-making: A psychological analysis of conflict, choice and commitment.* New York: Free Press.

JANZ, T. (1982). Manipulating subjective expectancy through feedback: A laboratory study of the expectancy-performance relationship. *Journal of Applied Psychology, 67,* 480–85.

JURAN, J. M. (1988). *Juran on planning for quality.* New York: Free Press.

JUSTER. F.T.(1975). Education, income, and human behavior: Introduction and summary. In F. T. Juster (Ed.), *Education, income, and human behavior.* New York: McGraw-Hill.

KAHNEMAN, D. (1973). *Attention and effort.* Englewood Cliffs, NJ: Prentice Hall.

KANFER, F. H. (1970). Self-regulation: Research issues and speculations. In C. Neuringer & J. Michael (Eds.), *Behavior modification in clinical psychology.* New York: Appleton-Century-Crofts.

KANFER, F. H. (1974). Self-regulation: Research, issues, and speculations. In C. Neuringer & J. Michaels (Eds.), *Behavior modification and clinical psychology.* New York: Appleton-Century-Crofts.

KANFER, F. H. (1975). Self-management methods. In F. H. Kanfer (Ed.), *Helping people change.* New York: Wiley.

KANFER, F. H. (1980). Self-management methods. In F. H. Kanfer & A. P. Goldstein (Eds.), *Helping people change: A textbook of methods.* New York: Pergamon Press.

KANFER, F. H., & PHILLIPS, J. S. (1970). *Learning foundations of behavior therapy.* New York: Wiley.

KANFER, R. (1987). Task-specific motivation: An integrative approach to issues of measurement, mechanisms, processes, and determinants. *Journal of Social and Clinical Psychology, 5,* 251–78.

KANFER, R., & ACKERMAN, P. L. (1988). Motivation and cognitive abilities: An integrative aptitude-treatment interaction approach to skill acquisition. Department of Psychology, University of Minnesota, unpublished manuscript.

KANFER, R., & ZEISS, A. M. (1983). Depression, interpersonal standard setting and judgements of self-efficacy. *Journal of Abnormal Psychology, 92,* 319–29.

KAPLAN, R., & ROTHKOPF, E. Z. (1974). Instructional objectives as directions to learners: Effect of passage length and amount of objective-relevant content. *Journal of Educational Psychology, 66,* 448–56.

KAROLY, P., & KANFER, F. H. (1982). *Self-management and behavior change: From theory to practice.* New York: Pergamon Press.

KATERBERG, R., & BLAU, G. J. (1983). An examination of level and direction of effort and job performance. *Academy of Management Journal, 26,* 249–57.

KAUSLER, D. H. (1959). Aspiration level as a determinant of performance. *Journal of Personality, 27,* 346–51.

KAVANAGH, D. J., & BOWER, G. H. (1985). Mood and self-efficacy: Impact of joy and sadness on perceived capabilities. *Cognitive Therapy and Research, 9,* 507–25.

KAY, E., FRENCH, J. R. P., & MEYER, H. H. (1962). A study of the performance appraisal interview. Behavioral Research Service, General Electric Co.

KAZDIN, A. E. (1974). Reactive self-monitoring: The effects of response desirability, goal setting and feedback. *Journal of Consulting and Clinical Psychology, 42,* 704–16.

KENT, G., & GIBBONS, R. (1987). Self-efficacy and the control of anxious cognitions. *Journal of Behavior Therapy and Experimental Psychiatry, 18,* 33–40.

KERNAN, M.G., & LORD, R. G. (1988). Effects of participative vs. assigned goals and feedback in a multi-trial task. *Motivation and Emotion, 12,* 75–86.

KERNAN, M. G., & LORD, R. G. (in press). The effects of explicit goals and specific feedback on escalation processes. *Journal of Applied Social Psychology.*

KIESLER, C. A. (1971). *The psychology of commitment.* New York: Academic Press.

KIM, J. S.(1984). Effect of behavior plus outcome goal setting and feedback on employee satisfaction and performance. *Academy of Management Journal, 27,* 139–49.

KIM, J. S., & HAMNER, W. C. (1976). Effect of performance feedback and goal setting on productivity and satisfaction in an organizational setting. *Journal of Applied Psychology, 61,* 48–57.

KINCEY, J. (1983). Compliance with a behavioural weight-loss programme: Target setting and locus of control. *Behavior Research and Therapy, 21,* 109–14.

KIRMEYER, S. L. (1987). Job demands, productivity, and type A behavior: An observational analysis. Presented at the American Psychological Association meeting.

KIRSCH, I. (1978). Tangible self-reinforcement in self-directed behavior modification projects. *Psychological Reports, 43,* 455–61.

KIRSCH, I., SACCONE, A. J., & VICKERY, A. R. (1981). The effects of norms and self-reward on goal setting and subsequent behavior. *Cognitive Therapy and Research, 5,* 217–19.

KIRSCHENBAUM, D. S. (1985). Proximity and specificity of planning: A position paper. *Cognitive Therapy and Research, 9,* 489–506.

KIRSCHENBAUM, D. S., & FLANERY, R. C. (1984). Toward a psychology of behavioral contracting. *Clinical Psychology Review, 4,* 597–618.

KIRSCHENBAUM, D. S., HUMPHREY, L. L., & MALETT, S. D. (1981). Specificity of planning in adult self-control: An applied investigation. *Journal of Personality and Social Psychology, 40,* 941–50.

KIRSCHENBAUM, D. S., MALETT, S. D., HUMPHREY, L. L., & TOMARKEN, A. J. (1982). Specificity of planning and maintenance of self-control: 1 year follow-up of a study improvement program. *Behavior Therapy, 13,* 232–40.

KIRSCHENBAUM, D. S., TOMARKEN, A. J., & ORDMAN, A. M. (1982). Specificity of planning and choice applied to adult self-control. *Journal of Personality and Social Psychology, 42,* 576–85.

KLEIN, G. S. (1973). Applying management by objectives to plan and measure program goals. Paper presented at National Plant Engineering and Maintenance Conference.

KLEIN, H. J. (1988). Further evidence for the integration of goal setting and expectancy theories. Faculty of Management and Human Resources, Ohio State University, unpublished manuscript.

KLEIN, H. J., & MULVEY, P. W. (1988). The setting of goals in group settings: An investigation of group and goal processes. Faculty of management and Human Resources, Ohio State University, unpublished manuscript.

KLEIN, H. J., WHITENER, E. M., & ILGEN, D. R. (1988). The role of goal specificity in the goal setting process. Faculty of Management and Human Resources, Ohio State University, unpublished manuscript.

KLEINBECK, U. (1986). Effects of goal-setting on motivation and performance in dual-task situations. Presented at the 21st International Congress of Applied Psychology.

KLIEBHAN, S. J. M. (1967). Effects of goal-setting and modeling on job performance of retarded adolescents. *American Journal of Mental Deficiency, 72,* 220–26.

KLINGER, E. (1987). Current concerns and disengagement from incentives. In F. Halisch and J. Kuhl (Eds.), *Motivation, intention and volition.* New York: Springer–Verlag.

KLOCKMANN, L. J. (1985). An examination of the relationship between subjective probability of success, self-efficacy, and performance in a goal setting study. Department of Psychology, Bowling Green State University, unpublished master's dissertation.

KOCH, J. L. (1979). Effects of goal specificity and performance feedback to work groups on peer leadership, performance, and attitudes. *Human Relations, 32,* 819–40.

KOLB, D. A., & BOYATZIS, R. E. (1970). Goal-setting and self-directed behavior change. *Human Relations, 23,* 439–57.

KOLB, D. A., & BOYATZIS, R. E. (1981). Goal setting and self directed behavior change. In D. A. Kolb, I. M. Rubin, & J. M. McIntyre (Eds.), *Organizational psychology: A book of readings.* Englewood Cliffs, NJ: Prentice Hall.

KOLB, D. A., WINTER, S. K., & BERLEW, D. E. (1968). Self-directed change: Two studies. *Journal of Applied Behavioral Science, 4,* 453–71.

KOMAKI, J., BARWICK, K. D., & SCOTT, L. R. (1978). A behavioral approach to occupational safety: Pinpointing and reinforcing safe performance in a food manufacturing plant. *Journal of Applied Psychology, 63,* 434–45.

KOMAKI, J., COLLINS, R. L., & PENN, P. (1982). The role of performance antecedents and consequences in work motivation. *Journal of Applied Psychology, 67,* 334–40.

KOMAKI, J., HEINZMANN, A. T., & LAWSON, L. (1980). Effect of training and feedback: Component analysis of a behavioral safety program. *Journal of Applied Psychology, 65,* 261–70.

KONDRASUK, J. N. (1981). Studies in MBO effectiveness. *Academy of Management Review, 6,* 419–30.

KOPELMAN, R. E. (1982). Improving productivity through objective feedback: A review of the evidence. *National Productivity Review, 2,* 43–55.

KOPELMAN, R. E. (1986). Objective feedback. In E. A. Locke (Ed.), *Generalizing from laboratory to field settings.* Lexington, MA: Lexington Books.

KORMAN, A. K. (1976). Hypothesis of work

behavior revisited and an extension. *Academy of Management Review, 1,* 50–63.

KOSLOWSKY, M., KLUGER, A. N., & YINON, Y (1988). Predicting behavior: Combining intention with investment. *Journal of Applied Psychology, 73,* 102–6.

KOTTER, J. P. (1982). *The general managers.* New York: Free Press.

KRACKHARDT, D., McKENNA, J., PORTER, L. W., & STEERS, R. M. (1981). Supervisory behavior and employee turnover: A field experiment. *Academy of Management Journal, 24,* 249–59.

KUHL, J. (1986). Action control: The maintenance of motivational states. In F. Halisch and J. Kuhl (Eds.), *Motivation, intention, and volition.* New York: Springer-Verlag.

LABICH, K. (1988). Big changes at big brown. *Fortune,* January 18, 56–64.

LAPORTE, R. E., & NATH, R. (1976). Role of performance goals in prose learning. *Journal of Educational Psychology, 68,* 260–64.

LATHAM, G. P. (1983). The role of goal setting in human resource management. *Research in Personnel and Human Resources Management, 1,* 169–99. Greenwich, CT: JAI Press.

LATHAM, G. P. (1986). Job performance and appraisal. In C. L. Cooper & I. T. Robertson (Eds.), *International review of industrial and organizational psychology.* Chichester, England: Wiley Ltd.

LATHAM, G. P. (1988). Human resource training and development. *Annual Review of Psychology, 39,* 545–82.

LATHAM, G. P. (1989). The reliability, validity, and practicality of the situational interview. In G. Ferris & R. Eder (Eds.), *The employment interview: Theory, research, and practice.* Newbury Park, CA: Sage.

LATHAM, G. P., & BALDES, J. J. (1975). The "practical significance" of Locke's theory of goal setting. *Journal of Applied Psychology, 60,* 122–24.

LATHAM, G. P., EREZ, M., & LOCKE, E. A. (1988). Resolving scientific disputes by the joint design of crucial experiments by the antagonists: Application to the Erez-Latham dispute regarding participation in goal setting. *Journal of Applied Psychology* (Monograph), *73,* 753–72.

LATHAM, G. P., & FINNEGAN, B. J. (1987). The practicality of the situational interview. Presented at the Academy of Management meeting.

LATHAM, G. P., & FRAYNE, C. A. (1989). Self-management training for increasing job attendance: A follow-up and a replication. *Journal of Applied Psychology, 74,* 411–16.

LATHAM, G. P., & KINNE, S. B. (1974). Improving job performance through training in goal setting. *Journal of Applied Psychology, 59,* 187–91.

LATHAM, G. P., & LEE T. W. (1986). Goal setting. In E. A. Locke (Ed.), *Generalizing from laboratory to field settings.* Lexington, MA: Lexington Books.

LATHAM, G. P., & LOCKE, E. A. (1975). Increasing productivity with decreasing time limits: A field replication of Parkinson's law. *Journal of Applied Psychology, 60,* 524–26.

LATHAM, G. P., & LOCKE, E. A. (1979). Goal setting: A motivational technique that works. *Organizational Dynamics, 8,* 68–80.

LATHAM, G. P., & MARSHALL, H. A. (1982). The effects of self-set, participatively set and assigned goals on the performance of government employees. *Personnel Psychology, 35,* 399–404.

LATHAM, G. P., & MITCHELL, T. R. (1976). Behavioral criteria and potential reinforcers for the engineer/scientist in an industrial setting. *JSAS Catalog of Selected Documents in Psychology, 6,* 83 (MS. No. 1316).

LATHAM, G. P., MITCHELL, T. R., & DOSSETT, D. L. (1978). Importance of participative goal setting and anticipated rewards on goal difficulty and job performance. *Journal of Applied Psychology, 63,* 163–71.

LATHAM, G. P., & SAARI, L. M. (1979a). Importance of supportive relationships in goal setting. *Journal of Applied Psychology, 64,* 151–56.

LATHAM, G. P., & SAARI, L. M. (1979b). The effects of holding goal difficulty constant on assigned and participatively set goals. *Academy of Management Journal, 22,* 163–68.

LATHAM, G. P., SAARI, L. M., PURSELL, E. D., & CAMPION, M. A. (1980). The situational interview. *Journal of Applied Psychology, 65,* 422–27.

LATHAM, G. P., & SAARI, L. M. (1982). The importance of union acceptance for productivity improvement through goal setting. *Personnel Psychology, 35,* 781–87.

LATHAM, G. P., & SAARI, L. M. (1984). Do people do what they say? Further studies on the situational interview. *Journal of Applied Psychology, 69,* 569–73.

LATHAM, G. P., STEELE, T. P., & SAARI, L. M. (1982). The effects of participation and goal difficulty on performance. *Personnel Psychology, 35,* 677–86.

LATHAM, G. P., & STEELE, T. P. (1983). The motivational effects of participation versus goal setting on performance. *Academy of Management Journal, 26,* 406–17.

LATHAM, G. P., WEXLEY, K. N., & PURSELL, E. D. (1975). Training managers to minimize rating errors in the observation of behavior. *Journal of Applied Psychology, 60,* 550–55.

LATHAM, G. P., & WEXLEY, K. N. (1977). Behavioral observation scales for performance appraisal purposes. *Personnel Psychology, 30,* 255–68.

LATHAM, G. P., & WEXLEY, K. N. (1981). *Increasing productivity through performance appraisal.* Reading, MA: Addison-Wesley.

LATHAM, G. P., & WINTERS, D. W. (1989). Separating the cognitive and motivational effects of participation on performance. Graduate School of Business, University of Washington, unpublished manuscript.

LATHAM, G. P., & YUKL, G. A. (1975a). A review of research on the application of goal setting in organizations. *Academy of Management Journal, 18,* 824–45.

LATHAM, G. P., & YUKL, G. A. (1975b). Assigned versus participative goal setting with educated and uneducated woods workers. *Journal of Applied Psychology, 60,* 299–302.

LATHAM, G. P., & YUKL, G. A. (1976). Effects of assigned and participative goal setting on performance and job satisfaction. *Journal of Applied Psychology, 61,* 166–71.

LAWLER, E. E. (1970). Job design and employee motivation. In V. H. Vroom & E. L. Deci (Eds.), *Management and motivation.* Baltimore: Penguin.

LAWRENCE, L. C., & SMITH, P. C. (1955). Group decision and employee participation. *Journal of Applied Psychology, 39,* 334–37.

LAWRENCE, P. R., & LORSCH, J. W. (1967). *Organization and environment.* Boston, MA: Harvard Business School Press.

LAZARUS, R. S., & FOLKMAN, S. (1984). *Stress, appraisal, and coping.* New York: Springer.

LEANA, C. R., LOCKE, E. A., & SCHWEIGER, D. M. (in press). Fact and fiction in analyzing participation research: A critique of Cotton, Vellrath, Froggatt, Lengnick-Hall, and Jennings. *Academy of Management Review.*

LEE, C. (1988). Effects of goal setting and self-efficacy on female field hockey team performance. College of Business Administration,

Northeastern University, unpublished manuscript.

LEE, C., BOBKO, P., EARLEY, P. C., & LOCKE, E. A. (1988). An empirical analysis of a goal setting questionnaire. College of Business Administration, Northeastern University, unpublished manuscript.

LEE, C., & EARLEY, P. C. (1988). Comparative peer evaluations of organizational behavior theories. College of Business Administration, Northeastern University, unpublished manuscript.

LEE, C., EARLEY, P. C., HANSON, L. A. (1988). Are type A's better performers? *Journal of Organizational Behavior, 9*, 263–69.

LEE C., LOCKE, E. A., & EARLEY, P. C.(1988). Preliminary empirical analysis of a goal setting measure. *Eastern Academy of Management Proceedings*, 128–30.

LEE, C., & NIEDZWIEDZ, E.(1983). The effects of goal setting under different levels of task interdependence. University of Maryland, unpublished manuscript.

LEE, T. W., LOCKE, E. A., & LATHAM, G. P. (1989). Goal setting theory and job performance. In L. Pervin (Ed.), *Goal concepts in personality and social psychology*. Hillsdale, NJ: L. Erlbaum.

LEE, T. W., & MOWDAY, R. T. (1987). Voluntarily leaving the organization: An empirical investigation of Steers and Mowday's (1981) model of turnover. *Academy of Management Journal, 30,* 721–43.

LEIFER, R., & McGANNON, K. (1986). Goal acceptance and goal commitment: Their differential impact on goal setting theory. Presented at Academy of Management meeting.

LENS, W. (1986). Goal setting, future time perspective, and strength of motivation. Presented at International Congress of Applied Psychology.

LEVINE, M. (1971). Hypothesis theory and non-learning despite ideal s-r reinforcement contingencies. *Psychological Review, 78,* 130–40.

LEVINE, M. (1975). *A cognitive theory of learning: Research on hypothesis testing.* Hillsdale, NJ: L. Erlbaum.

LEWIN, K. (1943). Forces behind food habits and methods of change. *Bulletin of the National Resource Council, 108,* 35–65.

LEWIN, K. (1947). Frontiers in group dynamics. *Human Relations, 1,* 5–42.

LEWIN, K. (1951). *Field theory in social science.* New York: Harper & Row.

LEWIN, K. (1952). Group decision and social change. In T. Newcomb & E. Hartley (Eds.), *Readings in social psychology.* New York: Holt, Rinehart & Winston.

LEWIN, K. (1958). Psychology of success and failure. In C. L. Stacey & M. F. Demartino (Eds.), *Understanding human motivation.* Cleveland: Howard Allen.

LEWIN, K. (1961). Intention, will and need. Reprinted in T. Shipley (Ed.), *Classics in psychology.* New York: Philosophical Library. (This article originally appeared, in German, in *Psychol. Forsch.,* 1926.)

LEWIN, K., DEMBO, T., FESTINGER, L., & SEARS, P. S. (1944). Level of aspiration. In J. McVHunt (Ed.), *Personality and the behavior disorders,* Vol. 1. New York: Ronald.

LICHTMAN, R. J., & LANE, I. M. (1983). Effects of group norms and goal setting on productivity. *Group and Organization Studies, 8,* 406–20.

LIKERT, R. (1961). *New patterns of management.* New York: McGraw-Hill.

LIKERT, R. (1967). *The human organization.* New York: McGraw-Hill.

LOCKE, E. A. (1965a). A test of Atkinson's formula for predicting choice behavior. *Psychological Reports, 16,* 963–64.

LOCKE, E. A. (1965b). Interaction of ability and motivation in performance. *Perceptual and Motor Skills, 21,* 719–25.

LOCKE, E. A. (1965c). The relationship of task success to task liking and satisfaction. *Journal of Applied Psychology, 49,* 379–85.

LOCKE, E. A. (1966a). A closer look at level of aspiration as a training procedure: A reanalysis of Fryer's data. *Journal of Applied Psychology, 50,* 417–20.

LOCKE, E. A. (1966b). A preliminary study of some cognitive factors in boredom. American Institutes for Research, Report AIR-R&D-3/66-TR.

LOCKE, E.A.(1966c). Relationship of task success to satisfaction: Further replication. *Psychological Reports, 19,* 1132.

LOCKE, E. A.(1966d). The relationship of intentions to level of performance. *Journal of Applied Psychology, 50,* 60–66.

LOCKE, E. A.(1966e). Relationship of task success to task liking: A replication. *Psychological Reports, 18,* 552–54.

LOCKE, E. A. (1967a). Further data on the relationship of task success to liking and satisfaction. *Psychological Reports, 20,* 246.

LOCKE, E. A. (1967b). Motivational effects of knowledge of results: Knowledge or goal setting? *Journal of Applied Psychology, 51,* 324–29.

LOCKE, E. A. (1967c). Relationship of goal level to performance level. *Psychological Reports, 20,* 1068.

LOCKE, E. A. (1967d). Relationship of success and expectation to affect on goal-setting tasks. *Journal of Personality and Social Psychology, 7,* 125–34.

LOCKE, E. A. (1968a). Effects of knowledge of results, feedback in relation to standards, and goals on reaction-time performance. *American Journal of Psychology, 81,* 566–74.

LOCKE, E. A. (1968b). Toward a theory of task motivation and incentives. *Organizational Behavior and Human Performance, 3,* 157–89.

LOCKE, E. A. (1969a). Goals, probability of success (expectancy), and anticipated affect as determinants of performance level. In E. A. Locke, N. Cartledge, C. S. Knerr, & J. F. Bryan, (1969), *The motivational effects of knowledge of results.* Silver Spring, MD: American Institutes for Research, Report No. R69–2.

LOCKE, E. A. (1969b). Purpose without consciousness: A contradiction. *Psychological Reports, 25,* 991–1009.

LOCKE, E. A. (1969c). What is job satisfaction? *Organizational Behavior and Human Performance, 4,* 309–36.

LOCKE, E. A. (1970a). Job satisfaction and job performance: A theoretical analysis. *Organizational Behavior and Human Performance, 5,* 484–500.

LOCKE, E. A. (1970b). The supervisor as "motivator": His influence on employee performance and satisfaction. In B. Bass, R. Cooper, & J. Bass (Eds.), *Managing for accomplishment.* Lexington, MA: Heath Lexington.

LOCKE, E. A. (1971). Is "Behavior Therapy" behavioristic? (An analysis of Wolpe's psychotherapeutic methods.) *Psychological Bulletin, 76,* 318–27.

LOCKE, E. A. (1972). Critical analysis of the concept of causality in behavioristic psychology. *Psychological Reports, 31,* 175–97.

LOCKE, E. A. (1973). Satisfiers and dissatisfiers among white-collar and blue-collar employees. *Journal of Applied Psychology, 58,* 67–76.

LOCKE, E. A. (1975). Personnel attitudes and motivation. *Annual Review of Psychology, 26,* 457–80.

LOCKE, E. A. (1976). The nature and causes of job satisfaction. In M. D. Dunnette (Ed.),

Handbook of industrial and organizational psychology. Chicago: Rand McNally.

LOCKE, E. A. (1977). The myths of behavior mod in organizations. *Academy of Management Review, 2,* 543–53.

LOCKE, E. A. (1978). The ubiquity of the technique of goal setting in theories of and approaches to employee motivation. *Academy of Management Review, 3,* 594–601.

LOCKE, E. A. (1980a). Attitudes and cognitive processes are necessary elements in motivational models (Debate). In B. Karmel (Ed.), *Point and counterpoint in organizational behavior.* Hinsdale, IL: Dryden.

LOCKE, E. A. (1980b). Behaviorism and psychoanalysis: Two sides of the same coin. *Objectivist Forum, 1*(1), 10–15.

LOCKE, E. A. (1980c). Latham versus Komaki: A tale of two paradigms. *Journal of Applied Psychology, 65,* 16–23.

LOCKE, E. A. (1981). Comment on Neider: The issue of interpretation of experiments. *Organizational Behavior and Human Performance, 28,* 425–30.

LOCKE, E. A. (1982a). The ideas of Frederick W. Taylor: An evaluation. *Academy of Management Review, 7,* 14–24.

LOCKE, E. A. (1982b). Relation of goal level to performance with a short work period and multiple goal levels. *Journal of Applied Psychology, 67,* 512–14.

LOCKE, E. A. (1984). Job satisfaction. In M. Gruneberg and T. Wall (Eds.), *Social psychology and organizational behavior.* Chichester, England: Wiley Ltd.

LOCKE, E. A. (1986a). *Generalizing from laboratory to field settings.* Lexington, MA: Lexington Books.

LOCKE, E. A. (1986b). Job attitudes in historical perspective. In D. Wren (Ed.), *Papers dedicated to the development of modern management.* Academy of Management.

LOCKE, E. A. (1987). How to motivate employees. *State Legislature, 13*(1), 30–31.

LOCKE, E. A., & BRYAN, J. F. (1966a). Cognitive aspects of psychomotor performance: The effects of performance goals on level of performance. *Journal of Applied Psychology, 50,* 286–91.

LOCKE, E. A., & BRYAN, J. F. (1966b). The effects of goal-setting, rule-learning, and knowledge of score on performance. *American Journal of Psychology, 79,* 451–57.

LOCKE, E. A., & BRYAN, J. F. (1967). Performance goals as determinants of level of performance and boredom. *Journal of Applied Psychology, 51,* 120–30.

LOCKE, E. A., & BRYAN, J. F. (1968a). Goal-setting as a determinant of the effect of knowledge of score on performance. *American Journal of Psychology, 81,* 398–406.

LOCKE, E. A., & BRYAN, J. F. (1968b). Grade goals as determinants of academic achievement. *Journal of General Psychology, 79,* 217–28.

LOCKE, E. A., BRYAN, J. F., & KENDALL, L. M. (1968). Goals and intentions as mediators of the effects of monetary incentives on behavior. *Journal of Applied Psychology, 52,* 104–21.

LOCKE, E. A., & BRYAN, J. F. (1969a). Knowledge of score and goal level as determinants of work rate. *Journal of Applied Psychology, 53,* 59–65.

LOCKE, E. A., & BRYAN, J. F. (1969b). The directing function of goals in task performance. *Organizational Behavior and Human Performance, 4,* 35–42.

LOCKE, E. A., CARTLEDGE, N., & KOEPPEL, J. (1968). Motivational effects of knowledge of results: A goal-setting phenomenon? *Psychological Bulletin, 70,* 474–85.

LOCKE, E. A., CARTLEDGE, N., & KNERR, C. (1970). Studies of the relationship between satisfaction, goal-setting and performance. *Organizational Behavior and Human Performance, 5,* 135–58.

LOCKE, E. A., CHAH, D. O., HARRISON, S., & LUSTGARTEN, N. (1989). Separating the effects of goal specificity from goal level. *Organizational Behavior and Human Decision Processes, 43,* 270–87.

LOCKE, E. A., FEREN, D. B., McCALEB, V. M., SHAW, K. N., & DENNY, A. T. (1980). The relative effectiveness of four methods of motivating employee performance. In K. D. Duncan, M. M. Gruneberg, & D. Wallis (Eds.), *Changes in working life.* London: Wiley Ltd.

LOCKE, E. A., FITZPATRICK, W., & WHITE, F. M. (1983). Job satisfaction and role clarity among university and college faculty. *Review of Higher Education, 6,* 343–65.

LOCKE, E. A., FREDERICK, E., BUCKNER, E., & BOBKO, P. (1984). Effect of previously assigned goals on self-set goals and performance. *Journal of Applied Psychology, 69,* 694–99.

LOCKE, E. A., FREDERICK, E., LEE, C., & BOBKO, P. (1984). Effect of self-efficacy, goals, and task strategies on task performance. *Journal of Applied Psychology, 69,* 241–51.

LOCKE, E. A., & HENNE, D. (1986). Work motivation theories. In C. Cooper & I. Robertson (Eds.), *International review of industrial and organizational psychology.* Chichester England: Wiley Ltd.

LOCKE, E. A., & LATHAM, G. P. (1984a). *Goal-setting: A motivational technique that works.* Englewood Cliffs, NJ: Prentice Hall.

LOCKE, E. A., & LATHAM, G. P. (1984b). Goal setting for individuals, groups, and organizations. In F. E. Kast & J. E. Rosenzweig (Eds.), *The modules in management series* (2-34). Chicago, IL: Science Research Associates.

LOCKE, E. A., & LATHAM, G. P. (1985). The application of goal setting to sports. *Journal of Sport Psychology, 7,* 205–22.

LOCKE, E. A. & LATHAM, G. P. (in press). Work motivation: The high performance cycle. In U. Kleinbeck, H. Thierry, H. Haecker, and H. Quast (Eds.), *Work motivation.* Hillsdale, NJ: Lawrence Erlbaum.

LOCKE, E. A., LATHAM, G. P., & EREZ, M. (1988). The determinants of goal commitment. *Academy of Management Review, 13,* 23–39.

LOCKE, E. A., MENTO, A. J., & KATCHER, B. L. (1978). The interaction of ability and motivation in performance: An exploration of the meaning of moderators. *Personnel Psychology, 31,* 269–80.

LOCKE, E. A., MOTOWIDLO, S. J., & BOBKO, P. (1986). Using self-efficacy theory to resolve the conflict between goal-setting theory and expectancy theory in organizational behavior and industrial/organizational psychology. *Journal of Social and Clinical Psychology, 4,* 328–38.

LOCKE, E. A., & SCHWEIGER, D. M. (1979). Participation in decision-making: One more look. In B. M. Staw (Ed.), *Research in organizational behavior, Vol. 1.* Greenwich, CT: JAI Press.

LOCKE, E. A., SCHWEIGER, D. M. & LATHAM, G. P. (1986). Participation in decision-making: When should it be used? *Organizational Dynamics, 14*(3), 65–79.

LOCKE, E. A., SHAW, K. M., SAARI, L. M., & LATHAM, G. P. (1981). Goal setting and task performance: 1969–1980. *Psychological Bulletin, 90,* 125–52.

LOCKE, E. A., & SHAW, K. N. (1984). Atkinson's inverse–U curve and the missing cognitive variables. *Psychological Reports, 55,* 403–12.

LOCKE, E. A., SIROTA, D., & WOLFSON, A. D. (1976). An experimental case study of the successes and failures of job enrichment in a government agency. *Journal of Applied Psychology, 61,* 701–11.

LOCKE, E. A., & SOMERS R. L. (1987). The effects of goal emphasis on performance on a complex task. *Journal of Management Studies, 24,* 405–11.

LOCKE, E. A., & TAYLOR, M. S. (in press). Stress, coping and the meaning of work. In A. Brief & W. Nord (Eds.), *The meaning of work in America.* Lexington, MA: Lexington Books.

LOCKE, E. A., & WHITING, R. J. (1974). Sources of satisfaction and dissatisfaction among solid waste management employees. *Journal of Applied Psychology, 59,* 145–56.

LOMBARDO, T., HULL, D. B., & SINGER, D. C. (1983). Variables affecting achievement of direct service goals of mental health center outpatient services. *Administration in Mental Health, 11,* 64–66.

LONDON, M., & OLDHAM, G. R. (1976). Effects of varying goal types and incentive systems on performance and satisfaction. *Academy of Management Journal, 19,* 537–46.

LOPES, L. L. (1976). Individual strategies in goal-setting. *Organizational Behavior and Human Performance, 15,* 268–77.

LORD, R. G., & HANGES, P. J. (1987). A control system model of organizational motivation: Theoretical development and applied implications. *Behavioral Science, 32,* 161–78.

LORD, R. G., & KERNAN, M. C. (1987). Scripts as determinants of purposeful behavior in organizations. *Academy of Management Review, 12,* 265–77.

LUGINBUHL, J. E. R. (1972). Role of choice and outcome on feelings of success and estimates of ability. *Journal of Personality and Social Psychology, 22, 121–27.*

LUTHANS, F., & KREITNER, R. (1975). *Organizational behavior modification.* Glenview, IL: Scott Foresman.

LYMAN, R. D. (1984). The effect of private and public goal setting on classroom on-task behavior of emotionally disturbed children. *Behavior Therapy, 15,* 395–402.

MACE, C. A. (1935). *Incentives: Some experimental studies.* Industrial Health Research Board (Great Britain), Report No. 72.

MACKWORTH, N. H. (1950). Researches on the measurement of human performance. *Medical Research Council Special Report Series* (Great Britain), No. 268, 119–31.

MAHLMAN, R., VANCE, R. J., COLELLA, A., WAUNG, M., & URBAN, M. (1988). A dynamic test of

cognitive processes in goal setting. Psychology Department, Ohio State University, unpublished manuscript.

MAHONEY, M. J. (1974). Self-reward and self-monitoring techniques for weight control. *Behavior Therapy, 5,* 48–57.

MAHONEY, M. J., MOURA, N. G., & WADE, T. C. (1973). The relative efficacy of self-reward, self-punishment, and self-monitoring techniques for weight loss. *Journal of Consulting and Clinical Psychology, 40,* 404–7.

MALONE, T. W. (1981). Toward a theory of intrinsically motivating instruction. *Cognitive Science, 4,* 333–69.

MAMIS, R. A., & PEARLSTEIN, S. (1988). Company doctor Q. T. Wiles. *Inc.,* February, 27–38.

MANDERLINK, G., & HARACKIEWICZ, J. M. (1984). Proximal versus distal goal setting and intrinsic motivation. *Journal of Personality and Social Psychology, 47,* 918–28.

MARCH, J. G., & SIMON, H. A. (1958). *Organizations.* New York: Wiley.

MARROW, A. J., BOWERS, D. G., & SEASHORE, S. E. (1967). *Management by participation.* New York: Harper & Row.

MARTIN, J. E., DUBBERT, P. M., KATELL, A.D., THOMPSON, J. K., RACZYNSKI, J. R., LAKE, M., SMITH, P. O., WEBSTER, J. S., SIKORA, T., & COHEN, R. E. (1984). Behavioral control of exercise in sedentary adults: Studies 1 through 6. *Journal of Consulting and Clinical Psychology, 52,* 795–811.

MASLOW, A. H. (1954). *Motivation and personality.* New York: Harper.

MASSIE, J. L. (1965). Management theory. In J. G. March. (Ed.) *Handbook of organizations.* Chicago: Rand McNally.

MASTERS, J. C., FURMAN, W., & BARDEN, R. C. (1977). Effects of achievement standards, tangible rewards, and self-dispensed achievement evaluations on children's task mastery. *Child Development, 48,* 217–24.

MATHERLY, T. A. (1986). Effects of prior success or failure on performance under varying goal conditions. *Journal of Social Behavior and Personality, 1,* 267–77.

MATHEWSON, S. B. (1931). *Restriction of output among unorganized workers.* New York: Viking Press.

MATSUI, T., KAKUYAMA, T., & ONGLATCO, M. L. (1987). Effects of goals and feedback on performance in groups. *Journal of Applied Psychology, 72,* 407–15.

MATSUI, T., OKADA, A., & MIZUGUCHI, R. (1981). Expectancy theory prediction of the goal theory postulate "the harder the goals, the higher the performance." *Journal of Applied Psychology 66*, 54–58.

MATSUI, T., OKADA, A., & KAKUYAMA, T. (1982). Influence of achievement need on goal setting, performance, and feedback effectiveness. *Journal of Applied Psychology, 67*, 645–48.

MATSUI, T., OKADA, A., & INOSHITA, O. (1983). Mechanism of feedback affecting task performance. *Organizational Behavior and Human Performance, 31*, 114–22.

MATSUI, T., OKADA, A., & KAKUYAMA, T. (1983). Feedback mechanism: A basis of connecting goal setting and achievement motivation theories. Graduate School of Applied Sociology, Rikkyo University (Tokyo), unpublished manuscript.

MAURER, S. D., & FAY, C. (in press). Effect of situational interviews, conventional structured interviews, and training on interview rating agreement: An experimental analysis. *Personnel Psychology.*

MAYER, R. C. (1989). Examination of the multidimensionality of organizational commitment. College of Business Administration, University of Notre Dame, unpublished manuscript.

MAYFIELD, E. C. (1964). The selection interview—A re-evaluation of published research. *Personnel Psychology, 17*, 239–60.

McCARTHY, M. (1978). Decreasing the incidence of "high bobbins" in a textile spinning department through a group feedback procedure. *Journal of Organizational Behavior Management, 1*, 150–54.

McCAUL, K. D., HINSZ, V. B., & McCAUL, H. S. (1987). The effects of commitment to performance goals on effort. *Journal of Applied Social Psychology, 17*, 437–50.

McCAUL, K. D., & KOPP, J. T. (1982). Effects of goal setting and commitment on increasing metal recycling. *Journal of Applied Psychology, 67*, 377–79.

McCLELLAND, D. C. (1961). *The achieving society.* Princeton, NJ: Van Nostrand.

McCLELLAND, D. C., ATKINSON, J. W., CLARK, R. A., & LOWELL, E. L. (1953). *The achievement motive.* New York: Appleton-Century-Crofts.

McCLELLAND, D. C., & WINTER, D. G. (1969). *Motivating economic achievement: Accelerating economic development through psychological training.* New York: Free Press.

McCORMACK, P. D., BINDING, F. R. S., & CHYLINSKI, J. (1962). Effects on reaction-time of knowledge of results of performance. *Perceptual and Motor Skills, 14*, 367–72.

McCORMACK, P. D., BINDING, F. R. S., & McELHERAN, W. G. (1963). Effects on reaction-time of partial knowledge of results of performance. *Perceptual and Motor Skills, 17*, 279–81.

McCUDDY, M. K., & GRIGGS, M. H. (1984). Goal setting and feedback in the management of a professional department: A case study, *Journal of Organizational Behavior Management, 6*, 53–64.

McCULLOUGH, D. (1977). *The path between the seas.* New York: Simon & Schuster.

McGREGOR, D. (1960). *The human side of enterprise.* New York: McGraw-Hill.

McLAUGHLIN, T. F. (1982). Effects of self-determined and high performance standards on spelling performance: A multi-element baseline analysis. *Child and Family Behavior Therapy, 4*, 55–61.

MENTO, A. J., CARTLEDGE, N. D., & LOCKE, E. A. (1980). Maryland vs Michigan vs Minnesota: Another look at the relationship of expectancy and goal difficulty to task performance. *Organizational Behavior and Human Performance, 25*, 419–40.

MENTO, A. J., & LOCKE, E. A. (1989). Studies of the relationship between goals and valences. Loyola College, Baltimore, manuscript in preparation.

MENTO, A. J., STEEL, R. P., & KARREN, R. J. (1987). A meta-analytic study of the effects of goal setting on task performance: 1966–1984. *Organizational Behavior and Human Decision Processes, 39*, 52–83.

MERCIER, P., & LADOUCEUR, R. (1983). Modification of study time and grades through self-control procedures. *Canadian Journal of Behavioral Science, 15*, 70–81.

MERTON, R. K. (1957). Bureaucratic structure and personality. In R. K. Merton (Ed.), *Social theory and social structure.* Glencoe: Free Press.

MEYER, H. H., KAY, E., & FRENCH, J. R. P. (1965). Split roles in performance appraisal. *Harvard Business Review, 43*(1), 123–29.

MEYER, J. P., & GELLATLY, I. R. (1988). Perceived performance norm as a mediator in the effect of assigned goal on personal goal and task performance. *Journal of Applied Psychology, 73*, 410–20.

MEYER, J. P., KONAR, E., & SCHACHT, B. (1983). Goal setting effects on motivation: A VIE theory explanation. Presented at American Psychological Association meeting.

MEYER, J. P., SCHACHT-COLE, B., & GELLATLY, I. R. (1988). An examination of the cognitive mechanisms by which assigned goals affect task performance and reactions to performance. *Journal of Applied Social Psychology, 18,* 390–408.

MEYER, W. U. (1987). Perceived ability and achievement-related behavior. In F. Halisch and J. Kuhl (Eds.), *Motivation, intention and volition.* New York: Springer-Verlag.

MICHELS, R. (1962) *Political parties.* New York: Collier.

MIGLIORE, R. H. (1977). *MBO: Blue collar to top executive.* Washington, D.C.: Bureau of National Affairs.

MILES, R., & SNOW, C. (1978). *Organizational strategy, structure and process.* New York: McGraw-Hill.

MILGRAM, S. (1974). *Obedience to authority.* New York: Harper & Row.

MILLER, D., & FRIESEN, P. (1978). Archetypes of strategy formulation. *Management Science, 24,* 921–33.

MILLER, G. A., GALANTER, E., & PRIBRAM, K. H. (1960). *Plans and the structure of behavior.* New York: Henry Holt.

MILLER, H. E., & STEELE, D. L. (1984). Boundary conditions on goal-setting: An examination of goal difficulty effects under two incentive schedules. Industrial Relations Center, University of Minnesota, unpublished manuscript.

MILLER, J. G. (1960). Information input overload and psychopathology. *American Journal of Psychiatry, 11,* 695–704.

MILLER, K. I., & MONGE, P. R. (1986). Participation, satisfaction and productivity: A meta-analytic review. *Academy of Management Journal, 29,* 727–53.

MILLER, L. (1965). The use of knowledge of results in improving the performance of hourly operators. Management Development and Employee Relations Services, General Electric Co.

MINER, J. B. (1977). *Motivation to manage.* Atlanta: Organizational Measurement Systems Press.

MINER, J. B. (1980). *Theories of organizational behavior.* Hinsdale, IL: Dryden.

MINER, J. B. (1984). The validity and usefulness of theories in an emerging organizational science. *Academy of Management Review, 9,* 296–306.

MINTZBERG, H. (1983). *Power in and around organizations.* Englewood Cliffs, NJ: Prentice Hall.

MISCHEL, W. (1977). The interaction of person and situation. In D. Magnusson and N. S. Endler (Eds.), *Personality at the crossroads: Current issues in interactional psychology.* Hillsdale, NJ: L. Erlbaum.

MITCHELL, T. R. (1973). Motivation and participation: An integration. *Academy of Management Journal, 16,* 670–79.

MITCHELL, T. R. (1974). Expectancy models of job satisfaction, occupational preference, and effort: A theoretical, methodological, and empirical appraisal. *Psychological Bulletin, 81,* 1053–77.

MITCHELL, T. R. (1979). Organizational behavior. *Annual Review of Psychology, 30,* 248–81.

MITCHELL, T. R., ROTHMAN, M., & LIDEN, R. C. (1985). Effects of normative information on task performance. *Journal of Applied Psychology, 70,* 48–55.

MITCHELL, T. R., & SILVER, W. S. (1989). Individual and group goals when workers are interdependent: Effects on cooperation, competition and performance. Department of Management and Organization, University of Washington, unpublished manuscript.

MIZES, J. S., & SCHULDT, W. J. (1981). Effects of explicit and implicit achievement standards on performance. *Psychological Reports, 48,* 305–6.

MOBLEY, W. H. (1982). *Employee turnover: Causes, consequences and control,* Reading, MA: Addison-Wesley.

MOBLEY, W. H., & LOCKE, E. A. (1970). The relationship of value importance to satisfaction. *Organizational Behavior and Human Performance, 5,* 463–83.

MOLZ, R. (1987). Managing organizational goals. In H. Babian & H. Glass (Eds.), *Handbook of business strategy.* Boston: Warren, Gorham & Lamont.

MONTAGUE, W. E., & WEBBER, C. E. (1965). Effects of knowledge of results and differential monetary reward on six uninterrupted hours of monitoring. *Human Factors, 7,* 173–80.

MORGAN, C. D. (1984). Exploring the processes through which feedback affects productivity. University of Houston, unpublished doctoral dissertation.

MORGAN, M. (1985). Self-monitoring of attained subgoals in private study. *Journal of Educational Psychology, 77,* 623–30.

MORSE, J. H., & LORSCH, J. W. (1970). Beyond theory Y. *Harvard Business Review, 48*(3), 61–68.

MOSSHOLDER, K. W. (1980). Effects of externally mediated goal setting on intrinsic motivation: A laboratory experiment. *Journal of Applied Psychology, 65,* 202–10.

MOTOWIDLO, S. J. (1977). Relationships between expectancy theory and goal setting theory. University of Toronto, unpublished manuscript.

MOTOWIDLO, S. J., LOEHR, V., & DUNNETTE, M. D. (1978). A laboratory study of the effects of goal specificity on the relationship between probability of success and performance. *Journal of Applied Psychology, 63,* 172–79.

MOWDAY, R. T., PORTER, L. W., & STEERS, R. M. (1982). *Employee-organization linkages.* New York: Academic Press.

MOWEN, J. C., MIDDLEMIST, R. D., & LUTHER, D. (1981). Joint effects of assigned goal level and incentive structure on task performance: A laboratory study. *Journal of Applied Psychology, 66,* 598–603.

MUELLER, M. E. (1983). The effects of goal setting and competition on performance: A laboratory study. University of Minnesota, unpublished master's thesis.

MURRAY, E. A. (1979). A commentary on Mintzberg's organizational power and goals: A skeletal theory. In D. Schendel & C. Hofer (Eds.), *Strategic management.* Toronto: Little, Brown.

NAYLOR, J. C., & ILGEN, D. R. (1984). Goal setting: A theoretical analysis of a motivational technology. In B. Staw & L. Cummings (Eds.), *Research in organizational behavior,* Vol. 6. Greenwich, CT: JAI Press.

NEALE, M. A., & BAZERMAN, M. H. (1985). The effect of externally set goals on reaching integrative agreements in competitive markets. *Journal of Occupational Behavior, 6,* 19–32.

NEALE, M. A., NORTHCRAFT, G. B., & EARLEY, P. C. (1987). Working hard vs. working smart: A comparison of anchoring and strategy-development effects of goal setting. Kellog School of Management, Northwestern University, unpublished manuscript.

NEBEKER, D. M. (1987). Computer monitoring, feedback, and rewards: Effects on workstation operators' performance, satisfaction and stress. Navy Personnel Research and Development Center, San Diego, unpublished manuscript.

NELSON, J. K. (1978). Motivating effects of the use of norms and goals with endurance testing. *Research Quarterly, 49,* 317–21.

NEMEROFF, W. F., & COSENTINO, J. (1979). Utilizing feedback and goal setting to increase performance appraisal interviewer skills of managers. *Academy of Management Journal, 22,* 566–76.

NESS, R. G., & PATTON, R. W. (1979). The effect of beliefs on maximum weight-lifting performance. *Cognitive Therapy and Research, 3,* 205–11.

NEWELL, A., & SIMON, H. A. (1972). *Human problem solving.* Englewood Cliffs, NJ: Prentice Hall.

NUTTIN, J. (1984). *Motivation, planning and action.* Hillsdale, NJ: L. Erlbaum.

NUTTIN, J. (1985). *Future time perspective and motivation.* Hillsdale, NJ: L. Erlbaum.

O'CONNELL, A. N. (1980). Effects of manipulated status on performance, goal setting, achievement motivation, anxiety, and fear of success. *Journal of Social Psychology, 112,* 75–89.

ODIORNE, G. S. (1965). *Management by objectives: A system of managerial leadership.* New York: Pitman.

ODIORNE, G. S. (1978). MBO: A backward glance. *Business Horizons,* October, 14–24.

OLDHAM, G. R. (1975). The impact of supervisory characteristics on goal acceptance. *Academy of Management Journal, 18,* 461–75.

OLDHAM, G. R. (1976). The motivational strategies used by supervisors: Relationships to effectiveness indicators. *Organizational Behavior and Human Performance, 15,* 66–86.

OLDS, J. (1958). Self-stimulation of the brain. *Science, 127,* 315–23.

OLIVER, R. L., & BRIEF, A. P. (1983). Sales manager's goal commitment correlates. *Journal of Personal Selling and Sales Management, 3* (1), 11–17.

ONGLATCO, M. L. (1988). *Japanese quality control circles.* Tokyo: Asian Productivity Organization.

O'REILLY, C., & CHATMAN, J. (1986). Organizational commitment and psychological attachment: The effects of compliance, identification and internalization on prosocial behavior. *Journal of Applied Psychology, 71,* 492–99.

ORGAN, D. W. (1977). Intentional vs. arousal effects of goal-setting. *Organizational Behavior and Human Performance, 18,* 378–89.

ORGAN, D. W. (1987). *Organizational citizenship*

behavior: The good soldier syndrome. Lexington, MA: Lexington.

ORNE, M. T. (1962). On the social psychology of the psychological experiment with particular reference to demand characteristics. *American Psychologist, 17,* 776–83.

OSTROW, A. C. (1976). Goal-setting behavior and need achievement in relation to competitive motor acitivity. *Research Quarterly, 47,* 174–83.

PACKER, E. (1985a). *The art of introspection.* New York: Objectivist Forum.

PACKER, E. (1985b). *Understanding the subconscious:* New York: Objectivist Forum.

PAPANDREOU, A. G. (1952). Some basic problems in the theory of the firm. In B. Haley (Ed.), *A survey of contemporary economics,* Vol. 2. Homewood, IL: Irwin.

PARSONS, H. M. (1974). What happened at Hawthorne? *Science, 183,* 922–23.

PARSONS, T. (1960). *Structure and process in modern societies.* New York: Free Press.

PAYNE, R. B., & HAUTY, G. T. (1955). Effects of psychological feedback upon work decrement. *Journal of Experimental Psychology, 50,* 343–51.

PEARCE, J. A., & DAVID, F. (1987). Corporate mission statements: The bottom line. *Academy of Management Executive, 1,* 109–16.

PEARLMAN, K. (1982). The Baysean approach to validity generalization: A systematic examination of the robustness of procedures and conclusions. Department of Psychology, George Washington University, unpublished doctoral dissertation.

PERKINS, D. N. T., NIEVA, V. G., & LAWLER, E. E. (1983). *Managing creation: The challenge of building a new organization.* New York: Wiley.

PERROW, C. (1961). The analysis of goals in complex organization. *American Sociological Review, 26,* 854–66.

PERROW, C. (1970). *Organizational analysis: A sociological view.* Belmont, CA: Wadsworth.

PETERS, L. H., CHASSIE, M. B., LINDHOLM, H. R., O'CONNOR, E. J. & KLINE, C. R. (1982). The joint influence of situational constraints and goal setting on performance and affective outcomes. *Journal of Management, 8,* 7–20.

PETERS, L. H., O'CONNOR, E. J., POOYAN, A., & QUICK, J. C. (1984). The relationship between time pressure and performance: A field test of Parkinson's law. *Journal of Occupational Behavior, 5,* 293–99.

PETERS, T. J., & WATERMAN, R. H. (1982). *In search of excellence.* New York: Harper & Row.

PHILLIPS, J. S., & FREEDMAN, S. M. (1988). The task-related competency and compliance aspects of goal setting: A clarification. *Organizational Behavior and Human Decision Processes, 41,* 34–49.

PINDER, C. C. (1984). *Work motivation.* Glenview, IL: Scott, Foresman.

PODSAKOFF, P. M., & FARH, J. (1989). Effects of feedback sign and credibility on goal setting and task performance. *Organizational Behavior and Human Decision Processes, 44,* 45–67.

PODSAKOFF, P. M., & SCHRIESHEIM, C. A. (1985). Field studies of French and Raven's bases of power: Critique, reanalysis, and suggestions for future research. *Psychological Bulletin, 97,* 387–411.

PODSAKOFF, P. M., & WILLIAMS, L. J. (1986). The relationship between job performance and job satisfaction. In E. A. Locke (Ed.), *Generalizing from laboratory to field settings.* Lexington, MA: Lexington Books.

POFFENBERGER, A. T. (1928). The effects of continuous work upon output and feelings. *Journal of Applied Psychology, 12,* 459–67.

PORTER, L. W., AND LAWLER, E. E. (1968). *Managerial attitudes and performance.* Homewood, IL: Irwin.

PORTER, L. W., STEERS, R. M., MOWDAY, R. T., & BOULIAN, P. V. (1974). Organizational commitment, job satisfaction, and turnover among psychiatric technicians. *Journal of Applied Psychology, 59,* 603–9.

POSNER, B. G., & BURLINGHAM, B. (1988). The hottest entrepreneur in America. *Inc., January,* 44ff.

POWERS, W. T. (1973). Feedback: Beyond behaviorism. *Science, 179,* 351–56.

PRINCIPATO, F. R.(1983). Effect of goal setting with feedback on productivity in a sheltered workshop. *Education and Training of the Mentally Retarded, 18,* 141–44.

PRITCHARD, R. D., BIGBY, D. G., BEITING, M., COVERDALE, S., & MORGAN, C. (1981). Enhancing productivity through feedback and goal setting. Air Force Human Resources Laboratory, Brooks Air Force Base, Texas. AFHRL-TR-81-7.

PRITCHARD, R. D., & CURTIS, M. I., (1973). The influence of goal setting and financial incentives on task performance. *Organizational Behavior and Human Performance, 10,* 175–83.

PRITCHARD, R. D., JONES, S. D., ROTH, P. L., STUEBING, K. K., & EKEBERG, S. E. (1988). Effects of group feedback, goal setting, and incentives on organizational productivity.

Journal of Applied Psychology (Monograph), 73, 337–58.

PRITCHARD, R. D., MONTAGNO, R. V., & MOORE, J. R. (1978). Enhancing productivity through feedback and job design. Air Force Human Resources Laboratory, Brooks Air Force Base, Texas. AFHRL-TR-78-44.

PROTHERO, J. & BEACH, L. R. (1984). Retirement decisions: Expectation, intention, and action. *Journal of Applied Social Psychology, 14,* 162–74.

PRUITT, D. G. (1983). Achieving integrative agreements. In M. H. Bazerman & R. J. Lewicki (Eds.), *Negotiation inside organizations.* Beverly Hills, CA: Sage.

PUNNETT, B. J. (1986). Goal setting: An extension of the research. *Journal of Applied Psychology, 71,* 171–72.

QUICK, J. C. (1979). Dyadic goal setting and role stress: A field study. *Academy of Management Journal, 22,* 241–52.

QUINN, J. B. (1980). *Strategies for change.* Homewood, IL: Irwin.

RAIA, A. P. (1965). Goal setting and self-control: An empirical study. *Journal of Management Studies, 2,* 32–53.

RAIA, A. P. (1966). A second look at management goals and controls. *California Management Review, 8*(4), 49–58.

RAKESTRAW, T. L., & FLANAGAN, M. (1984). The effects of goal presentation style on performance satisfaction. Management Department, Youngstown State University, unpublished manuscript.

RAKESTRAW, T. L., & WEISS, H. M. (1981). The interaction of social influences and task experience on goals, performance, and performance satisfaction. *Organizational Behavior and Human Performance, 27,* 326–44.

RALIS, M. T., & O'BRIEN, R. M. (1986). Prompts, goal setting and feedback to increase suggestive selling. *Journal of Organizational Behavior Management, 8,* 5–18.

RAND, A. (1964). The Objectivist ethics. In A. Rand (Ed.), *The virtue of selfishness.* New York: New American Library.

RAND, A. (1969). *Introduction to Objectivist epistemology.* New York: The Objectivist.

RAVEN, B. H., & RIETSEMA, J. (1957). The effects of varied clarity of group goal and group path upon the individual and his relation to his group. *Human Relations, 10,* 29–45.

REBER, R. A., & WALLIN, J. A. (1984). The effects of training, goal-setting, and knowledge of results on safe behavior: A component anal-

ysis. *Academy of Management Journal, 27,* 544–60.

REYNOLDS, R. E., & ANDERSON, R. C. (1982). Influence of questions on the allocation of attention during reading. *Journal of Educational Psychology, 74,* 623–32.

REYNOLDS, R. E., STANDIFORD, S. N., & ANDERSON, R. C. (1979). Distribution of reading time when questions are asked about a restricted category of text information. *Journal of Educational Psychology, 71,* 183–90.

RICHARDS, C. S. (1976). When self-control fails: Selective bibliography of research on the maintenance problems in self-control treatment programs. *JSAS: Catalog of Selected Documents in Psychology, 8,* 67–68.

RICHARDS, M. (1986). *Setting strategic goals and objectives.* St. Paul, MN: West.

RIEDEL, J. A., NEBEKER, D. M., & COOPER, B. L. (1988). The influence of monetary incentives on goal choice, goal commitment, and task performance. *Organizational Behavior and Human Decision Processes, 42,* 155–80.

ROBERSON-BENNETT, P. (1983). The relation between need for achievement and goal setting and their joint effect on task performance. College of Business and Management, University of Maryland, unpublished doctoral dissertation.

ROBERTS, G. C., & HALL, H. K. (1987). Motivation in sport: Goal setting and performance. Department of Kinesiology, University of Illinois, unpublished manuscript.

RODGERS, R. C., & HUNTER, J. E. (1989). The impact of management by objectives on organizational productivity. School of Public Administration, University of Kentucky, unpublished manuscript.

RODGERS, R. C., HUNTER, J. E., & RODGERS, D. H. (1987). The impact of management by objectives on job satisfaction. Department of Management, University of Texas at Austin, unpublished manuscript.

ROETHLISBERGER, F. J., & DICKSON, W. J. (1956). *Management and the worker.* Cambridge, MA: Harvard University Press.

RONAN, W. W., & PRIEN, E. P. (1971). *Perspectives on the measurement of human performance.* New York: Appleton-Century-Crofts.

RONAN, W. W., LATHAM, G. P., & KINNE, S. B. (1973). Effects of goal setting and supervision on worker behavior in an industrial situation. *Journal of Applied Psychology, 58,* 302–7.

ROSS, C. C. (1927). An experiment in motivation. *Journal of Educational Psychology, 18,* 337–46.

ROSSWORK, S. G. (1977). Goal setting: The effects on an academic task with varying magnitudes of incentive. *Journal of Educational Psychology, 69,* 710–15.

ROTHKOPF, E. Z., & BILLINGTON, M. J. (1975). A two-factor model of the effect of goal descriptive-directions on learning from text. *Journal of Educational Psychology, 67,* 692–704.

ROTHKOPF, E. Z., & BILLINGTON, M. J. (1979). Goal-guided learning from text: Inferring a descriptive processing model from inspection times and eye movements. *Journal of Educational Psychology, 71,* 310–27.

ROTHKOPF, E. Z., & KAPLAN, R. (1972). Exploration of the effect of density and specificity of instructional objectives on learning from text. *Journal of Educational Psychology, 63,* 295–302.

RUST, J. O., STRANG, H. R., & BRIDGEMAN, B. (1977). How knowledge of results and goal setting function during academic tests. *Journal of Experimental Education, 45*(4), 52–55.

RYAN, T. A. (1947). *Work and effort.* New York: Ronald Press.

RYAN, T. A. (1958). Drives, tasks, and the initiation of behavior. *American Journal of Psychology, 71,* 74–93.

RYAN, T. A. (1970). *Intentional behavior.* New York: Ronald Press.

RYAN, T. A., & SMITH, P. C. (1954). *Principles of industrial psychology.* New York: Ronald Press.

SAARI, J. (1987). Management of housekeeping by feedback. *Ergonomics, 30,* 313–17.

SAARI, L. M., & LATHAM, G. P. (1981). Hypotheses on reinforcing properties of incentives contingent upon performance. Technical Report GS-11, N00014-79-C-0680,Office of Naval Research.

SACKET, T. R. (1947). The effect of knowledge of scores on learning a simulated tracking problem. *American Psychologist, 2,* 299 (abstract).

SAGOTSKY, G., PATTERSON, C. J., & LEPPER, M. R. (1978). Training children's self-control: A field experiment in self-monitoring and goal-setting in the classroom. *Journal of Experimental Child Psychology, 25,* 242–53.

SALANCIK, G. R. (1977). Commitment and the control of organizational behavior and belief. In B. M. Staw and G. R. Salancik (Eds.), *New directions in organizational behavior.* Chicago: St. Clair Press.

SALES, S. M. (1970). Some effects on role overload and role underload. *Organizational Behavior and Human Performance, 5,* 592–608.

SANDELANDS, L. E., GLYNN, M. A., & LARSON, J. R. (1988). Task performance and the "control" of feedback. Columbia University, unpublished manuscript.

SASHKIN, M. (1984). Participative management is an ethical imperative. *Organizational Dynamics, 12*(4), 5–22.

SASHKIN, M. (1986). Participative management remains an ethical imperative. *Organizational Dynamics, 14*(4), 62–75.

SCHACTER, S. (1982). Recidivism and self-cure of smoking and obesity. *American Psychologist, 37,* 436–44.

SCHACTER, S., ELLERTSON, N., McBRIDE, D., & GREGORY, D. (1951). An experimental study of cohesiveness and productivity. *Human Relations, 4,* 229–38.

SCHAFER, L. C., GLASGOW, R. E., & McCAUL, K. D. (1982). Increasing the adherence of diabetic adolescents. *Journal of Behavioral Medicine, 5,* 353–62.

SCHENDEL, D. E., & HOFER, C. W. (1979). *Strategic management.* Toronto: Little, Brown.

SCHMIDT, F. L., HUNTER, J. E., McKENZIE, R. S., & MULDROW, T. W. (1979). The impact of valid selection procedures on work force productivity. *Journal of Applied Psychology, 64,* 609–26.

SCHMIDT, F. L., & HUNTER, J. E. (1983). Individual differences in productivity: An empirical test of estimates derived from studies of selection procedures utility. *Journal of Applied Psychology, 68,* 407–14.

SCHMIDT, F. L., HUNTER, J.E.,OUTERBRIDGE, A. N., & TRATTNER, M. H. (1986). The economic impact of job selection methods on size, productivity, and payroll costs of the federal work force: An empirically based demonstration. *Personnel Psychology, 39,* 1–29.

SCHMIDT, K-H, KLEINBECK, U., & BROCKMANN, W. (1984). Motivational control of motor performance by goal setting in a dual-task situation. *Psychological Research, 46,* 129–41.

SCHRODER, H. M., DRIVER, M. J., & STREUFERT, S. (1967). *Human information processing.* New York: Holt, Rinehart & Winston.

SCHULDT, W. J., & BONGE, D. (1979). Effect of self-imposition and experimenter imposition of achievement standards on performance. *Psychological Reports, 45,* 119–22.

SCHUNK, D. H. (1983). Developing children's self-efficacy and skills: The roles of social comparative information and goal setting. *Contemporary Educational Psychology, 8,* 76–86.

SCHUNK, D. H. (1984). Enhancing self-efficacy and achievement through rewards and goals: Motivational and informational effects. *Journal of Educational Research, 78,* 29–34.

SCHWARTZ, J. L. (1974). Relationship between goal discrepancy and depression. *Journal of Counseling and Clinical Psychology, 42,* 309.

SCHWEIGER, D. M., ANDERSON, C. R., & LOCKE, E. A. (1985). Complex decision-making: A longitudinal study of process and performance. *Organizational Behavior and Human Decision Processes, 36,* 245–72.

SCHWEIGER, D. M., & LEANA, C. R. (1986). Participation in decision making. In E. A. Locke (Ed.), *Generalizing from laboratory to field settings.* Lexington, MA: Lexington Books.

SCOTT, W. E. (1966). Activation theory and task design. *Organizational Behavior and Human Performance, 1,* 3–30.

SEARFOSS, D. G., & MONCZKA, R. M. (1973). Perceived participation in the budget process and motivation to achieve the budget. *Academy of Management Journal, 16,* 541–54.

SEARS, P. S. (1941). Level of aspiration in relation to some variables of personality: Clinical studies. *Journal of Social Psychology, 14,* 311–36.

SEASHORE, S. E. (1954). *Group cohesiveness in the industrial work group.* Ann Arbor: Survey Research Center, Institute for Social Research, University of Michigan.

SHALLEY, C. E., & OLDHAM, G. R. (1985). Effects of goal difficulty and expected external evaluation on intrinsic motivation: A laboratory study. *Academy of Management Journal, 28,* 628–40.

SHALLEY, C. E., OLDHAM, G. R., & PORAC, J. F. (1987). Effects of goal difficulty, goal-setting method, and expected external evaluation on intrinsic motivation. *Academy of Management Journal, 30,* 553–63.

SHAPIRA, Z. (1977). Goal difficulty and goal setting as determinants of task motivation. School of Business, Hebrew University, unpublished manuscript.

SHAPIRA, Z. (in press). Task choice and assigned goals as determinants of task motivation and performance. *Organizational Behavior and Human Decision Processes.*

SHAW, K. N. (1984). A laboratory investigation of the relationship among goals, strategies, and task performance. College of Business

and Management, University of Maryland, unpublished doctoral dissertation.

SHEPPARD, B. H., HARTWICK, J., & WARSHAW, P. R. (1988). The theory of reasoned action: A meta-analysis of past research with recommendations for modifications and future research. *Journal of Consumer Research, 15,* 325–43.

SHETTY, Y. K. (1979). New look at corporate goals. *California Management Review, 22,* 71–79.

SHRAUGER, J. S., & ROSENBERG, S. E. (1970). Self-esteem and the effects of success and failure feedback on performance. *Journal of Personality, 38,* 404–17.

SIEGEL, S., & FOURAKER, L. E. (1960). *Bargaining and group decision making.* New York: McGraw-Hill.

SIEGFRIED, W. D., PIEMONT, J., McCARTER, R., & DELLINGER, D. (1981). Motivational consequences of using performance goals. *Psychological Reports, 48,* 835–40.

SILVER, H. C., & GREENHAUS, J. H. (1983). The impact of goal, task and personal characteristics on goal-setting behavior. *Eastern Academy of Management Proceedings,* 11–13.

SIMON, H. A. (1964). On the concept of organizational goal. *Administrative Science Quarterly, 9,* 1–22.

SIMON, K. M. (1979). Self evaluation reactions: The role of personal valuation of the activity. *Journal of Cognitive Therapy and Research, 9,* 111–16.

SIMON, K. M. (1988). Effects of self-comparison, social comparison, and depression on goal setting and self-evaluative reactions. Psychology Department, Stanford University, unpublished manuscript.

SINGER, R. N., KORIENEK, G., JARVIS, D., McCOLSKEY, D., & CANDELETTI, G. (1981). Goal-setting and task persistence. *Perceptual and Motor Skills, 53,* 881–82.

SINGH, J. P. (1972). Some personality moderators of the effects of the repeated success and failure on task-related variables. University of Akron, unpublished doctoral dissertation.

SKINNER, B. F. (1953). *Science and human behavior.* New York: Macmillan.

SLOAT, K. C. M., THARP, R. G., & GALLIMORE, R. (1977). The incremental effectiveness of classroom-based teacher-training techniques. *Behavior Therapy, 8,* 810–18.

SMITH, K. G., LOCKE, E. A., & BARRY, D. (in press). Goal setting, planning and organizational performance: An experimental simulation. *Organizational Behavior and Human Decision Processes.*

SMITH, P. C. (1953). The curve of output as a criterion of boredom. *Journal of Applied Psychology, 37,* 69–74.

SMITH, P. C. (1976). Behaviors, results and organizational effectiveness: The problem of criteria. In M. D. Dunnette (Ed.), *Handbook of industrial organizational psychology.* Chicago: Rand McNally.

SOMERS, R. L., LOCKE, E. A., & TUTTLE, T. (1985–86). Adding competition to the management basics. *National Productivity Review,* Winter, 7–21.

SORCHER, M. (1967). Motivating the hourly employee. Personnel and Industrial Relations Services, General Electric.

SPIELBERGER, C. D. (1965). Theoretical and epistemological issues in verbal conditioning. In S. Rosenberg (Ed.), *Directions in psycholinguistics.* New York: Macmillan.

STAW, B. M. (1976). Knee-deep in the big muddy: A study of escalating commitment to a chosen course of action. *Organizational Behavior and Human Performance, 16,* 27–44.

STAW, B. M. (1981). The escalation of commitment to a course of action. *Academy of Management Review, 6,* 577–87.

STAW, B. M., & FOX, F. (1977). Escalation: Some determinants of commitment to a previously chosen course of action. *Human Relations, 30,* 431–50.

STEDRY, A. C. (1962). Aspiration levels, attitudes, and performance in a goal-oriented situation. *Industrial Management Review, 3*(2), 60–76.

STEDRY, A. C., & KAY, E. (1964). The effects of goal difficulty on performance. Management Development and Employee Relations Services, General Electric.

STEDRY, A. C., & KAY, E. (1966). The effects of goal difficulty on performance: A field experiment. *Behavioral Science, 11,* 459–70.

STEEL, R. P., & OVALLE, N. K. (1984). A review and meta-analysis of research on the relationship between behavioral intentions and employee turnover. *Journal of Applied Psychology, 69,* 673–86.

STEERS, R. M. (1975). Task-goal attributes, *n* achievement, and supervisory performance. *Organizational Behavior and Human Performance, 13,* 392–403.

STEERS, R. M. (1976). Factors affecting job attitudes in a goal-setting environment. *Academy of Management Journal, 19,* 6–16.

STEERS, R. M., & PORTER, L. W. (1974). The role of task-goal attributes in employee performance. *Psychological Bulletin, 81,* 434–52.

STEVENSON, M. K., KANFER, F. H., & HIGGINS, J. M. (1984). Effects of goal specificity and time cues on pain tolerance. *Cognitive Therapy and Research, 8,* 415–26.

STONE, E. F. (1986). Job scope–job satisfaction and job scope–job performance relationships. In E. A. Locke (Ed.), *Generalizing from laboratory to field settings.* Lexington, MA: Lexington Books.

STRANG, H. R. (1981). The effects of challenging goal instructions upon goal setting and performance on a reaction-time task. *Journal of Psychology, 107,* 241–46.

STRANG, H. R., LAWRENCE, E. C., & FOWLER, P. C. (1978). Effects of assigned goal level and knowledge of results on arithmetic computation: A laboratory study. *Journal of Applied Psychology, 63,* 446–50.

SUGALSKI, T. D., & GREENHAUS, J. H. (1986). Career exploration and goal setting among managerial employees. *Journal of Vocational Behavior, 29,* 102–14.

SWELLER, J. (1983). Control mechanisms in problem solving. *Memory and Cognition, 11,* 32–40.

SWELLER, J., & LEVINE, M. (1982). Effects of goal specificity on means-ends analysis and learning. *Journal of Experimental Psychology, 8,* 463–74.

SWITZKY, H. N., & HAYWOOD, H. C. (1974). Motivational orientation and the relative efficacy of self-monitored and externally imposed reinforcement systems in children. *Journal of Personality and Social Psychology, 30,* 360–66.

TATUM, B. C., & NEBEKER, D. M. (1986). A model of work strategies. Presented at American Psychological Association.

TAYLOR, D. W., BERRY, P. C., & BLOCK, C. H. (1958). Does group participation when using brainstorming facilitate or inhibit creative thinking? *Administrative Science Quarterly, 3,* 23–47.

TAYLOR, F. W. (1967). *Principles of scientific management.* New York: Norton (originally published in 1911).

TAYLOR, M. S. (1981). The motivational effects of task challenge: A laboratory investigation.

Organizational Behavior and Human Performance, 27, 255–78.

TAYLOR, M. S., LOCKE, E. A., LEE, C., & GIST, M. E. (1984). Type A behavior and faculty research productivity: What are the mechanisms? *Organizational Behavior and Human Performance, 34,* 402–18.

TENOPYR, M. L., & OELTJEN, P. D. (1982). Personnel selection and classification. In M. R. Rosenzweig & L. W. Porter (Eds.), *Annual review of psychology.* Palo Alto, CA: Annual Reviews.

TERBORG, J. R. (1976). The motivational components of goal setting. *Journal of Applied Psychology, 61,* 613–21.

TERBORG, J. R. (1978). Motivation and the goal setting process: An attempt at clarification. Presented at Academy of Management Meeting.

TERBORG, J. R., & MILLER, H. E. (1978). Motivation, behavior and performance: A closer examination of goal setting and monetary incentives. *Journal of Applied Psychology, 63,* 29–39.

TERRACE, H. (1979). *Nim: A chimpanzee who learned sign language.* New York: Knopf.

THOMPSON, J. D. (1967). *Organizations in action.* New York: McGraw-Hill.

THORNDIKE, E. L. (1917). The curve of work and the curve of satisfyingness. *Journal of Applied Psychology, 1,* 265–67.

TJOSVOLD, D. (1987). Participation: A close look at its dynamics. *Journal of Management, 13,* 731–50.

TOLCHINSKY, P. D., & KING, D. C. (1980). Do goals mediate the effects of incentives on performance? *Academy of Management Review, 5,* 455–67.

TUBBS, M. E. (1986). Goal-setting: A meta-analytic examination of the empirical evidence. *Journal of Applied Psychology, 71,* 474–83.

TUSHMAN, M. (1974). *Organizational change: An exploratory study and a case history.* Ithaca: New York State School of Industrial and Labor Relations, Cornell University.

TVERSKY, A., & KAHNEMAN, D. (1974). Judgment under uncertainty: Heuristics and biases. *Science, 185,* 1124–31.

UHLINGER, C. A., & STEPHENS, M. W. (1960). Relation of achievement motivation to academic achievement in students of superior ability. *Journal of Educational Psychology, 51,* 259–66.

ULRICH, L., & TRUMBO, D. (1965). The selection interview since 1949. *Psychological Bulletin, 63,* 100–116.

UMSTOT, D. D., BELL, C. H., & MITCHELL, T. R. (1976). Effects of job enrichment and task goals on satisfaction and productivity: Implications for job design. *Journal of Applied Psychology, 61,* 379–94.

VANCE, R. J., & COLELLA, A. (1988). Effects of feedback on cognitive processes in goal setting: Assigned vs. personal goals. Department of Psychology, Ohio State University, unpublished manuscript.

VANDERSLICE, V. J., RICE, R. W., & JULIAN, J. W. (1987). The effects of participation in decision-making on worker satisfaction and productivity: An organizational simulation. *Journal of Applied Social Psychology, 17,* 158–70.

VROOM, V. (1964). *Work and motivation.* New York: Wiley.

WAGNER, J. A. (1988). Another look: Does participation's form really effect its efficacy? Michigan State University, unpublished manuscript.

WAGNER, J. A., & GOODING, R. Z. (1987). Shared influence and organizational behavior: A meta-analysis of situational variables expected to moderate participation-outcome relationships. *Academy of Management Journal, 30,* 524–41.

WAGNER, R. (1949). The employment interview: A critical summary. *Personnel Psychology, 2,* 17–46.

WALTERS, R. W. (1975). *Job enrichment for results: Strategies for successful implementation.* Reading, MA: Addison-Wesley.

WARD, C. H., & EISLER, R. M. (1987a). Type A achievement striving and failure to achieve personal goals. *Cognitive Therapy and Research, 11,* 463–71.

WARD, C. H., & EISLER, R. M. (1987b). Type A behavior, achievement striving and a dysfunctional self-evaluation system. *Journal of Personality and Social Psychology, 53,* 318–26.

WARNER, D. A., & DEJUNG, J. E. (1971). Effects of goal setting upon learning in educable retardates. *American Journal of Mental Deficiency, 75,* 681–84.

WARNER, D. A., & MILLS, W. D. (1980). The effects of goals on the manual performance rates of moderately retarded adolescents. *Education and Training of the Mentally Retarded,* April, 143–47.

WATSON, C. (1983). Motivational effects of feedback and goal-setting on group performance. Presented at American Psychological Association meeting.

WATSON, J. B. (1924). *Behaviorism*. Chicago: University of Chicago Press.

WEBSTER, E. C. (1964). *Decision making in the employment interview*. Montreal: Eagle.

WEED, S. E., & MITCHELL, T. R. (1980). The role of environmental and behavioral uncertainty as a mediator of situation-performance relationships. *Academy of Management Journal, 23,* 38–60.

WEEKLEY, J. A., & GIER, J. A. (1987). Reliability and validity of the situational interview for a sales position. *Journal of Applied Psychology, 72,* 484–87.

WEINBERG, G. M., & SCHULMAN, E. L. (1974). Goals and performance in computer programming. *Human Factors, 16,* 70–77.

WEINBERG, R., BRUYA L., & JACKSON, A. (1985). The effects of goal proximity and goal specificity on endurance performance. *Journal of Sport Psychology, 7,* 296–305.

WEINER, B. (1986). *An attributional theory of motivation and emotion*. New York: Springer-Verlag.

WEINGART, L. R., & WELDON, E. (1988). The impact of an assigned group goal on the performance of individual group members. Kellogg School of Management, Northwestern University, unpublished manuscript.

WEISS, H. M. (1982). Criterion aggregation in personality research: Self-esteem and goal setting. Department of Psychological Sciences, Purdue University, unpublished manuscript.

WEISS, H. M., & RAKESTRAW, T. L. (1988). Effects of social influences and task experience on goals, expectancies for goal attainment, and performance level attractiveness. Department of Psychological Sciences, Purdue University, unpublished manuscript.

WEITZ, J. (1966). Criteria and transfer of training. *Psychological Reports, 19,* 195–210.

WELCH, J. B., & PANTALONE, C. (1985). Changing goals to increase stock price. *Journal of Business Strategy, 6,* 74–77.

WELDON, E., & WEINGART, L. R. (1988). A theory of group goals and group performance. Presented at Academy of Management meeting.

WEXLEY, K. N., & BALDWIN, T. T. (1986). Post-training strategies for facilitating positive transfer: An empirical exploration. *Academy of Management Journal, 29,* 503–20.

WEXLEY, K. N., & LATHAM, G. P. (1981). *Developing and training human resources in organizations*. Glenview, IL: Scott, Foresman.

WEXLEY, K. N., & NEMEROFF, W. F. (1975). Effectiveness of positive reinforcement and goal setting as methods of management development. *Journal of Applied Psychology, 60,* 446–50.

WEXLEY, K. N., SANDERS, R. E., & YUKL, G. A. (1973). Training interviewers to eliminate contrast effects in employment interviews. *Journal of Applied Psychology, 57,* 233–36.

WHITE, F. M., & LOCKE, E. A. (1981). Perceived determinants of high and low productivity in three occupational groups: A critical incident study. *Journal of Management Studies, 18,* 375–87.

WHITE, R. W. (1959). Motivation reconsidered: The concept of competence. *Psychological Review, 66,* 297–333.

WHITE, S. E., MITCHELL, T. R., & BELL, C. H. (1977). Goal setting, evaluation apprehension, and social cues as determinants of job performance and job satisfaction in a simulated organization. *Journal of Applied Psychology, 62,* 665–73.

WHYTE, W. F. (1955). *Money and motivation: An analysis of incentives in industry*. New York: Harper.

WILLIAMS, L. J., & HAZER, J. T. (1986). Antecedents and consequences of satisfaction and commitment in turnover models: A reanalysis using latent variable structural equation methods. *Journal of Applied Psychology, 71,* 219–31.

WILSTED, W. D., & HAND, H. H. (1974). Determinants of aspiration levels in a simulated goal setting environment of the firm. *Academy of Management Journal, 17,* 172–77.

WINETT, R. A., KAGEL, J. H., BATTALIO, R. C., & WINKLER, R. C. (1978). Effects of monetary rebates, feedback, and information on residential electricity conservation. *Journal of Applied Psychology, 63,* 73–80.

WOFFORD, J. C. (1982). Experimental tests of the goal-energy-effort requirement theory of work motivation. *Psychological Reports, 50,* 1259–73.

WOLF, W. B. (1968). Toward the development of a general theory of management. In P. LeBreton (Ed.), *Comparative administrative theory*. Seattle: University of Washington Press.

WOOD, R. E. (1986). Task complexity: Definition of the construct. *Organizational Behavior and Human Decision Processes, 37,* 60–82.

WOOD, R. E., & BAILEY, T. C. (1985). Some unanswered questions about goal effects: A recommended change in research methods. *Australian Journal of Management, 10,* 61–73.

WOOD, R. E., & BANDURA, A. (in press, a). Impact of conceptions of ability on self-regulatory mechanisms and complex decision-making. *Journal of Personality and Social Psychology.*

WOOD, R. E., & BANDURA, A. (in press, b). Social cognitive theory of organizational management. *Academy of Management Review.*

WOOD, R. E., BANDURA, A., & BAILEY, T. (in press). Mechanisms governing organizational performance in complex decision-making environments. *Organizational Behavior and Human Decision Processes.*

WOOD, R. E., & LOCKE, E. A., (1987). The relation of self-efficacy and grade goals to academic performance. *Educational and Psychological Measurement, 47,* 1013–24.

WOOD, R. E., & LOCKE, E. A. (in press). Goal setting and strategy effects on complex tasks. In B. Staw and L. Cummings (Eds.), *Research in organizational behavior,* Vol. 12. Greenwich, CT: JAI Press.

WOOD, R. E., MENTO, A. J., & LOCKE, E. A. (1987). Task complexity as a moderator of goal effects: A meta-analysis. *Journal of Applied Psychology, 72,* 416–25.

WOODWORTH, R. S. (1918). *Dynamic psychology.* New York: Columbia University Press.

WRAPP, H. E. (1967). Good managers don't make policy decisions. *Harvard Business Review, 45*(2), 8–21.

WREN, D. A. (1987). *The evolution of management thought.* New York: Wiley.

WRIGHT, P. M. (in press). A test of the mediating role of goals in the incentive-performance relationship. *Journal of Applied Psychology.*

WRIGHT, P. M. (1989). Goals as mediators of the relationship between incentives and performance: A test of the goal commitment hypothesis. College of Business Administration, University of Notre Dame, unpublished manuscript.

WRIGHT, W. R. (1906). Some effects of incentives on work and fatigue. *Psychological Review, 13,* 23–34.

WYATT, S., FROST, L., & STOCK, F. G. L. (1934). *Incentives in repetitive work.* Industrial Health Research Board (Great Britain), Report No. 69.

WYER, R. S., & CARLSTON, D. E. (1979). *Social cognition, inference and attribution.* Hillsdale, NJ: L. Erlbaum.

WYER, R. S., & SRULL, T. K. (1980). The processing of social stimulus information: A concep-tual integration. In R. Hastie, T. Ostrom, E. Ebbeson, R. Wyer, D. Hamilton, & D. Carlt-son (Eds.), *Person memory: The cognitive basis of social perception.* Hillsdale, NJ: L. Erlbaum.

WYER, R. S., SRULL, T. K., GORDON, S. E., & HARTWICK, J. (1982). Effect of processing objectives on the recall of prose material. *Journal of Personality and Social Psychology, 43,* 674–88.

YATES, J. F., & KULICK, R. M. (1977). Effort control and judgments. *Organizational Behavior and Human Performance, 20,* 54–65.

YUKL, G. A. (1989). *Leadership in organizations.* Englewood Cliffs, NJ: Prentice Hall.

YUKL, G. A., & LATHAM, G. P. (1978). Interrela-tionships among employee participation, in-dividual differences, goal difficulty, goal ac-ceptance, goal instrumentality, and performance. *Personnel Psychology, 31,* 305–23.

ZAJONC, R. B., & TAYLOR, J. J. (1963). The effect of two methods of varying group task diffi-culty on individual and group performance. *Human Relations, 16,* 359–68.

ZANDER, A., FORWARD, J., & ALBERT, R. (1969). Adaptation of board members to repeated failure or success by their organization. *Organizational Behavior and Human Performance, 4,* 56–76.

ZANDER, A., & MEDOW, H. (1963). Individual and group levels of aspiration. *Human Relations, 16,* 89–105.

ZANDER, A., & NEWCOMB, T. (1967). Group levels of aspiration in United Fund campaigns. *Journal of Personality and Social Psychology, 6,* 157–62.

ZANDER, A., & ULBERG, C. (1971). The group level of aspiration and external social pres-sures. *Organizational Behavior and Human Performance, 6,* 362–78.

ZEGMAN, M., & BAKER, B. (1983). The influence of proximal vs. distal goals on adherence to prescribed calories. *Addictive Behaviors, 8,* 319–22.

ZEITHAML, C. P., & FRY, L. W. (1984). Contextual and strategic differences among mature businesses in four dynamic performance sit-uations. *Academy of Management Journal, 27,* 841–60.

ZULTOWSKI, W. H., ARVEY, R. D., & DEWHIRST, H. D. (1978). Moderating effects of organi-zational climate on relationships between goal-setting attributes and employee satisfac-tion. *Journal of Vocational Behavior, 12,* 217–27.

NAME INDEX

Cornelius, E. T., 128
Cosentino, J., 53–54, 93–94, 180, 181
Cotton, J. L., 169–70
Coverdale, S., 209, 243
Cox, J., 324
Crawford, K. S., 43, 128, 209, 243
Crawley, S. L., 181–82
Creedon, C. F., 169
Crowell, C. R., 195
Cummings, L. L., 112
Curry, J. P., 250, 266
Curtis, M. I., 43, 128, 140, 141, 143, 201, 203
Cyert, R. M., 324, 326–29

Dachler, H. P., 38, 70, 116, 123, 145, 147, 153, 169, 210, 264
Daft, R. L., 325
Dansereau, D. F., 304
Das, B., 37, 44, 96, 129, 140, 141, 181, 194
David, F., 320
Dean, D. L., 214–15
Deane, D. H., 317
Deci, E. L., 55–58, 143
DeJong, W., 57
Dellinger, D., 167
Dember, W. N., 168–69
Dembo, T., 110
Deming, Edward, 98
Denny, A. T., 18, 30, 328
Dent, J. K., 322
Dermaris, O., 289
Dess, G. G., 323, 335
Dewhirst, H. D., 217, 245
Dickerson, E. A., 169
Dickson, W. J., 124, 136, 185, 255, 258, 288
Dockstader, S. L., 181, 194
Doman, M., 195
Donaldson, G., 325, 326, 330
Donnelly, J. H., 243
Dossett, D. L., 17, 43, 44, 112, 128, 134, 156–61, 179, 181, 194–95, 201, 203, 213–14, 216, 217, 243, 255, 275, 280, 289, 308–10
Dowling, W. F., 16
Dowrick, P. W., 119, 137
Driver, M. J., 296

Drucker, Peter F., 15, 324
Dubbert, P. M., 59
DuBose, P. B., 217
Duda, J. L., 87, 211
Dulany, D. E., Jr., 18, 187
DuMont, P. F., 128, 129, 147
Dunnette, M. D., 16, 65, 170, 277
DuPont, Pierre, 14–15
Duttagupta, D., 154
Dweck, C. S., 303

Earley, P. C., 31, 36, 43, 44, 46–48, 72–74, 89, 91–92, 97, 99–102, 104–6, 118, 125, 126, 128, 129, 134–37, 146–48, 162, 165, 167, 203, 204, 211–14, 245–46, 254, 255, 258, 260–62, 292, 297–99, 304–6, 308–13, 315, 316, 319, 330
Ebbesen, E. B., 94
Eden, D., 224
Edmister, R. O., 55
Eisler, R. M., 215
Ekeberg, S. E., 188, 244
Ekegren, G., 104, 260, 299, 306, 309–12
Ellerton, N., 136
Ellis, D. S., 167
Emery, G., 235
Emurian, H. H., 144, 145
England, G. W., 322
Epstein, S., 224
Erbaugh, S. J., 43, 88
Erez, M., 31, 37, 43, 51–54, 98, 122, 124, 125, 128–31, 135, 140, 145–47, 162–67, 169, 170, 190–92, 211–13, 254, 257–59, 262, 280, 309, 316, 318, 326
Ericsson, K. A., 307
Ernst, G. W., 311
Etzioni, A., 321, 327

Farh, J., 70, 73, 112, 118, 134, 199, 203
Farris, G. F., 119, 135, 258
Faucheux, C., 172
Fay, C., 273

Feather, N. T., 83
Feder, R. B., 184
Feeney, 190, 195
Fellner, D. J., 18, 44–45, 161, 187, 195–97
Feltz, D., 70
Feren, D. B., 18, 30, 328
Ferris, G. R., 138–39
Festinger, L., 110, 111, 117–18, 167
Finnegan, B. J., 273–74
Fishbein, M., 8, 24, 117
Fisher, C. D., 174, 204, 249, 251, 265–66, 302
Fitts, P. M., 97
Fitzpatrick, W., 228, 238, 265
Flanagan, J. C., 272
Flanagan, M., 229
Flanery, R. C., 292
Folkman, S., 227, 265
Ford, R. N., 17
Forward, J., 44–45, 114, 119, 135, 136
Foster, L. W., 48, 89, 148
Fouraker, L. E., 92
Fowler, P. C., 37, 191, 259, 318
Fowler, R. L., 169
Fox, F., 290
Frank, J. D., 110–112, 117, 122–23
Frayne, C. A., 268, 279–80
Frederick, E., 27, 64, 67, 68, 70, 73, 74, 100, 112, 116, 120, 128–30, 147, 148, 206, 207, 255–57, 259, 302, 313
Frederickson, J. W., 304, 305, 331
Freedman, S. M., 140, 141, 214, 236
French, J. R. P., 13, 44–45, 124, 133, 135, 154, 162, 203, 217, 257
French, W. L., 16, 277, 281
Frese, M., 24–25
Friedman, A., 288
Friesen, P., 330
Frogatt, K. L., 169–70
Frost, C. F., 16
Frost, L., 238
Frost, P. J., 37–38, 128, 190, 204
Fry, L. W., 330

SUBJECT INDEX